W9-BLO-030

YALE SERIES IN ECONOMIC HISTORY

A STUDY OF THE
FLORENTINE CATASTO OF 1427

DAVID HERLIHY AND
CHRISTIANE KLAPISCH-ZUBER

YALE UNIVERSITY PRESS
NEW HAVEN AND LONDON

Originally published in France as *Les Toscans et leurs familles. Une étude du Catasto florentin de 1427.*
© 1978. Editions de L'Ecole des Hautes Etudes en Sciences Sociales. Presses de la Fondation Nationale des Sciences Politiques.

Designed by Sally Harris,
and set in Galliard type.
Printed in the United States of America by
Murray Printing Company, Westford, Mass.

Library of Congress Cataloging in Publication Data

Herlihy, David.
Tuscans and their families.

Abridged translation of: Les Toscans et leurs familles.
Bibliography: p.
Includes index.
1. Florence (Italy)—Economic conditions—Sources.
2. Florence (Italy)—Social conditions—Sources.
3. Florence (Italy)—History—1421–1737—Sources.
4. Florence (Italy)—Census, 1427. I. Klapisch-Zuber, Christiane. II. Title.
HC308.F6H4713 1983 945ʼ.51 84–40195
ISBN 0–300–03056–8 (cloth)
0–300–04611–1 (pbk.)

10 9 8 7 6 5 4 3 2

Contents

Figures

Tables

Maps

Preface to the English Edition

In preparing this English translation of *Les Toscans et leurs familles,* we have reduced the original text by about one-half, in the hope of rendering our book accessible to a larger audience. We condensed considerably those parts of the French text (chapters 1, 2, 3, and 5) dealing with the history and the technical character of the Catasto. These materials are of interest chiefly to specialists and can be readily consulted in the French edition. We abridged less heavily, but rearranged substantially, the parts devoted to the demographic, administrative, and economic history of Tuscany in the period of the Catasto (chapters 4, 6, 7 and 8–11). We have omitted the last two chapters of the French edition (19 and 20), which view the Tuscan family largely through literary materials, but have transferred some of their content into relevant chapters of this edition. Along with conserving space, this arrangement brings the literary records and the statistical data into closer relationship. Finally, we omitted the documentary and statistical appendices. We remind our English readers that copies of the machine-readable edition of the Catasto can be procured at nominal cost from the Data Program and Library Service of the University of Wisconsin, Madison. The availability of the raw data seemed to us to obviate the need to publish lengthy statistical tables.

However, we have kept largely intact those portions of the French edition which deal directly with the Tuscan household (chapters 12 to 17, forming 5 to 10 in this edition). In our notes and bibliography, we make reference to several important publications that have appeared since 1978. These recent studies did not, however, in our estimation, require substantial revisions of our own analysis. Our interpretations of the character and history of the Tuscan household thus remain largely as we formulated them in preparing the original edition.

We would again like to express our thanks to the numerous institutions, scholars, and friends that have aided us in this research. They are mentioned in the Avant-Propos of the French edition. Here we single out only the directors and staffs of the State Archives of Florence and of Pisa, of Villa I Tatti (The Harvard University Center for Renaissance Studies) at Florence, and of the Center for Advanced Study in the Behavioral Sciences at Stanford, California. We are also grateful to the National Science Foundation in the United States and the Centre National de la Recherche Scientifique in France, which provided the needed financial support. We hope that this new English edition of our book will prove worthy of the generous help we have received, from many persons and institutions, over many years.

David Herlihy
Christiane Klapisch-Zuber
February 1983

Introduction

"Men who wish to show their superiority over other animals should make every effort not to pass through this life silently, as do sheep." In 1443, a notary of the Florentine commune placed this proud sentence at the head of a list of children and wards, whom their fathers or guardians had emancipated. He found the phrase in the writings of the ancient historian Sallust, but clearly he was making the sentiment his own. These words might have better served to introduce the great Florentine census known as the Catasto. Florence in 1427 undertook an exhaustive survey of its subjects and their properties: What other state or authority in Europe, saving only the Venetian, might have then attempted to illuminate systematically the human "flock" subject to its staff, down to the youngest baby?

Thanks to the clerks of the fiscal office and their diligent labors, all are there: the humble and the powerful, with all their belongings, squalid or splendid. The lowly, despised peasants and artisans have their voices recorded, alongside the proud patricians. They randomly complain of the wickedness of tenants or the greed of landlords, boast of high mercantile reputations, and lament the miseries caused by war, old age, or failed harvests. Of all regions of Europe in the fifteenth century, Tuscany seems unique in possessing this minute description. The Catasto scans the land, like the rays of a summer sun.

An impressive size, wide diversity, and adequate precision of the data set the Catasto apart from many contemporary fiscal surveys. The Catasto captures about 60,000 households, and it enumerates more than 260,000 persons. It meticulously inventories movable and immovable possessions, for which it supplies systematic assessments. This monument of the Florentine and Italian Renaissance thus preserves, in the same registers, homogeneous information on the wealth, the economic activities, and the demographic characteristics of an entire region.

In the pages that follow, we describe the character of the document, analyze its content, and interpret its data within spatial, social, temporal, and cultural contexts. The Florentines themselves had much to say about the place of the individual in relation to family, profession, and community. We therefore also attempt a reading of some of their many writings in the light of what the Catasto tells us of the realities of contemporary life. Social history, even quantitative history, ought not to be divorced from the study of values. And the use of numbers in historical argument ought not to obliterate individuals, to drown them in a faceless crowd, to change them into sheep. Rather, it ought to show the range of individual experiences, of choices and constraints, which in the past confronted human beings as they aged. Our hope is that this work will both stimulate further research in the fertile terrain of Tuscan history and illustrate the value of new approaches to the age, through disciplines not much recognized by historians, still less by medievalists, such as historical demography or social anthropology. The Tuscans in this great period of their history bequeathed to us enormous quantities of data. We should cultivate the imagination, perhaps even the daring, to use this legacy well.

1
The Document and the Data

Salus nostra in ordine pecunie consistit. . . .

Our safety depends on money. . . .

—Giovanni di Andrea Minerbetti, 1426

The Catasto is a fiscal record, created in 1427 out of the monetary needs of the Florentine commune. Our use of it for social history requires that we examine Florentine public finance in the years preceding 1427. The techniques of assessment that the Florentines adopted not only generated, but also colored, the enormous wealth of data that the Catasto has preserved. We see our Tuscan families through the spectacles of tax collectors. We must determine what they marked clearly, and what they ignored.

I. The Florentine Fiscal System, ca. 1250–1427

Since the middle thirteenth century, the dominant trend in public finances at Florence, as widely across Europe, was growth—astonishing growth, which continued in the face of plague, war, financial crashes, and acute demographic decline. According to the earliest surviving statement of account, dated March and April 1240, the communal treasurers received 4,300 pounds in revenue.[1] In May and June 1301, the comparable figure was 130,000 pounds—an increase of thirteen times in terms of

1. Guidi, 1981, 2:233–311, provides a useful review of the principal financial institutions of the Florentine commune in the period of the Catasto. On Florentine fiscal history, Barbadoro, 1929, is old but still fundamental. Fiumi, 1957, examines direct taxes in several Tuscan communes. For public finances at Pisa, Violante, 1966, is basic; and for Siena, Bowsky, 1970 and 1981. Herlihy, 1964, provides a partial list of the revenues of the Florentine commune from 1240 to 1427. Further information and much valuable comment on the development of Florentine public finances may be found in the many works of Marvin Becker, especially 1965, and 1966–67. Becker's fascination with the cultural implications of financial and credit practices is also reflected in his recent interpretation of medieval Italian culture, 1981. For Florentine finances in the early fifteenth century, see Molho, 1971b.

the silver value of the coins. Florence's yearly income was then an estimated 780,000 pounds, or roughly 338,000 gold florins. During the fourteenth century, Florence endured many disasters, but not a diminution of revenues. During the twelve months that passed between February 1, 1424, and January 31, 1425, income drawn from the city and *contado*, or county of Florence, reached the sum of about 770,000 florins. And the total of taxpayers in 1427 was probably only 30 percent of what they had numbered in ca. 1300. How did the government, the *Signoria*, of Florence extract from its citizens and subjects these gigantic sums?

DIRECT AND INDIRECT TAXES

In the thirteenth century, the principal wealth held by both citizens and rural residents for the most part consisted of holdings in land. Accordingly, the single, most remunerative tax which the government imposed weighed upon real properties, both in countryside and city. This direct tax on real estate was commonly called the *Estimo*. But already in the waning years of the thirteenth century, and still more in the fourteenth, the growth of Florentine industry, commerce, and banking was creating important sums of liquid capital, which largely escaped the direct tax on land. To capture some return from this new form of wealth, the commune had recourse more and more to indirect taxes, *gabelle* or gabelles.

This change in fiscal policy is quite striking. Giovanni Villani, writing before 1348, alludes to an epoch, which he dates before 1293, when no gabelles at all were collected at Florence.[2] In contrast, by 1338, indirect taxes furnished three quarters of all government revenue. Returns from the Estimo were simultaneously declining. The direct tax was suspended altogether in the city in 1315, and the sporadic efforts to reestablish it (during despotic regimes, in 1328 and again in 1342–43) succeeded only in linking direct taxes with tyranny in the popular mind.

The Estimo was retained in the countryside, but its total capital value—roughly measuring the contado's ability to support taxes—fell continuously.[3] It stood at approximately 30,000 pounds at the end of the fourteenth century, and slid to 25,000 in the early 1400s. By August 1425, it had further declined to a modest 16,450 pounds. Several factors account for this steep drop: the fall in rural population, consequent upon plague, fiscal oppression, and flight; spreading impoverishment in the countryside; and a growing concentration of rural lands in the grasp of city dwellers, who claimed exemption from the Estimo.

2. Villani, 1823–25, bk. 8, chap. 2. On the role of gabelles in Florentine public finance in the fourteenth century, see especially La Roncière, 1968.

3. The totals may be found in ASF, Provv. 115, f. 1, 3 April 1425 (20,000 pounds); ibid. 117, f. 1, 27 March (17,000 pounds); ibid., 117, f. 157, 29 August 1426, (16,450 pounds)

These taxes yielded to the Florentine government large and steady revenues that were more than adequate to meet its ordinary expenditures. But one purpose they could not serve: they could not yield the extraordinary sums of money that the government required at the outbreak of every war. For example, the most remunerative of the city taxes was the tariff collected at the town gates. But the government could not raise it suddenly and substantially without hurting commerce, upon which Florence's prosperity—and ultimately its power—depended. In 1424–25, when the costly war against Milan was raging, the communal government dared raise the tariff by a meager 3.7 percent.[4] How could the gigantic sums which war demanded and consumed be found without provoking the city's ruin?

The government responded to this pressing problem through an ingenious fiscal strategy: it required that its citizens lend the needed moneys; and it promised to pay interest on the sums it took, and ultimately to repay the loans themselves, when peace and prosperity allowed.

FORCED LOANS

In the felicitous phrase of the fifteenth-century humanist Poggio Bracciolini, rich citizens served their government and community as "barns of money."[5] Even as barns of wheat sustained the populace in seasons of dearth, so the rich citizens assured the government an abundance of cash. In return for the sums which the government borrowed, citizens received shares in the funded public debt. The debt, and the office which administered it, were called the *Monte* or "mountain," in the sense of "big amount." Established in 1345, the Monte quickly assumed a central role in Florentine fiscal administration.[6] It managed the ever growing debt, paid interest on the outstanding balances (usually 5 percent), and at times repaid the loans. Payments of interest and occasional repayments of principal replenished the private fortunes of the city. The barns of money had to be restocked—in expectation of the next fiscal famine—and the government helped in the harvest.

Forced loans were imposed only within the city of Florence, and the citizens contributed roughly in proportion to their fortunes. "Each one pays," Gregorio Dati explained in 1409, "more or less according to his means, and the man without resources pays nothing beyond the ordinary gabelles . . . "[7] The forced loan, which preceded the first Catasto in 1427

4. ASF, CC, Provedditori, 29, f. 345. The "rincrescimento" of the tariff returned 3,495 florins. The previous income from the tax was 94,723 florins.

5. "De Avaritia," Bracciolini, 1964, p. 15.

6. The Monte is discussed in most of the works on Florentine public finance cited in n. 1 above. See also Brucker, 1957. By 1427 four separate funded debts existed at Florence. For their names and the value of their individual shares, see ASF, AC, 2, f. 58.

7. Dati, 1902, p. 42.

(and would replace it in 1434), was called the *novina*.[8] In distributing the loan, the government first assigned a particular sum to each of the city's wards or *gonfaloni*. These sums themselves roughly reflected the distribution of wealth throughout the city. Within each ward, nine separate boards of assessors independently set an assessment for each household. To reach the final assessment, the three highest and the three lowest figures were excluded, and an average was taken of the middle three. The assessments of all households were then adjusted, so that their total exactly equalled the assigned amount.

This method of assessment was simple, quick, and cheap, but it also had serious shortcomings. In spite of safeguards, powerful citizens could still manipulate assessments: they protected themselves, rewarded friends, and punished enemies. In the words of a contemporary, Giovanni Cavalcanti, fairness could never be achieved in assessments "as long as men, and not law, imposed them."[9] Worse yet, from a fiscal point of view, the assessments were at best approximate, and the sums collected almost always disappointing. In the years immediately preceding 1427, the forced loans never yielded more than 85 percent of the anticipated revenue.[10] The first "big loan" (*prestanzone*) distributed in March 1425 yielded only 70 percent of what the government had expected. Giovanni Rucellai, who appears in the Catasto, once likened assessments based on the novina to "guessing in the dark."[11]

FISCAL CRISIS, 1423–1427

Florence's long struggle against Milan flared again in 1423, and the government once more had to meet huge demands for money. Over the five years from 1423 to 1428, the Florentine commune imposed upon the city no fewer than 114¼ prestanze or prestanzoni, in 73 distributions.[12] None of them returned the anticipated amounts, and the returns of all of them tended to slide rapidly with each new imposition. The government ordered several new surveys to be made (in August 1422, February 1425, and June 1426), but the pattern was always the same: the initial returns stayed below the targeted sums; and the yields slid with each new collection. The government tried to improve the returns by threatening draconian penalties, even death, for those who failed to pay, or through offering higher interest and quick

8. A complete description of methods of assessment under the novina may be found in ASF, Provv. 125, f. 100, 31 May 1434, which established the rules for taking a new survey of the city, to replace the Catasto.

9. Cavalcanti, 1838–39, 1:196.

10. A list of the sums returned by these forced loans may be found in Herlihy and Klapisch-Zuber, 1978, Appendix 1, Table 2, pp. 624–25.

11. Rucellai, 1960, p. 9: ". . . al buio per openione . . . ."

12. Listed in Herlihy and Klapisch-Zuber, 1978, Appendix 1, Table 2, pp. 624–25.

repayment to those who paid promptly.[13] These measures succeeded neither in raising income nor in convincing the public that the assessment procedures were fair. Already in the summer of 1426, a governmental commission chosen to examine the fiscal situation declared that it "was impossible to live and to remain subject to impositions distributed in this fashion."[14] In the government councils, orator followed orator in condemning the inefficiency and the injustice of the functioning system, which was driving numerous worthy citizens to ruin or flight. Inadequate revenues further threatened the independence of the city. The acerbic social commentator Giovanni Calvalcanti lamented how members of the finest families had been thrown into the "shameful and stinking prisons of the Stinche," as he was himself, for inability to pay their taxes.[15] The number of citizens caught in the "mirror" of tax arrears (*in speculo*) shows a spectacular increase from 1424.[16] The Preamble to the law of the Catasto makes vivid reference to this widespread despondency: "Neither pen nor tongue can describe the number and quality of the citizens, whom unfair taxes have stripped of their properties, forced into exile, and reduced to near despair. . . ."[17]

From 1424 the defeats suffered by the Florentine armies confirmed that the war against Milan would be long and costly. Within the government councils, numerous speakers raised the plea for fiscal reform. The principles they advocated can be summarized under three headings: (1) all forms of property, both real and movable, and shares in the public debt, should be liable to assessment, wherever they were found, in city, county, subject territories, or outside the Florentine domains; (2) the assessment of each household should be based no longer on opinion, but on an exact inventory of possessions; (3) each household should be held responsible only for its own fiscal charges, and not for the arrears of neighbors.

Within these lengthy and impassioned debates, one other reform was occasionally mentioned: the extension to the subject cities and their territories of the same methods of assessment used at Florence.[18] The speakers

13. For the death penalty imposed on tax delinquents (but never in fact exacted), see ASF, Provv. 117, f. 22, 12 April 1426, confirming the deliberation of 23 March. For extraordinary loans carrying short terms and high interest (8 to 10 percent), see ibid. 116, f. 254, 27 December 1425. These special loans were called *accatti*. Molho, 1971b, provides an extended discussion of the role of forced loans in Florentine finances.

14. The commissions's report, from ASF, Pratiche, is cited in Berti (ed.), no. 2, 4 July 1426.

15. Cavalcanti, 1838–39, 1:203.

16. The number of citizens declared ineligible for service in the *Tre Maggiori*, the three highest offices of the commune (priors, twelve good men, and sixteen standard-bearers), jumped from nine in 1423 to 42 in 1424. See Herlihy and Klapisch-Zuber, 1978, Table 1, p. 46.

17. ASF, AC 2, f. 1.

18. See the words of Giovanni di Andrea Minerbetti in Berti (ed.), 1860, p. 46 urging that Florence, like Venice, adopt a Catasto "covering all the world." This would assure that "we shall gain the help of our subjects."

argued that the territorial integration of the fiscal system would raise revenues and convince taxpayers that their assessments were basically fair. This reform was never fully implemented, as we shall see. Still, even in proposing that all persons—rich and poor, rural and urban, citizens and subjects—be taxed in the same manner, these speakers can claim to be numbered among the early advocates of modern fiscal methods.

On May 24, 1427, under pressures generated by protracted war, an exhausted treasury, and an exasperated citizenry, the Florentine government promulgated the "law of the Catasto." In the words of a later text, the great reform seemed to promise "the salvation and preservation of the Florentine republic, of its estate and of its liberty."[19]

II. Loans and Taxes

In embarking upon the *via Catasti*, the Florentine government could take advantage of both its own long tradition of fiscal surveys in city and countryside and the experience of other Italian cities, notably Venice, in developing efficient systems of taxation.

PRESTANZA AND ESTIMO

Within the city, the administration of the forced loan and of the Monte provided the communal government with a preliminary list of taxpayers, a rough estimate of their relative wealth, and an exact accounting of their holdings in the public debt. (Inscription in the forced loans was both obligation and proof of citizenship.) In the countryside, the Estimo, which had been imposed since at least the thirteenth century, was also based on the principles that surveys should be comprehensive and that assessments should indicate the ability of all households to support taxes.

Under the Estimo, the sum assigned to each household in the tax lists did not represent the true worth of its holdings.[20] Rather, it indicated relative ability to pay, in relation to its neighbors. At first, the basis of imposing the rural Estimo had been community opinion, but in the countryside as in the city, well before the adoption of the Catasto, increasing fiscal burdens made necessary more exact methods of assessment. As early as 1318 the Estimo of the rural commune of Poggibonsi included lists of properties owned by the villagers and an assessment of their value; the practice was subsequently adopted everywhere in the contado.[21] After 1394, all the rural parishes had to describe the possessions of their residents. Moreover, from

19. ASF, AC 2, f. 80, from the preamble to the law of 10 January 1458.

20. On the development of the Estimo, see especially Fiumi, 1957 ; Sorbi, 1962; Barbaro, 1929; and Conti, 1966, pp. 6–11 and 16–17.

21. Conti, 1966, p. 15.

1371, the communal government required that the local officials, called consuls or rectors, record the names, sex, and ages of family members. The lists showed the number of able-bodied, adult males in the village, called "heads" or *teste*, who were subject to a special head tax. The lists also allowed the government to track migrants from village to village.[22] No one should escape its fiscal scrutiny.

The description of households, their members, and their properties in the rural Estimo thus became ever more detailed and precise over the course of the fourteenth century. Moreover, between 1394 and 1422, chief responsibility for preparing the declarations passed from the village, or its consuls or rector, to the individual heads of households.

A rural Estimo—the last, in fact, before the introduction of the Catasto—had been undertaken in 1422. Many difficulties slowed its redaction, but it was finally deposited in the communal treasury in August 1424. Its registers are not extant, and we cannot compare their contents with the Catasto declarations.[23] Still, the ties between the two surveys were doubtless very close. All household heads who appeared in the Estimo were also required to submit declarations for the Catasto, and to state the amount of their earlier assessment. The frequent imposition of the Estimo by locally elected officials helped assure that a man's holdings would already be, in significant measure, public knowledge. This enhanced the accuracy and comprehensiveness of the new survey.

On the other hand, heavy reliance on prior surveys led to one curious fault in the finished Catasto. Eager to swell the lists of taxpayers, the local officials sometimes added to the Catasto names and declarations of persons found in the earlier Estimo, without inquiring into their present status. A few such persons had already registered for the Catasto under a slightly different name. Others had left the village altogether. The results of this zeal were predictable: the finished Catasto contained a fairly large number of duplicate declarations. For example, the tax rolls of the commune of Santo Stefano a Pozzolatico carry the names of Papi di Stefano and Iacopo di Stefano as distinct heads of households.[24] Over the course of a little more than two years, the two declarations were copied and recopied, and assessments calculated. Only then was it recognized that Papi and Iacopo were the same person. This kind of error was particularly common in the

22. In preparing the Estimi, the government inquired into those who remained (the stanti), departed (the usciti), arrived (the tornati), or were simply located (trovati) within the rural villages. Two volumes of such scrutinies, apparently used in the preparation of the Estimo of 1422–26, have survived, but are misfiled in the Catasto archives. See ASF, AC 106 (rural quarter of Santo Spirito) and AC 166 (San Giovanni).

23. Besides the preparatory volumes cited in n. 22 above, only the summary lists of assessments have survived in ASF, Archivio del Estimo, 261, 280, 289 and 301.

24. AC 307, f. 603 and f. 606.

subject territories, notably Pisa. Still today, some 361 households (0.6 percent of all households) are duplicates and not identified as such in all redactions of the survey.[25]

The *distretto* or district (that is to say, all the cities and territories subject to Florence's dominion that were not integrated into its contado) also possessed a long tradition of fiscal assessments, differing somewhat from the Florentine. In 1402, when it was still an independent city, Pisa had taken a census of its urban population, and again in 1412, six years after it had become a Florentine dependency.[26] In 1416 and 1427 Florence imposed a tax on Pisan countryside, under methods of assessment similar to those followed in its own territory. This latter impost envisioned two methods of assessment. Either the tax officials could themselves determine the assessment of each household, on the basis of an inventory of possessions; or, "if they judged it more equitable and if they thought that the peace and unity of the inhabitants might thus be better served," they could assign a global sum to the parishes, with the requirement that the local officials divide it among the residents. The latter method is essentially that of the Florentine Estimo of 1422–26; the former anticipates the rules of the Catasto. In the Pisan countryside, one system of assessment passed almost imperceptibly into the other.

From the city of Pistoia, an "Estimario" has survived from 1415.[27] The Catasto itself makes repeated allusions to an Estimo of the city of Arezzo. Redacted in 1422–23, this latter survey enumerated 1,166 hearths. For the *cortine* or near countryside, of Arezzo, a survey was redacted a little before 1427 and has survived in the Catasto archives.[28] Judged by these records, the methods of assessment at Pisa, Pistoia, and Arezzo were considerably less rigorous than those practiced at Florence. Household members were not listed separately. Often local officials or commissions (sometimes even local *signori* or magnates) would prepare a collective declaration, listing family heads and estimating their relative wealth.

The subject cities, when ordered in 1427 to collect declarations from their citizens, stubbornly resisted.[29] But in spite of their initial opposition to the policy of centralized taxation, the cities had every reason to render the survey as complete as possible, and to raise the comprehensiveness of the reporting. Every household omitted from the survey laid a heavier burden on those that remained.

25. Corrections of this sort were made only in the official clean draft of the survey, the campioni, not in the summary volumes supposedly recapitulating the results. On these versions, see below, p. 22.

26. Analyzed in Casini, 1957–58 and 1959–60.

27. Archivio di Stato di Pistoia, Provv. 699, Estimario della città. The survey contains 1,090 declarations.

28. AC 243, Catasto del comune di Arezzo. On Arezzo in 1427, see Varese, 1924–25.

29. See below, p. 24.

THE EXAMPLE OF VENICE

The Catasto was a development of, not a departure from, prior practices of tax assessment in Tuscany. But the Florentines also sought new methods of assessment to assure that burdens would be distributed "with open eyes on a certain basis," in the phrase of Rinaldo degli Albizzi.[30] The speakers in the Florentine councils praised one city above all others for its efficient fiscal management: Venice, "said to be the city better ruled and governed than any other."[31] To tax its citizens, Venice used a Catasto. What did the Florentines owe to Venetian precedent? They borrowed from Venice the word itself, "Catasto," and they adopted many techniques associated with it.[32] Unfortunately, no Venetian survey has survived, but we do possess, in the regulations of the Venetian Senate, dated 1411, a lengthy description of the methods by which the survey was taken.[33]

The Venetians assessed in their own Catasto all forms of wealth held by their urban residents—real property, coined money, merchandise, precious metals and stones, and shares in the public debt. The value of real property was calculated on the basis of rent received. Prudently, however, the Venetian statesmen did not wish to provoke the flight of ruined citizens, nor to injure their capacity to produce. They therefore exempted from the assessment the value of the taxpayer's domicile, the tools which supported him, and the furniture which served him. The family head could also deduct 200 pounds from his total assessment "for each legitimate son and daughter, male and female grandchild or nephew, who remained in his house at his expense."[34] Under these wise measures, the weight of taxes fell upon income-producing land and commercial capital, not upon productive labor.

The regulations of the Florentine Catasto are so similar to these provisions as to indicate conscious imitation. Like the Venetians, the Florentines included in their survey nearly all forms of wealth, but they did not assess property which yielded no immediate return. They exempted from assessment the family home and its furnishings, and also the tools which supported the taxpayer in productive employment. They gave favorable treatment to plow animals in the countryside and beasts of burden everywhere. They even allowed deductions for the costs of maintaining farm buildings

30. In Berti (ed.), 1860, no. 4, 7 March 1427.

31. Ibid.

32. The word "Catasto" had become widespread in Tuscany and Umbria well before 1427. For its history at Perugia, see Mira, 1955a and 1955b; Grohmannn, 1981, 2:1009–19, who publishes the legislation concerning the "catastri" of 1481. The word apparently derives from the Greek *kata-stikhos*, "lines reading down," in the sense of "list." See Du Cange, *Glossarium Graecum, ad verbum*. The etymology suggests that the Venetians themselves borrowed the word, and perhaps the methods of assessment, from Byzantine practice.

33. See *Commissione*, 1912, p. clxxxvi.

34. Loc. cit.

and fertilizing fields—at least in theory, as only urban landlords seem to have benefited from this provision.[35] Finally, every citizen of Florence was allowed to subtract 200 florins from his total assets for every family member—a figure strongly reminiscent of the 200-pound exemption permitted in Venice. (At Pisa, a personal exemption of 50 florins was allowed.) Finally, resident servants, apprentices and employees were not counted as household members in either the Venetian or the Florentine surveys.

The Venetian Catasto seems not to have included a head tax on adult males. In this, the Florentines departed from their presumed model. In both city and countryside they imposed a tax upon every able-bodied male, between the ages of 18 and 60 at Florence and Pisa, and between 14 and 70 elsewhere.[36]

Venetian experience, and the tradition of fiscal surveys in Tuscany itself, thus equipped the Florentines with effective methods of surveying and judging the wealth of their subjects. Without doubt these policies affected, and were meant to affect, behavior. The generous personal deduction allowed at Florence perhaps encouraged a higher birth rate. And the exemptions accorded domicile, tools, and work animals sustained workers everywhere in their productive efforts. The Florentine Catasto is not only a mine of social data; it is also an early example of the manipulation of fiscal policies to achieve desired social goals.

III. The Via Catasti

The law of May 24, 1427, conferred chief responsibility for the redaction of the survey on a commission of ten officials, the *Diece Ufficiali del Catasto*. They were chosen according to the complicated procedures—which combined drawings by lot, personal scrutinies, and elections—by which the Florentines regularly recruited the members of their high administration.[37] The electoral rules stipulated that eight of the ten officials (two from each quarter of the city) should be "greater" (*maggiori*) citizens, that is, members of one of the seven major guilds who were eligible for election to the Signoria. The two others were to be "lesser" (*minori*) citizens, belonging to one of the fourteen minor guilds and could be residents of any urban quarter. All were to be at least 30 years of age, and no citizen chosen for this office could decline to serve. The ten were promised a salary of 8 florins per month, but each of them was threatened

35. AC 2, f. 5, cap. 1; f. 57, cap. 26; and f. 53, cap. 16.

36. The legislation defining who should be counted as heads at Florence is found in AC 2, f. 7, cap. 33 (Karmin ed., 1906, p. 28). For rural heads, see ibid., f. 23, cap. 75, provision dated 27 May 1429. For Pisa, see ibid. f. 26, Casini ed., 1964, pp. 431–33.

37. The procedures are minutely described in AC 2, f. 1 (Karmin ed., 1906, pp. 2–14).

by a fine of 1,000 florins if their joint work was not accomplished within one year.

The first officials entered into office on May 28, 1427. Chosen for one year, they nonetheless served for a slightly longer time. In April 1428, recognizing that they could not finish their work by the stipulated date, they requested and obtained an extension of their term in office until the end of June.[38] The officials of the Catasto who succeeded them served for exactly twelve months, from July 1 through June 30 respectively, during the years 1428–1429 and 1429–1430. The administration of the Catasto was continued in this form up to 1434. But the first three boards accomplished the larger part of the labor, carrying to completion this first Catasto, which remained the basis for all later surveys of the fifteenth century.

The law of May 1427 directed the office of the Catasto to prepare within one year six surveys of Florentine citizens, subjects, and institutions. These surveys were to include, respectively: the *cittadini*, or residents of the city of Florence; inhabitants of the contado; priests and religious (*preti*); residents of the district (*distrettuali*); foreigners (*forestieri*); and guilds (*arti*). Of the six surveys, only the first was completed within the original schedule of one year, and it alone was prepared in close conformity with the law as promulgated on May 24, 1427. The officials were to take a new survey in the city every three years, and in the contado every five. Before the office was abolished in 1434, they were able to take two new surveys of the city, dated 1430 and 1433, and they began, but seem not to have finished, a new Estimo in the countryside (1434).

UNITS OF ASSESSMENT

Every Florentine citizen and subject who was liable for the payment of the forced loan in the city or the direct tax elsewhere was obligated to submit to the office of the Catasto a declaration (*portata*), describing in detail both his possessions and the "mouths" (*bocche*) which made up his household. No prior exemptions from fiscal charges were to be honored, but residents of the city were allowed to submit their declarations in whatever gonfalone they wished.[39] On the other hand, the law was quite obscure concerning the obligations of the clergy and of foreigners—persons traditionally exempt from the forced loans. Principally for this reason, these latter surveys remained confused in design and were never really completed.

Within the lay population, the basic unit of assessment was the "fiscal hearth," or, perhaps better, "the taxpaying household." (Some fiscal hearths might consist exclusively of an inheritance, without living members.) In

38. ASF, Provv. 119, ff. 3–4, 26 April 1428.
39. AC 2, f. 52, cap. 11, 4 July 1427.

fiscal terminology, this was the *fuoco* or the *partita*; in everyday language it was the *famiglia*. The family included

> all the "mouths" or "heads" who reside at the expense of the person or persons in whose name the value of the declared properties is registered, whether they be of masculine or of feminine gender, and whatever might be their age, condition or quality, with this one exception, that no deduction [of 200 florins] be allowed for the mouths or heads of any salaried person, whether servant, nurse, clerk, employee or apprentice.[40]

Adult servants, even when resident in their masters' households, were to submit their own declarations; young servants or apprentices would be included in the households of their natural parents. Slaves were listed among the properties of the household and were not regarded as mouths. However, sons or close relatives who were living abroad would usually be counted as members of their parents' or brothers' households at Florence.[41] In describing members of the household, the declaration was to state their names, ages, relationship to the head, occupations, and even their state of health, as this affected the number of heads, or able-bodied males, attributed to the family.

In a strict sense, the household as defined in the law of the Catasto was not a coresidential unit; servants actually resident were counted elsewhere, and some absent sons or relatives were considered present. Rather, the household was viewed as an association of persons related by blood or marriage, and bound together by obligations of mutual support. The Catasto officials very strongly resisted arbitrary combinations of domestic units, and still more their divisions, in order to gain some fiscal advantage. For example, persons living together might declare themselves separate families, in order to multiply the number of exempt domiciles. To counter this and similar manoeuvers, the officials insisted that households appear as they had been described in previous surveys [42]. In particular, wives were not allowed to declare separately from their husbands; husbands had to assume fiscal responsibility for their wives, and sons for their widowed mothers.[43]

In spite of these stipulations, the officials showed some ambiguity in assigning certain types of persons to the proper household. For example, what was the status of orphans "held for the love of God" by persons who

40. AC 2, f. 7, cap. 30.
41. AC 2, ff. 56–57 cap. 24.
42. AC 3, f. 11, 8 September 1427, recopied in AC 2, f. 54, cap. 23.
43. AC 3, f. 12, 11 September 1427, recopied in AC 2, f. 52, cap. 13.

were not their relatives? At times they were counted as true members of the household and at times they were excluded. Widowed mothers of adult and married children also resisted easy assignment. Frequently, the widow had a claim against the property of an adult son for the return of her dowry, and this confusion of possessions was strong reason for counting her in the son's household. On the other hand, she might still hold property in her own name, which rendered her independent of her offspring. Sometimes, in their zeal that none should escape assessment, the officials counted the same woman twice, once with a married son, and again as an independent family. A close study of the declarations of Pisa shows that some 30 households (4 percent of the total) and 65 persons (0.8 percent) appear twice; the ambiguous status of widows is the most important, single reason for such duplications.[44] The repetition, even more than the omission, of data is the Catasto's standard error.

Servants appear rarely among the duplicated hearths and never among the duplicated households. The missing servants doubtlessly reduce the observed size of the fiscal unit below its true membership. Since most young servants were registered in the countryside, their omission from their households of residence lowers by some small measure the size of the observed populations in the urban centers.

These divergences between the fiscal household and the true household cannot, however, be regarded as authentic distortions. The coresidential household (as indeed the entire population of the city) was extremely fluid. Servants were hired and dismissed; sons departed and returned. Unable to control these movements, the Florentine surveyors based their definition of the household on the stable bonds of blood relationship and of mutual obligations before the law. Provided that historians retain that definition in mind, they can very well utilize the taxpaying household of the Catasto for the purposes of social history.

THE MEASUREMENT OF WEALTH

The declarations were to contain a complete inventory of all forms of wealth (*sostanze, valsente*): real estate, animals deemed "worthy of value," coined money, merchandise, credits, and shares in the public debt. For each piece of land or unit of cultivation, landlords had to give its location, boundaries, size, and rents received; they had also to furnish a "just estimate" of its market value. However, certain categories of property were declared exempt: the family's domicile; furnishings (*massarizie di casa*);

44. We would like to express our gratitude to Dott. Michele Luzzati of the Scuola Normale, Pisa, for sharing with us the results of his patient examination of the declarations of the Catasto of Pisa in 1427.

tools; and "beasts for one's own use."[45] Landlords were also authorized to deduct from the value of the rents received one florin for every team of oxen given to their tenants to work the land, and 5 percent of the costs of fertilizing the fields.[46]

Such was the law. But the officials, or their clerks, applied these provisions with considerable laxity. The deduction supposedly allowed for the family domicile offers the most striking example of inconsistency. The residents of Florence were accorded this deduction without question. However, in 1427–28, in calculating the assessments of taxpayers in the Florentine contado and at Pisa and its county, the second officials ignored this provision. Perhaps they thus expected to speed up the survey and raise assessments. Several times the Florentine government ordered the officials to respect the law, but not until October 29, 1429, after the third officials had taken office, was the deduction finally allowed. The third officials had to recalculate the assessments of some 32,000 families resident in the Florentine countryside and at Pisa.

The Catasto officials apparently also refused to recognize deductions by landlords resident outside the city for the sums expended in maintaining farm buildings or in fertilizing the land. From one year to the next, and from one region to another within Tuscany, the Catasto regulations were applied in differing ways or not at all.

In keeping with the basic spirit of the reform—that laws and not men should set the fiscal burdens—the regulations of May 24, 1427 established exact and elaborate procedures for estimating the worth of property. These new procedures were supposed to replace the "just estimate" of a property's value, which, under the Estimo, the owner or neighbors provided. The basis for calculating the land's taxable value was the rent or return it yielded. For agricultural lands, a rent was considered to represent one-half of the total harvest, the usual arrangement, for example, under the widespread *mezzadria* form of land lease. A peasant who directly worked his own property—"with his own hand" in the language of the document—was therefore fiscally accountable for only one-half of his total harvest. The property owners were required to draw up an exact list of the rents or returns received from each piece of property over the preceding three years. When the rents were in produce, as was usual in the countryside, the clerks of the Catasto office had to estimate their monetary value in pounds of small Florentine deniers. To aid them, the officials drew up elaborate schedules, listing the normal prices of the principal agricultural products;

45. AC 2, f. 5, cap. 20.

46. AC 3, f. 13, 15 December 1427, recopied in AC 2, f. 57, cap. 26; ibid. f. 53, 1 December 1428.

the prices reflected both the quality of the commodities and the distance from markets.[47] The rent or return was assumed to represent 7 percent of the capital value of the property. The calculation of this last sum required that the clerks convert the value of the rent into gold florins (the basic monetary unit in the Catasto), and multiply the sum by approximately 14.3. The number of fields and vineyards for which this burdensome calculation had to be done numbered in the tens of thousands.

How did the values obtained by the laborious procedures compare with those reached by the traditional methods of the Estimo? Some few select comparisons of the two estimates suggest the following conclusions.[48] Usually, estimates based on rents fell below the market value, assigned to the property by its owner or by assessors. The divergence between the two values was particularly pronounced in areas close to cities. A farm or villa near Florence, for example, was worth substantially more than the income it returned might indicate. The value of lands owned by the residents of other Tuscan towns—and these were for the most part close to the city walls—seems to have been similarly inflated. Only in regions remote from the towns, where much property remained in peasant hands, was the opposite true. However, here too the officials were not consistent in the methods they followed. The first officials, who finished the survey of Florentine citizens, scrupulously respected the regulations, and assigned values on the basis of capitalized rent. But the second officials, who were committed to finishing the survey of the Florentine contado, utilized the market value supplied by owners and neighbors. This method was easier and quicker and seems usually to have set a higher figure on the worth of property. The third officials, perhaps because they were less hurried and harried, returned once more to the stipulated regulations.

Landed properties, in sum, were for the most part underassessed in the Catasto, and the fiscal burden weighed so much the heavier on movable possessions and on shares in the public debt.

MOVABLE POSSESSIONS

To assess movable property, the surveyors simply entered what they considered to be its fair market value; if the owner protested, the officials themselves settled the issue by a form of agreement (*composizione*). The more difficult problem in regard to movables was detection and control.

Of all forms of liquid assets, the easiest to survey were the shares in the

47. AC 3, f. 18, 26 May 1428, recopied in AC 2, f. 58–60, cap. 27. Conti, 1966, pp. 44–47, summarizes these prices in a convenient table. For the schedule of prices used at Volterra, see AC 2, f. 71, 18 May 1430.

48. See the comparison made by Conti, 1966, p. 81, on the basis of 90 declarations from five villages, and our own extended discussion, Herlihy and Klapisch-Zuber, 1978, pp. 65–67.

public debt. "The credits in the Monte are certain," declared Rinaldo degli Albizzi in the Florentine councils.[49] Immediately after taking office, on June 17, 1427, the first officials appointed three clerks to compile a list of the commune's creditors from the archives of the Monte.[50] The officials set the fair market value of a Monte share at 50 percent of its face value—a generous estimate of its true worth.[51]

Coined money (which the chronicler Cerretani estimated at 2 million florins in the city), personal or commercial credits, and *traffico*, or merchandise, were more difficult to locate, but the officials hoped to ferret them out through several means. The surveyors could demand to see the ledgers kept by most merchants in the city and by many in the countryside. Merchants frequently included copies of their account books with their declarations, to vouch for the honesty of their claims.

If a merchant was suspected of fraud, the clerks of the Catasto office immediately proceeded against him. They entered and searched his house for concealed money, merchandise, or foodstuffs; above all, they insisted on examining his account books. The books gave them records of creditors and debtors, of sales and purchases of goods, property, and animals. Moreover, the great urban merchants were invariably involved in complex partnerships and companies, and this made their business affairs a matter of nearly public knowledge. "Coined money," Rinaldo degli Albizzi explained, "is unknown, but in a short time, as others have said, it will be found through the companies."[52]

A second means of assuring accurate disclosure of movables was the comparison (*riscontro*) of the respective claims of debtors and creditors. According to a ruling of 1430, those sums "placed among the deductions of the debtor must also appear among the assets of the creditor."[53]

The great merchants of Florence, keeping careful accounts, and involved in numerous partnerships, could not easily conceal movables. In the countryside, on the other hand, where the population was dispersed, the officials doubtless encountered much greater difficulties in uncovering hidden wealth. Moreover, as the amounts of concealed wealth in rural hands were comparatively paltry, the officials did not probe into fortunes with the same rigor they applied in the affluent city. It is likely, therefore, that the

49. Berti (ed.), 1860, no. 4, 7 March 1427.

50. AC 3, f. 1.

51. Rinaldo Albizzi, in the speech cited above, n. 49, assumed that the total value of Monte holdings reached 3 million florins. His estimate was close to the figure of 2.8 million florins which is the value of all shares held by laymen and registered in the Catasto. However, soon after the redaction of the survey, many citizens protested that they could not sell their shares at one-half their face value—their purported value in the Catasto. The protests are found in AC 4 and 5, passim.

52. Berti (ed.), 1860, no. 4, 7 March 1427.

53. AC 2, f. 67, cap. 40, 14 May 1430.

Catasto slightly exaggerates the amount of liquid wealth in the urban centers, and slightly underrepresents the quantity of similar wealth in the countryside. Still, hidden capital could not be active capital. The Catasto, we may conclude, gives a reasonably accurate picture, perhaps not of all movable wealth, but at least of the active capital in the hands of Florentine citizens and subjects.

The household head also included in his declarations those obligations (*incarichi*) for which he claimed deductions from his total assets. This intelligent provision not only helped measure a family's true worth but also provided an effective means of controlling the accuracy of credits reported elsewhere. Commercial debts were generally admitted, on condition that commercial assets had also been clearly described. Certain types of debts were, however, almost always disallowed: loans contracted between members of the same household, tax arrears, debts owed to Jewish moneylenders, salaries due to servants, bequests to religious institutions, and debts owed by a sharecropper to his landlord. The taxpayer who rented his family domicile was permitted to deduct the capitalized value of the yearly rent, assumed to be 7 percent of the house's worth. This effectively extended to renters the same deduction for the family residence which owners enjoyed.

The difference between assets and liabilities constituted the taxable wealth, the surplus or *soprabondante*, of the household. This was the wealth regarded as not essential for maintaining the life and productivity of the taxpayer. This division between essential and nonessential possessions had the effect, perhaps unexpected, of promoting certain kinds of investments. For example, the exemption of the family domicile encouraged the building of elegant palaces at Florence and of sumptuous villas outside the city.[54] The furnishings and the decoration of these palaces similarly escaped the tax collector's scrutiny, as they were regarded as massarizie di casa. These exemptions had the pernicious effect of channeling capital away from commercial enterprises. But the policy certainly aided the building industry and the production of art at Florence. It thus may have contributed to the city's artistic efflorescence in the quattrocento.

THE REPRESSION OF FRAUD

The law of May 24, 1427, threatened heavy penalties on those who did not file declarations or who did not do so honestly. Those who failed to file lost the protection of the law in both civil and criminal matters.[55] Taxpayers

54. On the building of palaces at Florence in the Quattrocento, see Patzak, 1913, and, more recently, Goldthwaite, 1972 and 1980. Goldthwaite, 1980, gives comments on the Catasto (pp. 82–83), but does not discuss the fiscal aspects of palace construction.

55. AC 3, f. 15, 14 January 1428, recopied in AC 2, f. 54, cap. 18. The exclusion did not, however, apply to those persons whom the Catasto officials declared to be miserabiles.

apprehended in the concealment of wealth had to pay to the communal treasury one-half of the value of the undeclared possessions, as well as all delinquent taxes due from them. If the household head added a fictitious member to his family, he lost the deduction of 200 florins he was claiming, and another 200 florins were added to his assets. To uncover fraud, the officials invited both open and secret denunciations. *Notificatores*—that is, those who denounced the tax evaders—were promised one-forth of the value of the undeclared possessions, and one-half of the penalties collected. Moreover, the failure to declare a piece of land called into question the legal title to it. Owners might be willing to assign artificially low values to their lands, but few took the risk of concealing them altogether.

However, these stern penalties proved to be self-defeating. They frightened the taxpayers from freely admitting omissions and errors in their declarations, once the survey had been officially closed. Several times the Signoria extended the period of grace, during which additions could be made without prejudice or penalty.[56] The draconian measures envisioned by the enabling legislation of 1427 were thus applied with considerable flexibility and discretion.

PAYMENTS

After verifying the declarations, the clerks of the Catasto office set about calculating the charge against each household. This was called, like the survey itself, a catasto. At Florence, the charge was reckoned at 0.5 percent of taxable assets; at Pisa, 0.25 percent; and in the contado, 0.19 percent.[57] In the countryside, this sum was expressed not in gold florins but in Florentine pounds, doubtless for the reason that little gold circulated in rural areas. The varying rates partially offset the differences in the deductions allowed for household members across the Florentine domains (200 florins per person at Florence, 50 at Pisa). The practical result was to make the Catasto a strongly graduated tax at Florence, particularly burdensome for the very rich. The great households rarely included sufficient "mouths" to offset entirely or substantially their enormous fortunes. Elsewhere, both assets and deductions were modest, and the tax weighed more evenly across social categories.

The payment also included a head tax levied upon every able-bodied,

56. AC 4, f. 10, recopied in AC 1, f. 20, 7 July 1428. It was to be publicly announced that all inhabitants of the city, countryside, and district, including religious, could present or change their declarations up until 15 September. See also AC, 2, f. 18, cap. 38, allowing later additions to the declarations. Still other delays for purposes of adding properties were allowed on 23 December 1428 (AC 1, f. 22, and AC 2, f. 20) and on 18 March 1429 (AC 1, f. 24, and AC 2, ff. 22–23). A comparable concession made to the contadini on 2 and 19 July 1428 (AC 3, f. 11).

57. ASF Provv. 119, ff. 63–64; AC 2, ff. 16–17, 7 June 1428.

adult male member of the household. At Florence, males between 18 and 60 years of age were assessed from two to six gold solidi. Males elsewhere, between 15 and 70 years, paid one to four solidi of debased silver per head.

The large deduction at Florence of 200 florins per household member assured that many families of modest means—some 8,600, in fact—showed no taxable wealth in the final accounting. They were not for that reason exempted from payments. According to the enabling legislation, they were supposed to present themselves to the Catasto office, in order to set by agreement an equitable tax. The hope that these taxpayers would appear voluntarily proved illusory. On June 7, 1428, the officials lamented that many household heads "refused to support, by composition, whatever charge there might be for the safety of the fatherland."[58] The officials gained from the government the right to impose a tax charge on these delinquent citizens, even without their agreement. The officials were further authorized to declare as *miserabili* those men or women whom age or infirmity rendered incapable of earning a living. The miserable were exempt from taxes, but not from the obligation to file a return. This category gathered in the infirm, the aged, minor orphans, and, above all, widows. The miserabili of the city were usually totally destitute, while those of the countryside often possessed some modest belongings. Common to miserable households everywhere was the absence of an adult male member.

The catasto thus represented the amount which every household had to contribute, every time the state imposed a loan or tax. Unlike the methods of assessment, methods of payment were never standardized across the Florentine domains. Payments in the city above a certain amount were still regarded as loans. In the Florentine contado, the new survey was utilized much as the old. It was used, for example, for imposing direct taxes *ad libram* (that is, in proportion to the wealth registered), and also for distributing quantities of salt across the countryside, which the families were obligated to purchase in proportion to their size and their wealth. The new survey of the contado, redacted in 1434, which replaced the Catasto, is referred to without distinction as a *catastum seu extimum*.[59] The fiscal innovations which marked the Catasto in the city of Florence did not change by very much the fiscal policy pursued in the countryside.

The use made of the Catasto in the district seems to have been only

58. AC 2, f. 65, 30 June 1428. On traditional Florentine policy toward the "non habentes," see Fiumi, 1957, pp. 338–39, and Barbadoro, 1929, p. 402.

59. The new survey was underway by April 1434. ASF, Provv. 125, f. 57, 29 April 1434, mentions the obligation to conduct a new survey of the contado five years after the preceding survey had been finished (July 1429). The new survey was apparently finished before January 1435, as a document mentions "in distributione catasti seu extimi nuper finita"; ibid., f. 194, 19 January 1435.

partial and sporadic. The surveys of Pisa's city and countryside were certainly used to distribute salt.[60] In February 1429, the Florentine government with a view to reducing its debts, imposed a special tax of one penny per pound of fiscal assessment, per year; it was to be collected for the following three years from all families registered in the Catasto of the contadini, the distrettuali, the foreigners, and the clergy.[61] This is, to our knowledge, the only time the Florentine government attempted to collect, on the basis of the Catasto, a uniform tax over all its territory. (Residents of Florence had to pay, at a different rate, during the same period, a *catastum ad perdendum*, that is, a true tax for which no repayment was promised.) In spite of the energies and moneys expended in its redaction, the Catasto of the district seems never to have been utilized in the routine collection of taxes. The subject cities continued as in the past to collect their own taxes, to pay the Florentine officials who were sent to rule them, and to contribute to the costs of military contingents in time of war. In the fifteenth century, the fiscal machinery of the Florentine state functioned largely as in the past. The architects of the great reform of May 1427 had clearly envisioned a uniform, integrated, fair, and efficient fiscal system, extending over all the Florentine domains. But in the final reckoning, they could not overcome the weight of tradition.

IV. The Making of the Survey

Between 1427 and 1430, when the Catasto was principally redacted, 31 citizens (one died in office) served as the *Dieci Ufficiali.* They were granted a generous budget, and were aided in their work by a small army of notaries and clerks.

THE STAFF

The officials themselves show an average age of about 48 years; they were, by Florentine standards, mature men, close to the apex of their careers. They were not, however, recruited from the richest households. None belonged to the 50 wealthiest families (according to the Catasto itself); only two belonged to the hundred richest households; and twelve to the top 500.[62] Their private fortunes show a rough balance between holdings in

60. ASF, Provv. 119, f. 317, 27 September 1429: "Salis distributio in civitate et comitatu Pisarum," with an explicit reference to "quilibet descriptus in catasto civitatis Pisarum."

61. ASF, Provv. 120, f. 26, 6 March 1429: "Impositio trium catastorum ad perdendum et denarii unius pro libra pro diminutione montis." The text of the provision mentions the "catasto districtualium forensium et clericorum," even though all of these surveys were still being redacted.

62. For the names, ages, and rank in wealth of these thirty-one officials, see Herlihy and Klapisch-Zuber, 1978, Appendix 2, Table 2, p. 630.

land and liquid assets. This indicates that most were engaged in some commercial activities. The Catasto was not, as we have seen, favorable to mercantile capital, but its administration required mercantile skills.

To accomplish their mission, the Dieci needed the help of a large office and staff. From July 1, 1427 they leased the Davizi Palace.[63] They stocked it with furniture, torches, candles, tallow, and stationery. In September, they employed Lorenzo di Palla di Nofri Strozzi as treasurer—a son of the city's richest citizen, who was not yet 22 years old (he was born November 8, 1405). Ironically, Lorenzo was himself to fall into tax arrears in 1431, as did his father shortly after.[64] At various times, they sought the help of other specialists—accountants (*rationerii*), assessors (*stimatores*), and lawyers. The normal term of employment did not exceed two months, and the size of the staff consequently varied in relation to the kind of work it was accomplishing. In June 1429, as the office rushed to complete the census of the Florentine contado and of Pisa, 78 clerks were employed, some at 6 florins per month and others at 5. Presumably, the staff was even larger under the third officials (1429–30), who were finishing the survey of the district and correcting the numerous errors uncovered in the other sections of the document. Unfortunately, the loss of the administrative records for 1429–30 precludes us from watching this great bureaucratic enterprise at its busiest moment.

The clerks who prepared the document were drawn from several sources. Some were notaries, and many of them came from rural villages. Apparently, they were accustomed to moving temporarily into the city, whenever their services were required. But many more clerks did not have formal notarial training. Their ranks included many young men like Lorenzo Strozzi, some with famous Florentine names, who had only recently embarked on a business career. Service at the office gave them a salary and an opportunity to observe the ways of merchants.[65] The ability of the government to recruit such large numbers of clerks is a tribute to the high levels of literacy and of arithmetical training in Florentine society.

The staff fulfilled numerous functions. On the basis of the original declarations submitted by the taxpayers, the clerks prepared clean and corrected copies and entered them into large registers (*campioni*). They performed the laborious calculations required to determine the tax assessment. And they

63. Between 28 May and 30 June 1427, the Office was located at Santa Maria Novella. The Davizi palace was rented for 45 florins per year (AC 3, f. 33, 17 June 1427)—later raised to 60 florins (AC 9, f. 3, 1 July 1432).

64. On 28 August 1431, in a drawing for the sixteen standard-bearers, Lorenzo di messer Palla di Nofri Strozzi was declared to be "in speculo." ASF, Tratte, 198, f. 91.

65. See the extended discussion of the recruitment of personnel in Herlihy and Klapisch-Zuber, 1978, pp. 80–84. Along with beginners in a business career, older but poor businessmen seem to have supplied many clerks for the Catasto Office.

copied out the principal results into summary volumes (*sommarii*) They checked the veracity of the declarations. They investigated denunciations made against taxpayers. And they sought, as best they could, to correct the numerous errors which became visible as the survey progressed. In fact, the clerks succeeded in maintaining only the campioni, and not the summaries, reasonably correct. For this reason, the campioni, even more than the other versions of the survey, must be regarded as the true Catasto.

COLLECTING AND CORRECTING

In the city of Florence, the work progressed with relative dispatch. Many urban declarations bear a date from late June or early July—particularly July 12, 1427. During the ensuing twelve months, the clerks prepared sixteen volumes of campioni (one for every ward) and the four summaries (one for every quarter). While this work continued, citizens were allowed to amend their declarations. They added brides or babies and cancelled members who had passed out of the household either by marriage or by death. These changes make of the urban Catasto a register—doubtless crude, but nonetheless instructive—of population movements over one year (July 1427 to June 1428). The Catasto of the city of Florence was formally deposited at the public treasury and officially closed to further changes on June 30, 1428—only one month behind the official schedule.

To be sure, errors were discovered almost at once in the completed survey, especially in the four summaries, which seem to have been hastily redacted. This is perhaps the reason only one of the four registers has survived.[66] The officials had to allow changes in the supposedly closed registers. But in spite of some omissions and inaccuracies, the redaction of the urban Catasto had been done thoroughly and well, and very nearly on schedule.

The redaction of the remaining five surveys posed much more formidable problems. The first officials had begun collecting declarations from residents in the contado and in many parts of the district, including the territories of Pisa, Arezzo, the Val di Nievole, and the Val d'Arno di Sotto. But the declarations proved to be gravely deficient. On July 2, 1428, immediately upon entering office, the second officials ordered that the inhabitants of all the above regions either correct their declarations or submit them anew; if they had hitherto failed to provide a declaration, they had to do so before August 8, 1428.[67] Confusion in the countryside meant that the surviving registers of portate contain many duplicate declarations. Characteristically, the clerks chose as the basis for the official version the portata

66. The summary is preserved in AC 298.
67. AC 4, f. 3, 2 July 1428.

which showed the larger quantity of wealth. Consequently, the "family photographs" of Tuscan rural households preserved in the Catasto were taken over the duration of some thirteen months, from July 1427 to August 1428. Usually, it is not possible to know the exact date that these rural declarations were prepared and filed.

From August 1428, the clerks prepared the rural campioni and calculated the assessments. While they labored, residents of the rural areas were allowed to amend their declarations, and to note births, marriages, and deaths which altered the composition of their households. Some volumes of campioni show many changes, and others almost none.[68] Presumably, the first volumes completed were subject to the most corrections, while those finished late could not be altered. In the countryside, as in the city, these references to births, deaths, and marriages illuminate—even if poorly—vital movements in the rural population. By dint of great effort, the second officials were able to deposit in the communal treasury the Catasto of the Florentine contado on June 30, 1429.

The preparation of the Catasto of the district suffered even further delays. On July 30, 1428, the second officials ordered residents of the district to submit new or corrected declarations before September 15.[69] They succeeded in finishing the Pisan registers and deposited them in the treasury on June 30, 1429, as their term of office expired. But the second officials could not complete the survey in other areas of the district. Several subject cities—San Gimignano, Colle, Castiglione Fiorentino, Cortona, Montepulciano, and above all, Volterra—stubbornly refused to submit declarations. But through a combination of threats and reassurances that traditional privileges would be respected, most regions of the district filed their declarations by July 1429. By then, only Volterra and the Florentine Romagna, a mountain region over which Florence exercised a loose control, still remained unsurveyed.

An inventory prepared on June 30, 1429, as the second officials were leaving office, shows exactly the progress of the survey two years after its inception:[70]

68. For example, AC 307, the first of four registers containing the declarations from the rural quarter of Santo Spirito shows numerous corrections, while AC 310, the last of the group, reveals very few. Presumably, AC 307 was the first to be finished and was thus subject to numerous, later corrections. It also may be that the survey of the entire countryside began in the second year with the quarter of Santa Croce. At all events, the addition of brides is especially abundant in this part of the countryside.

69. AC 4, f. 16, 30 July 1428, letter addressed "universis et singulis rectoribus districtus fiorentini."

70. AC 1, ff. 26 ff. The inventory is printed in full in Herlihy and Klapisch-Zuber, 1978, Appendix 3, Document 1, pp. 632–36. The inventory does not in fact mention the Catasto of the city, which had been completed and closed a year earlier.

1. The Catasto of the city, consisting of the portate, sixteen volumes of campioni, and four summaries, had been finished and closed to changes one year earlier, on June 30, 1428.

2. The Catasto of the Florentine contado included seventy-seven volumes of portate, thirty-one of campioni, and four summaries, and had been officially closed on June 30, 1429. It was, however, soon to be subject to additional corrections.

3. The Catasto of Pisa and of its "former county," which included eighteen volumes of portate and ten campioni, had similarly been finished and closed on the above date. But here, too, additional corrections had to be allowed. For other areas of the district, the office had gathered "writings and registers," but the assessments had not yet been "either finished or closed." This survey had to remain open for another year.

4. The survey of the clergy and of religious institutions consisted of six volumes of "writings and registers." The clerks had not yet begun to calculate the assessments.

5. The survey of guilds consisted of only a single volume.

6. The survey of foreigners similarly included only a single volume.

The last three surveys were well behind schedule, but in spite of their comparatively small size, the officials gave them scant attention.

The chief task of the third officials was to bring to completion the Catasto of the district. The effort provoked an armed rebellion at Volterra in October 1429.[71] In suppressing the uprising, Florence also finally wrung from the population the long-demanded declarations. On June 30, 1430, the third officials deposited the registers of Volterra and its former territory. The great survey of the lay population was finished.

How complete was the survey?[72] Only two parts of the Florentine domains largely, or entirely, escaped assessment. The Florentine Romagna, lying beyond the Apennine watershed, had recently been devastated by war, and the Signoria had reestablished its authority only with grave difficulty (1427–30). Perhaps 15,000 persons inhabited this mountainous frontier. Within the Florentine domains, descendants of great feudal families—the Conti Guidi, the Ubertini, or the Fibindacci—and their retainers held fiefs in the rugged terrain between Pratomagno and Monte Falterona. To judge from the extent of these privileged enclaves (nearly 300 square kilometers) and their population as recorded in the Grand Ducal census of 1555,

71. On the resistance at Volterra, and its complicated connections with Florentine domestic politics, see Herlihy and Klapisch-Zuber, 1978 pp. 40–42, and pp. 92–94.

72. The following estimates of omissions from the Catasto are based on the extended discussion in Herlihy and Klapisch-Zuber, 1978, pp. 137–64.

they probably contained, in 1427, some 6,000 or 7,000 persons. In all, in rough estimate, probably between 20,000 and 25,000 Florentine subjects escaped assessment because of the lands they inhabited.

Other exempt groups were far smaller. We would place the number of foreign visitors to Florence between 400 and 500, and foreign mercenaries between 12,000 and 19,000. Residents who claimed special exemptions from taxes and Jews who lived under special fiscal arrangements were still required to file declarations, although much confusion surrounds their status. Their numbers were at all events small; for example, we have declarations only from some ten Jewish households scattered across the small Tuscan towns. By far, the largest group of exempt persons was the clergy. From the number of parishes and religious institutions in Tuscany, we would estimate their size at some 7,000 or 8,000 men and women. Together with their servants and wards—orphans and abandoned children, the impoverished, the sick and the aged in hospitals—the ecclesiastical population may have reached 10,000 or 11,000 persons.

In all, the true population of those living under Florentine rule in 1427 may have been as much as 20 percent greater than the 260,000 persons registered in the Catasto. Still, as with property so with persons: the Catasto registers not every Tuscan, but the active, settled members of the lay population—those who by their labors supported society, and with their numbers filled out its families and households. These are the people whom the redactors of the Catasto investigated with maximum rigor and admirable success. These too are the people on whom our own analysis will concentrate.

During their tenure the third officials also corrected the registers of the Florentine contado and of Pisa. On August 2, 1429, they drew up a list of sixteen common errors which required correction: garbled names; families placed in the wrong village; deceased or aged males wrongly charged with a head tax; numerous priests counted in their paternal families; foreigners taxed though legally exempt; properties listed twice; and so forth.[73] The officials constantly examined their own work, and their administrative records, which survive only partially, illuminate those areas where the great survey tended to be inaccurate or incomplete.[74]

In prosecuting fraud, the officials uncovered numerous instances of deception in declaring possessions, especially in rural areas, where the new methods of assessment departed from traditional ways and were received

73. AC 1, ff. 31 ff. The list of errors and methods to be followed in correcting them is printed in full in Herlihy and Klapisch-Zuber, 1978, Appendix 3, Document 2, pp. 637–40.

74. For the errors and frauds which the officials most frequently observed, see the tables presented in Herlihy and Klapisch-Zuber, 1978, pp. 95–99.

with scant enthusiasm. The listings of household members seem reasonably complete. A large family was likely to mean low taxes for its head. Many households probably wished to hide adult males or to falsify their ages, in order to avoid or reduce the tax upon the teste. We shall examine this distortion at length in chapter 6. In sum, the officials of the Catasto were able to complete a comprehensive survey of Florentine citizens and subjects, as the law of May 24, 1427, had directed them.

PRESERVATION AND ANALYSIS

In a strict sense, the reform of 1427 must be reckoned a spectacular failure. The Florentine government never again undertook a systematic survey of all its domains. Within the city of Florence, between July 9, 1428, and June 12, 1434, the Signoria collected on the basis of Catasti no fewer than 53 imposts.[75] But the old patterns soon recurred. Returns rapidly diminished after the first collection. Particularly after 1430, the number of citizens in tax arrears soared.[76] Dissatisfaction mounted, and the system was abandoned in May 1434. Several times in the fifteenth century, in 1458, 1469, and 1487, the government sought to tax the city on the basis of exact surveys, but the policy was never rendered permanent. The adoption of an assessment based exclusively on land rents, the Decima, in 1495, wrote a permanent *finis* to this grand experiment in fiscal reform.

The government's failure ever to redo the survey of 1427 had one happy result; it lent the document a lasting utility, and this helped assure its survival. The employees of the fiscal offices assiduously consulted this first Catasto in all subsequent surveys of the fifteenth century. Today, losses sustained by the Catasto archives remain minimal: two of the thirty-one campioni of the Florentine contado and another pertaining to the district; two volumes of the portate from the contado and one from the district; three summaries from the city, one from the mountains of Pistoia, and several from the northern contado of Arezzo and parts of the Val di Nievole and the Vald'Arno di Sotto are the only apparent losses.[77] As the survey exists in three versions, it is almost always possible to reconstruct lost parts of one version from the information preserved in the other two.

We have called the first Catasto a complete survey, but in one important

75. For the loans imposed, see Herlihy and Klapisch-Zuber, 1978, Appendix 1, Table 3, pp. 626–27.

76. The number of citizens declared ineligible to serve in the Tre Maggiori for reason of tax arrears rose from 25 in 1428, to 72 in 1429, to 71 in 1431, to 137 in 1432. See Herlihy and Klapisch-Zuber, 1978, Table 1, p. 46.

77. The volumes are preserved in ASF, AC, and in ASP, UFF. The thousand and more volumes in the Florentine deposit are described, but with many errors, in an inventory prepared in 1948. The best introduction to the Archives of the Catasto is now Conti, 1966. For a description of the Catasto of the city of Pisa, see Casini, 1964.

respect this is not so. To our knowledge, no contemporary cited, and none presumably knew, the grand totals—the sum of households and of persons it described and the amount of wealth it inventoried. Even the energetic Florentines had not the will or the means to make these interminable additions. But the data carried in this rigorously systematic survey are today easily convertible into machine-readable form and quickly analyzed by that versatile jinni of modern research, the computer. Even we, in preparing the Catasto's data for computer processing, had to limit our choices. We surveyed all households, and entered demographic information concerning all persons, but we carried the names only of the household heads. We did not register the inventories of possessions which the declarations preserve, but only the total value of properties grouped into three large categories (real estate, liquid assets, and shares in the public debt). In spite of these economies, our partial, machine-readable edition of the Catasto offers the computer a huge amount of data, in which to search for patterns.[78]

More than a century ago, in *The Civilization of the Renaissance in Italy*, Jacob Burckhardt called Florence of the quattrocento the "cradle of statistical science".[79] Today, the remarkable compatibility of the Catasto and the computer confirms the insight of this great historian.

78. Copies of this machine-readable edition of the Catasto are available at the University of Wisconsin, Madison; at Harvard University, Cambridge; and at the Ecole des Hautes Etudes en Sciences Sociales, Paris, and may be utilized by all interested scholars.

79. Burckhardt, 1929, 1:95.

2

Territory and Settlement

. . . Delle quali, essendo principale, la città è come il centro, posta nel mezzo di tutte. La quale essendo cinta di mure et di belli borghi, sono poi li borghi circundati dalle ville, et da esse ville similmente l'altre terre et castelli, le quali tutte chose sono come da uno magiore circulo da l'ultima circunstante regione circundate.

Within these concentric circles, the city is the first, placed at the center in the middle of all. The city is surrounded by walls and by lovely suburbs, and the suburbs themselves are encircled by villas. These enclose more distant villages and fortified places. And all this is surrounded, as in a larger circle, by outlying regions.

Leonardo Bruni, *Panegirico della città di Firenze*, 1403

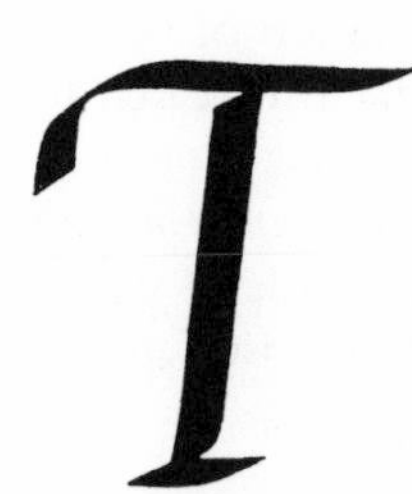

he Catasto offers historians a highly detailed, but still static picture of the Tuscan community in 1427. To use this treasury of data properly, we must inquire into its territorial and chronological setting. How extended were the Florentine domains in 1427 and how were they acquired and settled? And what were the demographic and social experiences of the Tuscan people in the tumultuous years preceding and following 1427? In this and the following chapter, we attempt to capture the historical moment, when the great survey was redacted and thus to impart movement and life to its massive statistics.

I. The Florentine State in the Fifteenth Century

In 1427 the Florentine commune ruled nearly the entire northern half of what is today the province of Tuscany. But the frontiers of the fifteenth-century principality show frequent divergences from those of the modern province.

BORDERS

To the northwest, Lucca and its territory remained an independent principality until 1847. Nearly the whole of the Garfagnana (the upper valley of the Serchio river), except Barga and Sommocolonia, escaped Florentine control. So also did Lunigiana, the small mountainous region set between Tuscany and Liguria on the Tyrrhenian coast. To the north, Florentine Tuscany in 1427 extended into the Apennines above Pistoia and Prato almost as far as the modern province. Toward the east, it pushed into the mountains well beyond the watershed to claim, in considerable measure, the northern slope of the Romagnole Apennines. To the east, departures from the modern frontier were even more frequent. Florence ruled the slopes of the Apennines as far as Lake Trasimeno in modern Umbria. Part of the upper valley of the Tiber river, including the town of Anghiari, was Florentine, but Borgo San Sepolcro was still a free commune in 1427. In this entire zone of mountains, the limits of Florentine rule rarely coincided with the watershed. The frontier strode across valleys and mountains, blithely ignoring the direction of ridges and the flow of waters. And numerous feudal enclaves, set within these frontiers and claiming special status, lent an especially complex design to the eastern borderlands.

To the south, between Lake Trasimeno and the sea, the frontiers of Florentine Tuscany show the largest deviations from those of the modern province. In 1427 Siena and its territory remained independent, and were not to be absorbed into the Florentine state until 1557. But Florence did rule over many towns that are now part of the province of Siena: Montepulciano, Radda, Castellina in Chianti, Colle, and San Gimignano. Toward the southwest, Florence claimed all the present territories of Pisa and of Volterra, as far as Campiglia; but Piombino on the coast, Suvereto, and the province of Massa Marittima lay beyond its sovereignty.

LANDSCAPES

This domain, which covered more than 11,000 square kilometers (about the size of the state of Massachusetts) was large for a medieval Italian principality.[1] Laid out in an arc, it included the entire length of the Arno valley. Hills, which give their unique stamp to the Tuscan landscape, occupied more than one-half its extent. They especially dominated the southern half of the Florentine territory. To the north, mountainous ridges, and the valleys or basins over which they towered, molded the landscape.

These parallel ridges, running from northwest to southeast, splintered the province into small territories (*paesi*), which long clung to independence. The county of Pisa, rimming the Tyrrhenian shore, occupied the lowest part of the Florentine territory in 1427. The ridge closest to the sea, formed in the northwest by the Ligurian mountains and the stately Alpi Alpuane, was continued in the Florentine domains by the Monti Pisani, "for which the Pisans cannot see Lucca." This ridge pressed the Pisan

1. By way of comparison, the duchy of Milan included in 1542 about 7,200 square kilometers, according to Beloch, 1937–61, 2: 201. The Genoese Republic claimed 6,000 square kilometers; Lucca, 1,100, ibid. pp. 362 and ff. Conti, 1965, pp. 237–39, places the area of the Florentine contado at 4,930 square kilometers. He also gives a map of the Florentine contado showing the modern borders of communes. For a description of northern Tuscany see Seronde *et al.*, 1970, pp. 3–6. See also the discussion regarding a classification by altitude of Tuscany into four zones by the Istituto Centrale di Statistica in Barbieri, 1966, pp. 28–30. For Orvieto, see Carpentier, 1962, p. 29; for Siena, Bowsky, 1981, pp. 1–22.

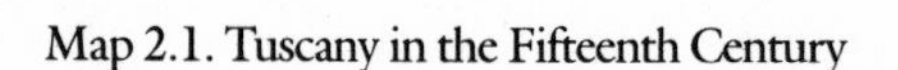

Map 2.1. Tuscany in the Fifteenth Century

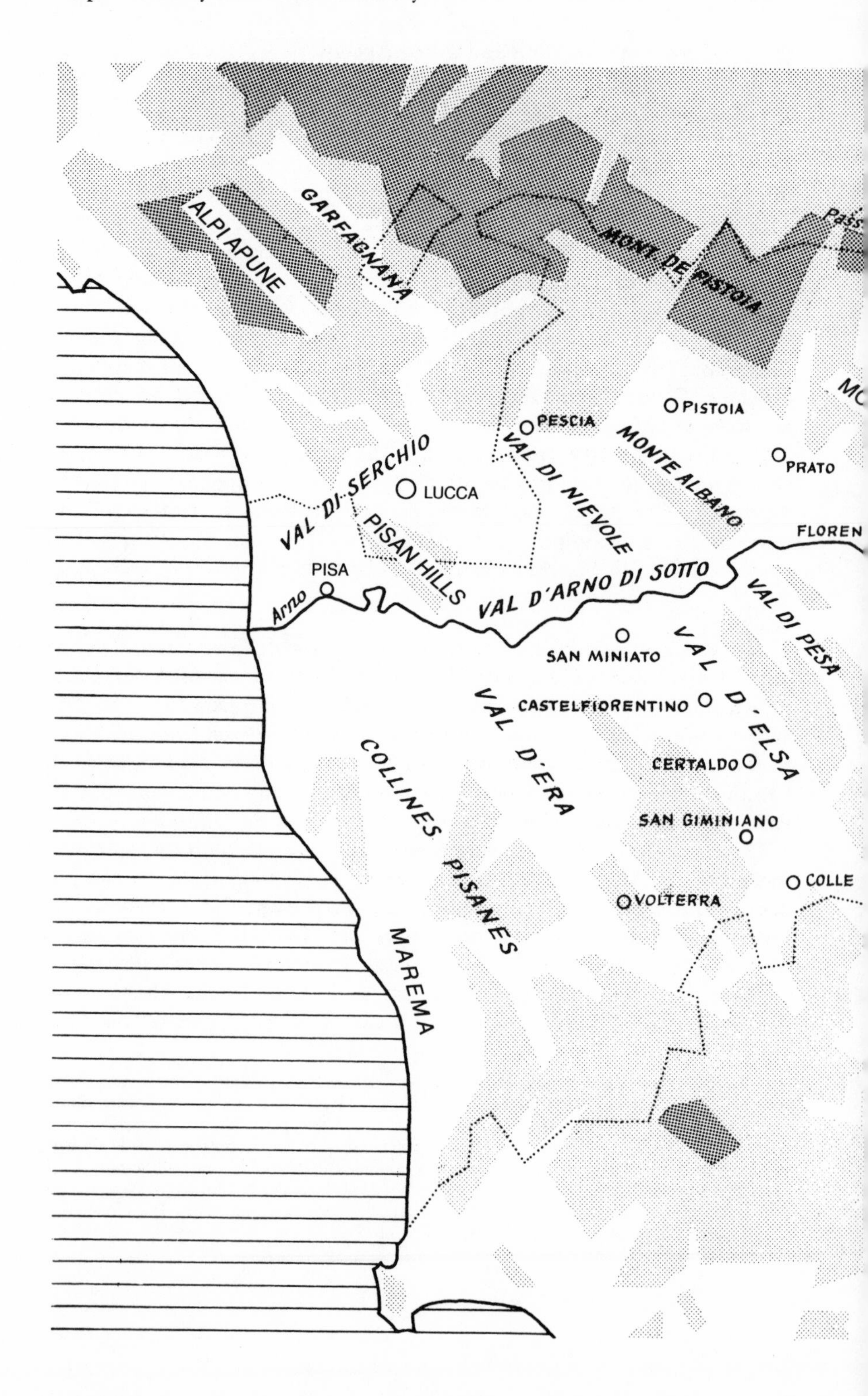

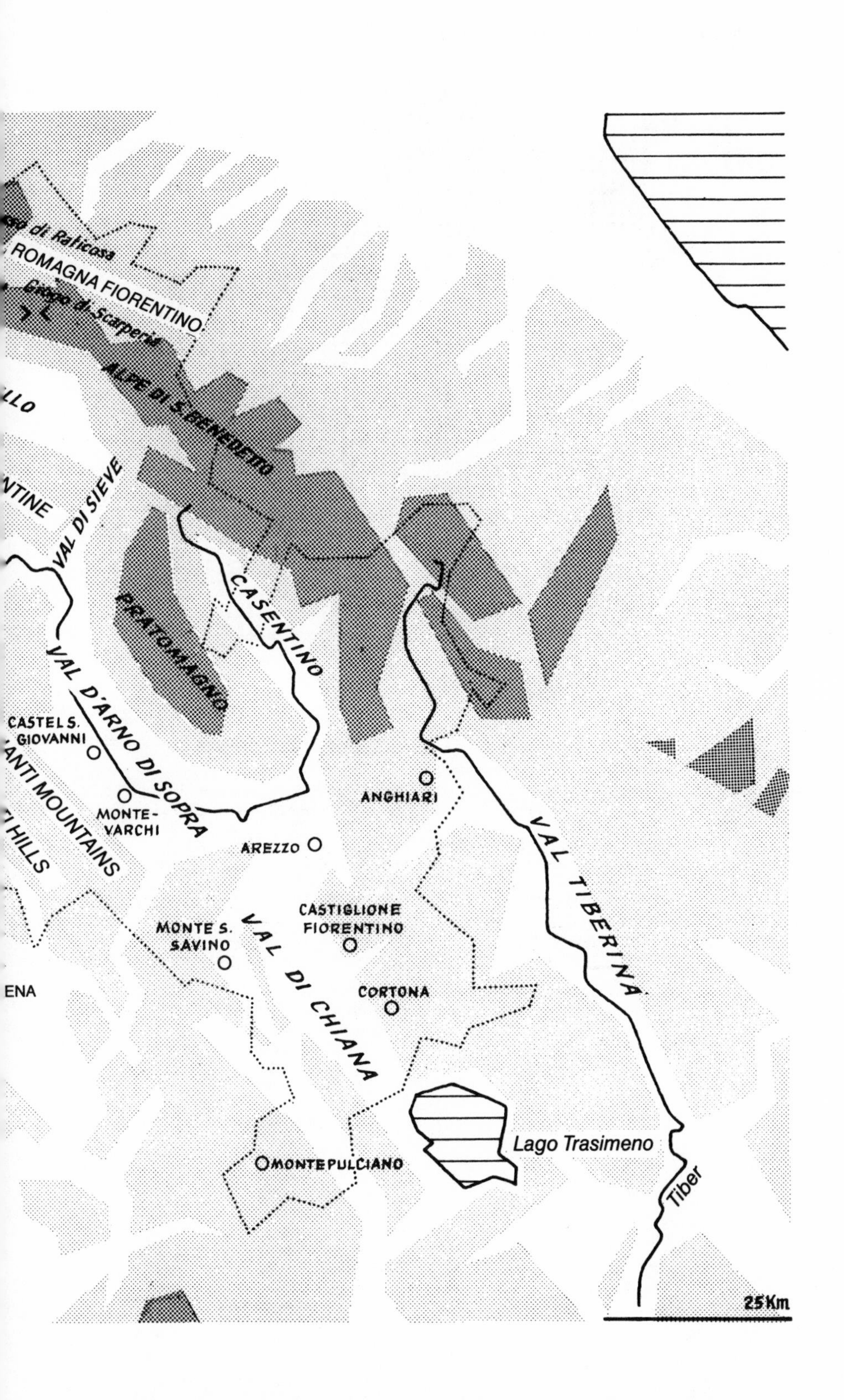

ROMAGNA FIORENTINO
Giogo di Scarperia
ALPE DI S. BENEDETTO
VAL DI SIEVE
CASENTINO
PRATOMAGNO
VAL D'ARNO DI SOPRA
CASTEL S. GIOVANNI
MONTE-VARCHI
ANGHIARI
AREZZO
VAL TIBERINA
CASTIGLIONE FIORENTINO
MONTE S. SAVINO
VAL DI CHIANA
CORTONA
Lago Trasimeno
MONTEPULCIANO
Tiber
25 Km

Map 2.2. The Administrative Divisions of the Florentine State, 1427

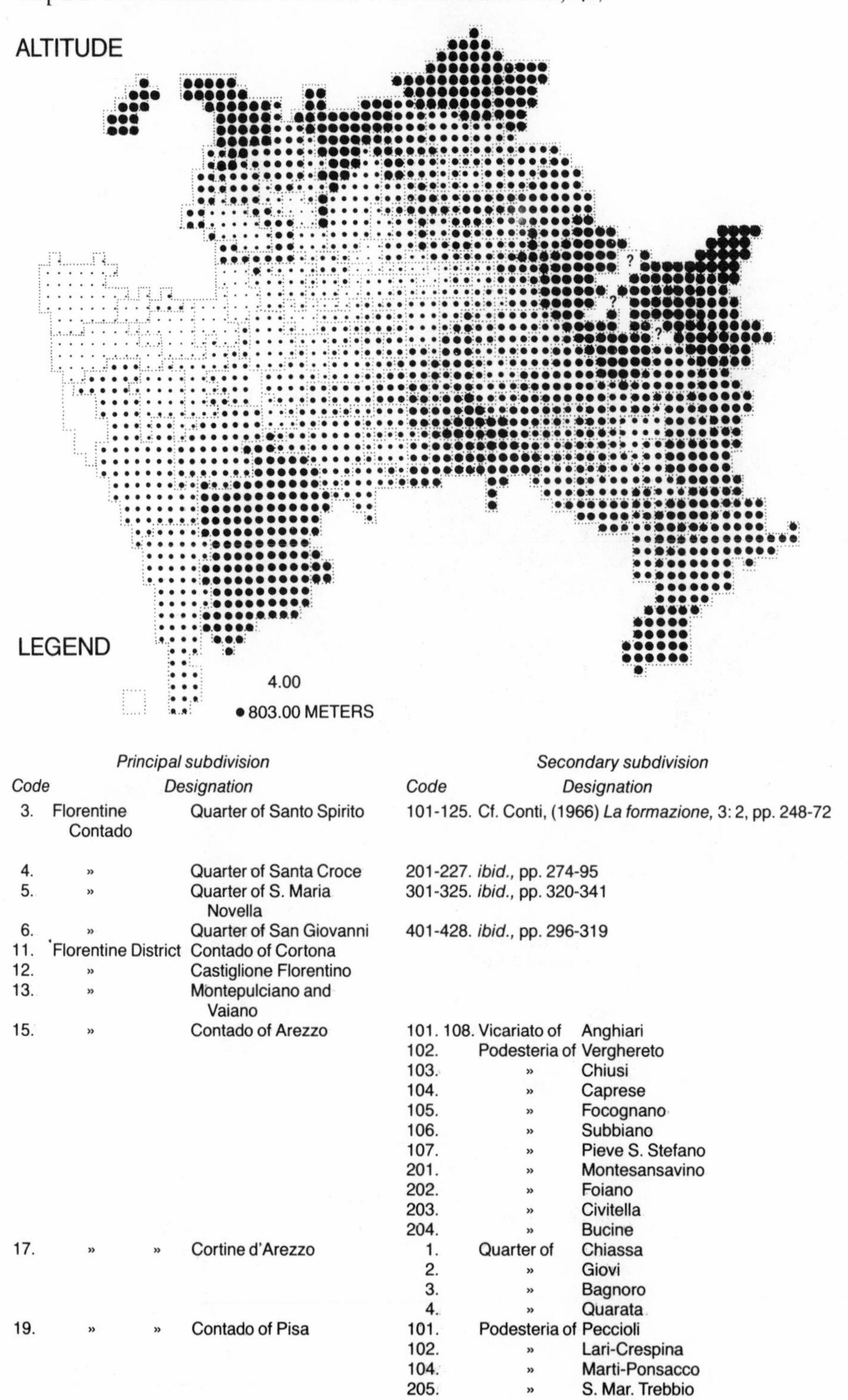

Principal subdivision			Secondary subdivision	
Code		Designation	Code	Designation
3.	Florentine Contado	Quarter of Santo Spirito	101-125.	Cf. Conti, (1966) *La formazione,* 3: 2, pp. 248-72
4.	»	Quarter of Santa Croce	201-227.	*ibid.,* pp. 274-95
5.	»	Quarter of S. Maria Novella	301-325.	*ibid.,* pp. 320-341
6.	»	Quarter of San Giovanni	401-428.	*ibid.,* pp. 296-319
11.	Florentine District	Contado of Cortona		
12.	»	Castiglione Florentino		
13.	»	Montepulciano and Vaiano		
15.	»	Contado of Arezzo	101. 108.	Vicariato of Anghiari
			102.	Podesteria of Verghereto
			103.	» Chiusi
			104.	» Caprese
			105.	» Focognano
			106.	» Subbiano
			107.	» Pieve S. Stefano
			201.	» Montesansavino
			202.	» Foiano
			203.	» Civitella
			204.	» Bucine
17.	» »	Cortine d'Arezzo	1.	Quarter of Chiassa
			2.	» Giovi
			3.	» Bagnoro
			4.	» Quarata
19.	» »	Contado of Pisa	101.	Podesteria of Peccioli
			102.	» Lari-Crespina
			104.	» Marti-Ponsacco
			205.	» S. Mar. Trebbio

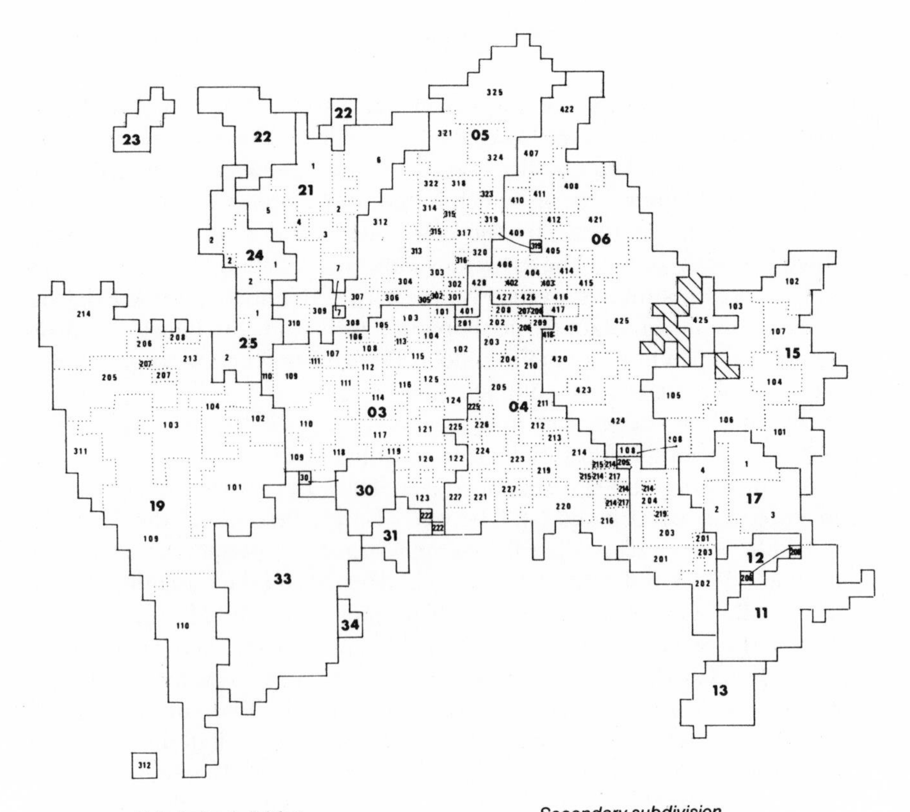

Principal subdivision			Secondary subdivision		
Code		Designation	Code		Designation
19.	Florentine district	Contado of Pisa (cont)	206.	»	Calci
			207.	»	Cascina
			208.	Commune of	Valle di Buti
			109.	Podesteria of	Rosignano
			110.	Capitanato of	Campiglia
			311.	Commune of	Livorno
			312.	Commune of	Castiglione d. Pescaia
			213.	Podesteria of	Vico Pisano and Pontedera
			214.	»	Ripafratta
21.	»	» Circonstanze and Contado of Pistoia	1.	Circ.	Porta S. Andrea
			2.	»	Porta Guidi
			3.	»	Porta Caldatica
			4.	»	Porta Lucchese
			5.	Podesteria of	Larciano
			6.	»	Tizzana
			7.	»	Montale
22.	»	» Mountains of Pistoia			
23.	»	» Garfagnana			
24.	»	» Val of Nievole	1.	Podesteria of	Buggiano
			2.	»	Pescia
25.	»	» Val d'Arno di sotto	1.	»	Castelfranco
			2.	»	Fucecchio
30.	»	» San Gimignano			
31.	»	» Commune of Colle			
33.	»	» Contado of Volterra			
34.	»	» Communes of Silliano and Montecastelli			

territory hard against the sea. Further inland, a second line of highlands, the Monte Albano, closes off the lower Arno valley from Florence, and is continued toward the southeast by the rugged Chianti mountains. Still further inland, the mountainous massif, which looms over Florence from the north, is continued in the southeast by the heavy mass of Pratomagno. To swing around this steep barrier, the Arno must flow in a great loop between Arezzo and Florence. Continuing to the east, the massifs dominating the Val di Chiana carry this line of ridges to the shores of Lake Trasimeno. Finally, the main ridge of the Apennine mountains follows the same orientation, although this is at times obscured in the complex quilt of landscapes.

Between these ridges run long valleys or eroded basins (*conche*). For much of the Middle Ages they remained ill-drained and marshy, forming fever-ridden sinks and obstructing travel. Thus, the marshes of Altopascio and Fucecchio overlay the land between Lucca, Pescia, and the Arno. In the middle Arno valley, marshlands approached the peripheries of Pistoia and Prato. The Val d'Arno di sopra, near Arezzo, and the Casentino, or the valley of the upper Arno, contain similar landscapes. The Mugello, too, or valley of the Sieve river to the north of Florence, shares this characteristic, as does the Val di Chiana between Arezzo and Lake Trasimeno.[2] To the south of the Arno river, its tributaries—the Era, the Elsa, and the Pesa—were likewise set between long bands of hills. These ill-drained bottom lands set the obvious limits to jurisdictions in medieval Tuscany.

Thus, between the coast punctuated by few good ports, the Apennines traversed by difficult passes, and the zone of hills and unhealthy valleys, Florence in 1427 ruled a land of contrasts. To examine how these lands were ruled requires a brief review of the reasons for which, and the ways by which, Florence acquired them. Here, too, geography exerted a powerful influence.

THE GATHERING OF THE TUSCAN LANDS

In extending its domains, the Florentine goverment aimed at two principal goals: control of the Apennine passes guarding the approaches to the city from the north and east, and the acquisition of ports on the Tyrrhenian coast. The absorption of Prato (1350), Pistoia (1351), Arezzo (1384), and Cortona (1411) carried the Florentine domains deep into the mountainous hinterland of Tuscany. To reach the sea, Florence established a protectorate over Volterra (1361) and purchased Pisa (1406) and Livorno (1421).

The network of roads within Tuscany itself also affected the expansion of the Florentine state. The road system that had grown up in ancient times

2. On the reclamation of plain lands along the Ombrone and the Bisenzio, see Conti, 1965, pp. 63–74.

continued to serve Tuscany well into the thirteenth century.[3] The one great loss was the Via Aurelia. This highway had paralleled the coast south of Pisa through lands which in the early Middle Ages became infested with marshes and exposed to pirates. The Aurelian way was abandoned. These ancient routes had converged not on Florence, but on the older Etruscan centers of Fiesole, Arezzo, and Volterra.

From the thirteenth century, a "road revolution" occurred in Tuscany, as Johann Plesner observed some years ago.[4] It had two dimensions. Roman roads tended to follow the crests of ridges; they were high, dry, and easily maintained and defended, but they rarely went from station to station in a straight line. Road builders were now challenging the ill-drained bottom lands and tracing their routes in straight and short segments from town to town.

Moreover, the attraction of the Florentine metropolis was warping the traditional network of roads. In the early Middle Ages, interregional traffic predominantly followed two lateral axes, oriented as the terrain, from northwest to southeast. To the east, the ancient Via Flaminia Minor joined Arezzo to Bologna, traversing the Mugello and the Casentino. It linked Bologna directly with Rome. In suppressing the feudal clans perched on the Apennine slopes (the Conti Guidi in particular), Florence gained control over a segment of this highway and turned the traffic toward itself. At the other extreme of Florentine territory, a new interregional and international highway, the Via Francigena, or Strata Romea, had grown up in the early Middle Ages, replacing the now abandoned Via Aurelia. It linked Rome with France, and crowds of pilgrims and petitioners moved across it. Descending from the north along the Tyrrhenian shore, it passed Lucca and then swung inland to Altopascio and Fucecchio, where it again turned south. It crossed the Arno and proceeded up the Elsa valley to Siena.[5] In the fourteenth century, Florence gradually acquired dominion over the many communes of the Elsa valley, located near or on this great pilgrim highway—San Miniato al Monte, Castelfiorentino, Certaldo, San Gimignano, and Colle.

In absorbing segments of these routes, Florence drew to itself a flourishing traffic. Through this "commercial displacement," in the phrase of Federigo Melis, Florence became a principal entrepôt in the lucrative trade flowing between northern Europe and the lands of the eastern Mediterranean.[6]

3. See M. Lopes-Pegna, 1971; Repetti, 1833–64, 5: 709–40.

4. Plesner, 1938. See also the revisions proposed in this thesis by Thomas Szabo in his "Presentazione" to the new edition published in Florence, F. Papafava ed., 1980, pp. i–xiv. See also idem, 1977.

5. Lopes-Pegna, 1971, pp. 58–67; Fiumi, 1961, pp. 28–33.

6. F. Melis, 1966, pp. 206–13.

II. *Administration*

In 1427 the shape of the administrative divisions within the Florentine state and the statute under which they were governed still reflected the age and phases of Florentine expansion. The Florentine administration rested upon a triple distinction among the city, the county, and the district. The archives of the Catasto itself are faithful to this tripartite division.

THE CITY OF FLORENCE

In 1427 the city of Florence was enclosed in the *terzo cerchio*, its third circle of walls—some 8.5 kilometers in length, surrounding an area of nearly 5 square kilometers.[7] The second circle of walls, laid out in the late twelfth century, had sufficed for barely 100 years in this period of rapid expansion. The new walls, erected in stages between the late thirteenth century and 1333, were designed with an eye to further growth. That growth, in medieval times, never came. The terzo cerchio embraced numerous empty spaces, gardens, orchards, vineyards, and the like. In 1427 the now greatly diminished urban population floated within these walls like a child in a suit of armor.

The walls visibly ringed the urban community, but they did not cleanly and consistently separate urban and rural jurisdictions. They did not, for example, follow ecclesiastical boundaries. Within Tuscany, certain ancient churches had a traditional right to administer baptisms and perform all principal religious functions. Such a church was called a *pieve* (Latin *plebs*), and the territory it served was its *piviere*. With time, numerous small parishes grew up in the vicinity of the ancient pievi. These were called "peoples" or *popoli*; they served the rural population as centers of worship, but they could not administer baptisms.

The city of Florence formed a part, but not the whole, of the piviere of San Giovanni, which extended some 5 kilometers beyond the city walls and included some 30 rural parishes. Moreover, 10 urban parishes stretched beyond the circle of walls and contained several hundred rural hearths. The largest extensions pushed westward from the city along the banks of the Arno; there, the valley, pressed between hills upstream from Florence, widened into a plain and invited suburban settlement. Still, the number of families (398, with 1,770 persons) settled in these rural extensions of urban parishes represented only 3.8 percent of the 10,172 hearths of the city. The city floated within its oversized armor, and hardly anywhere strained against it.

Florentine fiscal tradition—both the earlier Estimo and the Catasto

7. For the history of Florence's walls, see Davidsohn, 1962, 7:475, 479–85.

itself—treated those parts of the piviere of San Giovanni located "outside the walls," as belonging to the countryside. In this measure at least, the terzo cerchio adequately defined the fiscal city.[8]

The city itself, at the end of the twelfth century, had been divided into six wards, called *sesti* or sestieri. They were named after city gates and their origins are probably associated with the construction of the second circle of walls. These divisions were retained until August 1343. The expulsion of the would-be despot, the Duke of Athens, in that year, gave occasion to an administrative reform. So also, probably, did the growth of the city and the recent completion of the third circle of walls.

The new dispensation divided the city into four quarters, which no longer took their names from gates, but from the principal religious sanctuaries they contained.[9] To the south, the old sestiere of Oltrarno was renamed the quarter of Santo Spirito; this undoubtedly reflects the recent, prodigious growth of this part of the city. To the west, the sestieri of Borgo and of San Pancrazio formed the quarter of Santa Maria Novella—named for the great church of the Dominican friars. To the east, a smaller quarter of Santa Croce was laid out between the river, the walls, and a limit defined by the streets of Calimala and Por Santa Maria—the ancient *cardo maximus* of the Roman town. Named for the principal Franciscan church, this quarter completely absorbed the old sestiere of San Piero Scheraggio.[10] Santa Croce included all the political centers of the city, the palace of the podestà and the communal palace. The religious heart of the city—the cathedral and the baptistry—lay within the last quarter of San Giovanni. It absorbed the former sestieri of Porta Duomo and of Porta San Piero, with the exception of a fringe of territory along its southern confines, which was assigned to Santa Croce. San Giovanni was the only quarter that did not abut the river. The two largest quarters were Santo Spirito and San Giovanni. In 1427 Santa Croce contained only 17.7 percent of the urban households, and Santa Maria Novella contained 20 percent.[11] In these latter

8. Still in the 1450s, the baptismal registers of San Giovanni consistently note if the parents of the newborn baby lived outside the walls.

9. On the old organization by quartieri, then by sestieri, see Stahl, 1965, pp. 97–98. On the nature of the reform in 1343, see Plesner, 1938, p. 83. Guasti and Gherardi (eds.), 1866–93, 2:57, publish the text instituting the quarters, dated 11 August 1343. G. Villani, 1845, bk. 18, 4:37–40, also gives a description. Donato Velluti, 1914, pp. 163–65, gives, together with a description of the old sestieri, an account of the prevailing political atmosphere at the time of the reform. Apparently, the grandi and the popolani of the sestiere of Oltrarno thought that they were not receiving their just share of communal offices. Velluti was himself a member of the commission which effected the reform.

10. Guasti and Gherardi, 1866–93, 2:57. On the limits of the quarter in the eighteenth century, see *Stradario*, 1913.

11. Out of 9,781 hearths in the city, Santa Croce contained 1,731 and Santa Maria Novella, 1,952.

quarters the fabric of urban settlement remained loose; the plain allowed the population to spill outside the walls.

The basic urban community was the parish, the popolo or *cappella*, although only the baptistry of San Giovanni and the cathedral could baptize and perform all religious services. Still, the parishes provided a place where neighbors and relatives could gather, discuss, and organize.[12] Giovanni Villani counted 57 of them in about 1340—a number which remained the same a century later.[13] However, the Catasto of 1427 did not divide the urban population according to parishes, although it frequently alluded to them. A larger communal subdivision, the gonfalone, had from the thirteenth century gradually replaced the parishes for purposes of administrative, military, and political organization. Each gonfalone possessed an armed company of popolani who were first organized to enforce the antimagnate legislation of the thirteenth-century popular commune. Each had its own banner and heraldic symbol. The number of gonfaloni passed from 20 to 19 in 1306; the reform of 1343 reduced the number to 16—4 per quarter. The gonfalone cut across parish boundaries; in the absence of the needed, painstaking research, their exact limits in 1427 remain unknown.[14]

The administrative divisions within the city thus manifest a double ordering: the old parishes grouped together in the pieve of San Giovanni, and the newly formed secular gonfaloni and quarters. The decision, in 1427, to base the urban survey on the newer divisions registers to some extent the laicization of administrative practices in the fifteenth century. Elsewhere, though not everywhere, in Tuscany a comparable tendency is evident: the government counted its people according to secular units and dispensed with ancient ecclesiastical divisions.

Several Tuscan cities grouped the urban parishes or wards into quarters, as in the capital. Thus, the eight contrade or *ottavi* of Prato, named after the eight gates of the city, were joined into quarters.[15] Eight *contrade* (previously, three *terzieri*) made up the city of Volterra in 1429. Pistoia, San Gimignano, Arezzo, and Pisa similarly adopted, at various times, division into quarters.[16] But other towns remained divided into sestieri or terzieri. This was the model which Florence itself had followed up to 1343. It appears with particular frequency in the southern and eastern regions of the Florentine domains. Cortona, Castiglione Fiorentino, and Pisa (before the thirteenth century) retained the tripartite division, found also at Siena.

12. On parishes as communities, see Cohn, 1980; and Davidsohn, 1962, 5:276–81.

13. Villani, 1823–25, 6:185.

14. See Herlihy and Klapisch-Zuber, 1978, p. 123, Table 7, for the correspondence between parishes and gonfaloni.

15. Fiumi, 1968, pp. 31–33.

16. On the appearance of the quarter of Kinzica at Pisa, see Cristiani, 1962, p. 164. On Pistoia, see Herlihy, 1967, p. 58. On San Gimignano, see Fiumi, 1961, p. 151.

The Catasto grouped the town populations of Tuscany into widely differing units. At Prato, it respected the contrade but ignored the quarters; at Pistoia, it recognized both the quarters and the popoli; at Florence, as we have seen, it used the quarters and the gonfaloni, but not the popoli, at least not systematically; and at Arezzo, no subdivision was retained. Differing local traditions partially explain this diversity. But above all it indicates the incomplete standardization of administrative and fiscal procedures across the Florentine territory.

CONTADO AND DISTRETTO

In 1427 the old county or contado of Florence contained no more than 40 percent of the lands it governed. At one time the contado had closely corresponded with the territories of the twin bishoprics of Florence and Fiesole, over which the commune had successfully established its direct rule. But from the 1330s into the early fifteenth century, Florence, in its expansion, brought under its rule lands belonging to other Tuscan and even Umbrian dioceses. All or much of the vast diocese of Arezzo to the southeast, of Pistoia to the northwest, and of Pisa and Volterra to the west passed under Florentine domination. To the south, the Florentine state further absorbed several Sienese parishes, and also the lands of San Miniato, Fabbrica, and Monterappoli, formerly under the jurisdiction of the archbishop of Lucca.

In 1427 the district included, in whole or in part, eight different dioceses. The communes which Florence had progressively subjugated from the late thirteenth century had usually brought an endowment of lands—*corti*, for the smallest towns; contadi elsewhere. Much like Florence itself, these communes had gradually extended their authority over these rural regions between the eleventh and thirteenth centuries. The corti or contadi of San Gimignano, Colle, Castiglione Fiorentino, or Montepulciano were very tiny, claiming an average size of only 100 square kilometers. But Cortona with some 350 square kilometers, Volterra with 800, or Pistoia with almost 900 brought big rural areas into the Florentine domain. Finally, through the annexation of Arezzo in 1384, and of Pisa in 1406, Florence absorbed two huge territories, with areas of some 1,500 and 2,000 square kilometers respectively; they were the largest counties in Tuscany, after Florence's own.

The distinction which the Florentines maintained between contado and distretto remained, in the epoch of the Catasto, ambiguous. In a strict sense, the contado designated the countryside stretching beyond the walls of Florence, but certain jurists gave it a much larger meaning, assigning it nearly all the territories subject to Florence.[17] In the Catasto, the distinction

17. Kirshner, 1971, pp. 226–64, especially pp. 240–42.

primarily reflected the traditional fiscal status of the territory: lands subject to the Florentine rural tax, the Estimo, formed the contado; lands free of that burden did not. Accordingly, the varying terms under which the subject cities had accepted Florentine rule affected their status. For example, the inhabitants of Prato—Florence purchased the city for 175,000 florins in 1351—were regarded as *comitatenses originarii*. This facilitated the territory's integration into the contado. San Gimignano, on the other hand, submitted to Florence by treaty; it claimed special rights of self-government and exemption from direct Florentine taxation.[18] Similar pretensions sustained Volterra and Cortona in their violent opposition to the introduction of the Catasto in 1428–29.

The status of Pisa and its countryside was especially complicated. The Florentine government repeatedly sought to integrate "the former county of Pisa" into its own contado and then relented.[19] The government thus joined the regions of the Pisan county north of the Arno to the Florentine rural quarter of Santa Maria Novella; lands to the south were given to the quarter of Santo Spirito.[20] Portate from the Pisan countryside (though not the campioni) occasionally allude, in 1427–30, to this attempted annexation.[21] This policy of assimilation doubtlessly also prompted the provision of May 23, 1429, which extended the Catasto to Pisa and its countryside. In contrast, the city of Pisa enjoyed a distinct status; alone among the towns of the district, its citizens could claim a personal deduction for the mouths of household members, as did the residents of the capital.

In regard to Volterra, Florentine policy also showed shifts and inconsistencies. After suppressing the uprising of 1429, Florence punished the rebellious town by annexing its countryside.[22] Its inhabitants were required to submit their portate, "like the other inhabitants of the county of Florence." In 1431 the Florentines relented and returned the countryside to Volterra's jurisdiction. This was equivalent to a restoration of fiscal privileges, as the inhabitants were no longer subject to the Florentine Estimo.

18. Ibid., pp. 256–58. The agreements regulating the submission of these communes may be found in Guasti and Gherardi, 1866–93, passim.

19. The usual phrase in the portate of 1427 is: "del contado per l'adietro di Pisa" or "de comitatu olim Pisarum," sometimes with the addition, "nunc de comitatu Florentie."

20. In 1416 a commission, utilizing methods closely resembling those of the Florentine Estimo, examined and assessed the sostanze of peasants in the "former county of Pisa." The Estimo immediately preceding the Catasto survey was similarly applied to the Pisan contado. See Molho, 1971, p. 35, n. 30.

21. These scattered references from the portate are limited to declarations from the lower Arno (podesterie of Peccioli, Marti, S. Maria a Trebbio, Vico, and Cascina) and are never transcribed into the campioni.

22. The names of the localities of Volterra joined to the county of Florence are given in Provv. 120, f. 406, 23 Dec. 1429. The provision regarding Volterra is only partially reproduced in AC 2, f. 37.

In sum, at the start of the fifteenth century, the distinction between subjects of the district and those of the county was less a matter of law and constitutional theory than of fiscal practice. To belong to the Florentine contado meant primarily to be subject to the Estimo. In the fifty years preceding the Catasto, Florence made sporadic efforts to enlarge its own contado and thus to integrate its subjects under a common fiscal regimen. This process of integration and assimilation was still far from complete in 1427.

CONTADI AND THEIR DIVISIONS

The large contadi incorporated into the Florentine state were commonly divided into small circumscriptions, which were charged with judicial, military, or fiscal functions. Their number and names often represented projections of urban divisions over the surrounding rural lands. Thus, the largest territorial unit of all, the Florentine contado, was, like the city, initially divided into quarters. In the early thirteenth century the city was redivided into sestieri, as was the county, even though the rural sestieri were strikingly unequal in area.[23] In this epoch the administrative and economic bonds linking urban and rural sestieri seem to have been especially close and authentic. Numerous immigrants were entering the growing city, and they preferred to settle in the urban sestiere closest to their rural homes. Usually, they retained close ties with their native villages. Curiae, or courts within the sestieri, assumed various juridical functions for their subjoined rural sixths.

This administrative framework grew obsolete by the middle of the fourteenth century with the continuing growth of the city and shifts in the road routes. The return in 1343 to a division by quarters, in both city and countryside, further reflects a new taste for symmetry. The new rural quarters (and the urban as well) were laid out in roughly equal size. Florence remained at their point of intersection and the focus of the jurisdictional pattern. But the intimate ties between urban and rural zones, characteristic of the thirteenth-century commune, were now greatly loosened. The new rural quarters were left largely without social, administrative, or ceremonial functions. By then the urban population was fixed in size and would soon suffer catastrophic losses. Decreasing immigration doubtlessly weakened contact with the countryside.

The quarter of Santa Maria Novella, about 1,200 square kilometers in size, extended to the northwest and included even Prato and its county.

23. Plesner, 1938, pp. 78–83, shows that this reorganization by sestieri aimed at a fairer distribution, at the local level, of the responsibilities for the maintenance of the road network inherited from antiquity.

The Arno river formed its southern limit and separated it from the quarter of Santo Spirito. Santa Maria Novella claimed the chief lowlands of the Florentine county—the plain stretching from Florence to Pistoia and, beyond the Monsummano, to the Val di Nievole. It also embraced stretches of the Apennine hinterland, climbing up the mountains to the pass of Raticosa behind Firenzuola. The road from Florence to Borgo San Lorenzo and to Firenzuola roughly defined its eastern border. This fact alone illustrates a basic distinction between these new jurisdictional units and those which had preceded them. Since antiquity, administrative divisions had overlapped important stretches of major roadways, particularly across difficult terrain and had assumed principal responsibility for their maintenance. The new rural quarters were, in contrast, set between the principal highways.

North of this road, the vast quarter of San Giovanni (about 1,600 square kilometers in area) also climbed the Apennines and stretched well beyond the watershed, embracing a large, thinly settled, mountainous zone. It included the high valleys of the Lamone, the Senio, and the Santerno—streams which flowed toward the Adriatic. San Giovanni also claimed much of the valley of the upper Arno. Its boundaries toward Arezzo cut across the massif of Pratomagno and brought within its area the high valley of the Casentino (the upper Val d'Arno) between Bibbiena and Dicomano—a region dotted with feudal enclaves.

Laid out along the left bank of the Arno, the remaining two quarters of Santa Croce and Santo Spirito were smaller in size, about 950 and 1,100 square kilometers respectively. The road running south into the Chianti roughly marked their mutual border. These quarters showed a considerably less variegated landscape than the regions to the Arnos's north. The hills which formed most of their terrain ran from the northwest to the southeast, steadily gaining in height up to the pinnacle (800–900 meters) formed by the Chianti mountains. Of the two, Santa Croce was the hillier; the terrain of Santo Spirito rarely surpassed an altitude of 200 meters.

Several other regions surveyed by the Catasto repeated this division into quarters. Around Pistoia, the boundaries of the four suburban circumscriptions, the *circonstanze*, formed a cross with the city at its center. So also did the cortine of Arezzo. Typically, these rural jurisdictions bore the names of urban quarters or of principal urban gates. Many Italian regions—Perugia, Orvieto, and Siena, for example—show this projection of urban divisions into the countryside.[24] But this linkage of urban and rural units remained no more than superficial in the epoch of the Catasto. The citizens of Santa

24. On Perugia, see the extensive treatment of its urban form in Grohmann, 1981, 1:27–67; for Orvieto, Carpentier, 1962, p. 29; for Siena, Bowsky, 1971, and more recently, 1981.

Croce, for example, inhabited an urban sector north of the Arno, while the rural quarter of the same name was laid out to the south. In the countryside, smaller, more vital units than the sprawling quarters subsumed the chief administrative functions.

PIVIERI AND PODESTERIE

Between the large rural quarter and the tiny popolo or commune, several jurisdictional units, differing markedly in origin, function, and size, were interposed. In 1419 officials known as the "cinque ufficiali del contado e del distretto," drew up a list of the circumscriptions in the entire Florentine domains, excepting only San Gimignano, Colle, Montepulciano, and Volterra.[25] Ten vicariates (*vicariati*) divided up the some 11,000 square kilometers governed by Florence, and were in turn divided into 85 *podesterie* and 3 *capitanati*. Forty-seven units of these diverse types covered the Florentine county alone.

The center of the Florentine territory was distinguished by the dominance of pivieri, of which there were 94 in 1427. Apparently replicating the ancient *pagus*, this rural community took care of roads and bridges.[26] The pivieri's unexpected shape at times bears witness to their "pontifical" or "bridge-making" functions. Occasionally, they spanned rivers around an important bridge. More often, they straddled a ridge and commanded both slopes. Their central churches were thus often located on top of ridges along the course of Roman roads, which characteristically avoided valleys and lowlands. In the thirteenth century the reclamation of valleys and the rerouting of highways carried traffic away from these ancient centers, usually to the lowland fringes of their territories. At the same time they lost their functions as military zones. From 1293 the rural peoples came to be grouped under a captain into large units, called *leghe* or leagues, which typically included several pivieri.[27] But for all its archaism, this ancient grouping survived, and in surveying its own contado in 1427, Florence adopted it as its basic fiscal unit. We too have retained it as the basis for the maps we present, rather than the small, subordinate popolo.

In the thickly settled regions around Florence, the pivieri formed a dense matrix of small territories. At the contado's periphery, on the other hand, they could attain imposing size. There, too, several ecclesiastic pivieri were sometimes combined to form still larger, totally secular jurisdictions. Thus Dicomano, in the quarter of San Giovanni, included the pievi of S. Maria a Dicomano, S. Detolo, S. Bavello, and Corella.

25. ASF, Miscellanea repubblicana, CII, insert. 1, ff. 1–180. The list sets the authorized expenditures in each circumscription of Florentine territory, from the vicariati to the popoli.

26. Mengozzi, 1914. Plesner, 1938, p. 20, gives a different interpretation.

27. Davidsohn, 1962, 4, pt. 2:365–67. Plesner, 1938, p. 24, 74.

Toward the end of the thirteenth century, Florence fused these ancient territorial divisions into larger and more homogenous administrative units.[28] We have already mentioned the military leagues in the countryside. In the thirteenth and fourteenth centuries, Florence further established units of civil administration, the podesterie, under peace officers, the podestà. These military and juridical divisions gradually fused, and their importance continued to grow after 1427, largely at the expense of the ancient pivieri.

In the district, the counties of San Miniato and Prato similarly included several pievi, but the Catasto did not make systematic use of these ecclesiastical divisions in surveying the population. The officials preferred to group the people into larger units; podesterie or vicariati. The same practice prevailed in the corti of San Gimignano, of Colle, and in the counties of Castiglione Fiorentino, of Cortona, and of Volterra. A close inverse relation existed between density of settlement and size of the preferred administrative unit. This is most apparent in the Apennine districts commanding the passes to Lombardy and Emilia. There, the huge vicariates of Firenzuola and of Podere Fiorentino and the capitanate of Castrocaro were comparable in area to the contado of Cortona or the province of the Val di Nievole.

Thus, in 1427, the Florentine government shepherded the residents of its domains into vastly different administrative units. Within its own contado, it largely respected the ancient ecclesiastical divisions into pivieri. In the more thinly settled district, it preferred larger, essentially secular circumscriptions. In both town and countryside, across the Florentine domains, administrative units remained in 1427 unsystematized. In fact two administrative cadres, one inherited from the Church and the other of purely secular origins, overlaid the land.

RURAL POPOLI AND COMMUNES

The same ambivalence is apparent on the lowest administrative level, that of the tiny rural community, the popolo and the rural commune. Comparable in character to the pivieri, of which it formed the body, the popolo contained a small chapel or church and honored the name of a titular saint—some even preserved the titles of churches which had been abandoned or had vanished.

The popolo had very early assumed important secular functions. Above all, those who prepared the rural Estimo—the substantial residents of the

28. See the list drawn up in 1419 by the *Cinque ufficiali del contado e del distretto*, in which 35 out of 85 podesterie are called "podesteria e lega di. . . . " (ASF, Miscellanea repubblicana, CII, insert. 1). Three others, the leghe of Tagliaferro, Cintoia, and Gangalandi, are not clearly identified as podesterie. For a list of leghe in 1415, see *Statuta*, 1778–81, 3:693–706.

village—worked within its area.[29] The local priest often aided the illiterate peasants in preparing their inventories, and the village chiefs—rectors or *massai*—helped collect the declarations, verify data, enter deaths and births, and explain absences. They formed essential wheels in the Florentine fiscal mechanism.

The popoli at times included only a few families, and at times were large agglomerations of more than 100 hearths. On the average, their households numbered between 10 and 15.[30] Most centers which attained or passed the figure of 80 or 100 hearths were not called popoli, but *comuni*.[31] (A comparable, usually smaller aggregation of hearths was the *villa*.) The rural communes might contain only a single parish or, as at San Miniato and Empoli, might collect several. They appeared at times as a federation of villages, which, individually, had developed as popoli. The commune of Gangalandi thus gathered together 5 distinct popoli, and Carmignano collected 6 *stanze* or scattered villages. Borgo San Lorenzo was composed of 7 *opere*; at the beginning of the fifteenth century they still had not fused into a single community.[32] The regions which counted the largest number of comuni and ville were found in the western limits of the Florentine county and in the mountainous districts to the north and east. There, nearly 8 percent of rural settlements were called ville, and between 12 and 13 percent comuni.[33] These were, on the whole, prosperous regions, once governed by important free communes such as Prato and San Miniato. They claimed a long tradition of self-government, which explains the proliferation of rural comuni and ville within them.

So also, in the large counties of Pistoia, Pisa, Arezzo, Volterra, the lower Val d'Arno, and the province of the Val di Nievole, the rural population was principally distributed into communes, with some rare ville interspersed among them. The villa remained the basic division in territories belonging to the smaller communes—San Gimignano, Colle, Cortona, and Castiglione Fiorentino.

The Catasto of 1427 thus shows successive layers of administrative cadres—laid down in different ages, serving different purposes, and finally

29. Conti, 1966, pp. 4–5.

30. The Catasto includes, for example, 107 popoli or ville with fewer than ten hearths in the sole quarter of Santo Spirito. Some communes are equally tiny, such as Leporaia, with one family, or Coiano, with nine. The big popoli are usually urban parishes, like those of Empoli or San Miniato.

31. To take another example from Santo Spirito, 6 communes out of 36 had more than 100 families.

32. Communes of the mountain regions, such as Valle Fiorentina or Palagio Fiorentino, in the piviere of Gropina in the east of the contado, were similarly comprised of a scattering of localities with their own parishes.

33. 11.5 percent of comuni in Santo Spirito and 13.8 percent in Santa Maria Novella.

adapted to meet Florence's fiscal needs. The most venerable was the lattice of popoli gathered into pivieri, which were in turn ghosts of ancient pagi; but also visible were the new secular units, the urban gonfaloni and quarters, and the corresponding rural divisions. These cadres not only recalled the past, but they also certainly reflected different types of settlement and different traditions of political organization and forms of public life.

III. Settlement

In 1427, as the following chapter will further illustrate, the Tuscan population had recently plunged to its late-medieval nadir, stabilized, and would not grow again for another 40 years. The Catasto shows us the Tuscan community even as it was adjusting to enormous losses and seeking a new equilibrium.

DENSITIES

Viewed across the major administrative divisions, the balance of regional settlement appears highly clustered. Florence's own contado, with 42 percent of the land, held 62 percent of the population. Even if the capital is excluded, some 56 percent of the people inhabited the Florentine county, leaving only 44 percent to the surrounding district.

Also notable is the small but visible displacement of population toward the western half of the Florentine domains, that is, toward the sea. The quarters of Santa Maria Novella, Santo Spirito, and the territories set between them and the coast held, without regarding Florence, 59 percent of the population. Still, the position of Florence was not eccentric. Inhabitants living north of the Arno (50.5 percent of the total) only slightly exceeded those south of the river (49.5 percent). The capital very nearly held the fulcrum, where the weight of population in all directions balanced.

The maps accompanying this chapter illustrate these distributions, but they require some initial comment. The distributions regard only the lay population, not the clerics, whom the Catasto omitted. Some zones are left blank, or carry a question mark, in order to indicate that the relevant data are either lacking or defective. The drawing of boundaries raised special difficulties. Almost always for our period, they are unknown and were probably shifting. In laying them out, we resorted to surmises seasoned by prudence. For the most part, the lines we drew follow the modern boundaries of provinces and communes whenever the redrawings of the nineteenth and twentieth centuries did not completely obliterate their ancient course. The communes of today seem rather often to replicate the territory of an ancient piviere or podesteria.[34] When we could not utilize this guidance, we followed orthographic divisions—ridge tops and valley bottoms. These conjectures regarding boundaries affect the calculations of densities, but not the rates and percentages which our maps carry; these are independent of area.

DISTRIBUTIONS

Map 2.4, illustrating densities of rural settlement, excludes agglomerations with more than 1,000 inhabitants. Colle is not represented on this map because its rural and urban inhabitants are all but indistinguishable in the survey. Map 2.5 reintroduces the inhabitants of towns with more than 1,000 residents. When these towns do not comprise an independent jurisdiction represented on the map the population is shown as if distributed across the surrounding lands, which correspond often enough to the territories of the present communes.

The overall density of the lay population in the Florentine domains falls between 24 and 24.5 persons per square kilometer. The small margin of uncertainty reflects our indecision whether or not to include in the calculations the large (210 square kilometers) area of marshy land downstream from Pisa. Without the Florentine metropolis, the density falls to 21 persons per square kilometer. If we add the estimated ten or eleven thousand ecclesiastics missing from the survey, the overall density still scarcely attains 25 inhabitants per square kilometer.

The most significant concentrations of rural population were located to the west and the northwest of Florence, within the triangle Florence—Empoli—Pistoia. There, the Monti della Calvana beyond Prato, the Monte Albano to the west, and the hills to the Arno's south mold the rim of a large basin. The plain forming the floor of this basin was of comparatively recent settlement. Still, in 1427, densities there could reach as high as 140–60 persons in the immediate environs of the city of Florence itself (the pivieri of San Giovanni, Brozzi, and Santo Stefano in Pane); they then fell progressively to 60–80 in the eastern areas of the elongated piviere of Signa. At the confines of Pistoia and Prato, rural densities ranged from 30–50 persons—considerably higher than the general mean. The basin of the middle Arno supported a comparatively thick population.

Other segments of the Val d'Arno formed axes of dense settlement: the lower Val d'Arno from Pontedera to Pisa, down river from the capital, and in the opposite direction, the valleys from Florence to Pontassieve and from Castel San Giovanni to Bucine. Densities in these zones ranged from

34. In the maps published here, we have used the piviere as the base for illustrating various spatial distributions.

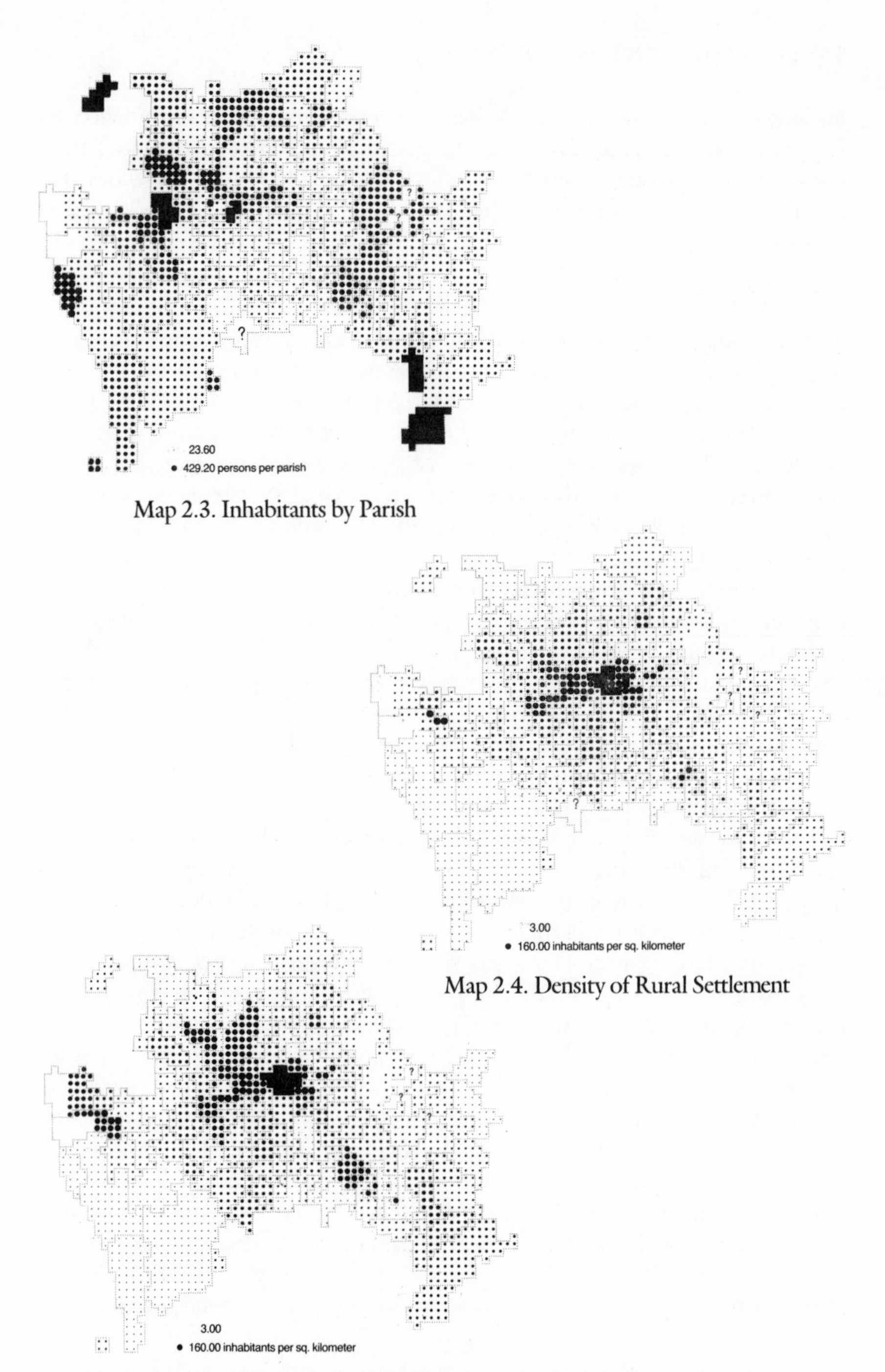

Map 2.3. Inhabitants by Parish

Map 2.4. Density of Rural Settlement

Map 2.5. Density of Settlement (Cities Included)

50 to 100 and were, for the most part, higher in the western than in the eastern sectors.

The western hills and the slopes of the interior basins also constituted regions of relatively dense settlement, at least equal to the overall average. To the southwest of Florence, the repeated ranges which formed nearly all the quarter of Santo Spirito and the counties of San Gimignano, Colle, and San Miniato, supported a population at densities higher than the average (25–40). So also did the hills which stretched across the quarter of Santa Croce, southeast of Florence, up to Figline in the upper Val d'Arno, and the heights which dominated the city from the north (the pivieri of Cercina, Petroio, and Larciano). On the other hand, in the contado's south, densities fell below 25 persons per square kilometer in the mid-Chianti region (the pivieri of Gaville, Monteficalli, Panzano, and Santa Maria Novella) and in the southern pivieri of the quarter of Santo Spirito (the pivieri of San Lazzaro, San Appiano, and San Donato in Poggio). To the east, the steep slopes of Prato Magno, the narrow Val di Sieve running up from Pontassieve into the Mugello, the low hills surrounding Arezzo, the eastern rim of the Chiana depression, the regions of Cortona, Castiglione Fiorentino, and Montepulciano, and finally the hills which looked over Pisa and the lower Val d'Arno all supported densities slightly below the regional average. All were ridges or hills dominating an interior depression—a basin or valley. These formations were among the more typical features of the Tuscan landscape.

Areas within the Florentine contado of still lower densities (between 10 and 20 inhabitants per square kilometer) were the zones of high hills and rugged mountains: in the Chianti, the pivieri of Sant'Agnese, Spaltenna, and San Giusto in Salcio; the Monte Morello up from Florence, and the massif which separated the city from the Mugello to the north; the vicariates of Firenzuola and of Podere Fiorentino, laid out on the slopes of the Apennines beyond the basins of the Mugello and the Casentino; and the Alpe di San Benedetto above Dicomano. Densities at this low level marked even bigger stretches of the district: the Pisan hills of Lari, Marti, Buti and Vico, the northern half of the county of Arezzo, and the mountains of Pistoia and of Barga.

Regions of lowest settlement (fewer than 10 persons per square kilometer) were the mountain of Verghereto to the north of the county of Arezzo, the monti del Chianti properly so called, to Florence's south, and the territories facing Siena (San Polo in Rosso, San Leonino, and San Marcellino). These are all border zones, often ravaged by mercenary bands. To the west, the two counties of Pisa (density 12.7 persons) and of Volterra (density 8.9 persons) appear almost deserted over large stretches of their territories, particularly in their coastal zones, the Maremma.

Scrutiny of these maps shows the marked contrasts in settlement densities across the Florentine domains: between regions close to the capital and outlying mountains, and between the contado as a whole and the thinly populated district. The territories of the subject towns attained densities comparable to the Florentine only in San Gimignano and Colle (26 persons on the average). Still, the county of Pistoia, where plain and mountain were sharply contrasted, shows again the attractiveness of the lowlands. The county claims a density of 18.5 persons, or 22.5 if the mountains are excluded. The *circuitus* or *provincia* of the Val d'Nievole and the Val d'Arno di Sotto, with a density of 20.8 persons, shows a similar pattern. Two factors, in sum, seem to have influenced powerfully movements of rural settlement in the period of the Catasto: a preference for lowlands, and a tendency for population to cluster around the Florentine metropolis.

CLUSTERED AND DISPERSED SETTLEMENT

In some Tuscan regions, the inhabitants gathered into large villages, the relative weight of which, in relation to the surrounding countryside, remained imposing in spite of the sharp drop in human numbers. Elsewhere, they lived in scattered hamlets or farms, the isolation of which seems all the greater when many—two out of three—were deserted and marked for disappearance.

In the center of the Florentine contado, the regions of *mezzadria* (sharecropping) were distinguished by dispersed settlement around a tiny center. The inhabited core of these popoli melted, so to speak, as its population scattered across the compact and isolated farms, the *poderi*, on which the sharecroppers had to reside under the terms of the contract.[35] The concentration of parcels into single, compact, dispersed poderi reflects the search for improved productivity. The old system of working scattered parcels, usually without the help of animals, was a form of subsistence agriculture, using little capital investment; it drew habitations into one or several villages within the communal territory. The spread of the mezzadria provoked an inverse movement of people, a dispersal out of the old, small centers, even while maintaining overall dense settlement on the land. Despite demographic decline, moderate or high rural densities continued to characterize most of the regions where the mezzadria was common. Those regions display, besides a tight network of old and tiny parishes, an administrative framework formed of remarkably small units, often devoid of real centers.

35. On rural settlement see Conti, 1965, especially chap. 1. See also Klapisch, 1972c; Jones, 1968, p. 232; Cherubini and Francovich, 1973. For deserted hill villages at Pistoia, see Herlihy, 1967, p. 71.

How closely do the numerous large communes found beyond the Florentine contado or within the outlying and mountainous zones reflect not just administrative convenience, but real patterns of settlement? The data from the Catasto are often ambiguous, and do not readily allow a judgment whether the population assigned to a big commune really inhabited a big center. The clerks, for example, often attributed a place of origin, "da N. ," to a family head.[36] Does this indicate recent immigration into the administrative center, or continued habitation in place N.? We can take as an example Caprese, in the county of Arezzo. The Catasto presents it as a big commune of 275 hearths and 1,100 persons. But examination of the numerous references to places of origin shows that significant numbers of the population lived scattered across some 30 hamlets, villages, or isolated farms. Many, even among those who called themselves "from Caprese," inhabited cabins or shacks—often destroyed and often rebuilt—in the open country, although they kept a permanent house in the central castello. In these shacks they stored grain and sometimes sheltered animals, and they fled to their protected homes in times of war and epidemic. But usually, reference to a place of origin among the family heads of Caprese identified those who did not own a house or refuge in the fortified center. For this reason, the registered population of central villages probably ought to be somewhat reduced, and some residents counted as belonging to the countryside.[37] For this reason too, it is difficult to judge the degree to which the inhabitants of these large jurisdictions also lived in big and concentrated villages.

The example of Caprese thus recommends prudence when we examine a map of settlement drawn on the basis of the Catasto. Examples of a double residence could be multiplied, especially in the eastern regions, in the county of Arezzo, where war had worked havoc shortly before the Catasto was redacted.[38] Even in a prosperous province, such as the Mugello, peasants might multiply their residences to take advantage of the protection offered by fortified centers.[39] Caprese, Anghiari, and many other localities

36. See the discussion of this problem in Emery, 1952, pp. 43–50; and R. Lopez, 1954, pp. 6–16.

37. Particularly at Colle, Caprese, Gangalandi, Carmignano, Borgo San Lorenzo, Palaia, and San Gimignano.

38. For example, at Anghiari, the castle served as a refuge for numerous members of the commune who lived in cabins in the open country (see AC 242, f. 161, 190, passim). Although half destroyed, the castelli and castellari of Pulicciano, Pieve a Quarto, and Libbia in the cortine of Arezzo, performed a similar service. At San Nastagio, one inhabitant out of three or four held a house or palazzo in the circuitus of a place called Mulinelli, "la quale habita a tempo di guerra." Other examples would be, in the mountainous zones of the contado of Arezzo, the castelli of Baldignano, Valsavignone, Montoto, and Sigliano, which gathered in the residents of the burnt and destroyed villages of Collelungo and Sitignano. For further examples drawn from the Catasto, see Jones, 1968, p. 223, n. 4.

39. See the comments of Morelli, 1956, p. 101.

strikingly illustrate this phenomenon of shifting domiciles, characteristic of the closing Middle Ages. Peasants hesitated between the rationalization of their labors, which required settlement close to their fields, and security, which the old circle of walls still promised. The continuing attraction of fortified places is especially evident, in 1427, in zones which had recently been exposed to military operations and to the depredations of the mercenary bands. These were the counties of Pisa and of Arezzo, and the Romagnole mountains. The destruction and the fear which frontier zones (and those areas disputed for decades by Florence and its neighbors) painfully and repeatedly experienced, worked to slow the diffusion of the mezzadria, which required dispersed settlement.

Map 2.3 presents a simplified picture of the average size of the administrative units—popolo or commune—by piviere. Variations in the size of these units are quite striking. The zones of high rural density are also those where the localities are the smallest. People grouped themselves into villages which were so much the larger as their number was fewer. But the exceptions to this overall pattern are also interesting. The Arno valley, an axis of dense settlement, also supported big localities both upstream and downstream from the city. Conversely, some regions of thinly populated hills carried a scattering of tiny settlements: the hills and mountains of the Chianti, the cortine of Arezzo, the countrysides of San Gimignano and of Castiglione Fiorentino, the massif which separates Florence from the Mugello, and the mountains of the Podere lying to the north.

Moreover, large villages and small towns lay like beads on the slopes above valleys and basins. The strings they formed stood out against the even scattering of the tiny popoli in the hill zones. Villages with more than 400 or 500 inhabitants thus followed one another in a vast crescent which ran from Vico, in the territory of Pisa, up to Pescia, in the Val di Nievole. Parishes with more than 200 or 300 inhabitants—big by Tuscan standards—were laid out with regularity along the lines dividing the slopes from the plains: between Florence and Pistoia, on the flanks of the Mugello, above the upper Arno valley, and on the gentle heights which rise above the Val di Chiana.

Roads also influenced the location of these large villages; like the villages themselves, they avoided the marshy and menacing depths of the valleys. Altitude also had an unmistakable influence. The quarter of San Spirito, the greatest part of which (over 90 percent) fell below 200 meters in altitude, counted the largest number (66 percent of the total) of tiny centers and the fewest communities claiming more than 200 inhabitants (11.1 percent). Santa Maria Novella contained numerous large villages (47.5 percent of all villages with from 101 to 800 inhabitants). Their presence primarily reflects the quarter's extended stretch of mountains.

URBAN CENTERS

In examining regional variations in settlement densities, we have usually regarded towns as localities with more than 1,000 inhabitants. On that basis, they are limited, to the number of 18, in the distribution of Tuscan settlement.[40] This threshold is, of course, artificial. Many large villages or small towns, containing 800–1,000 inhabitants, were already urban agglomerations; they differed hardly at all from small communities counted as towns—from Anghiari, for example, an administrative and military center, or Castiglione Fiorentino, a small gathering of rentiers and of administrators standing close to an important highway. Places occupying the margin between village and town are San Godenzo (824 inhabitants), Bibbiena (830 inhabitants) and Caprese (968 inhabitants at most)—all three set at the confines of lands of the feudal *conti*. Joined with them too should be Terranuova (914 inhabitants) in the upper Val d'Arno; Foiano (956 inhabitants) near Montesansavino, on a stretch of the via Cassia in the Val di Chiana; Lamporecchio (884 inhabitants) where the Monte Albano met the marshy plain of Fucecchio; Fucecchio itself (858 inhabitants), where the Via Francigena crossed the Arno; and finally Barga (916 inhabitants), a small administrative and industrial center of the Garfagnana. A wide gap separates these towns from smaller communities. Only Agliana, a large agricultural village on the plain of Pistoia, falls in the next lower category—communities with 700–800 inhabitants. Does this indicate that the character of communities changed once they surpassed 800 residents?

To investigate this hypothesis, we made use of a standard technique developed by geographers to study the distribution of communities within regions.[41] We entered on a graph (see Figure 2.1) the size of communes along the horizontal axis, using a logarithmic scale. The vertical axis is measured according to a Gaussian scale, that is, it reflects the distribution of values in the normal, bell-shaped probability curve. On this scale are represented cumulative percentages of the towns classified by increasing order of size. If the distribution of the size of the communes is "log normal," then the cumulative percentages ought to be distributed along a straight line. This would indicate that there exists a constant relation between the rank of the localities and the logarithms of their size. The graph

40. We did not, however, follow this division in subsequent tables. Urban communities are usually taken to be Florence, the six principal cities, and 18 or 20 minor towns. The number of the latter varies, according to whether Montepulciano and Castiglione Fiorentino are included or not; this we indicate in the tables.

41. See Berry, 1961, pp. 573–88, on the application of this method to cities with more than 20,000 inhabitants; Prost, 1965, pp. 117–59; Haggett, 1973, pp. 115–23. On the distribution of communes with fewer than 300 inhabitants, see Biraben, 1973, pp. 19–21. We thank Dr. Biraben for aiding us in applying this test to Tuscany.

allows us to identify homogeneous groups of localities. In this instance, it should help us determine the threshold at which Tuscan communities form a new group. The group which includes the largest Tuscan cities may be classified as urban.

The graph we have constructed shows an unmistakable break in the line at the class of localities possessing 700 to 800 inhabitants; here, we believe, is the decisive transition from rural village to small city. Communities above this threshold were fulfilling authentically urban functions. Their services (chiefly tertiary in character—administration, education, legal work, and the like) gave them a certain independence from their nearby, surrounding territory.

URBAN AND RURAL BALANCES

Let us then take the figure of 800 inhabitants as the line of separation between rural and urban communities. With this division, the ratio between urban and rural populations, 1:1.92, shows an urban sector of extraordinary size. Towns contained some 34 percent of the total population. Even if we consider only the population of the ten largest cities of the Florentine domain, as many authors have done, then still nearly 27 percent of the Tuscans would have to be regarded as city dwellers; the ratio of urban to rural inhabitants then becomes 1:2.7.[42]

In J. C. Russell's estimate, the proportion of city dwellers (taken to be residents of the ten largest cities) in the Tuscan region was some 26 percent before the great pestilence. (The region, as he defines it, spread well beyond the Florentine state of 1427, toward the south and southeast).[43] Still according to Russell, a comparable measure of urbanization could be found only in the regions of Venice and Milan (23.4 and 19.1 percent respectively). Even in the territory of Ghent in Flanders, one of the most urbanized areas of medieval Europe, only 14.1 percent of the population lived in cities. Tuscany seems to have been the most urbanized region of medieval Europe, among the many studied by Russell. Moreover, the portion of its people living in towns remained remarkably stable from the middle of the fourteenth century to 1427.

To consider a narrower zone than Russell's region, the ratio between hearths in the city of Florence and those in its contado may be estimated at about 1:2.8 before the Black Death. Nearly a century later, the area of the contado had grown considerably. Still, if we continue to count by hearths, the ratio remained fixed at 1:2.7, taking into account only the city of Flor-

42. Towns with more than 1,000 inhabitants constitute close to 31 percent of the total population and show a ratio of 1:2.25 to the rural population.

43. Russell, 1972, p. 235, Table 32.

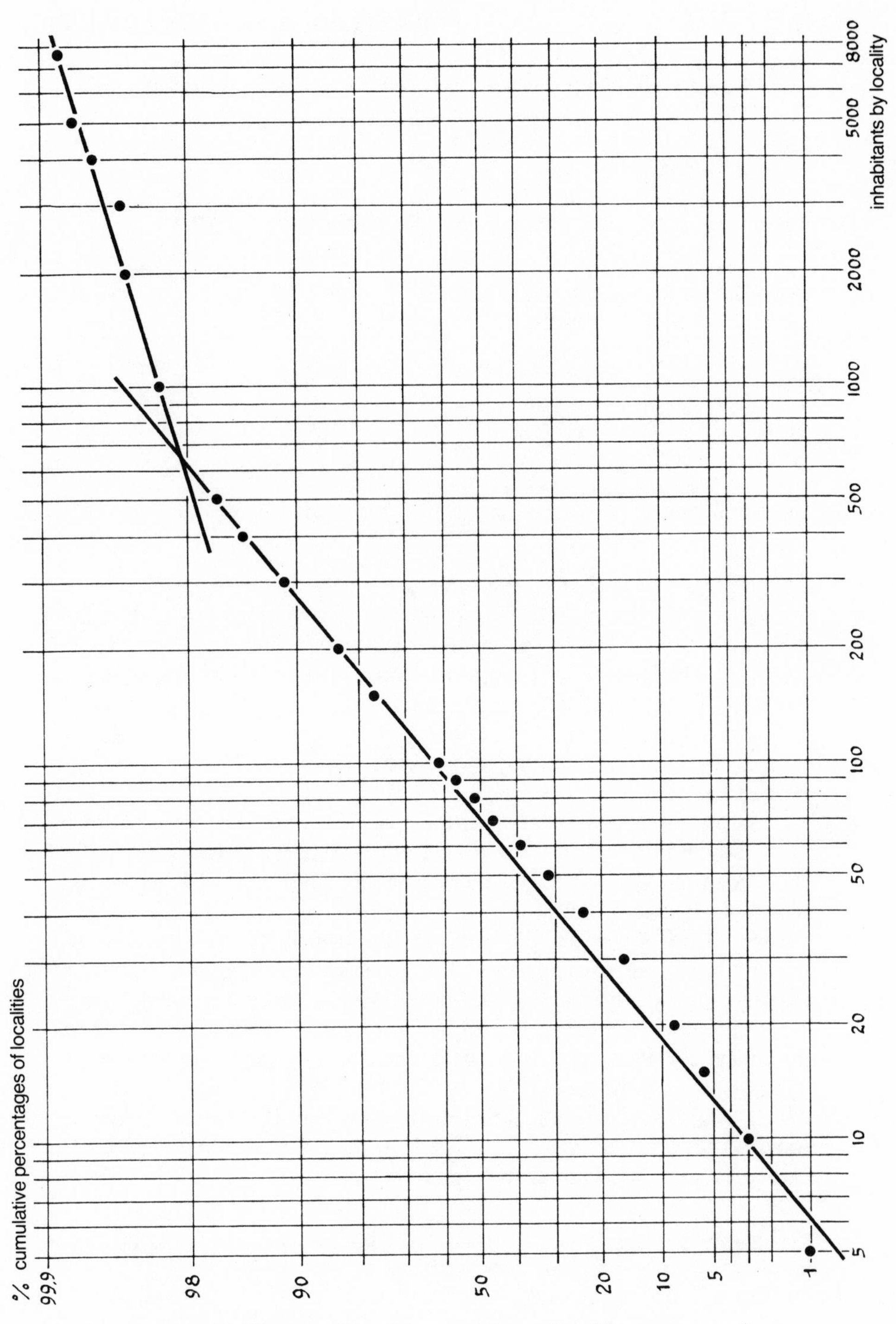

Fig. 2.1. Distribution of Localities according to Size (Tuscany, 1427–30)

Table 2.1. Relation between Urban and Rural Populations according to Regions in 1427

	Inhabitants			*Inhabitants*		
Province	*a* *of the first city*	*b* *of the remaining territory*	*Ratio a/b*	*c* *of the cities over 800 inhabitants*	*d* *of the remaining territory*	*Ratio c/d*
Florence	37,246	126,831	1:3.4	49,322	114,755	1:2.32
Florence and Prato	40,808	123,269	1:3	—	—	
Pisa	7,333	18,100	1:2.47	7,333	18,100	1:2.47
Pistoia	4,412	11,737	1:2.65	5,296	10,853	1:2.05
Arezzo	4,152	19,397	1:4.7	8,213	15,336	1:1.87
Volterra	3,342	3,864	1:1.16	3,342	3,864	1:1.16
Cortona	3,246	4,636	1:1.42	3,246	4,636	1:1.42
Pescia	1,529	6,037	1:3.95	2,387	5,179	1:2.17
Pescia	1,529	3,252	1:2.12	1,529	3,252	1:1.12

NOTE. The rural population compared to Pescia is that of the Val di Nievole and of the Vald'Arno di sotto in the first instance, and that of the Val di Nievole alone in the second.

ence. (If Prato is included, the ratio falls to 1:2.5). The place held by the Florentine population, and still more by the two chief towns, had only sightly diminished within an enlarged contado.[44] But if we consider the situation of Florence in relation to the entire territory which it governed in 1427, the ratio of those living in the capital to those outside the capital falls to 1:5.9. Florence, which alone claimed 27 percent of the population of its territory in 1336–38 held only 14 percent of the inhabitants of its vast, territorial state in 1427.

Table 2.1 gives, for most of the provinces of the Florentine domain, ratios showing the relationship between the size of the principal city and all towns with more than 800 inhabitants, to the number of residents found in their respective counties.

If we regard only the population of the principal city, then the east, with the county of Arezzo, appears to be the most rural region of Florentine Tuscany; on the other hand, if account is taken of secondary towns, Arezzo and its province emerge as one of the most highly urbanized. In contrast, the county of Pisa appears to have been an essentially rural zone, but capped by an important city.

If we compare these indices of urbanization with the comparable figures from the previous century, then clearly several Tuscan towns had lost in relative weight. San Gimignano, for example, in 1332, contained two times

44. See the following chapter, pp. 64–65 and 67–69, for a examination of the size of Florence's population in city and countryside before the Black Death.

the number of rural hearths (1,687 to 852, or a ratio of 1.98:1). In 1428, it held no more than 314 hearths and 1,677 inhabitants, against 250 hearths and 1,503 inhabitants in the countryside. The ratio had thus fallen to 1.26:1 for hearths and 1.11:1 for persons.[45] Pistoia may have fallen from an index of 2.2:1 before 1340 to 2.65:1 in 1427.[46] As in the Florentine contado, the subject cities were diminishing in relation to the surrounding rural world. Still, the high level of urbanization is beyond doubt the trait which most distinguished this region within contemporary Europe.

RANKINGS

In Tuscany of the quattrocento, culture radiated from the cities. And yet the chief towns among them were all located far from Florence. By keeping a respectful distance, they emphasize the capital's preeminence. Their distribution looks to be, in effect, very unequal and, with the exception of Prato, all were found beyond a radius of 30 kilometers out of Florence. The two most important cities of the Tuscan region, Florence and Pisa, were set apart, each in the center of true urban deserts, broken only by Prato, an industrial satellite set in the plain some 20 kilometers from Florence. But Pisa itself seems quite isolated at the western extremity of the Florentine territory. To be sure, the great highways—the via Francigena or Romea to the west and the via Cassia to the east—and the Arno valley formed the basic axes of this distribution. Still, the distribution seems remarkably unbalanced when judged by size. The ratio of population between Pisa and Florence was 1:5. If the distribution of cities according to size follows the rule devised by Auerbach and Zipf, then the second city of a region ought to contain a population equal to half that of the principal center.[47] In Florentine Tuscany, this rule did not apply.

Table 2.2 makes at once apparent the demographic dominance, and loneliness, of Florence. The other salient trait of the Tuscan distribution is the plethora of secondary towns falling behind, but not much behind, Pisa. Florence's lead over the other towns is so great that it obscures any correlation between rank and size. But even if we take Pisa as our base, as is done in the last vertical column of the table, no clear and consistent relationship emerges.

In his book Russell accepts, in modified form, the rank-order rule which geographers have proposed.[48] He then proceeds to define the medieval regions, the cities of which follow the predicted rankings and ratios of size. The enterprise is imaginative, but the effort fails when applied to Tuscany.

45. Fiumi, 1961, pp. 173–74.
46. Herlihy, 1967, p. 76.
47. Stewart, 1959, pp. 240–56; Auerbach, 1913; Zipf, 1949.
48. Russell, 1972.

Table 2.2. Rank Order of Tuscan Cities, 1427

Rank	*City*	*Number of Inhabitants*	*Predicted Index*	*Florence Index*	*Pisa Index*
1	Florence	38,000	1000	1000	—
2	Pisa	7,330	525	193	1000
3	Pistoia	4,411	356	117	601
4	Arezzo	4,143	270	109	565
5	Prato	3,517	220	93	480
6	Volterra	3,342	195	88	455
7	Cortona	3,251	170	86	445
8	Montepulciano	3,191	142	78	435
9	Colle	2,657	127	70	362
10	San Gimignano	1,677	115	44	229

NOTE. Montepulciano includes the population of the villa di Montepulciano, some 693 inhabitants. The population of Colle is doubtlessly overstated, because of the inclusion of rural households in its census.

Thus, Pisa, the second city of the Florentine domains, qualifies by virtue of its small size only for fifth place within the theoretical Tuscan hierarchy. To fill in the missing places, Russell must look in the direction of Rome, Bologna, Perugia, or Orvieto. To accept the reality of this greater Tuscany, we would have to know the principles which generate the rankings and ratios of size. Russell does not offer an explanation, and his obliteration of historic (in some sense, too, of geographic) frontiers is consequently unacceptable.

The demographic preeminence of Florence within Tuscany was based perhaps less on its role as a regional metropolis, and more on the interregional and international functions it assumed. Thus, the activities of Florentine merchants, bankers, and diplomats extended far beyond Tuscany, even the bigger Tuscany envisioned by Russell. Florentines traversed Europe. Tuscany of the quattrocento perhaps most closely resembles regions of the world today where, within a tight geographic structure, large cities with a developed commercial sector look to international markets, even while remaining set within a traditional agricultural system.

This interplay between regional and international functions explains the unequal distribution of small urban centers. There was no city of any significant size (with the exception of Prato) within a radius of 30 kilometers around Florence. In this zone of mezzadria, agricultural production was directly tied to the consumption demands of the metropolis. There was no need (or opportunity) for the development of small centers of exchange or rural markets with some commercial importance. Beyond that limit, on the other hand, out of the shadow of Florence, market villages and small intermediate cities enjoyed some growth. They attracted and redirected agricultural produce and raw materials, partially to Florence, and partially toward the outside world.

Tuscany thus was marked by the demographic preeminence of its great city and by the multiplication of secondary towns (far behind it in size), which in turn dominated a plethora of villages. This is the land as we see it in 1427. What, in turn, was the demographic experience of the Tuscan community over the last two centuries of the Middle Ages?

3
Population Movements, 1300–1550

. . . era istimato che in Firenze avesse in quel tempo [1348] 120 mila anime che ne morirono, cio è de' corpi, ottantamila. Pensate se fu fracasso!
It has been estimated that at that time [1348] there were 120,000 souls in Florence, of whom 80,000 suffered bodily death. Think of the bedlam!

—Giovanni di Pagolo Morelli, *Ricordi* (written between 1393 and 1411)

uropean peoples in the fourteenth and fifteenth centuries endured a series of disasters of exceptional fury. The Catasto catches the Tuscan community and families even as they sought to adjust to radically altered conditions of life.

I. Decline, Stability, Recovery

An inquiry into the size and state of Tuscan populations during the late Middle Ages faces one principal obstacle. Both before and after 1427, comprehensive surveys, comparable to the first Catasto, are lacking. Before 1427 surviving surveys illuminate only limited areas of the Florentine domains, and none approach the Catasto in wealth of reported data. Between 1427 and the end of the century the surveys (including later Catasti) are large and detailed, but still not as comprehensive as the first Catasto in the populations that they included. Not until the census of the Grand Duke Cosimo II, dated 1552, can we again study the entire population of the Florentine territories, and even that census gives, for Florence, only the total number of household members, but not their ages. For areas beyond the city of Florence it supplies only the total population found in each commune.[1]

These surveys, before and after the first Catasto, also pose formidable problems of interpretation. The precise boundaries of the communities included are rarely stated, and there is no assurance that those boundaries

1. See P. Battara, 1935b.

remained fixed over centuries, or even decades.[2] It is not always clear who is, and who is not, counted in the enumerations.

Several recent studies have illuminated population movements in regions of Tuscany from as early as the thirteenth century. The historian who has worked most productively on Tuscan demography of the Middle Ages is certainly Enrico Fiumi.[3] Our own reconstruction of demographic movements before 1427 will make large use of the data which Fiumi has indefatigably gathered from numerous Tuscan archives.

PRATO, CITY AND COUNTRYSIDE

Prato, located less than 20 kilometers to the northwest of Florence, possesses probably the richest series of censuses dating before 1427, for both the city and the countryside. With Fiumi's guidance, we shall use these censuses as a measure of Tuscan population movements in the late Middle Ages.

Many of the oldest surveys of Prato—they extend back into the thirteenth century—are fragments; only a few urban quarters and rural villages are included in them. Most enumerate the households, but not their members. To estimate the total population, therefore, we must determine average household size, or the household "multiplier".[4]

Table 3.1 presents both the partial data and our estimates of Prato's likely total population based upon them. When average household size cannot be calculated on the basis of a particular survey, we have taken the figure from the survey closest to it, which allows such a calculation. If the defective survey falls between two dates when multipliers can be known, we have assumed that the change in average size was linear over time, and have estimated the figures through standard methods of interpolation. Table 3.1 gives these interpolated multipliers in brackets. When a survey included only part of a community, we assumed that the relationship of the given part to the entire community remained the same as that discernible in the closest complete survey. In order to extend our projections, we have combined several of the highly fragmented earlier surveys when they are dated over a short span of years. Finally, in order to facilitate comparison, index figures have been added, indicating the changes both in the number of households and in the total population. The numbers of households and persons given in the Catasto of 1427 serve as base figures, with the value of 100. The average annual rates of change are determined according to the

2. On the problem of boundaries, see above, chap. 2, pp. 46–47.

3. Fiumi, 1962, 1:251–90; idem, 1950; idem, 1957–59; idem, 1961; idem, 1968.

4. On the problem of the multiplier in the interpretation of hearth lists, see the remarks by Heers, 1968.

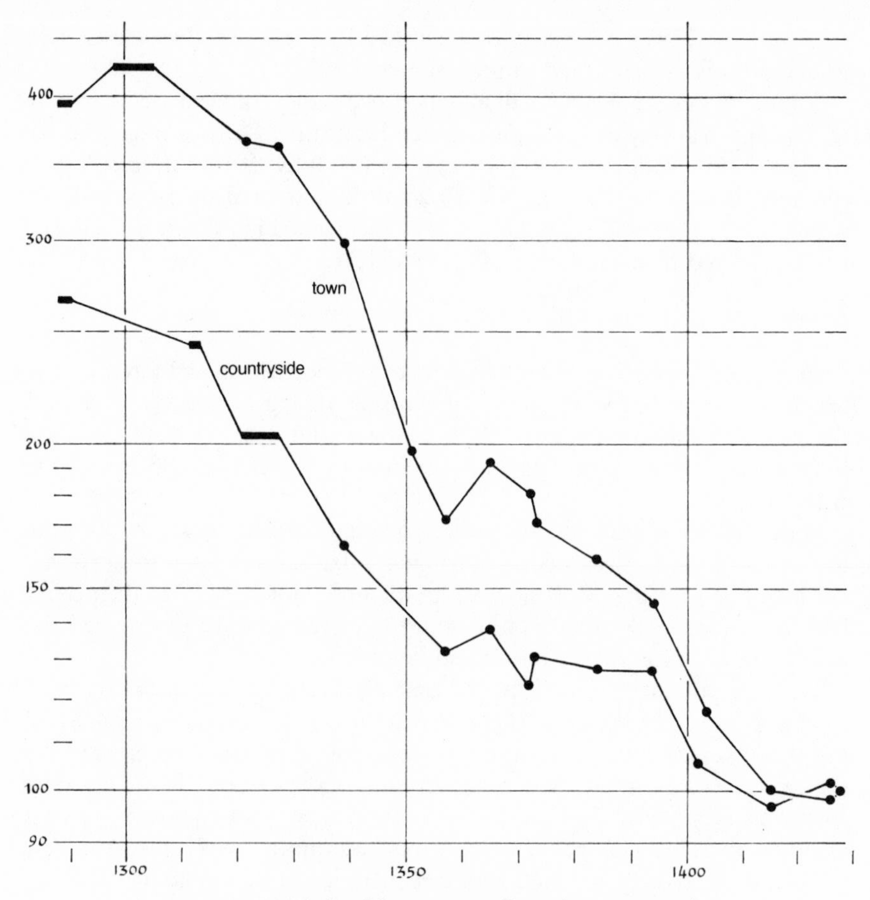

Fig. 3.1. Population Movements at Prato (ca. 1290–1427)

rules for calculating compound interest. Figure 3.1, based on this table, shows the movement of population at Prato from the end of the thirteenth century until the period of the Catasto.

In both city and countryside, the population of Prato sustained stunning losses between ca. 1300 and 1427. Its urban population collapsed to 23.6 percent of its former size; this represents an average annual rate of decline of 1.0 percent, measured from 1288, and of 1.24 percent since 1339. Losses in the countryside were only slightly less appalling. Some 62.5 percent of the rural population disappeared; the rate of decline was 0.71 percent per year from 1300, and 0.56 percent from 1339. By the early fifteenth century, the

Table 3.1. Population Movements at Prato, 1288–1427

	City						*Countryside*						*Total*		
	Hhlds	*Index*	*Ave. Size*	*Ppltn*	*Index*	*Ave. Annual Change*	*Hhlds*	*Index*	*Ave. Size*	*Ppltn*	*Index*	*Ave. Anual Change*	*Hhlds*	*Ppltn*	*Index*
1288–90	*(1460)* (3396)	357.1	[4.1]	(13924)	394.1		*(207)* (2241)	237.7	[5.6]	(12550)	266.6		(5637)	(26474)	321.3
1298–1305	*(1040)* (3477)	365.6	4.1	(14996)	424.3	+0.20			5.6			−0.40	(5645)	(26486)	321.4
1312–13							*(136)* (2168)	229.9	[5.3]	(11490)	244.1				
1322	*(871)* (3214)	338.0	[4.0]	(12856)	363.9	−0.73						−1.49			
1321–27							*(1090)* (2042)	216.5	[4.7]	(9597)	203.9		(5256)	(22453)	272.5
1327	3275	344.4	[3.9]	(12773)	361.6							−1.47			
1339	2762	290.4	3.9	10559	298.9	−1.57	1786	189.4	4.3	7690	163.4		4548	15107	183.3
1351	*(232)* (1837)	193.2	[3.8]	(6981)	197.6	−3.39						−1.16			
1357	1686	177.3	[3.6]	(6070)	171.8	−2.32	1356	143.8	[4.6]	(6238)	132.5	+0.50	(3042)	(12308)	149.4
1365	1952	205.3	[3.5]	(6832)	193.4	+1.49	1381	146.4	[4.7]	(6491)	137.9	−1.51	(3333)	(13323)	161.7
1372	1806	189.9	3.5	6405	181.3	−0.92	1241	131.6	4.7	5835	124.0	+0.25	3047	12240	148.5
1373	1724	181.3	[3.5]	(6034)	170.8	−1.09	1314	139.3	[4.7]	(6176)	131.2		(3038)	(12210)	148.2
1384	1604	168.7	[3.5]	5614	158.9	−0.81	1252	132.8	[4.8]	6010	127.7	−0.04	2856	11624	141.1
1394	1478	155.4	[3.5]	5173	146.4	−2.45	1222	129.6	[4.9]	5988	127.2	−2.40	2700	11161	135.4
1402	1178	123.9	[3.6]	4241	120.0	−1.34	1017	107.8	[4.9]	4932	105.9	−0.61	2195	9173	111.3
1415	988	103.9	[3.6]	3557	100.7		911	96.6	[5.0]	4555	96.8		1899	8112	98.4
1426	940	98.8	[3.7]	3478	98.4	−0.06	946	100.3	5.0	4730	100.4	+0.27	1886	8208	99.6
1427	951	100.0	3.7	3533	100.0		943	100.0	5.0	4707	100.0		1894	8240	100.0

Figures for average household size given in brackets are interpolations.
Italicized figures in parentheses are from incomplete surveys.
Roman figures in parentheses are projections of the total population based on the incomplete surveys.
SOURCE: The basic data is taken from Fiumi, 1968 pp. 35–111. Interpolations, projections and estimates are our own.

entire territory claimed less than one-third (31.1 percent) of the inhabitants it had supported a century before.

These horrendous losses were, however, distributed very unevenly across the span of years from 1300 to 1427. The population appears to have been relatively stable at high levels from 1290 (and probably before) until 1320 or 1330. It then fell precipitously, victimized by the notorious pestilence of 1348. A period of relative stability—marked by a brief recovery, then by moderate losses—ensued, lasting until the 1390s. Then again the curve plunged sharply; here, the epidemic of 1400 worked the chief havoc. From approximately 1410 the population once more stabilized, but now at very low levels.

How well do population movements at Prato reflect trends in other Tuscan areas? In one respect Prato was distinctive. From an early stage its urban community had to face the powerful commercial and industrial competition of its great neighbor Florence. This doubtlessly contributed to the precocious decline of its urban population, noticeable even before 1340. On the other hand, its rural areas benefited from the growing Florentine demand for agricultural products and industrial raw materials. People moved out of the commercial and industrial sectors of the economy into the agricultural. In ca. 1300 approximately 56.6 percent of the Pratese population lived in the city; by 1427 the urban segment had fallen to 42.9 percent. This shift from one sector of production to another continued after the epoch of the Catasto. According to the calculations of Fiumi, the urban population (excluding religious) grew between 1427 and 1551 by 59.8 percent; but rural dwellers (here including some few religious and priests) increased by 78.1 percent.[5] An analogous decline of regional urban centers is evident also at San Gimignano, Pistoia, and Volterra, as we have already seen.[6] Florence was claiming an ever greater share of urban functions within the Tuscan province.

THE FLORENTINE CONTADO

Estimates of population size in the Florentine contado, for the period before 1348, rest principally on the numbers, of uncertain and disputed meaning, supplied by the contemporary chronicler Giovanni Villani.[7] Villani affirms that in 1300 the Florentine contado could muster 70,000 men capable of bearing arms; by 1338 it could summon to war 80,000 men.

5. Fiumi, 1968, p. 154.

6. See above, p. 56–57.

7. Villani's figures are examined with much insight by Fiumi, 1950. But Fiumi wrote the article when the amount of information concerning late-medieval population movements in Tuscany was still quite limited. His own subsequent research has shown that the losses were more substantial then he himself concluded in 1950.

Unfortunately, it is not known what extent of territory Villani understood by the term contado. At all events, the Florentine domains had grown between 1300 and 1338. In 1327–29, for example, Florence annexed, besides Pescia, six communes on the low hills of the Monte Albano. Formerly belonging to Pistoia, they were officially declared parts of the Florentine contado in 1336.[8]

Moreover, it is difficult to judge the ratio between those males able to bear arms and the entire population. Many historians, including Fiumi, have adopted a multiplier of 3.5. The figure may not, however, give sufficient weight to the extraordinary number of small children and of adults incapable of of armed service that was characteristic of traditional populations. In the opening decade of the fifteenth century, a Pistoiese chronicler utilized a multiplier of 4.0 as the ratio between *uomini d' arme* and mouths or bocche.[9] To judge by the Catasto of 1427, the ratio between rural males of ages 15 to 70 years—the years of service for rural militiamen—and the total population lay between these two figures (3.7). We shall thus use both multipliers (3.5 and 4.0) in order to arrive at two estimates, high and low, of the total population.

By the use of these multipliers, the inhabitants of the Florentine countryside in ca. 1338 may be estimated as between 280,000 and 320,000 persons. In 1427 the Florentine contado contained 26,681 households and 128,370 persons.[10] But the contado by then included a substantially larger territory than it possessed in 1338. Table 3.2 enumerates the pivieri which, in the larger part of their areas, were absorbed into the Florentine contado after 1338.[11]

If reduced then to its approximate boundaries of 1338, the Florentine contado in 1427 would have contained only some 21,000 households and 104,000 persons. It had lost, in other words, between 62.9 and 67.5 percent of its preplague size—approximately two-thirds. This represents an average rate of decline of from 1.11 percent to 1.25 percent per year. These losses are distinctly larger than those which affected the countryside of Prato, where the population decline began earlier and was initially sharp, but slowed in the period reviewed here (1339–1427). Again, Prato seems to have benefited

8. Guasti and Gherardi, 1866–93, 1, no. 3:5.

9. Luca Dominici, 1933, p. 9; Beloch, 1937–61, 3:343, proposes a multiplier of 3, which is certainly too low.

10. Totals of households taken from the Catasto will vary sightly, depending o whether or not we include hearths that contain no members (corporations and the like) or no listed members (incomplete data). The figures cited here include 118 "incomplete" hearths, for which the declarations list no members.

11. None of these pievi is included in the oldest surviving rural Estimo, dating from 1350. See Fiumi, 1950, pp. 90–93.

Table 3.2. Additions to the Florentine Contado, 1338–1427

Region	*Hhlds* (1427)	*Persons* (1427)
San Miniato al Tedesco	765	3,544
Fabbrica	481	2,290
Prato (city)	951	3,562
Prato (countryside)	943	4,707
Firenzuola	673	3,007
Vicariato del Podere	262*	1,087*
Bibbiena	1,361	5,527
Total	5,436	23,724

* Partial figures corresponding to the part described in the Catasto.

SOURCE: Fiumi, 1950.

by the strong Florentine market, which attracted and sustained a comparatively large rural population.

The Estimi of the Florentine contado dating from this period indicate a rhythm of decline similar to that observed at Prato. The total number of rural households fell gradually between 1350 and 1384, passing from 32,700 to 30,000 households—a decrease of 0.30 percent per year.[12] The slow but relentless decline continued from 1384 to 1427, reaching the figure of about 26,000 found in the Catasto, an average annual decrease of 0.27 percent. The number of chargeable male heads shows a more precipitous drop, going from 40,711 in 1404 to 36,444 in 1414 (a decrease of 1.10 percent per year) and 36,199 in 1427 (0.05 percent annually).[13] Stabilization in population numbers thus seems to have come in the second decade of the fifteenth century.

In sum, Florentine rural population lost approximately two-thirds of its numbers between the early fourteenth and early fifteenth centuries. The periods of greatest loss centered on the two plague years of 1348 and 1400, and were separated by three or four decades of moderate decline or of

12. Fiumi, 1950, gives the total of rural hearths over comparable territories for the years 1343, 1350, 1356, 1365, 1375, and 1384; in his late article, 1957, p.476, he acknowledged that the figures he attributed to 1343 belonged to 1470. Conti, 1966, p.13, has added further correctiions to the totals; they were needed because the fascicules belonging to the various surveys have been preserved in a disordered state. Conti's figures are the following (Fiumi's are provided in parentheses): 1356–57: 32,700 (32,463): 1365: 29,313; 1372: 30,822 (30,110); 1384: 30,012. See also Pardi, 1916 and 1921a.

13. Molho, 1971, p. 26, has interpreted these figures, the "numerum personarum, que dicuntur le teste," as referring to taxable heads of households. But see the Provvisione of 27 April 1414, that states explicitly that the totals refer to teste, that is, men between ages 15 and 70, and not to family heads. ASF, Provv. 103, ff. 13–15. "Nova distributio extimi comitatus, diminutio summae."

relative stability. The size of population reached a new floor, now very low, in the second decade of the fifteenth century.

FLORENCE

Estimations of the Florentine urban population before 1348 are beset by special difficulties. Not only is the documentation sparse, but it also appears to be contradictory. Here, too, we shall develop high and low estimates of the urban population in the early fourteenth century. The low estimate is based upon Giovanni Villani's famous description of the city in ca. 1338. He claims that Florence then possessed upwards of 90,000 "mouths of men, women and children".[14] He expressly excludes foreigners, visitors, and soldiers (he gives their number as approximately 1,500 persons), and also members of religious orders (1,500–1,600 persons). If these people are included in the count, we reach a total figure of 93,000. Villani also observes that the city could call to arms 25,000 men between the ages of 15 and 70. If we use the same multipliers previously applied to the rural population (3.5 and 4.0 respectively), then the population of Florence would fall between 87,500 and 100,000 persons. So far, Villani's figures appear consistent.

The most perplexing data supplied by Villani concern the number of babies christened each year at the central baptistry of San Giovanni. As noted previously, nearly all babies born within the confines of the piviere of San Giovanni would have been brought for baptism to this sanctuary. Any priest, or even a layman, could administer the sacrament, but only when the infant was in grave danger of death. The number of babies baptized thus should approximate the number born within the jurisdiction. Villani learned from the presiding priest of San Giovanni that each year between 5,500 and 6,000 babies were baptized in his church, and that males outnumbered females by some 300 to 400 babies.[15]

In pages which have become a classic of Florentine historiography, Niccolò Rodolico attempted, in 1905, to utilize these figures to estimate the total population of the city.[16] He assumed that the crude birth rate would be 45 per 1,000 persons, and concluded that the 5,500 to 6,000 babies baptized each year would correspond to a total population of 125,000 persons. (His estimate should really have been between 122,000 and 133,000 persons). Referring to Villani's figure of 90,000 mouths, Rodolico acutely observed: "Either the number of births which [Villani] states is inexact, or the number of the population is higher than 100,000 persons."[17]

14. Villani, 1823–25, bk. 11, chap. 94.
15. Loc. cit.
16. Rodolico, 1905, pp. 18–21.
17. Ibid., p. 19.

Rodolico's own methods elicit some criticisms. The crude rate of 45 baptisms per 1,000 persons, which he utilized, appears high for the Florentine population. Rodolico took as his model the high birth rate of certain workers' quarters in Naples and Berlin in the 1890s, on the dubious assumption that Florentine workers in 1338 were comparably fertile. And he took no account of babies who died before they received solemn baptism. Marco Lastri, the erudite Florentine who in the eighteenth century first called attention to the importance of the baptismal registers of San Giovanni, proposed a rate of 40 baptisms per 1,000 persons as typical of the Florentine population.[18] He noted that in 1767, when Florence had a known population of 78,635, those baptized numbered 2,878, which he rounded to 4 babies per 100 persons (the exact ratio is only 3.6 per 100, or 36 per 1,000).[19] The use of a lower birth rate (for example, Lastri's figure of 40 per 1,000) has the result of substantially inflating the estimate of the total population. Villani's stated number of baptisms would correspond to a population between 137,500 and 150,000 persons. Rodolico, we suspect, adopted the high birth rate in order to avoid exactly this—pushing the estimate of the total population beyond the bounds of the credible.

A further adjustment is required here. The piviere of San Giovanni, as we saw in the previous chapter, extended beyond the city walls to include a substantial number of rural households. In 1427 the total population of the piviere was 44,068 persons, of whom 6,928—or 15.7 percent—lived outside the circle of walls. If this distribution was the same in 1338, then the population within the walls, helping to produce 5,500 to 6,000 babies, should range between 115,900 to 126,450 persons if the baptismal rate was 40 per 1,000. Florence, in sum, may very well have counted a population of 120,000 inhabitants before the plague.[20] Villani's estimate of total population, "da 90,000 bocche," looks to be a particularly low minimum, perhaps limited to bread consumers in the population. (The consumption of wheat is the apparent basis for his estimate.)

A population of about 120,000 persons before the Black Death corre-

18. Lastri, 1775.

19. At Pavia in the seventeenth century, the birth rate oscillated between 36.9 and 42.5 per 1,000; at Venice in 1601–10, it was only 33. For these and other examples of birth rates in traditional communities, see Reinhard, Armengaud, and Dupâquier, 1968, p. 165.

20. Fiumi, 1950, p. 86, and other scholars have argued that many inhabitants of the countryside brought their babies for baptism to the city, in order to confer upon them the advantages of citizenship. But the soundings we took of the baptismal registers from November 1450 to November 1451 show that only 1.9 percent of the babies baptized (33 in number) in fact derived from rural families. Presumably, this distortion should have also affected the registrations in the eighteenth as well as the fourteenth century. In sum, the figure of 40 per 1,000, proposed by Lastri, already included these rural babies and needs no further adjustment.

sponds well with other figures bearing upon Florence's size. Giovanni Morelli, a Florentine writing in the first decade of the fifteenth century, believed that the city possessed 120,000 inhabitants before the great plague.[21] Several writers—Matteo Villani, Giovanni Boccaccio, Marchionne di Coppo Stefani, and Morelli himself—number the victims of the plague of 1348 as falling between 80,000 and 100,000. Such figures would be entirely fanciful if the urban population was in fact only 93,000.[22]

If this estimate of 120,000 persons residing in the city in ca. 1338 is acceptable, then by 1427 Florence had lost 69 percent of its former numbers. Expressed in indices, the urban population fell from 323 in 1338 to 100 in 1427—an average annual decrease of 1.25 percent. These results closely parallel the figures calculated for Prato on the basis of more yielding sources. Prato, between these dates, also lost two-thirds of its people and registered an annual average decline of 1.24 percent. But unlike the pattern discernible at Prato, the losses within the city of Florence were very close to those suffered by the rural population—between 62.9 and 67.5 percent, in our estimate. In consequence, as we noted previously, the populations of Florence and its countryside retained a stable relationship in spite of their steep downward movements.

At Florence as elsewhere, the years of heaviest losses cluster around the plague dates of 1348 and 1400. According to surveys (perhaps incomplete) taken of urban households in 1352 and 1355, the city counted slightly fewer than 10,000 hearths.[23] If we adopt a multiplier of 4.19 (the known mean size of Florentine households in 1380), then Florence immediately after the plague of 1348 had a population of some 42,000 persons. But it also seems to have partially recovered from its losses and retained a population of about 60,000 persons over the last decades of the fourteenth century. In his description of the plague of 1374, the chronicler Stefani notes that "there were then in the city 60,000 or more".[24] An estimo dated 1379 enumerates 13,779 households in the city.[25] In 1380, another survey yields the slightly smaller sum of 13,074 households, with 54,747 persons.[26] A chronicler of

21. Morelli, 1956, p. 290, cited in the heading to this chapter.

22. Rodolico, 1905, p. 32, rightly makes this argument and calls to witness the various estimates of plague mortalities. Villani and Stefani both assert that 96,000 persons died; Boccaccio rounds the figure to an exact 100,000.

23. The exact figures are 9,955 hearths in 1352 and 9,904 in 1355, taken from the "Libri della Sega," ASF, Estimi, reg. 306 and 307. On their character, see Fiumi, 1950, p. 106; Barbadoro, 1931, pp. 7–18.

24. Cited in Rodolico, 1905, p. 32

25. ASF, Archivio delle Prestanze. "Libri dell' estimo del 1379," reg. 366–69. See Rodolico, 1905, p. 39.

26. The totals are given by Ildefonso di San Luigi, 1778, 10:123–24, and reprinted in Rodolico, 1905, p. 41.

Pistoia observes that Florence contained 60,000 persons before the plague of 1400, and had never been so "triumphant in numbers."[27]

After perhaps forty years of overall stability, the plague of 1400 brutally claimed at least 12,000 victims. If we can assume that the Florentine population followed the same curve traced by the city of Prato, then it reached its late-medieval floor about 1410–15, even though losses had moderated from about 1405. The population which appears in the Catasto had thus been stable at very low levels for about a decade.

THE DISTRICT

Beyond the Florentine contado, two regions of Tuscany have attracted special studies of their populations: San Gimignano and Pistoia. In his detailed reconstruction of population movements at San Gimignano, Fiumi has again amassed some remarkable, even shocking, statistics.[28] The total population of the city and of its tiny territory fell from an estimated 13,000 persons in 1332 to 3,138 in 1427—a loss of 75.9 percent. Although it is difficult to separate town from countryside in this small community, the number of urban households seems to have collapsed by 84.4 percent (representing an annual rate of decline of 1.75 percent). Numbers in the countryside diminished by a comparatively moderate 70.7 percent, at an annual decrease of 1.28 percent. The urban rate of decline at San Gimignano is thus much higher than that discernible at Prato. This pattern would seem to confirm our previous observations: during this period of heavy demographic contraction, the Tuscan population tended to collapse around the Florentine capital and the outlying towns suffered the most pronounced losses.

For Pistoia, Table 3.3 illustrates population movements in the countryside from the middle of the thirteenth century until 1427.

Between the middle of the thirteenth and the early fifteenth century, the population of the Pistoiese countryside fell by somewhere between 62.3 and 68.7 percent. These losses are close to those sustained by the countryside of Prato (62.5 percent between 1290 and 1427), but were not as severe as at San Gimignano. The pattern of demographic decline observable at Pistoia suggests the same contraction of settlement around the city of Florence noted elsewhere. But this ring of thin settlement also began rapidly to grow once the demographic recovery began. Already between 1404 and 1427 the curve of population in Pistoia's countryside registered a fairly pronounced upward movement. This was the early phase of a resurgence of Pistoia's rural

27. Dominici, 1933, 2:9.
28. Fiumi, 1961, pp. 154, 171, 174.

Table 3.3. Population Decline in Rural Pistoia, 1244–1427

Year	*Est. Ppltn*	*Index*	*Year*	*Est. Ppltn*	*Index*
ca. 1244	37,598	336.5	1401	10,027	85.4
1344	23,964	196.4	1404	8,969	76.5
1383	14,178	120.7	1427	11,172	100.0
1392	11,364	96.5			

SOURCE: Herlihy, 1967, p. 70. The estimate of 31,220 rural residents in ca. 1244, made in 1967, was calculated with a household multiplier of 4.65 persons per hearth—a figure taken from the Catasto and applied to the survey of that date known as the *Liber focorum,* which enumerates 6,714 households. But this average size is a minimal estimate. If we rather use the multiplier of 5.6 found in the rural census of the region of Prato closest in time to the *Liber,* then the estimated rural population of Pistoia becomes 37,598, and the index 336.5. The subsequent estimates are based not on hearth lists but on the number of salt consumers, adjusted to compensate for those persons, age 0 to 4, who were not subject to the salt tax. The assumed ratio between the total population and the population without these young children is 1.22—a proportion found in the nearby countryside of Prato in 1372 and also in 1427, in the same contado of Pistoia.

population, which would gain considerable momentum in the sixteenth century. The swing of population, down and up, was not quite so extreme in the rural areas closer to Florence.

The pattern of population movements discernible in the Pistoiese countryside probably approximates the experiences of rural areas still more remote from Florence, such as the counties of Pisa and Arezzo. Through the promise of tax exemptions, the Florentine government in the early fifteenth century tried to attract new settlers into these areas; the drop in population must have been alarming.[29] Although hard data are lacking, the cities of the district seem to have suffered even greater and more enduring losses than did the rural areas. Thus, if the population of the city of Pisa had fallen to the same extent as the Florentine (here we utilize our high estimate of Florence's population in ca. 1338 of 120,000 inhabitants), then its peak population before the Black Death would have been about 24,000 persons. The figure is, however, almost certainly too low; Pisa at its peak medieval size in the thirteenth century probably numbered 40,000 inhabitants.[30] In other words, between ca. 1300 and 1400, Pisa's population must have fallen even more drastically than Florence's. On the other hand, if Pisa's losses had been proportionately the same as Prato's, then its maximum size at the end of the thirteenth century would have been 31,440 inhabitants. This is a reasonable estimate. By the same reasoning, if Arezzo had suffered losses comparable to the Florentine losses,

29. See above, chap. 2. Almost nothing is known concerning the population of the Pisan contado in the fourteenth century. See Tangheroni, 1973, p. 192.

30. Rossi, 1945–47, pp. 5–62; Herlihy, 1958, pp. 35–53. Cristiani, 1962, p. 168.

then its peak size before the plague would have been 13,615 residents, a figure which again appears too low. To judge from its circle of walls, the city probably possessed about 20,000 inhabitants in the thirteenth century.[31] Had it declined to the same extent as did Prato, then it would have possessed 18,000 at its medieval peak. The population of Pistoia is difficult to follow, but on the basis of an oath taken by its citizens in 1219, to confirm a treaty with Bologna, its population was then about 11,000.[32] Presumably it grew in the later years of the thirteenth century, but it is impossible to judge by how much. In 1427 the city possessed 4,478 residents. If its decline had been proportionate to Prato's, then it would have claimed 19,000 at its peak size before the plague. It thus appears that Pisa and Arezzo had declined very substantially since 1300; losses at Pistoia, on the other hand, may have been a bit less brutal.

Pisa in particular sustained heavy losses and continued to do so into the fifteenth century. According to surveys, it counted 2,816 hearths in 1407, 1,779 in 1412, and 1,752 in 1427.[33] The five or six years immediately following its annexation by Florence (1406) were especially devastating. The average annual loss over the years 1407–12 was a staggering 8.78 percent, apparently due principally to the flight of oppressed taxpayers. In the twenty years preceding the Catasto, Pisan hearths diminished at the lower but still horrendous rate of 2.34 percent per year. Arezzo fared better, at least in comparative terms. Lists of taxpayers (*allirati*) indicate that hearths decreased from 1,776 in 1390 to 1,166 in 1423, then recovered slightly to the 1,183 (4,143 members) found in the Catasto. Between 1390 and 1423–27, the average annual rate of decline was between 1.27 and 1.09 percent.[34] Pistoia, on the other hand, seems to have enjoyed a slight recovery in the second decade of the fifteenth century. The Estimario of 1415 counts only 1,090 hearths, and the Catasto enumerates 1,247. If the Estimario was exhaustive (and this is not certain), then Pistoia's hearths would have increased in numbers between the two dates by an annual rate of 1.12 percent.[35]

In the thirteenth century, these secondary Tuscan towns had competed vigorously against one another, and also against Florence. Their subsequent steep demographic slide allowed Florence to consolidate its economic and political hegemony and to assume the status of a regional metropolis.

31. Beloch, 1937–61, 2:170–72, followed by Russell, 1972, p. 44.

32. Herlihy, 1967, p. 73. The number of adult males participating in the oath was 3,206.

33. The figures from the tax of 1402 and 1412 and from the prestanza of 1407 are published in Casini, 1957–58, pp. 156–272; idem, 1959–60, pp. 90–318.

34. See Varese, 1924–25, pp. 17 ff. Varese's figures were taken by Beloch, 1937–61, 2:170–73. Taxpayers with an assessment lower than one-tenth of a *libra* in 1390, and one-fiftieth in 1423, seem to have been excluded from the lists.

35. Herlihy, 1967, pp. 75–76.

Table 3.4. The Population of the Florentine Contado, 1427–1551

Year	*Households*	*Multiplier*	*Ppltn*	*Index*	*Mean Annual Change*
1427	26,681	4.83	128,370	100.0	
1459–60	22,434	[5.15]	(115,535)	89.7	−0.33
1469–70	23,851	5.26	(125,375)	97.3	0.61
1487–90	25,395	[5.39]	(136,900)	106.2	0.49
1552	36,922	6.14	226,698	176.5	0.82

SOURCE: The totals for 1427 are taken directly from the Catasto of that year. The totals for the Estimi from 1459 to 1490 are from Canestrini, 1862, pp. 346–48, and from Conti, 1966, p. 78. The Totals for 1552 come from Fiumi, 1950, p. 101, which are based on Repetti, 1843, pp. 566–69. We have, however, corrected them to adjust for changes in the Florentine domains between 1427 and 1552.

STABILITY AND RECOVERY

Between 1427 and 1494 the Florentine commune imposed several Estimi or Catasti on its countryside, and in 1552 the government of the Grand Duchy took a comprehensive census of the entire domain. Table 3.4 shows the population of the Florentine contado which these records reveal. The figure for 1469–70 is based on a 10 percent sample of households, numbering 2,121, taken from the full unpublished survey. Multipliers enclosed in brackets represent interpolations from the figures for previous and subsequent surveys.

To judge from the Estimo (or Catasto) of 1457–60, the population of the Florentine contado declined by about 10 percent in the 30 years following 1427. However, the government had granted exemptions from the direct tax to areas of the contado recently ravished by war; Conti sets the number of exempt rural households as about 1,200 in ca. 1470.[36] Moreover, these later surveys were not carried out with the rigor shown by the assessors of 1427. The totals for the rural Estimo of 1459–60 should certainly be adjusted upward. The population of the Florentine countryside between 1427 and 1459 was either experiencing a continuous, slow decline, or, in the most optimistic interpretation, remained largely stable, moving along a very low floor.

After 1460 the countryside entered a period of substantial demographic growth, which was probably most vigorous in the first two decades of the sixteenth century. By 1552 the residents of the countryside had increased from a base index of 100 in 1427 to 176.6. This expansion of three-quarters of its initial size was achieved by an average annual growth rate of 0.46 percent.

36. He bases his estimation on the number of rural communes, for which the total of hearths is not given in the "Tavola antica di tutti i popoli e comunità dello Stato fiorentino," published with the incorrect date of 1343 by I. di San Luigi, 1788, 13:207–88 (see above, n. 26). The list was in fact prepared for the Estimo of 1469–71. See Conti, 1966, p. 77, n. 13.

Table 3.5. The Population of the City of Florence, 1427–1552

Year	*Households*	*Multiplier*	*Ppltn*	*Index*	*Average Annual Change*
1427	9,780	3.80	37,144	100.0	
1441	8,722	[4.25]	(37,036)	99.7	0.0
1458–59	7,753	4.82	(37,369)	100.6	0.06
1469	8,250	4.89	(40,332)	108.6	0.76
1480	7,998	5.20	(41,590)	112.0	0.28
1552	9,527	6.21*	59,191	159.3	0.49
1427–1552					0.37

* If institutions and artificial households (*convivenze*) are excluded, the multiplier is 5.66.

SOURCE: The totals for 1427 are taken directly from the Catasto of that year. The totals of the surveys between 1441 and 1480 are from G. Pardi, 1916, pp. 78–79. The multipliers for 1458 and 1469 respectively are calculated on the basis of 10 percent samples of the households. The totals for 1552 come from P. Battara, 1935, p. 33. Clergy, religious, and servants are included in the last figure.

The remarkable baptismal registers of San Giovanni, which begin in November 1451, can help fill the long gap in the series from 1480 to 1552. Lastri published his totals in the eighteenth century, and here we utilize his figures.[37] Figure 3.2 shows their movement in absolute numbers from 1451 to 1600. Figure 3.3 illustrates the residual values of this series after removal of the trend. The first graph identifies the years when growth in the city was most pronounced; the second shows the periods when the number of births was especially high in relation to the total population.

In contrast with the countryside, the city shows virtually no signs of even a moderate decline between 1427 and 1459, but neither are there any indications of growth. On the basis of the number of baptisms, it is possible to discern two periods in which the growth of the city was probably most rapid. The first period corresponds closely with the years of political stability in Italy between the Peace of Lodi (1454) and the French invasions (from 1494). Later writers, such as Francesco Guicciardini, remembered these times as prosperous and happy.[38] Under the leadership of Lorenzo the Magnificent, Florence then attained perhaps its highest levels of cultural creativity. The beginning of prolonged warfare in Italy from 1494, the Savonarola episode, and the plagues which struck in the last years of the century, apparently halted further growth. Florence witnessed a second period of expansion after the Medici restoration (1512), but this ended with the plague of 1527 and the protracted siege of 1529–30. Only

37. Lastri, 1775.
38. Guicciardini, 1929, 1:2.

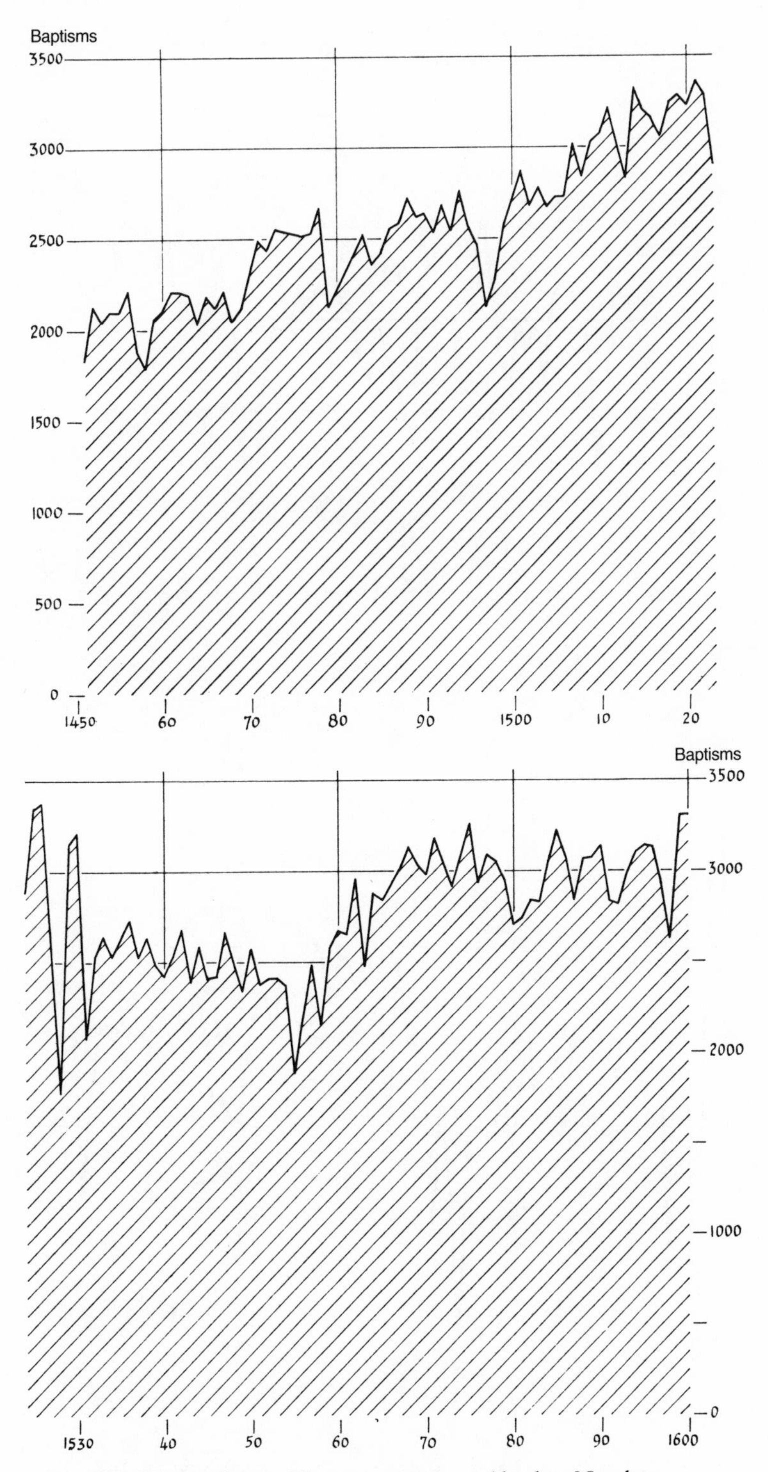

Fig. 3.2. Baptisms at Florence, 1451–1600: Absolute Numbers

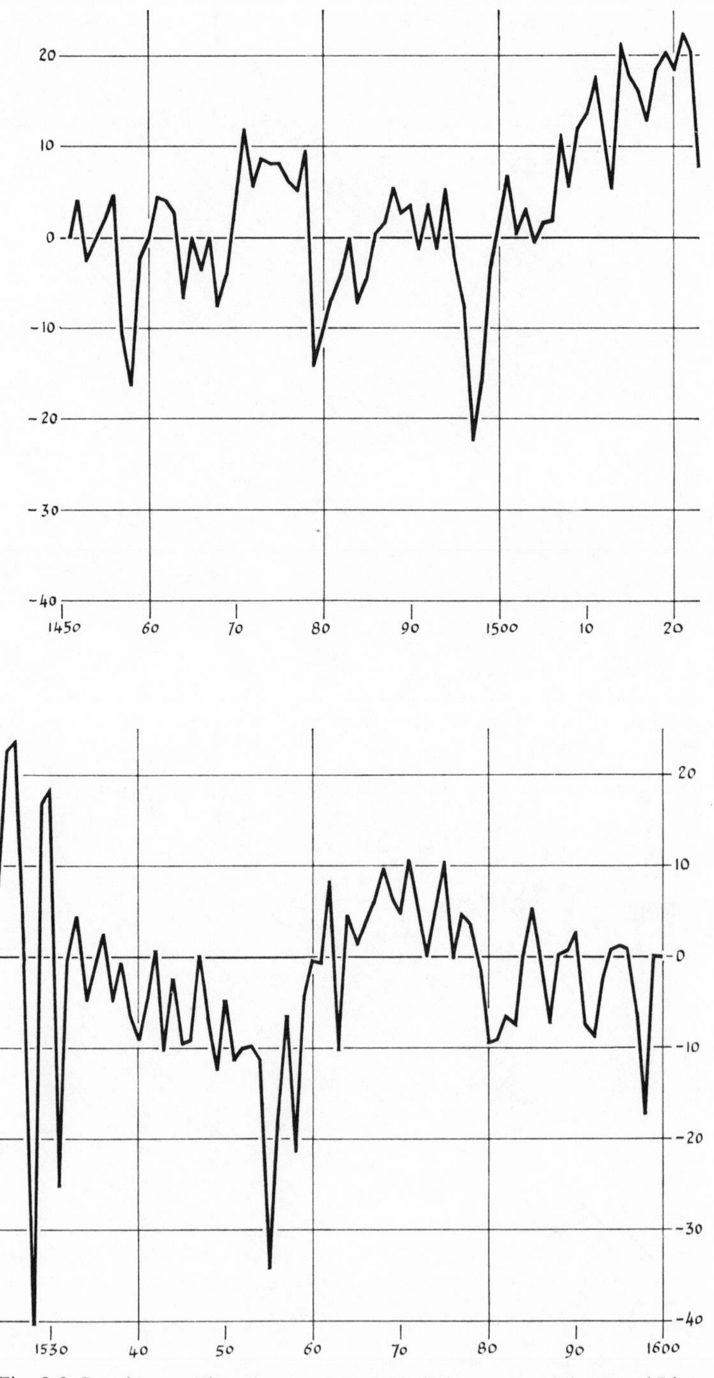

Fig. 3.3. Baptisms at Florence, 1451–1600: Variations around the Trend Line

after 1560 are there indications that the population had begun again slowly to increase.[39]

Outside of the traditional county of Florence, the population upsurge of the late fifteenth and sixteenth centuries was again particularly strong in rural areas. At Pistoia, between 1427 and 1552, the rural population grew from 11,744 to 32,498 persons, from a base index of 100 to 276.7. The average annual rate of increase was an im impressive 0.82 percent. Much in contrast, the city of Pistoia moved from 4,478 residents to 6,168, from index 100 to a low 137.8; its rate of growth was only 0.26 percent per year. Within these same chronological limits, the Pisan contado, in its 1427 boundaries, gained from index 100 to 201.7 (in absolute numbers, from 18,330 to 36,972 inhabitants respectively), registering an average annual growth rate of 0.56 percent. But again, the city of Pisa lagged behind. With 7,410 residents in 1427 and 11,849 in 1552 (index, 161.5), it grew at an annual rate of 0.38 percent. The total population of the Florentine domains in 1427 was 262,450 persons (clergy excluded); in the same area, adjusting for the expansion of the Florentine domains with the acquisition of Siena, we count 507,869 persons in 1552. Our yardstick of indices shows an increase from 100 to 193.5; this corresponds to an average annual growth rate of 0.53 percent.

The population thus nearly doubled in size. But the pattern of Tuscan settlement was also changing. Rural areas did better than cities, and regions remote from Florence, the biggest losers in the previous population plunge, now emerge as the biggest gainers. When the population was falling, the ring of dense settlement contracted close to Florence; as the total population once more expanded, growth was most pronounced in the more distant zones, in the regions partially deserted in 1427. The small towns, on the other hand, fared poorly. As Fiumi observes in regard to Prato, much of their increase was attributable to the great growth in the numbers of religious.[40] Servants also proliferated. Economically and demographically these were inactive groups. Neither in terms of size nor in terms of economic functions did the small Tuscan towns come again to resemble the vigorous commercial centers of the thirteenth century.

A final observation may be made concerning Florence, the regional metropolis. Between 1427 and 1552, it expanded in size by two-thirds, but it

39. Pardi, 1916, pp. 191–96, calls the years from 1531 to 1564 a "periodo di ristagno." The figures from 1552 are taken from Battara, 1935b, p. 33. A certain confusion surrounds the date of this census, which is often given as 1551. The date of the survey for the city is 25 February 1551, Florentine style, corresponding to 1552 in the modern calendar. We here follow Battara, 1935b, p. 3.

40. Fiumi, 1968, p. 153.

also lost relative position among the principal cities of Italy. According to the best estimates, Florence was the third city of Italy in number of inhabitants before the plague of 1348; only Venice and Milan were larger. But by the middle of the sixteenth century, Florence had sunk to seventh or even ninth position among Italian cities.[41] This substantial drop in relative size points unmistakably to a corresponding decline in Florence's economic importance. Florentine merchants, bankers, and manufacturers were losing ground to foreign competitors, especially Lombards and south Germans. A pioneer in the commercial recovery of Europe from the doldrums of the early Middle Ages, Florence let leadership pass to other cities, other peoples.

II. Cycles of Life

Although the documentation yields only occasional glimpses, it still shows beyond a doubt that the population losses of the middle and late fourteenth century were frightful. It is harder to discern how this demographic disaster touched individual lives.

DEADLY YEARS, DEADLY SEASONS

It seems certain that the plagues wreaked their principal havoc in the big cities. Florence has left good records through which to watch a community battling for survival against devastating epidemics. The Dominican convent of Santa Maria Novella gives historians two necrologies, both beginning at the end of the thirteenth century. The first and larger commemorates the names and dates of death of 1,758 laymen buried in the church cemetery. The second records the names and dates of death of 602 friars, postulants, and lay brothers (*conversi*).[42] To these numbers of reported dead, we add some 531 references to departed relatives, taken from twenty-one published family memoirs.[43] In all, this composite file of the dead includes 2,891 names.

41. Battara, 1935b, p. 78, places Florence in seventh place with a population of 59,191 inhabitants in 1552. But the censuses of the two following cities (Rome, with 53,887 inhabitants, and Verona, with 53,280) date respectively from 1527 and 1577. Both cities may have been larger than Florence in 1552.

42. "Nomi di uomini e di donne seppelliti in S. Maria Novella, tratti da un Libro di cartapecora esistente nelle mani de' Fratri di detta chiesa," I. di San Luigi, 9:123–203; *Necrologio*, 1955.

43. Corsini, 1965; Dati, 1969; Rucellai, 1960; Landucci, 1883; Morelli, 1956; Velluti, 1914; Masi, 1906; dell'Antella, 1843; Oderigo di Credi, 1843, reprinted in Castellani, 1956, 2:804 ff.; Rinuccini, 1840; Pitti, 1905; Rospigliosi, 1909, this book comes from Pistoia; Monaldi, 1845; Macinghi-Strozzi, 1877, these are letters, but contain occasional references to vital events; Naddo da Monte Catini di Val di Nievole, 1784; Salviati, 1784; Bernardo Machiavelli, 1954; Niccolini, 1969; Giovanni di Lemmo da Comugnori, 1876, this journal concerns the lower Arno valley; *Diario di anonimo*, 1876; Giovanni di Iacopo and Lionardo di Lorenzo Morelli, 1785, does not carry useful information for our purposes. For a recent, though still partial, bibliography of family memoirs, see Pezzarossa, in Anselmi et al., 1980, pp. 93–149, with 330 entries.

Table 3.6. Deaths by Months: Plague Years and Other Years, 1251–1500

	Plague Years		*Other Years*	
	Deceased	*Percent*	*Deceased*	*Percent*
January	15	1.60	139	8.61
February	15	1.60	125	7.74
March	25	2.66	130	8.05
April	66	7.03	146	9.05
May	107	11.40	111	6.88
June	197	20.98	134	8.30
July	244	25.99	150	9.29
August	139	14.80	188	11.65
September	51	5.43	142	8.80
October	29	3.09	132	8.18
November	31	3.30	120	7.43
December	20	2.13	97	6.01
Totals	939	100.00	1614	100.00

SOURCE: Necrologies and memoirs cited in n. 43 above.

Our composite necrology identifies the following years as marked by high mortalities: 1340, 1348, 1363, 1374 to 1375, 1383 to 1384, 1390, 1400, 1417 to 1418, 1423 to 1424, 1430, 1437, 1449, 1457, 1479, and 1495 to 1499. Table 3.6 shows the monthly distribution of burials in these years of incremented mortality and compares this with the monthly distribution of burials in other years, from 1251 to 1500.

In periods of high mortalities, deaths show a pronounced tendency to cluster in the hot summer. As Table 3.6 illustrates, during the plague years the numbers of deaths in July surpassed by fifteen times the recorded burials of January or February. Contemporaries were well aware of this phenomenon. Giovanni Morelli writes:

> And know that with February [plague] begins to make itself felt within the city, and proceeds to gather strength through the entire month of July. And after middle July it attacks honorable people and those who live regular lives; fewer people then die, but they are of the best.[44]

The marked seasonal character of the plague allows us to construct a crude index of its relative severity. If deaths were distributed evenly throughout the year, then 8.5 percent should occur in the 31 days of July. Before 1348 July claimed 8.9 percent (74 out of 830) of the recorded burials. The plague seems to have been unknown at Florence before 1348; not even the many deaths of 1340 can be attributed to it. From 1348 until 1400 July deaths soared to 20.9 percent of the total (274 out of 1,313). In those 53 years, one out of five Florentines died in July. The plague wanes in the first half of the fifteenth century when July deaths account for 10.1 percent of all deaths (25

44. Morelli, 1956, p. 294.

out of 248), but shows renewed power in the second half of the century when July burials represent 13 percent (21 out of 161) of the total.

Are cyclical movements discernible in occurrences and recurrences of plague? In collaboration with Perry Gluckman and Mary Pori, both formerly of the staff of the Center for Advanced Study in the Behavioral Sciences at Stanford, California, we subjected the composite record of deaths in the city of Florence to spectral analysis, which is essentially a means of searching for cycles in time-series data. The results of this analysis suggested a principal cycle with a period of approximately 43 years, and secondary cycles showing periods of approximately 32, 25, and 15 years respectively. While the results cannot command complete confidence, they suggest some hypotheses. The mortalities caused by the late medieval epidemics were to some extent age-specific. The most numerous victims were children and young adults; mature people who lived through one or more epidemics were not likely to fall victim to a later pestilence. The immediate impact of epidemics was to "age" the population, which also obviously now consisted of plague survivors. For this reason the population gained a certain immunity from an early recurrence of a major epidemic.

The population also rebounded from its terrible losses in distinctive ways. As we show in the following section, massive deaths raised fertility levels among the survivors, which in turn led to the formation of a large cohort of babies relative to the total population. With time, this enlarged cohort moved up the scale of ages. From approximately age 15, the girls in the cohort would begin to marry, and these girls would reach their maximum fertility (their mean age of motherhood) at approximately age 26. (This was the mean age of mothers with babies less than 1 year of age in the city of Florence in 1427.) However, the girls had to find husbands within a smaller and much older age cohort of males. Consequently, many girls would be unable to marry, and this would lower the gross rate of reproduction for the cohort as a whole. By age 30 the young men in the enlarged cohort would be marrying in large numbers, and they reached their maximum rate of reproduction (their mean age of fatherhood) at approximately age 40. In sum, the large cohort, generated in response to the mortalities of a major plague, would be most actively reproducing itself (of course with the aid of women found in younger cohorts) approximately 40 years later, and at that time would be making its most substantial additions to the total population. This was likely to create another "baby bubble" and set it moving up the scale of ages, but it would also give the population large numbers of young people and increase its vulnerability to another major epidemic. Plague occurrences, in other words, may have been strongly influenced by the cycles of marriage and births, observable at Florence in the fifteenth and sixteenth centuries.

MORTALITY AND FERTILITY

These hypotheses imply that deaths, marriages, and births at Florence were tightly linked. Examination of the marital behavior of the ancestors of Giovanni Morelli show clearly that plagues encouraged marriages.[45] Giovanni's eldest uncle, also named Giovanni, did not marry until he was past age 40. The reason for the delay was apparently the survival of his father, who, in those good years before the Black Death, lived until 1347, when Giovanni was 38 or 39. Giovanni took a wife "because he was the eldest [son]" in 1349, 2 years after the death of his father and 1 year after the Great Pestilence. It took another pestilence to prompt any of his brothers into marriage. The plague of 1363 carried off Giovanni and two other brothers, sparing the youngest, Pagolo, father of our author. Pagolo was now obligated, in the interest of family survival, to take a wife, which he did in January 1364. The Florentine family memoirs show a flurry of marriages in the years following major epidemics. Matteo di Niccolò Corsini, for example, was probably married in 1364, following the epidemic of 1363 (his first child was born in 1365).[46] His daughter Francesca and son Giovanni were both married in 1401, following the plague of 1400, and another daughter married in 1403. Giovanni in turn arranged the marriage of one daughter in 1418, following the plague of 1417, and another in 1425, after the plague of 1424.

In encouraging marriages, the high levels of mortality also encouraged births. Presumably, the younger persons who now married would be more fertile than the older couples they replaced. The age pyramid of the countryside of Prato in 1371–72 reveals an extraordinary demographic reprise over the 8 years since the last major epidemic. Children younger than 8 years of age made up nearly 38 percent of the total population.[47] Morelli relates that Florentine women in the period before the great epidemics, in spite of good health and longevity, bore in the course of their lives usually four to six children. In contrast, the wife of his contemporary, Niccolo Corsini bore 20 babies in 24 years (1365–89), of whom only eight survived childhood.[48] Another contemporary remarked how fertile the women of Florence became after the plague of 1400: "At that time many women became pregnant; for a long time they weren't making babies."[49]

Massive deaths stimulated births principally because they took a particu-

45. Ibid., pp. 138–42.

46. Corsini, 1965, passim.

47. See below, chap. 6, pp. 187–88.

48. Morelli, 1956, p. 112: ". . . e aveano in tutto il più quattro o sei figliuoli." Corsini, 1965, p. 82. Another Corsini wife, Tita, spouse of Matteo di Giovanni, bore 17 babies between 1435 and 1457.

49. Luca Dominici, 1933, 1:197. "In questo tempo [1400] sono ingrossate molte donne chè gran tempo non ne feceno fanciulli. . . . "

Table 3.7. Plagues and Baptisms in the City of Florence

	1457		*1479*		*1497*		*1527*	
	Bapt.	*Index*	*Bapt.*	*Index*	*Bapt.*	*Index*	*Bapt.*	*Index*
Years from plague								
−4	2,046	100.0	2,536	100.0	2,548	100.0	1,899	100.0
−3	2,100	102.6	2,512	99.1	2,760	108.3	2,885	99.5
−2	2,100	102.6	2,539	100.1	2,565	100.7	3,342	115.3
−1	2,207	107.9	2,664	105.0	2,468	96.9	3,377	116.5
0*	1,882	92.0	2,126	83.8	2,137	83.8	2,645	91.2
1	1,781	87.0	2,215	87.3	2,269	89.1	1,777	61.3
2	2,058	100.6	2,337	97.2	2,578	101.1	3,148	108.6
3	2,105	102.9	2,412	95.1	2,704	106.1	3,208	110.7
4	2,206	107.8	2,515	99.2	2,871	112.7	2.070	71.4

(o= Plague Year)*

SOURCE: M. Lastri, 1775.

larly heavy toll of the very young. A chief reason why parents have shown restraint in procreating children has always been other children.

To illustrate still more precisely the stimulus which deaths exerted on births, Table 3.7 records the movements in the number of baptisms at Florence over the four years preceding and following major epidemics.

In all these plague years, baptisms, and presumably births, fell by an average of 12 percent. Many families were doubtlessly fleeing Florence, and some babies were consequently born and baptized outside the city. The drop in baptisms was still greater in the year following the epidemic—more than 18 percent on the average. Deaths disrupted many marriages, and at times carried off both partners. Moreover, the fear was common that sexual intercourse heightened the risks of infection. Finally, these traumatic events, and the famines which often accompanied them, may have induced temporary sterility.[50] But thereafter, the number of baptisms and births rebounded to equal or surpass the levels maintained in the years immediately preceding the plague. The most remarkable recovery followed the most severe of the epidemics—that of 1527. The plague then carried off probably one-third the population, and yet the crop of babies in 1529 and 1530 was nearly as large as the numbers born each year from 1523 to 1526. (The sharp drop of births in 1531 results from the long siege of the city by the forces of Emperor Charles V, from October 1529 to August 1530.) This feat of producing babies is the more remarkable, as the plague itself was not lenient toward young adults of

50. The relation between amenorrhea and famine has been demonstrated in Le Roy Ladurie, 1969, pp. 1589–1601. Famine often accompanied plague and no doubt plague itself caused an equivalent psychological anguish.

marriage age.[51] In spite of huge losses, the community strove to keep constant its yearly birth rate, usually with success.

DURATION OF LIFE

To develop even a crude picture of changes in the life cycle across these centuries, the most serviceable sources would seem to be the family memoirs, which many Florentines and Tuscans composed and preserved from the late thirteenth century. To be sure, these memoirs present many difficulties. The published ricordanze are numerous for the fourteenth and early fifteenth centuries, but after 1450 they decline in number. Moreover, the manner in which these ricordi were kept introduced subtle distortions into the data. The authors were nearly all male, and this affected their perspectives. The tragic passing of a young wife or daughter was far more likely to be noticed than the death of an aged and solitary widow.[52] The recorded deaths of women thus seem to show a bias toward lower ages. Moreover, beyond the circle of his immediate family and present generation, the author was likely to possess and report information primarily for male relatives; almost always, they would be adults who had gained some social visibility. The reported ages of male deaths thus favor higher ages.

The published ricordi give dates of birth and of death for 157 men and 63 women, who lived in the period from 1250 to 1500. The average duration of life was 37.2 years for the men and 33.14 for the women. Because of the biases previously described, these figures represent at best only an order of magnitude. Very roughly then, the duration of an average life over the course of these two centuries was about 35 years.[53] Contemporaries themselves regarded this age as a threshold beyond which death was not unexpected; at years younger than 35, death seemed untimely and tragic.[54] Table 3.8 illustrates the average duration of life for 25 year periods, from the years 1276 to 1500. For each quarter-century, we calculated the average duration of life both for those who were born and for those who died within the period; we also give a composite estimate, or an average of the two averages, of life expectancies. This serves to smooth the estimates and to reduce the influence of particular epidemics upon them.

About 1300 the average duration of a human life at Florence was approximately 40 years. But over the following 100 years, amid the fury of pestilence, it collapsed to only one half that figure (an average of only some 20

51. See below, chapter 9, p. 273.

52. Distortions of this type also affect the use of gravestone inscriptions in judging average duration of life. See Henry, 1957, pp. 149–2 , and idem, 1959, pp. 327–29.

53. The figure is higher than the life expectancies of English peers over the same period (30–31 years), probably because the death of babies is insufficiently noted in the ricordi.

54. Gilbert, 1967, pp. 7–32.

Table 3.8. Average Duration of Life, 1276–1500

Years	*Persons Born*	*Average Life*	*Persons Died*	*Average Life*	*Composite*
1276–1300	17	38.72	5	24.00	31.41
1301–1325	36	40.56	7	39.71	40.14
1326–1348	20	23.90	14	50.64	37.27
1349–1375	17	36.12	56	36.95	36.54
1376–1400	37	19.49	27	16.44	17.97
1401–1425	39	29.15	41	19.59	24.37
1426–1450	24	31.33	17	24.41	27.87
1451–1475	11	38.82	22	43.41	41.12
1476–1500	7	27.71	14	50.07	38.89

SOURCE: *Ricordi* cited in n. 43 above.

years). In the fifteenth century the average duration of life grew more extended, especially after 1450, to regain the summit of 40 years. These estimates, while evidently crude, parallel Russell's calculations of the duration of life of the princes of the English royal family over the same period. Among them, life expectancy from birth fell by one third between 1300 and 1400, passing from 30 years to 20 in one century.[55]

A perusal of the Florentine family memoirs leaves the impression that men lived to an old age in the thirteenth century, even if claims that some survived to age 100 and older must be viewed with skepticism.[56] Among the direct ancestors of Giovanni Morelli, his great-great-grandfather Giraldo, born about 1199, "lived a long time, according to the age at that time." Giovanni does not, however, give his exact age at death, for fear that "I might be telling a falsehood."[57] Giraldo's son, Morello, born about 1255 or 1256, "lived a long time, more than 80 years," and died not long after 1334. Continuing down the line of his ancestors, Morelli cites his grandfather Bartolomeo, born about 1287; he died in 1347 at the age of about 60 years. The advent of the great epidemics from mid-century had a visible impact on the longevity of Giovanni's relatives. Pagolo, Giovanni's father, was born in 1335 and died, a victim of the plague of 1374, when he was younger than 40 years. His three brothers were cut down by the plague of 1363, at the ages of 55, 54, and 40 years respectively. Giovanni himself concluded that babies born in the twelfth and thirteenth centuries "were of good and strong constitution and lived a long

55. Russell, 1948, p. 180. The average duration of life reached 30.22 years before the Black Death; fell to 17.33 years between 1349 and 1375; 20.53 between 1376 and 1400; then slowly lengthened, 23.78 years between 1401 and 1452, and 32.76 between 1426 and 1450.

56. See, for example, Niccolini, 1969, p. 56: "vivette circa cento trenta anni." Giovanni di Lemmo da Comugnori, 1876, p. 169: "habebat annos centum et ultra." Velluti, 1914, p. 72: "vivette bene CXX anni."

57. Morelli, 1956, pp. 118–19.

Table 3.9. Average Duration of Life in Religion: Friars of Santa Maria Novella

Period	*Friars*	*Average Years*
1276–1300	32	31.78
1301–1325	56	30.07
1326–1350	155	27.46
1351–1375	65	26.22
1376–1400	36	26.51

SOURCE: Necrology of Santa Maria Novella, see n. 31 above.

time." In his belief, 40 years of life passed in former times were the equivalent of 25 or 30 years in his own day and age.[58]

The lowering of life expectancy affected all other principal events in the life cycle—age of entry into adult careers, age of marriage, age of parenthood, and, because of early death, the duration of service in careers and the duration of marriages. The career which best illustrates these phenomena is service in the religious life. The plague of 1348 alone carried off 77 friars from the Dominican convent of Santa Maria Novella, and the subsequent epidemics of 1363–64 and 1400 were nearly as devastating.[59] According to a contemporary, the need to admit large numbers of young and untrained novices to replace the departed was a disaster for the convent, both economically and spiritually:

> As the chief men died and novices replaced them, the religious orders themselves fell to ruin. How painful it is, whenever men have been trained for many years and with great effort, that they pass away in scarcely one hour. All that diligence, which men previously applied in preparing and supporting outstanding careers, is rendered vain and useless.[60]

The surviving necrology of friars from Santa Maria Novella allows us to calculate exactly how lowered duration of life affected careers in religion; for friars who died before 1400, the necrology usually mentions not only the date of death, but also the date of profession (see Table 3.9).

In the last quarter of the thirteenth century the average elapsed time spent in the order, between profession and death, was 32 years; it fell to 26 years over the course of the next 100 years—a contraction of roughly 20 percent. A comparable necrology from Christchurch, Canterbury, in England, shows nearly the same decline in the duration of life in religion, from 30.6 years in the early fourteenth century to 27.6 years at its close.[61] The mean duration of

58. Ibid., pp. 110, 111–12.
59. The figures are taken from Giovanni di Carlo, 1698, p. 407.
60. Loc. cit.
61. Cited in Russell, 1948, p. 180.

this career, and surely most careers, endured substantially less contraction in this troubled age than did the mean duration of an entire life, or even of an adult life—to judge from English evidence. The reason for this seems apparent. To compensate for losses from the plague, the convent recruited men younger, on the whole, than those who had died. The mean age of the friars was thus reduced, and their apparent life expectancy increased. This partially compensated for the shortened duration of life experienced in the population as a whole. In more general terms, in order to maintain needed or desired services, society attempted to keep the numbers performing those services as stable as possible. With falling population, the sole means of accomplishing this was to admit into a given career younger persons and in larger numbers. Often, as at Santa Maria Novella, this swing towards youth would affect the character and the quality of the services performed.

MARRIAGE

It might be predicted that the ages at first marriage would follow the same trend as ages of entry into other careers; when life expectancy decreased, the mean age at first marriage should fall, and with it the mean age of parenthood. Morelli included in his memoirs several remarkable comments about the marital practices of the Florentines in past and present.[62] He affirms that the usual age of first marriage for men in the twelfth and thirteenth centuries was 40 years, and he tells his reader not to be surprised. He expected his own descendants to marry between 20 and 25 years, or before age 30 at the latest.[63] Still, according to Morelli, girls in these days married between the ages of 24 and 26; his own contemporaries, he says, were reluctant to wait until their daughters reached age 15 before giving them to a husband.[64] Other writers of this epoch shared the opinion that men and women were much older at first marriage in the thirteenth century than in later periods. A chronicler from Rimini, writing in 1354, claimed that men in the days of Emperor Frederick II, who died in 1250, postponed marriage until age 30.[65] The delay clearly struck him as remarkable. The Florentine domestic chronicler, Lapo di Giovanni Niccolini de' Sirigatti, writing in the early fifteenth century, noted with similar surprise that three of his uncles, living the early fourteenth century, were still bachelors at age 40, and then only one took a wife.[66]

Although the surviving ricordi yield only sparse data, they would seem to support the thesis that the advent of the great epidemics and the short-

62. Morelli, 1956, pp. 111–12.
63. Ibid., p. 207.
64. Loc. cit.
65. Battagli da Rimini, 1913, p. 10.
66. Niccolini, 1969, p. 57.

Table 3.10. Estimated Age at First Marriage: Tuscany, Fourteenth and Fifteenth Centuries

	City of Prato			*City of Florence*		
	1372	*1427*	*1470*	*1427*	*1458*	*1480*
Male Age	23.8	26.9	29.6	30.3	30.5	31.4
Female Age	16.3	17.6	21.1	17.6	19.5	20.8
Difference	7.5	9.3	8.5	12.7	11.0	10.6

	Countryside of Prato			*Countryside of Florence*	
	1372	*1427*	*1470*	*1427*	*1470*
Male Age	22.3	24.0	24.4	25.7	27.7
Female Age	15.3	17.3	19.5	18.4	21.0
Difference	7.0	6.7	4.9	7.3	6.7

SOURCE: Estimo of 1372 and Catasti of 1427, 1458, 1470, 1480; data from the last three surveys come from a sample of 1/10 of the households. Calculations for the countryside of Prato concern only 13 villages out of 43; the ages of adults were not recorded in the others.

ened duration of life acted to depress ages at first marriage for both men and women. Of 16 marriages contracted between 1251 and 1350, the average age of the groom was 30.1 years; in 13 marriages between 1351 and 1400, the average age was only 23.9 years. In the fifteenth century, under less severe epidemiological conditions, the age of male first marriage again moved upward, to about 30 years.[67] Unfortunately, the memoirs do not yield sufficient references to the bride's age at first marriage to establish a pattern. But it remains very likely that her age also fell under the conditions of short life expectancy.

Estimi of the fourteenth century (we make particular use of surveys from Prato, dated 1372) and Catasti of the fifteenth century offer an exceptional opportunity to observe shifts in ages at first marriage for both sexes. To calculate those ages, we make use of a method devised by J. Hajnal, which can be applied to any census giving ages and marital status of the population.[68] The results are presented in Table 3.10. to come here.

The example of Prato confirms that the age at first marriage reached its lowest point in the period when the expectation of life was also at its nadir, about 1372. And it responded to improving conditions of life by moving upward. At Prato, between 1372 and 1427, the male age at marriage increased by two or three years, and this movement continued in the city, though not in the countryside, over the course of the fifteenth century. At Florence, to judge from the ricordi, the male age advanced rapidly from the fourteenth into the fifteenth century, but after 1427 stabilized at approximately age thirty. Florentine girls, on the other hand, between 1427 and

67. The data are presented for both men and women in Herlihy and Klapisch-Zuber, 1978, Table 23, p. 205.

68. Hajnal, 1953. See below, Chapter 7, p. 207, for an explanation of the method.

1480 delayed their marriages by an additional three years. Seemingly everywhere in Tuscany of the fifteenth century, marital age for girls advanced more rapidly than that for males. This delay in contracting a first marriage would tend to slow the formation of new families, dampen the birth rate, and brake the upward surge in the numbers of people.

Changes in the duration of life affected not only ages of marriage, but the proportions marrying—and those remarrying. In crowded Prato of 1325 and 1329, women without a spouse appear as household heads more frequently than they do in 1372 and 1427. Most were probably widows, but some may have been that rarity in Tuscan society, spinsters. After 1348 almost all Tuscan girls who did not enter religion married. At Prato in 1372, 98.5 percent of women between age 15 and 30 were married or widowed. The proportion of those marrying (and remarrying) continued high in 1427. Again at Prato, in 1427 with the generation of women centering upon age 50, only 5.4 percent had apparently never married. At Florence in the same year, the comparable group of permanent spinsters made up 3.8 percent of the feminine population; in the countryside, 1.7 percent; and in the total population, 2.4 percent.[69] By 1470 the proportion had fallen to 0.9 percent in the entire contado, but at Florence it fluctuated between 2.9 percent in 1458 and 4.3 percent in 1480. The proportions of unmarried women were doubtlessly much bigger, as ever larger numbers of girls were flocking into, or were herded into, convents.[70] In sum, a lengthening span of life and demographic recovery not only pushed upward ages at first marriage, but discouraged or prevented many young people from marrying at all.

POSITIVE AND PREVENTIVE CHECKS

What factors were regulating the size of the Tuscan community at the close of the Middle Ages? Demographers since Thomas Malthus have distinguished between "positive checks" and "preventive checks" on population growth.[71] Positive checks include plagues, famines, wars, and all natural and social disasters—all the dread horsemen of the Apocalypse. Populations also control their own growth through preventive checks limiting marriages and births.

Contemporaries were well aware that plagues and famines were barriers to further expansion of dense populations. Morelli offered this extraordinary explanation for the carnage of 1348:

> The reasons were in part these. . . . Florence was at that time very filled with people, more than it had ever been before. The previous

69. Only the lay population is included in these figures.
70. On the growing numbers of women in the religious life, see Trexler, 1972.
71. Discussed in the second chapter of Malthus, 1798/1970.

year [1347] there had been a great famine at Florence, and out of every hundred persons, I don't believe there were twenty who had bread or any cereal. . . . They lived on herbs and on the roots of herbs and on vile plants . . . and they drank water, and the entire countryside was filled with persons who went about grazing like cattle on the grass. Think how their bodies were affected. . . . For these reasons they were dying continuously.[72]

A century or so later, Niccolò Machiavelli cast the same observation in more abstract terms:

It is natural that such scourges (epidemic, famine and flood) should rage . . . . Like most simple bodies, nature, when it is burdened by an excess of matter, shakes itself repeatedly and undergoes a purge which is the cure of this great body. Thus . . . when the world has a surplus population and the earth cannot nourish them . . . when human malice and duplicity are at their height, nature, to purge itself, makes use of one of these three scourges, so that men, thus reduced to small number and depressed by sorrow, can more easily find subsistence and become better.[73]

That positive checks, in the form of plague and famine, operated against the swollen Tuscan population of the early fourteenth century seems unquestionable. On the other hand, a purely Malthusian explanation of the fourteenth century crisis leaves many questions unanswered. The plague was unknown at Florence, as elsewhere in Europe, before 1348. Morelli himself noted its novelty:

At Florence they did not know this evil (I mean to say, the whole of the population), because it had not appeared since very long.[74]

In the absence of pestilence, the region was able to support a population the size of which would not be attained again before the eighteenth or even the nineteenth century. We do not know why the plague appeared in the middle fourteenth century, but it seems at once to have imposed a new and lower ceiling on the size of the Tuscan community. For three centuries and more after 1348, the city of Florence was several times to challenge, but never to penetrate, a limit of 60–70,000 inhabitants. Not even malnutrition can explain the high susceptibility of the Tuscan population to this new disease. By 1427 the population had been reduced by two-thirds; food seems to have been reasonably cheap and abundant. And yet the plague

72. Morelli, 1956, pp. 291–92.
73. Machiavelli, s. d., bk. 2, chap. 5, p. 308.
74. Morelli, 1956, p. 291.

lingered. Medical factors, rather than social or Malthusian, seem to have been crucial here, but they remain difficult to analyze. Here is a task for future research.[75]

HEARTHS AND RESOURCES

The Tuscan population did not, however, remain a passive victim to these devastating epidemics. We have seen that marriages here played an central role in promoting or repressing population growth. Marriages resulted in the formation of new families and, usually, of new hearths. To understand the nature of the preventive checks operating in Tuscany, we must inquire into the relationships linking the number of hearths, their average size, and (insofar as we can judge its character) the level of available resources.

In the fourteenth and fifteenth centuries, the violent swings of the population affected both the number of households and their average size, but not in the same manner. The "leading variable," in the sense of the one which initially showed the greater sensitivity to population change, was average household size. The "trailing variable," the one which manifested the greater inertia in regard to population movements, was the total number of hearths.

At Prato, for example, in the earliest phases of the population collapse, the number of people between ca. 1290 and 1325 fell by 15.3 percent. But the number of hearths slipped by only 6.7 percent. Average household size over the same period sank from 4.7 to 4.3 persons—a loss of 8.5 percent. On the other hand, when the population began to grow during the fifteenth century, average household size was the first, and for long the only, value to reflect the demographic upswing. At Prato, it passed from 3.73 in 1427 to 4.26 in 1470, while the number of households remained exactly the same. At Florence, the multiplier was a low 3.78 in 1427, but it reached 4.72 in 1458, although the number of hearths continued to slip.

Thus, the growth of population was reflected only belatedly in the an increased number of hearths. At Florence, the stability in the number of households between the middle fourteenth and the middle sixteenth century is especially striking. Urban households were 9,555 in 1352, 9,780 in 1427, and 9,527 in 1552. Between these last two dates, the urban population increased substantially, from 38,000 to 59,000 inhabitants. At Pistoia, the number of urban hearths declined slightly between the same two years (from 1,247 in 1427 to 1,139 in 1552), even though its population grew from 4,478 to 6,168 persons.[76]

Is this a purely Tuscan phenomenon? It would seem not. Table 3.11

75. See Le Roy Ladurie, 1973, pp. 627–96.
76. The population for 1552 is taken from Repetti, 1833–64, 5:568.

Table 3.11. Households and Household Size at Verona, 1425–1502

Year	*Hhlds*	*Index*	*Size*	*Index*	*Ppltn (est.)*	*Index*
1425	3,866	100.0	3.68	100.0	14.225	100.0
1456	4,078	105.5	5.20	141.3	20,800	146.2
1502	7,142	184.7	5.89	160.0	42,000	295.3

SOURCES: Veronese Estimi in the Archivio di Stato of Verona. See D. Herlihy, 1973b.

shows movements in the number of hearths and average household size in the city of Verona in the fifteenth century.

The urban population of Verona was nearly 50 percent larger in 1456 than in 1425. But the number of households had grown by only a little more than 5 percent. This substantial population growth was initially reflected almost exclusively in average household size. Thereafter, average household size stabilized, and the number of households became the more sensitive register of continuing population increase.

Why was the number of households so slow to reflect the decline or growth of the population? The plague rarely swept away entire families. Rather, it left in its wake large numbers of truncated households. At Florence in 1427, a fifth of the households (20.1 percent) contained only a single person. So also, in periods of growth, many young persons delayed their departure from their family of origin until they achieved economic independence; if jobs were not available, many would not depart at all.

Most fundamentally, at Florence as elsewhere, the number of hearths seems to have been a function of economic resources. In the countryside, it depended on the number of family farms; in the city, the count of households reflected the availability of basic jobs remunerative enough to support a family. The balance between population and resources thus fixed the total number of "economic units," and worked to stabilize them even when the population suffered serious losses or was registering vigorous gains. In periods of population decline, landlords, employers, and the government—all those who as members of the dominant classes controlled the flow of salaries and benefits—sought to keep hearths occupied, that is to say, jobs filled in the city and farms worked in the countryside. Failure to do so would have meant radical losses in their own revenues, rents, profits, or taxes. By offering low rents, good salaries, favorable terms of tenure or employment, and tax concessions, they also encouraged marriages and the formation of new families. Linked to farms and jobs, the number of hearths also set a kind of floor to the demographic decline. As the population approached that floor, various mechanisms were called into play to encourage marriages and births. These processes emptied the established hearths of their younger members of marriage age and lowered average household size. To be sure, the great epidemics were certainly powerful enough to drag the total population even below this floor. But the strong opposition to the abandonment of farms and jobs, and the resulting encouragement of marriages and births, usually assured a quick recovery.

On the other hand, the number of hearths worked to impose upward limits on population growth. At Florence in the sixteenth century, the decline of industrial and commercial initiative limited the number of basic jobs needed to support a household. Mechanisms were set into motion which delayed marriage for the young or excluded it altogether. Many young men, unable to win economic independence and thus prevented from marrying, lingered on in the households of their parents, and swelled their average size. Many unmarriageable girls were placed in the bulging convents. In 1552 the Florentine hearth was among the most crowded in all Italy—a testimony not to vigorous demographic expansion, but to limited opportunities for the young. These "impacted" hearths thus slowed to a halt the growth in Tuscan population. Continued expansion would have required an economic upsurge, which the torpid state of Tuscany in the sixteenth century could not originate or sustain.

In this perspective, the very structure of the Tuscan domestic group acted as a brake upon the demographic recovery of the late fifteenth and sixteenth centuries. In stimulating or retarding its own growth, the Tuscan community thus betrays the unmistakable traits of a homeostatic, "self-regulating" system. Preventive, even more than positive checks, kept the population within the limits which its resources, and initiative, could support.

4
Wealth and Enterprise

Tertio ad civitatis tutelam natura utitur naturali posse, quod maxime consistit in tribus: primo in denariis, secundo in vectualiis, tertio in gentibus.

In the third place, nature offers three natural means for the preservation of the city: first of all, money; secondly, provisions; finally, people.

Bernadino of Siena, *De conservatione et custodia civitatum*

s an inventory of property, as well as a census of people, the Catasto reveals how resources were divided between cities and countryside, among Florence and its subject cities, and also up and down the social scale. In attributing places of origin and occupations to many household heads, it helps identify who created this wealth, and how.

I. Distributions of Wealth

As we noted in chapter 1, the law of the Catasto distinguished among several kinds of property.[1] Certain possessions, regarded as essential to the family's survival and productivity—its residence, tools, and work animals—were exempt. Agricultural lands were assessed on the basis of one-half their harvests; the other half was presumably reserved for the support of the peasant family. Usually, therefore, agricultural properties carried an assessment below their true market value. The Catasto thus displays in an homogeneous way the distribution not of all forms of properties, but of those producing surplus income—"d'avanzo alla vita," not needed for life. The picture of wealth and its accumulations emerging from the Catasto, is incomplete, but it retains great interest. This was the wealth which supported all undertakings beyond subsistence living: prayer and politics, art and war. It assured Florence's importance among the states of Italy and sustained its brilliant culture.

1. See above, pp. 13–14.

Table 4.1. Regional Distribution of Wealth in Tuscany according to Residence *

	Florence	*Six Large Cities*	*Fifteen Towns*	*Countryside*	*Total*
Nmbr Hhlds	9,946	6,724	5,994	37,266	59,890
Percent	16.2	11.2	10.0	62.2	100.0
Nmbr Prs	37,245	26,315	24,809	175,840	264,210
Percent	14.1	10.0	9.4	66.5	100.0
Real Pprty	4,128,024	1,137,466	614,446	2,178,253	8,058,189
Percent	51.2	14.1	7.6	17.0	100.0
Movables	3,467,707	585,357	170,245	223,792	4,447,101
Percent	78.0	13.2	3.8	5.0	100.0
Public Debt	2,573,378	3,438	1,888	1,337	2,580,041
Percent	99.7	0.1	0.1	0.1	100.0
Total Wlth	10,169,109	1,726,261	786,579	2,403,382	15,085,331
Percent	67.4	11.4	5.2	15.9	100.0
Ddctns	2,504,041	332,763	135,341	321,205	3,293,350
Percent	76.0	10.1	4.1	9.8	100.0
Txble Wlth	7,665,068	1,393,498	651,238	2,082,177	11,791,981
Percent	65.0	11.8	5.5	17.1	100.0

* Values are in gold florins. Figures do not include the personal deduction of 200 florins per person allowed at Florence and 50 florins at Pisa.

REGIONAL DISTRIBUTIONS

Table 4.1 shows the distribution of the principal forms of wealth across the four "environments," into which we have crudely divided the Tuscan population.[2]

All the properties assessed in the Catasto were thus evaluated at close to 15 million florins before deductions, and, after them, at 12 million florins. Ecclesiastical properties are, to be sure, missing from these totals. According to Canestrini, the Church's possessions, chiefly real estate, were worth about 1.5 million florins, or about 11 percent of Tuscany's total taxable wealth.[3] The estimate seems conservative. By Fiumi's calculations, ecclesiastical properties constituted 25.7 percent of all assessed holdings at San Gimignano in 1419, and 29 percent at Prato in 1472.[4] The Catasto officials, as we saw, were casual in checking the ecclesiastical declarations. Then, too, the Church's lands benefited from the fiscal policy favoring agricultural holdings. For these two reasons, Canestrini's estimate is probably low, but beyond our powers to correct.

2. Small differences in the totals carried in our several tables are due to the inclusion or exclusion of certain categories of taxpayers—those with incomplete declarations, those subsequently added in 1428–29, declarations of institutions, and so forth. These small variations have no effect on proportions and percentages.

3. Canestrini, 1862, p. 151. Canestrini assesses clerical property at 1,423,992 florins, and the patrimonial possessions of the clergy at 69,950 florins, but he does not state the source of his information.

4. Fiumi, 1961, p. 220; and idem, 1968, p. 168.

Table 4.2. Population and Movable Wealth in the Tuscan Cities (in gold florins)

Town	*Population*	*Average Investment Per Household in Movables*	*Proportion of Urban Wealth in Movables*
Florence	37,245	609.87	59.6
Pisa	7,333	153.55	42.7
Pistoia	4,412	69.46	27.1
Arezzo	4,152	81.08	33.5
Prato	3,517	43.79	25.0
Volterra	3,342	75.83	39.0
Cortona	3,246	42.78	24.0
Montepulciano	2,498	36.06	24.7
San Gimignano *	1,677	99.37	31.6
Castiglione Fior.	1,524	25.86	14.8

* Colle is not included, because of the difficulty of distinguishing households in the town from those in the countryside. Presumably it would closely resemble San Gimignano in its investments.

The net wealth held by laymen—some 12 million florins—thus represented an average capital support for each of the 60,000 households of some 200 florins. The figure is striking. The minimum living wage in 1427, needed to support a worker, was about 14 florins. At the rate of 7 percent adopted by the fiscal office, this sum would represent the yearly return on a capital of 200 florins. (The sum of 200 florins was also the individual deduction allowed to residents of Florence.) In other words, a Tuscan family possessing an average share of the social capital could hope to survive on a 7 percent return, no matter what salary it received.

But in fact this wealth was very unevenly distributed, both geographically and socially. Florence in 1427 included only 14 percent of the total lay population, but it claimed two-thirds of the region's wealth. A Florentine household possessed, on the average, a patrimony of 1,022 florins before, and 790 florins after, deductions. The individual living in the capital enjoyed an average worth of 273 and 208 florins, gross and net figures respectively. The comparable averages for households in the secondary cities were 257 and 207 florins (for individuals, 66 and 53 florins respectively). Households and persons in these cities show barely a quarter of the wealth claimed by their counterparts in Florence. Finally, the gross and net assets of rural households were 66 and 57 florins; of rural persons, 14 and 12 florins. The poor but numerous rural families at the bottom of the ladder of wealth were worth, on the average, only a fourth as much as households in the secondary towns, and their wealth was only a twentieth of that claimed by families resident in the Florentine metropolis.

The Florentine domination of Tuscan resources was particularly overwhelming in regard to commercial investments and shares in the public debt. Florentines owned a comparatively modest 51 percent of the taxable real estate in Tuscany. In contrast, they controlled 78 percent of movable property and business investments, and they owned virtually the entire public debt.

Although poor by Florentine standards, the secondary Tuscan towns still retained significant proportions of their wealth in liquid investments. The percentage of their wealth held in movables also helps identify those towns which were able to retain an important role in commercial exchanges and in the industries of their regions.

Within the towns, the share of wealth held in movables tends to fall, albeit irregularly, with the size of the urban population. With more than a third of their wealth in movables, Pisa and Volterra reveal a commercial activity of considerable importance. Among the smaller towns, tiny San Gimignano was exceptional in the size of its commercial investments. This rough hierarchy underscores the importance of the towns found in the western half of the territory and in particular those which lay close to the sea, and to the old land links to France and the north.

Map 4.1, which shows the distribution of average net wealth (all forms) by household in rural districts, reveals an evident concentration in those regions that were most open to the outside world: near Livorno, a port; in the Val di Nievole and the Val d'Arno di sotto; around San Gimignano; and, in a certain measure, around Arezzo.[5] If we regard only movable assets, then the households of the Florentine contado possessed, on the average, more substantial holdings than elsewhere, even though their total fortune by household was smaller. The deductions allowed by the Catasto office also show the special importance of liquid wealth in areas close to Florence (see Map 4.2). There, the proportions of families burdened with obligations, and also the size of those obligations, were notably large. That quintessential urban creation—credit—percolated through the Florentine environs.

The economic domination of town over countryside was less pronounced outside the Florentine core. Together, residents of Florence and Prato owned 75.7 percent of the land in their surrounding countryside. In the district, the inhabitants of the principal towns held only about 46 percent of the rural properties.[6] Rural residents of the district also held a comparatively greater share of the movable wealth than did the rustics of the Florentine contado—16 as opposed to 4 percent respectively. The bour-

5. Based on average wealth per piviere in the center of the territory, and per podesterie at the periphery. See chap. 2 for discussion of these units. Data on Colle should be ignored, for reason given in Table 4.2.

6. For a detailed analysis of the distribution of landed property in contado and district, see Herlihy and Klapisch-Zuber, 1978, Table 31, p. 249.

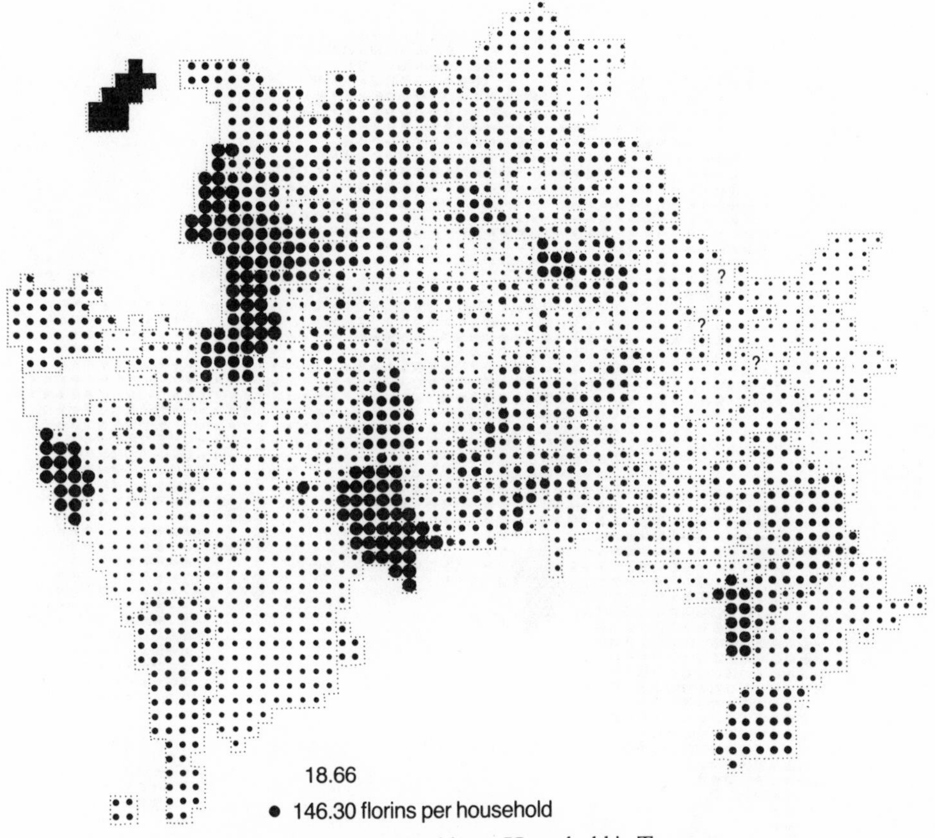

Map 4.1. Average Wealth per Household in Tuscany

geoisie of these towns lagged far behind the Florentines in their ability to appropriate the wealth of their regions.

SOCIAL DISTRIBUTIONS

Florence was thus a blazing sun of affluence, surrounded by dim planets of wealth in the smaller Tuscan cities—all of them set within a dark, nearly destitute rural space. Still, it would be wrong to imply that this affluent metropolis contained only, or chiefly, or even many, affluent households. Figure 4.1 shows the distribution of wealth within Florence and within the six large cities in 1427. In constructing the graph, we rearranged the urban households in descending order of total wealth. The households were then divided by centiles, and the wealth of each centile was calculated for our three forms of property. The figures for each

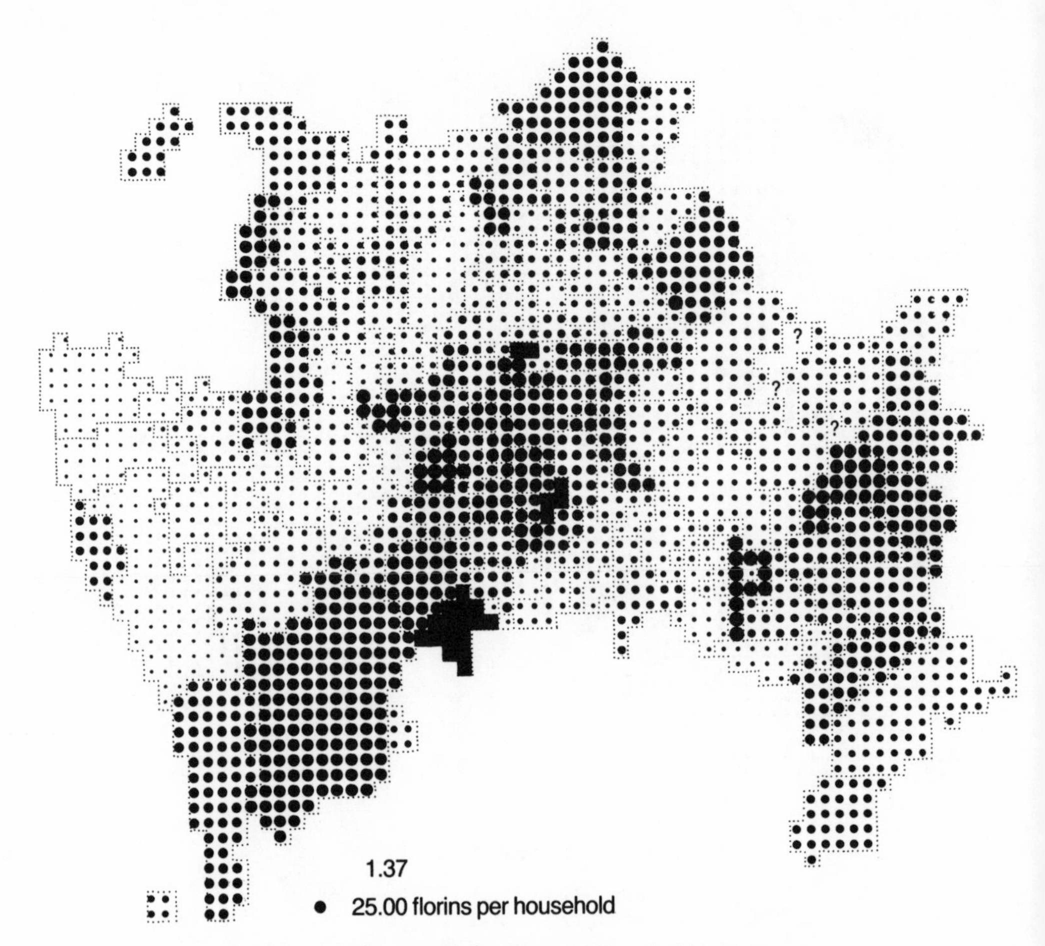

Map 4.2. Average Deductions per Household in Tuscany

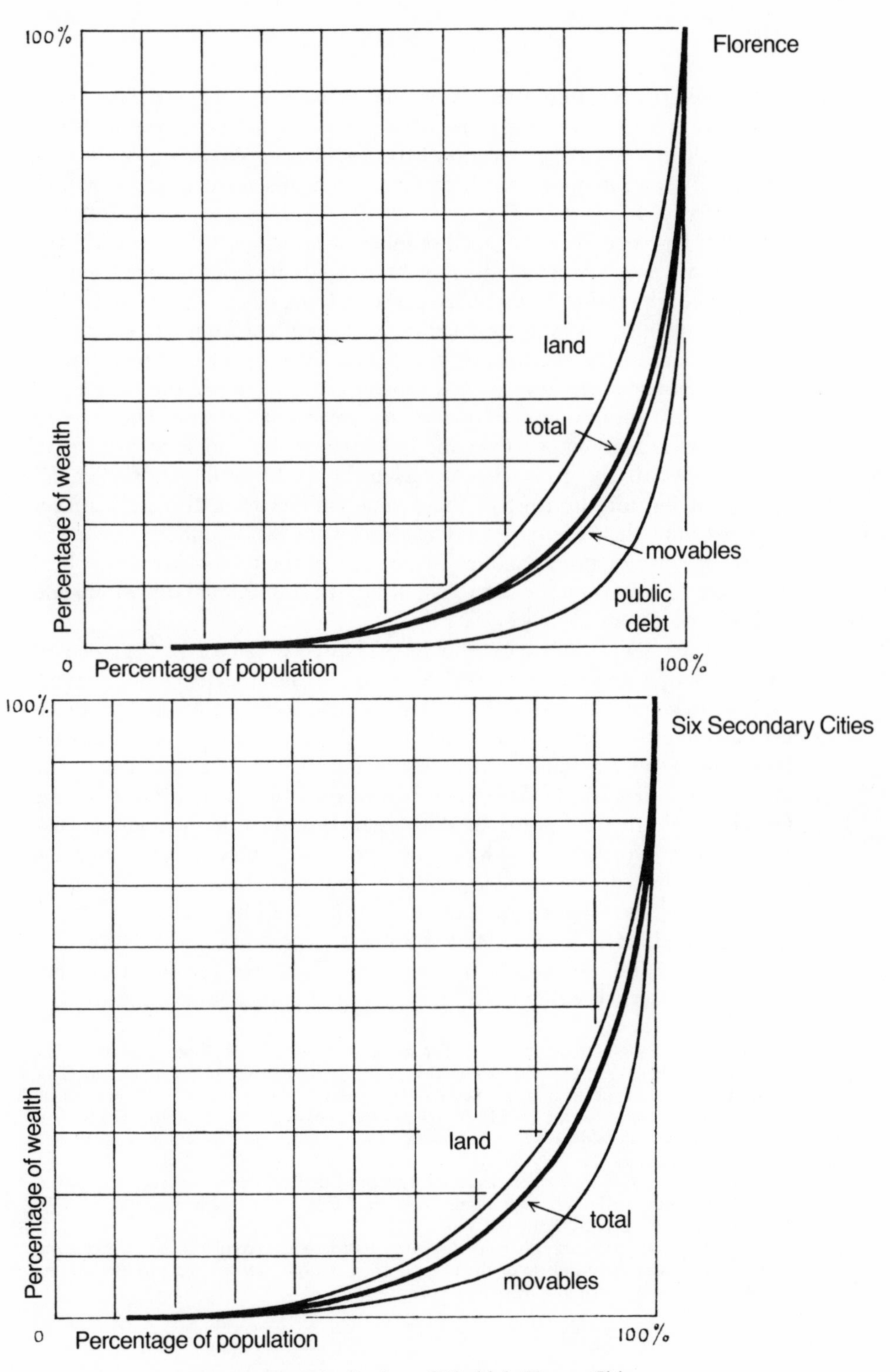

Fig. 4.1. The Distribution of Wealth in Tuscan Cities

centile were then accumulated; from the lowest to the highest. The curves presented in Figure 4.1 thus show what part of landed, movable, or taxable wealth fell to a particular portion of the population. We also give the Gini indices of concentration, which facilitate comparisons among the various forms of wealth.[7]

Within Florence in 1427 a small number of households disposed of large possessions, and a large number of households had but little.[8] About 14 percent of Florentine households possessed no taxable assets; after the allowable deductions were taken, the proportion climbs to 31 percent. At the other end of the social scale, the richest 1 percent of the urban households—about 100 families—owned more than a quarter of the city's enormous wealth, about one-sixth of the total wealth of Tuscany. The share of these families was bigger than the holdings of the poorer 87 percent of their fellow citizens; it likewise surpassed the wealth of the 37,000 families who lived outside the towns. These same families were also substantially more wealthy than the entire population of the six secondary cities. The richest 3,000 Florentine families—5 percent of the total—themselves held more than the remaining 57,000 Tuscan households, found both within and without the city of Florence.

Still, even the richest households of Florence cannot be regarded as entirely independent entities. They were bound together into various groupings based on relationship, marriage, and common political and economic interests.[9] Here, we consider only those clusterings of households based on blood relationship, manifest in the sharing of a common family name. In this regard, the Strozzi—a name borne by 53 families listed in the Catasto—held the first position. With each constituent household enjoying a patrimony worth 3,724 florins (average value), they alone owned 2.6 percent of the total net taxable capital of the city. They were followed by the 60 Bardi (holding 2.1 percent of the total wealth), the 31 Medici (1.9 percent), and, at a distance, the 18 Alberti (1 percent), the 24 Albizzi (1 percent) and the 28 Peruzzi (1.1 percent). These six groups of families together possessed close to 10 percent of the taxable wealth in 1427.

7. The index ranges from 1 to 100. The score of 1 indicates that every centile of the population holds 1 percent of the total wealth; 100 signifies that the richest 1 percent of the population owns all the wealth. In calculating the index, a "Lorenz curve" is drawn, which shows what percentage of the population owns what percentage of the wealth. The index is the ratio of area under this curve to the area that would be defined if wealth were distributed with absolute equality.

8. Goldthwaite, 1980, pp. 59–66, has recently argued that at Florence in 1427, "wealth was distributed among a relatively large number of men." It is hard to see how this view can be reconciled with the data from the Catasto.

9. On faction at Florence in the period of the Catasto, see the recent analysis of Dale Kent, 1978. She identifies the members of the two principal factions (Medici and anti-Medici) and examines the bonds which lent them their cohesiveness.

To be sure, some of the 214 household heads counted above were in reality the impoverished relatives of the truly affluent.[10] But even the destitute and those of middling means basked in the glory of a famous name. Often this association also conveyed material assistance: jobs, loans, gifts, and bequests. Alongside these compact and united family groups, which were set apart by numbers, wealth, and aggregate power, the firmament of Florentine society held some secondary, less sizeable constellations, with a few shining members.[11] There were also some brilliant, lone personalities, survivors of past greatness, or new to the Florentine universe. The two brothers Panciatichi, immigrants from Pistoia, alone possessed 1.7 percent of the city's wealth; the two Bischeri, or even a single Tornabuoni, claimed about 0.6 percent of total urban assets.

So also, in the secondary towns, the concentration of wealth was highly skewed. Few hands grasped much real property and many movables, in proportions closely resembling the Florentine. To be sure, gross wealth in the subject cities was slightly more evenly spread across the population than at Florence, for two evident reasons. The subject towns had no share in the funded public debt—the form of wealth which, at Florence, accrued principally to the very rich. And a lower percentage of households (11 as against 14 percent at Florence) was completely destitute. But another indicator uncovers a difference between the apparently similiar distributions. At Florence, a scant 2.5 percet of the taxpayers owned one-half of the commercial or industrial investments. But this "minimum majority," as statisticians call it, is even smaller outside the capital.[12] In spite of the extremely uneven distribution of total wealth at Florence, a larger segment of its people than in the smaller towns invested some capital, however modest, in industrial and commercial ventures.

Florence shows another distinctive trait. The composition of the patrimonies varied with the level of wealth more widely than in smaller cities or the countryside. (See Figures 4.2 and 4.3).

In the cities, "little people," worth between 1 and 200 florins and forming 60 percent of the households, invested between 15 and 20 percent of their assets in commerce and industry. Above this threshold of 200 florins, the middle class and the "fat people" of these secondary towns (about 25 to 30 percent of the taxpayers) invested proportionately larger parts of their assets in nonagricultural enterprises as their wealth increased. At Florence,

10. Among the Strozzi, only 5 heads of family (10 percent) held more wealth than the mean for the group; the same figure for the Medici was 3 (10 percent), for the Bardi 12 (20 percent).

11. For example, the 5 Portinari, 6 Rinuccini, 5 Soderini, 4 Lamberteschi, 6 Giugni, 6 Macinghi, and 5 Morelli. On these secondary groups and their relationships, see F. W. Kent, 1977, pp. 63–117.

12. The "minimum majorities" are 2.5 at Florence, 2.1 in the towns of the contado, 1.5 in those of the district, and 1.6 and 2.0 percent in their respective countrysides.

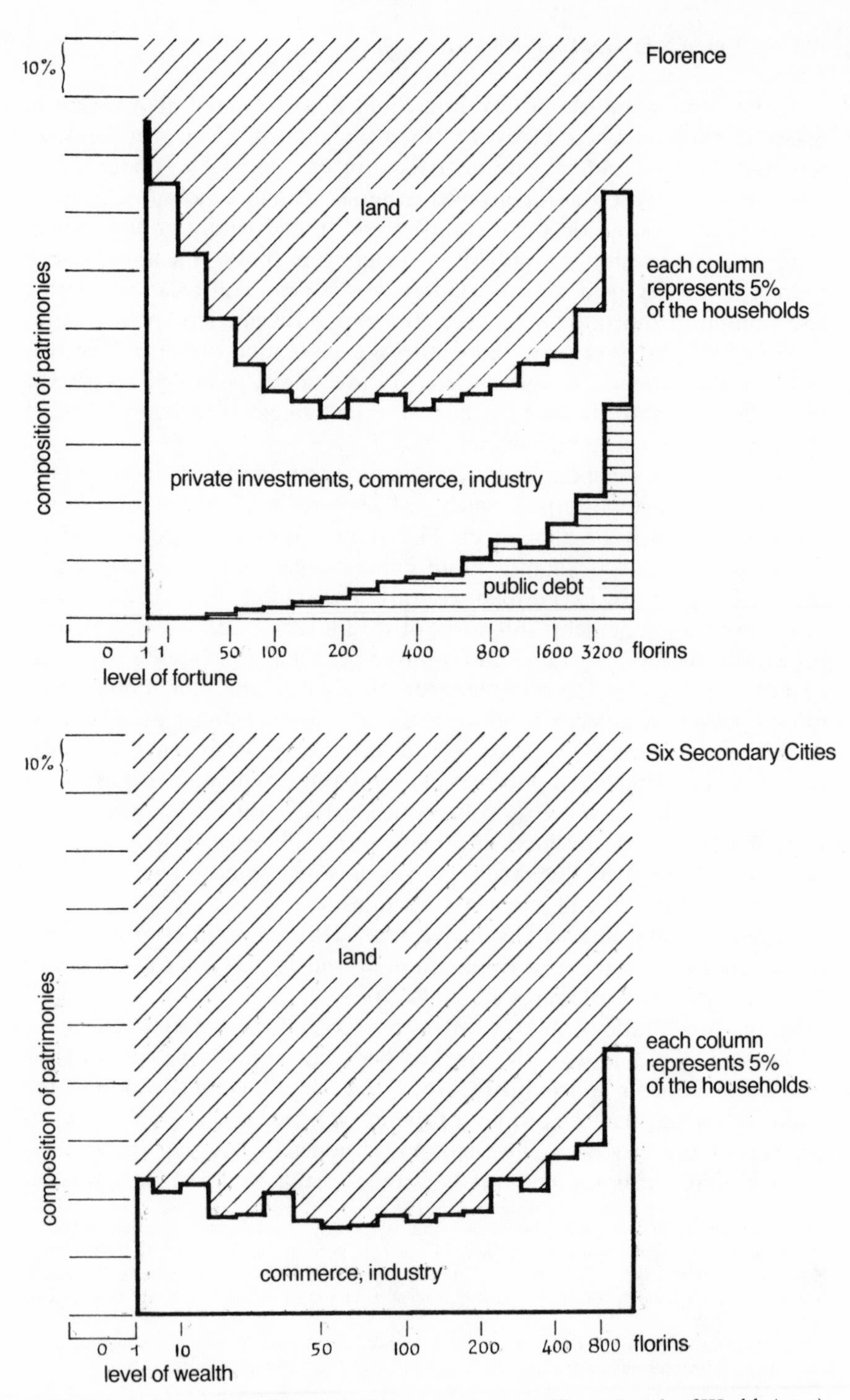

Fig. 4.2. Composition of Household Patrimonies according to Levels of Wealth (1426)

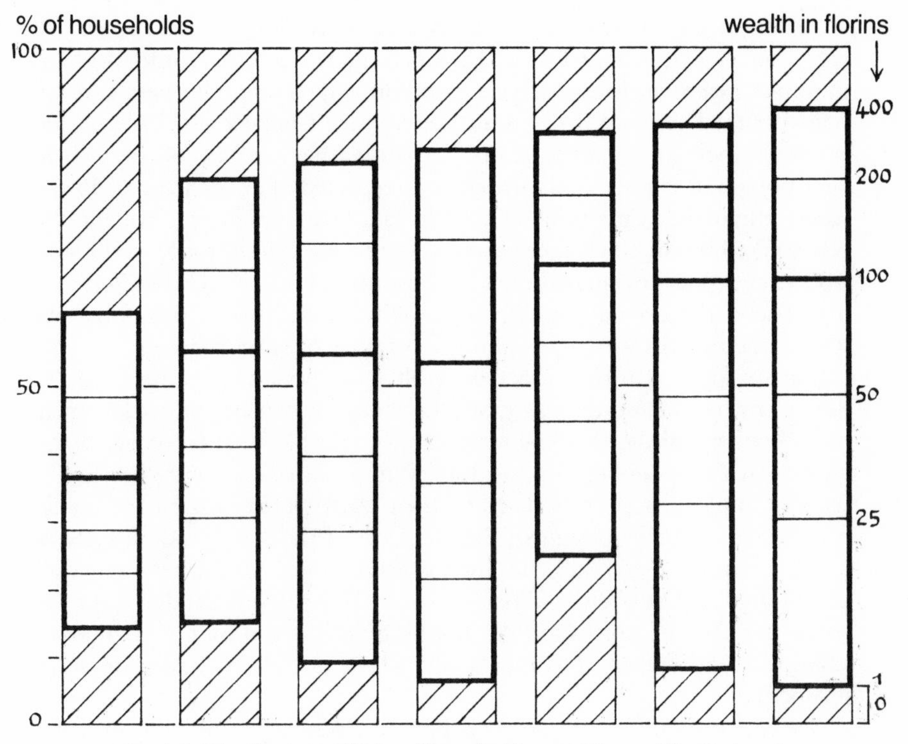

Fig. 4.3. Distribution of Urban Households according to Wealth (1427)

on the other hand, the middle classes look to be much less uniform in behavior. A whole group of small possessors, worth below 60 florins and making up 15 percent of the households, had hardly any holdings in land. Further up the scale of wealth, the large group (60 percent of the households) with assets from 56 to 2,310 florins, were remarkably homogeneous. Land holdings account for 55 to 60 percent of this group's assets. Only the highest 10 percent of the Florentine taxpayers gave a decisive advantage to movable investments and to shares in the public debt. Finally, at the very top of the ladder of fortunes, the richest 2 to 3 percent placed less than a third of their wealth in land, invested another third in business and industry, and with their remaining assets they gained the dubious honor of serving as the commune's principal creditors. The portfolio of the wealthiest households thus appears remarkably balanced.

The six secondary cities did not form an entirely homogeneous group. The proportion of families with no taxable assets varied on a scale of 1 to 4, according to city. It was low at Cortona, Arezzo, Volterra, and Pistoia.[13] But it reached 15.4 percent at Pisa and 25.8 percent at Prato. Except for Volterra, movable wealth is found largely concentrated among the best endowed households. There are, to be sure, differences. Cortona and Volterra look similar in their social composition; they lacked big numbers of very rich and very poor households. This structure is repeated at Arezzo and at Pistoia, where the higher categories of wealth had, however, greater weight. Pisa was marked by the small numbers of those on the middle rungs of the social ladder, and Prato by an inordinate proportion of households holding nothing. There, the average household wealth fell well below 50 florins; elsewhere, the median was twice as high, between 51 and 100 florins.

Can we locate, on the ladder of wealth, the poor and the powerful, the minori, mediocri, and the maggiori, to whom the contemporary documents make frequent allusion? Social rank was not a simple function of wealth, and wealth itself is an ambiguous measure. Within the cities, numerous families, without apparent resources, lived on their salaries better than many humble people with some belongings. The mezzadri of the countryside usually declared no property at all, but they enjoyed other advantages—especially capital provided by their landlords—which the small independent cultivator could not claim. Deprivation did not necessarily mean misery, and possessions were not proof that the family which held them basked in secure prosperity.

The recent work of Charles de la Roncière suggests a different yardstick: endebtedness .[14] At Florence, debts completely obliterated the assets of the lowest 30 percent of the taxpayers. From the next 20 percent of households (with average gross wealth of 60 to 210 florins) debts subtracted 40 percent from their patrimonies. The free capital they enjoyed (about 80 florins) might have yielded an annual return of scarcely 6 florins— hardly sufficient to support a single person.[15] In all, probably half the city fell within, or on the margins of, the minori. The next category of taxpayers, with 20 percent of the households, enjoyed, by a similar calculation, a return from unencumbered capital of 8 to 30 florins. With an average patrimony of 600 florins and average debts of about 200, a Florentine could then be assured of a modest standard of living, with a return equaling the salary of the lowest paid worker.[16] Beyond this threshold of 600 florins gross worth,

13. The exact values are 5.9, 6.3, 8.5 and 9.1 percent respectively.

14. La Roncière, 1974, pp. 661–745, especially p. 690.

15. The figure is calculated on the basis of a 7 percent return regarded by the Catasto office as the normal yield on capital.

16. See for example the Pisan salaries cited by Casini, 1965, pp. 556–64. Cherubini, 1968a, identifies the poor at Pisa as the 288 miserabili of the city, as well as 906 families with assets under 100 florins before deductions. Given the generally lower salary levels, standard of living, and capital holdings at Pisa, one could escape poverty with relatively smaller wealth than at Florence.

debts consumed on the average no more than a quarter of the family's possessions. The richest 30 percent of Florentine households made up the middle or great bourgeoisie. Their average debts far outweighed their assets, and their investments included in roughly balanced measure all types of assets: land, business capital, and shares in the public debt.

In the six large towns, endebtedness, also measured as a proportion of gross assets within each centile, fell more rapidly than at Florence. Debts exceeding the family's wealth burdened only 8 percent of the households; 62 percent of the families (in contrast to 50 percent at Florence), bore charges against their holdings which amounted to less than 40 percent of their assets. To be sure, patrimonies were also considerably less substantial than in the capital. Smaller debts did not mean that the poor fared better in the secondary towns. Rather, they indicate that social differentiation, among the minori, mediocri, and maggiori, had not progressed as far in these small urban centers as it had at Florence.

Within the framework of the regional economy, the concentration of wealth within the city of Florence could only enlarge the pull of its market and the power of its investors. In the sixteenth century, a Florentine official, Giovanni Battista Tedaldi, in a description of Pistoia and its countryside, described the region's production chiefly in terms of what it exported to Florence.[17] Then, too, the meager supplies of capital available in the small towns conferred on Florentine investors a dominant voice in commercial and industrial enterprises. They were particularly interested in products easily sold at Florence: iron taken from the isle of Elba and smelted in the Apennines; lumber and wood from the same regions; cattle and animal products (including soap) from the plain of Pisa; sheep which followed the routes of transhumance between the mountains and the Maremma; and earthenware from Arezzo, Impruneta, Volterra, and Pisa.[18]

The importance of the Florentine market and the weight of Florentine capital advanced what could be called the regional integration of the Tuscan economy. In the thirteenth century numerous, free communes had engaged in ferocious competition in the same economic sectors. But the growth of the political and, above all, the financial power of Florence undercut this often wasteful competition and encouraged an evolution toward a more coordinated and rational use of regional resources.

17. For Tedaldi's analysis, see Minuti, 1892, pp. 302–31.

18. On the important investments of Florentine families in the Pisan countryside, see Mallett, 1968, pp. 441–42. Lorenzo the Magnificent invested in iron foundries in the Pistoiese mountains, see de Roover, 1963, pp. 165–66. On the influence of the Florentine market on a particular Pistoiese commercial house, the Partini, see Herlihy, 1967, pp. 168–71. On the growth of a specialized silk industry at Pescia "in the shadow of Florence," see Brown, 1982, especially, pp. 60–125.

THE CIRCULATION OF CAPITAL

But the skewed distribution of capital, especially liquid assets, also created problems. The flow toward the city and its fat people abundantly stocked the barns of the wealthy, but it threatened the little people with monetary famine. In response, the humble could sell their lands and possessions, but growth in the numbers of the destitute, under whom Tuscany groaned in 1427, only sharpened the hunger for cash. The system threatened to immobilize capital in the coffers of the wealthy and to stifle effort and initiative within the lower social orders.

In the countryside the Tuscan tenant usually paid his rents in kind, but he had need of coin to meet his taxes and to purchase at market the few indispensable goods he could not produce at home. Good husbandry also required substantial capital outlays for the acquisition of animals, seed, fertilizer, and materials used in construction or repair. Money also provided protection against the typically erratic yields of the Tuscan harvests. A countryside drained of money could not maintain adequate levels of productivity. Further, heavy burdens of debt and taxes provoked peasants into flight and aggravated the already pressing problem of deserted lands and farms. The wealth concentrated within the hands of a few Florentine families threatened their city with the curse of Midas: Florence risked starvation amidst accumulated gold.

The welfare of the rural economy thus demanded that some liquid capital be constantly recycled and redirected from city to countryside. The famous sharecropping arrangement, the mezzadria, channeled capital, in diverse ways, back from town to land.[19] The contract stipulated that, in return for a rent of one-half the produce, the "host" or landlord would provide the tenant not only with a podere (a farm of sufficient size to support a family) but also with most or all of the stock or capital he needed to work it—oxen, seed, and fertilizer. Moreover, the host frequently made loans to his cultivator. These prestanze helped tie the laborer to the soil, but they seem rarely to have been repaid.[20] The Catasto officials refused to consider loans of this sort as authentic obligations on the part of tenants, or as taxable assets on the part of landlords. They were equivalent in the fiscal perspec-

19. Jewish moneylenders were allowed to settle only in remote areas of the Florentine contado and in the subject cities, that is to say, in regions where the mezzadria was almost totally absent. See Cassuto, 1918, and Molho, 1971a, p. 108, n. 18. Between 1406 and 1410 they were allowed to reside in the communes of Pescia, San Miniato, Arezzo, Prato, Colle, Castiglione Fiorentino, Montepulciano, Volterra, and San Gimignano (the only one of these towns whose territory was cultivated in mezzadria since the fourteenth century).

20. Bernardo Machiavelli, for example, often tried to recover the loans given to his lavoratori; Machiavelli, 1954, p. 165. Bernardo also granted a loan to a peasant with the open intention of luring him away from another oste, ibid., p. 11. See also at Pistoia the complaints against sharecroppers, who allegedly desired the loan but not the lease, Herlihy, 1967, p. 137.

tive to loans contracted among members of the same household; the officials would also not accept these as genuine obligations. The links between host and laborer thus appear almost familial.

Indeed, the landlord was supposed to be the patron and protector of his sharecroppers, providing them counsel and help in difficult times.[21] The sharecroppers in turn gave gifts to their patron, and also, supposedly, honor and love.[22] When Giovanni Morelli lost his eldest son, he counted among the mourners the contadini who worked his land.[23] The system of the mezzadria lent a strong flavor of paternalism and of a "gift economy" to Tuscan society, that supposed bastion of early capitalism.

Within towns, too, the skewed distribution of wealth favored the development of patronage systems and of factions and parties based upon them. Cosimo dei Medici supposedly cultivated popular and political support through granting loans to, and paying the debts of, citizens who had fallen into misery.[24]

But everywhere, the deprived workers, eking out a living on the margins of subsistence, had little incentive to better their plight; strenuous efforts might win them greater income, but this would largely benefit others—the host claiming one-half the harvest and repayment of loans; or urban creditors. Many in Tuscan society were too poor to generate much demand for the products of the regional economy. Feeble local demand for goods of mass consumption was probably a principal reason why the Tuscan economy, so well endowed with skills, so promising in the late Middle Ages, could not break through to new forms of industrial organization and toward industrialism.[25]

The chronicler Giovanni Calvacanti points to still another curious effect of this skewed distribution of wealth. He attributes this perception to the prominent oligarch, Rinaldo degli Albizzi.[26] According to Rinaldo, the poor artisans, the shopkeepers, the recent immigrants to the city—the popolo minuto in sum—saw a solution to their desperate need for money in advocating war. Although they paid taxes continuously to the government, their poverty exempted them from the weight of extraordinary levies.

21. Thus, in January 1482, the sharecropper of Bernard Machiavelli told him that he lacked bread and could no longer work the land if Bernardo did not advance him bread and cereals. Machiavelli, 1954, p. 164.

22. Morelli, 1956, p. 236, advised his descendants not to cultivate close ties with their lavoratori, but he also implied that most landlords expected presents from them.

23. Ibid., p. 457.

24. See the accusations made against Cosimo by Rinaldo degli Albizzi, according to Cavalcanti, 1838–39, 1:502, that he was using his wealth to cultivate political support. Dale Kent, 1978, concludes that the accusation is well-founded.

25. For further comment, see Herlihy, 1977c, pp. 155–57.

26. Rinaldo supposedly delivered this "bella diceria" before an assembly of Florentine patricians shortly before the introduction of the Catasto. Cavalcanti, 1838–39, 1:74–90.

When war broke out, the rich, and not the poor, had to disgorge their accumulated wealth. The popolani allegedly reasoned: "when there are wars the city is always filled by a multitude of soldiers [who] must buy all their needs; artisans grow rich and are well rewarded. . . . "[27] Rinaldo explained to his fellow magnates:

> War is their profit and their wealth, and thus through your deprivation comes their abundance . . . your ruin is their glory and exaltation. War among the wolves has always been and is today peace among the lambs. [The popolani] say that they are the lambs and you are the wolves.[28]

The fiscal system, designed as a preparation for war, fleeced the lambs of the city; fittingly, the waging of war fed them. Not only did the distribution of wealth in Tuscany weaken the stimulants of economic growth and block the development of a strong local demand for cheap wares, it also introduced elements of instability into political and social life.

THE ETHICS OF AFFLUENCE

The presence of these enormous urban fortunes attracted the comments of contemporary moral philosophers. As we have already noted, Poggio Bracciolini (or his presumed spokesman, Antonio Loschi) praised the great fortunes as the city's strongest ramparts. Rejecting traditional suspicions, he further affirmed that accumulations of moneys were the foundation of civilization. Destroy the great fortunes and . . .

> you will destroy all the splendors of cities, the ceremonies and the embellishments which art supplies; no one would any longer construct churches and porticoes, all activity would cease. . . . [29]

Avarice, not a deadly sin, was a living virtue, keeping men productive. "For no one would then sow more than he strictly needed, to feed himself and his family".[30]

Of the many humanists to proffer advice to the affluent perhaps the most eloquent was the Neapolitan Giovanni Pontano.[31] Advocating an almost completely secular code, he instructed the rich to cultivate the virtues of generosity, beneficence, magnificence, splendor (meaning their dwellings should be large and luxurious), and hospitality. They should respond to the

27. Loc. cit. Goro Dati has the same opinion. Dati, 1902, bk. 9.
28. Cavalcanti, 1838–39, 1:79.
29. "De Avaritia," in Bracciolini, 1964, p. 13. On his view that the wealthy were "barns of money," see above, p. 3.
30. Loc. cit.
31. Pontano, 1965. On definitions of "nobility" in humanist thought, see Tateo, 1967, pp. 358–63.

needs of the deserving poor, especially girls lacking dowries and boys who gave indication of special talent.[32] In Pontano's view, a contemporary of the Catasto, Cosimo dei Medici, was the model of proper behavior:

> In our days Cosimo the Florentine imitated the magnificence of the Ancients through constructing temples and villas and through founding libraries. He was not content, it seems to me, to imitate them, but he was the first to revive the custom of dedicating private wealth to the public welfare and to the embellishment of the fatherland.[33]

The rich, in sum, ought to dispense their wealth among the needy with no reward in mind saving a good conscience. Pontano's essays may look like scholastic exercises, studded with classical allusions but remote from social realities. In fact, this advice to the rich to keep their moneys moving responded to an authentic social need. The wealthy but stingy citizen was not merely a shameful figure; he was a social disaster. The Florentine affluent were thus constantly importuned to display liberality: through extending loans to the state in times of war; helping clients; adopting a seigneurial style of life; enlivening social life by banquets, feasts, and ceremonies; beautifying the patria by palaces and churches; and patronizing learning. In its distribution and in its circulation, wealth thus deeply affected the culture of the Florentine Renaissance.

II. The Producers

We now look at the makers of this wealth, the Tuscan peasants, artisans, merchants, professionals: where they came from and what they did. As to their origins and movements, two forms of data yield some information. In the countryside, the tax officials tried to identify those who remained in the village since the last survey (the *stanti*), those who had departed (the *usciti*), and those who had newly arrived (the *tornati*). We have two registers showing such movements in two rural quarters, Santo Spirito and San Giovanni, approximately between 1412–15 and 1425.[34] Then, too, many household heads appear in the Catasto bearing a name of origin.

Unhappily, these latter references to place prove to be a defective indicator of migratory flows. The names are not always supplied. The two registers previously mentioned show that, over roughly a decade (1415–25), 26.7 percent of the families in the quarter of Santo Spirito, and 22.7 in San

32. "De liberalitate," Pontano, 1965, p. 37.
33. "De magnificentia," ibid., p. 101.
34. AC 106 and 166.

Giovanni, were newly arrived. For the same quarters the Catasto identifies places of origin for a trifling 2.6 percent of the households.[35] Even if we assume that the figure represents movements only since the Estimo of 1425–26, it still seems much too low.

There is this further, crippling distortion. Place of origin interested the tax officials because it allowed them to locate the previous, and sometimes still official, residence of the household head. But it quickly fell from use when the emigrant no longer retained possessions in his former village. The name of origin is above all the mark of landowners large and small. They are thus most frequently found in regions where small peasant property or perpetual leases prevailed. When and where peasants were landless, they had little reason to state, and the clerks little reason to record, from whence they came. In particular, households in the zone of mezzadria encircling the city almost never show a place of origin.[36] And yet sharecroppers were certainly among the most mobile of rural inhabitants.

The Catasto's data retain greater precision in regard to artisans, merchants, and other professional persons who carried their occupation with them. However, here too, a name of origin tells us nothing about the time of immigration. Many such references came to serve as family names and were retained permanently over generations, when links to the original place had become frayed and forgotten.

FOREIGNERS

The flow of people to and from outside regions is perhaps the easiest to discern. In the ten largest towns, 2.2 percent of the families (as against 0.7 percent of rural households) carry the name of a foreign country. On the other hand, 1 percent of urban families (and 0.3 percent of rural households) are reported abroad at the time the Catasto was redacted. The balance of exchange thus appears positive, though it concerns only a minuscule part of the population.

Florence itself hosted a good hundred families from Italian states, and a compact group of Germans comprising 87 families in 1427.[37] Other nationalities had slim representation: Frenchmen or Provençaux, Flemings, Spaniards, Slavs, Hungarians, and so forth, to a grand total of 24, who had lived long enough in the city to be counted among the other taxpayers. The

35. For a detailed breakdown of the use of these names in rural Tuscany, see Herlihy and Klapisch-Zuber, 1978, Table 37, p. 305.

36. Ibid., Table 38, p. 307, for a detailed breakdown of the use of placenames by various occupational groups.

37. On immigration into Florence from abroad, especially from Germany, during the late Middle Ages, see the interesting observations by Cohn, 1980, pp. 91–113.

Table 4.3. Proportion of Migrant Households in the Towns and Rural Zones of Tuscany

Town	*Stable Hhlds*	*Hhlds from Tuscany*	*Hhlds from Abroad*	*Gone elsewhere in Tuscany*	*Gone abroad*	*Total*
Florence	7,921	992	211	475	123	9722
Percent	81.5	10.2	2.1	4.9	1.3	100.0
Pisa	1,152	326	77	139	35	1729
Percent	66.6	18.8	4.5	8.1	2.0	100.0
Pistoia	1,124	88	17	14	2	1245
Percent	90.4	7.0	1.4	1.1	0.1	100.0
Arezzo	1,019	131	17	14	8	1189
Percent	85.7	11.0	1.4	1.2	0.7	100.0
Prato	900	21	11	6	5	943
Percent	95.5	2.2	1.2	0.6	0.5	100.0
Cortona	808	41	19	2	7	877
Percent	92.1	4.7	2.2	0.2	0.8	100.0
Volterra	715	52	14	11	2	794
Percent	90.0	6.6	1.8	1.4	0.3	100.0
Montepulciano	631	43	38	1	8	721
Percent	87.5	6.0	5.3	0.1	1.1	100.0
Castiglione Fiorentino	357	26	5	3	0	391
Percent	91.3	6.6	1.3	0.8	0.0	100.0
San Gimignano	342	17	4	4	2	369
Percent	92.5	4.6	1.2	1.2	0.5	100.0

German preponderance in the foreign population of Florence remained notable a generation later; in 1450–51, of 38 fathers of infants baptized at San Giovanni, who declared a non-Italian origin, 34 were Germans and their children accounted for 1.9 percent of the baptisms. The presence of Germans was large not only at Florence, but was equally notable in Florentine zones north of the Arno and in the towns laid out along the via Francesca.

Certain Tuscan towns assumed the role of asylum cities. Thus, at Montepulciano, families coming from Siena, Perugia, or nearby regions constituted 5.3 percent of the population. Pisa, with 4.5 percent of its families coming from abroad, perhaps reflects the moderate success of Florentine policy, encouraging immigration to the depopulated coastal zones. But Pisa (and Livorno) also show significant outward migration (see Table 4.3). This emigration in the years immediately preceding the Catasto prolonged the demographic anemia which had emptied the city since passing under Florentine rule in 1406.[38]

38. On the phases of this population decline after the establishment of Florentine rule, see Casini, 1957–58, and idem, 1959–60, pp. 90–318; Silva, 1909–10, pp. 285 ff.; and Mallett, 1968, pp. 403–41.

MIGRANT WORKERS

Although the phenomenon is more difficult to discern, exchange among regions and rural emigration toward the cities seems to have involved a much larger number of people. The registers of 1425 indicate a flow from the southwest periphery of the Florentine contado (pivieri of Fabbrica and San Lazzaro, that is, the zones of San Miniato and of Castelfiorentino) toward the center of the Florentine state. But notable proportions also moved from the high western country to the lowlands, as far as the Pisan Maremma. The seasonal flow of animals along the same course, between the Apennines and the coast, seems also to have carried men in its wake.[39] A drift of poor montagnards toward lower and richer lands seems an perennial feature of Mediterranean life.[40]

The population movements most difficult to assess are exchanges between countryside and towns. Still, on a relative scale, the proportion of immigrants was most pronounced at Pisa (Table 4.3), where almost a fifth of the families bear names indicating origins outside the town. At Arezzo and Florence, recent immigration supplied at least one-tenth of the families. Elsewhere, between 5 and 6 percent of urban families bear names of generally rural origin. Everywhere, the separate countrysides surrounding the towns were the great providers of immigrants. Between 1415 and 1425, 46 percent of the men emigrating from the rural quarter of San Giovanni, and 34 percent of those from Santo Spirito, headed for Florence.

MIGRATIONS BY SEX, AGE, AND STATUS

What traits of sex, age, and status distinguished these migrant groups? The vast majority of emigrants were men. Female mobility was nonetheless pronounced, but difficult to ascertain. The census takers observed women only casually because they were not subject to the head tax. Many young girls of rural origins entered household service in the city. Their masters often promised to provide a dowry "when they come of age".[41] The close ties which urban landlords maintained with their sharecroppers facilitated these displacements. Under the prevailing, patrilocal system of marriage, rural brides joined their husbands' households. Given the small size of many rural parishes, girls usually had to seek and find husbands in different, even distant, villages. Rural women moved more frequently and farther than the Catasto indicates. Only when, as widows, they assumed con-

39. These impressions come from the entries in AC, reg. 246, f. 59, 63, 105, 121, 161, 170, 181, 183, 184, passim.

40. See the now classic observations of Braudel, 1979, 1:34–47, 76–93.

41. As shown by numerous examples in the Catasto, these young servants received support, but no salary, and the promise of a dowry when they attained marriage age. For the same arrangement at Toulouse in the fourteenth century, see Laribière, 1967, pp. 335–62

trol over their own households do their movements achieve visibility.[42] Many returned to their places of origin, even passing beyond the Florentine frontiers. The surveys of the border regions register a high proportion of women emigrating abroad. Economic difficulties often followed hard upon the death of a breadwinner; many widows had to seek employment as servants. Entire families thus dispersed at the death of a father: the widow to Florence, the girl to a market town, the boy to the household of a neighboring peasant.[43]

Age also distinguished the migrants. Among women, widows, usually elderly, achieved, as we have mentioned, a novel visibility. But the young still constituted the most mobile group. A distribution of household heads by age shows that the number of emigrants decreases as age advances.[44] The preponderance of young males and old women reduces the size of the transient family. In the piviere of Impruneta in 1425, stable families supported on the average 6.1 members; the newly arrived, 4.7; and the departed, 4.5 persons.[45] The pattern is repeated in other villages we have studied—at Gangalandi and, in 1412, at Santa Maria a Campoli.[46] To judge from the registers of Santo Spirito (1425), the sons of sharecroppers, probably surplus boys on the poderi, typically departed to seek their fortunes in the city. More than two-thirds of the emigrants from this rural quarter were young men; and males under the age of 45 account for 90 percent of the total. The proportion of emigrants under age 45 is lower for San Giovanni—71 percent. Probably the greater diffusion of the mezzadria in the quarter of Santo Spirito explains these differing proportions.[47]

And what about the wealth of the migrants? Did poverty engender mobility? Within the countryside, at Impruneta in 1425, 87 percent of stable households (and 82 percent of those at Gangalandi) turn up again two years later in the Catasto. And the Catasto shows that stable families were indeed the wealthier, not only at Impruneta, but at Gangalandi and at San Lorenzo al Corniolo in the Mugello.[48] In the contado of Pisa in 1427, half of the 100 men, who had left their villages in the years immediately preced-

42. Women appear more frequently at the head of migrant households than of stable households, nearly everwhere in Tuscany. For the figures, see Herlihy and Klapisch-Zuber, 1978, p. 322, n. 43.

43. Thus, AC 250, f. 39; 255, and f. 517.

44. Migrant households also contain a larger proportion of heads for whom no age is stated than do stable families. They are 3 percent in the latter group, but 6–7 percent among urban immigrants, 13 percent among urban emigrants, and 18 percent among rural emigrants.

45. The figures for Impruneta are from Herlihy, 1973c, p. 54.

46. At Gangalandi, the average size of the three types of households (stanti, tornati and usciti) are 6.05, 4.4 and 5 persons respectively; at Campoli, 4.8, 2.9 and 2.8 respectively.

47. AC 250, 255.

48. On Impruneta, see Herlihy, 1973c, pp. 41–56. At Gangalandi, 82 percent of the stanti in the survey of 1415–25 are found in the Catasto, but only 75 percent of the poorer tornati.

ing the Catasto, belonged to the poorest strata of the population. Poverty and misery churned up the rural inhabitants and kept them circulating among the villages.

Within the towns, the impact of poverty was less consistent. According to a famous study by J. Plesner, the upper strata of rural society primarily provided immigrants to Florence in the late thirteenth century, a period of exuberant urban growth.[49] To assess the character of rural immigration to Florence for the fifteenth century, we shall look again at the sample of the two countryside quarters, San Spirito and San Giovanni. In 1427 the median wealth of the 72 families who had recently settled in Florence was a paltry 16 florins. Even the 68 families who had settled in the secondary towns and important villages of the Florentine dominion were better off, with an average wealth of 33 florins. Those migrants, 24, who remained within the countryside were the poorest of all with only 3 florins. Close scrutiny of the migrants to Florence shows that the metropolis attracted the extremes: the destitute poor and some of the truly rich. Immigration elsewhere was homogeneous.

Thus, at the beginning of the fifteenth century, Florence was attracting predominantly poverty-stricken rustics, humble folk adrift in the world, seeking the city's public or private charity, or young workers hoping to gain, even without fortune, a better lot. But Florence and other towns continued to attract a few families from the contado with some resources. Among them the notaries figured prominently.[50] In 1293 at Pisa, two-thirds of the notaries were recent immigrants; in 1427, 41 out of 69 in the same city still carried a name of origin. In the gonfalone of Scala, at Florence, 9 of 23 notaries in 1427 (close to 40 percent) similarly indicate recent immigration from the countryside. These and other skilled and resourceful immigrants hoped to enlarge their capital and to rise in the social and political hierarchy of the towns. The *novi cives*, however, were usually recruited from important villages and secondary towns, not from the open countryside. Plesner's thesis, while not inapplicable to the fifteenth century, accounts for only a small part of a complex phenemonon.

In zones of the Florentine contado where the mezzadria reigned supreme, emigrants were principally sons and brothers, surplus workers not needed to work the land. In regions where *appoderamento*, the formation of compact farms, was still proceeding, they were likely to be small landowners and tenants dislodged and deprived of roots through the agrarian changes. In remote areas still untouched by these transformations, emigra-

49. Plesner, 1934.

50. On the Pisan notaries, see Volpe, 1902, pp. 177–203; Banti, 1964–66, pp. 131–86; Herlihy, 1958, p. 41. On the notaries of 1427, Casini, 1964, p. 462.

tion seems more directly linked to subsistence crises, to bad times engendered by epidemics wars and famine. Vagabondage and military service absorbed some of those shaken loose, but the towns, it would appear, drew the larger numbers.

The collapse of the population after 1348 accentuated these human movements. In indirect ways it hastened the formation of new relations of production. Increased investment in the countryside, growing concentrations of land under the control of urban landlords, and the accelerated diffusion of the mezzadria were all linked, closely or remotely, with demographic changes. In more direct terms, the crisis disrupted many families and constrained surviving members to disperse for their own survival after the death of the family head. Young male laborers, dislodged from ancestral holdings and attracted by high urban wages; young and aging peasants forced to look for work after the breakup of their families; widows in search of sustenance—all these gravitated to the towns, especially Florence, to help maintain their human numbers.

III. Occupations

The Catasto registers the professional activities of the taxpayers with considerably less precision than their wealth, though with more precision than their origins. According to the enabling legislation, the clerks of the Catasto office were to "examine with diligence the industry and occupation" of every adult male Tuscan. But many did not bother to declare a profession, or the clerks saw no particular purpose in recording it.[51] Still, the thousands of professions mentioned in the Catasto are surely representative of the spread of skills within Tuscany. The Catasto illuminates, even if partially, in the words of a contemporary, the "many occupations needed by the human community, peasants who hoe the earth, carpenters, masons, sculptors, painters, tailors, armorers, weavers, drapers, changers, silk dealers, merchants, and a thousand others".[52]

PEASANTS

Nearly one out of three families certainly, and three out of five probably, lived primarily by working the land.[53] Peasants almost never bear an occupational title, but the declarations usually allow us to identify who they were and what were the terms under which they worked the land. In 1427 more than one-half the rural families (56.6 percent) lived in their own

51. Karmin (ed.), 1906, pp. 28, 33.
52. Dominici, 1860, p. 182, written ca. 1400–05.
53. Probable peasants are those living in the countryside without apparent occupation.

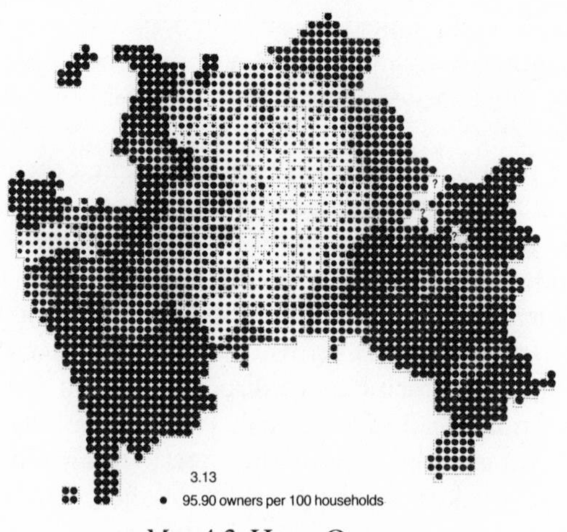

Map 4.3. Home Owners

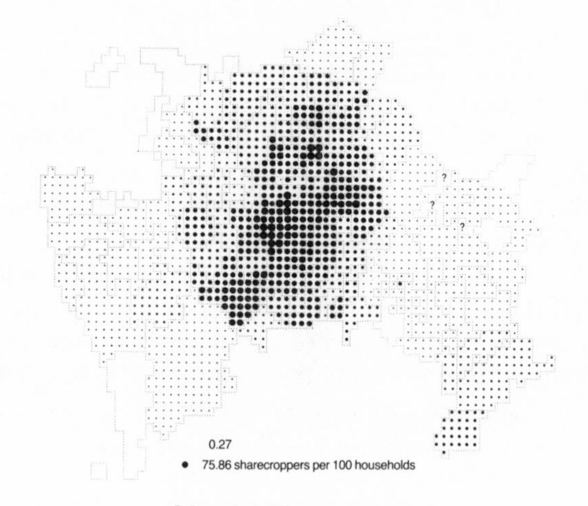

Map 4.4. Sharecroppers

homesteads; though they often leased additional plots, they are best regarded as independent cultivators. Some 18.9 percent of the peasant families (minimal estimate) were sharecroppers, while a small number (4.3 percent) leased their houses and farms for fixed rents. Maps 4.3 and 4.4 show the distributions of these families of independent cultivators and of sharecroppers. Not surprisingly, the maps are mirror images of each other.

The mezzadria was frequent in 1427 at the center of the Florentine territory, especially to the south of Florence. This was an area, as we previously saw, of comparatively small parishes, and dense though scattered settlement. Sharecropping dominated the regions from Florence to San Gimignano, as far as the Elsa river. It grew rare toward the southeast, in the Chianti hills and toward the upper Val d'Arno. To the north of Florence, it prevailed in the Mugello, where many Florentines owned land. It quickly vanished to the west and northwest of Prato, and beyond the suburbs of Pistoia. Rare outside the Florentine contado, it was all but totally absent from the Maremma, and from mountainous zones everywhere. In these regions, peasant landowners continued to live in large, clustered villages, and to work countless plots of land scattered about them, often at great distances from their homes.[54]

Many factors, both technical and social, contributed to the diffusion of the mezzadria in late medieval Tuscany. But the chief impetus to its spread came from the flow of urban capital into the countryside. Money from the city underwrote the costs of gathering separate plots into compact poderi and of building the *case coloniche* upon them. It also provided the needed *bestie*, and often seed and fertilizer. This influx of urban capital seems to have swelled considerably after the Black Death. Flexible rents gave the cultivator a measure of protection against erratic harvests, and helped to attract and hold workers in a period of demographic decline and scarcity of labor.

To be sure, the diffusion of the mezzadria was far from complete in fifteenth-century Tuscany. Table 4.4 measures its progress between the years 1427 and 1469.

Between 1427 and 1469 the frequency of sharecropping contracts increased with particular vigor to the northwest of Florence, in the quarter of Santa Maria Novella. The relative numbers remained fairly stable in the quarter of San Giovanni to the northeast. Over forty years and two generations, the mezzadri thus passed from a fourth of the rural households to close to 30 percent, registering an increase of 4 points over their initial proportion.

54. On the formation of compact poderi, see especially Conti, 1966, vol. 1. On the spread of the mezzadria, see Imberciadori, 1951; idem, 1971, "Economia corso-maremmana nel'400." On the northern contado of Arezzo, see Cherubini, 1972a; idem, 1972b, pp. 26–36. See also Jones, 1968, pp. 227–34, and idem, 1954, p. 176.

Table 4.4. The Diffusion of the Mezzadria, 1427 and 1469

Quarter	1427 Number Hhlds	1427 Total	1427 Percent	1469 Number Hhlds	1469 Total	1469 Percent
S. Spirito	2,518	7,452	33.7	191	486	39.3
S. Croce	1.247	4,851	25.7	119	406	29.3
S. Maria Nov.	1,629	7,271	22.4	190	586	32.4
S. Giovanni	1,334	6,992	19.1	106	568	18.6
Totals	6,728	26,566	25.3	606	2046	29.6

SOURCE: Catasto of 1427 and a ten percent sample of households surveyed in the rural Estimo of 1469.

SHARECROPPERS

The *Georgofili* ("friends of agriculture," who formed an academy at Florence) and many other writers on agriculture, from the eighteenth century on, praised the mezzadria as a nearly ideal arrangement, linking capital and labor.[55] They stressed the harmony and the cooperative spirit which the system elicited from both the host and the cultivator. The balanced contribution spread social contentment even as it fructified the land.

The picture of sharecropping that the Catasto provides departs from this ideal picture. The podere was supposed to be big enough to assure the support of the peasant family. But the Catasto shows that one-quarter of the mezzadri retained some properties which they worked. The retention of additional lands in the heart of the zone of the mezzadria suggests that the podere itself did not always fully support its resident family.[56] Of the sharecroppers, 14.3 percent continued to live in their own houses—another indication of the possible inadequacy of the landlord's casa colonica. Moreover, landlords frequently balked at making repairs in the farm buildings, as more than a single account book and complaints to the fiscal office make apparent.

Did the landlord at least provide the *bovi*, the oxen, which productive husbandry required?[57] Unfortunately the Catasto does not allow an exact count of the number of mezzadri who worked their land with the aid of oxen. Those who owned cattle, or who received them under the peculiar form of lease known as the *soccida* are, to be sure, readily visible. But the declarations also make frequent reference to loans in florins, from host to peasant, without specifying the uses to which the money was put. Fre-

55. Imberciadori, 1951; Bologna, 1924; Luzzatto, 1948; Imberciadori, 1957.

56. Imberciadori, 1957, reaches similar conclusions.

57. On the various types of soccida, see La Roncière, 1973, pp. 118–20.

Table 4.5. The Status of Farms and the Presence of Oxen in the Tuscan Countryside, 1427

Status	*No Mention*		*Oxen Leased*		*Oxen Owned*		*Total*	
	No.	*Perc.*	*No.*	*Perc.*	*No.*	*Perc.*	*No.*	*Perc.*
Peasant Proprietors	3,207	48.9	173	2.6	3,175	48.4	6,555	100.0
Leaseholders (fixed rent)	841	52.8	105	6.6	646	40.6	1,592	100.0
Sharecroppers	4,640	64.6	1,041	14.5	1,499	20.9	7,180	100.0

SOURCE: Catasto of 1427.

quently, even usually, the peasant used the loan to purchase oxen, but the Catasto does not report this. Moreover, as the pair of oxen used in the cultivation of a podere was tax exempt, the Catasto office was not scrupulous in recording their presence. As a census of animals, the Catasto leaves much to be desired. Though the count is incomplete, Table 4.5 shows the distribution of bovi across the various kinds of tenancy.

Table 4.5 makes evident that, of all the peasants, the mezzadri were by far the least likely to own cattle in their own name. Conversely, they were more likely than either the peasant proprietors or the leaseholders (*affituari*) to hold cattle a soccio or under any form of lease. In 60 percent of the contracts of soccida to which the Catasto refers, the recipient of the animals is a sharecropper. Of all peasants, the mezzadri were most dependent on investments from outside. We would like to know how the nearly 50 percent of sharecroppers, who appear on farms without evidence of animals, secured, if they did secure, bestie. But here the Catasto does not yield a precise response.

So also, the image of reigning harmony between host and laborer may need retouching. In the fourteenth and fifteenth centuries, the host seems invariably to have made a loan to his sharecropper when the latter took possession of the farm. These advances consisted of cattle (or of the money needed to purchase them) and of grain—for seed or for nourishment over the hungry months until harvest. We encounter these loans frequently in the Catasto, though its record is not complete because the fiscal officers refused to recognize the loans as true assets or liabilities. They could at times reach impressive amounts. Palla di Nofri Strozzi listed in his declaration 122 such loans, for a total of 3,200 florins. He claimed to have granted many more to peasants now dead or "gone with God." He did not bother to list them, "for fear of boring" the tax officials.[58]

These advances were designed to attract tenants and to bind them tightly to the land. They tended to grow from year to year (especially in periods of

58. AC 76, f. 169 ff.

dearth), and loomed over the peasant, threatening him with harsher terms each time the contract was renewed.[59] Rather than engendering gratitude and harmony, they could provoke the flight of the sharecropper, especially in areas where landed property of his own did not tie him to the spot. These desertions seemed betrayals to the landlords; the Catasto itself contains numerous complaints against the faithless fugitive peasants.

The zone of mezzadria, surrounding Florence, may look to be a region of debt and depression, where the cultivators owned only a tiny fraction of the lands they worked. But this in turn may be too harsh a picture. Even the debts indicate that some capital circulated in the countryside. This credit did not necessarily work to the benefit of the subject peasantry, but at least it gave to the economy of the central region a vitality which seems altogether lacking in the more lethargic peripheral zones. Despite his occasional rancor against the peasants, the owner of a podere had little choice but to supervise it closely and, however reluctantly, to contribute to its maintenance. The monastery or magnate who lived on perpetual rents from mountain plots may have exploited their hereditary tenants less rigorously, but they also extended little support to them and their enterprises. The mezzadria, hardly an idyllic contract in human terms, sustained in central Tuscany a reasonably well-managed agriculture.

PEASANT FLOCKS

Though laconic concerning the bestie present on the podere, the Catasto offers a marginally better illustration of other forms of animal husbandry. Even here, however, herds and flocks belonging to urban owners appear in urban declarations. Only a special study of pastoral activities in Tuscany, and an integration of rural data with the widely scattered information from the urban Catasti, might yield us a reasonably complete census of livestock. The following impressions are based exclusively on data from the rural declarations.

Several factors contributed to the importance of stock raising in fifteenth-century Tuscany. The decline in population and the contraction of the zones of dense settlement increased the lands which could be given over to pasturage. The highland pastures of the Apennines complemented the wet lowlands of the Tyrrhenian shore and invited transhumance. The prices of wool, cheese, and meat reached a relatively high level in Tuscany, as in many parts of Europe.[60] Finally, the diffusion of the mezzadria itself

59. For an example of sharecroppers from the commune of Valiano near Montepulciano, see Herlihy and Klapisch-Zuber, 1978, p. 278.

60. On price movements in northern Europe, see Abel, 1978. For Tuscan prices in the fourteenth century, see La Roncière, 1976; Goldthwaite, 1975; Pinto, 1978. The problem of prices and wage rates is discussed at length in Goldthwaite, 1980, pp. 317–50.

created a demand for cattle, as many of the central poderi did not produce enough fodder to raise their own.

A comparison of select regions allows us to distinguish zones where animals contributed to the farm economy from those more truly pastoral areas where they were raised primarily for sale and profit. San Gimignano offers an example of the first form of animal husbandry. There, nearly four out of five of the 203 households living in the open countryside were raising animals. These heads of cattle were both numerous, some 760 at least, and valuable, ranging from 5.8 to 7.1 florins. To them were added large flocks of sheep, goats, and swine. Almost all the inhabitants of the region owned an ox, and they raised one pig at least which, often, a townsman had left to be fattened. In sum, few peasants were deprived of animals in this region where the mezzadri seem to have been exceptionally prosperous.

As an example of pastoral zones, we can take two Pisan podesterie, Rosignano and Campiglia, located at the borders of the Maremma; and, at the other end of the trail of transhumance, the podesterie of Subbiano and Pieve Santo Stefano in the mountains above Arezzo. In these infertile upland zones, livestock was an important, perhaps the principal form of wealth. Roughly one-half (54 percent) of the families definitely owned animals. Many more doubtlessly gained employment tending the flocks of urban owners, which do not appear in the rural declarations. In the Maremma, inventoried heads of cattle (again we only see those belonging to local residents) numbered upwards of 2,400. The average value was, however, quite low (3.25 florins), indicating that the animals were young and probably semiwild. The raising of small animals also held an important place in the total pastoral economy of the Maremma. Oddly, goats and pigs formed a larger part of this livestock than sheep. The swine—2,800 head—might number more than 400 in a single herd, though the average drove was counted in the 30s.

On the whole, however, the Catasto leaves the strong impression that, at the end of the Middle Ages, animal husbandry in Tuscany was still not a highly specialized and capitalized enterprise; it remained of limited importance for the rural population. Even in areas suitable for it, such as the mountains above Arezzo, it remained only part of a traditional subsistence economy founded upon mixed agriculture. Serious obstacles—the lack of capital, the lack of markets, and above all the need to achieve self-sufficiency in domestic outputs—limited the peasant commitment to this form of rural enterprise.

RURAL ARTISANS AND MERCHANTS

Fewer than 6 percent of rural families declared a nonagricultural occupation. Moreover, most of them were engaged in transporting or transforming the produce of the land, including its livestock. They were animal dealers, butchers, shoemakers, innkeepers (who often doubled as butchers), sellers of wine (*vinattieri*), millers, and grain dealers. Shoemakers alone numbered 151, nearly a fifth of all who worked in Tuscany. Their importance underscores the wide use of leather in peasant clothing. All these groups together numbered close to 600 persons—more than a fourth of all Tuscan artisans performing comparable services.

Processors of raw materials—ironmongers, wood workers, lime burners, and brick makers—were also numerous in the countryside.[61] Foundries or *fabbriche*, set in the Apennines, took advantage of the abundant wood, which yielded charcoal, and the racing mountain streams, which pumped their bellows.[62] Mills of many kinds were built along the rivers, sawing wood, grinding grain and chestnuts, fulling cloth, and crushing olives. Artisans working in wood were concentrated in forested areas, such as the Garfagnana and the mountains of Pistoia. In all, 16 percent of Tuscan artisans, working in wood and stone, lived in the countryside. Given the defective reporting of professions in the Catasto, the estimate must be viewed as minimal.

Rural notaries numbered 114, some 13.5 percent of the entire corps of notaries who appear in the Catasto as household heads. Their numbers had probably been steadily declining since the early fourteenth century.[63] Finally, the Catasto mentions here and there activities dependent upon the textile industries of the city. Still, apart from 100 or so weavers, most rural textile workers have left little trace in the survey. There was scant reason to mention salaried laborers working with small investments and few tools; this was women's work too, and thus more easily ignored.[64]

The diversity (if not the number) of country artisans is enough to show that the population was not closed within endless cycles of agricultural labor; a noticeable movement of goods and of people enlivened rural life. Still, if most Tuscans lived in a country setting, residents of cities put together the great accumulations of wealth which made Tuscany the economic marvel of contemporary Europe.

URBAN OCCUPATIONS

Occupational activities can be known only for a minority of the urban households. At Florence, family heads who did not declare or give evidence

61. On the construction industry in both city and countryside, see most recently Goldthwaite, 1980.

62. On mills, see Muendel, 1972.

63. The number of surviving chartularies from rural notaries in the Florentine State Archives drastically declines after the Black Death.

64. References to feminine labors "colla rocca," "with the distaff," are common. See AC 933, f. 874: "Lavoro a opere aiutando altrui e cholla rocha fa la donna." AC 938, f. 845, ". . . chol filato delle mie fanciulle mi vengho sostenando." Both references are from the Catasto of 1469. On wool spinning in the countryside, a poorly paid feminine labor, see Melis, 1966, pp. 518–19.

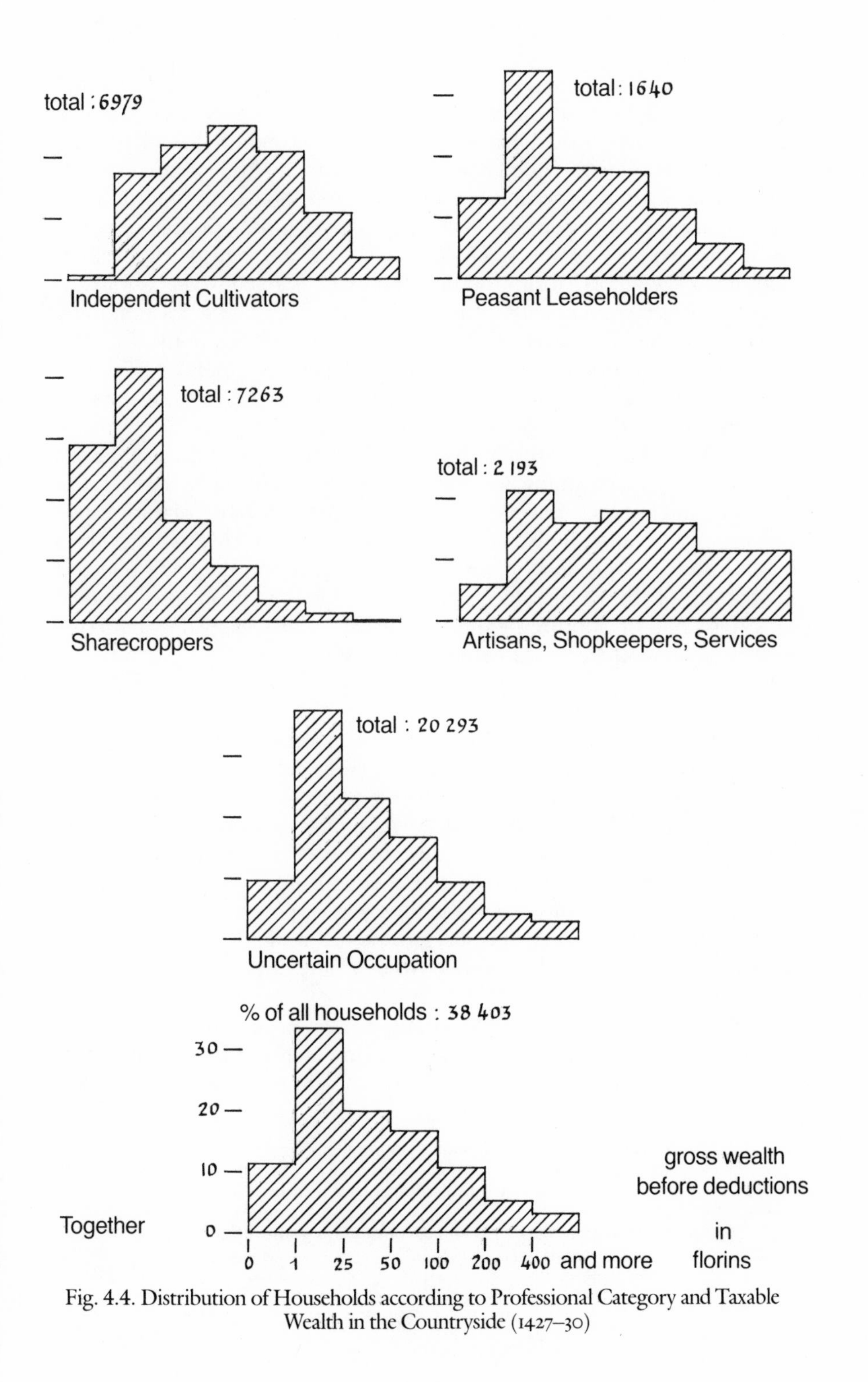

Fig. 4.4. Distribution of Households according to Professional Category and Taxable Wealth in the Countryside (1427–30)

of an occupation were 43.5 percent of the total, and at Pisa, 44.6 percent.[65] Female household heads, who filled the poorest urban classes and who seem to have participated hardly at all in the economic life of the city, contributed substantial numbers to this category. At Florence, widows made up a quarter of those without profession, and the proportion was even higher (up to 32 percent) in the secondary towns.[66] Collectors of land rents, and workers of the soil, who went each day outside the walls to cultivate a few plots, form another important segment. The cumulative proportion of taxpayers without profession stands in inverse relation to the total size of the population: the smaller the town, the more the the countryside impinged upon its society. Finally, the richest heads of household often did not declare a profession, probably because their investments and interests cut across many economic sectors.

The Florentine constitution distinguished three occupational groupings.[67] Seven greater guilds dominated the government: with the exception of judges and notaries, they were chiefly engaged in manufacture for export and in long-distance trade. Fourteen minor guilds, with limited political rights, organized production for the local market and the retail trade. At the bottom of the social ladder were the *sottoposti*, disenfranchised workers subject to one or another of the recognized guilds. Does distribution of wealth correspond to this distribution of power?

Figure 4.5 shows that it does. The greater guilds, represented by close to 900 taxpayers, claimed a concentration of the wealthiest families—households which surpassed, often by much, the urban average of about 1,000 florins. Few of these househols were heavily in debt, and the distribution remains almost as skewed whether based on gross or net assets. Households with no declared occupation show a similar concentration of wealthy families, but also many of the destitute. Impoverished widows, as we mentioned, figure prominently among those without profession.

Equally clustered, but now in the direction of poverty, were the households of the sottoposti. At this level, debts had a significant impact. Once charges were deducted, close to two-thirds of the taxpayers were left without a florin.

Finally, the spread of wealth among the lesser guilds, that is, small shopkeepers and independent artisans, seems at first glance quite equal. Still, even this prosperity was fragile. Once debts were subtracted, more

65. Here as elsewhere, only heads of families are counted.

66. At Florence, female heads of households number 1,536, or 15.7 percent of the total; 72.8 percent of these women do not state a profession, either their own or that of their deceased husband.

67. The fundamental study of the Florentine constitution in the fifteenth century is Rubinstein, 1966. Now see also Guidi, 1981.

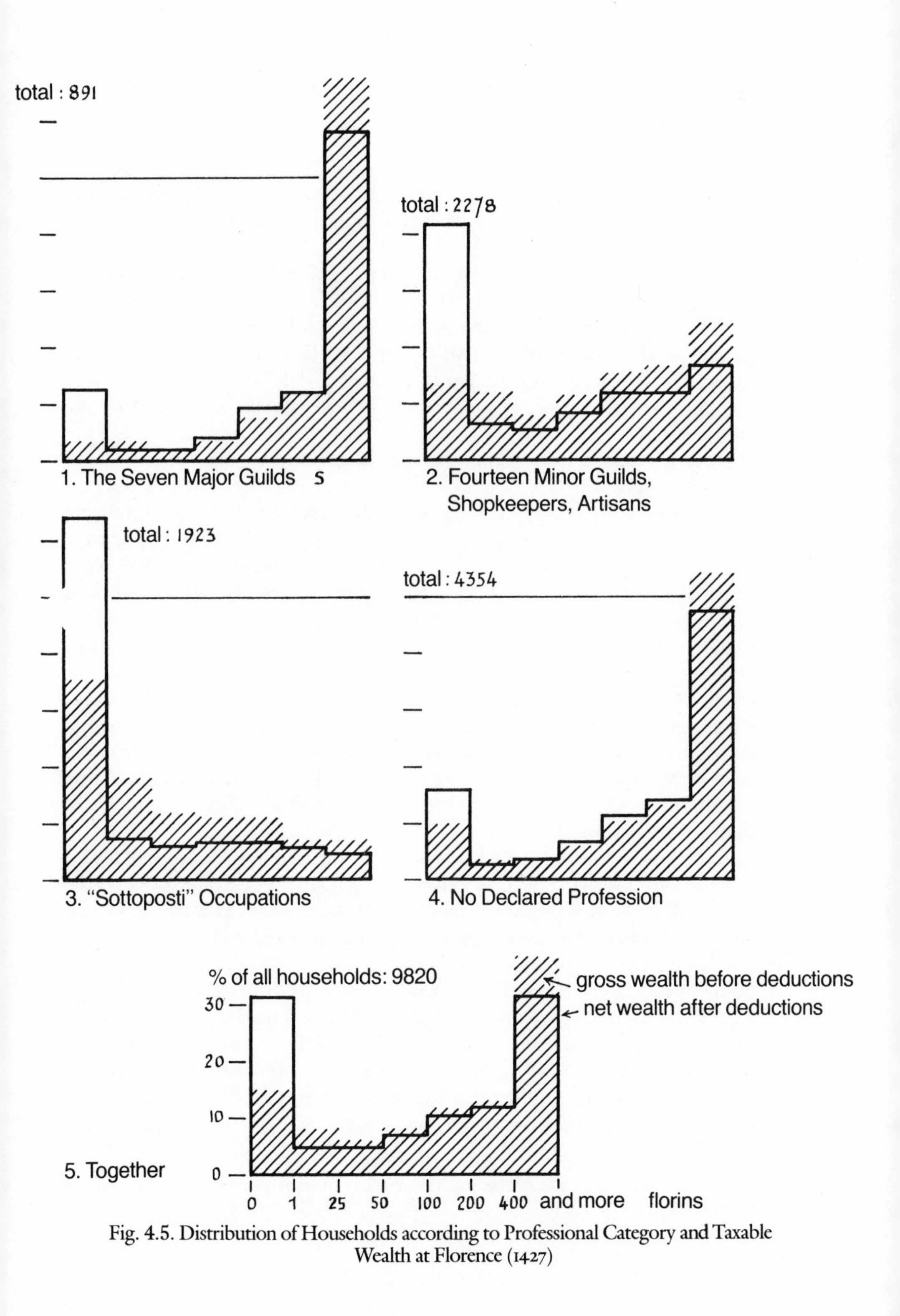

Fig. 4.5. Distribution of Households according to Professional Category and Taxable Wealth at Florence (1427)

than 40 percent of these small tradesmen appear hardly better off than the humblest laborers.

REGIONS

Declared professions also allow us to judge, albeit crudely, the relative importance of various economic activities across the Tuscan towns (see Table 4.6).

Table 4.6 hightlights the special vitality of the Florentine economy. Some 56 percent of its households earned their support through a named skill, as opposed to 30–50 percent in the four following cities, and 20–23 percent in the smaller towns. An exception here is San Gimignano, where 30 percent of the household heads declared a skill. We have already seen that commercial and business investments were also large in this tiny but vigorous city.

Table 4.7 shows, for all the principal urban centers, the ten most common occupations.

The distribution of professions listed in Table 4.7 shows an advancing regional specialization. Florence is the only city of Tuscany to possess a large industrial population, and it dominated the manufacture of woolen cloth. Four of its most numerous professions consisted of textile workers (weavers, combers, carders, and dyers). No fewer than 76 percent of Tuscan households supported by wool manufacture (and 74 percent of those working in other textiles) were found in Florence. On the other hand, the small towns claimed a role in the sale and distribution of cloth; *lanaiuoli* were numerous in Prato, Arezzo, Cortona, Volterra, San Gimignano, and even Montepulciano. As a shipbuilding center, Pisa produced sailcloth, ropes, and tackle. Arezzo was engaged, though on a small scale, in cotton manufacture. Colle, with its fifteen paper makers, was the center of that industry in Tuscany.[68]

Pisa, close to well-watered lowlands, held the lead in the leather industry, followed by Pistoia, Prato, Florence, and Arezzo; 9.3 percent of its households—double the relative numbers found elsewhere—lived by curing and working leather. The metal industry was principally concentrated in the five largest cities—Florence, Pisa, Pistoia, Arezzo, and Prato. Pistoia, aided by nearby supplies of wood and charcoal from its mountains, maintained a traditional visibility in iron manufacture. Construction marked the largest towns, Florence and Pisa. As Tuscany's principal port, Pisa consumed much wood in shipbuilding and ship repair. Residents of still tiny Livorno also showed interest in the maritime trades. Some twenty Livornesi owned shares in vessels. They were not, to be sure, active sailors, and, by their

68. Arezzo held 10 of the 11 Tuscan cotton workers or *bambaciai*. On the paper works of Colle, see Dini, 1902.

Table 4.6. The Distribution of Occupations in the Principal Tuscan Cities

	Florence	*Pisa*	*Pistoia*	*Arezzo*	*Prato*	*Volterra*	*Cortona*	*Small Towns*
No declared occupation	4,266	765	780	736	565	398	631	3,086
Percent	43.9	44.6	62.6	61.8	59.9	50.1	17.9	49.3
Cultivators	24	102	52	10	89	223	49	2047
Percent	0.3	6.0	4.2	0.8	9.4	28.1	5.6	32.7
Food Services	464	101	27	57	42	14	27	116
Percent	4.7	5.9	2.2	4.8	4.5	1.8	3.1	1.9
Woolens	1,580	120	57	86	62	33	35	133
Percent	16.3	7.0	4.5	7.2	6.6	4.2	4.0	2.1
Other Textiles	458	59	13	26	6	7	7	31
Percent	4.7	3.4	1.0	2.2	0.6	0.9	0.8	0.5
Paper	13	3	0	1	0	0	0	15
Percent	0.1	0.2	0.0	0.1	0.0	0.0	0.0	0.2
Leather, furs	554	159	78	63	54	24	30	162
Percent	5.7	9.3	6.3	5.3	5.7	3.0	3.4	2.6
Spices	113	34	20	13	13	4	14	44
Percent	1.2	2.0	1.6	1.1	1.4	0.5	1.6	0.7
Metals	272	54	62	46	26	10	21	119
Percent	2.8	3.2	5.0	3.9	2.8	1.3	2.4	1.9
Wood, Stone	387	85	33	34	21	18	9	66
Percent	4.0	5.0	2.7	2.9	2.2	2.3	1.0	1.1
Services	1,591	232	125	119	65	63	55	443
Percent	16.3	13.5	10.0	10.0	6.5	7.9	6.3	7.1
Total	9,722	1714	1246	1191	943	794	878	6262

Table 4.7. The Ten Most Numerous Occupations in the Tuscan Towns

	Florence	*Pisa*	*Pistoia*	*Arezzo*	*Prato*	*Volterra*	*Cortona*
1	Notary 307 (8.3)	Shoemaker 76 (10.4)	Shoemaker 50 (11.3)	Shoemaker 54 (13.1)	Pleasant p. 43 (12.2)	Peasant t. 116 (34.7)	Peasant p. 45 (13.8)
2	Adminis. 261 (7.0)	Notary 62 (8.5)	Peasant 48 (10.9)	Wool d. 39 (9.5)	Wool d. 36 (10.2)	Peasant t. 82 (24.6)	Wool d. 26 (8.0)
3	Weaver 261 (7.0)	Peasant p. 44 (6.0)	Notary 47 (10.7)	Notary 29 (7.0)	Sharecr. 34 (9.7)	Wool d. 27 (8.1)	Shoemaker 22 (6.8)
4	Shoemaker 244 (6.6)	Tanner 41 (5.6)	Iron wor. 32 (7.3)	Iron wor. 21 (5.1)	Shoemaker 33 (9.4)	Notary 25 (7.5)	Notary 17 (5.2)
5	Wool d. 222 (6.0)	Peasant t. 39 (5.3)	Wool d. 21 (4.8)	Doublet m. 17 (4.1)	Notary 19 (5.4)	Sharecr. 21 (6.3)	Spice d. 14 (4.3)
6	Comber 202 (5.4)	Wool d. 33 (4.5)	Spice d. 17 (3.9)	Barber 16 (3.9)	Spice d. 18 (5.1)	Miller 10 (3.0)	Dry Goods 11 (3.4)
7	Carders 188 (5.1)	Spice d. 31 (4.2)	Barber 13 (3.0)	Spice d. 12 (2.7)	Miller 15 (4.3)	Dry goods 6 (1.8)	Iron wor. 11 (3.4)
8	Carpenter 169 (4.3)	Barber 31 (4.2)	Carpenter 13 (3.0)	Carpenter 11 (2.7)	Spice d. 13 (3.7)	Furnace 6 (1.8)	op. Religious 10 (3.1)
9	Linen d. 149 (4.0)	Broker 25 (3.4)	Worker 11 (2.5)	Food d. 11 (2.7)	Carpenter 13 (3.7)	Carpenter 5 (1.5)	Food d. 8 (2.5)
10	Dyer 117 (3.1)	Goldsmith 23 (3.1)	Barrel m. 10 (2.3)	Butcher 11 (2.7)	Peasant t 10 (2.8)	Miller 5 (1.5)	Harness m. 6 (1.9)

NOTE: The first number in each column gives the absolute number of household heads declaring the occupation. The number in parenthesis shows the rate per 1000 households; p= proprietor, t= tenant, d = dealer, m= maker.

Table 4.8. Occupational Hierarchy at Florence, Pisa, Pistoia and Arezzo *

Occupation	*Florence*		*Pisa*		*Pistoia*		*Arezzo*	
	Rk	*Wlth*	*Rk*	*Wlth*	*Rk*	*Wlth*	*Rk*	*Wlth*
Banker	1	8748.4	1	1734.8	—	—	—	—
Wool mer.	2	3301.0	2	1213.4	2	853.3	1	930.8
Other Txtls	3	1696.2	4	490.3	1	1253.8	2	478.6
Lawyers	4	1079.2	9	228.2	3	434.0	4	315.0
Spice mer.	5	1019.1	5	429.5	5	411.6	3	404.6
Paper makers	6	598.7	7	278.7	—	—	—	—
Dctrs, brbrs	7	460.9	18	82.2	7	235.1	7	197.3
Leather mer.	8	427.9	6	427.5	4	415.4	15	87.5
Potters	9	384.8	15	92.8	6	268.5	14	89.0
Food Services	10	379.1	10	152.8	9	220.0	9	169.4
Artists	11	348.0	8	235.2	18	86.2	18	71.0
Metal workers	12	314.7	13	123.3	15	100.2	8	173.1
Leather workers	13	290.9	20	71.6	11	156.4	6	204.1
Wood workers	14	228.1	14	95.6	10	172.9	17	82.7
Masons	15	168.7	24	50.6	13	114.9	20	52.4
Cultivators	16	166.6	17	83.7	16	94.8	19	53.7
Metal mongers	17	164.9	3	507.6	12	136.2	13	98.0
Religious	18	160.8	12	131.7	—	—	16	85.3
Tailors	19	154.6	11	137.8	8	232.9	11	154.1
Servants	20	109.5	22	63.8	14	110.4	21	51.8
Transporters	21	105.6	23	61.8	—	—	10	159.0

* Average wealth expressed in florins.

own admission, vagaries of weather and the threat of coastal pirates limited their maritime ventures.

The making of pottery was actively pursued at Arezzo and Volterra, centers of the art since ancient times. Pisa too, through large exports of decorated pottery, was acquiring a reputation for earthenware, extending well beyond Tuscany. Stone was dressed at Florence, Pisa, Pistoia, Arezzo, and Volterra, although only at Pisa and Pistoia did it achieve more than ordinary importance. "Service" occupations (administration, health, law, and banking) were heavily concentrated at Florence and, in a lesser measure, at Pisa. But notaries were everywhere in Tuscany, sometimes in surprising numbers.

One other specialization distinguished the two largest centers: traffic in luxuries. Of 123 Tuscan goldsmiths, 92 were Florentine and 23 Pisans; the two groups together account for 92 percent of the cadre. They also gathered in the great majority of silk merchants (88.7 percent) and of furriers (81.3 percent). Surely the great concentrations of wealth at Florence attracted these tradesmen. If Pisa was poor, its port offered ready access to imported luxuries, and it gave hospitality to colonies of foreign merchants. Florence's prominence in the production of art work is closely tied to its stature in the luxury trade.

Table 4.8 shows, for the four largest towns, the hierarchy of principal occupations, ranked according to average wealth.

The occupational groups in the subject towns consistently show a lower average wealth than the corresponding Florentine trades. Whether we consider spice merchants, doctors and barbers, the food dealers, the masons and builders, the cultivators and, right at the bottom of the ladder, the textile workers and civil servants, Florentine preeminence holds throughout.

Bankers head the list, where they are found, and wool merchants everywhere are close to the top. These are usually followed by traders and manufacturers involved with other textiles, and, a little further down the ladder, by traders in spices and drugs. The most interesting variations involve sectors where the secondary towns were able to preserve their specializations. Thus, leather merchants held sixth place at Pisa and fourth at Pistoia. Manufacturers and merchants dealing in metals held a low position at Florence, but were in third place at Pisa, twelfth at Pistoia, and thirteenth at Arezzo.

The growth of regional specializations in Tuscany, apparent everywhere in our occupational listings, doubtlessly reflects the distribution of natural resources, but it shows as well the power of the Florentine market, and of Florentine investments. And Florence itself emerged as the great beneficiary of this regional integration of the Tuscan economy. It retained the most remunerative activities and professions. For economic as well as fiscal and political reasons, it appropriated an overwhelming share of the region's endowment, in both material and human capital.

5
Men and Women

Aggiugni a queste che ottimo sarà indizio se la fanciulla si troverà copia di fratelli tutti maschi, imperochè di lei appresso di te potrai sperare sarà simile alla madre.

Add to these [qualities to be sought in a bride] that it is an excellent sign if the girl has numerous siblings all of them males. You can thus hope that when she joins you she will be similar to her mother.

—Leon Battista Alberti, *Della famiglia*, ed. Grayson, p. 112

he Catasto not only shows us households, the wealth that they owned, and the work that they did; it also opens the doors of Tuscan homes and reveals who were resident within. In this and the following chapter, we look at these family members and at their distributions by sex and by age.

I. Sex and Registrations

As early as the middle of the fourteenth century, the chronicler Giovanni Villani observed that out of the 5,500 to 6,000 babies baptized at Florence every year, the males outnumbered the females by some 300 to 500 infants. To be sure, the methods of registering the sex of the newborn were hardly rigorous. The priest performing the baptisms simply cast in some sort of receptacle a black bean for a boy and a white bean for a girl, and later counted the accumulation.[1]

These figures evoke a problem, which students of traditional populations frequently encounter. Are these imbalances in the sex ratio, favoring males, to be attributed to faulty registrations? Or do they indicate that within the given society baby girls did not survive as well as their brothers? Not only the newborn raise this problem of skewed sex ratios. All through life, in traditional populations, that ratio is likely to show mysterious swings. And again the researcher must ask: Do these variations principally reflect divergent life expectancy for men and for women? Or are they characteristic of the record itself, the way in which the information was gathered and pre-

1. Villani, 1823, bk. 11, chap. 94: p. 184.

served? In a document as old as the Catasto, the suspicion hangs heavy that defects in collecting and recording the data, rather than the real conditions of social life, gave the male sex a majority.[2] In studying distributions by sex in Tuscan society, we are thus obligated first to ask: What portion of the observable variations in the sex ratio up and down the scale of ages can reasonably be attributed to faulty registration?

The Catasto allows us to identify the sex of nearly all the persons it surveys. Only in some forty cases does the given name or title (or other evidence) fail to indicate the gender of its bearer. In these few instances, age is specified, but the declared name, "Andrea," for example, can be either masculine or feminine. In the absence of conclusive evidence, the sex of the person was entered into our "edition" as uncertain.[3] The 532 other individuals whose sex is unknown were registered as groups. For some few communes, the declarations, in both rough and clean drafts, have been lost; we had then to rely on summaries, which give the total number of mouths in each family, but tell us nothing about sex, age, marital status or relation to the household head.[4] However, the number of such losses is so small (only 0.2 percent of the population) that we felt safe in excluding them from most of our tables. They do, however, figure in the calculation of mean household size.

MALE AND FEMALE

Viewed in its totality, the population subject to Florence for which sex is stated shows a ratio quite unfavorable to females. For every 100 women entered in the survey there are about 110 men.[5] The balance is puzzling. In most known populations the sex ratio stands at 105 males to females at birth, but thereafter diminishes. Males usually do not survive through

2. Henry, 1967, p. 37, and 1972, pp. 30–31.

3. The most frequent ambiguous names have endings in "a" (Andrea above all, but also Battista, Laudomina, Luca, Pasqua, Ventura or Buonaventura, Vangelista, and Zaccaria) and also in "e" (Bice, Felice, etc.). The scribe occasionally notes their ambiguity and tries to overcome it, for example "Vangelista . . . è femina" (AC 272. f. 80). or "Andrea . . . maschio" (ibid., f. 86). Elsewhere, uncertainty prevails. For example, AC 272, f. 99, two Andrea's, of 2 and 4 years respectively, are most likely girls. This kind of name raised serious problems for the priest of San Giovanni who drew up the baptismal registers from 1450. Many errors in adding the sexes appear in the totals by page or by month, and seem due to the presence of these names (the errors are reproduced by Lastri, 1775, and Zuccagni-Orlandini, 1848–54). The priest quickly adopted the practice of giving the second name of the baby, in these instances at least.

4. The communes for which only summaries have survived are Montemurlo, Doccia, Monterappoli, and Fabbrica.

5. In exact figures, men are 137,994 and women 125,645, giving a ratio of 109.8, which increases to 110.3 if we omit persons of uncertain age, who are chiefly female (persons of known age are 136,103 males and 123,398 females). Males thus constituted 52.4 percent of the population.

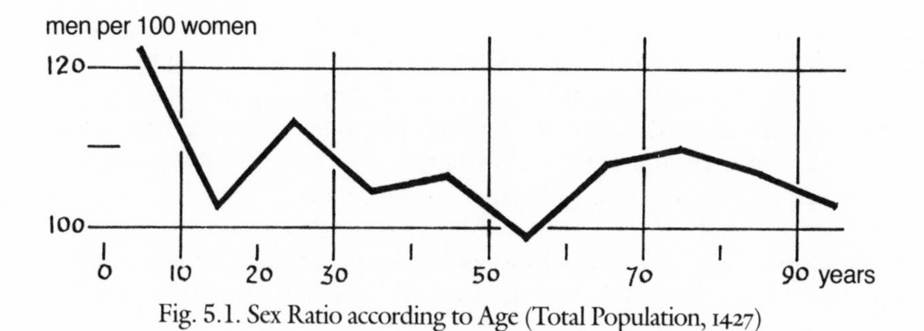

Fig. 5.1. Sex Ratio according to Age (Total Population, 1427)

childhood as well as females, and women in modern populations typically constitute a majority. But in Tuscany in 1427, men seem to outnumber women by nearly 13,000.

From early childhood through old age the male sex holds a nearly constant advantage. The age groups which depart from this pattern are exceptional (see Figure 5.1). Between the ages of 15 and 20 there are more females among the young people of Tuscany; and again between the years 40 to 60 women come to hold a slight numerical advantage over men; thereafter they fall to a short-lived equality with males. After age 60 the number of women declines more rapidly than their male partners.[6] In sum, the deficit of females is especially marked in childhood and (after an interruption during adolescence) during the years of young adulthood.

EARLY CHILDHOOD

The pyramid of ages, constructed on the basis of the registrations, shows a marked irregularity at its base. Babies less than 1 year of age are fewer than those reported as age 1, and those as age 3 and 4 are nearly as many. The small number of children of less than one year (or exactly one year) may indicate significant underregistration of young babies. But it is also possible that the number of children born in 1426–27 was lower than it had been in the immediately preceding years.[7]

Predominant in all the years of childhood, males hold a particular advantage among infants. Up to 15 years of age, there are nearly six males for every five females, representing a sex ratio of 119.4. The proportion is roughly the same for children under 5. But among infants in their first year

6. Henry, 1967, p. 59. After 55 years "the sex ratio of a population subject to a constant mortality rate of 30 years life expectancy" falls below 100 to reach 74.2 between 80 and 84 years.

7. For variations in the birth rate in the years before 1427, see below, chap. 8, p. 237.

of life (under age one), the figure climbs still higher, to 128.1. This count is clearly at odds with the expected sex ratio at birth, about 105.[8] Indeed, later in the century, the registration of baptisms at Florence, beginning in 1450, yields balances at birth close to normal. The ratio of males to females baptized at San Giovanni between November 1450 and November 1451 was 107.4; over the decade 1451 to 1460 it averaged 104.3.[9] Nearly a century before the redaction of the Catasto, Villani's count of baptized babies gives a figure close to 116.[10] The high ratio approximates the Catasto's. But again the issue of reliability confronts us. Can we trust the chronicler and his source, the priest sorting his beans?[11] Could the sex ratio have been so skewed in ca. 1338, when Villani was writing, and again in 1427, only to sink to normal levels after the middle of the fifteenth century? Variations in so fundamental a datum are perplexing. The suspicion is inescapable that extraneous factors were undermining the accuracy of the registrations. They could have been of several types: mistakes in recording or transcribing the names or ages, rounding of ages, or conscious fraud.

One of the most common errors in registering children is the confusion of months and years in reporting ages. Sometimes the busy scribe, in drafting the declaration, wrote "11 years" when he meant to put, or should have put, "11 months." Irregularities in the order by which the members of a household are listed occasionally reveal such errors. Usually, the household mouths are listed in descending order of ages. When a child supposedly 6 years of age follows a baby of 2 years, it is almost certain that the scribe miscopied years for months. It remains, however, difficult to judge, without independent documentation, how many errors of this kind were really made. So also, in copying out the clean version of the declarations from the rough drafts, the often hurried clerks of the Catasto office were prone to similar mistakes. A comparable error, which we shall discuss later in the chapter, was the tendency to enter or copy names in their masculine forms; to write, for example, "Giovanni" for "Giovanna." Mistakes in copying the ages or names of young children were likely to remain unnoticed and uncorrected; their exact age and even their sex did not affect the charge

8. Henry, 1967, p. 37. Variations around the mean (105) of more than 5 points indicate that the birth registrations for one or the other of the sexes are faulty.

9. Lastri, 1775, pp. 15, 104–05. Lastri counts 925 males and 861 females baptized between 4 November 1459 and 3 November 1461. A. Zuccagni-Orlandini, 1848–54, 1:435–55; S. Somogyi, 1950, p. 465. According to Luzzati, 1976, between 1457 and 1476 the sex ratio of the babies baptized at Pisa was 111.9.

10. At Siena, the sex ratio of babies baptized was 119.4 for the period 1386 to 1390; 110.9 for 1415 to 1419; 125.4 for 1425 to 1429. See Ottolenghi, 1903.

11. At least in the late fourteenth century, as all our surviving ricordi indicate, babies were baptized within a few days after birth.

laid upon their families. We noted many such mistakes as we routinely checked the clean campioni back against the rough portate. We corrected these ages and names when we encountered them in our edition of the document; this was one of the rare instances in which we took the portate, rather than the campioni, as the basis of our entries. But no doubt many errors of transcription escaped notice. This kind of mistake would work to reduce the apparent number of children under one year of age, and, in lesser measure, older children whose ages were still given in months. And it would obviously affect sex ratios in those periods of life, such as early childhood, when sex had no relevance to the fiscal assessment.

The rounding of ages, a classical distortion in primitive censuses, also worked against the accurate reporting of infants. As we shall presently see, household heads tended to round off the ages of their children to the nearest birthday.[12] For older children, this error was, in a crude way, self-correcting. Persons lost to the next higher age were replaced by those gained from the next lower. But this compensation obviously did not affect the cohort of children in their first year of life; the practice was thus likely to produce a substantial reduction in their declared numbers. Also, the rounding of ages was especially marked in regard to women—at every age. Female babies less than one year old were thus more likely than male infants to be pushed up to age one; this practice helps to explain the skewed sex ratio of the newborn.

Prevailing attitudes toward children, of both sexes, also led to oversight and confusion. Adults tended to ignore, neglect, and forget their offspring; infants in early life possessed a kind of transparency. It may be that their slim chances for survival prompted adults to keep a certain distance from their infants, to avoid cementing emotional attachments with them until their chances of survival substantially improved.[13] Moreover, it is probable that the scant value accorded female babies multiplied the instances of simple oversight. The underreporting of female infants may thus be further evidence of the negligence or indifference with which a father of this epoch regarded his daughter. The custom of placing babies soon after birth with often distant wetnurses increased the chances that the father or guardian would fail to remember their existence and report their names. And girls

12. See below, chap. 6, pp. 165–66.

13. Klapisch, 1973a, especially pp. 104–05, on the sentiments regarding girls, expressed, for example, in the formulas reporting their births in the ricordi. Morelli, 1956, p. 173, reflects this tendency to forget or ignore daughters. After naming the sons of a cousin, he says of the daughters: "There is no need here to make mention of the females, since they are very young; when they are old enough to marry, if they reach that age, then we shall mention them, if it pleases God. . . . "

were more likely to be sent for nursing outside the home than were their brothers. As the rich committed their infants to external wetnurses more frequently than did the poor, the practice had a particular impact on the sex ratios within the families of the wealthy. The affluent, to be sure, had a strong reason to produce an exact count of family members, as the law allowed a personal deduction for every dependent.[14] And yet the preponderance of male infants is even more pronounced among the rich than among the poor. Were the missing female infants in the homes of nurses?

In sum, a whole range of attitudes regarding children compromised the accuracy with which the very young were reported and entered into the census. The low esteem accorded female offspring, common in patrilineal societies, made the registration of girls especially defective. Underregistration of babies is common in primitive censuses, and the redactors of the Catasto were not immune from this classic error.

CHILDREN IN SERVICE

For children between 3 and 12 years of age, the sex ratio remains above 121 for the Tuscan population as a whole; in Florence, it stands at 116.2 for the age group 3 to 7, and 118.4 up until age 13. One reason why girls in these age ranges were omitted from the survey is their early entry into household service. Children still of tender years were often placed in service outside the family.[15] The Catasto offers a limited sample (it is hard to judge how representative) of servants. Their status remained ambiguous, and some household heads listed them among the family members. A rough count of the ages of these servants shows that 41.5 percent of the men and 34.2 percent of the women were still children or adolescents, between 8 and 17 years of age.[16] Tuscan families also frequently declared children "kept for the love of God".[17] These were orphans, sometimes foundlings, whom hospitals placed with a family to be nursed and reared. Some were children sent into service (in fact often abandoned) by their natural parents. In this category girls were much more numerous than boys—testimony to the fragility of their roots within the family.[18] For their part, the serving girls

14. In spite of the deduction, the sex ratio of the newborn rises with wealth. Thus, the sex ratio at age 1, for families with no taxable assets, is 128.5; for families with 401–800 florins, 132.1; and for those with more than 1600 florins, it soars above 160—five boys for three girls.

15. Klapisch, 1973a, pp. 111–14.

16. Of the 456 male servants identified as such in the Catasto, 6.3 percent are between 3 and 7 years, 25.8 percent between 8 and 12, and and 15.7 percent between 13 and 17. The corresponding percentages for the 280 women servants are 3.5, 19.6 and 14.6 percent respectively.

17. Tamassia, 1911, p. 255, pp. 369–70; Klapisch, 1973a, p. 113.

18. Girls were 137 and boys 79. Three quarters of these "tenuti per Dio" (159 out of 216) are counted as bocche having a right to a personal deduction, while only 36.2 percent of the servants (266 out of 736) gain the same benefit for their patrons. Sometimes infants were placed with a wetnurse by their parents, and then abandoned. See AC 251, f. 328 and f. 682.

sought above all else to amass a dowry; their employer frequently pledged himself to pay "at the required age" a dowry suitable "for their station." Sometimes he provided, in lieu of salary for their years of service, the necessary bed and trousseau.[19] Marriage, at age 16 or 17, far from returning girls to their families of origin, placed them under the authority of their husbands and severed all bonds with their paternal home. Many *fantine* of lower-class background thus permanently departed from their families at the time of their first employment.

Young boys in service or in "preapprenticeship" remained more closely linked to the paternal hearth. Their earnings were returned to the parents, who were likely to retain great interest in their professional future. The boys continued to be heirs to the paternal wealth, and not uncommonly they succeeded to the profession of the father. These obligations and expectations tightened the linkages between parents and sons and improved the chances that the father would remember his son and report him as a household member, even if he was temporarily living outside the family. Fathers did not have the same reasons for remembering their absent daughters.

Reasons for overlooking girls were present even among the more prosperous urban classes. Here, the educational system played a major role. At the beginning of the fifteenth century, girls received their education primarily in the bosom of the family and in convents. It seems that girls no longer attended public schools, as Villani says they did in the early fourteenth century.[20] While still quite young, sometimes only 7 years of age, they entered the convent. There they remained until they were of an age to make a personal commitment to the religious life (9 to 10 years of age) and then to pronounce their vows (12 to 13 years).[21] Of the cloistered nuns listed in the ecclesiastical Catasto, for whom ages are given, 24 out of 122—nearly a fifth of the total—were between 5 and 18 years of age. And many girls who did not enter the religious life still remained in the convent until the time of marriage, between 15 and 20 years of age. Under these conditions, the household head—perhaps an uncle or a grandfather—describing a large family, with many *nipoti*, probably often neglected to mention one or another of these girls not currently in residence.[22] Here too, the size and complexity of the wealthier households may have made these oversights more common than in the simpler, smaller families of the poor. The underregistration of females certainly does not alone explain the imbalance in the

19. The Catasto gives many examples. These young serving girls received no salary, but were guaranteed a dowry. They would be placed, this time with a husband, at the end of their term of service. See Klapisch, 1980b. The same practice occurs at Toulouse in the fourteenth century. See Laribière, 1967.

20. Villani, 1823, bk. 11, chap. 94, pp. 183–88.

21. Trexler, 1972, p. 1343.

22. On the composition of extended families, see below, chap. 10.

sex ratio for children, but it is one of the factors which gave an exaggerated preponderance to the record of young boys before adolescence.

ADOLESCENCE

The ratio, extremely high in the beginnings of adolescence, drops markedly during the next range of years, from ages 13 to 22. At this stage in their life cycles, men reached the age of personal and fiscal responsibility. Florentine and Pisan males between 18 and 60 years of age, and male residents elsewhere between ages 15 and 70, were obligated, at least in theory, to a head tax (*testatico*). Household heads now had much to gain by falsifying the ages of male family members; the temptation was strong to report them as too young or too old to be subjected to the head tax. On the other hand, the clerks of the Catasto office zealously checked the reported ages in order to eliminate fraudulent claims. Indeed, the scribes were themselves accused of a complementary error: they allegedly attributed exaggerated years to young boys in order to draw the largest possible number into their fiscal net.[23] However, the depressed sex ratio in the years just past the critical thresholds of 15 or 18 years shows that these maneuvers were not altogether successful. They did not entirely prevent the concealment of males, the heaping of names in the exempt ages, and other practices designed to hide from the assessors taxable male heads.

Table 5.1 shows that the relative decrease in the number of adolescent boys is most obvious in the rural areas of both Florence and Pisa. (In the table, the number in the year when the testatico was first applied is assigned the base value of 100; shifts around the threshold year are illustrated both by the sex ratio and by the relative number of boys in the surrounding ages.) In regions of the district, where the age of fiscal responsibility was also supposed to be 15, disagreements over fiscal reforms within the subject towns delayed the full application of the law; the assessments therefore did not take into consideration the number of heads. Thus, the size and sex composition of the age group 15 to 19 shows a reduced sensitivity to the looming menace of the testatico. Finally, in Florence and in Pisa the fiscal age was reckoned from 18 years. The cohort of those aged 1 to 17 continues to show the high sex ratio typical of Tuscan children. Its decline in the following age group is also less marked than in the countryside, which may mean that in the large towns the clerks were more conscientious in checking reported ages. On the other hand, in the two cities, the heaping of boys at age 16 is very visible, and the sex ratio itself falls at age 18, exactly when

23. One of the sixteen errors cited in August 1429 as frequent in the Catasto of the countryside and of the Pisans was that the testatico was imposed "ad altri che non sono d'età legitima . . . ad altri che anno passato l'età d'anni LXX. . . ." AC 1, f. 31, 2 August 1429.

Table 5.1. Variations in Sex Ratios at Adolescence

Age	Florence and Pisa (testatico at 18 yrs)					Countryside of Florence and Pisa (testatico after 14 yrs)					District (testatico after 14 yrs)				
	Men		Women		SR	Men		Women		SR	Men		Women		SR
	No.	I	No.	I		No.	I	No.	I		No.	I	No.	I	
10						2,018	192	1,780	123	120	967	183	712	110	136
11						855	81	659	48	130	442	84	354	55	125
12						1,611	153	1,702	124	95	916	174	804	124	114
13	409	115	342	82	120	783	75	808	59	97	455	86	441	68	103
14	459	129	345	82	133	1,473	140	1,421	104	104	599	113	735	113	81
15	386	108	334	80	115	1,049	100	1,369	100	77	528	100	651	100	80
16	465	131	419	100	111	1,051	100	1,788	130	59	546	103	737	113	74
17	318	90	223	53	143	572	55	595	43	96	326	62	258	40	126
18	356	100	419	100	85	1,482	141	1,732	126	86	842	159	747	116	111
19	268	75	133	32	202	429	41	204	15	210	231	44	130	20	177
20	456	128	464	111	98										
21	203	57	98	23	207										
22	428	120	350	84	123										
10–14						6,740		6,269		108	3,379		3,046		111
13–17	2,037		1,663		123										
15–19						4,583		5,688		91	2,473		2,533		98
18–22	1,711		1,464		117										

Abbreviations: I = Index (year of initiation of head tax taken as base 100). SR = Sex Ratio.

the head tax was imposed.[24] Even in the towns, the clerks could not suppress all deception in the reporting of male ages.

The initiation of the testatico thus affected the balance of the sexes, or rather, their reported numbers. What exactly was occurring? One plausible explanation of these shifting numbers is the following: from birth to adolescence the count of boys and girls had been subject to systematic error, and this error was at last corrected when the advent of the testatico made accuracy important to both taxpayers and tax collectors alike. We must remember that our knowledge of the sex of the Tuscan resident is primarily based upon the form of the name. In the city of Florence, as in the countryside, illiterate heads of families (and even many who had a knowledge of letters) dictated their declarations to a notary, priest, landlord, or neighbor, who knew how to write. These intermediaries probably did not pay careful heed to the names dictated to them. They knew the importance of registering all children, in order to qualify for deductions, or to plead for mercy, but the sex of children under age 15 or 18 was of no significance in setting the final assessment.

Moreover, the predominance of the male pronoun in the Italian language obliterates the sex of grouped or unnamed individuals. A father who did not give the names of his children tended to describe them in exclusively male terms: "un suo fanciullo," or "i suoi figliuoli." Working under pressure of time, the scribes of the Catasto office were little inclined to verify unessential information such as the names of young children. The tracking of names across the various versions of the survey shows a drift towards masculine forms. Thus, Bartolomea in an early version is copied as Bartolomeo, Iacopa changes into Iacopo, and so forth. A widow from the Florentine countryside, Antonia di Luca, found herself recopied in the summary as Nanni di Luca, for no apparent reason.[25] Scribes seem to have regarded masculine forms as normal and the standard, and feminine names as some sort of deviation from the rule. The imposition of a head tax on women is cited in August 1429 as one of the sixteen common errors in the rural Catasto.[26] The clerks were directed to correct these mistakes, but did they catch them all?

24. It is true that at Florence the sex ratio drops markedly to 85 (356 men and 419 women) at age 18. But the heaping of women at this age—the preferred age of marriage for girls, and very nearly the maximum age for the richest classes—obscures the true extent of the male desertion. For this reason we have preferred to consider ages over five-year periods, in groups that are less sensitive to age heaping.

25. AC 307, f. 461. The error was corrected in the summary on 26 January 1429. One of the errors cited in August 1429 concerned names: "alcuni altri sono errati i nomi. Dice Antonio, vuol dire Attaviano e simili errori." AC 1, f. 31.

26. Loc. cit. The personal tax had been imposed on "alcune che sono femine." Many female heads of family bore the testatico, especially in Pisa and Arezzo. See, for example, AC 329, f. 269, Nanna fu di Battista Catenacci with her three sons between 16 and 25 years, four teste; AC 330, f. 207, Mattea di Giovanni, 50 years, and her sister, 40 years, one testa. . . .

Once the population reached the age of 16 or 18, the sex of a household member attained full relevance, both for the head of the family and for the Florentine officials who counted up dependents and calculated the tax assessment. The heads of families stood to gain if they reported as girls their boys who had reached the fiscal age. But the clerks of the Catasto office had strong reasons also to verify their claims. The new attention paid to the sex of adolescents and the verifications required explain why the number of girls between the ages of 15 and 19 suddenly spurted in the countryside; not only did they then surpass in number boys of the same age, but they also formed a larger cohort than did the girls a little younger than themselves.[27]

Still, even these two prominent distortions do not offer an entirely satisfactory explanation for the swings in the sex ratio.[28] Other factors also contributed. For example fathers were prone to misstate slightly the true ages of their nubile daughters. Girls tend to cluster around the age of 18, the modal age of first marriage for Tuscan women. Fathers apparently kept their maturing daughters at that favorable age in order to prolong their chances of attracting a husband. Typically, when they thought they could do so without detection, they reported to their own best advantage the ages and sex of their children.

Corrections in the registers show the many small dishonesties through which family heads sought to delay, if only for a little while, a further increase in their fiscal burdens.[29] The simplest, crudest way of deceiving the tax office was omission; the father failed to declare the presence in his home of males liable to the head tax. This type of fraud was also difficult to uncover whenever the tax officials did not have access to earlier surveys. At least in certain areas, particularly in the contado of Pisa, fathers deliberately tried to hide sons. In this region, young people were especially mobile; many of them wandered, fought, or sailed abroad and their frequent absences facilitated fraudulent reporting.[30] In the course of the two years which followed the original redaction of the Pisan survey, the clerks reintroduced many young people into the lists of household members. It is, of

27. This phenomenon is not quite so pronounced at Florence and at Pisa in the age group 18–24, since the numbers of both men and women show a decline from those in younger ages. Still, the size of the masculine cohort falls more substantially than that of women.

28. We would have to suppose that an error of this type affected some 4,000 of the 96,000 names of Tuscan children (4 percent of the total), in order to account for the skewed sex ratio.

29. The following comments are based on a systematic screening of the errors which the redactors of the Catasto discovered and corrected in the survey of the Pisan county, both at the time of transcribing the portate to the campioni and in the campioni, through later investigations.

30. Persons added were 157, of whom 128 were registered as teste (82 percent of corrections). Of the teste, 93 were between ages 14 and 25 years, 32 between 26 and 70. The tendency to register these boys as age 18 may reflect the Florentine origins of the scribes, as 18 was the fiscal and military age of maturity in the capital.

course, difficult to tell whether paternal repentance, or the severity and efficiency of the official controls, prompted these additions.[31] But how many of the unreported males were successfully rediscovered, registered, and assessed? We have no basis for judging; by their very nature errors of omission are the most difficult to control, both for contemporaries and for historians.

A less flagrant, but doubtlessly more common, method of deceiving the tax office was to claim that sons were younger than they truly were, and hence not yet liable to the tax.[32] This kind of distortion has important repercussions on our statistical measurements. To be sure, in the countryside, the loose reporting of ages and the tendency to state them in rounded or even numbers were independent sources of distortion. Thus, age 14 is highly favored; on the other hand, in both Florence and Pisa, the population shows a strong aversion against number the 17.[33] Also, ambiguities regarding the definition of the fiscal age in the contado (were 14 year olds liable or not?) allowed the assessors to pull large numbers of young boys under the head tax. Uncertainty in the interpretation of the law caused household heads to lower even more drastically the declared ages of their children.[34] In Table 5.1, the repercussions of this practice on the size of age groupings become abundantly clear. Many males, almost surely age 14 or older, were being assigned younger years. They especially fill the two, even-numbered years right before the threshold age of 14.

None of the practices described here can alone account for the increase in reported females and the decrease in males between 13 and 22 years of age. But, taken as a whole, they do confirm that the Florentine clerks, in correcting the declarations, were fully conscious of the kinds of deception that household heads were prone to practice. Thus, to look again at the survey of the Pisan countryside, the clerks succeeded in identifying 206 new heads, not represented as such in the original declarations. Of these corrections, 4 percent involved the "remasculinization" of pretended daughters; 35 percent were rectifications of declared ages; and 61 percent were the addition of omitted teste. In only 12 percent of the changes were the ages of old men

31. Some were "ritrovato dal podestà," probably on the basis of the Estimo of 1426–27. Others were added by an *aggiunta* or addition by the household head, but under what pressures?

32. Within the Pisan contado, 68 percent of the various corrections affecting ages (73 out of 116) were "useful," and subjected to the head tax males who had previously eluded it.

33. On favored and unfavored years, see below chap. 6.

34. The definition of the age of fiscal responsibility at Florence was "d'anni diciotto o vero maggiore non passando l'età di sessanta," and in the countryside, "maggiore d'anni quattordici nientedimeno minore d'anni settanta," Karmin, 1906, p. 28. Conti, 1966, p. 77, points out that, in the surveys following that of 1427, men aged 14 and 70 were included, in contrast with the first Catasto, where these ages were supposed to be excluded. In fact, in the countryside, boys of 14 years were usually taxed in 1427, as were men of 70 years who were not ill or infirm.

lowered to bring them back under the regime of the head tax. Either the clerks had mercy on the old, or they had no sure way of establishing the true ages of the elderly. However, in 33 percent of the delared ages of children, the clerks added one to three years and in 55 percent they added four to twelve years. They thus pushed the children over the borders into the domain of fiscal liability. But the numbers of reported boys continued to show irregularities. In the final analysis, the vigilance of the clerks could not entirely offset the maneuvers of the Tuscan taxpayers. In matters of tax payment and evasion, their ingenuity knew no bounds.

MATURITY AND AGE

After adolescence the sex ratio once more moves upward and hovers around 105; men continue to outnumber women until both sexes reach their 40s. Then the relative number of men noticeably declines. By age 50, fewer men than women are found in the Tuscan population—an extraordinary fact, not witnessed earlier, save in the suspect domain of early adolescence. But then, suspiciously, as our population continues to age, the relative number of males swells again. For people older than age 60, through the last decades of life, between 105 and 110 males are matched with 100 females. This ratio flies in the face of modern experience and raises questions concerning the reliability of the data.

Some comment is required. The dip and then the return to dominance of males over the years of early adolescence make one point irrefutable. Their temporary fall in numbers reflects not a social but a fiscal reality—the government's efforts to catch rising adolescents in the net of the head tax and the population's attempts to move its male youngsters slowly and evasively through the fiscal waters.

The increased numbers of males among those in advanced years is more surprising. Men, to be sure, had a good reason to reach old age sooner than women; a reported age of over 60 or 70 liberated them from the infamous head tax.[35] Undoubtedly, this zeal to show advancing years inflated the ranks of elderly men and eroded male cohorts in their 40s and 50s. But another factor was working here, perhaps of greater impact. The very old and the very poor are often overlooked in primitive censuses, and old women are more likely to be forgotten than old men. The widow in Tuscan society was often solitary and usually ignored. Amid high mortalities, an old woman might have no close surviving relatives, or none who cared. She often passed her final days in poverty. Because of the ambiguous

35. An age of 60 years at Florence and Pisa, and 70 years elsewhere, brought fiscal exemption. The "rejuvenation" imposed by the fiscal administration on the presumed over-aged is marked in the Pisan contado, as elsewhere (see above, note 34).

fiscal rules, many widows were not counted in the households of their married children, even when they lived with them. Some, as we have seen, were counted twice, but many more, we must assume, were not counted at all. In checking the membership lists included in the early declarations, the clerks were able to catch some of these omissions; they added the names and declarations to the supposedly finished surveys of many parishes and villages. But the frequency of these additions argues forcefully that many aged women, particularly within the poorest stratum of the population, were never noticed. Inevitably, the officials gave their chief attention to profitable corrections; like tax collectors in every age, they pursued the solvent. Destitute widows interested them little.[36] If we could assume that as few as 300 aged and pauper women were missed in the survey, over all Tuscany, then the sex ratio of the eldest Tuscans, registered without wealth, would fall to equilibrium.[37] An addition of 1,300 would similarly even out the ratio on the levels of modest wealth. The rich present no problem; women there predominated. In 1427 there were more impoverished women in Tuscany than the Catasto registers.

The count of sexes within the lay population was thus subject to numerous distortions. We have sought to identify the several reasons why household heads deliberately falsified the ages, sex, or existence of their dependents. In general, these many small deceptions resulted in an inflation in the numbers of one or the other sex during particular periods of life. Besides these efforts at evasion, certain habits of mind, even the cultural preference for particular numbers, worked in a largely random fashion to tilt the sexual balances. But whatever their roots, these errors in distinguishing the sexes either become visible in our aggregated figures (during adolescence, for example, or extreme old age) or they are in some measure self-compensating. At all events, the numerous factors pulling the count in one direction or another argue that a consistent underregistration of females was not the exclusive cause of the usually high sex ratio. It is impossible to believe that the recording of women would have been uniformly poor at nearly every level of life. Rather, it appears incontrovertible that the Tuscan population was marked by a true deficit of females. Social factors of some sort must have deprived girls of their normally better chances of survival.

36. In this sensitive age group of older persons, the sex ratio among paupers reaches 129.4 (1,422 men to 1,099 women), but it falls among the wealthy to 98.7 (1,017 men to 1,030 women). No natural movement of the population can explain this discrepancy, particularly since women tended to become poorer as they aged. One would expect that the sex ratio among the poorest, oldest Tuscans would fall, not rise.

37. The addition of 300 women older than 65 years to the lowest wealth category (0 florins) reduces the sex ratio from 129.4 to 101. The addition of 1,300 women to the wealth category ranging from 1 to 400 florins, from 114 to 100.

II. Sex and Survival

ABANDONMENT

In several recent studies, Richard Trexler has illuminated one important social factor which eroded the ranks of little girls more than boys: infanticide and abandonment.[38] Infanticide, the stealthiest of sins, and its impact are hard to evaluate, although the crime attracted much attention from both ecclesiastical and civil authorities. Abandonment is more visible. At the beginning of the fifteenth century, two Florentine hospitals—La Scala, founded in 1316, and San Gallo, dating from the end of the thirteenth century—received, besides the sick and infirm, foundlings. At the time of the Catasto, these institutions were no longer able to provide for the swelling numbers of the abandoned. Moved by a new compassion for these unfortunates, the Florentine commune in 1419 determined to establish a special hospital for the *trovatelli* or *gittatelli*, the abandoned babies of the city.[39] Known appropriately as the hospital of the *Innocenti*, it did not actually open until 1445, and its inauguration seems at once to have encouraged abandonments. This was a harbinger of what would be a major bane of early modern society.[40] At all events, in the period of the Catasto, the abandonment of babies was already a frequent recourse, particularly when famine, plague, or war raised the costs of supporting a family.[41] Significantly for our inquiry, the admission registers of San Gallo over the years 1404 to 1413 show that 61.2 percent of the children accepted by the hospital were girls.[42] For La Scala, the ecclesiastical Catasto provides a census of its personnel and of the foundlings in its care. Of children under the age of 15, 43 were boys and 98 were girls; of those under age 5, 26 were boys and 62 were girls.[43] Girls thus constituted 70 percent of the foundling population.

Substantial numbers of the abandoned babies were the offspring of unequal unions, of liasons between a master (or the friend of the master) and his slave. The mother's servile status (and consequent inability to support a child) was the reason given for 22 percent of the admissions to San Gallo between 1430 and 1439. In 1445 a good third of the first hundred admissions to the newly opened Innocenti were the children of women slaves.[44] The registers are surprisingly frank in identifying the personal status of the

38. Trexler, 1973–74a; 1973–74b. Older but still useful is the work of Passerini, 1853a, pp. 33 ff.

39. Klapisch, 1973a, p. 121; Trexler, 1973–74b p. 261.

40. Trexler, 1973–74b, pp. 263–64; 1973–74a, p. 102; Passerini, 1853a, pp. 685 ff.; 1853b.

41. See the texts cited in nn. 56, 57.

42. Trexler, 1973–74b, pp. 266–68.

43. AC 185, f. 528 ff. For the newborn less than one year of age, the proportion of girls (27 of 35) attains 77 percent.

44. Trexler, 1973–74b, pp. 266–68.

mothers. Apparently, the mother's servile status alone justified her decision to give up her baby.[45]

It is, moreover, painfully evident that the fathers of these illegitimate children were more likely to retain them and rear them in their own households if they were males. In the Catasto, the sex ratio of illegitimate children in the household declarations runs strongly to the advantage of boys: among declared bastards under age 13, boys are twice as numerous as girls.[46] So too, the abandonment of illegitimate girls born to slave mothers helps to explain the imbalance between the sexes in the wealthier classes. The rich alone harbored female slaves in their households. These "domestic enemies" were easy sexual prey for their masters.[47]

Among the poor, the dearth of illegitimate children is a bit puzzling. Perhaps the less advantaged had a different understanding of illegitimacy than the rich, or less interest in declaring it. After all, questions of inheritance did not much concern them. It may be that the systematic practice of infanticide, or secretive abandonment, has obscured the true dimensions of illegitimacy among the impoverished. At all events, there can be no doubt that the primary motive for the abandonment of babies among the poorer classes was destitution.[48] It was not the only motive, at least in the view of some contemporaries. The directors of the hospital of San Giorgio at Pistoia blamed sexual passion, enkindled "because courtly young girls are always in blossom, like hazel trees".[49] Other foundling hospitals must have noticed a correlation between the surge of war and plague, shortly before the Catasto, and the contemporaneous rush of abandoned children into their care.[50] War and famine marked the decade between 1430 and 1439, and in this period of crisis, to judge from the entry lists of San Gallo, the number of abandoned baby girls grew even more substantially than that of boys.[51]

45. Ibid., p. 271.

46. The Catasto identifies 94 male bastards under age 13, as opposed to 46 girls. Their sex ratio was thus 204. Cf. the identiical conclusions in Trexler, 1973–74b, p. 267 and n. 52.

47. On slaves, especially at Florence, see Zanelli, 1885; Origo, 1955. The subject is treated *in extenso* in Verlinden, 1977.

48. Trexler, 1973–74b, p. 274.

49. "A le volte cie n'à quatro o se' o otto a balia, che grazia a Dio no'cene al presente tanti, ma possimo sperare d'averne ongni dì perchè le chortesi filgluole stanno sempre in fiori come i nocciuoli." AC 198, f. 38, San Giorgio di Pistoia.

50. The number of abandoned babies seems to have grown in the years preceding the Catasto, as the directors of the Misericordia of Prato affirm, AC 197, f. 48. They had to find wetnurses for 10 to 12 babies.

51. Trexler, 1973–74b, pp. 266–68. On the other hand, the opening of the Innocenti in 1445 seems to have lowered the sex ratio of abandoned babies, doubtless for the reason that parents became more willing to forsake their male babies, as they were assured that a new hospital would care for them. The baptismal registers of San Giovanni show a drop in the sex ratio of abandonned children after 1450. Of the 84 infants, wards of the hospitals, baptized in 1450–51, we count 44 boys and 40 girls, for a sex ratio of 116.

NURSING

Abandonment especially threatened the newborn, for whom it often meant a disguised or delayed infanticide. The deserted baby might not be rescued in time to save its life. Even in the hospital, its chances of survival were notoriously bad. The hospital had at once to procure a wetnurse for the baby, if there was none in residence, and then to commission, supervise, and pay her. Some parents, in abandoning their child to the Innocenti, pleaded that the hospital keep it and not send it to an outside nurse. They were acutely aware that the sending of a child to a remote nurse placed its survival in jeopardy. Apparently, the directors of the hospital subjected little girls to this risk more commonly than little boys. Perhaps they were responding to the pleas of the parents, who spoke out for their male babies more often than for their females.[52] Perhaps they recognized that girls, who would require a dowry, cost more to rear than boys, who could be placed in shops and become self-supporting at an early age. But likely too their policy reflected the low esteem in which they held their little girls.

There is this further cause of attrition. Among prosperous or even wealthy families, the parents were more likely to place their daughters, rather than their sons, with a distant nurse.[53] While the sex ratio for all children age 0 to 3 stands at a high 120, it is only 103 among the 234 babies of that age group who, according to the Catasto, had been placed with a outside nurse.[54] Moreover, the Florentine family memoirs leave no doubt that the fathers were well aware of the risk of placing babies outside the home. They often railed against the wetnurses, and warned that through their carelessness they might cause the deaths of children placed in their charge.[55] Baby boys, nursed at home more frequently than their sisters, thus gained an inestimable advantage in the struggle. And they

52. Trexler, 1973–74a, p. 102; 1973–74b, p. 272.

53. We here reckon as wealthy those with more than 400 florins in gross assets. If the Catasto can here be trusted, only about a dozen nurses lived in Florentine households, and two-thirds of them with families above this level of wealth. Usually, babies were placed with rural wetnurses. See the salaries for them laid down in the Statutes of 1415, *Statuta*, 1778–81, 2: 267–70. Salaries diminished with distance from the city. Taxpayers often make mention of moneys paid to wetnurses, in the vain hope of gaining deductions. See Klapisch, 1980b.

54. Of the 234 babies placed with nurses, 144 (61.5 percent) came from families with more than 400 florins gross wealth. The number of babies, aged 0–3, in the same category of wealth form only 12.5 percent (4,379 out of 35,275) of that age group.

55. Morelli, 1956, p. 452, for example, expresses his suspicions on the death of a baby at Ripoli, "pensammo l'affogasse. . . ." See also Corsini, 1965, p. 147, about a boy who died in 1457: "ucciselo la balia che fu Piera donna di Chaio, in San Chasciano vixe." On suffocation by nurses, see Trexler, 1973–74a, p. 103 ff. Bernardino of Siena shows awareness of the reduced chances of survival, which children placed with outside nurses endured. He writes: " . . . satis evidens est iudicium Dei, ut qui ad lactandum aliis filios tradunt pauciores minoresve filios habeant, quam mulieres ceterae proprios filios nutrientes." "De pudicitia coniugali," 1950–, 1:220. See also Klapisch 1980b.

probably continued to enjoy better care throughout childhood. According to Paolo da Certaldo, who wrote at the end of the fourteenth century, fathers were expected to supervise the diet of a boy more attentively than the nourishment of a girl.[56]

THE PLAGUE

Did other factors meting out death to women reduce their numbers still further? Historians of the early modern world have observed that epidemics sometimes took higher tolls of women than of men, most noticeably in the seventeenth century.[57] Plague deaths thus sustained a high sex ratio in the surviving population. The data on deaths that we have gathered in regard to Florence, which we shall later examine in detail, show, on the other hand, a rough equality in the registered deaths of males and females.[58] But here again, the deaths of girls may have been less conscientiously recorded than those of boys. Moreover, medical opinion, expressed at the close of the Middle Ages, held that the plague was more dangerous to women than to men. The Florentine Marsilio Ficino, a physician as well as a philosopher, opined that: "Children and women are particularly vulnerable to the plague . . . as they are full of corruptible humors and live without order or measure".[59] Our present state of knowledge does not exclude this possibility: the repeated plagues at the end of the fourteenth and the beginning of the fifteenth century may have especially thinned the ranks of women. Plague recurrences perhaps helped produce a lasting disproportion between the sexes within the Tuscan population.

At all events, the sex ratio continued to change from the Black Death until the beginning of the sixteenth century. Unfortunately, our observations must be based exclusively on limited urban samples, which is to say, on populations that cannot be regarded as closed. In the city of Prato, the sex ratio moved from 97.9 in 1372, to 106.6 in 1427, to 107.3 in 1469. Its value in 1552 is unknown, but by 1622 it had fallen to 91.7.[60] Florence in the fifteenth century experienced a similar movement toward a greater masculine preponderance in the urban population. The sex ratio, to be sure, remained high over the entire course of the 1400s. But it reached its apparent apogee toward the century's close. Thus, it went from 118.9 in 1427, to 123.8 in 1458, to 126.7 in 1480, and then fell again to 89.2 in 1552.[61] This

56. Paolo da Certaldo, 1945, pp. 126–27.
57. Delille, 1974.
58. See below, chap. 9, and Table 9.3.
59. Ficino, 1522, f. 5, verso. See also the text cited below, p. 257.
60. On Prato's population in 1662, see Fiumi, 1968, p. 177.
61. The figures for 1458 and 1480 are based on our sample of one-tenth of the population. For 1552, see Battara, 1935b, pp. 31 ff. At the last date, with servants and religious, the Florentine population included 26,821 men and 32,370 women, for a ratio of 82.9. Without the religious, 26,380 men and 29,584 women, ratio 89.2; without both religious and servants, 23,608 men and 23,466 women, ratio 100.6. In no instance does the ratio climb much above 100.

evolution, common to the two cities, seems largely attributable to the constant growth of the ratio among adults and the aged.[62] Thus, at Prato, women, who were in the majority at the end of the fourteenth and beginning of the fifteenth century, were progressively eclipsed by their male counterparts in the second half of the 1400s.[63] These movements offer some support for the hypothesis that the recurrence of plague outbursts affected the sex ratio; specifically, plague mortalities may have permanently held down the number of women, who were allegedly more susceptible to infection. On the other hand, these were not closed populations; immigration of women to the cities almost certainly increased in the sixteenth century, as the ranks of female servants and religious were growing. The fluidity of the population precludes any firm conclusions about differential mortalities linked to sex. It is, at all events, certain, that in 1427 social as well as epidemiological factors were chiselling away at the feminine side of the age pyramid.

STATUS AND MOBILITY

The balance between the sexes was not the same at all levels of the social hierarchy (Table 5.2). Certain factors affected the ranks of the poor more powerfully than those of the rich. For example, the underregistration of young males entering upon the age of the head tax was especially pronounced among the poorest classes. Families with gross wealth under 800 florins struggled desperately to escape the testatico on their male members by all the devices we have previously described. On the other hand, households with more than 800 florins of gross taxable assets found the head tax less onerous and the need to elude it less pressing; properties and not persons set the tax burden among the prosperous. The fraudulent concealment of males in the age group 10 to 19 was thus relatively attenuated; also, fairly affluent households had less incentive than the poor to present males in their 50s as already past the age of fiscal responsibility. The wealthiest Tuscan taxpayers (with more than 3,200 florins in assets) are the only group in the community in which old women were more numerous than old men, as is the normal situation. Omissions and fraud varied inversely to the household's wealth.

62. But we should also note that the sex ratio of children (0–14 years of age) at Prato moves from 117.3 in 1372 to 133.6 in 1427, only to return in 1469 to its level at the end of the fourteenth century (115.2).

63. Women seem also to remain in the majority in the group of ages 15–64 in the Florentine countryside, and particularly in the contado of Prato, for the entire fifteenth century. But fraudulent reporting of the sex of boys had become so common a practice in the countryside (see below, chap. 6, p. 192) that the data on children and young people in 1469 are all but useless. Old women on the other hand seem to have been greatly underregistered. The sex ratio among the aged (65 years and up) climbs in the Florentine contado to 173.1 in 1469 and to 287.5 in the countryside of Prato.

Table 5.2. Sex Ratios according to Wealth

Wealth in Florins	*0*	*1–25*	*26–50*	*51–100*	*101–200*	*201–400*	*401–800*	*801–1,600*	*1,601–3,200*	*3,201 +*	*Total*
Florence	106.9	119.5	108.0	104.9	107.3	110.3	125.7	127.3	134.0	135.9	118.9
Territory	114.7	106.6	107.6	107.7	108.1	111.5	114.7	113.3	118.6	128.3	108.9
Total	113.4	107.1	107.6	107.6	108.1	111.3	118.2	121.3	129.7	134.7	110.3

SOURCE: Catasto of 1427–1430.

But in spite of their generally more complete and accurate declarations, wealthy Florentines (and Tuscans) declared in their households substantially fewer women than did the poor, and urban families also showed fewer females than do homes in the countryside. At the richest levels of urban society, during young adulthood and middle age, men hold a truly extraordinary preponderance over women, as Table 5.2 and Figure 5.2 illustrate.

Already on the middle rungs of the scale of wealth, within families with a gross fortune between 400 and 800 florins, the number of men in the age group between 20 and 50 greatly exceeds that of women. Their numerical superiority grows even weightier as we climb higher up the ladder of wealth. Within the richest households (for the most part Florentine), among members giving ages in the 30s, we encounter no fewer than 174 men for every 100 women.

It is difficult to believe that the rich were simply failing to report their women. They had, in the deduction of 200 florins allowed for every household member, good reason to declare them conscientiously. Moreover, carelessness in reporting is usually associated with a low cultural or educational level. But the Florentine wealthy were the best educated of all social groups, and most of them retained a deep interest in the management of their families and properties. During childhood, the sex ratio of the wealthy is not markedly different from that of the poor. In adolescence, when males became responsible for the head tax, the ratio does not lurch downward as with the poor; at least in this instance, the rich were not prone to practice fraud. In old age, rich women surpass old men in number, as in most known populations. Why then were there so few wealthy women between the ages of 30 and 60?

The span includes the years of childbearing, and this biological function had to have had some impact on the survival of women. The wealthiest women, as we shall see, were the most fecund within the population. They could afford to place their babies with wetnurses, but they lost the protection against another pregnancy which nursing partially provides. And they seem not to have engaged quite as much in the primitive contraceptive practices to which the preachers of the day make frequent allusion. Their wealth allowed them more easily to respect the Church's command that sexual intercourse be always open to procreation. Wealthy married women were thus more likely to risk bearing children than those of a lower social order. Still, it would have required a veritable massacre of child-bearing women to account for a sex ratio of higher than 150.

Another, less obvious social phenomenon was also working, not to kill women, but to drain them out of the ranks of the wealthy. Because of inflated dowries and a shortage of suitable marriage partners, many wealthy girls had to accept grooms from lower levels of the social hierar-

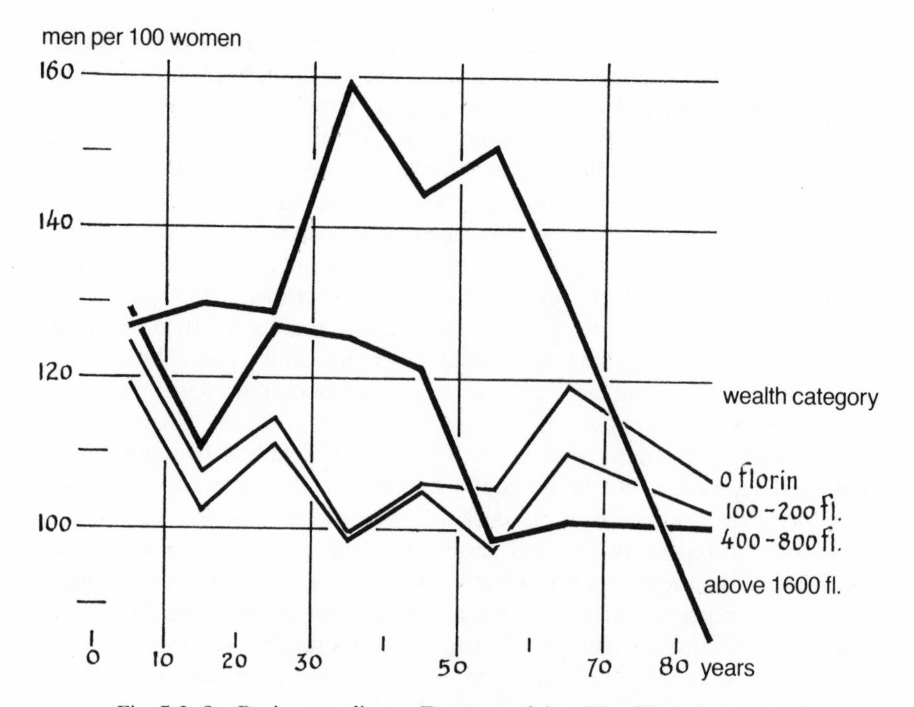

Fig. 5.2. Sex Ratio according to Fortune and Age (Total Population, 1427)

chy. As we shall see when we examine Tuscan marriages, rich girls tended to marry down.[64] Conversely, males tended to marry up. These currents effectively substituted upwardly mobile males for downwardly mobile females in the upper echelons of society.

Closely related to the disadvantaged position of Tuscan women on the marriage market is the loss of many of them from the lay Catasto through entry into the religious life. To be sure, if we only consider the population of the city of Florence (the community best illuminated in our sources), and if we restore to it the estimated numbers of clerics and religious, the impact on the overall sex ratio is scarcely impressive.[65] The number of females in the population is augmented a bit more than the number of males; and the sex ratio drops, but only by one-tenth of 1 percent.[66] On the other hand, if we define more precisely those social sectors, from which clerics and religious were recruited, then their inclusion in the lay popula-

64. See below, chap. 7, pp. 226–28.

65. On the clerical population, see above, p. 25, and Herlihy and Klapisch-Zuber, 1978.

66. Men pass from 19,544 to about 20,600, and women from 16,441 to 17,340 approximately. The sex ratio is only sightly affected, as it changes from 118.9 to 118.8.

tion becomes meaningful. The data assembled by Richard Trexler, and our own soundings, indicate that Tuscan nuns, and Florentine nuns in particular, were in the vast majority drawn from "established families," belonging to the city's middle and upper classes.[67] Most of the nuns bear well-known family names.[68] They thus derive from those same parts of the urban population where the deficit of women is most obvious. We can attempt to correct the sex ratio of the Florentine middle and upper classes by restoring to them the number of women given to religion. This adjustment is, however, based on two assumptions, both of which could be questioned. We do not know the exact number of nuns at Florence, as the Catasto provides membership lists for only a few of the convents. On the basis of this partial information, we can make a reasonable estimate of their total numbers, but we cannot be entirely sure of its accuracy. Then too, our assessment of the social origins of the nuns is also based on a sample, which might be quite unrepresentative of nuns as a whole.

With these cautions in mind, we shall try to adjust the sex ratios of the middle and upper classes of the Florentine population. We have estimated that there were in the female monasteries of the city and its immediate environs roughly 900 to 935 nuns, including lay sisters.[69] Two-thirds appear to have come from the substantial or wealthy classes, from households with at least 1,600 florins of gross assets.[70] The addition of 600 women to the lay population, found within these categories of wealth, lowers the sex ratio from 135 to about 115. The correction, in other words, brings the sex ratio to a figure comparable to that prevailing in the rest of the Florentine population.[71]

Against this adjustment there is, however, one evident objection. In increasing the number of wealthy women, should we not raise the number of men as well?[72] We think not, for the following reason. Males in religion seem to have much more heterogeneous social origins than do the females. They do not often show the well-known Florentine names borne by many nuns. Male religious orders, particularly the mendicants, drew their members from a wide territorial circuit, far exceeding the limits of the Florentine domains.[73] Foreigners were common among the friars, but are rarely

67. Trexler, 1972.

68. Ibid., p. 1338.

69. For these estimates, see Herlihy and Klapisch-Zuber, 1978, p. 15.

70. Trexler, 1972, p. 1339. The median rank in order of wealth, by quarter, held by the fathers of nuns is 66, but three–quarters of consecrated nuns come from these families.

71. The 4,644 men would then be balanced by 4,040 women (ratio is 114.9), instead of 3,440 (ratio is 114.9).

72. See above, n. 69.

73. At the Carmine of Pisa, for example, three of the twelve friars and one famiglio came from Lucca or Nice, AC 196, f. 558.

Table 5.3. Sex Ratios in Successive Age Groups according to Wealth: Florence, 1427

	0 florins			*1600 florins and over*		
Age Group	*Men*	*Women*	*Sex Ratio*	*Men*	*Women*	*Sex Ratio*
0–9	100	100	118	100	100	122
10–19	53(a)	61	103	70	62	138
20–29	95	78	125	60	63	131
30–39	81	100	100	83(b)	68	173
40–49	96	101	95	67	77	151
50–59	82	77	102	71	69	156
60–69	97	100	98	63	70	140
70 and over	63	65	95	50	85	81

The figures given under the columns for men and for women are indices, with those in the cohort 10 to 19 assigned the value 100. The sex ratios are, however, calculated on the real numbers of men and of women in each cohort.
(a) Note the sharp drop in the number of males as they enter the age of liability for the head tax.
(b) On the inflated number of rich males in this age range, when they became eligible for public office, see the following chapter.

found, insofar as we can judge, among the female religious. For this reason, we chose to distribute the male ecclesiastics across the entire range of the Florentine population. Unlike the nuns, they do not come predominantly from the middle and upper classes. Affluent parents tended, much more frequently than the poor, to place their daughters in religion; this is one reason (among several) for the severely skewed sex ratio in the middle and upper levels of Florentine adolescence and the decade of the 20s. This was the period in life when single girls either married or lost all hope of winning a husband. The ranks of adult women thus became singularly rarified in comparison with their male counterparts. Table 5.3 shows the reduction in the relative number of women, by decades, as the population ages. To show the influence of wealth, we give comparable figures for the totally destitute and for the comfortable—families with 1,600 florins or more in gross assets. The table shows that the fall in the number of women is especially marked before 30 years of age in the upper levels of Florentine society. The attrition thereafter subsides; the convents, we can assume, were already filled. The pattern is markedly different among the poor. There is no consistent tendency for the sex ratio to rise immediately after the marriage period for women. And for nearly all age levels, women are relatively more numerous among the poor than among the rich. Here again, we note a linkage between poverty and the female sex.

The impact of ecclesiastical recruitment on sex ratios outside of Florence is very difficult to judge. Even the number of clergy and religious living in the countryside can only be crudely estimated. The inclusion in the lay population of the estimated number of ecclesiastics—priests, friars, and nuns—in the contado and the district raises the sex ratio from 109 to roughly 111. Outside the cities, the number of female religious was small.[74] Recruitment into the religious life primarily affected the sex ratios in the propertied classes of Florence, where women show a numerical inferiority to men much more markedly than in the total population.

REGIONAL VARIATIONS

The sex ratio not only shifts with wealth, but it varies significantly according to region. Map 5.1 shows that men and women were distributed differently across the Florentine domains. The map presents a pattern of broad diagonal bands, indicating areas of marked male predominance, which are oriented from northeast to southwest. This layout with "sashes" crossing the map is found in other representations of statistical data drawn from the Catasto.[75] The eastern borders and the Val di Chiana (the regions of Cortona, Castiglione Fiorentino, part of the cortine and contado of Arezzo) are areas of high sex ratio. They contrast with the western half of the county of Arezzo, the Casentino (the high valley of the Arno), and the eastern parts of the rural quarter of Santa Croce (the mountains of Chianti). Women are frequent in these last areas, and the sex ratio often falls below 100. Still another sash, further to the west, is the region which runs toward the southwest, from the mountains dominating the Mugello, embracing the environs of Florence, the entire rural quarter of Santo Spirito, the county of Volterra, and the Pisan Maremma. Here, the number of men almost everywhere exceeds that of women, and their preponderance is increasingly accentuated as one descends toward the sea. Finally, the middle and lower valley of the Arno (including the plain of Florence as far as Prato), the Val di Nievole, the Pisan hills, and the immediate environs of Pisa are marked by a stronger female presence. But the sex ratio rises again in another strip to the west, which includes the mountains to the north of Pistoia and Prato. The clearest impression emerging from this rapid overview of Tuscany is the singularity of the lower Arno valley, its plains and hills, and of the east-central zone, stretching from the Casentino to the Chianti. These are all "feminine" regions, in which men are comparatively rare. Was it immigration to the towns which drained these territories of significant numbers of male inhabitants?

Taken as a whole, the towns show a sex ratio (112) higher than that of the countryside (109). The concealment of adolescent boys, more pronounced

74. If we add to the rich of the territory (those with gross assets surpassing 400 florins) two-thirds of the nuns, as we did at Florence, under the supposition that recruitment here too primarily affected the wealthy, then the sex ratio within this wealth category passes from 115.5 to 104.3 (7,917 men and 6,880 women, plus 732 nuns).

75. See, for example, Map 4.2.

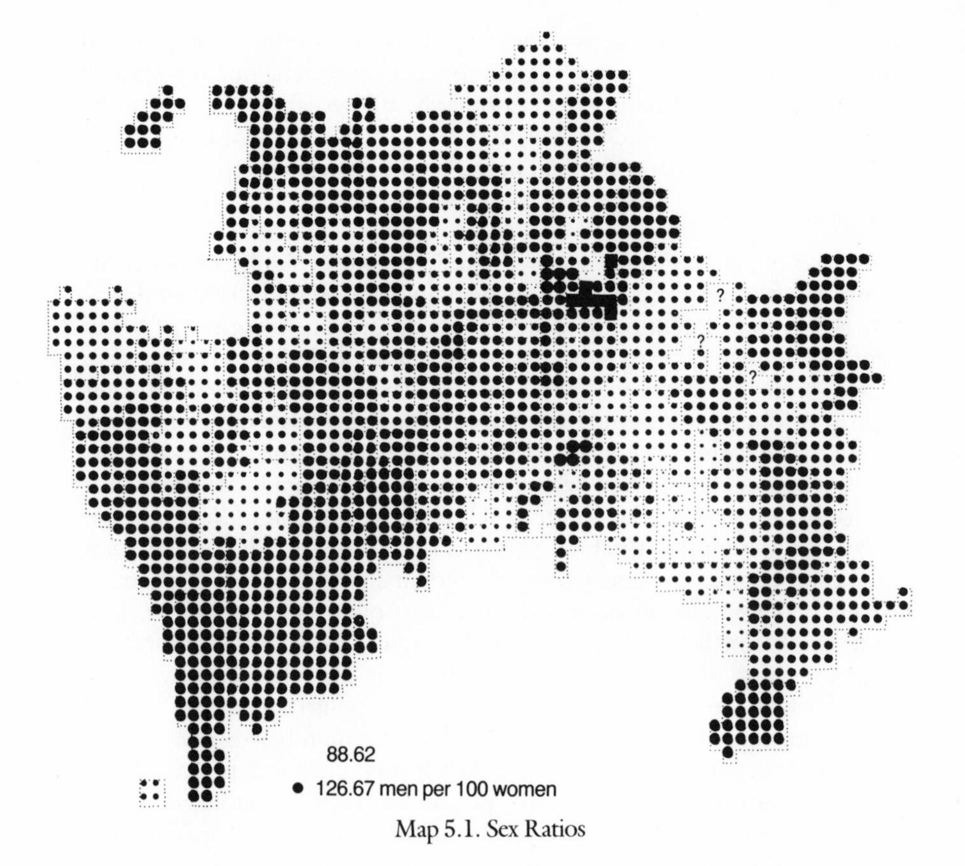

Map 5.1. Sex Ratios

in rural than in urban communities, explains this in part. But the twelve principal towns of Florentine Tuscany also show marked differences among themselves. These are illustrated in Table 5.4.

The two primary cities, Florence and Pisa, show a substantial plurality of males over females; so also do San Gimignano, Colle, Pescia, and Montepulciano, among the secondary towns. On the other hand, women are distinctly more numerous, though still less than a majority, at Pistoia, Arezzo, Prato, Volterra, and Castiglione Fiorentino. Only Cortona possessed a true majority of women.

By superimposing the age pyramid of the countryside on that of the towns, we can investigate how immigration affected the Tuscan sex ratios at different stages of life. (see Figure 5.3.) Migration into the towns reduced

Table 5.4. Sex Ratios according to Residence

	Towns			*Rural Territories* *		
Residence	*Men*	*Women*	*Sex Ratio*	*Men*	*Women*	*Sex Ratio*
Florence	19,953	16,956	117.6	58,224	53,442	108.9
Pisa	3,873	3,447	112.3	9,346	8,738	106.9
Pistoia	2,235	2,176	102.7	5,748	5,098	112.7
Arezzo	2,140	1,979	108.1	8,255	7,773	106.2
Prato	1,808	1,709	105.7	2,836	2,455	115.5
Volterra	1,737	1,603	108.3	1,821	1,539	118.3
Cortona	1,603	1,648	97.3	2,417	2,219	108.9
Montepulciano	1,677	1,514	110.7	—	—	—
Colle	1,436	1,219	117.8	—	—	—
San Gimignano	877	774	113.3	823	677	121.5
Castiglione F.	778	746	104.2	905	793	114.1
Pescia	806	716	112.5	3,087	2,947	104.7

* The rural territories included are the respective contadi, towns excluded, of each city: for Pescia, the two provinces of the Val di Nievole and of the Val d'Arno di Sotto. We did not include figures for Montepulciano, the rural population of which consisted of two villages, nor for Colle, where it is difficult to distinguish the urban from the rural population.

the number of young adult males in rural areas, enlarged their numbers in the cities, and worked overall to even out the rural sex rations. As Figure 5.3 shows, the towns were lacking in girls and young women, but claimed numerous young males, many of them immigrants. The pattern changes in later life. The influx of males into the towns slackened, but that of females increased. Old, often widowed, women from the countryside sought out the amenities and services which towns provided more readily than villages. Some looked for employment as domestics, others came for alms, and still others may have wished only for companionship.[76] The attractiveness of cities to older women is a near constant of social history.

Sex ratios thus show much variation, according to wealth and residence, in Tuscany in 1427. Our critical examination of the document itself supports this conclusion: neither the variations themselves, nor the nearly constant numerical superiority enjoyed by males, can be solely attributed to ignorance or fraud. They are not, in other words, exclusively the product of the record, or of the fiscal system. Negligence, fraud, and clerical mistakes helped to swing the ratios and usually favored males. Behind many of these documentary distortions there lurked an attitude slighting the female sex and discounting its importance. But apart from faults in the record, we would argue that demographic, social, and economic factors did indeed reduce the numbers of Tuscan women in the early fifteenth century. The care they received was less attentive, especially in childhood, and the nourishment given to them was less sustaining. Their parents abandoned them

76. See above, chap. 4, pp. 112–13.

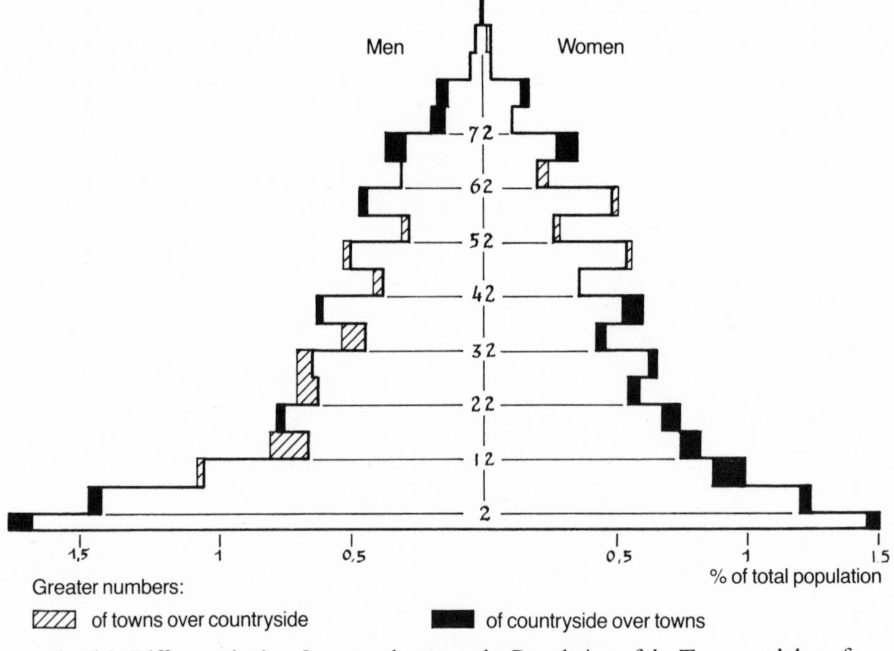

Fig. 5.3. Difference in Age Structure between the Population of the Towns and that of the Countryside (Tuscany, 1427–30)

more readily than they did their sons, and tolerated more easily their absence from the home, in the care of wetnurses, or their early commitment to a convent. They also accepted more readily the marriage of daughters beneath their station. The inferior treatment meted out to girls resulted in an erosion of their numbers, especially in early childhood. Yet, the biological experience of women was not entirely bleak. In the last stages of life, women seem to have survived better than males. But this advantage, characteristic of many societies, only belatedly affected sexual balances within the Tuscan population.

In conclusion, the sex ratio does not merely reflect the close attention that the fiscal administration accorded male taxpayers in its zealous quest for augmented returns. And it does not translate the efforts made by the population to escape close scrutiny. Rather, it teaches us to look for the social practices which affected feminine mortality and visibility at every stage of life and for the material interests and cultural values which often lay behind them.

6
The Young and the Old

L'ora, el dì, il mese e l'anno, e anche il luogo si noti, et in sui nostri domestici commentarii e libri secreti si scriva subito che'l fanciullo nacque, e serbisi tra le care cose.

Let the hour, the day, the month and the year be noted as well as the place of birth, and may these be written down in our household commentaries and secret books as soon as the child is born, and kept with other precious goods.

—Leon Battista Alberti, *Libri della Famiglia*

till in the fourteenth century, the citizens and subjects of the Florentine commune did not have to keep an exact count of their years in order to meet the requirements of civil life. The Church, for its part, had traditionally set age thresholds for the reception of some sacraments: the Eucharist, penance, marriage, and Holy Orders. But the Church never expected or demanded documented proof of age; manifest physical and mental maturity was sufficient evidence that a young man or woman could licitly receive these sacraments.[1] Similarly, a young peasant robust enough to shoulder arms was likely to be recruited into the communal militia no matter what his true age. So also, evident senility or decrepitude, rather than the exact threshold of 70 years, freed an elderly man from military service.

At Florence a crude estimate of years sufficed for most social purposes until approximately the last three quarters of the fourteenth century. By then, the government, for both fiscal and political reasons, began to insist that its citizens and subjects keep track of their passing years with greater accuracy. No longer was the government content to classify its subjects by large categories with fluid margins—children, youth, and the aged. Even the peasant in the countryside, like the resident in the capital, had to learn that the years he had lived were a significant and changing personal attribute; duration of life affected the taxes he paid, the military service for which he was liable, and his chances for government employment.

How could the Tuscans of this epoch accurately monitor their own passing years? They certainly recognized that the population diminished as

1. See Esmein, 1929–35, p. 212.

it aged. The death of contemporaries alone made them aware of that time-related attrition, which modern demographers measure through age pyramids and life tables. But perhaps the more arresting evidence of aging was not diminishing numbers but changing qualities, which the generations displayed as they grew older. Since ancient times, philosophers and sages had divided the span of life into distinct "ages," and attributed to each stage its own physical, moral, and spiritual qualities.[2] More than the dry count of surviving numbers, the passage from one "age of man" to another and the physical, mental, and spiritual changes which marked the transition—observed in others and felt in oneself—measured the passing years and the movement of generations. Tuscans had a sense, still confused, of this endless march from birth to death. The moral hierarchy of the "ages of man," portrayed in popular songs, as well as formal literature, depicted this process on an abstract level. The contrasting qualities segregating the generations allowed the Tuscan to find his or her approximate location on the passage through life.

The appearance of the earliest baptismal registers, which survive sporadically across Tuscany from the last decades of the fourteenth century, greatly extended the opportunities for measuring the duration of life exactly.[3] Also, in the secular world, numerous Florentine (and Tuscan) citizens were keeping detailed family memoirs, beginning in the early thirteenth century. In them they scrupulously recorded all events, both public and private, which influenced the family. In particular, they entered the births and baptisms of children; the government accepted these entries as proof of age, needed, for example, if a male wished to enter a career of public service.[4] Numerous frescoes, depicting the life of John the Baptist show women presenting the naked infant to his father Zachary.[5] Zachary inspects the sex of the child and then is shown writing in a great book—probably noting the event in his family memoirs A new view of age was taking hold in Tuscan society: age was not a function of variously paced biological processes, but was a duration of time which could be measured exactly on the basis of written records.

This need and urge to count the exact years of life continued to spread in the period of the Catasto. Still, ancient habits of reckoning, and the symbolic value ascribed to certain numbers, long slowed this movement to-

2. On the ages of life, see the bibliography in Boll, 1913; Aries, 1973, pp. 1–22.

3. Baptismal registers have survived at Siena from 1381; and at Pescia from the end of the fourteenth century. Elsewhere in Tuscany, they begin usually from the second half of the fifteenth century: Florence, 1450; Pisa, 1457; Pistoia, 1471. See Corsini, 1974; and Ottolenghi, 1903. Lastri, 1775, gives the totals for Florence.

4. See Alberti's extended exhortation to fathers that they carefully keep their "secret books," 1960, 1:119–20. The communal government accepted entries in ricordanze as proof of age. See ASF, Tratte, 1093, giving a list of birth dates of Florentine citizens redacted in 1429. Many carry the comment: "Produsse il libro di . . ."

5. For example, in Giotto's fresco in the Peruzzi chapel, Santa Croce.

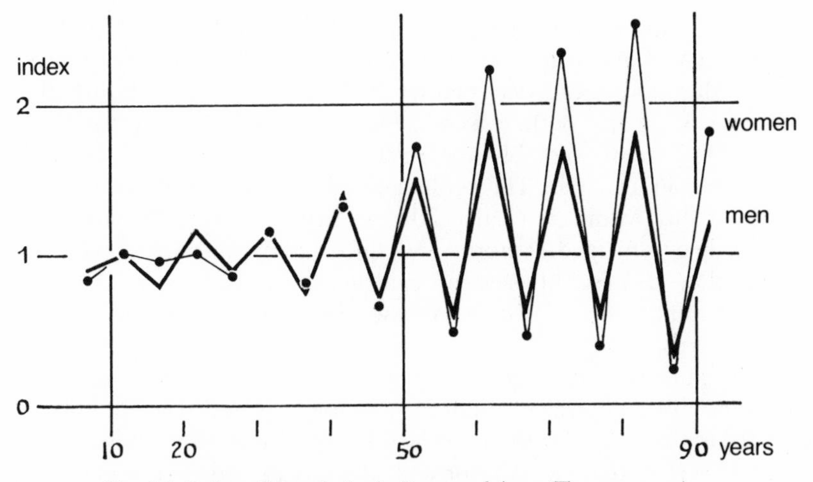

Fig. 6.1. Index of Regularity in Reported Ages (Tuscany, 1427)

ward precision. The age pyramid (Figure 6.3), representing the lay population of 264,210 souls, bristles with long protrusions and is pitted by deep indentations; its shape alone proclaims that Tuscans in 1427 had only a vague knowledge of their own ages or were loath to report them accurately. A scant 259 people affirm that they are 39 years of age; an equally derisory number—253—say they are 41. In marked contrast, the number who declare themselves age 40 is 11,200. In the age pyramid the size of the groups near figures divisible by 10 are excessively large by comparison to those divisible by 5, as can be shown through the results of a simple test (Figure 6.1).[6] Moreover, a fiscal census like the Catasto is likely to contain numerous other biases—intentional deformations designed to reduce assessments. We have already observed the effort of males to escape the head tax by pretending to be younger or older than they really were. The full use of these reported ages for demographic analysis requires that we first distinguish between errors willfully introduced into the Catasto and those deriving from unconscious attitudes and habits.

I. The School of Precision

There are many reasons why the ages recorded in the Catasto often lack precision. The various parts of the survey were not

6. The test establishes the ratio between a given group of ages and the average of the two groups which encompass it. If the results differ greatly from 1, then the ratio shows that the ages are probably rounded. See Henry, 1972, pp. 30–31.

made at one time and its redaction required an extended period of three years. The Catasto in consequence does not yield truly simultaneous data. Although most declarations had been collected during the summer of 1427, many portate were added in the following years. Certain parts of Tuscany—notably the region of Volterra—were surveyed only very late, in 1429–30. The prolonged labors, needed to collect and record the data, would not affect the structure of ages if birth and death rates had remained uniform and unchanging. But we cannot assume that they did in this age of epidemics. In accordance with the place and timing of the redaction, the data reflect differing demographic moments.[7]

The addition of persons neglected or absent at the time of the first draft also muddles chronological relationships. Individuals added to the survey naturally bear their ages at the time of the emendation. They join others whose ages were noted one, two, or even three years earlier. For example, three elder sons of a barber of Arezzo returned from military service in 1429, two years after their father had submitted his declaration.[8] Their father dutifully added them to his household, but understandably attributed to them the ages they had in 1429, not in 1427. This phenomenon also affects our judgments concernig the ages at which women became mothers. The scribes often append the names of the newborn to the declarations. But at the birth of their babies the mothers are no longer the age they had previously declared. Efforts to correlate maternal ages with new births are thus encumbered with these slight inconsistencies.[9]

AGE: AN APPROXIMATION

Still, these distortions, artifacts of the three-year period over which the Catasto was redacted, have only a slight repercussion on the age structure. They render it somewhat more difficult to relate two categories of persons, infants and their mothers, who were not surveyed at the same time. But, clearly, these faults cannot account for the heaping of ages at particular years, so evident in our age pyramid.

The declarations themselves make clear that the years declared were often, even usually, approximations. With commendable scrupulosity, the heads of families often indicate their inability to specify the exact ages of household members. The best they can offer are approximations: "past 90,"

7. On the delays accompanying the redaction of the Catasto, see above, chap. 1, pp. 22–26.
8. AC 330, f. 313; 210, ff. 819, 821.
9. This affects some 28 percent of all mothers of babies added to the original list. See below, chap. 8, p. 233.

"around 50," "6 or 7," "75 or over". . . . The wonder may be not that the Tuscans could give only approximate ages, but that they even attempted to assign ages to nearly the whole population.[10]

The very old were particularly prone to give rough estimates for their ages. Thus, the proportion of centenarians is surely inflated. The Catasto enumerates 89 persons of more than 100 years in the lay population, or 33.7 for every 100,000, one for every 3,000. This would make old Tuscany a rival of present-day Georgia, which is famed for the exceptional longevity of its population, with 39 centenarians for every 100,000 inhabitants. According to the Catasto, more women than men (49 of the 89) and more residents of the countryside than of the city (36 and 28, respectively, for each 100,000 inhabitants) reached these advanced years. However, as we shall see, neither women nor peasants were renowned for the accuracy with which they stated their ages.[11] Some Tuscans lept nimbly over the century mark to land at ages 103, 104, 105 and even 110 years.[12] On the other hand, no one in 1427 reported totally incredible ages. In 1372, for example, probably baffled by the reform of the Estimo which required that he state an age, a peasant claimed, perhaps with a touch of humor, that he had "nothing [to declare] but 130 years".[13] The large number of centenarians in 1427 may also be a function of the big population that inhabited Tuscany before the Black Death of 1348. At all events, the number of declared centenaries diminishes after 1427. Ages as incredible as 130 have already vanished from the Catasto of 1427, and the reporting of ages in the subsequent fifteenth century makes manifest a progressive apprenticeship to accuracy. In 1470 no more than one centenarian for each thousand of the population appears in the survey within the Florentine contado. (This is equivalent to one centenarian per 5,000 population.) There may have been no one of such venerable years within the city of Florence in 1458 and 1480.[14] Surely advancing accuracy in age reporting, rather than shifts in life expectancies, explains the almost total disappearance of centenarians in Tuscany.

The manifest distortions in age reporting, which the Catasto of 1427 reveals, still constitute an appreciable advance over previous performance. The Catasto illuminates an interesting moment in the cultural evolution of

10. On the 4,686 persons for whom no age is stated (1.78 percent of the population), see below, p. 165.

11. See below, p. 171. There should be added to the 49 women over age 100 a Franciscan tertiary, resident of Cortona, who appears in the ecclesiastical Catasto, AC 292, f. 161.

12. For example, 103 years (ASP, UFF 1542, f. 143); 105 years (ibid. f. 207: "sta nel lecto . . . ."); 104 years (AC 251, f. 710); 110 years (AC 242, f. 236); and so forth.

13. Conti, 1966, p. 103: "nichil habet nisi CXXX annos."

14. None appear in the 10 percent samples that we took from these different Catasti; a small number of centenarians may have escaped this partial scrutiny.

Tuscan society, at least in rural areas. Since 1371 the Florentine commune had obliged the taxpayers of the contado to declare their ages, as well as those of their household members. But if a survey of the town of Prato and the villages of its countryside done in 1371–72 is typical, then adult peasants responded poorly to this demand.[15] In two-thirds of the villages, only children were endowed with an age. In all, 44 percent of the population, including heads of families, their spouses, their older relatives, and generally their children past adolescence, appear without a count of years. In the town of Prato, on the other hand, only one of the eight districts surveyed shows similar omissions. For the most part, the urban taxpayers were apparently able to find adequate reference points from which to derive an approximate age for all persons described, adults as well as children.

In sum, from the last quarter of the fourteenth century, citizens displayed a greater aptitude for estimating their ages than did villagers. And their performance continued to improve in the following century. In 1427 at Prato, only 28 percent of reported ages are stated in multiples of ten; in 1371 the comparable figure had been 38 percent. Accuracy continued to improve after 1427; in the Catasto of 1470 multiples of ten make up no more than 16 percent of the total reported ages. In like manner, even-numbered ages (apart from ten) go from 29.5 percent of the total in 1371 to 34.6 percent in 1427 and to 43.2 percent in 1470. The odd-numbered ages (apart from multiples of five) register a slower increase, passing from 15.9 percent to 21.3 percent and finally reaching a quarter of the total in 1470.[16]

Over the course of this century bracketing the Catasto, peasants also learned greater accuracy. This is particularly noteworthy. Only after 1371 were most of them thrown into the *terrae incognitae* of numbers and duration, where they had little in the way of traditional landmarks to guide them, and where they had much to master. In 1427 the peasants inhabiting the villages surrounding Prato show an age distribution quite similar to that of the city dwellers. Even before the institution of the first baptismal registers, the people of Tuscany, including its humblest members, thus underwent an apprenticeship in measuring time which was probably unique in Europe. Through the Catasto of 1427, we can glimpse the means by which the commune's authority encouraged this cultural revolution and we can discern the kinds of conscious or unconscious resistance which opposed the official demand for accuracy.

15. The data were collected in the last months of 1371 and the copy prepared at the beginning of 1372; ASF, Estimo 215, ff. 376–704.

16. Later in this chapter we examine at length these favored numbers. At Florence itself, reporting improves from a score of 60.5 in 1427 to 66.35 in 1480; the basis of this scoring is explained below, n. 39. See also Conti, 1966, p. 105.

ADMINISTRATIVE PRESSURES

The fiscal machinery set up by the law of 1427 exerted strong pressure on the heads of families, requiring that they attempt to assess accurately the ages of their mouths and adult male heads.[17] The figures they reported had also to appear reasonable to the tax officials. Taxpayers who did not specify the ages of their mouths were suspected of proposing fictitious family members. They thus risked losing anticipated deductions. The Catasto clerks occasionally note that "these mouths are not recognized, as the taxpayer gives neither names nor ages".[18] And indeed, only a minuscule proportion of the population (4,154 persons, or 1.6 percent) in the survey fails to show an age. Though slight, this failure to declare an age was twice as common in the cities as in the countryside, and was definitely more pronounced among the aged and the widowed than among the young. Isolated individuals of unknown marital status, rather than those integrated in a family group, were also more likely to omit their ages. The more mobile elements in the population seem to have been the worst offenders. In households that give no indication of recent movement, some 2.2 percent of male heads and 10.5 percent of female heads fail to report ages, but these proportions double and even triple among households that had recently changed residence.[19]

The Catasto officials made numerous corrections of declared ages, clearly in an effort to suppress fraudulent claims. However, some distortions in reported ages did not derive from conscious design. If we are to understand the involuntary distortions of the age structure, we must first determine what the declared ages exactly indicated: age at last birthday (or the number of completed years of life); at next birthday (or the current year of life); or finally, age at nearest birthday. Occasionally the family head entered into his declaration the exact dates of birth for his children, in order to establish the truth of the attributed years. This happens in the contado, but seemingly never in the district, apart from notices of newborn babies.[20] Here we take as the basis of our inquiry the declaration of a Florentine citizen, Guardo di Lapo Guardi.

Guardo was keeping careful record of the births of his own children and of his nieces and nephews, including—remarkably—the little girls. For six

17. The tiny numbers who do not declare ages are classified in relation to sex and marital categories in Herlihy and Klapisch-Zuber, 1978, Table 50, p. 355.

18. AC 72, f. 407, declaration of Francesco di Martino and his brother: "Non si mette perchè non sanno i nomi ne l'età di dette tre bocche." See also AC 2, ff. 32–34 (2 August 1429, "Errores corrigantur"): the tax on adult male heads was often wrongly imposed "ad altri che non sono d'età legitima . . . , ad altri che anno passato l'eta d'anni lxx . . . . "

19. See Herlihy and Klapisch-Zuber, 1978, Plate 10, Map 23, p. 409.

20. For example, AC 92, f. 759.

Table 6.1. Dates of Birth and Declared Ages: Declaration of Guardo di Lapo Guardi, Catasto of 1427

Sex	*Date of Birth*	*Completed Years on 12 July 1427*	*Declared Age*
Girl	16 July 1418	8	9
Boy	28 October 1419	7	8
Boy	9 January 1421	6	6 1/2
Girl	1 June 1422	5	5
Girl	30 March 1425	2	2 yrs 3 mnths
Boy	19 August 1426	0	1
Boy	9 February 1423	4	4
Girl	10 April 1425	2	2
Boy	1 July 1426	1	1

SOURCE: AC 36, f. 527 and 73, f. 101. The first six children are Guardo's, the last three are his nephews and nieces.

of the children he reported ages in completed years. But the proximity of the next birthday exerted an influence on the declared ages. The little boy born on August 19, 1426 was not yet 11 months old when Guardo drafted his declaration; nonetheless, he declares for him an age of exactly one. The eldest daughter had still a few days remaining until her ninth birthday, but she appears as already nine. The eldest son was three months removed from his eighth birthday, but is presented as eight years old. Although ages generally represented completed years, there remained a strong tendency to advance the count toward a coming birthday when it was only a few weeks or months away. The same tendencies are apparent in the countryside, to judge from the few instances in which we can compare birthdays and reported ages.[21] This rounding-off results in a slight exaggeration in declared ages. However, the phenomenon does not affect the general shape of the age pyramid, as persons lost to a higher age are themselves replaced by those transferred from a lower bracket. Except for children under one year of age, who are underreported by virtue of this rounding, the shape of the age pyramid is minimally affected.[22]

Unfortunately, the Catasto declarations only rarely carry birthdays, and we must resort to other records, here again primarily Florentine, if we wish to compare real and declared ages for substantial numbers of the popula-

21. Loc. cit. On the assumption that the declaration was drawn up in August 1427, a daughter born 11 February 1410 who had completed 17 years of life is registered as 17 years; another born 13 October 1408 who had passed her eighteenth birthday is given 18 years in the Catasto. On the other hand, a third, born 21 September 1418, is entered as 9 years, although she had completed only eight.

22. As rounding primarily occurred during the last month of the first year of life, a corresponding correction would reduce the size of those age 1 from an index of 127 to 118.5 (taking those under 1 year of age as the base of 100). However, as we shall see, it is also possible that there in fact occurred a fall in births in 1426–27

tion. Two sets of documents can help us in this investigation, although they concern only males and only those from the wealthiest strata of society. On August 12, 1429, the Florentine government determined that all male citizens who wished to hold office had to present exact proof of age; fathers were required to bring their family memoirs with the birth dates of their sons, so that names and ages could be recorded. The officials who collected this information were the notaries of the *Tratte* ("sortitions"), who supervised the lottery by which the commune filled its principal offices.[23] The Book of Ages redacted in 1429 (and those drawn up later in the century) captured no more than one-fourth the male population. The poor in particular fail to appear, since only the commune's creditors, holders of shares in the Monte, were eligible to hold high office.[24] There has also survived a partial listing of Florentine baptisms for the period from 1428 to 1435.[25] This too includes only males of the office-holding class. Perhaps officials of the Tratte also took this survey, but the two sources were redacted on different principles. The "Books of Ages" contain dates of birth, while this second listing is of baptisms; usually, baptism followed birth by one or two days.

The earliest exact birthdays reported fall in the year 1381, but only from 1384 do they become numerous. Usually citizens over 45 do not give their date of birth but only the years they have lived. Some are content with reporting that they have passed their forty-fifth year; attainment of age 45 made them eligible for all communal offices and exact age then lost its relevance. In most instances this approximate age seems to have been copied directly from the Catasto, even though more than two years had elapsed since the survey had been taken. The preservation of so many exact birthdays after the early 1380s confirms this assumption: almost every Florentine citizen of the middle and upper classes was by then keeping ricordi, in which he carefully inscribed the births of children. The commune itself was showing a comparable interest in ages; as we have several times mentioned, only a few years earlier, in the Estimo of 1372, the government had sought to record the ages of villagers.

Here we shall compare the birth dates of residents of Scala with the ages

23. ASF, Tratte 39. See also Tratte 1093, which represents a partial, rough draft of this survey.

24. Thus, the number of boys cited as born in 1427 is only 156; in 1428 and in 1429 (up to August) only 100. The usual number of male births at Florence was at least 400 to 500 every year. The number of boys less than 1 year old reached 581 in the Catasto of 1427, and those added in 1427–28 were 424. The survey of 1429 did not therefore include the larger part of the male population.

25. ASF, Mss 496. This volume is cited by C. A. Corsini, 1974, p. 698, n. 7 The frequent citation of the father's occupation in the list may mean that the list was somehow associated with guild matriculations.

Table 6.2. Some Male Ages Incorrectly Reported: Gonfalone of Scala, 1427

Name	*Date*	*Completed Years*	*Declared Years*	*Source AC 64*
Antonio di Niccolo Benozzo	11 Oct 1398	28	38	f. 248
Andrea di Amerigo da Verazzano	8 July 1398	29	33	347
Apollonio di Bartolo del Pancia	15 May 1397	30	32	202
Bernardo di Gherardo Canigiani	16 March 1399	28	32	60
Bernardo di Antonio da Uzzano	28 Feb 1399	28	33	403
Giovanni di Luigi Canigiani	8 Oct 1398	28	30	285
Iacopo di Gherardo Canigiani	18 June 1400	27	30	60
Lotto di Donato Quaratesi	8 Dec 1396	30	32	35
Ristoro di Carlo Canigiani	19 July 1398	28	31	366

SOURCE: Dates of birth taken from ASF, *Tratte,* 39.

attributed to them in the Catasto. (Scala is one of the sixteen Florentine gonfaloni, part of the quarter of Santo Spirito.) Although identifications are sometimes difficult and we have had to eliminate the dubious cases, the results are the following: some 26 residents appear with ages representing completed years of life, and nearly the same number, 28, reckon their ages by the coming birthday. This comparison between birthdays and declared ages shows an unexpected distortion. Florentine citizens approaching age 30 often tried to present themselves as age 30 or older. Table 6.2 provides some examples of this inflated reporting.

What did these Florentines gain by adding two to four years to their ages in order to appear older than 30 in the census? The apparent reason is that age 30 often served as the threshold of eligibility for high governmental functions. Clearly, many young men were eager to enjoy the salaries and the influence attached to these offices. The communal government, on its part, was quite aware of this petty fraud. Presumably for this reason it required, in August 1429, that proof of age be provided by all prospective office-holders. The government already possessed, in the Catasto itself, declarations of ages, but clearly it had little confidence in their accuracy.

This gravitation of a large number of male ages from the late 20s into the 30s deforms the urban age pyramid in a minor, but still perceptible way. A comparison of the male and female age groups, aged 25 to 29, with those aged 30 to 40, for Florence on the one hand and the countryside on the other, shows a marked heaping of urban males in the older group (see Table 6.3).

The number of Florentine males in their early thirties thus appears artificially inflated by more than ten index points. In contrast, males in the countryside, who did not aspire to public office, show a slight decline in numbers. The small increase in the numbers of women, evident in both city and countryside, attests to the powerful attraction of age 30 for the femi-

Table 6.3. Fictitious Aging of Florentine Citizens in their Thirties

Age Category (in years)	*Florence*				*Countryside*			
	Men		*Women*		*Men*		*Women*	
	No.	Index	No.	Index	No.	Index	No.	Index
25–29	1,320	100	979	100	5,192	100	4,887	100
30–34	1,486	111	1,011	103	5,089	98	5,084	104

nine population, both urban and rural. Here, we encounter the phenomenon of age heaping. The comparison of birth dates and declared ages in Table 6.3 shows that males were also prone to this practice. To be sure, in this group of young Florentine males from the privileged classes, the rounding of declared ages was not especially marked; but even these men show a tendency to raise rather than lower their ages, and to report them as multiples of 2 or 5.[26] Still, these young male citizens were not entirely representative of the population, as they had excellent reasons to appear in the Catasto older than they really were. Apart from these instances of fiscal or political fraud, a much more widespread form of distortion affected the age pyramid: the unconscious rounding of ages.

II. The Rounding of Ages

From the moment of a child's birth, the father began to reckon its age in rounded numbers; newborn babies in the Catasto are generally said to be 8, 10, 12, 15 or, 20 days old. The powerful attraction of certain numbers is apparent here. Could not the father have easily recalled the exact duration of elapsed time since the birth of his child? For older children or adults, the recollection of exact age was even more difficult. The majority of Tuscan families kept no written record of their births and had no recourse to baptismal registers, still a rarity in 1427. If the inhabitants of the countryside were by then accustomed to estimating ages, the practice seems to have been a total novelty for the residents of the district. The many Tuscans without written reminders of their birthdays could only give a rough estimate of their ages; they doubtlessly used the ages of near relatives—parents, siblings, children—as points of reference. Thus, the members of a single household set their ages in relation to the group, as all

26. Here are some examples drawn from this volume of the Tratte and from AC 64: Bindo di Francesco Canigiani, born 9 September 1413, 13 years completed, 15 declared (f. 238); Bartolomeo di Feo Ridolfi, born 12 August 1403, 23 years completed, 26 declared (f. 266); Luigi di Astorre Gianni, born 10 October 1403, 23 years completed, 25 declared (f. 207); Simone di Antonio Canigiani, born 27 December 1402, 24 years completed, 26 declared (f. 101); Viviano di Stefano Corsellini, born 16 October 1403, 23 years completed, 25 declared (f. 367).

were aging together. This consciousness of collective aging helped assure that no member was likely to declare an age totally inconsistent with reality.

As a result, the data on ages rarely show complete incoherence. And even the few evident errors are not always attributable to the taxpayers. Occasionally, the scribes themselves were guilty of introducing manifest absurdities into the survey.[27] The Catasto office, in reviewing their work, queried the most blatant anomalies.[28] They specifically challenged those which threatened the tax base by reducing the number of male heads.[29] Both the taxpayers and the treasury had an equivalent interest in recording accurately the ages of men which were near, at, or within the range of the head tax.[30] The largest errors in age reporting thus affected those males who were not, or were no longer, liable to the tax, and women to whom the tax did not apply. Thus, in two declarations separated by two years, a certain Cecco di Cecco of Arezzo passed normally from age 16 to age 18; his mother, on the other hand, went from 60 to 52.[31]

AGING AND ROUNDING

The survival of duplicate declarations allowed us to compare systematically the ages declared at two different dates. The test included about 70 households, comprising 363 persons of known age (196 men and 167 women), all residing in the district—around Arezzo, Cortona, Pistoia, Pisa, or Volterra. In the best examples, the two declarations are dated and the elapsed time between them obvious. When the declarations were not exactly dated (and most were not), we judged their order and the time between them by the regular aging of children.[32] For each pair of duplicates, we calculated the difference between the number of added (for occasionally subtracted) years

27. Thus, Puccetto di Puccio, a contadino of Pisa who claimed 72 years in his first declaration, and 44 in a later addition, was given the latter age by the tax office, as he thus became liable to pay the testatico. His wife continued to be reckoned as 60 years and his son as 36. ASP, UFF 1540, f. 387.

28. For example, ASP, UFF, 1538, f. 165: Nanni di Cecco is 50 years old, his mother 60.

29. An inspector was sent to Marti, in Pisan territory, to check the age of a Florentine merciaio settled there, who had given himself 8 years of age (a slip of the pen?) but claimed to be in his 80s, ASP, UFF 1537, f. 278, and 1542, f. 475: "Vorebesi mandare per Francescho di Iachopo da Firenze merciaio a Marti che cie na schritte parecchi viziate." Two inhabitants of the cortine of Arezzo are first declared to be in their 90s, and then both of them are transferred to the green 50s, AC 245, f. 155.

30. An example of corrected inaccuracy: a citizen of Arezzo presents together his "otto figliuoli," but afterwards adds "una maritata e una anni XIV. El magiure anni XV, il minore anni II"; another, corrected portata then replaced it in the register (AC 200, f. 843, 17 July 1429 and 329, f. 255, for the grouped description; AC 200, f. 729, 11 July 1427, copied into AC 329, f. 322).

31. AC 200, ff. 905, 906; 329 f. 393.

32. We eliminated five doubtful cases. The comparisons proved to be too incoherent to allow any analysis.

with the probable number of elapsed years separating the declarations. This duration rarely exceeds two and one-half years, as the earlier drafts were executed between the summer of 1427 and, for Volterra, the winter of 1429 to 1430, while the later and final declarations were finished before 1430.

Figure 6.2 shows how the differences between reported ages and probable ages varied for the two sexes, and for age groups. The height of the central point indicates the degree of correspondence between probable aging and the aging reported in the second declaration. Ideally, perfect correspondence should push this point up to 100 percent. In fact, however, the distribution of birthdays over the year precludes this result; even faultless reporting would more likely result in a score of about 66 percent, which is achieved for the age group under 14 years.

It is remarkable that this, our youngest group of ages, should already reveal an eccentric pattern for females. It would seem that fathers aged their daughters a little less precipitously than they did their sons—an artificial rejuvenation which indicates great paternal negligence in adjusting to the temporal changes affecting female offspring.[33] Between ages 15 and 24, declared years and probable years are better matched for women than for men, although a few young women passed over four years in a single stride in order to arrive at a multiple of five. The young woman owed this laudable precision to her father or a recently acquired groom: the father could use his other children as points of reference, the husband doubtlessly had "dated" his young wife during courtship. On the other hand, the aging of males is much more exaggerated, and the graph confirms what we have said above regarding the tendency of men between ages 20 and 30 to raise and round off their years for fiscal, legal, or political reasons. In adult life (25 to 59 years) males and females achieve equivalent accuracy; still, both sexes show a tendency to add several years (sometimes even five or more) at once in order to reach a multiple of five or ten. At this stage in life, the tendency toward excessive aging is stronger than that toward rejuvenation. After age 60, old people skip 3, 5, or 10 years without hesitation and there is hardly a single person who correctly registers the true lapse of time.[34] The figures reveal a slight habit of rejuvenation among women, who lose and gain decades at random; men, on the other hand, advance steadily toward patriarchal status, marching resolutely forward, five years at a time.

33. See for example the two declarations of Luigi di messer Giovanni Guicciardini, AC 788, f. 157 (a. 1458. and AC 906, f. 476 (a. 1469–70): his daughter Dianora passes from 6 1/2 years to 13 years, his son Giovanni, from 2 1/2 to 12. However, as the ricordanze show, names borne by deceased children were often given to subsequent children: the Dianora of 1469 is not necessarily the Dianora of 1458. On Tuscan naming conventions, see Klapisch, 1980a.

34. Aged males were the more prone to make these leaps when they landed on ages which gave them exemption from the head tax. See the further comments of Conti, 1966, pp. 103–04.

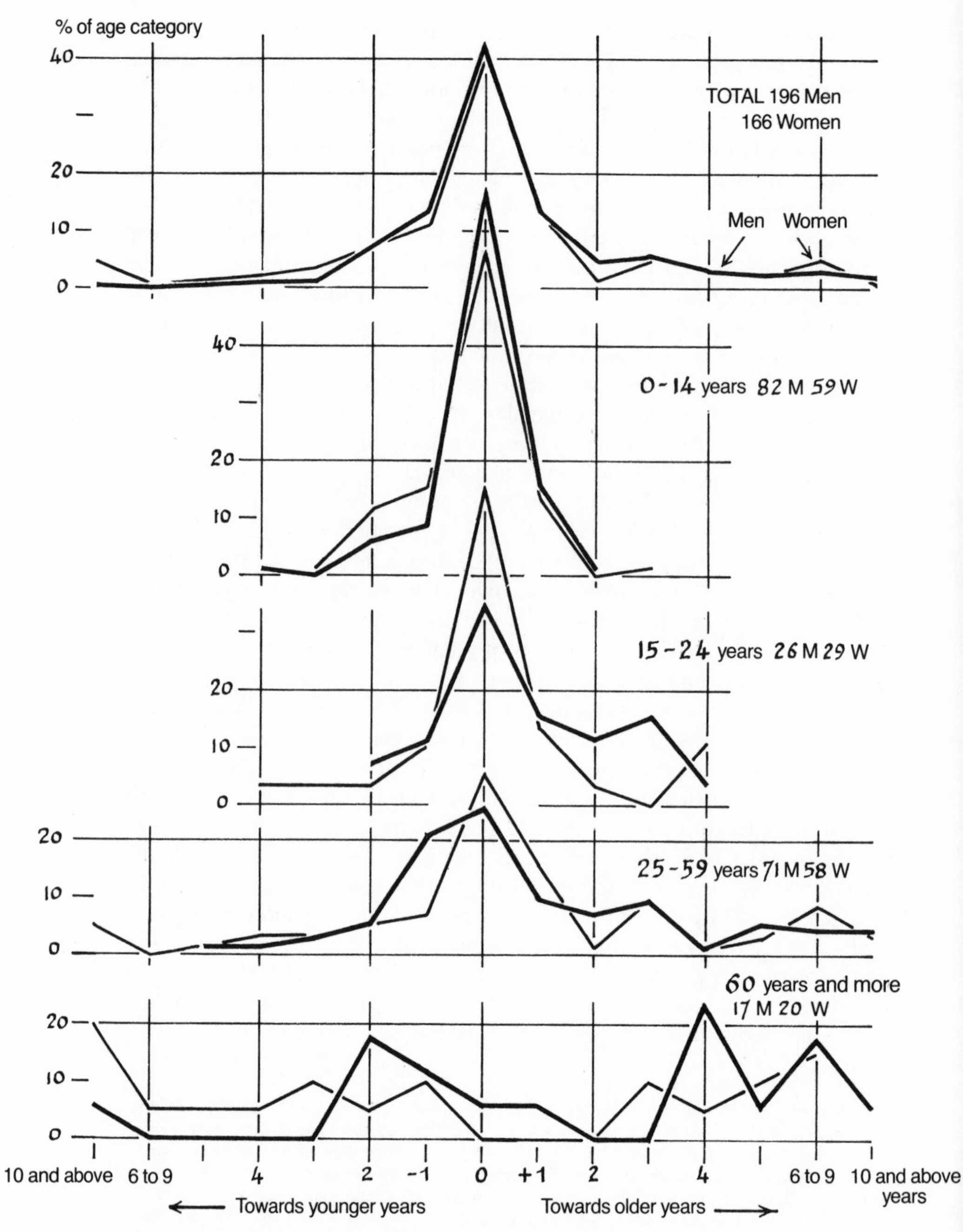

Fig. 6.2. Distribution of the Differences between Ages Reported in Two Successive Declarations, 1427–30

Table 6.4. Errors in Reporting Incremented Age: Tuscan Sample, 1427–30

Reporting Error	*Men (Percent)*	*Women (Percent)*
Younger than the Probable	24.1	30
Correct Age	42.4	40
Older than the Probable	33.5	30

SOURCE: 363 persons appearing in duplicate declarations redacted between 1427 and 1430.

Table 6.4 shows that men and women, in declaring ages, followed, *grosso modo*, the same tendencies. Men did, however, prefer premature aging to rejuvenation, and they are marginally more accurate than women in measuring the the passing of time.

FAVORED AGES

Age groups one or two years distant from one another (as, for example, 39, 40, and 41) show enormous variations in size. Still, this does not prove that the selection of declared ages was entirely whimsical. Our comparison of duplicate declarations has shown that rounding was likely to occur in consistent patterns. Through the detailed analysis of the age pyramid and the application of some elementary tests, we shall now try to determine the criteria by which Tuscans, in estimating their ages, selected some numbers and rejected others.

The pyramid for the total population (Figure 6.3) displays, after age 20, formidable projections at the decadal years and secondary pinnacles at ages ending in five. The largest grouping is not found, as we might have expected, between birth and one year, or between one and two years. Instead, the most crowded age is 50 for women and 40 for men. Odd-numbered ages on either side of the decadal figures lose their constituents quite early. Already at age 29 or 31, the numbers found are five or six times fewer than they ought to be. To illustrate the powers of attraction and repulsion characteristic of various numbers, we shall examine the population in moving intervals of five years. With accurate reporting, in a reasonably stable population, the middle year in any five-year interval ought to approach in size the average for the entire group. The ratio between the actual and the predicted size supplies a coefficient, which, when it exceeds or falls far below unity, testifies to the extent of rounding.[35]

The curves in Figure 6.4 illustrate the extent of age heaping in the population as it ages, and they show the relative attraction of numbers divisible by 10, of even-numbered ages (2 and 8, 4 and 6) and of odd-numbered ages (1 and 9, 7 and 3) respectively. In order not to clutter the graph,

35. The method was developed by the English statistician G. Chandle-Whipple; see Henry, 1949.

Fig. 6.3. Age Pyramids in Tuscany, 1427 (By One, Five and Ten Years)

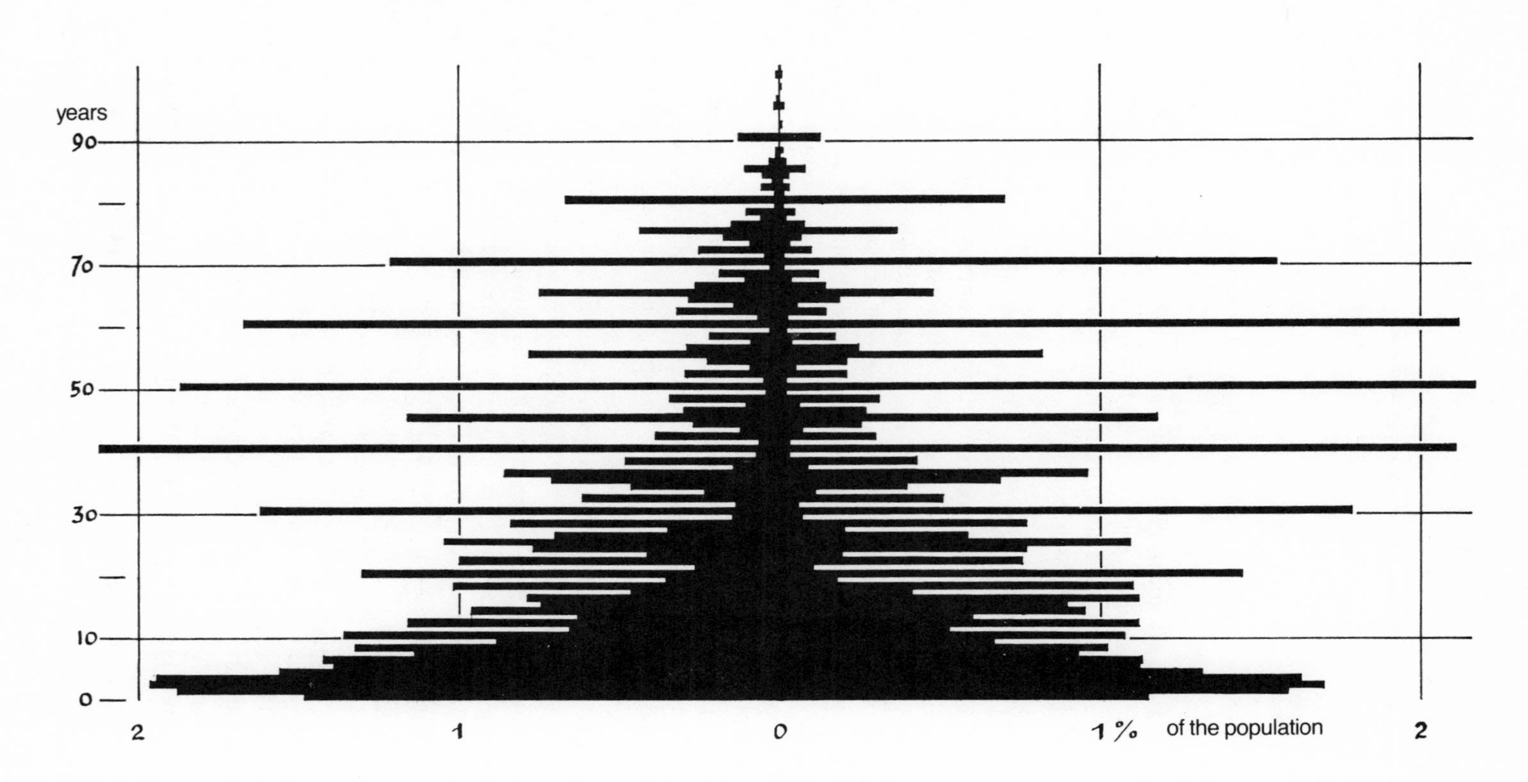

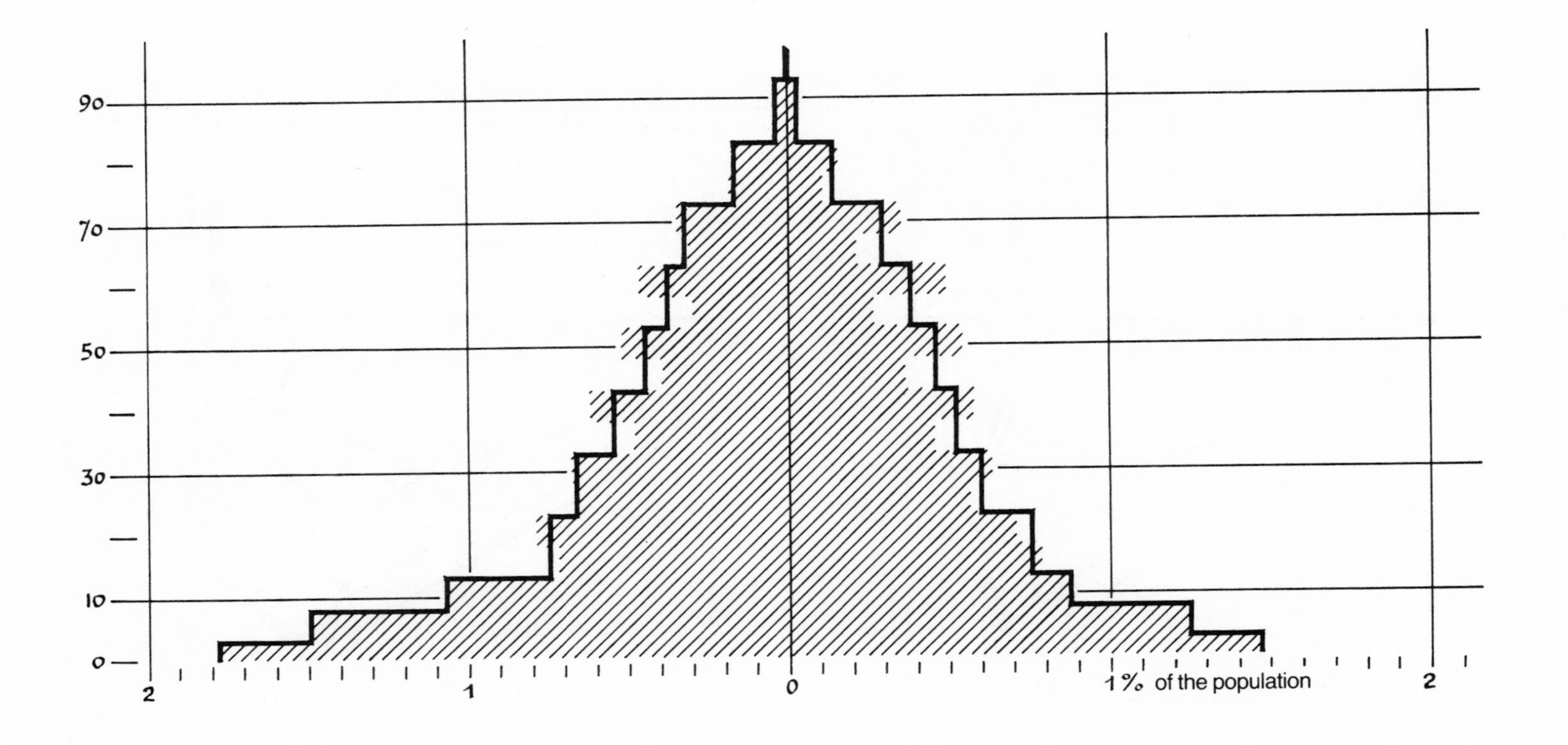
90
70
50
30
10
0
2
1
0
1 % of the population
2

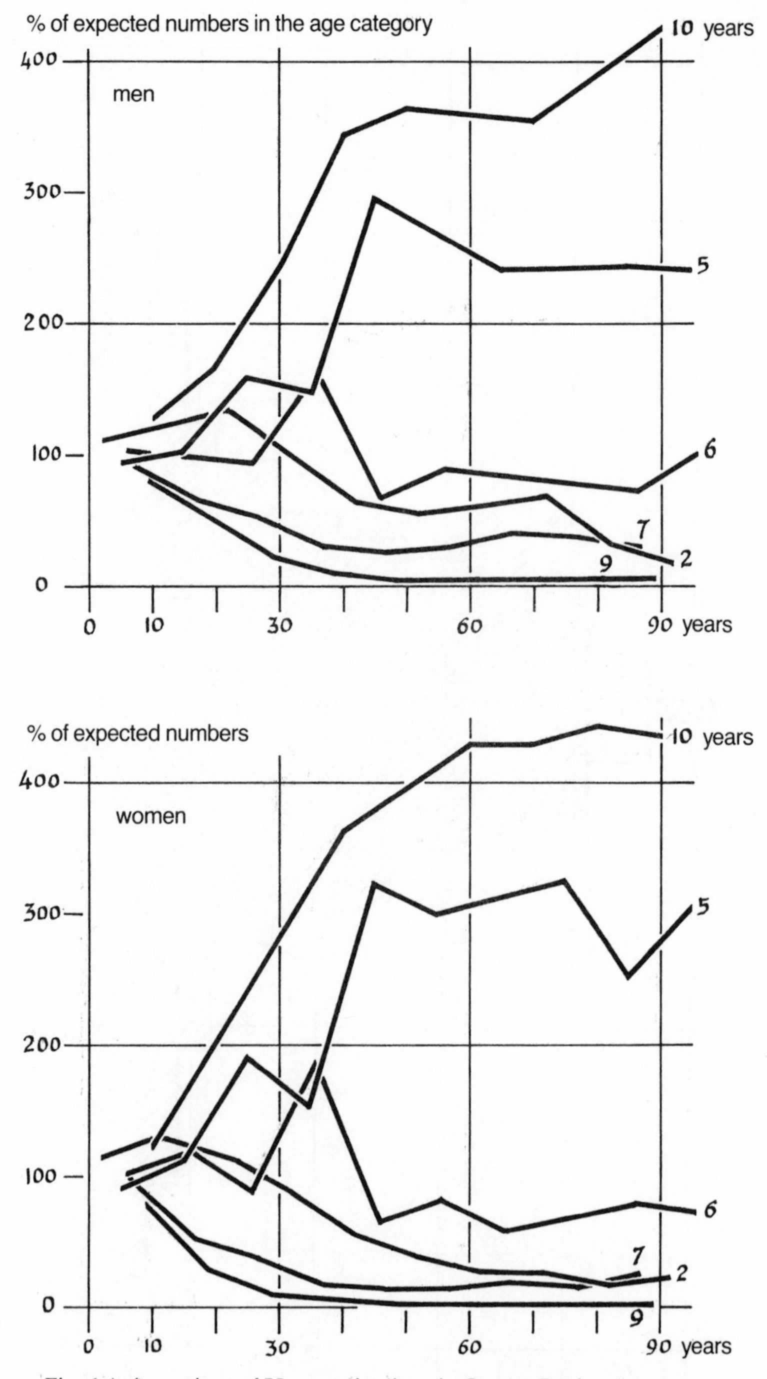

Fig. 6.4. Attractive and Unattractive Ages in Catasto Declarations, 1427–30

we have represented only 2, 6, 7, and 9; they closely resemble in their powers of attraction the unrepresented numbers 8, 4, 3, and 1 respectively.

It is striking to note the immediate, rapid decline, beginning in infancy, of odd ages, which dip far below the 1.00 line indicative of accurate reporting. By age 20, those declaring odd ages have shrunk to scarcely one-half the expected size. The categories ending in 1 and 9 lose their constituents most quickly and drastically; they are almost vacant after age 30. The curve for female odd ages, while tracing a course similar to the male, sinks to even lower levels.

What ages profit from this depletion of the odd-numbered years? The curves for ages ending in 2 or 8, 6 or 4, show that these years are the beneficiaries during childhood and adolescence. However, after age 30, rounding off toward even numbers slackens in turn, and then virtually ceases, to the advantage of ages terminating in 5 or 0. This phenomenon grows prodigiously stronger up to age 40; men claiming that year are three and one half times, and women four times, more numerous than the expected size. Thereafter, rounding at years ending in zero levels off, and even registers a slight decline for the male half of the population, only to be once more accentuated in extreme old age. For both males and females, age heaping then attains fantastic proportions—four to four and one-half times greater than the expected numbers. There exists, in sum, a systematic hierarchy of preferred numbers, which initially reduces the odd ages (and among these, primarily 1 and 9), then the even ages (4 and 6 more radically than 2 and 8 up to age 30, when, curiously, the situation is reversed), and then ages ending in 5; at the upper levels of the age pyramid, multiples of 10 hold the ultimate advantage.[36] The rounding of reported years is thus directly correlated with age, but its forms and preferences vary with the stages of life. It may also have been correlated with marital status, although it is difficult to distinguish these effects from those associated with age.

This schedule of preferred numbers, which unconsciously guided Tuscans in declaring ages, warps other counts contained in the Catasto. One such is the number of years separating married couples. These are a function not exclusively of the desired ages of husband and wife. The curve of Figure 6.5 shows that husbands estimated the number of years separating them from their spouses according to a comparable schedule of preferred numbers (10, 5, 15); this, in turn, must have affected the ages they attributed

36. This hierarchy is confirmed also over time. Improvement in precision in the city of Prato from 1371 to 1427 reduces 10 above all and then 5 (among men), while the other even numbers become considerably more common and the odd numbers slightly so. Between 1427 and 1470 even numbers increase among men, odd numbers among women.

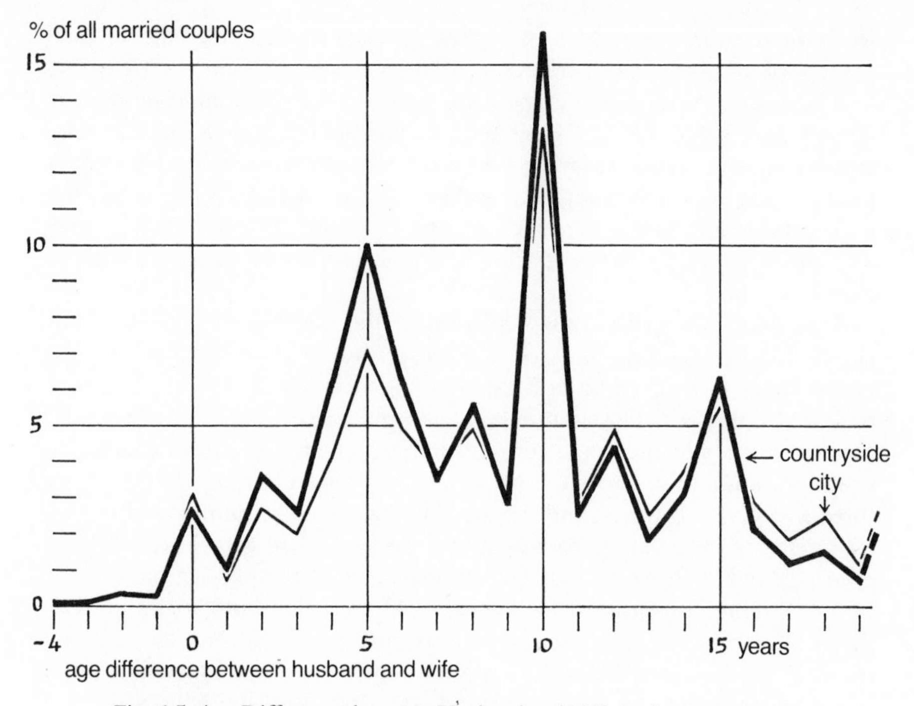

Fig. 6.5. Age Differences between Husband and Wife in the Catasto, 1427

to their wives.[37] This phenomenon is less pronounced in towns than in rural areas.

Particular ages in the declarations seem peculiarly inflated, and it would be interesting to know whether cultural traditions unique to Tuscany affected their selection. Age 36—a multiple of 6—attracts a particularly high number of men and even more women. Because of its proximity to 35, it weakens the expected attraction of the latter number, and disrupts the steady growth in popularity of ages ending in 5. Among even numbers, those ending in 6 seem systematically preferred by adults to those ending in 4; nevertheless, 84, another multiple of 6, has great magnetism. This phenomenon of rounding off to multiples of 6 seems to occur in other European communities: for example, in fifteenth-century Rheims, in the Franche-Comte, and in Burgundy. However, unlike

37. On marriage ages, see below, chap. 7.

these other communities, Tuscany in 1427 shows no particular affinity for ages 17 or 77.[38]

A deeper understanding of this phenomenon would require an explication of the symbolic meaning of the favored—and resisted—numbers. Then too, we should note that the number 36 appears in many set phrases in the Italian language. When queried about their ages, household heads may have spontaneously resorted to remembered phrases and expressed their ages by this familiar number. Only the wealthiest household heads (those possessing more than 3,200 florins in gross assets and best served by written reminders) managed to escape the attraction of age 36. The phenomenon of age heaping thus possesses an important cultural dimension. Clearly, many males in the community imparted a symbolic value to particular numbers; women doubtlessly did so too, but women were also more prone than men to express their ages in flat multiples of 10. (And most feminine ages in the Catasto came from masculine sources.) The phenomenon of rounding was further dependent upon the conventions of oral culture, which were much the more powerful where the use of writing was limited.

WEALTH AND RESIDENCE

There is another way of measuring the extent of age heaping, and to assess the strength of the practice across different regions and social classes.[39] In most known censuses, the odd-numbered ages, 1, 3, 7, and 9, are the least attractive. The Catasto is no exception to this general rule, as we have seen. Under conditions of perfect reporting, individuals claiming these ages ought to constitute 40 percent of the population. We can add up the number of Tuscans in these unpreferred categories and calculate how closely this sum approaches 40 percent of those declaring ages. The proportion between the true and expected numbers constitutes an index, which effectively measures the accuracy of age reporting across the aggregate population.

For the Tuscan population as a whole, the proportion is only about 47 percent—a score which would be typical today of underdeveloped communities.[40] But different sectors of the community register widely divergent scores. Men are more accurate in reporting their ages than are women (their respective scores are 52.6 and 43.2 percent). Town dwellers know their ages better than the residents of the countryside (54.4 and 44.1 percent respectively). The citizens of the capital are better informed than

38. On the rounding of ages in other European areas and the the preference for certain ages such as 17 or 77, see the studies cited in Herlihy and Klapisch-Zuber, 1978, p. 367, n. 37.

39. This method was developed especially by Smith, 1960, pp. 151–61.

40. Ibid. p. 155. The Egyptian population in 1947 shows a score of 47.5.

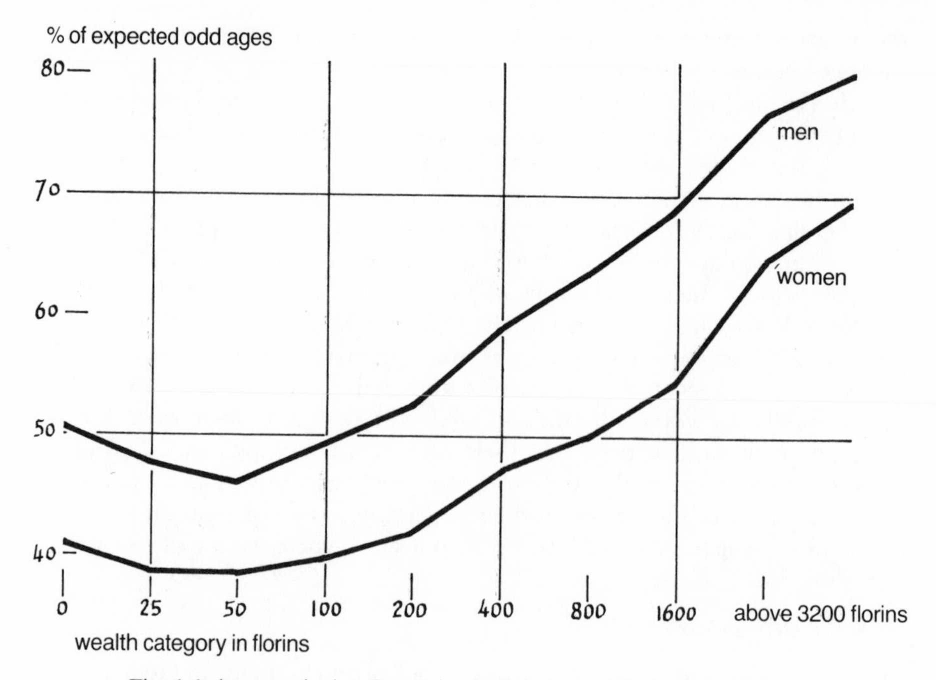

Fig. 6.6. Accuracy in Age Reporting in Relation to Wealth, Tuscany, 1427

those of secondary towns (62 and 52.4 percent Finally, the rich do better than the poor. Within families possessing more than 3,200 florins of capital, the index rises to 80.1 percent; in contrast, the urban destitute score hardly better than the peasants. The influence of wealth is more pronounced among women than among men. The curves in Figure 6.6 illustrate the differential scores separating the sexes, laid out along a scale of wealth. Feminine scores consistently trail those for males by fairly stable values; only among the wealthiest Florentines does the gap narrow.

Map 6.1 shows the spatial variations in accuracy, measured by this same index, across the rural population. There emerges a clear contrast between the west and northwest third of Florentine Tuscany and the eastern half, together with the Maremma of Volterra. The boundary between zones with high scores (and hence with better reporting) and those with low scores runs from the northeast to the southwest, across the two rural quarters of the Florentine contado, San Giovanni and Santa Croce. The zones of lowest scores are found along the territorial borders or those of

Map 6.1. Precision in Reporting Ages, Tuscany, 1427–30

major administrative units: in the lands facing Siena; in the mountains of Arezzo; and in the frontier regions between the counties of Florence and Arezzo.

The contrast between these two divisions of the Florentine territory doubtlessly reflects differing census traditions. The Florentine Estimo, recently extended to the Pisan countryside, had already habituated many Tuscans to the declaration of plausible ages. These prior surveys further provided the Florentine clerks with a means of verifying the data they collected. Map 6.1 throws into high relief the region of Volterra and the eastern part of the district, that is, the zones which were not deeply touched by the traditional Florentine methods of fiscal enumeration. It is here that accuracy is poorest.

But the rounding of years is also related to the average age of the population. The index we use to study the regional variations is based on the frequency of odd ages ending in other than 5, and these are vacated as the population grows older.[41] The accuracy of ages therefore strongly correlates with the proportion of youths in the population. On the other hand, as with other demographic phenomena, the precision of age reporting is less dependent on wealth in rural areas than in the towns.

The habit of rounding ages thus shows a strong, positive correlation with years of life, and negative correlations with wealth and residence. Sex also exerts a strong infuence.[42] Finally, the length of time regions had been exposed to the fiscal methods of the Florentine commune profoundly affected the spatial distribution of this phenomenon across the Tuscan countryside.

Tuscans as they aged soon lost firm control over the measurement of their own passing years. The pace with which they marched toward death was repeatedly thrown off cadence, through abrupt halts and forward lurches. Nevertheless, the stratification of generations, which emerges out of the Catasto, is not completely arbitrary. The rapid diminution of age categories ending in 0, after age 40 for men and age 50 for women (see again Figure 6.3), is smooth and consistent. Even illiterate peasants sensed a graded relation among these years of life. The claim to be 70, 80, or 90 years meant something more than "very old." Most were accustomed to bring the estimates of their own ages into line with those they declared for other members of their households. For fiscal and political reasons, men learned the value of accuracy sooner than did women, but women too profited from their apprenticeship. They used the ages of close male relatives as guidelines for their own. Most Tuscans in 1427–30 could give only a rough approximation of the duration of their lives; but the figures they supplied the Catasto officials were not random or gratuitous.

III. The Age Pyramid

The powerful effects of rounding preclude a direct, year-by-year analysis of the Tuscan age pyramid in 1427.[43] Is it possible to correct even partially the defects in the reported data? In order to smooth the distribution we did not, as is usually done, divide the pyramid into intervals introduced by multiples of five or ten (0–4, 5–9, 10–14, . . . , or

41. It is probable that an index based on rounding at 2, 4, 6, 8 would be more tightly tied to the proportion of adults in the population.

42. Sex is so much the more influential, as the husband usually declared his wife's age. The woman did not speak for herself until an advanced age, when she was widowed and had long since lost count of her years.

43. For the raw numbers entering into the age pyramids for Florence and for Tuscany, see Herlihy and Klapisch-Zuber, 1978, Appendix V, Tables 1 and 2, pp. 656–64.

0–9, 10–19, 20–29 . . .). Rather, we centered the intervals on the most populous years, those ending in 5 or 0. This strategy, to be sure, was not noticeably more successful than the usual method in overcoming the depressing effects of totally empty years, or in smoothing rates of attrition. However, it has the merit of forming the age categories around the popular years that were responsible for depopulating their neighbors. And the resulting cohorts, it could be argued, better correspond with natural associations in Tuscan society, with the many, for example, who thought of themselves as vaguely "age 40," or "age 45."

Classification by these five-year groups smooths out the rough edges of the pyramid. This operation makes the pyramid easier to read, and we can smooth it still further by taking a running average over several five-year intervals. Still, even these procedures are not powerful enough to offset heaping at years ending in 0 after age 30. To read the pyramid as a whole for adults and the elderly, we must have recourse to ten-year groups, or take further running averages over several five-year intervals. Unfortunately, these smoothing procedures obliterate real as well as artificial contrasts in the age distributions. In particular, they wipe out the special characteristics of cohorts born before 1400, which suffered through the devastating epidemic of that year. Heaping at the upper age levels thus obstructs refined analysis. But even our defective pyramid can illuminate the recent past of the Tuscan population.

DISTRIBUTIONS BY SEX AND AGE

The most striking characteristic of the Tuscan age pyramid in 1427 is the dearth of adolescents and adults. Young adults appear crushed between a plethora of old people and a swarm of little children. A breakdown into age groups highlights the exceptional importance of the elderly (see Table 6.5). Of older Tuscans, 14.6 percent claimed to be age 60 or over; and 9.5, age 65 or above. These proportions resemble those found in a modern population, with low birth and death rates. For example, at the beginning of the nineteenth century, France could count no more than 7 percent of its people as elderly persons age 60 or older; the proportion climbed to 9.9 percent toward the middle of the century, and attained 12.6 percent only in 1911. Today it approaches 16 percent. In developing countries, like the lands of the Maghreb, old people make up only about 7 to 11 percent of the population.[44] These comparisons make the number of old people found in

44. Reinhard, Armengaud, and Dupâquier, 1968, especially pp. 329, 654. At Venice in 1600, persons over 60 years of age form 10.7 percent of the total population; at Sorrento in 1561, 7.5 percent, and those more than 64, 4 percent (ibid. p. 116). In the United States in 1880, then in full demographic growth, the proportion of aged 65 and over was only 3.4 percent and, in 1966, still only 9.4 percent. See Petersen, 1969, p. 68.

Table 6.5. Division by Age Groups: Total Population, 1427

Age Groups	*Men*		*Women*		*Unknown*	*Total*		*Sex Ratio*
	No.	*Prct.*	*No.*	*Prct.*	*Sex*	*No.*	*Prct.*	
Youths (0–19 Yrs)	60,951	44.8	53,405	43.2	38	114,394	44.2	114.6
Adults (20–59 Yrs)	55,302	40.7	51,863	42.0	1	107,166	41.3	106.6
Aged (Over 59 Yrs)	19,754	14.5	18,209	14.8	1	37,964	14.6	108.3
Chldrn (0–14 Yrs)	52,090	38.3	43,644	35.3	38	95,772	36.9	119.4
Active (15–64 Yrs)	70,733	52.0	68,300	55.3	1	139,034	53.6	103.8
Old (Over 64 Yrs)	13,184	9.7	11,533	9.4	1	24,718	9.5	114.1
Totals:	136,007	100.0	123,477	100.0	40	259,524	100.0	110.3

SOURCE: Catasto of 1427–1430. Only population with stated ages is included.

Tuscany at the beginning of the fifteenth century seem extraordinary. But Tuscany in this regard does not appear to have been unique in Italy. At Verona in 1425, a partial survey covering more than one-half the population shows nearly identical proportions of the aged (15.2 percent 60 and over, 8.8 percent 65 and over).[45] To be sure, naive estimates of age and fiscal fraud (in Tuscany at least) certainly added some additional numbers into the ranks of the elderly. But ignorance and deception cannot alone explain the inflation of the age pyramid in its upper levels. The Tuscan population at the beginning of the fifteenth century was "old," in the demographic sense.

The young were also numerous—indeed, very numerous—in Tuscany of 1427, though their number does not appear as exceptional as that of the aged. The proportion of those from birth to 19 years, 44 percent, resembles that found in Napoleonic France. In contrast, a town in full demographic growth, like Pozzuoli in 1489, shows an even larger proportion of youths under age 20—55.2 percent; at Pozzuoli, only 5 percent were old people over age 59, and 2.5 percent were over age 64.[46] Children under age 15 are also generously represented in quattrocento Tuscany. Among comparable communities, only Pozzuoli in 1489 supported a larger proportion of children.[47] In Verona, in 1425, the proportion of children (28.6 percent) and that of youths (36.7 percent) are much smaller than those of Tuscany.[48] The community described in the Catasto thus unexpectedly combines large numbers of elderly persons with swarms of children. The Tuscan population of 1427 resists simple description as whether "aging," or "young." It resembles neither traditional European populations marked by high fertility and mortality (and few aged members) nor even ancient or contemporary aging populations, with low birth rates and few children.[49] It is *sui generis*.

The Tuscan age pyramid, and, less sharply, the total pattern of relationships among the age groups, show in their irregularities the blows sustained by the population in its recent past. To judge those blows, we shall look at partial sets of data strung out over a century. Here Prato, in its

45. Herlihy, 1973b, p. 101.

46. For the figures cited, see Reinhard *et al.*, 1968, pp. 105, 111, 165, 223. In Napoleonic France, this proportion is also 44 percent (ibid., p. 329); in contemporary Sweden, 42.9 percent (ibid., pp. 213, 258).

47. Ibid., pp. 105, 111, 221, 228. The proportion at Pozzuoli is precisely 43 percent. Compare Bohemia in 1754 (32.6 percent); lower Austria in the eighteenth century (30 percent); Sorrento in 1561 (31.8 percent). In the United States in 1880, the proportion was 38.1 percent (Petersen, 1969, p. 77, Table 42).

48. Herlihy, 1973b, p. 101.

49. In particular, the proportion of young children less than 5 years (17.4 percent) gives the impression of a high natality in Tuscany of 1427. At Verona in 1425, this age group contains only 11 percent of the total (Herlihy, 1973b, p. 101); at Pozzuoli in 1489, 4.4 percent (Reinhard *et al.*, 1968, p. 105).

town and countryside, offers much illumination. Its Estimo of 1371, and the later Catasti of 1427 and 1470 capture at least partially the general movement of the population between the late fourteenth and late fifteenth centuries.[50] We shall also compare different age distributions for the fifteenth century in those parts of Tuscany which our soundings in the later Catasti illuminate.

The most notable conclusions to be drawn from Table 6.6, would seem to be the following:

1. The proportion of old people reached its maximum everywhere in Tuscany in 1427. It then slightly declined over the course of the fifteenth century. But at Prato in 1470 it still had not attained its level of one hundred years before. The aging of the population thus occurred largely before 1427. Florence itself seems to have been consistently less affected by this phenomenon of aging than its own countryside or the town of Prato. At all times, Florence contained lower proportions of the elderly and higher proportions of the young than other Tuscan communities.

2. The proportion of the young (age 0 to 19) had almost everywhere dipped to its lowest point by 1427. But at Prato, by 1470, it had climbed to higher levels than it had held in 1371. The proportion of children (age 0 to 15) looks high in 1427. But to judge from Table 6.6, it was then lower at Prato than it had been at the end of the fourteenth century. At both Prato and Florence, it was also lower in 1427 than it would be later in the century. (In the Florentine contado the underregistration of young children is obvious in 1470.) The increasing proportion of youths in 1470 is chiefly attributable to growing numbers of adolescents. Perhaps this indicates the better survival of young children between the plagues of 1449 and 1456.[51]

3. The proportion of adults (age 20 to 59) reached its lowest point at Prato in 1470, but the decline was largely anterior to 1427. The "active" population (age 15 to 64) did not change between 1427 and 1470. At Florence this group diminished slightly between 1427 and 1458, but had grown again by 1480. The contado, on the other hand, between 1427 and 1470 achieved an appreciable gain in the adult and working population.

In sum, in 1427 the Tuscan population on the whole claimed its highest proportion of the very old, even as its numbers of young adults fell to minimum levels. At the end of the fourteenth and beginning of the fifteenth century, the shifting relationships among the age categories indicate

50. Fiumi, 1968, does not analyze the age composition of the population. In interpreting the figures given here, it should be remembered that the Estimo of 1371–72 does not give adult ages for one of the eight quarters of the city and for some 30 villages.

51. On the plagues of the fifteenth century, see above, chap. 3.

Table 6.6. Changes in Age Distributions in Tuscany, Fourteenth and Fifteenth Centuries

(Percentages of population surveyed at the respective dates)

Age Category	*Prato*			*Contado of Prato*			*Florence*			*Contado*	
	1371a	1427	1470b	1371c	1427	1470b	1427	1458b	1480b	1427	1470
0–14 (Chldrn)	39.7	36.1	38.7	49.4	37.3	37.6	38.7	41.1	38.6	37.5	35.9
15–64 (Active)	56.5	54.3	54.2	46.9	55.0	56.7	54.5	53.2	56.6	52.5	57.5
Over 65 (Old)	3.8	9.5	7.1	3.3	9.7	5.3	6.8	5.7	4.8	10.0	6.7
0–19 (Youths)	45.3	42.5	48.5	54.7	43.9	49.8	46.0	49.4	49.2	44.7	45.9
20–59 (Adults)	46.2	42.3	41.7	38.6	40.9	40.2	42.3	41.4	43.4	40.3	43.8
Over 60 (Old)	8.5	15.2	9.8	6.2	15.2	9.7	11.7	9.2	7.4	15.0	10.3
Numbers surveyed	5729	3488	367	1890	5189	580	36131	3319	3824	125039	10675

a. Seven of eight quarters.
b. Based on 10 percent sample of households.
c. Thirteen villages with ages given.

that the Tuscan population was unstable; reeling under powerful blows, it was groping for a new equilibrium. Age pyramids from two towns, Prato and Florence, and from their countrysides, offer indirect but moving testimony of the terrible experiences through which these communities had passed.

The pyramid for the city of Prato in 1371 is large and regular at its higher levels. Two features strike the eye: the cohort aged between 23 and 47 years (consequently, those born between 1327 and 1347) shows a slight contraction at its base. This may mark the beginnings of demographic retrenchment, perhaps due to a diminution in births in the years immediately preceding the Black Death. Evidence from hearth lists suggests that the great plagues dramatically worsened, but did not initiate, the demographic collapse of the fourteenth century.[52] Then too, J. C. Russell has tried to demonstrate that the Black Death in England took particularly heavy tolls among elderly men aged 50 or over.[53] Did a comparable experience shape the pyramid at Prato? In 1372, men over 63, who were therefore over 40 at the time of the plague, do seem strangely absent.

The pyramid of 1371 of course shows deepest imprints from the "second plague" of 1363–64. The English called this the "children's plague".[54] In France too, according to the chronicler Jean de Venette and the physician Guy de Chauliac, the epidemic of 1360–61 especially attacked children and men more than women.[55] In central Italy, several chroniclers observed that high mortalities among children distinguished the second plague from its predecessor of 1348.[56] The pyramid for Prato confirms this huge loss of children. This epidemic may well have been a complex mix of diseases—typhus, measles, and influenza as well as bubonic and pulmonary plague.[57] At all events, in 1363, children between 5 and 15 years of age were among its favored victims. Seven or eight years later, the adolescent and young-adult population, reduced to hardly two-thirds its expected size, bears witness to this carnage of the young.

The pyramid of 1371 also shows in its upper levels a marked inequality between the sexes. After adolescence, women hold the advantage. In all cohorts born before 1358, the sex ratio runs between 80 and 100.[58] This feminine preponderance among the aged is the more remarkable as the

52. Fiumi, 1968, p. 104.

53. Russell, 1948, pp. 216 ff. See the discussion of these results in Shrewsbury, 1970, pp. 51–53.

54. Shrewsbury, 1970, pp. 127–30.

55. Guy de Chauliac, 1546, f. 22 Jean de Venette, 1843–44, 2:325–26.

56. See the *Cronaca senese* of Donato di Neri and his son, in *Cronache senesi*, 1934, p. 605. See also the "Discorso historico" of Orvieto, cited by Carpentier, 1962, pp. 208–09.

57. On the nature of this plague, see the remarks of Shrewsbury, 1970, pp. 128–33.

58. The exact figures are 82 for the general ratio and 102 between 0–3 years.

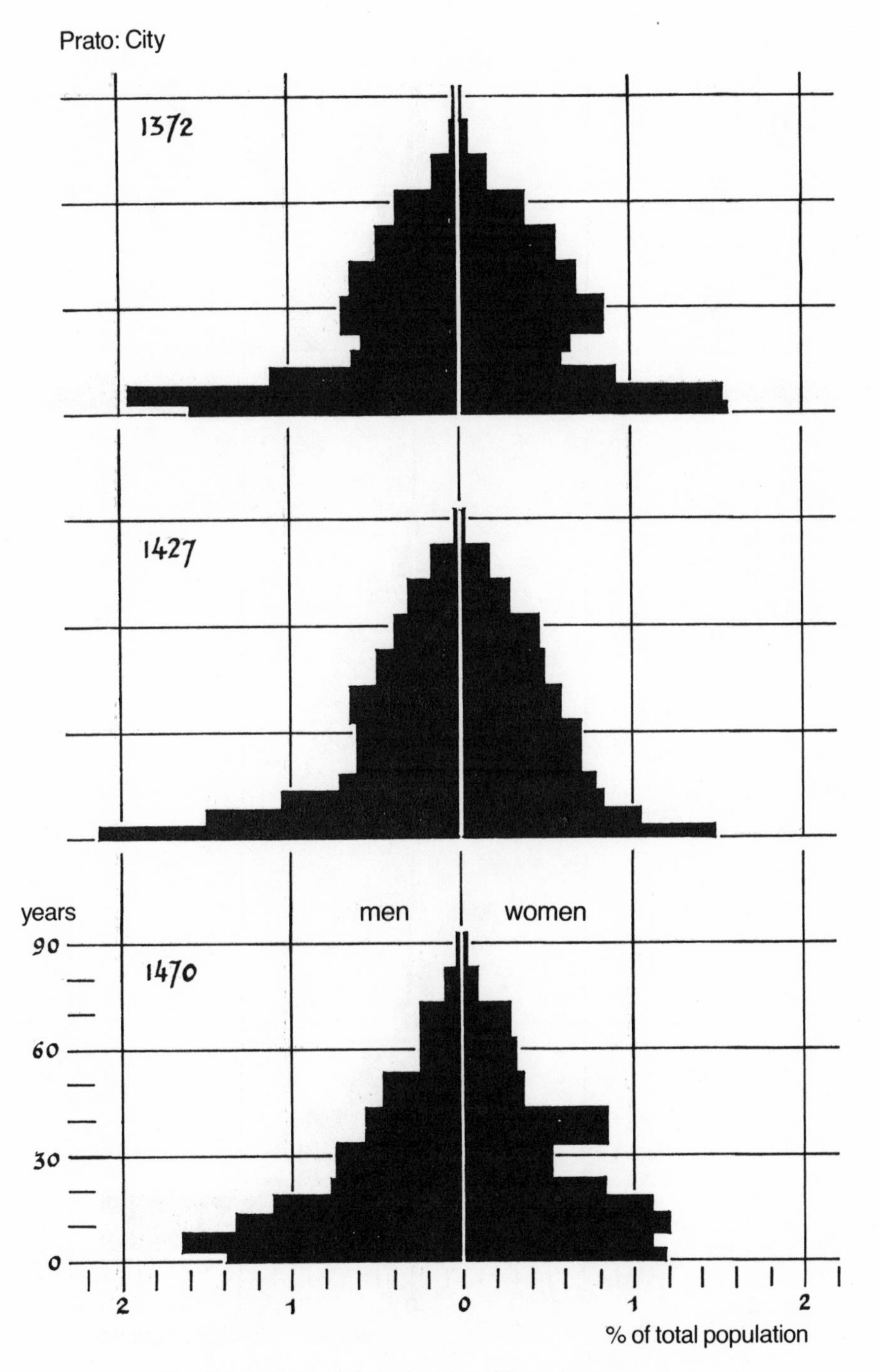

Fig. 6.7. Age Pyramids in the City of Prato (1372, 1427, 1470)

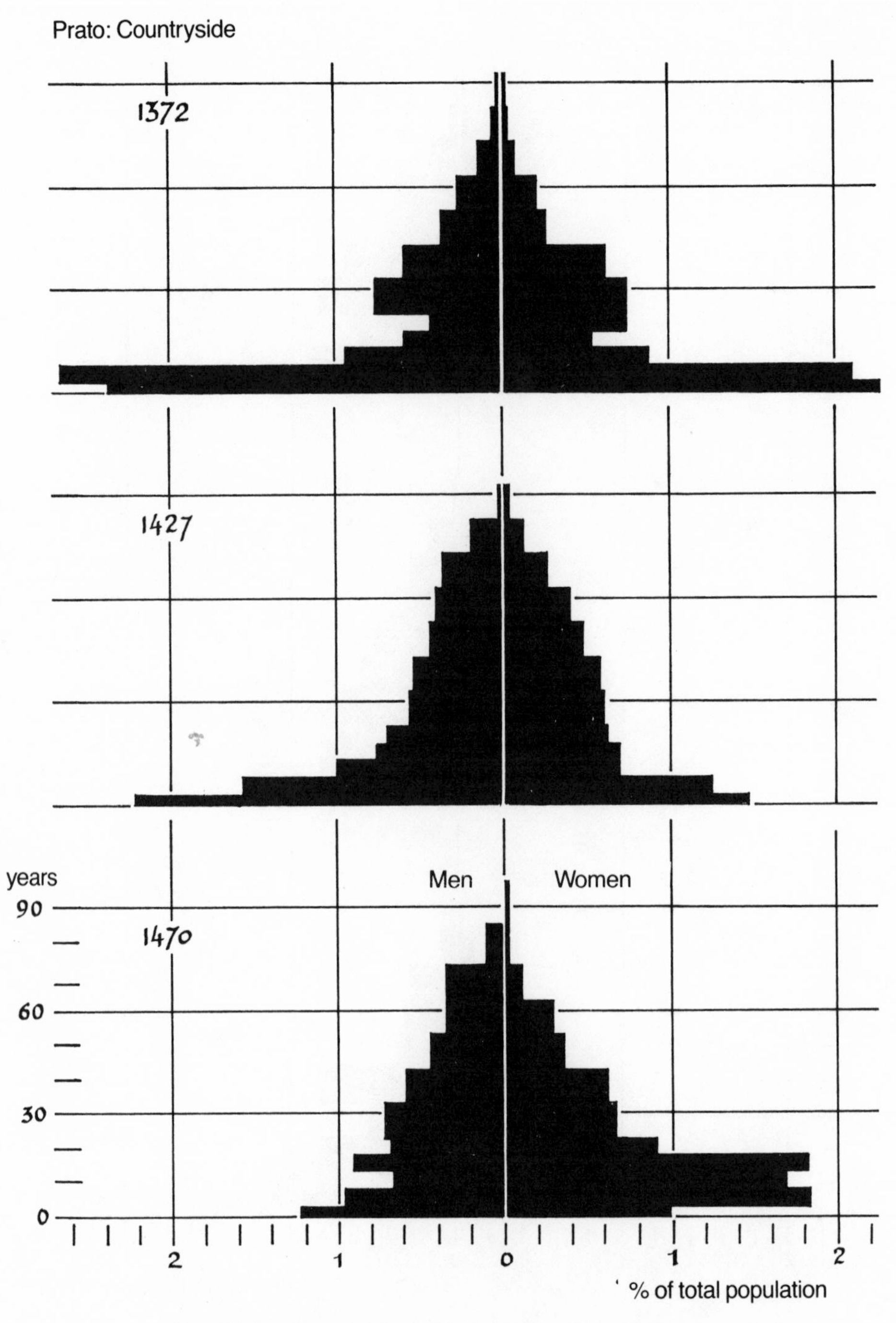

Fig. 6.8. Age Pyramids in the Countryside of Prato (1372, 1427, 1470)

ratio among children incontestably favors males. Indeed, it closely corresponds with the ratio among children registered in the Catasto of 1427.[59] And a high sex ratio among children seems to have been, as we previously argued, generally characteristic of the Tuscan population in the fifteenth century. At Prato, did more males than females fall victim to the plagues? We cannot give a definite answer. Depopulation within the towns may have induced much immigration from the countryside, and towns were attractive to older women.[60] The pyramid for 1371 reflects the age-specific impact of the plague seven years earlier: children, more than adults, were its prime victims. Its impact on the sexes must for the present remain an unresolved question.

In displaying large numbers of children younger than 8, the pyramid of 1371 illustrates the extraordinary recuperative powers of a population, the adult members of which had been relatively spared by the children's plague. The number of young children, conceived and born during the seven years preceding the census, stretches the base of the pyramid to incredible dimensions, particularly in Prato's countryside. This spurt in births explains why the population in 1371 shows so large a cohort of young children, bigger even than in 1427. This marked distortion of the age pyramid had powerful, long-term social consequences. Succeeding epidemics (1374, 1383, and 1400) seem to have been comparably costly for the very young. Numerous chroniclers affirm that *giovani e fanciulli,* were their special victims.[61] The operative principle seems to have been that those who lived through one epidemic had an improved chance of surviving the next. In decimating children and the young approximately every decade, the plagues obstructed the recovery of the population and modified the structure of ages for far into into the future. In the late 1300s and early 1400s, surviving children were not numerous enough to sustain the ranks of the young adults; the younger age categories could not therefore counterbalance the mass of old people, survivors of earlier, more populous cohorts. The population aged. The results of these processes are very visible in 1427.

By 1427 the pyramid for Prato has taken on a very different shape. Almost vertical in the middle, it is marked by a paucity of adults and adolescents, while children and old people predominate. No doubt the structure preserves the traces of recent events, particularly the plague of 1400, which helps explain the narrowness of the cohort born before that

59. On the sex ratio in 1427, see chap. 5 above. The ratio was 125 in 1371, for those 3–7 years and 118 for those 8–12 years.

60. Women, for example, age 43 to 52 years, were in short supply in the countryside of Prato; but they were more numerous than men in the city.

61. See ser Lapo Mazzei, 1880, 2:348; *Cronache senesi*, 1934, p. 654, cited above, n. 56; Naddo, 1784, p. 66; *Cronica urbevetana*, 1920 p. 208.

year (aged 27 and older in 1427). But the steep slopes of the pyramid for all cohorts born between 1395 and 1410 may attest still more to a deficit in the balance between births and deaths. That deficit seems not to have been corrected until the period 1413 to 1423, which contemporaries described as a time of peace and plenty.[62] The plague of 1422–24 put an end to this brief and happy interlude. But in turn it stimulated a spurt in births, of which the large number of children registered in the Catasto, aged two to four, give testimony.

Finally, in 1470, the population of Prato is distributed in a pyramid with roughly concave sides, an indication of a high birth rate. The survey shows obvious shortcomings in the registration of babies, little girls, and young men. Still, the general shape remains very different from those displayed in either 1371 or 1427. Population growth has filled in the terrible cavities dug out by the epidemics of the fourteenth century.[63] And the birth rate has been rising long enough to restock the ranks of adults.

Age pyramids from the Florentine countryside, dated 1427 and 1470, show comparable patterns. In the latter survey, underregistration has clearly removed many young children, and the feminization of boys, for fiscal motives, distorts the sex ratio.[64] But the spurious, hunchbacked pyramid of 1470 still shows a population which in its upper portions at least was regaining demographic equilibrium. In contrast, the pyramid of 1427 had been characterized, like Prato's, by a large base of children, a meager representation of young adults, and inflated numbers of the aged.

Florence itself retains certain idiosyncratic traits throughout the fifteenth century: asymmetry between the male and female halves, especially among adults; and a striking predominance of males in all three years, 1427, 1458, and 1480. The upper part of the pyramid takes on a more gentle slope over the course of the fifteenth century, and the sides thicken toward the base. Here again, the impression emerges of a population gaining in vigor across the last third of the century.

In the light of these partial examples, let us take another look at the pyramid for the total population of Tuscany in 1427 (Figure 6.3). We assume that the Black Death of 1348 did not take an extravagant toll of children—if only for the reason that there were probably fewer children in the population. Its effects were at all events too distant in 1427 to be visible in the pyramid. The second epidemic of 1363–64 seems to have established the patterns of decline, still visible in 1427.

The pyramid of 1427 seems particularly depleted for the age cohorts

62. Rucellai, 1960, p. 46.

63. It is necessary here to adjust upward the number of women between 23 and 33 years, who are depleted by the extravagant rounding at age 40.

64. Conti, 1966, p. 102, cites a contemporary law denouncing this fraud.

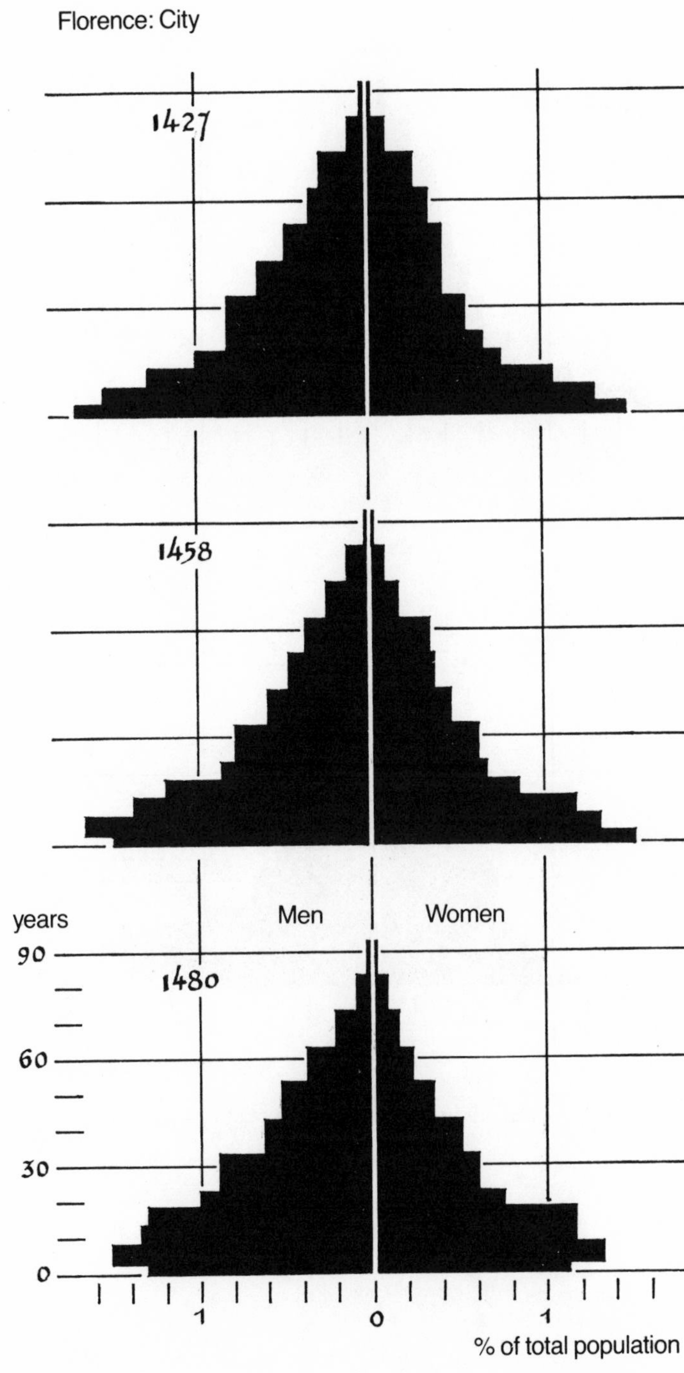

Fig. 6.9. Age Pyramids in the City of Florence (1427, 1458, 1480)

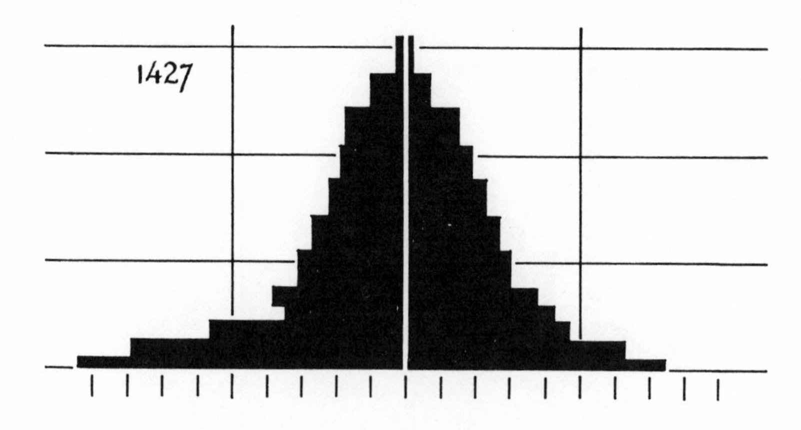

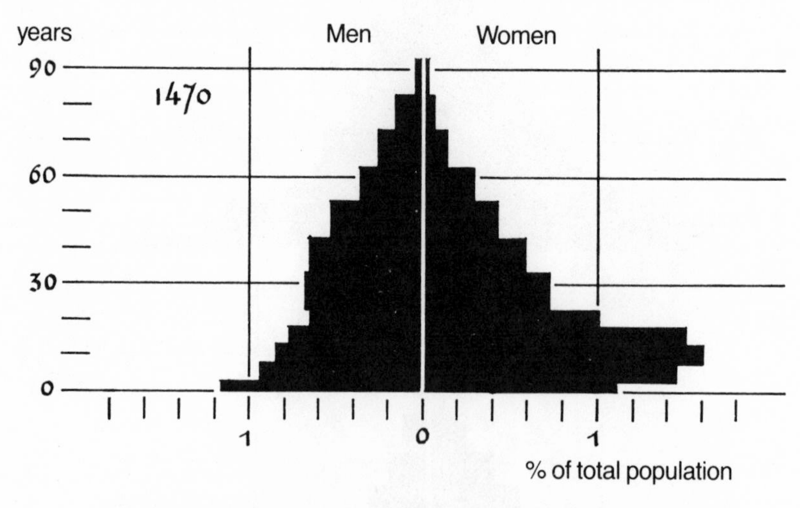

Fig. 6.10. Age Pyramids in the Florentine Contado (1427, 1470)

between 15 and 55 years of age. Adults older than 55 represent the survivors of those born before the second epidemic, before the rhythms of decline were fully established. In Tuscany as a whole, as in the small town of Prato, these empty cohorts and their descendants, born between 1375 and 1415, left the aged with a marked preponderance, and the pyramid would remain top-heavy for well into the fifteenth century. A population needs time to overcome the cyclic effects of big losses—especially when those losses are strongly age-specific. It cannot quickly recapture its initial equilibrium.[65] The Tuscan population needed nearly a century to overcome the frightful loss of children which it suffered between 1363 and 1400, and to reduce its burden of the aged. Not until well after 1400 was the birth rate high enough (and long enough sustained) to produce a balanced pyramid of ages. The lull in epidemics in the first decade of the fifteenth century may have been a turning point. At all events, by about 1470, the population seems close to achieving a new equilibrium.

Our age pyramids emphasize the instability of the Tuscan population described in the Catasto. At the same time, they reveal the obstacles involved in utilizing for historical purposes model life tables which are based on stable or stationary populations.[66] Their use requires a comparison of the age distribution of a given, supposedly stable or stationary population with several model tables. The model table which most closely approximates the real distributions also yields estimates concerning birth rates, death rates, and life expectancies. But the age pyramid of 1427 does not fit any of the theoretical distributions closely. To achieve an acceptable fit, we have to segment the population into homogeneous generational groups, characterized by different vital rates and different histories.[67] But this defeats the purpose of the tables—the generation of reasonable estimates of vital rates valid for the entire population. The assumption behind the model tables, that death and birth rates have remained constant over the life of the oldest members, is unrealistic when applied to a population molded by catastrophes.

SOCIAL AND REGIONAL VARIATIONS

The distribution of ages is not the same for all strata of society. For example, the mean age of the population in 1427 shifts remarkably according to level of wealth. For the entire population, it is roughly 29 years—a

65. The impact of a major disaster on age distributions remains visible in a population for about 150 years. See the analyses in Lotka, 1943; Coale, 1956; P. Lopez, 1961; and Le Bras, 1971.

66. See Coale and Demeny, 1966.

67. Samuel Kline Cohn Jr. attempted a comparison of the data and the tables and found that the younger generation under 25 looked like a growing population with increments ranging from 2 to 15 per 1,000 per year, but the generation above age 35 seemed to be shrinking at a yearly rate of −10 per 1,000.

little lower for men (28.54 years) and a little higher for women (29.33). But for both sexes it falls consistently as wealth increases (see Figure 6.10). If we look at the median age, which divides the population into two equal parts, the rich are considerably younger than the poor. In households with more than 1,600 florins in total assets, half the men are less than 17 years of age, and half the women are under 15. In poor households (under 25 florins gross assets), the median age is 25. In Florence in particular, only 50 percent of the men and women of the wealthiest families (possessing more than 3,200 florins before deductions) are over age 16 in 1427, as against 60 percent in the total population of the city and 61.4 percent in Tuscany as a whole.

A breakdown of the population by age categories allows a closer view of these differences. As Figure 6.11 illustrates, two sectors of society depart significantly from the mean. First, households with modest assets (one to 100 florins) appear with the fewest children (35 to 36 percent), but relatively large numbers of the old (more than 10 percent) and even of adults (more than 54 percent). Here, mean ages also slightly exceed those found in other categories of wealth. Totally destitute households, and those of moderate means (100 to 800 florins), flank this child-poor sector. In these two categories, the age structure approximates the mean, although the wealthiest among them are already showing a younger average age. At the upper end of the social scale households with more than 800 florins contain a decidedly younger population, and this tendency is the more marked as wealth increases. Households with 1,600 to 3,200 florins in total assets include almost as many children as adults; in this category, in its narrow upper fringe, the proportion of old people falls to exiguous size (3.5 percent). The wealthiest segment of the community resembles a population undergoing exuberant growth. These privileged classes, it will be recalled, also sustained the most flagrant imbalance between the sexes, manifested in a soaring sex ratio. This limited sector of the population thus carries the largest proportions of youths and children, and also of males. Their less-advantaged fellow citizens could justifiably regard, and dread, these families of "leading citizens" as hotbeds of insubordination and disorder. Their superabundant young males were impatient to achieve their fortunes and gain a stable niche in society.[68] The pressure they exerted against their elders is a frequent theme in the period's literature. And contemporaries seem to have sensed that the differing social classes had varying typical ages. They thus directly associated poverty and old age (and wealth and youth), and this affected many other social and religious attitudes regarding the stages of life.

68. Herlihy, 1972a, pp. 142–45.

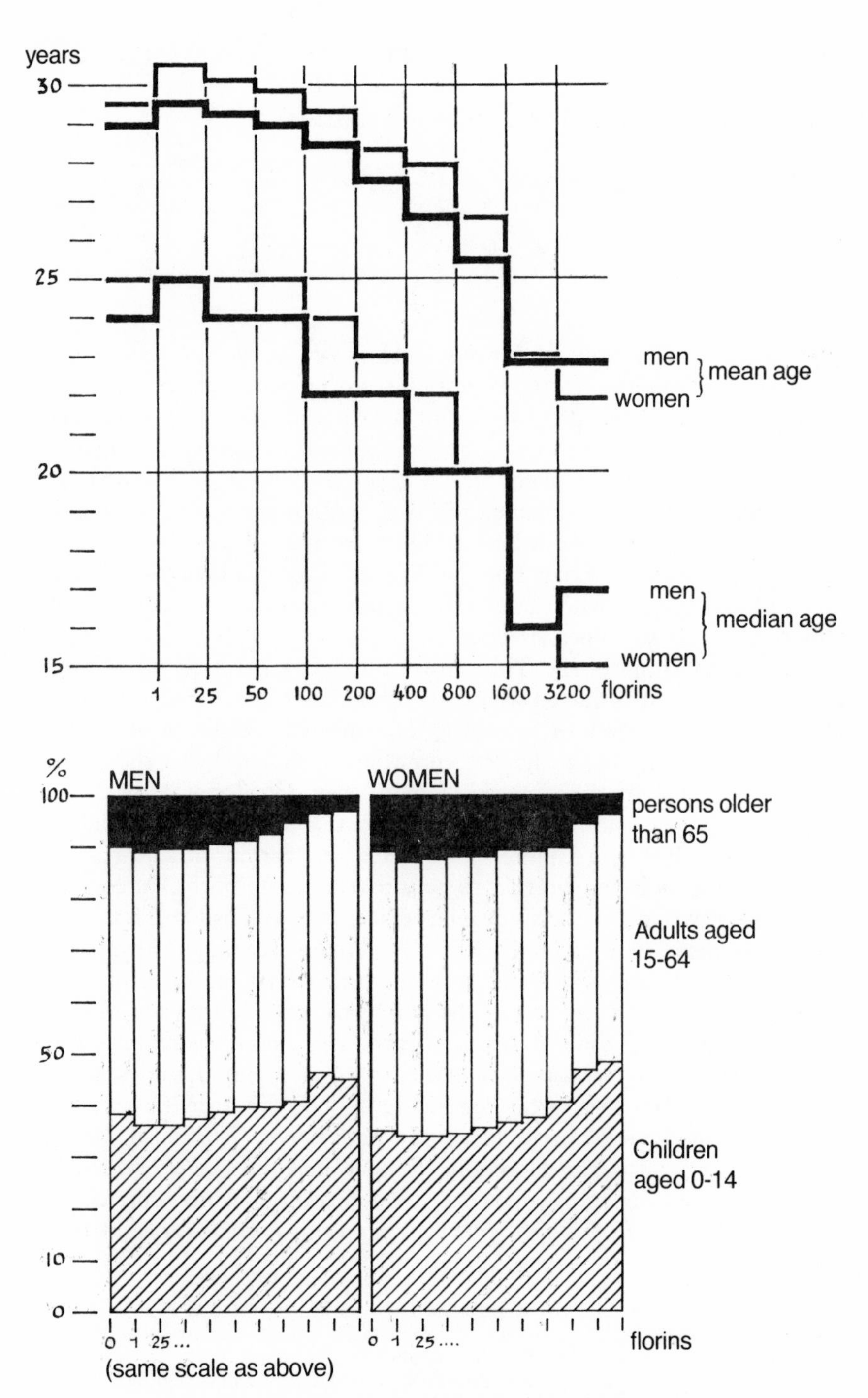

Fig. 6.11. Age according to Sex and Level of Wealth, Tuscany, 1427

Table 6.7. Division by Groups of Ages according to Habitat, 1427

		Towns				*Rural Zones*		
Age Ctgry	*Florence*	*Six Cities*	*Small Towns*	*All Cities*	*Flrntn Contado*	*West Dstrct*	*East Dstrct*	*All Zones*
0–14	38.7	35.5	35.4	36.8	37.7	37.3	33.7	37.0
15–64	54.5	54.1	54.4	54.4	52.3	53.0	57.2	53.1
Over 65	6.8	10.4	10.2	8.8	10.0	9.7	9.1	9.9

Do equally significant variations differentiate town and countryside? Taken as a whole, the towns, large or small, differed from the rural areas chiefly in their larger proportions of adolescents and adults, and their smaller proportions of the aged. But significant contrasts within the urban bloc set off the capital from the six cities and the smaller towns. The population of Florence contained relatively large numbers of children, and comparatively few elderly residents. Even the rural zones in the contado and district could not boast such an abundance of children. Not only the influx of young men, who came to the capital in search of employment, but also the relatively numerous children under age 15, gave the Florentine population its youthful tilt. This "man-eating" city fed itself not so much on the workers it attracted as on the children it bred. Their profusion attests to a high level of fertility.[69] The marked weight of children in Florence is mainly due to its concentration of well-to-do families. Of all residents of Tuscany who possessed more than 800 florins in wealth, 70 percent live in Florence. They made up more than a third of the population (35.3 percent), but their children constituted 41.3 percent of all urban children. Urban conditions did not, to be sure, encourage births. At comparable levels of wealth, the less advantaged in the towns had still fewer children than those in the countryside.[70] Florentine wealth, in other words, more than overcame the limits on fertility that cities normally imposed.

As for the six secondary cities, the two to the east, Arezzo and Cortona, and even the small town close to Arezzo, Castiglione Fiorentino, show particularly low proportions of children (31.6, 34.8, and 32.8 respectively).

As a whole, the rural areas register fewer children than Florence, but more than all the secondary cities and minor towns. They also show an interesting diversity. The Florentine contado and the western half of the district have similar age structures.[71] But the contrast which differentiates the eastern towns from all others crops up again in their rural surround-

69. See below, chap. 8, p. 238–39.

70. The proportion of children younger than 15 years remains fixed at Florence between 33.4 and 34.6 percent in all categories of wealth below 400 florins, except for taxpayers possessing between 51 and 100 florins, where it falls to 30.7 percent.

71. This includes the rural regions of Pisa, Pistoia, Volterra, and San Gimignano, the Val di Nievole and the Val d'Arno di Sotto, and finally the Garfagnana.

ings. The rural zones around Arezzo, Cortona, and Castiglione Fiorentino are as lacking in young people as are the towns themselves.

An examination of the population at the level of pivieri or podesterie confirms the youth of the middle regions. Maps 6.2–6.4 show the population in these rural divisions by age group. The central zones of the Florentine contado and its southwestern extensions (San Gimignano, Colle, and the Volterra) show large proportions of children.[72] Children, on the other hand, are scarce in the entire mountainous fringe to the east and northeast, in the greater part of the elevated areas in the Aretine contado, in the contado of Cortona, and the rural quarter of Santa Croce to the southeast. Only the Val di Chiana around Montesansavino, Foiano, and Montepulciano, differs by its youth from the remaining eastern district. To the west, the contrasts are even sharper: the Pisan hills and the southern slopes of the Arno valley are aging regions, while the territory of Volterra, the outskirts and the slopes of the Monte Pisano near Pisa, and even the countryside of Rosignano approach the mean.

The Florentine territory thus resembles an aging body with a youthful heart and weak extremities. Map 6.4 illuminates in particular the "senescence" of the eastern and southeastern regions; old people abound in the high zones of Santa Croce and San Giovanni. They are also numerous in the lower Arno valley, and on the periphery of the Fucecchio depression. The cartography of mean male and female ages yields a comparable pattern: the young collect in the middle region, while the old surround them like a halo.

The city of Florence, with its exceptional proportion of youths, is thus set within a countryside which manifests similar characteristics. The pattern seems consistent. The aging towns of the east, Arezzo and Cortona, dominate a similarly aging countryside, and the youthful towns of the west, Volterra and San Gimignano, look out over youthful villages.

The presence of a young population at the center of the territory merits all the more emphasis, as this geographic distribution closely follows that of the mezzadria in the Florentine contado. A comparison between Maps 6.2 and 4.4 (pp. 200 and 116) shows that the rural districts containing many sharecroppers also contained many children. This relationship cannot, to be sure, be affirmed for the peripheral zones where the mezzadria was still a rarity, but where children were legion. These would be the Val di Chiana, the Garfagnana, and the mountains of Pistoia. The diffusion of the mezzadria, in sum, did not alone assure a youthful population. But the rela-

72. At San Gimignano one can distinquish the urban from the rural populations, in which children constituted 36.5 and 46.9 percent respectively (combined, 41.5 percent); the proportion is the same at Colle (41.7 percent), where it is difficult to distinguish citizens from rural residents.

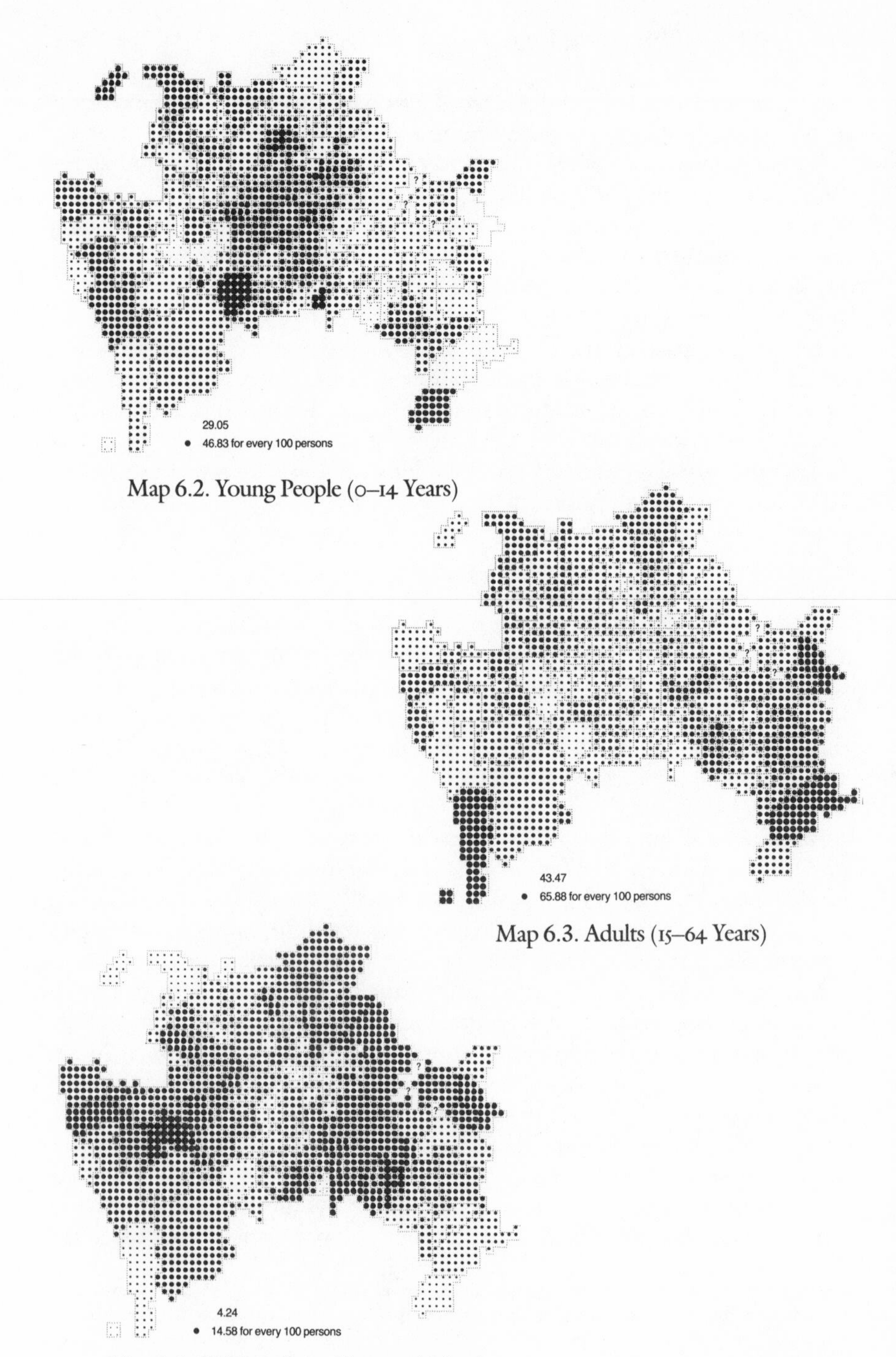

Map 6.2. Young People (0–14 Years)

Map 6.3. Adults (15–64 Years)

Map 6.4. Old People (64 Years and More)

tionship between the two deserves to be further explored, as this would surely illuminate the interactions between a particular social system and the demographic behavior of those involved in it.

We may safely regard the Tuscan population in its entirety as closed, with only insignificant exchanges with the outside world. But stability did not rule the relationships of communities within Tuscany itself. The large proportion of children and the even greater number of youths in the Florentine population of 1427 may indicate a recent rise in the urban birth rate. This increment in births was characteristic of the central and western zones of the territory, while in eastern areas the birth rate lacked buoyancy.[73] However, migratory exchanges between countryside and city were also operative here, and these the Catasto, as we have seen, does not illuminate well.[74] Florence and Pisa were certainly not closed populations; rather, they received immigrants in large numbers from the surrounding countryside, and from still farther afield. On the other hand, Pisa had recently lost many citizens through emigration for political or fiscal reasons. These movements inevitably affected the distribution of ages. In Florence, the influx of young men looking for work no doubt partly explains the high sex ratio among young adults; the ranks of urban youth grew inflated, while the relative size of adjacent age categories appears smaller. Inversely, in zones of emigration, such as the Chianti, the Casentino, the Pisan hills, or the lower Arno valley the sex ratio drops, as mainly men depart, and the proportion of old people grows as emigration principally involves the young. The distribution of ages is not exclusively a function of the demographic order prevailing in 1427 within a period of high instability. Ages also shed light on the internal movements which the community was experiencing, and on the forces which propelled them.

The Catasto illuminates no more than a brief moment in the history of a population struggling to regain stability after enormous losses. An unwieldly number of aged (the burden of the immediate past) and a large contingent of children (its hope for future recovery) kept it continuously off balance. The preponderance of males contributed further to this disequilibrium. We cannot examine directly the vital rates which produced these characteristics. But we can look at the broad patterns of demographic behavior: how Tuscans approached marriage, reared their families, and met with death in the fifteenth century.

73. Age distributions are more sensible to variations in fecundity than in mortality. See Schwarz, 1968.

74. See above, chap. 4, pp. 109–10.

7
Marriage

Se tutti gli altri uomini avessino auto la paura del tor donna come voi, sare' di già ispento el mondo.

If all other men were as afraid of marrying as you are [Filippo and Lorenzo, my sons] mankind would have long since been extinguished.

—Alessandra Strozzi, 1465

he Catasto, as a single census, does not permit a direct measurement of vital events. But it still yields data about them which, if almost always indirect, are nonetheless abundant. Other sources found in Tuscany's rich archives supplement our knowledge. We shall begin our inquiry into demographic deportment with a consideration of marriage. More than any other vital event, marriage created or transformed the Tuscan household, the Catasto's basic unit. The makers of the survey therefore gave it particular attention; so also did the numerous authors of the epoch who wrote on social matters.

I. The Tuscan Marriage Model

In a fundamental study, the English demographer J. Hajnal has identified what he calls the "West-European pattern of marriage".[1] The distinctive characteristics of this pattern are two: relatively late age at first marriage for both men (age 26 to 27 or older) and women (age 23 to 24 or older), and a high proportion of both men and women in the population who never marry at all. According to Hajnal, this pattern is unique to modern Western societies. When did it first come to govern matrimony in the West? Hajnal cites examples demonstrating that it was prevalent in European societies of the eighteenth, and occasionally of the sixteenth and seventeenth centuries. But he does not venture an opinion as to its earliest appearance. His comments regarding marital behavior in the medieval period are cautious:

1. Hajnal, 1965.

> It does not seem possible that the population of medieval Europe had the fully developed European marriage pattern; they must either have had a marriage pattern clearly identifiable as non-European, or else some mixture of the two types with a wider variation of age at first marriage than is found later.[2]

In order to illuminate the basic model of Tuscan marriages in 1427 we shall adopt the two criteria utilized by Hajnal: the age at first marriage for both men and women, and the proportion of persons in the population who did not marry at all.

AGE AT FIRST MARRIAGE

The Catasto provides several means for estimating the age at first marriage. Over a period ranging from 1 year in the city of Florence to 3 years in some areas of the contado and district, household heads were allowed to change their declarations, and, specifically, to register the addition or the loss of household members by reason of matrimony. If a girl married and departed from her household of origin, the household head, usually a father or elder brother, cancelled her name and often noted whom the girl had married and how much dowry had been paid or promised to her husband. The cancelled names of brides give us an obvious means of discerning their ages at first marriage, but some biases are present. First of all, the marriages declared are not all first marriages; widows often returned to the house of their father or brother and, if they remarried, they left their families in the same manner as a young girl at her first wedding. The number is small, but their ages tend to inflate slightly the mean age of feminine marriage. A second distorting factor concerns the accuracy of the declared ages. We have already considered the phenomenon of rounding, which affects even adolescent ages.[3] Then too, the age given to a girl cancelled for reason of marriage does not correspond to her actual age at the time of the wedding but rather to her years when the declaration was first prepared. When she left her father's house she had nearly always grown older by several months, or as much as a year, in relation to the age which the Catasto attributes to her.

More serious is the fact that the sample at hand concerns for the most part the daughters of wealthy families.[4] All taxpayers did not in fact have the same motivations for registering recently celebrated marriages. Household heads with sovrabbondante (that is, wealth remaining after all allow-

2. Ibid., p. 120.
3. See above, chap. 6, pp. 169–73.
4. Of the 41 brides living in the countryside, only 10 percent come from families owning more than 400 florins worth of property. But 76.7 percent of urban brides (120 cases), and 87.6 percent of the Florentines (81 cases) come from this category.

able deductions) were, as we know, taxed according to the real value of their surplus means; others, who possessed little or no net assets after deductions, were still obliged to reach a "compromise" with the Catasto administration, an agreement setting their tax assessment.[5] In the first instance, marriage made necessary a recalculation of the size of the tax assessment. In the second case, the household head had usually to await the next Catasto before the compromise with the tax office could be adjusted. Thus, a daughter's departure significantly affected the assessment of a wealthy father in two ways. In Florence and in Pisa, he lost the deduction (200 florins and 50 florins respectively) allowed for a household member. On the other hand, he could subtract the value of his daughter's dowry, whether paid or only promised, from his taxable goods. For wealthy families, the amount of the dowry almost always exceeded the value of the personal deduction. The rich therefore had strong reasons for registering their marriages; the poor, on the other hand, and even those of modest means, had nothing to gain by doing so, and even, at Florence and at Pisa, had something to lose in the girl's personal deduction. Few family heads in these latter categories bothered to declare their marriages.

The sample of Tuscan marriages derived from the cancelled names of young brides thus suffers from significant distortions; it gives disproportionate weight to the residents of Florence and Pisa, and to the wealthier sectors of urban society. Moreover, these cancellations reflect only the marriages contracted during the short periods of time when the Catasto was open to changes—only one year within the city of Florence. We cannot control for changes in behavior over time, which may have been significant.

The Catasto affords a second means of estimating age at first marriage. The groom's family (or the groom himself, if a household head) had in turn to register the new bride as a household member and add her dowry to the taxable assets, under the same conditions as the bride's father. These corrections in the declarations inform us not only of the bride's age, but the groom's also, and consequently the age difference separating the two (see Figures 7.1 and 7.2). These data suffer nevertheless from the same distortions mentioned above, and some others besides. Here it is even more difficult to determine whether the husband is marrying for the first time or remarrying. The additions state the real age at marriage for the young woman, while the husband retains the age he had when the declaration was first drafted, several months to a year previously.[6] The age difference between the spouses is thus surely understated. Finally, the addition of young brides, particularly

5. See above, chap. 1, p. 19.

6. Albiera, daughter of Luigi Benvenuti, appears as age 14 in the declaration of her father (AC 75, f. 114). but as 16 in the declaration of her new husband, Girolamo di Francesco dello Scarfa (AC 76, f. 296). It is possible that her husband had similarly grown older since the redaction of his declaration.

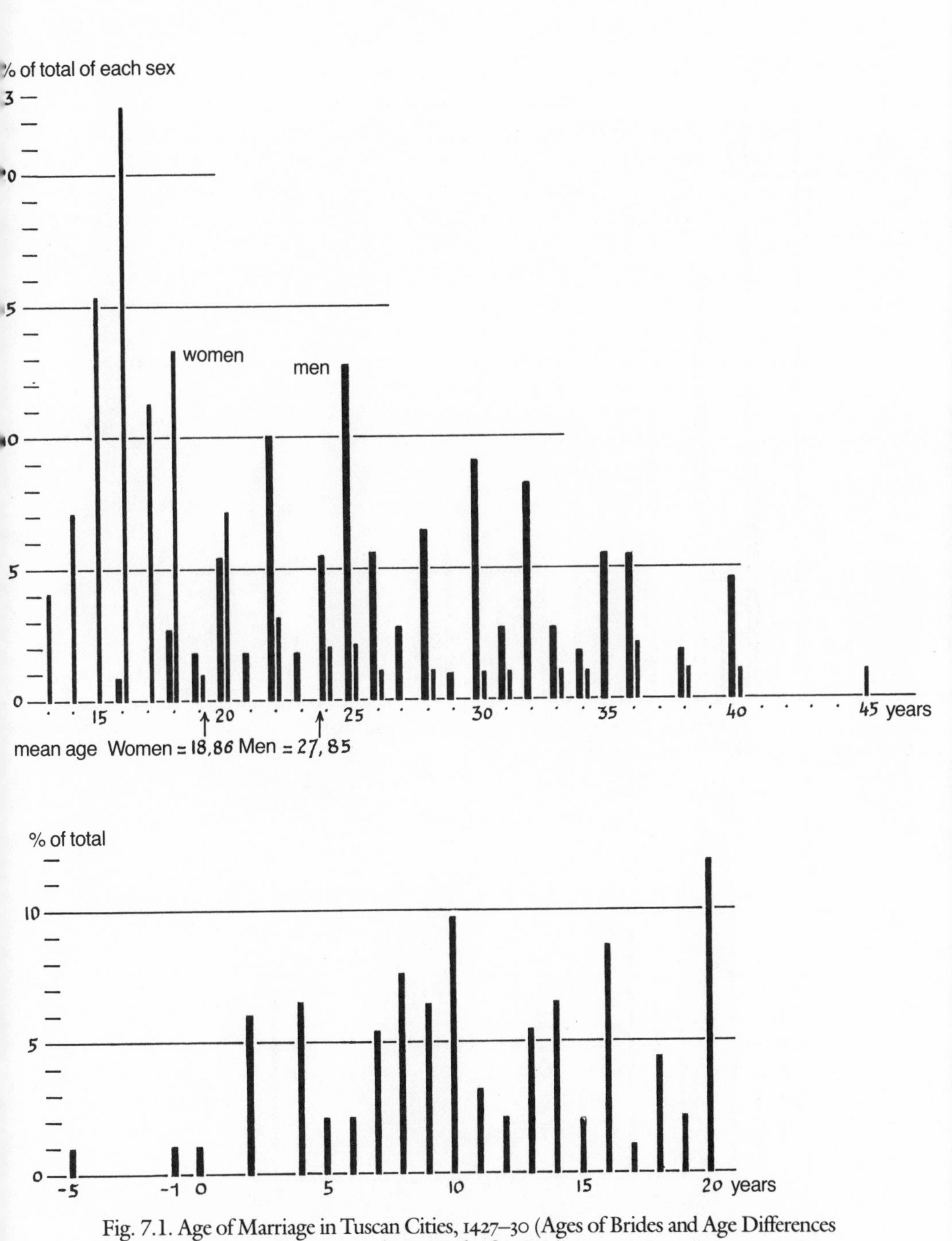

Fig. 7.1. Age of Marriage in Tuscan Cities, 1427–30 (Ages of Brides and Age Differences between the Spouses)

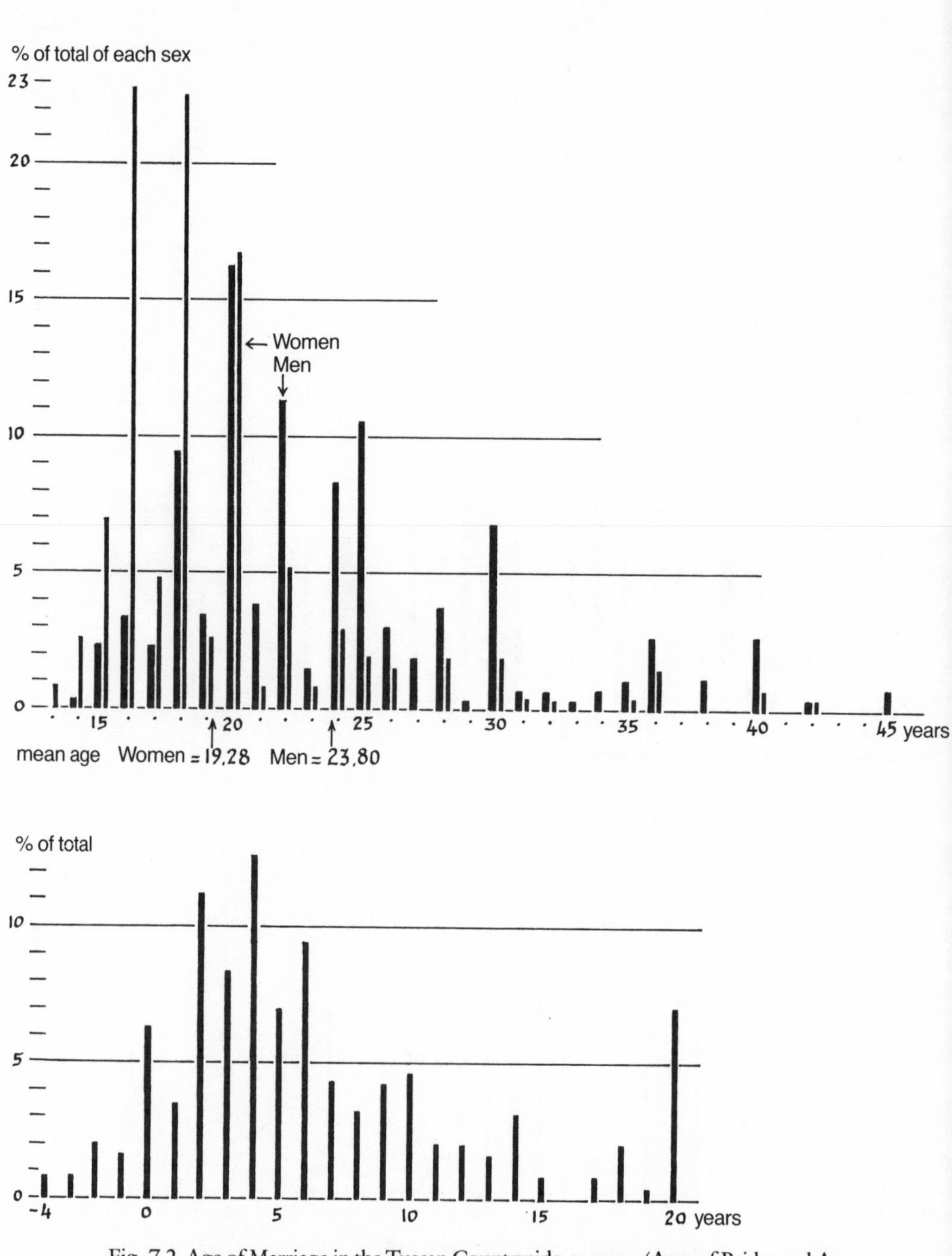

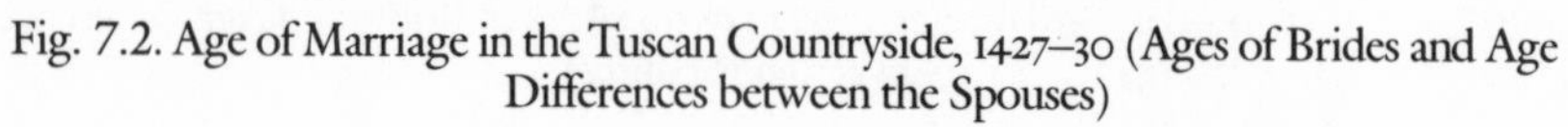
Fig. 7.2. Age of Marriage in the Tuscan Countryside, 1427–30 (Ages of Brides and Age Differences between the Spouses)

numerous in the city of Florence and in well-to-do families, only captures those unions celebrated during the short period in which the Catasto remained open to changes. The estimates of marriage age which the additions support must be regarded as rough approximations.

There remains a third method, this one indirect, which we have already used in determining the variations, by century, of age at first marriage.[7] The method was described by Hajnal in 1953.[8] Age at first marriage is estimated by the proportions of single men and women found in successive age groups within a census. The figures essentially show the average number of years which those who subsequently marry are likely to spend in single life before taking a spouse. This "expectation of single life" is analogous to life expectancy in standard life tables: marriage is treated in the former as death is in the latter. In applying this method, the researcher must select a cut-off year, or interval of years, at which time it may be assumed that those in the population who are still unmarried will never marry; we shall assume "permanent bachelors" to be those in the population, men and women, who are still unmarried at 48–52 years of age. Age groups at five-year intervals (13–17, 18–22, and so forth) are used in these calculations in order to compensate for the rounding off of ages ending in 0 and 5. We assume that men of indeterminate matrimonial status were in the immense majority bachelors.[9] It is likely that we overestimate slightly the proportions of temporary and permanent bachelors in the population, and this probably introduces a small upward bias in the estimates of male age at first marriage.

This method assumes that the population under consideration is closed, and does not take into account the death rate, which may have varied considerably from one generation to the next. We know of no way of correcting for these generational differences. The approximate ages which the method yields obliterate possible variations in marital practices across the generations represented in the survey. They provide a composite image of age at first marriage during the three and one-half decades studied. At least they have the supreme advantage of illuminating, if only in outline, those sectors of the population, notably the peasants and the poor, whose matrimonial characteristics cannot otherwise be determined from the Catasto's data.

As in chapter 4 (Table 4.1), we have divided the population of 1427 into several classes, each one characterized by a distinctive physical and social milieu: the metropolis of Florence itself; the six principal cities, Pisa, Pis-

7. See above, chap. 3, p. 87–88.

8. Hajnal, 1953.

9. See below, p. 216. On the other hand, we did not consider that women of uncertain marital status (who are at all events very few) were spinsters, as they seem for the most part to have been widows.

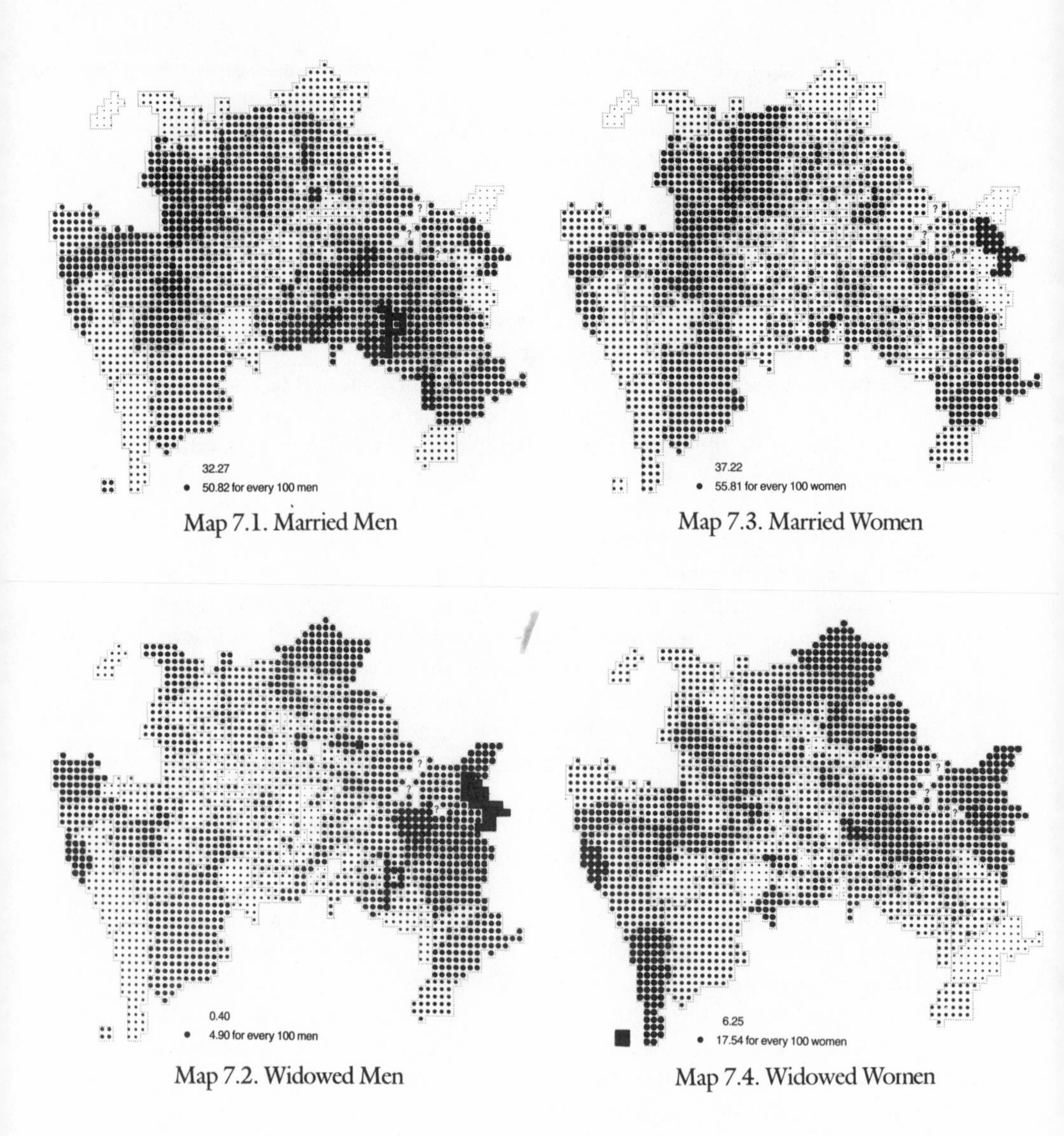

Map 7.1. Married Men

Map 7.3. Married Women

Map 7.2. Widowed Men

Map 7.4. Widowed Women

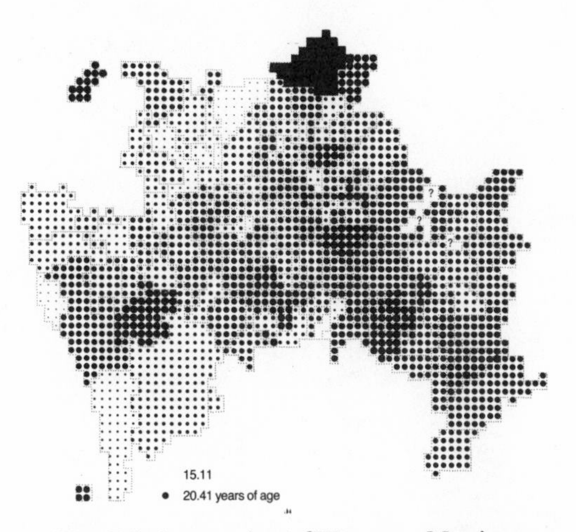

Map 7.5. Average Age of Women at Marriage

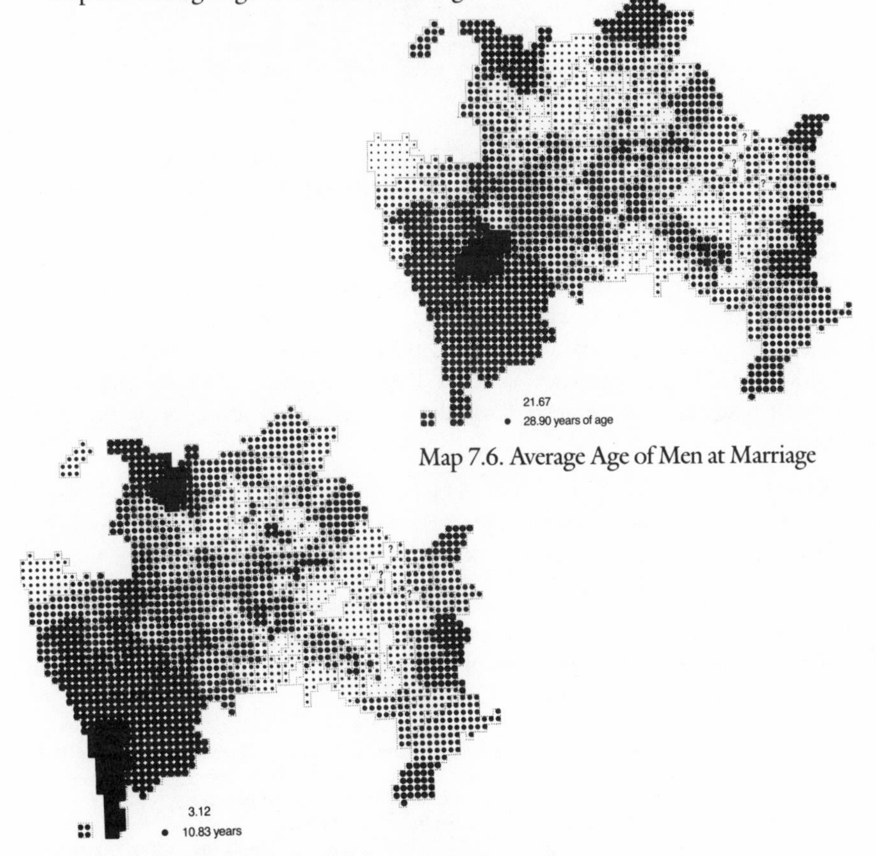

Map 7.6. Average Age of Men at Marriage

Map 7.7. Difference in Average Age at Marriage

Table 7.1. Observed Ages and Estimated Ages at Marriage

	Cities			Countryside		
	Florence	*Large*	*Small*	*Contado*	*District*	*Total*
1 Brides canceled from father's declaration.						
Number	67	29	11	26	15	150
Ave. Age	17.56	21.98	22.77	17.00	16.60	18.20
2 Brides added to husband's declaration.						
Brides:						
Number	55	16	26	245	26	369
Ave. Age	20.83	18.25	19.04	19.26	19.42	19.17
Grooms:						
Number	76	17	27	238	27	375
Ave. Age	34.41	29.15	25.80	23.42	25.37	25.03
Both Ages Known						
Number	51	14	26	228	26	345
Ave. Diff.	13.63	10.29	6.88	6.63	7.04	7.89
3 Estimate ages based on proportions of single persons.						
Women	17.96	17.92	17.93	18.36		
Men	29.95	27.40	26.39	25.63		
Ave. Diff.	11.99	9.48	8.46	7.27		

**Only persons with known ages are included.*

toia, Arezzo, Prato, Volterra, and Cortona; fifteen towns or large villages; and the population of the countryside, with contado and district examined separately.[10]

The three methods of estimating ages of first marriage utilized in Table 7.1 yield reasonably consistent results, especially for Florence and the Florentine countryside, for which our information is most abundant.[11] The bride was quite young when she first was given in marriage, in the countryside as well as in the city. When a Tuscan married, whatever his age or place of residence, he preferred to take as bride a girl under 20 years, even under 18.

> Take her as a child, if you wish to be happy with her, that she might be healthy and whole . . . let her be very young, and not at all neglected [by suitors], as girls become vicious when they do not receive what nature requires.[12]

This advice from Morelli corresponds well with the practice of his contemporaries. The most common age of marriage for women was 16 in both the countryside and the city (Figures 7.1 and 7.2).

10. The villages included are Empoli, San Miniato al Tedesco, Castelfiorentino, San Giovanni Valdarno, Montevarchi, Carmignano, Cerreto Guidi, Borgo San Lorenzo, San Godenzo, Terranuova, Bibbiena, Anghiari, Monte San Savino, San Gimignano, and Colle.

11. The category of those added to the declarations doubtlessly includes the largest number of second marriages, both of women and of men. This explains why brides and grooms here appear slightly older than in the the other categories.

12. Morelli, 1956, p. 210.

The groom was usually much older than his bride. Within the urban centers, the marriage age for males climbed rapidly with population size, while this factor had a negligible effect on the marriage age of urban girls.[13] Thus the age difference between the spouses, everywhere greater than six years, was double that amount in the capital. Regional variations, obscured by aggregate averages, were equally significant, particularly in the district. Maps 7.5 to 7.7 show these contrasts. Age differences between spouses were especially marked in the western territory where, except around Pisa, they hover around 10 years. In the east, except in the fringe of mountains behind Arezzo, the difference falls to 5 years (Map 7.7). The Florentine contado was more homogeneous, but it still juxtaposed zones in which the spread was considerable (south of the Arno except in the Chianti mountains, and in the northeast across Fiesole, Diacceto, and Dicomano) with regions where it fell to only a few years (Casentino, Chianti, and the area of Prato). Local variations do not, however, obliterate the fundamental characteristic of fifteenth-century Tuscan marriage: the great gap between the ages of husband and wife.[14]

Variations in this spread depended, moreover, primarily on factors affecting male behavior. Even in the countryside (Map 7.6) male ages show the most significant shifts. In contrast, the range of ages at first marriage for females, clearly higher in the eastern half of the territory and in the contado and its extension into the Pisan hills, still did not vary greatly and did not clearly set off city from countryside. An important conclusion follows: those forces in society which impeded or aided first marriages acted primarily upon males. When social conditions discouraged the formation of new households, men, rather than women, delayed marriage; conversely, factors favorable to marriage encouraged men, rather than women, to marry sooner. In 1427 the age of first marriage for women was comparatively unresponsive to shifting social conditions.

PROPORTIONS MARRIED AND UNMARRIED

Obviously, for a given population, the proportions of married and unmarried persons vary greatly with age. Table 7.2, represented graphically in Figure 7.3, shows the distribution of the Tuscan population according to sex, age, and marital status. Unfortunately, the indeterminate marital status of many adult men (some 15 percent of the male population) introduces a large note of uncertainty into the data. The declarations do not directly

13. The coefficient of correlation between the size of urban communities (Florence and the six principal towns) and masculine age at first marriage is 0.78, but for feminine age it is nearly 0. On the coefficient, see below, pp. 218–19.

14. It remains to be determined whether this marriage pattern ought appropriately to be described as "Mediterranean" or "medieval."

Table 7.2. Division by Sex, Age, and Marital Status of the Tuscan Population (Numbers per 1,000) by Age Category 1426–30, 1427–30

	Men				*Women*				*Both Sexes*			
Ages	Sngle	Nt Gvn	Mrrd	Wdw	Sngle	Nt Gvn	Mrrd	Wdw	Sngle	Nt Gvn	Mrrd	Wdwd
0–12	1000.0	0.0	0.0	0.0	999.3	0.1	0.5	0.1	999.8	0.0	0.2	0.0
13–17	995.0	0.1	4.7	0.2	839.2	3.4	157.4	1.0	912.5	1.9	85.0	0.6
18–22	27.1	826.9	143.5	2.5	163.0	11.7	821.0	4.3	91.9	438.0	446.7	3.4
23–27	16.4	512.7	462.7	8.2	26.3	7.7	946.5	19.5	21.1	277.2	688.2	13.5
28–32	10.6	286.2	683.5	19.7	14.0	9.0	946.9	30.1	12.3	150.4	812.5	24.8
33–37	9.0	166.2	795.9	28.9	10.8	8.1	923.9	57.2	9.9	89.6	857.9	42.6
38–42	5.7	98.4	867.1	28.8	7.0	11.6	883.1	98.3	6.3	56.6	874.8	62.3
43–47	4.3	66.5	897.6	31.6	4.5	15.7	848.1	131.7	4.4	41.9	873.6	80.1
48–52	4.5	59.7	902.4	33.3	5.1	18.4	744.1	232.4	4.8	38.5	820.9	135.8
53–57	4.6	50.2	904.5	40.7	5.0	22.3	686.8	285.8	4.8	36.8	800.0	158.4
58–62	3.4	49.6	899.7	47.3	3.5	32.7	504.9	458.9	3.5	40.9	695.4	260.2
63–67	3.2	45.6	891.5	59.7	7.3	32.1	431.9	528.7	4.9	40.0	700.1	255.0
68 +	5.1	56.4	798.2	140.3	8.2	49.6	191.8	750.4	6.5	53.2	510.4	429.9
Unknown	142.5	606.3	203.9	47.9	224.7	109.3	324.7	341.3	179.0	406.3	236.7	178.0
All Ages	422.9	149.4	403.8	23.9	405.6	13.6	446.6	136.2	414.1	86.3	422.3	77.3

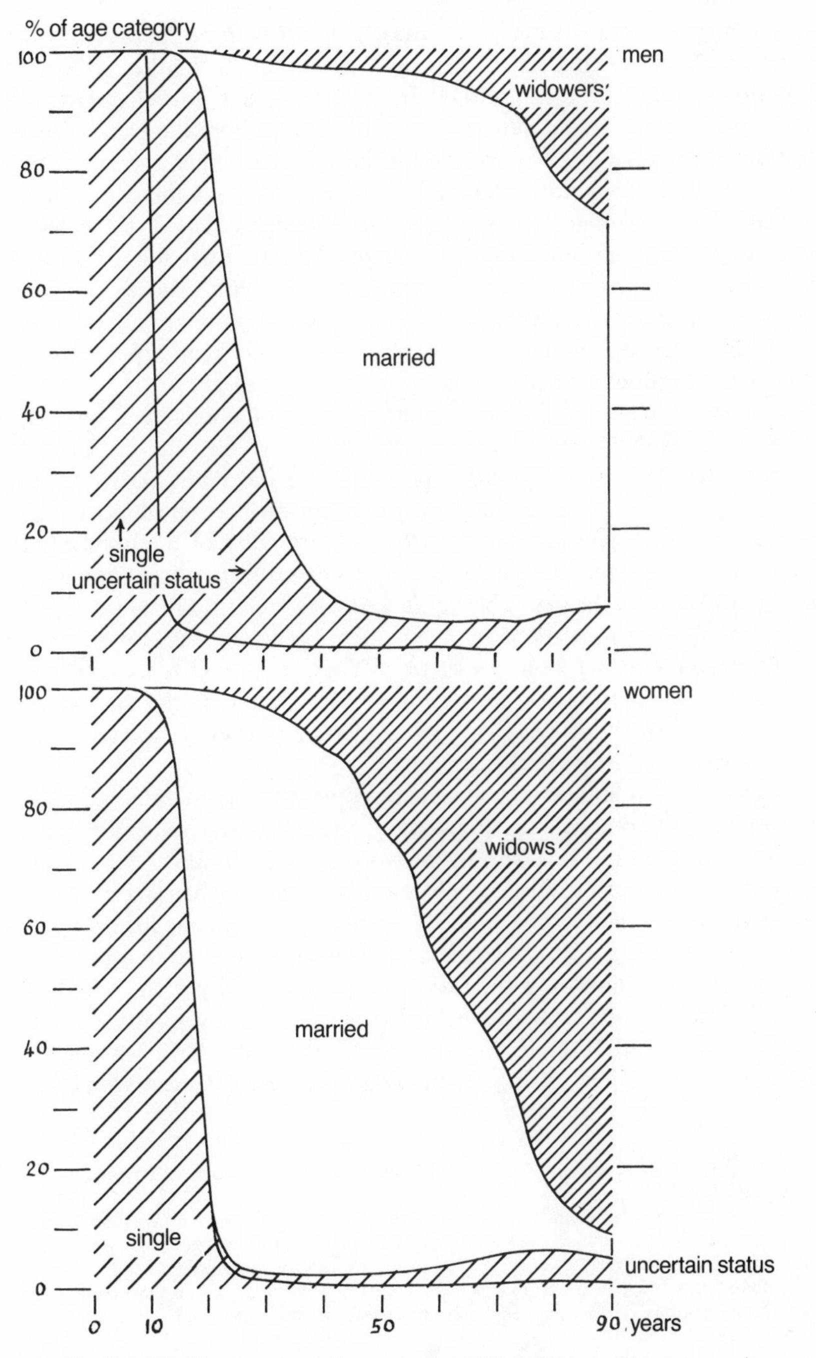

Fig. 7.3. Distributions according to Age and Marital Status (Tuscany, 1427)

state the marital status of males; we must judge that from the presence or absence of a wife and children. Under these conditions, a childless widower living alone cannot be distinguished from a permanent bachelor. On the other hand, women are easily classified. The woman bore the name of her father and her husband; we are usually also told whether the latter are living or dead. Uncertainty affects only 1.4 percent of the figures, ten times less than the percentage for men. This uncertainty is larger for elderly women (5 percent) and for those, often living on their own, for whom age is not stated (10.9 percent). We can suppose that the great majority of these were widows. Unmarried females in the lay population seem in fact to be limited, after age 40, to the minute proportion (less than 1 percent) of women unambiguously identified as single.

On the other hand, adult sons within a family or young men over 18, who were awaiting a propitious moment to marry, fill our category of indeterminates. It is possible that a part of these indefinite cases over 50 years of age are widowers, as the slight rise in the proportion of indeterminates after this age may indicate. At all events, stability of the number of indeterminate cases around the fiftieth year suggests that these men were indeed permanent bachelors. The figure provides at least a maximum estimate; all in all, near 50 years of age, permanent bachelors make up no more than 4.5 percent of the male population. These male and female permanently unmarried persons are thus quite few in relation to the number of single people in the "European" model of marriage, where at 50 years they considerably exceed 10 percent of the total.

As Table 7.2 also shows, if unmarried people, including children, comprise more or less one-half the population, the figure reaches 57.2 percent for men as against only 41.9 percent for women. Here, however, it is better to exclude children and consider only the population of marriageable age. If we take the canonical ages as starting points (12 years of age for girls and 14 for boys), the proportion of single adult women mounts to 16.15 percent, and of single men (including the indeterminates) to 32.3 percent.[15] Even if this latter figure is inflated by the inclusion of a few widowers, the number of single males greatly exceeds that of single females who have not entered the religious life.[16] Here again, the marriage pattern of Tuscan women is

15. In all Tuscany there are only some 20 girls married before 13 years, of whom 5 are 10 years old, and 13 are 12.

16. If we add to the lay population the estimated number of priests and religious (see above, chap. 1, p. 25), then the proportion of single women older than 12 rises to 18.5 percent, as against 36.9 percent of men over age 14. The proportions in relation to the total population rises for men from 57.2 percent to 61.8 percent, and for women from 41.9 percent to 44.2 percent. Thus religious celibacy has only a limited effect on the proportions of single people in the whole population.

markedly "non-European"; Tuscan males, on the other hand, show greater conformity to the modern model.

Although we cannot control for the effects of mortality and migration, we can still calculate the odds that a Tuscan, man or woman, of age 10, 15, 20 and so forth, would marry within the next 5 years. For women, the odds went from 13 percent at 10 years of age to 88 percent at 15; they then fell to 69 percent at 20 and to less than 33 percent at 25. A girl who had not married by age 30 and had not entered a convent had no more than 1 chance in 4 of finding a husband before age 35, and less than 1 chance in 10 of marrying after 35. Nearly 90 percent of fifteen-year-old girls did in fact marry before age 20, and 97 percent of women aged 25 were already married or widowed. In contrast, fewer than one-half the male cohort were married at this age. The odds that a boy would marry before 20 were low (about 15 percent), and then ranged between 40 to 45 percent from ages 20 to 35. Still at age 40, more than a quarter of the remaining bachelors were likely to marry in the following 5 years. Nearly 1 bachelor in 10 at age 45 would ultimately marry before his fiftieth birthday. For females, the chances of marriage were confined to a small extent of time; for males, the likelihood remained strong right up to the threshold of 50, when, in contemporary opinion, the groom was regarded as an old man.

These then are the principal characteristics in the marriage pattern of the Tuscans, evident in the Catasto: a young age at first marriage for women, with almost no permanent spinsters in the community outside the convents; an advanced age at first marriage for men, with a significant number of permanent bachelors; and, as a consequence of all this, a very extended age difference between husband and wife. In the cities in particular, male behavior corresponds well enough with the late marriage and propensity to remain single characteristic of the European model as described by Hajnal. But women diverged from this pattern significantly. Nearly all women who remained in the lay world married, and most were quite young when they took a husband. Clearly, to judge from the female half of the population, fifteenth-century Tuscany did not conform to the European model of modern times.

RESIDENCE AND SOCIAL STATUS

The characteristics of Tuscan marriages, which we have described in the aggregate, show significant differences from one locale or social milieu to another. Table 7.3 presents marital status in Florence, the six large towns, the 15 important villages, and the countryside. The proportion of adult men who remain single is large everywhere, but it climbs from less than a third in the countryside to more than one-half in Florence. High proportions of single men reflect the tardiness with which men entered marriage—be-

Table 7.3. The Marital Status of the Tuscan Population according to Residence, 1427

	Florence	*Cities*	*Towns*	*Countryside*
Men over Age 12				
Married	6,447	5,263	5,329	38,499
Percent	47.71	59.15	62.83	65.09
Widowed	544	322	280	2,162
Percent	4.03	3.62	3.30	3.66
Single*	6,523	3,312	2,872	18,484
Percent	48.27	37.22	33.86	31.25
Total	13,514	8,897	8,481	59,145
Women Age 12 and Over				
Married	6,468	5,290	5,356	38,574
Percent	53.45	57.72	61.58	65.05
Widows	3,041	2,211	1,804	10,046
Percent	25.13	23.81	20.74	16.94
Single	2,256	1,218	1,284	9,825
Percent	18.64	13.29	14.76	16.57
Indeterminate	336	446	254	856
Total	12,101	9,165	8,698	59,301

*Includes those of indeterminate status.

tween 26 and 30 years of age, according to our estimates—and the refusal of some to marry at all. In Florence, the proportion of presumably single men aged 48 to 52, whom we take to be permanent bachelors, reaches 12.1 percent. One man in eight did not marry in the city; or at least, among the survivors in the cohort born 50 years previously, one in eight seems never to have taken a wife. The corresponding figure for the countryside is much smaller (5.3 percent). The sharpest contrast set Florence apart from all other Tuscan communities; only at Florence do fewer than one-half the adult males appear with a spouse in 1427.

The behavior of women is quite different. The proportion of married women varies little across the differing environments, while their absolute number ranges from one-half that of single men in the countryside to two-fifths in Florence. The stability in the proportion of single women results from the relative inelasticity of their marital age and their high marriage rate; these characteristics remain largely constant in the different environments. The proportions of single males and single females increase considerably where men marry late, that is to say, in the big towns. Permanent spinsters (excluding nuns) make up an insignificant part (less than 2 percent) of the feminine population. In contrast, the proportion of widows varies radically with residence: it diminishes regularly as one moves from the capital to the towns, and from the important cities to the smaller villages. As a result, the proportion of married women consistently increases in passing from capital to countryside; so also does the relative number of married men, but for different reasons. Widowhood for women thus shows a certain symmetry with the prolonged or permanent bachelorhood of the males.

Widowers were a small group everywhere, although exact proportions are hard to specify, as a certain number of widowers are concealed among the indeterminate cases. The small proportion of widowers, largely constant in all environments, suggests that almost all males who lost a wife, in the city and in the villages, quickly took another. These same men who so cautiously approached their first unions showed no such hesitancy when considering second and later marriages. Even if we add to the declared widowers all the indeterminate cases, we would still count no more than 10 percent as widowers at 60 years of age; the proportion of widows is still twice as big.

Table 7.3 informs us that women were widowed early; 10 percent of women were already widows at 40; 25 percent at 50; and fully 50 percent after age 60. Widows particularly abound in the cities: in Florence, one adult woman in four was a widow in 1427, as against one in ten in the countryside. These figures would prove, if proof were needed, that widows remarried only reluctantly or with difficulty. The great majority, after the death of their first husband, viewed the prospects of a second marriage with about as much enthusiasm as men viewed their first. This hesitation was nonetheless subdued in the countryside; there, the proper management of a farm required male help. But it was very pronounced in the city, where widows could live independently, on salary, rent, or public charity.

The aggregate figures for the countryside mask considerable differences among regions. The center of the contado contains a high proportion of unmarried people, both men and women. This is clearly linked to the youth of the population (see Map 6.2).[17] The addition of men of unknown marital status to the group of single men widens this picture of rural bachelorhood. The zone in which it is significant extends toward the west, to include the Maremma, the whole southern contado of Pisa, and the countryside of Volterra. Remote and mountainous regions—the mountains above Pistoia, Barga, the Florentine Romagna, and the podesteria of Verghereto are, in contrast, regions where bachelorhood has less to do with youth, and more to do with the tendency of the resident males to delay their marriages (see Map 7.5).

The proportion of people married (Maps 7.1 and 7.3) is strongest in the least youthful regions. In fact, it is negatively correlated with male age at marriage (Map 7.6), the dominant variable of marital practice even in the rural zones. The distribution of widowers in the countryside shows a con-

17. See above, chap. 6, pp. 198–99.

centration toward the periphery and toward the east (Map 7.2); widows show a wider diffusion, towards the periphery of the contado, the northern county of Arezzo, the lower Arno valley, and the Maremma (see Map 7.4). For both males and females, widowhood is rarest in the zone of the mezzadria; the podere could not be readily managed by an incomplete family.

Although the Tuscan marriage pattern appears relatively uniform, nonetheless different sectors of the population register differences in both age of marriage and in the proportions marrying. What factors are at work here? As we have seen, life expectancy of the population played a role. In the epoch of the Catasto, the marriage age for males, while not as low as it had been 50 years previously, still had not reached the heights it would attain toward the end of the fifteenth century and in the beginning of the sixteenth.[18] But it was moving upward unmistakably in 1427; and this affected marital status within the population.[19] At Prato, for example, the proportions of married and of widowed men were already lower in 1427 than they had been in 1371.[20]

Perhaps even more than the long-term movements, factors having to do with environment, social status, or wealth molded the marital behavior of the Tuscans. The city discouraged males, both native born and immigrants, from assuming the burdens of matrimony early. Two-thirds of adult men were married in the contado in 1427, as against less than one-half in Florence itself. Urban conditions discouraged women from marriage too, but the effect is particularly noticeable in regard to second and subsequent, rather than first, marriages. The cities also attracted widowed women from rural areas who did not want a new husband, easily found in the countryside. Florence and the other Tuscan towns abounded in unattached adults, especially bachelor men and widowed women. Many urban households were truncated and biologically inactive, in the sense that they lacked a procreative couple. Hostile to the formation of new families, the urban environment further hampered their survival.

The analysis of correlation permits us to specify, and to some extent to measure, the strength of relationships linking marital behavior with sex, residence, and wealth. The coefficient of correlation varies between 1.0 and

18. See above, chap. 3; Litchfield, 1969, p. 199.

19. At Prato, in the age category 15–30, the proportion of married persons passes from 58.5 percent to 36.2 percent for men and from 88.6l percent to 77.2 percent for women, between 1371 and 1427. These proportions continue to fall over the fifteenth century, at least among women, reaching 39 percent and 67.6 percent respectively in 1469. In the countryside around Prato, married men have passed from 66.5 percent in 1371 to 44.3 percent in 1427, and married women from 98.6 percent to 83.5 percent.

20. Among males at Prato between 13 and 47 years, the proportions of married pass from 61.8 percent to 55.4 percent between 1371 and 1427, and among women, from 85.4 percent to 78.8 percent.

Table 7.4. Correlation Matrix: Sex, Residence, Wealth, and Marital Status (1427)

	Sex	*Residence*	*Wealth*	*Pprtn Married*	*Pprtn Widowed*	*Pprtn Single*
Sex	1.00					
Residence	0.0	1.00				
Wealth	0.0	0.0	1.00			
Pprtn Mrrd*	−0.03	−0.74	−0.46	1.00		
Pprtn Wdwd*	0.94	0.19	−0.06	−0.19	1.00	
Pprtn Single*	−0.90	0.18	0.25	−0.30	−0.88	1.00

*Both sexes.

−1.0, and basically indicates how closely, or how divergently, the two value fluctuate in relation to each other. There is, of course, an evident difficult here: we cannot assign precise numerical values to factors such as environment or sex. But we can attribute to the four "environments" defined above values which reflect their relative positions on a scale of urbanization.[21] These values can then be correlated with other values, which measure certain marital characteristics of the population. The matrix of correlations presented in Table 7.4 shows the relations between sex, residence, wealth, and marital status for the population of 1427.

Coefficients of correlation measure the linear relationship between the variables; they translate poorly, or not at all, other forms of association, however direct. Still, some of the strong correlations in Table 7.4, explaining more than one-half the variance, confirm what the preceding tables have shown.[22] The proportions of married men and women are everywhere the same, or nearly so.[23] Consequently, the coefficient of correlation between sex and proportion of persons married is zero, or nearly zero (−0.03). In contrast, the proportions of widowed persons or of those permanently single depend directly on sex: the great majority of those widowed are women (thus the positive coefficient, 0.94, as women have the value 2), and inversely, single people are for the most part men (thus

21. Florence is assigned the value 4, the six cities 3, the villages 2, and the countryside 1. Masculine sex receives the value 1 and feminine sex 2, on an artificial scale of femininity. The seven categories of wealth (0 florins, 1–25, 26–50, etc). were assigned the values 0, 1, 2, 4, 8 . . . since they follow a geometric progression.

22. The coefficient of determination, equal to the square of the coefficient of correlation, represents the proportion of the variance of the variable Y that is explained by variable X. In Table 7.4, the number of observations is 56; but these observations include the entire Tuscan population. If we were dealing here with samples, only coefficients higher than 0.27 would be significant at the 95 percent confidence level.

23. The coefficients of correlation calculated on the estimated ages of first marriage for men and for women, in regard to residence, show the strong influence of urbanization on the masculine age (r = 0.78); see above, n. 13. Its influence on the other hand is negative, and much weaker, for feminine ages (r = −0.33).

the negative coefficient, −0.90, as men have the value 1). These coefficients thus emphasize the close connections between the male sex and single life, and the female sex and widowhood, although the latter association is somewhat stronger than the former. The high negative coefficient (−0.88) well expresses the inverse variation between proportions widowed and proportions single in the population.

The influence of residence, or degree of urbanization, bears primarily on disposition toward marriage. The negative coefficient between proportions married and residence indicates that the inhabitants of rural areas are drawn earlier, and in greater numbers, into marriage than are the residents of cities. On the other hand, the correlation between the proportions of single or of widowed persons with residence seems weak, primarily because the two sexes gravitate toward single life or widowhood in opposite directions.

The influence of wealth on age at marriage and the proportions marrying is powerful in the cities, but apparently much weaker in the smaller towns and rural areas. In Florence, the wealthiest males were the most hesitant to marry; estimated age at first marriage ranges from 27.7 years among the destitute to 31.2 years among the wealthiest. Consequently, the correlation of age at first marriage for men with wealth is quite high at Florence (0.94). In the six large towns, the figure falls to 0.85; but it takes on weakly negative values in the important villages (−0.15) and in the countryside (−0.13).

In these last two instances, the coefficients of correlation do not fully show the complex ways in which wealth affected the Tuscan approach to marriage. The behavior of the wealthy was evidently not the same across the four environments. In Florence, 41 percent of the men belonging to families with more than 400 florins in taxable wealth were married, as against 60 percent of those without assets. In the Florentine countryside, the lowest percentage of married persons (63.5) is also found among the wealthiest, but this is considerably higher than levels at Florence. The wealthiest rural residents could not have included many workers of the soil, and they resemble the urban affluent in their behavior. Below them, well-to-do rural households (now including substantial peasants) register the highest proportions of married persons (68.3 percent in households with 100–200 florins; 67 percent in those possessing 200–400 florins). In this they surprisingly resemble their totally destitute neighbors (67.2 percent married). Wealth, measured in florins, did not have the same influence on nuptiality because it did not have the same meaning in the countryside as in the cities. Penniless peasants were chiefly mezzadri; their contractual obligations required that a complete family be available to work the podere. For their part, well-to-do peasants (with wealth of 100–400 florins), who owned the property they cultivated, required, as did the sharecroppers, the help of a large household. In both cases, marriage responded to the demand for labor and the desire to keep property productive.[24]

II. Motivations and Consequences

These contrasts across environments point to certain fundamental differences in the functions of the family in Tuscan towns and countryside.

In the countryside the family added to its biological and social functions—the procreation and education of children—an important economic responsibility, the management of an agricultural enterprise. In the peasant economy that dominated the Tuscan countryside of the quattrocento, as it did the major part of medieval Europe, the family, rather than the individual, formed the fundamental unit of labor.[25] One man, or one woman, could not easily manage a farm; he or she required, in the absence of salaried labor, the help of a spouse and eventually children or relatives. Thus, the young peasant who wished to attain economic independence had to marry. Once widowed, he promptly remarried, unless a young couple, perhaps his married son, already assisted him in working the land. Consequently, the countryside contained very few incomplete households, without at least one married couple.

In town, the family of course fulfilled the same biological functions in procreating and rearing children; but its economic role was markedly different. For the young man seeking to establish himself in an urban trade, the presence of a wife and children offered no particular advantage.[26] He had frequently to serve long years at low pay as an apprentice. He had to accumulate diligently his earnings and profits; capital alone permitted him to pursue his trade in his own right and name. Usually, he could not contemplate marriage until his mature years, when he was economically established; even then, the urban family was not cemented, as was the rural household, by close participation in a common economic enterprise. The Tuscan towns thus harbored a large, "maritally floating" population, comprised of single or widowed people. The cost of this system was the aggravated risk that urban lineages would not survive. In Tuscany, as elsewhere in Italy or in Europe, the city became the grave of many family lines.

As the family fulfilled different functions in the city and in the countryside, so the possession of property affected the formation of households in

24. See Klapisch and Demonet, 1972, pp. 886–87.

25. See Chayanov, 1966.

26. On the difficulties which the presence of a family caused for a wage-earning Florentine at the end of the fourteenth century, see La Roncière, 1974, pp. 675–77.

different ways. In the cities, rich young men approached marriage with far greater circumspection than did their poorer neighbors. The young man from a wealthy family, if he sought to make a career as a merchant, banker, or lawyer, had to wait even longer than the poor artisan to acquire enough wealth to found a new household suitable for his station in life. Moreover, marriage among the wealthy inevitably involved the conveyance of substantial sums of money through the dowry. Marriage also called for the sealing of family alliances, which affected the political and social position of all parties involved. The high stakes associated with marriage frequently led the wealthy young man, or his family, to search long for a suitable bride, and to protract the negotiations when she was found.[27]

The substantial peasant, usually owner of his farm, needed, for his part, a family which would render him as rich in harvests as he was in land. However, this does not mean that peasants in command of a solid patrimony did not exert some restraint upon the marriages of their children. The mean age of first marriage for the sons of rich peasants (201–400 florins) falls to 24.5 years, and, although it is the lowest found in Tuscany in 1427, it still conforms to the late ages of west-European marriages. Indeed, the characteristic trait of well-to-do rural families does not consist in the absence of bachelors; rather, it involves the almost constant presence of at least one married couple on the farm, and only rare occurrences of families led by a widow or a bachelor.[28] The rich young peasant could not marry at will, but he retained a better chance of marrying at a younger age, or of marrying at all, than his urban counterpart. Poorer inhabitants of the countryside—peasants who had to support themselves by working as hired hands—could not as readily take a wife. A spouse, and then children, might excessively tax their meager resources. But here too we must recall the singular exception of the mezzadri, who, without a penny of their own, worked farms which in principle were intended to occupy fully, and support, large families.

SOCIAL REPERCUSSIONS

The social implications of this model are considerable. The tendency of males to postpone marriage meant that the community would contain large numbers of unattached men, gathered especially into cities, who were denied legitimate sexual outlets for as long as two decades after puberty.

27. Morelli, 1956, p. 207, thus urges his male descendants to marry young, between 20 and 25 years, but he also advises that they wait until age 30 if they can gain thereby some advantage.

28. See below, chap. 10, p. 297.

Erotic tensions thus ran high in urban society, and the situation inevitably promoted both prostitution and sodomy, for which the Tuscan cities possessed a merited reputation.[29] The typical triad of many contemporary stories and dramas—the aged husband, beautiful young wife, and clever young man intent on seducing her—reflects a common domestic situation. These restless young men were uninhibited by responsibilities of a wife and family, and many were content to be so.[30] They were quick to participate in the factional and family feuds and battles, which were such frequent occurrences in the social history of the Italian towns.[31]

Delayed marriage for men inevitably affected the treatment and the fate of urban girls. In the wealthy classes, high mortality and inevitable shrinkage in the age pyramid at its upper levels reduced the number of men near age thirty who might take as brides girls between the ages of 15 and 20. The families of these young girls thus entered a desperate competition for grooms; this competition drove up the value of dowries to ruinous levels. It also persuaded many families to offer their daughters in marriage at still more tender ages, out of anxiety to settle their fate.

In the early fourteenth century, Dante deplores the excessive amounts that Florentine dowries had already attained.[32] The great collapse in population in the late fourteenth century, in facilitating marriages, probably kept the size of dowries reasonably stable, or at least slowed their inflation. Among the Corsini family, for example, Matteo di Niccolò, who married in 1352, received as dowry from his wife the sum of 600 florins.[33] In 1383, his own daughter, Caterina, was given in marriage with a dowry of 900 florins, and, when she was married for a second time in 1385, her dowry was 925 florins. But in 1401, Matteo's second daughter Francesca was wed with a dowry of 600 florins, and her sister Andrea, married in 1403, was given in marriage with an identical amount. Probably the great plague of 1400 facilitated the marriages of these two girls and enabled their father to marry

29. See Herlihy, 1969b, pp. 1348–49.

30. This is implied in both the complaints directed by Alberti against the young men of the *gente Alberti* and in the words of Alessandra Strozzi to her sons (see the epigraph to this chapter). The phenomenon also impressed an English observer at the end of the sixteenth century, Moryson, 1903, p. 409: "In Italy marryage is indeed a yoke, . . . as brethren no where better aggreeing yet contend among themselves to be free from marryage, and he that . . . will take a wife to continue their posterity shall be sure to have his wife and her honour as much respected by the rest, besyde their liberall contribution to mantayne her so as themselves may be free to take the pleasure of women at large. By which liberty they live more happily than other nations . . . and they make small conscience of fornication esteemed a small sinne and easily remitted by confessors."

31. See Herlihy, 1972a. For a parallel from the twelfth century, see Duby, 1964.

32. *Paradiso,* canto XV, verses 103–05. Villani, 1823–25, 2: 96, repeats this opinion.

33. Corsini, 1965, p. 5, and for the later marriages cited here, pp. 65, 81, 99.

them cheaply. The Niccolini family dowries confirm the relative stability of dowries in the second half of the fourteenth century.[34] But only an examination of notarial documents relating to marriage and the work in progress on the *Monte delle doti* will allow us to verify these impressions derived from the family memoirs.[35]

Near 1427 and, as in Venice, already for some time past, it seems that the sums paid for dowries had begun to rise.[36] The Catasto itself shows that within the Florentine patriciate, the average dowry had climbed to approximately 600 florins. In 1434 when Matteo Corsini married, he received a dowry of 1,000 florins.[37] The Corsini were, to be sure, among the city's leading families. But in 1464 the Florentine matron Alessandra Strozzi, in a letter to her two sons, called a dowry of 1,000 florins suitable only for an artisan.[38] In 1431 Giovanni Rucellai married the daughter of Palla di Nofri Strozzi, the wealthiest Florentine in the 1427 Catasto. The dowry was not more than 1,200 florins.[39] Some 35 years later, in 1466, his own son Bernardo would marry a Medici girl, who would bring a dowry almost double that amount, 2,500 florins.[40]

This unmistakable tendency for dowries to increase in value in Florence over the course of the fifteenth century becomes readily understandable when viewed in the light of contemporary movements in the age of first marriage for men. As we have seen, the improving life expectancy (and, perhaps also, diminishing economic opportunities) pulled upward the age of first marriage for men more strongly than that of women, lengthened the gap in age separating the spouses, and increased the plurality of women over men on the marriage market. Already weak in 1427, the negotiating position of the bride steadily deteriorated. This deterioration is reflected in the increasing costs, which the bride's family had to meet, to arrange her marriage.

The difficulties in dowering a daughte· preoccupied family heads and

34. The mother of Lapo di Giovanni Niccolini brought at her marriage in 1349 a dowry of 400 florins. Her granddaughter, Agnoletta di Niccolaio, was to bring, according to the will of her father (1383), 600 florins as dowry; in fact she brought 950 at her marriage in 1394. Lapo di Giovanni received as a dowry 700 florins in 1384, and his brother Filippo, 800 florins at the same date; at his remarriage in 1418, Filippo received only 500 florins. The dowry of their sister Monna attained 800 florins, a sum which also constituted the dowry of her own daugher Giovanna Folchi, in 1410. The daughters of Lapo, Lena and Giovanna, would receive 600 and 1,000 florins respectively in 1405 and 1409. Giovanna made a good match with an Albizzi, and this cost her father. See Niccolini, 1969, pp. 60, 69, 72, 89, 92, 100, 108, 112, 113, 134, 139. See also Klapisch, 1976b.

35. Julius Kirshner and Anthony Molho have undertaken a systematic analysis of this important archive. For a description of the project, see Kirshner and Molho, 1978.

36. See Chojnacki, 1975.

37. Corsini, 1965, p. 143.

38. Macinghi-Strozzi, 1877, p. 395.

39. AC 7, f. 6, 23 July 1431.

40. Rucellai, 1960, p. 28, mentions the marriage.

even the communal government. In many wills, heads of family enjoined their male heirs and executors to respect their provisions for dowering daughters. In one salient example, a paterfamilias in the tiny town of Colle ordered his four sons to pool their resources so that all his granddaughters might receive 100 florins in dowry. The girls, it appears, were not yet born, but the aspiring grandfather already recognized the difficulties they would face. "He who gives a daughter in marriage," he admonished, "gains greater honor in this world than he could have earned alone".[41] Many families looked to charitable donations in order to provide their daughters with a suitable dowry. The makers of wills often followed the recommendations of Paolo da Certaldo, who, in about 1370, deemed it preferable to endow generously one poor girl, rather than disperse bequests among several beneficiaries.[42] For those lower still on the social scale, one of the purposes of domestic service was to allow the young girl to accumulate a dowry for her eventual marriage.[43] Charitable confraternities also assumed among their most pressing obligations the provisioning of dowries to poor young girls, and in particular to those from good but impoverished families, the "shame-faced poor." The confraternity known as the *Buonomini di San Martino* would later in the century commission a painting of this charitable activity for the walls of their chapel at Florence.[44] The male reluctance to marry tended to increase dowries even at the lowest levels of urban society.[45]

To aid the hard-pressed parents who could neither marry off their daughters with their own resources nor borrow the necessary sums (cash was usually required), the Florentine commune decided in February 1425 to establish a special fund, the Monte delle doti.[46] By depositing in the Monte

41. AC 251, f. 655, 266. Filippo d'Alberto, one of the four brothers, had no daughters and found the paternal arrangement unsatisfactory, ibid. f. 266.

42. Paolo da Certaldo, 1945, pp. 148–49.

43. The young servant could count not only on her salary to constitute a dowry, but also contributions from her master. Many employers promised to provide a dowry when the girl reached marriage age, out of obligation or charity. See, for example, AC 250, f. 272: Giovanni di Bartolo declares in his incarichi: "Alla Tofana la quale è stata sua fante, alla maritata per l'amor di Dio, f. 6."

44. This confraternity was founded in 1442, under the auspices of St. Antoninus; the frescoes of the miniaturist Francesco d'Antonio del Chierico date from the 1470s. See Bargellini, 1972; Passerini, 1853a, pp. 501–15. There is a comparable depiction at the hospital of S. Maria della Scala at Siena, by Domenico di Bartolo, done probably in 1440–43.

45. The size of dowries among the poorer classes is not well known. To judge from entries in the Catasto, dowries ranged from 25 to 60 florins among rich peasants and the petty bourgeois, and from 6 to 15 florins for a servant.

46. Liquid sums, furniture, and clothing often formed the dowry, to judge from the Catasto. A certain Niccolo di Agnolo da Cortona registered the ten deposits he had received, some 36 florins, "per le figliuole delle sopradette persone, i quali ano a ristituire quando esse si mariterano de' quali gli tocha a ristituire la III. parte"; AC 252, f. 182. For recourse to Jewish lenders, see AC 266, f. 334: "A Liuccio giudeo per parte della dote di detta Monna C."

a sum of money at the birth of a daughter, the father could reclaim a substantially larger amount when the girl reached marriage age.[47] Like most funds under government control, the deposits were soon used by the state for other purposes. Nevertheless, contemporaries credited the Monte with enabling many young Florentines to marry.[48]

But despite these efforts and the help extended to marriageable girls, many of them, particularly in the higher social strata, had no statistical chance of finding a husband. For most of these, there was no alternative but the convent. In consequence, the number of religious women, at Florence and in other Tuscan cities, rose considerably after 1460 and continued to grow up to the middle of the sixteenth century.[49] As men delayed their first marriages, fewer women could marry at all.

Even the placing of a daughter within a convent required a form of dowry, albeit much smaller than that required for marriage. In 1412, when Giovanni Corsini put his eldest daughter, then nine years of age, in the convent of San Piero Maggiore, he paid 230 florins—a large sum, but still less than one-half the 600 florins which a marriage was likely to cost him.[50] It goes without saying that in this decision, the personal desires of the girls themselves counted for little. Bernardino of Siena, an exact contemporary of the Catasto, once described these unhappy girls, placed in convents because they were too poor, too homely, or too unhealthy to be married, as the "scum and vomit of the world".[51]

MARRIAGE AND SOCIAL MOBILITY

The great age difference separating the bride and groom, and the consequent imbalance in the numbers of men and women available for marriage at any given time had one other important consequence: daughters of rich families, able to offer large dowries, had a better chance of attracting a husband than did those of less wealthy families. But, given the shortage of grooms among their own social peers, they would often have to accept grooms from a lower social station. Thus through marriage, many women suffered a loss of status. On the other hand, the groom could look on marriage as a primary means of social advancement, not only by virtue of the dowry paid him, but also as a consequence of the connections—the *parentadi*—and the prestige that an alliance with a higher placed or richer

47. On the composition of this archive, see Molho, 1971, pp. 138–41. The earliest surviving volumes date from 1431 (ASF, Monte delle doti, 3733).

48. Dati, 1902, p. 153, gives this assessment. On the place of the Monte delle doti in the political and social life of the fifteenth century, see Becker, 1966–67, 2:236.

49. See Trexler, 1972, and chap. 1 above.

50. Corsini, 1965, p. 137. On the dowries of nuns, see Trexler, 1972.

51. ". . . quasi spumam vel vomitum saeculi," Bernardino da Siena, 1950–, 2:83.

girl brought him. "Strive to elevate yourself," Morelli expressly recommends to his descendants.[52] This was an additional reason for an ambitious young man to delay his first marriage. If he waited long enough, the chances improved that he could make a more favorable, perhaps even a brilliant match.[53]

The Catasto provides a means of verifying this assumption that women tended to marry down while men married up. In 1427–28, when the Castato remained open to changes, some 79 marriages were noted in the declarations, in which we can identify both brides and grooms according to their households of origin. This sample, as we know, probably favors the rich, but for our purposes this bias helps us to see even more clearly the marital practices of the Florentine patriciate. At first inspection, there is no apparent difference in relative social position, as measured by wealth, between the households of origin for the brides and grooms. In 41 of the 79 marriages, the household of the groom appears to be the richer. The mean value of the total taxable assets of the grooms' households was 2,869.5 florins, and for the brides, 2,897.6 florins. These figures would suggest that marriage involved a lateral movement in society, with brides joining households which were almost at the same levels in the pyramid of wealth as their own.

However, these sums represent the wealth of households after the payment of the dowry. Even if the declarations do not always clearly indicate that the dowry has been paid, the claim to payment, on the side of the groom, was itself a taxable asset. The average size of the dowry was approximately 600 florins, obviously a substantial sum relative to the average wealth of the households. One can easily understand the terror, described by Dante, which struck the hearts of fathers when they contemplated the marriage of daughters. If we correct for the dowry payment, it would appear that the average wealth of the bride's household had originally been some 1,200 florins greater than that of the groom.

Other documents confirm this fact. After the Catasto was officially closed in June 1428, the government still authorized certain adjustments to the declarations for weddings celebrated and dowries paid up to 1430.[54] In 44 of these later marriages we can again locate the two households of origin. This sample shows an even more marked bias in favor of the very rich, who took care to report their weddings: the average dowry reached 735 florins. But here there is no doubt that the declarations in the Catasto give the total amount of wealth before any addition or subtraction of the

52. Morelli, 1956, p. 208.
53. This is implied in the passage from Morelli, referred to above in n. 27.
54. AC 296, "Sceme di catasto di cittadini per dote date."

dowry. The direction of social movement generated by marriages is therefore clear: in 35 of the 44 cases, the bride came from the richer household. The average wealth of all the brides' households was approximately 5,050 florins, and the households of the grooms possessed on the average assets to the value of only 3,125 florins. Thus, the payment of a dowry represented for the former the surrender of about 14 percent of their property, while the latter augmented their wealth by nearly 23 percent.

It might of course be argued that the grooms, presumably much younger than the fathers of their brides, would consequently almost always appear to be poorer. Their wealth would, in other words, not accurately reflect their true social position but their age and the current stage of their careers. In reality, the families from which the young men came frequently possessed a complex structure. Some new husbands headed their own households, but most still lived as sons, younger brothers, or more distant relatives—under someone else's roof. Similarly, most young brides were daughters and under the jurisdiction of their fathers, but a few lived with a brother or were even heads of independent families. Finally, the relation between the wealth of a household and the age of its head is not linear, as we shall see. At the time of the first Catasto, at least among the wealthy households of Florence, women tended to marry down, and men to marry up. And this phenomenon no doubt became even more pronounced as marriage became more difficult in the late fifteenth and sixteenth centuries.

The tendency of upperclass women to marry down also meant that girls from the middle ranges of society saw their chances of marriage still further reduced. Many had no choice but to accept a life of religion. The long-term demographic trend of wealth, residence, and occupation thus profoundly affected the patterns of Tuscan marriage. And so also did the conscious strategies that the Tuscans adopted as they chose spouses, formed households, and sought to assure the survival of their family lines.

III. *In Praise of Matrimony*

In the traditional Christian and medieval (and even classical) view, marriage was an honorable state of life, but it was still regarded as inferior to celibacy and even to widowhood.[55] The responsibilities of the married state not only distracted from prayer and religious exercises, but in secular life marriage obstructed the study and meditation which the wise man ought to be pursuing.

55. See, for example, the typical appraisal in De laudibus virginitatis, Bernardino da Siena, 1950–, 4:470 ff.

Florentines of the fourteenth century fully shared these ancient prejudices against marriage. Giovanni Boccaccio, a notorious misogynist, considers in his biography of Dante whether the philosopher ought to marry, and uses the occasion to berate both matrimony and women.[56] After the death of Beatrice, Dante had supposedly fallen into profound melancholy. His concerned relatives, in hopes of reviving his spirits, persuaded him to marry. But Dante's wife was a second Xanthippe. She continuously nagged her husband and disrupted his meditations. Boccaccio draws the following moral: "Let philosophers leave marriage to the ignorant rich, to rulers, and to peasants; let them take delight in Philosophy, a better wife than any other".[57] Petrarch too, when he recommends a remedy for the sorrow caused by the death of a wife, rehearses the traditional list of marital ills from which the widower is now happily freed.[58]

But the society of late trecento Florence, slipping radically in numbers, could ill afford to recommend celibacy to its citizens. Amid the devastating epidemics of the late Middle Ages, a new and more affirmative attitude toward marriage emerged at Florence. Paolo da Certaldo at mid-century still manifested a harsh view of women, who were "vain, light, and inconstant".[59] Women were responsible for "all great scandals, shame, sins, and expenses".[60] Still, he registered among the five principal joys of life, if only in third position, the company and love of a good wife; her death enters too, at the same level, among life's five chief sorrows.[61]

At the century's close, the representatives of what is now called civic humanism at Florence totally rejected this traditional disparagement of marriage. In 1392 Coluccio Salutati, the dean of the civic humanists, composed a detailed refutation of the aspersions which Petrarch had cast against marriage.[62] He stressed that marriage sanctified the natural union of the sexes. Children born in wedlock alone assured the survival of the family and of society. The active citizen had necessarily to be a married man.

Leonardo Bruni of Arezzo, chancellor of the Commune at the time of the Catasto, spoke out with even greater eloquence in praise of matrimony. His own biography of Dante systematically refutes Boccaccio's earlier condemnation of the poet's marriage.[63] In his judgment, Boccaccio's arguments were decidedly "frivolous." The philosopher had to marry to promote the common good. Bruni's spirited words are worth quoting:

56. Boccaccio, 1965, pp. 580–81.
57. Ibid., p. 586.
58. Petrarca, 1867, 2:104–16.
59. Paolo da Certaldo, 1945, p. 105.
60. Ibid., p. 135.
61. Ibid., p. 159.
62. Salutati, 1891–1911, 2:365 ff., letter to Bartolomeo della Mella, dated 23 July 1392.
63. *Le vite di Dante e del Petrarca* (1436), Baron ed., 1928, p. 54.

> Man is a social animal, as all philosophers agree; the fundamental union, which by its multiplication makes the city, is that of husband and wife. Nothing can be accomplished when this union does not exist, and this love alone is natural, legitimate, and allowed.[64]

For Bruni, a "civic, whole, and learned life" required that the citizen not only live in a republic, but also with a wife.

The rehabilitation of marriage brought with it a reassessment of the quality and importance of conjugal love. The treatises on marriage written by clerics regarded conjugal love not as a requirement for, or even as a natural consequence of, marriage, but simply as a duty.[65] In the fifteenth century, lay treatises on marriage and the family rather regard conjugal love as the most natural, most generous, and most rewarding of human sentiments. Besides Bruni, Matteo Palmieri, Alberti, and many others play on this theme that marital love alone was natural. "Of all human associations giving rise to affection, none produces a nobler love, or more deeply rooted in nature, than the matrimonial union".[66]

The emphasis, which these and other authors place on the basis in nature of conjugal love, further reflects their concern with other forms of sexual expression, which they regarded as opposed to nature. Sodomy, as we have seen, was rampant in Tuscan and Italian towns. Bernardine of Siena identified sodomy, along with "vanities", the principal reasons for the disastrous fall in population.[67] Sins against nature provoked epidemics from an angered God and prevented the population from making good its losses. Marriage, in contrast, was the community's moral and social salvation.

One of the most enthusiastic of these eulogies to marriage dates from 1415 or 1416 and was composed by a young Venetian humanist, Francesco Barbaro. Barbaro had close ties with the Florentine civic humanists and he wrote his treatise, *De re uxoria*, on the occasion of the marriage of a Florentine friend.[68] The essay overflows with classical reminiscences, but this show of erudition does not tarnish the praise which Barbaro bestows on the married state:

> What greater pleasure is there, than to make common decisions, even as you are freed from domestic concerns? What greater pleasure, than to have a woman, a companion in days fair and foul, a wife and friend? To her you can confide your most intimate thoughts about the matters

64. Loc. cit.
65. *De matrimonio regulato, inordinato et separato,* Bernardino da Siena, 1950–, 8:57, 59.
66. Palmieri, 1825, p. 215.
67. See complaint about falling population in *De peccatis vanitatum,* Bernardino da Siena, 1950–, 2:83.
68. Barbaro, 1914–16.

> which concern you. Her sweetness and companionship offset all your worries and your pains. You so love her, that you think that a part of your life depends upon her welfare.[69]

To be sure, other writers, Alberti above all, present a view of marriage that remains thoroughly patriarchal. And we may doubt that many Florentine spouses achieved this "model of perfect friendship," which Barbaro envisions. After all, the first duty of the wife was to fear her husband, and that of the husband to instruct his wife "while keeping her in fright and dread".[70] The hope that love might develop between them not out of duty, but through close acquaintance and mutual appreciation, rested on slim foundations. How could a young girl easily become the "companion, wife, and friend" of a man, often older than she by more than a decade, occupied outside the home, distracted, absent, busy at the *bottega* or the *palazzo*, and at times spending years abroad? The mature man who married a young maiden saw little advantage in involving her in his affairs. Giannozzo Alberti, the chief figure in the third book of Alberti's *Libri della Famiglia*, mentions that he showed his young bride all the goods and supplies in his house, saving only the secret papers in his desk which she was never allowed to peruse. He urges his listeners never to share their secrets with their wives, nor with any women.[71] Women's tongues, dangerously loose, would soon divulge the information to the world at large. Condescension mixed with distrust constantly cooled relations between the marriage partners, even after the wife had gained in age and authority within her household.

Doubtlessly, few Florentine couples achieved in marriage the measure of love, companionship, mutual support, and appreciation that Barbaro envisioned. Historians must nonetheless record that such sentiments were at least expressed, and marriage warmly praised, seemingly for the first time, at Florence in the quattrocento.

69. Ibid., pp. 29–30.
70. Paolo da Certaldo, 1945, p. 105.
71. Alberti, 1960, 1:221.

8
Births

. . . quia licet appetere non plures proles habere quam possit nutrire. . . .

. . . as one may legitimately seek to have no more children than one can support. . . .

—Saint Antoninus, bishop of Florence, 1446–59

he Catasto contains little direct information on births and does not allow us to calculate precisely the birth rates which prevailed in 1427. However, it offers abundant information on the distribution of babies and children across the various social strata. It is possible to discern who in Tuscan society reared the greatest number of children and we can describe these successful parents in terms of residence, wealth, and age.

I. Children

The direct information the Catasto offers concerning births is slight, but worthy of brief comment. As we have seen, during a period which ranged from one year in the city of Florence to three years in certain parts of the Florentine district, the heads of households were permitted to change their declarations in order to register the births, marriages, and deaths of household members.[1] How complete are these primitive statistics of vital events?

REGISTRATION OF BIRTHS

Within the city of Florence, in the twelve months from July 1427 to June 1428, household heads added some 790 newborn children to their declarations. Within the entire Florentine domain, over a period approaching three years, family heads noted the births of 2,779 babies. Unfortunately, however, these additions do not represent a complete registration, or even

1. See above, chap. 7, pp. 203–04.

a random selection, of the births which had occurred either in Florence or throughout the Florentine territory.

At Florence itself, the 790 babies added in 1427–28 compare with 1,088 babies less than one year of age registered at the time of the initial survey, before July 1427. The small number of added babies suggests that, even within the city, new births were underreported by 25 or 30 percent. Not surprisingly, the poor in particular failed to register their full complement of newborn. This becomes apparent if we compare the distributions of these two sets of babies (those originally listed in the declarations and those subsequently added to them) across ten categories of wealth.[2] The coefficient of correlation between number of babies in the first set and relative wealth is 0.52. The greater the wealth of the family, the better the chance that a baby less than one year old would be found among its members. But among the second set—those added to the declarations—the coefficient jumps to nearly perfect correlation, to 0.97. It is impossible to believe that the affluent Florentines produced a bumper crop of babies in 1427–28, or that sterility suddenly descended upon the households of the poor. Rather, within the city, the richest parents carefully added to their declarations their newborn babies; those with lesser wealth did not. The additional family member represented a deduction of 200 florins, but this had limited interest for households of modest means.

In rural areas, where no deduction at all was allowed for household members, it is remarkable that the heads bothered to report any new births. But the obligations of the household affected the amount of head tax charged to each adult male, and rural families wanted to appear large and burdened with children. Still, those babies added to rural declarations clearly represent only a small fraction of the numbers born. In the four quarters of the Florentine contado, household heads added 1,589 babies to their declarations, from approximately 1427 to 1429; this number represents only about one-half the number of babies less than one year of age (3,040) originally listed in their declarations. Here too, the registration of new births is unequally distributed. It is relatively large in the entire rural quarter of Santa Croce (probably because the early completion of the survey here allowed time for many subsequent changes). But additions are negligible in the east, in the entire county of Arezzo and Cortona, and around San Gimignano. In these latter regions, the survey was finished only in the third year of the census. There was no opportunity for updating the data.

2. These wealth categories are based on gross taxable assets (i.e. before deductions) and are as follows: 0 florins, 1–25, 26–50, 51–100, 101– 200, 201–400, 401–800, 810–1,600, 1,600–3,200, 3,201 and above. In calculating the correlations, we assigned to these categories the following values: 0, 1, 2, 4, 8, 16, 32, 64, 128, and 256 respectively.

Although the pace at which the survey was completed affected the chances to make changes, it still emerges that the rich were more conscientious than the poor in reporting arrivals and departures to and from their households. In rural households without taxable assets the added babies constituted a scant 31 percent of those originally declared; the poor responded to the initial queries, but they did not spontaneously volunteer new information. In contrast, rural families with more than 400 florins in property eagerly advertized their fertility; the new babies they added constituted 85 percent of the numbers they had originally declared.[3]

Despite manifest omissions, these additions still retain some interest. They confirm, for example, that the rich prepared their declarations more carefully and more accurately than the poor, and that they kept the Catasto office informed of changes in their families. The additions also permit us to discern the ages at which many Tuscans became parents from 1427 to 1430. But this primitive register of births does not allow us to study variations in the birth rate across social strata. Here, as in many other records of the age, it is difficult to view the behavior of the humble over the broad and obstructive shoulders of the rich.

THE REGISTRATION OF CHILDREN

In contrast to later corrections, the original declarations were subject to the rigorous scrutiny of the Catasto officials; the data they contain therefore offer a reliable means for studying the distribution of babies and young children across Tuscan society. Of course, several months, sometimes a year, passed between the birth and registration of these children. The deaths sustained in the interval affected their distribution; so also did the movement of babies (such as adoptions) from one family to another. We can expect to identify not exactly the most fertile parents, but the most fortunate: those who were successfully rearing the new generation of Tuscans.

If we consider babies of less than one year (age 0) initially registered in the Catasto, the rounding off of their ages subjects the figures to a certain distortion. In all parts of the survey, but especially in rural areas, infants age 1 distinctly outnumber those age 0. In the population as a whole, there were 9,175 children age 1 and only 6,949 age 0.[4] Parents tended to report babies of 10 or 11 months as already age 1.[5] This rounding upward partially explains the preponderance of one-year-olds. The margin between age 0

3. In absolute numbers, 149 and 453 babies among the poor, and 113 and 133 among the rich.

4. In the entire population, families without assets count 722 babies age 0 and 923 age 1, for a ratio of the latter to the former of 1.28. Among families possessing more than 400 florins in taxable property, the corresponding figures are 1,012 and 1,131 babies, for a ratio of 1.13. Florence's population shows a similar ratio (1.12, with 1,088 and 1,221 babies in the respective ages).

5. See above, chap. 6, p. 166.

and 1 was unstable everywhere, but above all among the poor and the inhabitants of the countryside. Neither age can be regarded as an accurate index of the true distribution of infants across the community.

To compensate for this inconsistent reporting of the ages of infants in older censuses, historical demographers often group infants into larger age categories; conventionally, they have used the number of children between age 0 and age 4 as an index of the proportions of young children in the population. The relations between this number and the number of women of child-bearing age, or the "child-woman ratio," is at best a crude approximation of the fertility of women, since it is affected by the demise of infants and by the death and emigration of women. In spite of these defects, we have calculated this index; we take as the child-bearing years those between age 13 and age 47. The young age at which Tuscan women married recommends this interval; it also allows us to include preferred ages, such as 15 and 45, at the same time as the adjacent depleted ages. The effects of age heaping, which vary across different social sectors, are thus attenuated. We have also studied the proportions of children in the age groups 5 to 9 and 10 to 14, in order to develop a complete picture of the distribution of children in Tuscan society.

REGIONAL DISTRIBUTIONS

The distribution of newborn babies and young children differs markedly from that of adults. In regard to geography, the western regions of the Florentine territory, pinched between the sea and the middle valley of the Arno, show relatively large numbers of young children, and higher child-woman ratios, than the interior zones stretching toward the east. An examination of the population of Florence and of the six secondary cities clearly illustrates these regional contrasts.

The seven cities are characterized by extreme contrasts in their relative proportions of young children. Volterra, for example, counts 3 children under five years for every 2 found at Arezzo. Must we then conclude that the women of Volterra were bringing into the world 3 children for every 2 born at Arezzo? The child-woman ratio suggests that in 1427–30 the women of Volterra were, or recently had been, the most prolific of all urban women in Tuscany. Of course, differences in the structure of the female population according to age and marital status cannot be disregarded. At Volterra, 89.2 percent of the women were married, as against 78.8 percent at Arezzo. Then too, at Arezzo many women were widows, and the number of widows of child-bearing age doubtlessly lowered the reproductive capacities of the city. Nevertheless, even if we take into consideration only married women of child-bearing years, Arezzo still shows a substantially lower child-woman ratio than does Volterra.

Table 8.1. Children and Women in the Large Tuscan Cities, 1427

	Florence	*Pisa*	*Pistoia*	*Arezzo*	*Prato*	*Volterra*	*Cortona*
Ppltn	35,948	7,106	4,292	3,992	3,488	3,329	3,059
Chldrn 0–4	5,453	1,217	803	523	611	612	473
Prcnt	15.15	17.13	18.71	13.10	17.52	18.38	15.46
Wmn 13–47	7,035	1,378	891	816	765	612	611
Prcnt	19.55	19.67	20.76	20.44	21.93	18.38	19.97
Ratio 0–4/wmn 13–47	0.775	0.883	0.901	0.641	0.799	1.000	0.664
Mrrd wmn	5,704	1,091	796	643	616	546	545
Prcent	15.85	15.35	18.55	16.11	17.66	16.40	17.82
Ratio 0–4/mrrd wmn 13–47	0.956	1.115	1.009	0.813	0.992	1.120	0.877

Only persons of stated age are included.

The geographic distribution of high and low proportions of children and of high and low child-woman ratios confirms that the cities with the highest scores—Volterra, Pisa, and Pistoia—are all situated in the western part of the Florentine domain; the two cities with lowest proportions and ratios, Arezzo and Cortona, are found in the eastern regions. Florence itself and Prato occupy an intermediate position between these two groups of cities. These regions also show significant differences among themselves in their age structure. The proportions of children are highest where the population is most youthful; they are depressed in the east, where the population is generally older and where the elderly female contingent is especially large.[6]

How can we explain this plethora of babies in the western cities, and the asymmetrical age structure in the different regions? In the absence of precise registrations of births or of other sources of vital statistics, we can only propose tentative answers to these intriguing questions. It is usually assumed that prosperity and abundance stimulate births in traditional societies. But neither Volterra, nor Pistoia, nor Pisa seem to have been exceptionally prosperous in the years preceding the Catasto. Volterra had, in fact, been the site of violent disorders and had mounted a futile resistance against the imposition of the new survey. So also, the Pisan economy had long been troubled by the exodus of its wealthiest citizens.

The social and biological experience of these western cities shortly before the Catasto is, however, distinct in one respect. They all seem to have suffered, more seriously than the cities of the east, from the most recent epidemic, which struck Tuscany in the years 1423–24.

The literary references to this plague are unfortunately few and scattered.

6. See above, chap. 6, pp. 199–201.

The plague seems to have first attacked the western regions of the Florentine domain in 1423. In July of that year Buonaccorso Pitti refused the office of captain of Livorno because he had heard that a "great pestilence" was raging there.[7] Pistoia also suffered from a severe outbreak of plague in 1423; a late but well-informed historian, M. A. Salvi, affirms that it took numerous victims and that many citizens fled the town, which was allegedly emptied of its inhabitants.[8] The plague waned in the western regions during the following year; the infection in fact moved on to Florence. Many Florentines then sought refuge in the formerly infested western regions, which they now judged to be safe. Pitti fled with his family to Pescia, near Pistoia, because, he said, the plague had already devastated this area and had now departed.[9] Buoninsegni also affirms that the Florentines "fled in great numbers to Prato and Pistoia".[10] A contemporary historian from Pistoia, Sozomenus, likewise alludes to the "gigantic" plague which ravaged his city in 1423. When the disease abated in 1424, Pistoia attracted many Florentines; as the plague moved into their own city, they prudently moved out.[11]

In fact signs of the approaching epidemic were already evident at Florence in 1423, but it reached its full strength only in 1424.[12] Did it strike the eastern regions of the territory with equal severity? In 1424 Rinaldo degli Albizzi sought refuge in Pratovecchio, in the Casentino north of Arezzo.[13] His choice might indicate that the plague had either already departed from the eastern regions or had not yet arrived. In any case, when they mention a recent epidemic, the taxpayers of Arezzo mean the plague of 1417–18. These references, although scattered, seem to indicate that the plague hit the western regions hard in 1423; it attacked Florence first in 1423 and with still greater force in 1424. But the plague seems to have lost virulence as it moved to the east. We have no indication that its impact on the eastern regions was particularly severe.

Births, as we have seen, tended to fall during an epidemic and to remain low in the following year.[14] But in the second and third years after the plague, the number of births was likely to soar. The Catasto, in sum, catches the populations of the western towns and regions even as they were

7. Pitti, 1905, p. 244.
8. Salvi, 1656–82, 3:246.
9. Pitti, 1905, pp. 245–46.
10. Buoninsegni, 1637, p. 23.
11. Sozomeno, 1908, p. 14. The commune of Cerreto Guidi near Pistoia in 1423 asked for a tax reduction, for the reason that almost half its residents had died of plague. (ASF, Provv. 113, f. 179, 27 October 1423.)
12. Buoninsegni, 1637, p. 23.
13. Guasti (ed.), 1867–73, 2:950.
14. See above, chap. 3, p. 81.

Table 8.2. Children and Women in the Tuscan Population, 1427

	Florence	*Six Cities*	*Fifteen Towns*	*Countryside*
Total	35,984	26,266	24,806	172,414
Children Age 0	1,088	783	743	4,335
Percent	3.02	2.98	3.00	2.51
Children Age 1	1,221	842	914	6,198
Percent	3.39	3.21	3.68	3.59
Children 0–4	5,453	4,233	3,998	29,179
Percent	15.15	16.12	16.12	16.92
Children 5–9	4,714	2,546	2,434	19,398
Percent	13.10	9.69	9.81	11.25
Children 10–14	3,698	2,186	2,065	15,886
Percent	10.28	8.32	8.32	9.21
Women 13–47	7,035	5,174	5,111	36,953
Percent	19.55	19.70	20.60	21.43
Ratio	0.775	0.818	0.782	0.790
Married Women	5,704	4,237	4,169	29,521
Ratio	0.956	0.999	0.958	0.988

Only persons with stated ages are included. The category of "married women" includes widows and women separated from their husbands.

rebounding from from the plague of 1423. Here, as often, the plague emerges as the most powerful factor working to contort the structures of the Tuscan population.

CITY AND COUNTRYSIDE

We can now examine the proportions of young children in the various social environments, into which we have divided the Tuscan community. Table 8.2 presents the proportions of young children and of women for Florence, the six principal cities, the fifteen important villages, and the countryside.

The proportion of small children in the Tuscan population reaches truly impressive dimensions. Children between 0 and 4 years of age constitute from 15 to 17 percent of the total. The child-woman ratio also climbs to startling levels, much higher, it seems, than in other historical societies. Even in the little town of Pozzuoli, then experiencing rapid expansion in 1489, children age 0–4 constituted only a little above 14 percent of the community.[15] As we saw in chapter 6, the enormous numbers of the very young is the mark of a population struggling valiantly to retain its size in the face of repeated, devastating epidemics.

Table 8.2 also shows that the distribution of young children across our four environments is remarkably similar. Babies age 0–4 are more numer-

15. See the age pyramid constructed by J. Beloch and reprinted in Reinhard, *et al.*, 1968, p. 105.

ous in rural areas, where they constitute almost 17 percent of the population, than they are at Florence, where they barely exceed 15 percent. Still, given the reputation for sterility which the traditional city has long borne, this difference appears trivial. It is possible that the plague of 1423–24, which presumably extracted a greater toll from cities than from the countryside, also acted as a more powerful stimulus to births within the urban communities. Even if the plague of 1423–24 did obscure, to an extent difficult to judge, the normal contrasts between urban and rural birth rates, the weak correlation between residence and the number of small children in the Tuscan households remains unexpected and surprising.

Shall we therefore conclude from the data presented in Table 8.2 that urban or rural residence had negligible effects on births or on the successful rearing of children? Not at all; rather it would seem that the broad categories used in Table 8.2 obscure significant differences among the geographic and social sectors comprising the community. The countryside, for example, aggregates rural regions with profoundly different economic and social-structural characteristics. In all the categories of Table 8.2, the rich and poor are mixed in varying proportions. In the last analysis, the table does not so much prove uniformity in demographic behavior relating to birth rates, as it highlights the need for a closer and more detailed analysis of the data.

One part of the Florentine territory, the contado of Pistoia, invites a study of the contrasts within and among rural regions. Despite the ravages of the plague four years earlier, the countryside of Pistoia was fairly prosperous in 1427, and the rural population was destined to achieve remarkable growth in the later fifteenth and sixteenth centuries. Within its small space, the countryside of Pistoia contained two strongly contrasting areas, prime examples of Tuscan diversity. The plain and low hills around the city constitute a fertile zone permitting family-based agriculture. The high hills and mountains extending to the crest of the Apennines supported a radically different economy. The mountains offered as resources to their inhabitants groves of chestnut trees, pastures for cattle and small livestock, timber, and racing streams capable of driving mills; but they did not easily support cultivation, and highland inhabitants were usually very poor. Contemporaries fully appreciated these contrasts, and the surveyors of 1427 sensibly divided the countryside of Pistoia into the contado, with 58 communes located on the low hills and plain, and the montagna, with 11 highland villages.[16]

Here, constancy in the proportion of women across the total population allows the local contrasts in apparent fertility to emerge more clearly. The

16. On the economic geography of Pistoia, see Herlihy, 1967, chap. 1.

Table 8.3. Children and Women at Pistoia, 1427

Population	*City*	*Contado*	*Montagna*
Total population	4,292	9,162	2,376
Children, 0–4 years	803	2,012	430
Percent	18.71	21.96	18.10
Women, 13–47 years	891	1,917	489
Percent	20.76	20.92	20.58
Child-Woman Ratio	0.901	1.105	0.879

proportion of small children in the mountainous zone was considerably lower than that of the low country, even lower than that achieved in the city. The families of the contado were, on the other hand, far and away the community's best producers of children. Why were the montagnards so markedly infertile? In 1427 residents of the mountains show particularly high ages at first marriage (29 years) and a marked age difference separating groom from bride (more than 10 years). This delay in male marriages obviously dampens the birth rate, and has the effect of maintaining the population at a level proportionate to its resources. It seems clear that this brake was applied in the highlands and released in the low country. Additionally, the poverty of the montagnards forced them to emigrate, seasonally or for more extended periods of time, toward the more abundantly endowed lowland regions or to the towns. This necesssarily affected the stability and fertility of the married couples.[17] Even the poorest inhabitants of the lowlands, generally the mezzadri, had access to family farms established on fertile soil, which the urban landlords kept well stocked. The fiscal poverty of the mezzadri is very different from the poverty of starvation with which montagnards had to contend. Access to a productive farm allowed the sharecroppers to support numerous offspring. As Chayanov has written, "the peasant provides himself with a family in accordance with his material security".[18]

These characteristics of the Pistoiese countryside can be generalized over the entire rural area of the Florentine domains. With numerous local variations, the highlands of the Apennine periphery seem generally poorer in babies and in children than the zone of the hills. Above all, they fall behind the center of the contado, where the mezzadria was firmly entrenched. (See Map 6.2, "Young People, 0 to 14 Years", above, p. 200). Even if wealth measured in fiscal terms is less closely associated with a larger brood of offspring in the countryside than in the city, still, sufficient resources, or,

17. See Herlihy, 1972d.

18. Chayanov, 1966, p. 64. Chayanov still did not determine whether the peasant enlarged his family to correspond with the size of his holdings, or his holdings to correspond with his family. At all events, the two variables show a high correlation.

Table 8.4. Proportions of Children in the Tuscan Population in Relation to Wealth

Wealth (in florins)	*Florence*	*Six Cities*	*Fifteen Towns*	*Countryside*
0	13.77	16.89	17.33	17.61
101–200	14.64	16.01	16.36	17.29
401 and up	15.89	17.49	16.50	18.25

SOURCE: Catasto of 1427. The percentages are the proportion of children from 0 to 4 years in the total population, in the wealth category.

in Chayanov's words, "material security," remained a principal determinant of family size in rural areas.

Now we can consider the effects of residence on the distribution of children, at equivalent levels of wealth. Table 8.4 gives the proportions of children between ages 0 and 4 in the four environments we have already used several times previously, at three arbitrarily chosen levels of wealth.

Here, the influence of the urban environment on the proportions of infants is entirely clear. At each level of wealth the cities support fewer children than does the countryside. It is further evident that as the urban community grows and we pass from the important towns to the principal cities, and finally to Florence itself, the proportions of young children fall considerably. If we expanded this analysis to include the seven categories of wealth previously utilized, then the coefficient of correlation, between the level of urbanization and the proportions of children aged 0–4, turns significantly negative (−0.6.1).

How can we reconcile this conclusion with the data from Table 8.1, which demonstrated that the Tuscan cities in 1427 did not lag far behind the rural areas in the number of young children they were rearing? The answer has to do with the powerful influence which wealth exerted over household size and numbers of children. The cities possessed by far the greater part of Tuscany's wealthier families. These families tended also to be large and crowded with offspring; those rich in the goods of this world also abounded with children.

WEALTH

The influence of wealth on the distribution of children in the Tuscan population thus merits close examination. In general, wealth is associated with the presence of a large number of small children in both urban and rural households. Table 8.5 presents two matrices, showing the correlations between wealth and proportions of children in the Tuscan population. For the large cities, where the spread of wealth is far broader than in the countryside, we have used ten, rather than seven, categories of wealth.

The correlation between wealth and the proportions of infants is almost

Table 8.5. Correlation Matrices: Wealth and Proportions of Children in the Tuscan Population, 1427–30

	Wealth	*Proportions 0–4 Years*	*Proportions 5–9 Years*	*Proportions 10–14 Years*
A. Florence and the Six Cities (a)				
Wealth	1.00			
Prprtns 0–4	0.50	1.00		
Prprtns 5–9	0.78	0.23	1.00	
Prprtns 10–14	0.82	0.35	0.90	1.00
B. Villages and Countryside (b)				
Wealth	1.00			
Prprtns 0–4	0.47	1.00		
Prprtns 5–9	0.61	0.74	1.00	
Prprtns 10–14	0.74	0.67	0.86	1.00

(a) Number of observations: 20. Correlations above 0.38 are significant at the 95 percent confidence level.
(b) Number of observations: 14. Correlations above 0.53 are significant at the 95 percent confidence level.

identical in these two environments (0.50 for the large cities, and 0.47 for the villages and the countryside). But on closer scrutiny, the association of wealth and large numbers of children appears not to have been strictly linear. Table 8.6 shows the proportions of small children in the various wealth categories for Florence and the countryside.

In Florence, the relation between wealth and the relative number of infants in the population takes the form of a meandering line, which has no precise direction across the first seven categories of wealth, up to approximately 700 florins. These categories include nearly 65 percent of the population of the city. The disorganized course of the curve reflects the complexity of urban society and the existence of numerous truncated, incomplete households, some of them containing no more than a single person. These occur primarily across the middle categories of wealth. Beyond the threshold of 700 florins, the curve derived from these figures climbs dramatically, to level out only at the highest category, among families possessing assets in excess of 3,200 florins.

At Florence, therefore, substantial increments of wealth are needed before an association with the numbers of children becomes apparent. We can also calculate the average wealth of households with 1, 2, 3, and so on up to 10 children, and then calculate the slope of the regression line of average wealth against the number of children. The slope of the regression line comes out as 760 florins. This essentially is the difference in average wealth between households with n and $n+1$ children. It required money, and much of it, to rear children in the city. In the rural quarter of Santa Croce, which served us here as a sample of rural households, the difference in

Table 8.6. Proportions of Infants according to Category of Wealth: Florence and the Countryside

Wealth (in florins)	*Florence*		*Countryside*	
	Prcnt	*Index*	*Prcnt*	*Index*
0	13.77	100.0	17.61	100.0
1–25	15.97	116.0	16.31	92.6
26–50	16.61	120.6	16.26	92.3
51–100	13.14	95.4	16.50	93.7
101–200	14.64	106.3	17.29	98.2
201–400	13.90	100.9	18.38	104.4
401–800	13.55	98.4	18.25	103.6*
801–1600	15.08	109.5		
1601–3200	18.10	131.5		
3201 and above	17.29	125.6		

SOURCE: Catasto of 1427.
* Above 400 florins.

average wealth between households with *n* and *n*+1 children is a modest 28.4 florins. Although the possession of resources and the rearing of children are associated in both city and countryside, clearly the measure and meaning of wealth were radically different in the two communities.

In the rural areas of Tuscany, the correlations between wealth and proportions of children behave more coherently than at Florence, and they also trace a different line. The curve derived from Table 8.6 takes on the form of a supine "S." The relation is negative for the first three categories of wealth; over this range, proportions of children fall as assets increase. However, as we have already noted, the apparently destitute class of peasants includes the majority of sharecroppers. Access to a large and well stocked farm encouraged early marriages among them, and they also made prolific parents. In contrast, peasants belonging to the middle class of wealth possessed some few plots of land, but often wallowed in misery; their scant holdings did not allow them to support big households and families. Beyond the threshold of 50 florins, the correlation between wealth and the proportion of infants turns positive; the curve moves strongly upward after 100 florins, and thereafter levels off among the wealthiest rural residents. These may have cultivated a more urban style of life, which is to say, not especially favorable to procreation. However, their group still includes larger numbers of children than can be found in the city at comparable levels of wealth.

Within the six principal cities and the fifteen villages, wealth similarly shows a positive correlation with numbers of children, and the curve of relationship also takes the form of a supine "S." Wealth thus influences the distribution of infants across the entire Tuscan population; but it operates in conjunction with numerous other factors—the structure of the household, the occupation of its head, and so forth—which render the relationship singularly complex.

THE CHILDREN OF THE RICH

Table 8.5, which shows the correlation between wealth and the proportion of children in three age categories (0–4 years, 5–9, and 10–14) also illuminates a remarkable phenomenon: in all of Tuscany, in the cities as well as the countryside, as children grew older, they came to be concentrated in the wealthier households. In Florence, the correlation between wealth and proportion of children belonging to these respective age categories rises from 0.50 to 0.78 to 0.82. In the countryside, this concentration is only a bit less marked; the correlation passes from 0.47 to 0.61 to 0.74 across the respective categories.

How did the wealthier households gradually obtain larger numbers of children? The developmental cycle of the household, measured by the age of the household head, may offer an explanation.[19] Did households tend to accumulate, and later to lose, property and children, as their heads grew older?

The developmental cycle surely did affect the distribution of both wealth and children across society. Still, the relationship between these two distributions was not a simple one. Large segments of the population—the mezzadri, for example, and many artisans—acquired little or no wealth over the entire course of their marriages and their lives. Among other groups, the relationship between the age of the household head, his wealth, and the number of children in his home was highly complex. Extended families, with more than a single married couple, were common among both the urban rich and the peasants; the age of the male head here tells us nothing about the other married couples in the home or about their children.

To reduce the influence of the developmental cycle upon our data, we can study only those households at comparable stages in their histories under the direction of male heads of approximately the same age. The most fertile period, for the Florentine married couple, seems to have been reached when the husband was approximately age 40; this was the average age of the fathers of babies less than one year old registered in the Catasto. We shall therefore consider only those urban households with a married male head between age 38 and 42, and shall study the relationship of their wealth with the number of children found within them.

The coefficient of correlation between the number of infants age 0–4 and average wealth of the grouped households is already positive (0.53).[20] This is a weaker relationship than that which associates all children under

19. See below, chap. 10, on the developmental cycle.
20. The number of these hearths is 3,324.

age 16 with the average wealth of all households (r=0.75) Two conclusions follow. There is a tendency, of moderate strength, for the more propertied families to show the larger numbers of children from the moment those children first appear in the survey. But clearly, too, natural fertility was only one of several factors which constantly gathered children into the homes of the wealthy.

The child-woman ratio, crude as it is, also argues that rich women were either naturally more fertile than their poorer neighbors, or at least more successful in bringing their babies safely through the first months and years of life. Within the city of Florence, women in households with no possessions at all show a ratio of 0.648.[21] Women in households with 1,601 to 3,200 florins in taxable wealth, who apparently formed the most fertile group in the city, show a ratio of 0.980.[22] If possible contrasts in infant mortality can be ignored, then rich matrons were bearing approximately three babies for every two born to destitute mothers.

What other events, apart from births, gathered children into the affluent homes? Rich households were more likely than the poor to employ servants, some of whom would be children, and apprentices.[23] Of their numbers, the Catasto, which did not count servants in the households of their masters, gives us no measurement. Wealthy males were perhaps more likely than the poor to father illegitimate children, who are, at all events, predominantly found in the homes of the rich. Of 172 illegitimate children listed in the Catasto of Florence (128 boys and 44 girls), 148, or 86 percent, live with the richer half of the population.[24] This may imply that bastards born to the poor had reduced chances of surviving, or enhanced chances that their mothers would abandon them. But it might also be presumed that more bastards were born into rich households, where susceptible, vulnerable women, servants and slaves, abounded. Household heads with some resources, frequently out of charity, received into their homes orphans, often the children of near relatives, sometimes entirely unrelated. These children were usually said to be "held for the love of God." In 1340 the elder brother of Donato Velluti fathered an illegitimate daughter in Sicily; the mother was a woman of humble station, a *fornaia* or baker.[25] The child's parents never married, and both apparently fell victim to the pestilence of 1348. Donato learned of the plight of his niece and brought her to Florence in 1350, when she was ten years old. He never legally adopted the

21. This category includes 639 young children and 986 women age 13 to 47 years.
22. The young children are 697, the women 711.
23. On the age of servants, see above, chap. 5, p. 136.
24. So also in the entire population, the proportion of bastards found in households possessing more than 400 florins in assessed wealth is 81.6 percent of the total (206).
25. Velluti, 1914, p. 147.

child, but he reared her and provided her with a dowry when she was married in 1355. Amid devastating plagues, orphaned children proliferated in Tuscan society, and the wealthy were primarily able and willing to accept an additional mouth into their homes. Two-thirds of the Florentine children "held for the love of God" (a quarter of all those found in Tuscany) resided in the wealthiest hearths.

Negative factors too—infanticide, child abandonment, and infant mortalities—also affected the distribution of children. Especially in towns, impoverished families were often sorely tempted to abandon their newborn; the luckier among them would find a place in a foundling home.[26] So too, among the poor, the misery of their lives threatened the existence of their babies in the first few months, even the first years, of life. The progression in our coefficient of correlation between wealth and five-year age groups during childhood (Table 8.5) suggests that deaths whittled away the ranks of poor children and thus inflated, in relative measure, the numbers of the rich.

Wealth therefore affected the proportions of children found in Tuscan households, and its influence even intensified as the children aged. Access to resources affected all the ways by which the household took on new members or maintained its size—births; formal or informal adoptions; employment of servants, nurses, and apprentices; and doubtless also the health and longevity of family members. With time, in both city and countryside, the distribution of resources and the distribution of children moved toward a rough equivalence.

II. Parents

The Catasto informs us even more about the new parents than their children.[27] It is of course true that some babies died before they were registered in the survey and we cannot, consequently, identify all new parents. It is also true that some household heads rounded the ages of their babies less than one year old to exactly age 1, and those who did this are thereby excluded from the category of new parents as we define it here. Moreover, the declarations hardly ever distinguish stepmothers from natural mothers. It is therefore possible that some women who are accompanied by very young children are not their biological mothers. Nonetheless, the very young age of the nursing children we are considering here—less than one year— guarantees that stepmothers could not have been so nu-

26. On the difficult question of infanticide at Florence, see Trexler, 1973–74a, and see chap. 5 above, pp. 145–47.

27. In the following discussion, "new parents" refers to the mothers and fathers of babies less than 1 year of age registered in the census.

Table 8.7. Ages of New Parents, 1427–30

	Florence	*Six Cities*	*Fifteen Towns*	*Countryside*
A. Mothers				
Mean Age	27.13	28.52	29.16	29.93
Std. Dev.	7.06	7.36	8.15	8.94
Median Age	25	28	28	28
Modal Age	20	30	30	30
B. Fathers				
Mean Age	40.20	40.12	39.25	38.42
Std. Dev.	10.15	11.05	11.06	10.63
Median Age	38	40	38	36
Modal Age	40	40	40	40

merous as to be statistically significant. Thus, the age of the new parents, their residence, and their wealth can be studied with some precision. On these topics, the Catasto provides ample data for all sectors of the population at all levels of wealth.

AGES OF PARENTS

At what age did men and women usually become parents in Tuscan society? Table 8.7 presents three statistical measures of central tendency—mean or average age, median age (the value in the exact middle of the distribution), and modal or most common age—over our usual four environments. To shorten the calculations, we have used the residents of the four quarters of the Florentine countryside as an adequate proxy for the entire rural population. We should note that the age of both parents at the birth of a child should be reduced by several months, as the event took place in the year preceding the redaction of the Catasto.[28] These differences are, however, slight, and we have made no effort to adjust for them here.

Of these three measures of central tendency, the mean age best represents the time when Tuscan wives and husbands attained their maximum fertility. The standard deviation, which measures the dispersion around the mean, indicates how far the observed values deviate from it; the distance of two standard deviations, above and below the mean, delimits the range in which most observed values (about 68 percent in a normal distribution) appear.[29] We can use that distance here to define the period of high fertility, the span of years during which Tuscan mothers and fathers would have

28. Thus, for newborn babies added to the declarations at Florence in 1427–28, the average age of new mothers is 26.3 years, those of fathers, 39.6 years. These ages are slightly lower than the true ages, as they were entered into the Catasto usually a few months before the births of the babies.

29. The standard deviation is the square root of the variance, which in turn is the average of the squares of the differences between all observed values and their arithmetic mean.

most of their children. Thus, the period of high fertility for women in the city of Florence extended from approximately ages 20 to 34; the corresponding period for women of the countryside began a little later, because of a slightly later age at first marriage, and was slightly more prolonged (ages 21–38). However, the rounding off of ages to 40 artificially extends the apparent age of maternity. Tuscan males most frequently became fathers between 30 and 50 years in Florence, and between 28 and 49 in the countryside.

Table 8.7 suggests that the more urban the environment, the younger the new mother was likely to be, and the older the father. The differences between the parents' ages were therefore particularly extended in cities—13 years within Florence itself. To judge from the modal, or most common, age, the urban father, at 40 years, was sometimes twice as old as the urban mother; as much time separated the father from the mother, as the mother from their child.

A matrix of correlations (Table 8.8) allows us to examine the associations linking residence, wealth, and average age of motherhood. Another value becomes of relevance here: the average age of all married persons. This value reflects both the ages at which marriages were contracted and the ages at which they were dissolved through the death of a partner. The age of first marriage and the duration of time men and women remained within the married state directly determined whether or not they were "exposed to the risk," as demographers say, of becoming parents.[30]

These figures confirm that new mothers were distinctly younger in the more urban environments (−0.71), but so also were all married women (−0.45). This latter correlation reflects in part the earlier age at first marriage for women in the cities, but, perhaps even more, the fact that urban women, if they lost their husbands, did not remarry as readily as rural widows, and many did not remarry at all. By the statistical technique known as partial correlation we can measure the strength of the association between environment and mean age of motherhood, while holding constant the differences in the mean ages of married women. The results tell us, in effect, how environment would correlate with mean age of motherhood if women everywhere married at the same age and remained in the married state for the same duration of time. The partial correlation is −0.62. In other words, independently of earlier ages at first marriage, or of varying durations of marriage, the average urban woman bore her children

30. The standard deviation of the average age of marriage gives a useful indication of the time that most adults remained within the married state, but it says nothing about the average duration of individual marriages. We usually cannot tell whether the husband or wife had been married before.

Table 8.8. Correlation Matrix: Residence, Wealth, and Mean Age of Motherhood

	Residence	*Wealth*	*Mean Age New Mthrs*	*Mean Age Mrrd Wmn*
Residence	1.00			
Wealth	0.00	1.00		
Mean Age New Mthrs	−0.71	−0.27	1.00	
Mean Age Mrrd Wmn	−0.45	−0.66	0.55	1.00

Observations are 28; coefficients higher than 0.38 are significant at the 95 percent confidence level.

at younger ages than did women in a rural setting. Put another way, the fertility of urban women begins to decline relatively early in their married lives. Environment thus exerted a powerful influence upon the ages at which women bore children and upon the duration of time they were likely to remain fertile. The urban environment in particular seems hostile not only to the formation of new families, but also to their growth through natural reproduction.

RICH AND POOR PARENTS

Table 8.8 further indicates that wealthy women were slightly younger than poorer matrons when they became mothers ($r=-0.27$), and that they extended their period of high fertility over a slightly longer span. Wealthy men, on the other hand, were sightly older than poorer males when they became fathers ($r=0.21$), and their period of high fertility was also a little more extended ($r=0.14$). But none of these correlations is significant in a statistical sense; their weakness derives from the fact that the influence of wealth on the age of parents is everywhere quite complex. The correlations show that in an urban milieu the mean age of new mothers did not vary with wealth ($r=0.06$); on the other hand, married women were on the average much younger in wealthy households than among the poor ($r=-0.77$). If we calculate the partial correlation between wealth and mean age of motherhood, while controlling for the differences in the mean ages of all married women, then the coefficient turns significant: 0.56. This indicates that wealthy women reached their peak fertility, or maintained higher fertility, later or longer into the duration of their marriages. In other words, while the duration of time in the married state was distinctly abbreviated for wealthy women, they still matched women of lower social station in their long retention of high fertility.

Within the cities, new fathers tended to be older in wealthy households ($r=0.47$) and to beget children over a longer span of years ($r=0.32$). These correlations reflect late first marriages for wealthy urban males, but also their tendency to remarry quickly when widowed, their preference for young brides, and their continuing effort to sire new broods of children. Gregorio Dati, for example, married five times and fathered 28 children.

These correlations again indicate basic differences in the style of life differentiating rich and poor within the urban population. Cities tended to be, our data suggest, hostile to the formation and growth of families, but the rich and the poor reacted to that hostility in different ways. The time that rich women spent in marriage, under risk of pregnancy, was often cut short by the deaths of their older husbands, but, during their abbreviated married lives, they maintained high levels of fertility and produced numerous babies. In this social class there is no clear evidence that births were being artificially limited; the control of marriage was sufficient to hold the population within acceptable limits.

In the countryside, the influence of wealth on the average age of motherhood and of fatherhood is less clear than in the city. New mothers are indeed younger among the rich than among the poor ($r=-0.54$). But the correlation is weaker in rural than in urban areas. Again, taxable wealth emerges as a poor measure, in the countryside, of the material security of a family: the penniless mezzadri give evidence of comparatively high fertility, acting as if they really owned the farms they worked. Of all the inhabitants of the countryside, the families of sharecroppers show more children under age 14 for each married couple than any other social group.[31] Their large presence undermines the linear (though negative) relationship, which, in towns, connects wealth and the mean age of motherhood.

THE LIMITATION OF BIRTHS

Our analysis has so far shown that all segments of the population limited births through curtailing the duration of time men and women lived in the married state, primarily through discouraging and delaying first marriages for men and remarriages for women. But for one segment of the population there is also some evidence that births were being limited consciously and effectively within marriage itself. That segment consists of the middle and lower classes within the urban population.

Within the cities, women at the middle and low levels of the wealth pyramid appear in the survey with distinctly fewer babies than their rich neighbors.[32] The contrast is apparent even for the youngest babies less than

31. They show, on the average, 1.35 children, as against 1.15 among independent cultivators, 1.33 among leaseholders, and 1.01 among peasants of uncertain status.

32. Among married women at Florence, between 15 and 44 years, the child-woman ratio is 0.774 for those without property; and 1.214 for those found in hearths with between 1,601 and 3,200 florins. Among those belonging to the category 401–800 florins, the ratio remains low (0.857). Thus, only among the richest households, owning more than 800 florins in assets, does the ratio markedly increase.

one year in age; it does not seem likely that infant mortality alone can explain this concentration of infants in families of the affluent. Further, the deaths of infants, unless they occurred immediately after birth, would not explain why urban women of the middle and lower classes reached their peak fertility early in their marriages and bore most of their children over a short period of time.

How might the married couples of Florence have controlled their fertility? The nursing of the newborn may have had an influence. Rich mothers usually sent their babies forth from the home to be suckled; poor women nursed these babies for pay. Rich women thus lost the partial protection against a new pregnancy which nursing provides; the poor wet nurses had this period of relative infertility prolonged.[33] Also, couples burdened with children might have practiced continence in marriage; in the eyes of the Church, this was meritorious behavior. But couples used other methods as well, which the Church condemned. The great Franciscan preacher Bernardino of Siena commented explicity on the sexual mores of the Tuscans of his time. Without mincing words, Bernardino accused wives as well as husbands of acting against nature in order to prevent conception. In 1427, he condemned the women of Siena both for preventing conception and for procuring abortions:

> And this I say also to the women [he had just condemned sodomites] who are the cause that the children that they have conceived are destroyed; worse, who also are among those who arrange that they cannot conceive; and if they have conceived, they destroy them in the body. You (to whom this touches, I speak) are more evil than are murderers. . . . O cursed by God, when will you do penance? Do you not see that you, like the sodomite, are cause for the shrinkage of the world; between you and him there is no difference.[34]

Bernardino is even more explicit in castigating husbands who had intercourse with their wives in ways which were "against nature and against the proper mode of matrimony".[35] In the moral theology of the epoch, the phrase could refer to unusual positions during intercourse, or to interrupted intercourse.[36] In this passage, however, Bernardino seems to have

33. See Klapisch, 1980b.

34. Bernardino da Siena, 1880–88, p. 271. On the means and results of birth control in a traditional English community, see Wrigley, 1966.

35. Bernardino da Siena, 1880–88, p. 126.

36. Giovanni Dominici, 1860, p. 88, warns a Florentine woman against "unnatural" positions, "like a beast or a male." Contemporaries believed that these positions rendered the sex act infertile.

had foremost in mind sodomitic acts within marriage.[37] As an example of what he means, he tells of a beautiful married girl, who, after six years with her husband, remained a virgin; "she lived with him always in most grave sin against nature".[38] The desperate young woman, "consumed, moribund, pale, exhausted," had appealed for help to both the bishop and to the podestà, who responded that for them to act she had to bring proof of her husband's delinquency.

Bernardino observed that many young brides who went to their husbands did not know that such acts were sinful, but for him this was no excuse. The girls had a moral obligation to ask their mothers, and their mothers were bound to inform them. Many other married couples, according to the saint, were pretending that these sterile sexual acts within marriage were not sinful at all, or, if they admitted their guilt, they claimed to be too weak to renounce them.[39] These sinners did not even wish to hear the transgression mentioned in sermons. Bernardino himself considered that these practices were widespread in Tuscany, at least within the cities. Of every thousand marriages, he once remarked, 999 were of the devil.[40]

Bernardino marks an epoch in the history of moral theology in Tuscany. No preacher or writer before him so explicitly treats sexual practices, both inside and outside of marriage. Still, there are indications that the sexual practices he condemns had long been common in urban marriages. The Pisan preacher Giordano da Rivalto, who died in 1311, once affirmed that "out of 100 persons there was not one" who acted in marriage "according to nature, as God wishes".[41] A generation after Bernardino's death, another Sienese, Fra Cherubino, wrote a tract exclusively dedicated to the moral problems of marriage.[42] Clearly inspired by Bernardino's example, he describes at great length how husbands and wives either prevented conception or rid themselves of unwanted offspring. He repeats Bernardino's story of the young woman sodomized by her husband. He also explicitly condemns, as Bernardino apparently did not, husbands who practiced coitus interruptus, "as one who works the earth, and then throws the seed upon stone . . ."[43] Women too are condemned separately from the husbands, and among their crimes Fra Cherubino cites, as Bernardino does

37. Bernardino's admittedly guarded descriptions of contraceptive acts within marriage do not seem to refer to *coitus interruptus* but to sodomitic acts within marriage. He stresses the filth of this sort of intercourse in emphatic terms. See, for example, his condemnation of unnatural intercourse in Bernardino da Siena, 1880–88, p. 132.

38. Ibid., p. 140.

39. Ibid., p. 126.

40. Ibid., p. 95.

41. Giordano da Rivalto, 1839, 1:111.

42. Cherubino da Siena, 1888.

43. Ibid., p. 101.

not, infanticide.[44] Also in the middle of the fifteenth century, Saint Antoninus, bishop of Florence, allows husbands and wives to engage in fervent demonstrations of affection, even coitus reservatus, provided that neither the husband nor the wife is stimulated to the point where seed is released. This pastor of a sophisticated and troubled urban community, concerned for the souls of his flock, came close to separating the sexual debt and claim of marriage from procreation. "For one is not obligated," he explained, "to have more children than one can support".[45]

Moralists such as Bernardino depict in vivid language the sexual practices of fifteenth-century Tuscans; they leave no doubt that the prevention of births was known and widely practiced in Tuscan society. But these sources, no more than other documents, do not permit us to gauge the social impact of the practices to which they allude. We will hazard some conclusions by way of a preliminary assessment. The regulation of marriage and remarriage certainly constituted the most prevalent means of controlling births. But the fall off in fertility, apparently more precocious among urban women than in the countryside, implies that the former sought, in some way, to limit the size of their families well before the termination of their natural fertility. Of all groups of women encountered in urban society, the rich show the least inclination to limit births. Certainly the great families rigorously controlled their own expansion, but they achieved this primarily through the strict surveillance of the marriages of their sons and daughters. Once married, patrician women proved for the most part remarkably fertile. On the whole, they abided by the Church's moral precepts. Pregnancy, even if unwanted, was not for them a crushing economic burden.

The sectors of urban society in which the presumption of birth control seems most supported are the middle and lower classes, which, with fewer than 800 florins in wealth, are also marked by a dearth of young children. A low average age of motherhood and an abbreviated span of fertility—these are the almost classic indications that birth control is practiced within a community. Assuredly the nature of our sources precludes definite judgments. However, the moral commentators of the age typically associated these practices with poverty and the presence of many mouths asking to be fed. In sum, our data agree with the commentaries of Bernardino and

44. Ibid., p. 100.

45. Antoninus, 1474. "Si autem ante completionem actus se retrahit nec semen emittit eadem intentione non videtur mortale peccatum nisi sorte ex hoc mulier ad seminandum provocaretur. Sed si propter hoc omittit cognoscere uxorem ex communi consensu nec pagat debitum non videtur quod peccet etiam venialiter quia licet appetere non plures proles habere quam possit nutrire nec tantum ipse debitum petere nec actum inchoactum consumare nisi uxore petente. . . . " See the similar interpretation in the early fourteenth century by Peter de Palude, cited in Noonan, 1966, pp. 296–300.

Antoninus. Middle-class couples and the poor, laboring under economic constraints, rather than the rich with large resources, were prone to limit the number, risks, and burdens of pregnancies. These were the marriages which Bernardino and others regarded as the devil's own.

PARENTS AND CHILDREN

In a stimulating book Philippe Aries has argued that medieval people did not recognize childhood as a distinct period of life.[46] Of course they loved their offspring, but they tended to regard them as unformed adults and had little appreciation of the specific physical and moral attributes of the young.

The behavior of Tuscan parents lends some support to Aries's interpretation. Many among them did not really welcome the newborn baby into their hearths or hearts, at least not until it had survived the dangerous early years of life. Still, this attitude does not really prove that Tuscan parents were indifferent toward childhood and children. On the contrary, since at least the thirteenth century, the Tuscan cities were manifestly concerned with the education of children, if only because they needed persons trained in letters and in numbers to staff their shops and banks. From the thirteenth century, Tuscans and Italians generally were regarding childhood in distinctly sentimental tones.

This sentimental view of the child finds initial expression in the cult of the infant Jesus, which gains enormous popularity from the thirteenth century on. Many Tuscan and Italian (and indeed, Flemish) saints, chiefly but not exclusively women, aspire to fondle and play with the infant Christ. Thus, the Florentine widow Umiliana dei Cerchi, who died in 1246, prayed to the Virgin Mary to let her see "the child Jesus when he was three or four years old."[47] Mary granted here request, and Umiliana engaged the holy child in play and conversation. The nun Saint Agnes of Montepulciano, who died in 1317, expressed a similar desire to hold and caress the infant Jesus. Mary again delivered the sacred child to Agnes, who kept him through the night. When the mother of God returned to claim her offspring, Agnes did not want to surrender him, and the "pious contention" of the two women woke the convent.[48] Outside of Tuscany, Saint Francis himself set up the first Christmas crib, according to the *Legenda Gregorii*.[49] Saint Anthony of Padua, who died in 1231, was also observed one day fondling and kissing the child Jesus in his chamber.[50] In numerous depic-

46. Aries, 1965 and 1973.
47. ASS, Mai IV, p. 397.
48. ASS, Aprilis II, p. 797.
49. Tommaso da Celano, 1904, p. 67.
50. ASS, Junii II, p. 729.

tions across the late Middle Ages, Anthony is shown embracing the blessed child.

The cult of the child Jesus, flourishing at least since the thirteenth century, points to the presence of analogous attitudes towards children within the Tuscan homes. The little Jesus was innocent, humble, approachable, and a delight to contemplate and fondle—he was like every child. In playing with Jesus, Umiliana and Agnes were surely seeking the same emotional rewards that parents could expect to find with their own babies.

What explains this idealization of childhood and children? It may be that the pressures of living in bustling commercial centers led men and women to view childhood as a blessed period free from cares and troubles. Even the morose Morelli would later claim that nature itself made childhood the happiest period of life.[51]

By the time of the Catasto, these sentimental attitudes towards children find entirely secular expressions. Giovanni Dominici berates Florentine mothers who pass the day kissing and fondling their children, "licking" and tickling them constantly.[52] He even forbids the mother ever to smile at her little boy, "ever to show him a face which will cause him while still little to love women before knowing what they are."[53] Giovanni is here adapting an admonition out of the book of Ecclesiastes, which warned fathers not to smile at their daughters.[54] His exaggerated fear of sexuality is quite typical of contemporary religious authors. But this passage shows above all that Florentine mothers must have frequently delighted their children and themselves by repeated and warm signs of affection. Later, another Dominican, Savonarola, would underscore the purity and simplicity of the child, who brought joy to all who observed him.[55] Later still, this sentimental evaluation of the innocence of childhood found expression in the bands of young boys, who, under the friar's leadership, sought to direct Florence to a purer, holier life.[56]

How do the disasters of the late fourteenth and fifteenth centuries affect these attitudes toward children? We would say in two somewhat paradoxical ways. The horrible mortalities in the early years of life discouraged parents, we believe, from forming a deep emotional attachment with their

51. Morelli, 1969, p. 498: " . . . tempi più diletevoli alla natura."

52. Dominici, 1860, p. 151.

53. Ibid., 1860, p. 144.

54. Eccles., 7:24. Fra Paolino minorita, 1868, p. 90, repeats the counsel: "No mostrar ne faza allegra sovra d'esse." Morelli bitterly regrets that he never demonstrated his love for his dead son, but always showed him a stern countenance: "Tu non gli mostrasti mai un buon viso. . . ." Morelli, 1956, p. 501.

55. Savonarola, 1959, p. 63.

56. On the sodalities of boys at Florence and the ideal of youthful purity, see Trexler, 1974. The same author returns to the theme in his recent work, 1980.

newborn babies. This reluctance abetted the practice of dispatching the babies to wetnurses. But this same sense of their precarious hold on life led parents to lavish attention on the child when, from the age of approximately 2, its life chances were substantially better. Intense interest in the physical health as well as the moral training of the child permeates the domestic literature. Alberti devotes an entire book to the relations of the father with his son and to the specific needs, including medical, of the child as he ages. The menace to life, in other words, raised the moral and material investment which parents were willing to make in their children.

This concern with the welfare of the young affected even governmental policy. In 1421 the commune of Florence founded a hospital for the care of abandoned children, the Innocenti. Although no babies were received until a good 20 years had elapsed, the hospital was one of the first in Europe to be devoted exclusively to foundlings. In the iconography of the late Middle Ages, the figure of charity takes the form of a young woman nursing, embracing, and protecting children (previously her principal wards had been beggars and the poor).[57] Through the confraternities organized specifically for the young, the Church for its part sought better to serve their social and moral needs.[58]

If the thirteenth century had kindled an interest in the child's education and a sentimental assessment of its innocence and simplicity, the closing Middle Ages contributed a growing concern for its physical welfare. And society now gave unprecedented attention to the care of orphans and foundlings. If parents in this latter epoch were still hesitant and slow to form emotional ties with the newborn, the affection, solicitude, and material means they invested in the child, once accepted into their household, seem boundless.

57. Many authors have noted this new orientation toward children in the Quattrocento. See Bec, 1967, pp. 286–99; Klapisch, 1973a; Goldthwaite, 1972, pp. 109 –10.

58. R. C. Trexler, 1973–74b, p. 263.

9

Death

Corpora autem magis disposita ad recipiendum inpersionem huius pestis sunt indicative (=indicatione) sunta a virtute corpora debilia . . . indicatione sumpta ab aetate sunt pueri et adolescentes, a sexu vero feminae . . . indicatione sumpta ab anni temporibus sunt habentia autumnum calidum et humidum, indicatione sumpta ab arte sunt exercentia artes calidas multi laboris. . . .

These are the bodies chiefly prone to catch the plague: in strength, the weak; . . . in age, children and young people; in sex, women; . . . in time of year, those experiencing a hot and humid autumn; . . . in profession, those exercising strenuous trades requiring much exertion. . . .

—Anonymous Italian physician,
probably Florentine, late fourteenth century.

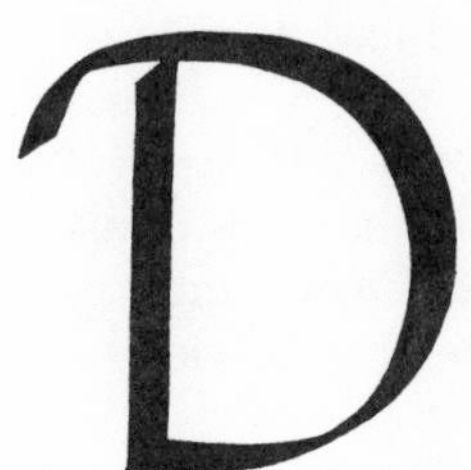

eath was present everywhere in Tuscan society in the early fifteenth century, but it remains, of all the vital events, the most difficult to investigate. The normal result of the termination of a Tuscan's life was his disappearance from the documents. The newly married and the newly born were likely to attract streams of documentary references as they lived out their lives; the dead, in contrast, did not long retain the attention of the living. We have in consequence only scattered and incomplete data on death in Tuscany, and we cannot rigorously study and compare mortalities in city and countryside, or among rich and poor. But in spite of this documentary void, we must attempt to reconstruct, at least in broad outline, how the high mortalities of the period affected Tuscan households and society.

I. Deaths in the Catasto

The Catasto, as we have often noted, was left open to corrections and changes for a period ranging from approximately one year in the city of Florence to three in certain areas of the district. The heads of households could report (and within the city were obligated to report) the deaths of family members, who were then cancelled from the declarations of the campioni.[1] For a limited period, therefore, the Catasto serves as a primitive register of deaths. How useful are the data it contains? Table 9.1

1. On the legislation concerning the declaration of mouths, see above, chap. 1, pp. 12–13.

Table 9.1. Persons Cancelled for Reason of Death in the Catasto, 1427–30

	Total Deaths	*Age Given*	*Mean Age*	*Median Age*	*Sex Ratio*
			Florence		
Men	209	193	35.6	30	143
Women	146	142	36.6	28	
			Contado		
Men	421	412	49.1	55	628
Women	67	64	43.5	50	
			District		
Men	241	222	50.8	58	287
Women	84	74	42.7	54	
			Totals		
Men	871	827	45.6	52	293
Women	297	280	38.8	45	

shows the total number of men and women whose names were cancelled on the registers after death, with their mean and median ages. It distinguishes among the principal administrative divisions of the Florentine territory, as their respective catasti were drafted at different dates.

It is at once apparent that these cancellations represent only a small fraction of the true numbers of deaths that occurred while the Catasto was open to corrections. The 1,168 deaths reported would have represented an incredibly low death rate of 4.4 per 1,000 persons in the population (the death rate in the United States in 1967 was 9.4 persons).

The reporting of deaths was especially defective in the Florentine countryside and in the district. These territories included some 86 percent of the Tuscan population, and the survey of the countryside and district was open to changes for a longer period than that of the capital. But this segment of the population accounts for only 68 percent of the reported deaths. The reason for this negligence seems apparent. In all subject territories save the city of Pisa, the household heads were allowed no deduction from their total assets for their mouths. Thus the officials of the Catasto did not press the taxpayers to inform them of the loss of family members.

The males in these territories between the ages of 14 and 70 were, however, subject to the head tax, and the household heads did have reason to report the demise of adult men. The imposition of the head tax unfortunately introduces strong and obvious biases into the registration of deaths. The sex ratio among the reported dead in the contado is a fabulous 628 men for every 100 women. In the district the figure is considerably smaller (287) because there the tax on adult men was not always calculated. Moreover, the ages of the deceased males are perceptibly bunched at the years 14 and 70.[2] Male

2. The number of boys of age 14 declared dead, 12 in all, surpasses the number of dead in the age group 8–13, 11 persons. The number of men age 70 declared to be dead (65) is also greater than those declared dead at age 60 (43) and at 80 (41).

adults liable to pay the testatico thus dominate the roll call of the dead in communities outside of Florence. As there is no way of removing this bias from the data, cancellations in the declarations unfortunately can tell us little concerning death in the Florentine contado; and their small number likewise precludes any exact study of mortalities in the district.

And what of the city of Florence itself? Citizens were obligated to report the death of all members of their households for whom they were claiming the deduction of 200 florins, but clearly many did not do so. We are aware, from other sources, of deaths which did not lead to the cancellation of names in the declarations.[3] The total of cancelled names, 355, would again represent an unbelievably low death rate of 9.3 per 1,000 in this city of aproximately 38,000. The poor in particular were negligent in reporting deaths. Of 55 deceased infants less than one year of age, 40 are found in households with more than 400 florins in total assets; in other words, 39 percent of the wealthiest households declared 73 percent of all infantile deaths.

The deaths reported in the city of Florence for 1427–28 are thus heavily biased in favor of the wealthy. The sex ratio among the deceased (143) also exceeds by far that of the total population (118). Here again, the head tax, imposed on males between 18 and 60 years of age within the city, doubtlessly prompted household heads to be more conscientious in reporting the deaths of males rather than of females.

It is, however, important to note that within the male population of the city, there is no evidence of bunching of the dead at ages 18 and 60. There is only one reported male death at age 18, and the number of men dead at age 60 is exactly the same as the number of deceased women at the same age—five persons. The personal deduction of 200 florins, which was granted to all urban residents, apparently assured that the reporting of male deaths would be reasonably well balanced with female deaths and representative of all ages. Moreover, the tax officials were prone to copy names from earlier to later surveys, often without inquiring whether the persons were living or dead. The prudent paterfamilias thus had strong reason for reporting the deaths even of male infants, lest in future years another adult male be ascribed to his family and an additional charge laid upon him.

We can, in sum, conclude that cancellations for reason of death in the urban Catasto are biased but perhaps still worth regarding. They illuminate the experiences of the rich much better than the poor, men better than women, and adults better than children.

3. According to ASF, Grascia, reg. 188, f. 101, Matteo di Agnolo, *famiglio de' Signori*, was buried on 25 October 1427, but his declaration (AC 64, f. 312. gives no notice of his death. Also, Giovanna di Matteo Salterelli, who died on 14 January 1428, does not have her name cancelled in the Catasto (AC 80, f. 399).

Within the city, if a household head took care to inform the Catasto officials of any deaths at all within his family, he was likely to do so without regard to the age of the deceased. Table 9.1 may therefore offer a fairly realistic picture of the mean and median ages of death at Florence, at least within the upper ranges of society, and at least for males. For them, the average age at death was 35.6 years, and the median age was 30. But it must also be remembered that Florence in 1427–28 was for the moment free from plague, and the plague, as we shall see, took particularly heavy tolls among children. Had the plague been raging in 1427–28, we would certainly be observing much lower mean ages of death. The ages of death, preserved in the Catasto, must therefore be regarded as high estimates of life expectancy at Florence in the early fifteenth century.

II. The "Books of the Dead"

If the Catasto, on the whole, disappoints as a register of the dead, the Florentine archives have preserved much larger censuses of the departed. These are the so-called *Libri dei morti*, or Books of the Dead.[4] Essentially, they are registrations, preserved from 1385, of the burials made within the city, principally but not exclusively by professional undertakers, the *beccamortui* or *becchini*.[5]

The decision to prepare such a register and the quality of the registrations themselves are intimately connected with the supervision of burials at Florence. The early history of the undertakers is obscure.[6] Before 1375, the becchini appear to have been loosely subject to the Guild of Spice Merchants and Physicians, the *Arte dei Medici e Speziali*. However, according to a text of 1375, not all the undertakers had been properly matriculated into the guild and many were ignoring its enactments.[7] Moreover, the populace was raising "endless complaints" against the "boundless extortions" which the avaricious undertakers were allegedly demanding for their services. In response, on December 23, 1375 the Guild of Spice Merchants and Physicians declared that all who had anything to do with the

4. On the Florentine Books of the Dead, see above all the study, which the author himself calls preliminary, by Parenti, 1943–49. On Italian *Libri dei Morti* see the general discussion in Corsini, 1974, 1:851–952. Burial registers exist elsewhere in Tuscany, notably at Arezzo, from 1373; their content has been analyzed by Varese, 1924–25; and utilized by Beloch, 1937–71, 2:170–73. A list of plague victims at Pistoia in 1400 appears in the chronicle of Luca Dominici, 1933.

5. It should be noted that these are civil, not ecclesiastical registrations, and they are among the oldest in Italy.

6. Boccaccio (*Decameron*, First Day, Introduction) dates the employment of the first undertakers from the terrible days of 1348, when families, neighbors, and friends would not, or could not, carry to the grave on their own shoulders the many who had died.

7. *Statuti*, 1922, , p. 286, "riforma" dated 23 December 1375.

burial of the dead should be subject to the Guild's authority.[8] A year later, on December 21, 1376 the Guild published a list of maximum charges which the undertakers could collect for their services—for the proclamation of the death throughout the city, the preparation of the body for burial, the invitation of mourners to the funeral, the funeral itself, and the interment. However, "considering especially the effort that must be sustained in the burials of famous men and those of high estate," the Guild waived these price ceilings in the burial of ecclesiastics, knights, judges, and medical doctors.[9] On the other hand, the becchini were exhorted to "exercise discretion" in the prices charged for burying "little boys and little girls and the poor."[10] A panel of eight guild members (two from each quarter of the city) was to hear complaints and to set a schedule of reasonable charges for the burials of children and of paupers. Finally, the undertaker in each quarter of the city was required "to notify the notary of the guild concerning the death of every person . . . before burial," under penalty of 50 pounds for each failure to do so.[11] Presumably, the Guild wished to know not only the identity of the deceased, but the status as well—whether or not it was one of the special categories in regard to burial costs. The becchini, in sum, probably reported who among the dead were very rich, very poor, or children.

The Guild of Spice Merchants and Physicians was not the only Florentine institution interested in burials. There was at least one other: the Office of the "Grascia," charged with assuring abundant food supplies for the city. The number of deaths, which constantly affected the number of consumers, partially determined the city's need for food.[12] According to its later, published statutes, the Office of the Grascia counted burials "in order to know the number of persons who inhabit the city of Florence . . . so as to be able to provide foodstuffs, which the said Office is supposed to provide."[13] In October 1377 the Florentine government, in an important reform, conferred a whole new set of responsibilities on the Office of the Grascia, including the holding of inquests regarding deaths and burials.[14]

8. Ibid., p. 286.
9. Ibid., pp. 290–93.
10. Ibid.
11. Ibid., p. 293.
12. The Statutes of 1348 already forbade citizens from accumulating more cereals than they had need of for their immediate families; the enforcement of this regulation meant that the government in one way or another had to keep a record of the size and age composition of urban households. See *Statutum*, 1934, p. 72, "De non emendo granum magis quam expediat emere pro sua familia."
13. Cited by Parenti, 1943–49, p. 292, n. 9, from the statutes of the Office dated 4 March 1579.
14. See the references to this reform of October 1377, in ASF, Grascia, 1, Statuti originali degli ufficiali di Grascia del 1378, f. 15r.

An inventory of the furnishings and possessions of the Office dated 1378 listed a "book of goatskin where the dead are inscribed."[15] As only one, presumably small book (it was written on expensive vellum) included all the registered dead, the decision to count burials was most likely taken shortly before October 1377.[16]

Both the Guild of Spice Merchants and Physicians and the Office of the Grascia thus began registering burials at approximately the same time (1376–78); it is highly probable that they collected essentially the same data in the same form. According to the communal Statutes of 1415, the becchini reported their burials to the "judicial officer of Or San Michele," who was responsible for enforcing all the regulations of the Office of the Grascia.[17] Failure to do so was again punished by a fine of 50 pounds.

Unfortunately, time has not treated these two registers kindly. Of the first, registrations have survived only from 1450.[18] These registrations are too late for our purpose, and we shall make no use of them here. The lists of burials associated with the Grascia Office have survived from 1385, but contain numerous large gaps (1413–22; 1431–38; 1450–56).[19] Moreover, these surviving lists are not always in strict chronological order and many folia and even entire fascicules are missing. These gaps in the series handicap our analysis, but, still, the total number of recorded dead is impressive. From 1385 until 1430, over the approximately 40 years before the redaction of the Catasto, the Books of the Dead enumerate 33,000 burials. However primitive and incomplete, these registrations still provide a vivid picture of various aspects of Florentine mortality in the late fourteenth and early fifteenth centuries.

ENTRIES

According to the Statutes of 1415, the undertaker was obligated to report the "name of the deceased with his surname (*pronomine*), quarter and parish."[20] In practice, he also invariably stated the place of burial and, up to 1412, his own name. The undertaker probably reported the burial in Italian, but the notary might write in either Italian or Latin. A typical entry for a deceased adult, dated July 20, 1426, is the following: "Bartolomeo di messer

15. *Statutum*, 1934, p. 254: "uno libro di carta di chavretti dove si scrivono i morti."

16. The Statutes of the Grascia of 1378 indicate that a further reason for investigating funerals and burials was enforcement of the sumptuary laws.

17. *Statuta*, 1778–81, 2:378, "Quod beccamorti notificent nomen defuncti." On the many functions of the *Officialis forensis Orti sancti Michaelis*, see *Statutum*, 1934, pp. 26–30.

18. ASF, Arte de' medici e speziali, reg. 244 ff. "Hic est liber sive quarternus continens in se notificationes mortuorum."

19. The inventory of the archives of the Grascia is printed in *Statutum*, 1934, p. 39.

20. *Statuta*, 1778–81, 2:378: "nomen defuncti cum suo pronomine, et quarterium, et populum . . . "

Palla di Nofri Strozzi, of the Strozzi family, parish of S. Maria Ughi, buried in S. Trinità."[21]

When the deceased was a child, the notary usually did not record the Christian name, but only the name of the father or the head of the household in which the child resided, as for example, in the following entry dated June 10, 1425: "A child of Giovanni di ser Nello, parish of San Lorenzo, buried in the said church. He drowned in the Mugnone."[22] The preferred terms used to identify children were *fanciullo*, *fanciulla* and their diminutives, or *puer* and *puella*. The only important departure from this practice occurred in 1430; then the notary usually gave the full names of the deceased, and did not consistently identify who among them were children.[23] Inconsistencies in the terminology and in the form of the entries make a rigorous analysis of these burials lists difficult, but do not entirely prevent it.

It should also be noted that in the years 1424, 1425, and 1430, and for some months in 1426 and 1429, the notary recorded the cause of death after the name of the deceased. As these were years in which the plague was either present or anticipated at Florence, the Office of the Grascia apparently sought this information in order to assess the severity of the plague and the rapidity of its development. We shall examine this information from the Books of the Dead later.

How useful are these data? Giuseppe Parenti concluded that the enumerated burials represented only a small part of the true number of deaths at Florence, principally because lay confraternities, hospitals, and religious houses were also engaged in burying bodies, and these interments supposedly escaped notice in the Books of the Dead.[24] He did not, however, examine the earliest registers from 1385 to 1430, perhaps because their disordered state made them difficult to study in a preliminary survey.[25] His criticisms need not necessarily apply to the earliest surviving burial lists, those redacted at a time when the statistical competence of the Florentines was probably at its peak.

The Statutes clearly require not only the professional undertakers, but all

21. The pagination of the Books of the Dead is not continuous even within the same register; citations here will be given by date alone. "Bartolomeo di messer Palla di Nofri Strozzi degli Strozzi, popolo di s. Maria Ughi, r(iposto) in s. Trinità." Grascia, 186.

22. Ibid. "Uno fanciullo di Giovanni di ser Nello, popolo di s. Lorenzo, r. in detta chiesa. Affogò in Mugnone."

23. In 1430 the number of masculine names given without further description is 1,192 out off 1,458 entries (81.8 percent). In the entire series, the proportion is only 47 percent (8,248 out of 17,568). This indicates that in 1430 the notary did not scrupulously distinguish children from adults. During this year of plague, he may have been too occupied to bother with this distinction.

24. Parenti, 1943–49, p. 294, affirms that the Books are reliable only after 1782.

25. His analysis commences only in 1458.

who had anything to do with burials to report them. The early registers show that religious houses, confraternities, and hospitals, as well as the becchini, did in fact report the burials they had made. For example, on January 29, 1398, an unnamed nun of the convent of "Sancta Maria mater" died and was buried by her religious sisters.[26] The members of his convent also buried Brother Bonacursus de Davino of the Carmelite order.[27] The surviving necrology of friars from the Dominican convent of Santa Maria Novella contains names which also appear in the Books of the Dead. Thus, Frater Franciscus Geri, who died on November 17, 1399, appears in the Book of the Dead under the same date; the entry notes that the Dominican friars had buried him.[28]

The schedule of maximum charges, dated 1376, mentions burials "in the tomb of a company."[29] This indicates that "companies" or lay confraternities often employed professional undertakers to perform their burials. The registrations also contain entries which almost certainly refer to burials by the brothers of a confraternity.[30] Finally, those who died in hospitals also appear among the departed, even when they were buried in the hospital's own cemetery.[31]

Were some Florentine dead buried privately, by families or friends, without engaging the help of undertakers or of institutions? For several reasons private burials, which might have escaped the notice of the undertakers, were all but impossible within the city. The communal Statutes require that the doors of a house in which a death had occurred be "opened," so that officials could enter and investigate whether the regulations concerning burials had been conscientiously followed.[32] The religious ethos of the age placed great value on prayers for the dead and burial in consecrated ground, which required that the body be taken through the city from the place of death to the place of interment. The same religious ethos also insisted that the youngest child or the meanest beggar was equal in spiritual dignity to the greatest citizen and had equal right to a Christian burial.

26. Grascia 186, 29 January 1398: "decessit quedam monacha de s. Maria matre de popolo s. Laurentii . . . sepulta fuit in dicta ecclesia per monacas."

27. Grascia 187, 28 August 1398: "Frater Bonaccursus de Davino ordinis fratrum carmeletanorum . . . per eos sepultus fuit."

28. *Necrologio*, 1955, 1:141: Frater Franciscus Geri; and Grascia 187, 17 November 1399, "unus frater Gieri ordinis fratrum predicatorum."

29. *Statuti*, 1922, p. 292: "Per riserrare ogni avello in che sepellissono il morto, soldi venti pic. Salvo se si sotterrasse il morto in avello di compangnia, non possino torre per uno più che soldi x. pic."

30. Grascia 187, 27 October 1398: "Advardus pontenarius populi s. Margherite . . . per fratres dicte ecclesie."

31. Grascia, 187, 13 June 1400: "decessit unus puer nomine Iohannes . . . in hospitale et ibi sepultus." Grascia 188, 17 June 1430, "Sandra una delle fanciulle dell'ospiedale della Scala."

32. *Statuta*, 1778–81, 2:387: "Quod aperiantur ostia domus, in qua fierent nuptiae vel esset mortuus"; this regulation clearly was connected with the enforcement of sumptuary laws.

Did those traditionally elusive segments of the population—beggars, prostitutes, criminals, foreigners, and immigrants—die without notice taken in the Books of the Dead? The Florentine underworld seems well represented in our city of the dead. In 1395 a Gualterius, "who roamed and begged for alms for the love of God," is entered among the departed, and in 1405 there appears a "maid of pleasure," otherwise unnamed.[33] Criminals, convicted and executed for capital offenses, are also registered, although not in large numbers: according to the entries from 1385 to 1430, only 18 Florentines, all of them males, paid the supreme penalty. In 1400 the ranks of the deceased include "a certain Iulianus, a foreigner who wished to go to Rome"; doubtless this luckless pilgrim had hoped to visit St. Peter's tomb in this year of jubilee.[34] In 1425 a foreigner from Flanders, named Cristiano, was buried; he sang in the episcopal choir and had probably come to Florence for that purpose.[35] In 1426 a pauper of unknown name and origins was found drowned in the Arno, perhaps a suicide; he was buried, the undertaker reported, "for the love of God".[36] In other words, even the departed whose names were known only to God still gained a notice in the Books of the Dead. Finally, the city of the dead has its army: 25 *stipendarii*, probably foreign mercenaries; and 21 *provisionati*, hired soldiers of presumably local origins. Firearms were already claiming casualties: in 1430 Agnolo di Francesco was killed by cannon, *di bombarda*, presumably in the war against Lucca.[37]

Although our tests are impressionistic, this survey of the Florentine dead reveals no systematic omissions. The becchini seem at pains to show how well they served the transient and the destitute, perhaps to refute the charge against them that they exploited the needy. But in burying bodies and recording names, did not the undertakers unconsciously favor certain segments of society—men over women, adults over children, the rich over the poor? Burial in consecrated ground was the hope of the dying and a duty for the living—the ultimate service and charity which Christians owed to all their departed brethren, even, and perhaps especially, the humblest. And the purpose of registering any burials—control of prices, or estimation of the number of grain consumers in the city—would have been defeated if the becchini had systematically underreported the deaths which were occurring in any particular social group.

33. Grascia 186, 3 January 1395: "decessit Gualterius qui ambulabat et petebat elimosinam per amorem Dei." Grascia 187, 19 August 1405: "famula de piacere."

34. Grascia 186, 11 May 1400: "decessit quidam Iulianus forensis qui volebat ire Romam."

35. Grascia 187, 30 July 1425: "Cristiano di Fiandra cantore in vescovado . . . affogò."

36. Grascia 188, 27 June 1426: "uno povero che affoghò in Arno risposto in s. Maria dei Magnoli pell'amore di dio."

37. Grascia 188, 29 May 1430: "Agnolo di Francesco legnaiolo popolo di s. Stefano a Ponte r. nella detta chiesa di bombarda."

How can we test our aggregated numbers of the dead for internal consistency and coherence, and look for indications of systematic omissions? From 1385 to 1430, in spite of many gaps, the Books of the Dead record the burials of 17,560 men and 15,341 women. This represents a sex ratio of 114 men per 100 women—not greatly different from the sex ratio of 118 prevailing in the city of Florence in 1427. There is, to be sure, a visible tendency in the Books of the Dead to masculinize the names of children, or, more commonly, the words used to describe them. For example, 1,781 male fanciulli are counted among the dead, and only 1,337 female fanciulle (the sex ratio, 133, also approaches that figure for the entire population of children entered in the Catasto).[38] The undertaker, or perhaps the hurried notary, seems to have described some dead children as boys when they were truly girls. The Catasto itself, as we noted in chapter 5, shows a comparable tendency to give the names of children, or references to them, in masculine form.[39] Apart from this apparent inaccuracy in reporting the sex of deceased children, there is no evidence that females were systematically omitted; as the sex ratio of 114 shows, women are, on the whole, well represented in the ranks of the departed.

Neither are there indications that the undertakers reported the deaths of adults more consistently than those of children. It is worth noting that even stillbirths are mentioned in the lists.[40] Even if no account is taken of the presumed inconsistency in identifying children in 1430, 41 percent of the total (13,513 persons) are explicitly described as children.[41] Another 5.3 percent (1,820) are presumably so, as they appear as dependent sons or daughters, or grandchildren, usually unnamed, in the households of their parents. We can also assume that the 154 persons described as apprentices or servants were children or adolescents. Finally, some 1,325 girls (some 4 percent of the deceased) bear names, but not the title *monna* given to married and widowed women; presumably they died before marriage.[42] Adding all these groups together, we arrive at a proportion of children and youths amounting to one-half (50.6 percent) of the dead (see Table 9.2). Although we must allow for wide margins of uncertainty in our estimates, we may still conclude that between 40 and 50 percent of the recorded dead are children or dependents.

38. See above, chap. 5, pp. 133–36.

39. See above, chap. 5, pp. 134; 140–141.

40. About a dozen in number; see below, Table 9.3.

41. See below, Table 9.2.

42. These girls are given a personal name but do not bear the title *monna* usual for married women and for widows; they were probably younger than the usual age of marriage for girls (18 years).

Are the poor and the destitute underrepresented in the lists of the dead? The undertakers frequently identified the paupers they had buried at low cost or entirely "for the love of God." Between 1385 and 1398 the number of deceased persons identified as paupers in the lists ranges between 10 and 20 percent of all the dead.[43] Women, many of them aged widows, predominate among the deceased paupers, as they did in the oldest levels of the urban population.[44] After the great plague of 1400, the number of paupers among the deceased falls and does not surpass 8 percent from 1401 to 1430. Various factors, not mutually exclusive, may explain this diminution of paupers. Perhaps the undertakers or the notaries were failing to provide this information, but perhaps too the plague itself had radically thinned the numbers of impoverished Florentines. Also, the plague may have allowed or persuaded widows to rejoin the hearths of their sons, which deaths had partially depleted.

Over the period 1385–30, the Books of the Dead pass these tests of internal consistency and coherence rather well. There is no evident underreporting of any segment of Florentine urban society. The Florentine undertaker, if he took the trouble to report burials. was likely to report them all. The lists of burials, in other words, may be considered an unbiased sample of all the deaths which occurred within the city. This encouraging conclusion does not, however, give assurance that the total number of burials, recorded in the Books, approaches the true number of urban deaths. We do not know whether all the undertakers in the city reported their burials, only that those who did so acted without apparent bias. Rather, in 1375, the Guild of Spice Merchants and Physicians complained that not all becchini were properly matriculated in the Guild and not all were obeying its regulations.[45] Can we then determine whether or not these registrations of the dead are complete?

NUMBERS

Both the Guild of Spice Merchants and Physicians and the Office of the Grascia seem to have encountered difficulty in securing compliance from all the Florentine becchini. The Office of the Grascia, for example, tried to impose an oath upon the undertakers that they would faithfully report all burials. But the number of becchini who took the official oath, usually twice a year, was always lower than the number of those who are known to

43. The proportion of paupers is 20.4 percent (23 out of 113 burials) in 1385, 20.5 percent in 1396 (53 out of 259) and 18.0 percent in 1398 (214 out 1187).

44. In 1385, for example, 16 percent of the deceased males were paupers, as against 30 percent of the women.

45. See above, n. 7.

Table 9.2. Burials Reported in the Florentine "Books of the Dead," 1385–1430

Year	*Men*	*Women*	*Total*	*Number Undertakers*	*Number Days*	*Estimated Totals*
1385	75	38	113	21	104	397
1386	218	143	361	25	279	472
1387	241	234	475	24	281	617
1388	460	414	874	34	328	973
1389	280	232	512	31	178	1,050
1390	508	373	881	42	325	989
1391	257	235	492	28	227	791
1392	95	105	200	28	149	490
1393	187	194	381	24	182	764
1394	423	421	844	28	314	981
1395	297	256	553	20	220	917
1396	145	114	259	27	98	965
1397	578	470	1,048	37	313	1,222
1398	619	568	1,187	34	364	1,190
1399	735	671	1,406	37	362	1,418
1400	5,741	4,665	10,406	51*	353	10,760
1401	362	339	701	39	295	867
1402	186	162	348	36	173	734
1403	198	172	370	41	183	738
1404	92	61	153	27	75	745
1405	383	317	700	40	308	830
1406	487	391	878	41	355	902
1407	264	265	529	34	319	605
1408	236	191	427	33	173	901
1409	349	287	636	40	177	1,312
[1410	4	4	8	5	3	973]
1412	247	202	449	48	137	1,196
1424	696	629	1,325		180	2,687
1425	508	437	945		362	953
1426	343	351	694		365	694
1427	257	267	524		313	611
1428	240	274	514		266	705
1429	399	347	746		364	748
1430	1,458	1,512	2,970		286	3,790

*No undertakers named after July.
SOURCE: ASF, Grascia, reg. 186–188.

have buried bodies in the city.[46] This implies that the supervision exerted over the undertakers remained lax, even after the reforms of 1375–76.

The Books themselves provide a partial index of the quality of the reporting. From 1385 until 1412 the entries record the names of the undertakers who reported burials, and we can judge from their numbers how effective was the Office in collecting data on urban burials.

Table 9.2 gives for each year from 1385 to 1430 the number of reported burials. The table also shows the number of undertakers who reported

46. Thus, in 1386, 16 undertakers took the oath, but 25 registered burials.

deaths from 1385 to 1412 (comparable information is unfortunately lacking from 1424 to 1430).[47] Because the record contains numerous gaps, we have also sought to estimate the true number of burials for those years in which the record of burials is incomplete. For each year, we added up the number of days represented in the lists. A day was considered missing only when evident physical damage to the Books deprived us of any reference to it. On the basis of the days represented, we calculated for each year a daily average of burials, and then multiplied the average by 365, in order to arrive at the estimate for total deaths in that year.

As Table 9.2 shows, the number of undertakers reporting burials fluctuated erratically from 1385 to 1396, and in the light of this instability we cannot place confidence in the total number of recorded burials. From 1397, however, the number of becchini named in the lists is high, consistently more than thirty, and remains relatively stable. Only in 1404 does their number fall to slightly below thirty, but this was a year during which many days, 290, are altogether missing from the record. Even if all Florentine burials were not perfectly reported, we can assume that after 1397 the estimated totals approach the true number of deaths, and that variations in the totals reflect actual movements of mortality levels at Florence.

The year of the major epidemic, 1400, does, however, present a special problem. The numerous burials required in the late summer and fall clearly exceeded the capabilities of the professional undertakers. Additional gravediggers were apparently hired to bury the thousands of plague victims.[48] From July 1400, until the waning of the onslaught in early 1401, the notaries no longer recorded the names of the undertakers, probably because no accurate record could be kept amid the carnage. Not surprisingly, the total number of burials entered in 1400—11,000—is almost certainly too low. Giovanni Morelli, who lived through this disaster, placed the number of victims at 20,000.[49] The huge mortalities associated with a major epidemic partially disrupted the Florentine system of supervising and recording burials. On the other hand, the system seems to have functioned reasonably well in normal years, when burials were generally less than 1,500.

MORTALITY RATES

What do these estimated totals of burials tell us about the death rate at Florence? We shall single out for special attention the years 1424–30, which embrace the date of the Catasto; it is of course difficult to judge whether or not these seven years were typical of the epoch. Moreover, we should note

47. Because of ambiguities in the names given, the number of undertakers given in the table is only an approximation.

48. The lists mention burials "per laboratores"; see reg. 187, 3 June 1400.

49. Morelli, 1956, p. 368: "morì circa di ventimila boche dentro . . . "

that during this period, the plague made its appearance in the city in 1424 and again in 1430; the two outbursts were of medium severity. During the seven years under study, Florence does not seem to have suffered extraordinary losses—surely nothing comparable to those it endured in 1400. But neither did the city enjoy complete immunity from plague, the bane of late medieval life. The annual mean of urban deaths (based on our estimates for complete years) is 1,445. As the city in 1427 had a population of some 40,000 persons (including clergy and religious), the number of burials would indicate an annual mortality figure of 36.4 deaths for every 1,000 inhabitants.

The true rate was almost certainly higher than this estimate. In a stagnant or slightly falling population, it must have equalled or exceeded the birth rate (40 per thousand and above) which probably prevailed in Florence in the fifteenth century.[50] Nonetheless, the minimal rate we have calculated still exceeds rates characteristic of other premodern societies also subject to epidemics.[51]

But perhaps more remarkable than this high average toll is the violence with which that toll could fluctuate from year to year (see Figure 9.1). Although the fluctuating numbers of becchini calls into question the completeness of the early registrations, especially for the plague year of 1390, nonetheless, for the subsequent years, the graph merits credibility.

During a major epidemic, such as that of 1400, the number of daily burials could soar to levels ten times greater than those registered during years of respite. Even during lesser contagions, as those of 1424 and 1430, daily burials were multiplied by a factor of 4 or 5. In 1430 the plague claimed at least one out of every 10 residents of the city. In 1400 the death rate may well have surpassed 300 per thousand, if contemporaries were correct in asserting, as they did, that one-third of the population died.

DEATHS BY AGE

Only rarely do the Books of the Dead supply the exact ages of the deceased, but usually they identify who among the departed were children. They also give indications of profession and, for women, marital status. As there was no strict compulsion to identify children, we must assume that those enumerated among the deceased represent minimal figures. Still, the proportions of dead children can illuminate mortality patterns at Florence in the period of the Catasto. Table 9.3 shows the distribution by presumed age categories of the deaths recorded over the entire range of the entries studied, from 1385 to 1430.

50. See above, chap. 3, pp 67–68.

51. In his study of Venice in the modern period, Beltrami calculated a general mortality rate for the last third of the sixteenth century of 30 per thousand; at Mantua in the early sixteenth century, the rate was also 30. See Reinhardt *et al.*, 1968, p. 114; Wrigley, 1968.

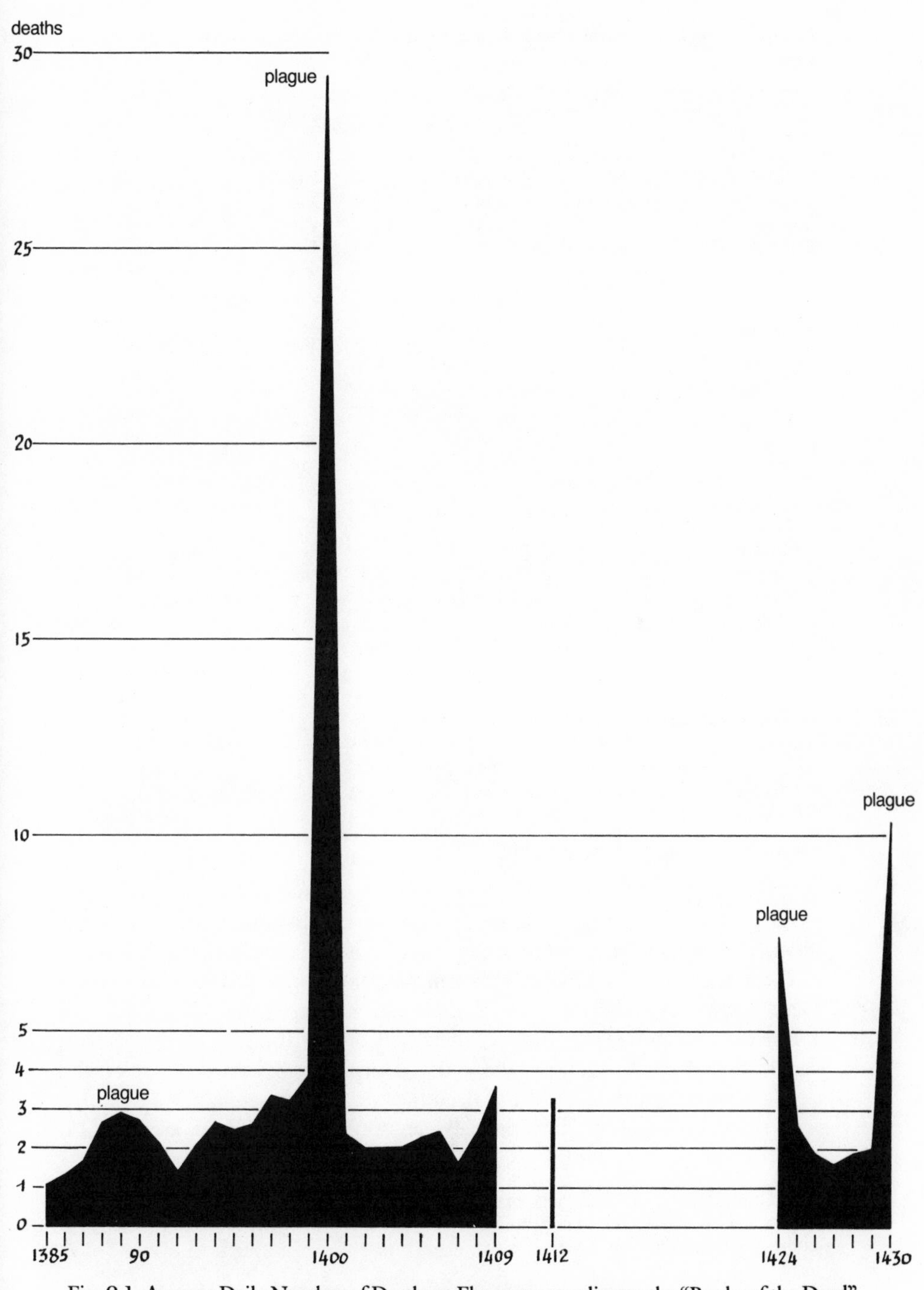

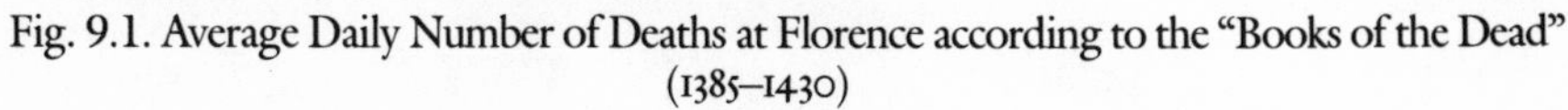
Fig. 9.1. Average Daily Number of Deaths at Florence according to the "Books of the Dead" (1385–1430)

Table 9.3. Florentine Deaths by Age Categories according to the "Books of the Dead," 1385–1430

Age Category	*Males*	*Females*	*Totals*
	I. *Little Children*		
Newly born	46	45	91
"Bambolino"*	29	27	56
"Parvulus"	348	246	594
"Infantulus"	299	189	488
"Fanciullino"	146	128	274
Totals	868	635	1,503
	II. *Children*		
"Fanciullo"	1,781	1,337	3,118
"Puer," "Puella"	4,744	3,994	8,738
Totals	6,525	5,331	11,856
	III. *Dependents*		
"Figlio"	806	952	1,758
"Nipote"	46	16	62
Totals	852	968	1,820
	IV. *Youths*		
"Discipulus"	4	14	18
"Garzonus"	42	—	42
"Iuvenis"	88	6	94
Totals	134	20	154
	V. *Adults*		
Undetermined	9,048	403	9,451
Presumed Single		1,325	1,325
Presumed Married		4,235	4,235
Widowed		2,287	2,287
Clergy and Religious	141	137	278
Totals	9,189	8,387	17,576
Grand Totals	17,568	15,341	32,909

*Feminine forms of most terms end in "a."

To be sure, we cannot assume that the descriptive qualifiers in the table identify children within precise age ranges. A deceased girl, aged 9 years, can still appear as an *infantula parvuncula*, and a male baby, dead at birth (*sopra parto*) is described as a *fanciullo*, rather than a *fanciullino* or *bambolino*.[52] These terms only crudely reflect distribution of the ages at death, but they do at least allow us to distinguish between adults and children in the great mass of the dead.

In making this gross division between adults and children, we can also

52. Grascia, 187, 1 July 1398: "una infantula Fagii tiratoris paupera parvuncula de viiii annis." Grascia, 188, 11 April 1425: "fanciullo del figliuolo del Barra sensale . . . sopra parto." The mother died the following day.

Table 9.4. Estimated Deaths of Female Children, Married Women, and Widows, 1397–1401

Year	*Female Children*	*Index*	*Married Women*	*Index*	*Widows*	*Index*
1397	230	100.0	132	100.0	113	100.0
1398	179	77.8	205	155.3	126	95.5
1399	301	130.9	230	174.2	88	66.7
1400	2,894	1258.3	985	746.2	260	197.0
1401	145	63.0	174	131.8	67	50.8

NOTE: Totals are adjusted for missing days.

seek to estimate the age specific death rates for children and adults in the years 1424 to 1427, when total population size is known through the Catasto.[53] The results of this exercise show the extreme volatility of death rates, especially for children. During the epidemic of 1424, fairly mild in Florence, the death rate for children soared to approximately 103 per thousand—nearly twice as high as the comparable rate for adults (53 per thousand). But in 1427, in the total absence of plague, the death rate for children was only 14 per thousand, even lower than that of adults (19 per thousand).

The volatility of the death rate for children implies that younger persons in the population were the plague's principal victims. We can test this assumption specifically for women. The marital status of deceased women gives us a rough indication of their ages. In 1427 the 6,443 married women in the urban population show an average age of 35.2 years; widows, on the other hand, were considerably older, with an average age of 59.5 years. How did the plague affect these three categories of urban women: children and unmarried girls, married women, and widows. Table 9.4 shows the number of deaths in each category before, during, and after the great epidemic of 1400.

Among widows, in the epidemic of 1400, the number of deaths increased by a factor of 2.25 over the average number of deaths recorded during the preceding three years. Among married women, the factor rises to 5.21, and among female children, to a remarkable 12.23. The younger the age cohort, the more volatile was its death rate, and the greater its vulnerability to plague. Several conclusions follow. If a Florentine lived through one major epidemic, she or he enjoyed improved chances of surviving the next. Age either conferred a certain immunity, or showed that the person already possessed high resistance to the infection. Those who resisted infection also earned improved chances of marrying and reproducing, and perhaps of passing on their good health to their children. Slowly and painfully, the

53. Estimated death rates for the years 1424–30 are given in Herlihy and Klapisch-Zuber, 1978, Table 73, p. 460.

Florentine community may have been building up its biological resistance to the disease which mercilessly flailed it in the fourteenth century.

SEX

Because of ambiguities in reporting the sex of children, it is difficult to speak with any assurance concerning the influence of sex in the early years of life. Superfically considered, the data presented in Table 9.2 suggest that little girls fared slightly better than little boys, as they died in smaller numbers. However, according to contemporary medical tracts, the plague was more dangerous for females than for males; the epidemic of 1424 at Florence seems, in fact, to have taken a greater relative toll of little girls than of little boys.[54]

Among adults, the reporting of sex in the list of burials is presumably accurate, but the base population—the Florentine urban community—is itself affected by immigration, which in turn influences death rates by sex. Women, for example, come to predominate in the oldest age levels in the city; the sex ratio among those 65 and older in the city is 89 men per 100 women. We have one indication that women were more successful than men in reaching, in old age, a natural termination of their lives. In listing the causes of death in 1424, 1425, and 1430, the undertakers noted that 92 men succumbed to "old age" (*vecchiaia*); the number of women who died for the same reason was an extraordinary 226. Again, it is impossible to adjust for the immigration of aged women into the city. But not even at the most advanced age levels does the sex ratio of the urban population dip to the low levels, 41 men per 100 women, found among the victims of old age. At least in the estimation of the becchini, women, far more frequently than men, were able to live out the full allotment of days that nature intended.

CAUSES OF DEATH

The undertakers over a period of several years (1424–30) give us a glimpse, episodically, of the major causes of death (in fact, relatively few Florentines died because of vecchiaia). They were particularly scrupulous in recording deaths from plague. The notary usually scribbled "di segno" ("with the mark") in the margin to the right of the burial entry, and added a large "P" in front of the name. Those among the dead who fell victim to the plague, at least in its bubonic form, are therefore easily identified. The becchini were, however, less concerned with reporting deaths from other causes, and these they give systematically only in 1424, when the plague was present in the city; in 1425, when it had abated but another outbreak was feared; and in 1430, when it struck once more. Deaths from the plague in

54. See, for example, the epigraph to this chapter, taken from Sudhoff, 1913, p. 314.

1424 and 1430 were so many as nearly to overwhelm all other causes of death. But for 1425, we are fortunate to have a list of fatal diseases at a time when the plague had nearly vanished from Florence.

The notations of the becchini, giving cause of death, highlight a recurrent theme in this study—the extraordinary devastation of the late-medieval epidemics, even the comparatively mild infections of 1424 and 1430. Over the seven years from 1424 to 1430, out of 7,718 recorded burials, 3,196 (41.4 percent) of the deceased were victims of plague. Even in the absence of major epidemics, two out of every five Florentines passed from this world with the mark of the plague upon their bodies. Within the population as a whole, the plague seems to have been indifferent to the sex of its victims; it accounts for 41.2 percent of male deaths and 41.5 percent of female deaths. Interestingly, however, little girls were more susceptible to plague infection than little boys, while adult women on the whole fared better than adult men.[55]

The notes of the becchini allow us to confirm and to refine the conclusion reached above, that the plague was particularly devastating for the young. In 1424, 604 out of 874 plague deaths, or 69.11 percent of all recorded deaths, were of children or dependents. Three out of every four children or dependents who died in 1424 succumbed to plague. Susceptibility to plague was thus a function of age, but here one nuance must be added. Comparatively few babies fell victim to plague, perhaps because many were being nursed in the countryside. In 1424, for example, among the 41 deceased little children, there are only 10 plague victims; among those described as children and presumably older, 590 out of 673, or a remarkable 76 percent, were victims. Of course babies, like the aged, may show relative immunity to plague because they were subject to so many other fatal illnesses. Still, from year to year, the deaths of babies remain considerably more stable than the deaths of older children, who were the preferred targets of plague attacks.

In Table 9.5 we have ranked the principal causes of death for both men and women. In interpreting the relative numbers of victims, it should be remembered that the deaths from plague are recorded for the entire seven years from 1424 to 1430, but deaths from other causes are given substantially only for the years 1424, 1425, and 1430.

It is useful for subsequent analysis to see also how deaths from these illnesses were distributed by months. This is done in Table 9.6.

The plague, as we have had occasion to note previously, was highly seasonal in its impact, claiming 77.5 percent of all its victims in the hot

55. From 1424 to 1430, among the victims of the plague are 237 fanciulli and 326 fanciulle, 148 figli and 184 figlie. Among the adults are 1,136 men and 1,030 women.

Table 9.5. Principal Causes of Death at Florence, 1424–30

	Men			*Women*		
Rank	*Cause*		*No.*	*Cause*		*No.*
1	Plague		1,620	Plague		1,576
2	Diarrhea			Old Age		226
	"bachi"	98		Diarrhea		
	"pondi"	93		"bachi"	77	
	"uscito"	7		"pondi"	59	
			198	"uscito"	5	
3	Fever		131			141
4	Old Age		92	"Long Illness"		79
5	"Long illness"		79	Fever		73
6	Smallpox		54	Natal deaths		
7	Natal deaths			"sconciatura"	8	
	"sconciatura"	2		"nato innanzi		
	"nato innanzi			il tempo"	22	
	il tempo"	23		neonatal	13	
	neonatal	20				43
			45	Epilepsy		39
8	Epilepsy		42	Smallpox		37
9	Violent and acci-			Childbed deaths		
	dental deaths		28	"sconciasi"	6	
10	Catarrh			"sopra parto"	26	
	"catarro"	1				32
	scesa	19		Pulmonary diseases		
			20	"tisico"	24	
11	Pulmonary diseases			"tossa"	1	
	"ambascia"	4				25
	"tisico"	12		Catarrh		
	"tossa"	1		"catarro"	6	
			17	"scesa"	12	
12	Hydropsy		7			18
13	Apoplexy		7	Hydropsy		10
14	Gout		5	Violent and acci-		
				dental deaths		8
				Apoplexy		5
	Totals		2,345			2,312

months of July, August, and September. Diarrhea, a chief symptom of gastrointestinal diseases, was also strongly and similarly seasonal in its appearance. Even the vaguely defined "long illness" shows a seasonal rhythm, suggesting that those members of the community who had long been sick were likely to fail in the summer. On the other hand, deaths from fever seem to have peaked in both summer and winter, in December and January, which suggests that different diseases were involved. Finally, deaths from old age were distributed with remarkable consistency throughout the year, showing only a slight increment in July and August—the most dangerous months for younger members of the community. The newborn disappear in greatest numbers in the hot months. This cannot be attributed to a seasonal rhythm of conceptions, as the deaths of women due

Table 9.6. Distribution of Deaths by Months at Florence, 1424–30

Month	*Plague*	*Old Age*	*Fever*	*"Long Illness"*	*Diarrhea*	*Natal Deaths*	**All Deaths*
Jan.	5	26	18	0	6	2	83
Feb.	5	24	3	7	14	4	72
March	10	28	12	3	18	4	96
April	28	18	17	5	13	14	115
May	92	28	15	15	12	5	201
June	277	27	28	13	19	12	412
July	679	36	22	32	40	18	893
August	906	31	26	30	110	11	1,177
Sept.	746	25	25	22	69	4	939
Oct.	374	26	16	14	18	4	485
Nov.	61	25	9	11	9	5	147
Dec.	13	24	13	6	5	5	91

*Totals of all deaths in period for which cause is stated.

to childbirth (not presented in the table) do not show an analogous fluctuation. Probably the newborn, like older children, were victims of gastrointestinal disturbances.

These fatal illnesses attacked men and women with different measures of severity. Distinctly more men than women succumbed to diarrhea, fever, smallpox, epilepsy, and gout (no women at all were killed by this last ailment). Men were also more likely than women to suffer violent or accidental death.[56] Women, on the other hand, were more commonly the victims of consumption and pulmonary diseases, and they were of course uniquely exposed to the dangers of the childbed. And, as we have noted, many more women than men died *di vecchiaia*,.

The risks of bearing children merit special attention. Adjusting for missing days in our lists of burials, we can estimate that 52 women died in childbirth in the years 1424, 1425, and 1430—an average of 17.3 deaths per year. Let us assume that approximately 1,200 babies were born in Florence in each of these years (in 1427, 1,088 babies are listed under one year of age, but this figure must be adjusted upward for reason of natal deaths and because of the tendency to report babies 10 or 11 months old as exactly age 1). The maternal mortality rate in the city of Florence then would be 14.4 deaths for every 1,000 births. Out of every 69 women who gave birth, one died from puerperal complications. About one-fifth of the deaths of married women in Florence seem to have been associated with childbearing.

56. The Catasto itself confirms these observations. Gout appears frequently in the western Florentine territory, in the towns, and affects only males. Amputations or crippling diseases, accidents, and mutilations are also almost exclusively male disabilities and are cited in order to gain exemption from the head tax. On the other hand, unspecified illnesses and old age are more usually attributed to women.

The lists of the dead also identify 33 babies who died shortly after birth, 45 who were "born before the time" (presumably premature), and even 10 *sconciature*, presumably aborted fetuses or stillbirths.[57] Adjusting for missing days in the lists, we can estimate that the total number of babies who died at, or shortly after, birth would be 142 for the three years in which reporting is good (1424, 1425, and 1430), an average of 47 per year. These estimates remain, however, difficult to interpret, as we do not know the exact number of births and the exact time of death, data necessary for evaluating neonatal mortality.

Among older children, plague was by far the most vicious killer, but our list of fatal illnesses identifies other major threats to a child's life. Gastrointestinal disorders, manifest in diarrhea, chiefly attacked children. After plague the most common cause of death for children was *mal di bachi*, "worms." All its 175 victims (98 males and 77 females) were children. The disease was attributed to the purported or real presence of worms in the intestines, which induced diarrhea and dehydrated the victim. Closely related to the mal di bachi was *mal di pondi*, or "illness of weights," so called because the infected persons, again suffering from diarrhea, felt as if they carried weights in their lower intestine. Of the 152 victims, 115 (93 males and 59 females), or more than 75 percent, were children. Similarly, five out of seven Florentines who died from *uscita*, still another word for diarrhea, were children.

Another killer preeminently of the young was *vaiolo* or smallpox. Alberti placed it first in the causes of infantile deaths, ahead of "eruptions and rashes and intestinal inflamations."[58] Of the 91 who succumbed to smallpox in the Florentine population, 68 (31 males and 37 females), or 75 percent, were children. Children were also the favored prey of the *malmaestro*, epilepsy, to which 81 Florentine deaths were attributed (23 males and 32 females, 78 percent of whom were children).[59] Fever, on the other hand, took an equal toll of children and adults. Apoplexy, consumption (*tisico*), hydropsy, gout, and the obscure "long illness" were predominantly, when not exclusively, diseases of later life.

This review of the causes of death highlights the importance of gastrointestinal disorders as a killer of children. These disorders were highly seasonal in their impact, peaking in the hot months of summer and early

57. The word scionciasi remains somewhat ambiguous; it isn't always clear whether the deceased is the mother or child. In the ten instances cited here, however, the baby is explicitly identified.

58. Alberti, 1960, 1:35.

59. The Catasto also attributes this disease more to children than to adults. In the region of Barga, and in certain zones of the county of Arezzo where the malmaestro is frequent, it is associated almost exclusively with children.

autumn (a pattern found as well in other premodern societies). Certainly a contaminated water supply was responsible for many of these deaths. It is, however, worth noting that widespread malnutrition in a population also makes its presence visible in intestinal disorders among the young. Moreover, it weakens the resistance of children to other forms of infection. Even today, in some poverty-stricken areas of Central America, "worms" are listed as a cause of children's deaths, when, according to nutritionists, the basic reason is acute malnutrition. We may suppose that the deaths allegedly from worms at Florence also reflected, in some measure, malnutrition among its poorer families. This hypothesis would help explain one distinctive characteristic of Florentine households. The cohort of urban children, as it aged, came to be more and more concentrated in the households of the advantaged, as we showed in the previous chapter. Perhaps one reason for this was that the children of the poor, in greater numbers than the offspring of the rich, fell victim to these murderous worms.[60]

Death thus reaped an ample harvest even in years such as 1424 and 1430, which did not witness major epidemics. Even then the plague was responsible for more than two deaths in five, and children and young adults made up the largest contingent of Florentine victims. Probably death depleted the ranks of the poor more severely than those of the rich: it seems especially to have thinned the ranks of children from destitute families. We have no way of measuring deaths in the countryside, but the village was probably healthier than the city; contemporaries at least fervently believed that this was so.[61] In sum, the mortalities that afflicted Florence and Tuscany in the epoch of the Catasto are notable above all for their violent annual fluctuations and for the occasional, brutal unleashing of a major epidemic. Under these conditions of mortality, as frightening as they were constant, Tuscans had to face the redoubtable task of assuring the stability, the prosperity, and the survival of their families.

60. See, for comparison, Neveux, 1968, giving data from Cambrai in 1377–1473.
61. See, for example, Alberti, 1960, 1:200.

10
The Hearth

Vorrei tutti i miei albergassero sotto uno medesimo tetto, a uno medesimo fuoco si scaldassono, a una medesima mensa sedesseno.

I would want that all my relatives live under the same roof, warm themselves at the same fire, and sit down at the same table.

—L. B. Alberti, *Libri della Famiglia*, III

The elementary group, which comprises the population surveyed in old censuses like the Catasto, is the hearth or household, that is to say, a coresidential unit. The census takers found it difficult to control groups of kin and affines that extended beyond the limits of the household. The analysis of old censuses thus allows us to observe, in the coresidential group united by blood relationship, one of the fundamental structures of society. Within it were carried out in whole, or in part, many essential functions: procreation, the socialization of children, consumption, and production. In taking up its study, we seek an understanding of this basic unit and, at the same time, we hope to discern, behind its variations and mutations, the interactions of kinship structure and the society at large.

But is the hearth our best point of departure? As residential units, hearths show different limits and functions from one society, from one epoch, even from one document, to another. Modern anthropology has learned to be sceptical of rigid definitions, inevitably incomplete, applicable here but inadequate there, or too diffuse and poorly reflective of reality.[1] Besides, several studies have recently reacted with vigor against the tendency to regard as everywhere valid the typology of residential groups emerging out of a single census, showing reality at a given moment, like a snapshot.[2] Despite the seeming immobility of their forms, residential groups are always changing. Variations of short or medium duration affect them; these are linked to the life cycles of individual members of the hearth. In combination, they shape the developmental cycle of the family,

1. See Goody, 1972.
2. See among others Berkner, 1975; Wheaton, 1975.

under which the household appears no longer as a fixed entity, but as a "process."[3] Long-term changes are important too; a population like that of Tuscany, hard hit by recurrent epidemics and suffering extraordinary losses prior to a slow recovery, cannot really maintain stability in its domestic units. Within them the position and importance of the members were constantly changing. Finally, differences across society reflect the adaptation of the various social sectors to their particular economic or cultural situations.

The domestic group obviously gives expression only to a small part of the kinship system, and it does not permit us to grasp the complete role which kinship plays in the total society. But the concentration of functions within this small group of relatives surely lends priority to its study; its composition also appears to be particularly sensitive to the changing conditions of demography and economy. We shall defer to the following chapter the analysis of the kinship system beyond the limits of the hearth.

I. The Tuscan Household in 1427

We argued in chapter 2 that the census unit of 1427, the fiscal or taxpaying household, ought to be regarded as a group of persons responsible, one for the others, before the treasury.[4] This interpretation is consistent with Florentine fiscal tradition. When, in 1371, Florence collected precise descriptions of the hearths of the contado for purposes of the Estimo, the scribe charged with the task in Sorniana, a village situated near Prato, interpreted the government's wishes in the following words:

> Here below [he writes] are inscribed all the men and all the persons of the town of Sorniana, in the district of Prato, men and women, adults and minors, the heads of each family, and the family of each head, with the name and the age of all those who stay and sleep together in one and the same residence and who survive together on the same bread and wine.[5]

This definition was faithful to that given for *fumanti* at the beginning of the fourteenth century.[6] The taxable unit of the rural Estimo was, without equivocation, the domestic community in which all members shared daily life under the same roof, living, sleeping, and consuming together. This

3. See Fortes's Introduction, in Goody, 1966; Hammel, 1972.

4. This explains why, in 1427–30, sons physically absent from the family were still included in the bocche of their fathers, who still supported them.

5. ASF, Estimo 215, f. 421.

6. On fumanti, focolari, and fuochi in the early fourteenth century, see Barbadoro, 1929, pp. 379–81.

defines the hearths listed in the Catasto some 55 years later, better, for example, than Alberti's contemporary description of the family: "the children, the wife, and all other *domestici*, servants, slaves."[7]

The composition of the residential group theoretically depends on the system of filiation and the rules governing the choice of residence of newlyweds. In Tuscany filiation is patrilineal at the end of the Middle Ages. The egalitarian rules of inheritance favored the male descendants to the detriment of dowered daughters. We shall return to this subject later on.[8] We note here only that dowered daughters leave their natal group at marriage to join that of their husbands; they lose, as do their children, the major part of their rights to the patrimony of their family of origin. As for the sons, their equal rights to the father's inheritance naturally gives them incentive to remain under his roof until his death and to bring their wives into the household. On the other hand, it does not prohibit them from leaving the household. Departed sons still can claim their part of the eventual inheritance upon their father's death. Patrilineal filiation is therefore classically associated with a tendency toward patrilocal residence; this principle need not, however, rigorously determine the composition of the domestic group.[9]

If this principle functioned as an absolute rule, we should expect to find, as a limiting case, many relatives gathered around Ego in his home: his parents, his paternal uncles and their children, his male descendants with their wives and their own children, his married brothers and their descendants, his single sisters and brothers. Ego's domestic group, in sum, should have been numerous, and endowed with a relatively complex structure. In reality, the residential group in 1427 only exceptionally includes all of these persons. Restrained by demographic and economic pressures, the system can never achieve free play. To understand the system as it operates under severe constraints, we shall first examine the diverse external characteristics of the household which the Catasto describes.

AVERAGE SIZE

The hearth of 1427 includes on the average only 4.42 persons for the entire Tuscan population (264,210 persons divided among 59,277 households).[10] The asymmetry of the histogram representing the distribution of house-

7. Alberti, 1960, 1:186.
8. See below, chap. 11.
9. See Fox, 1967; Murdock, 1948.
10. On the various possible ways of classifying households, see Laslett and Wall, 1972, pp. 39–40, 113. On the problem, largely now surpassed, of the ideal "multiplier" to apply to the medieval hearth, see Cuvelier, 1912, pp. lxix–lxxix, and the observations of Carpentier and Glenisson, 1962.

holds according to their size highlights the predominance of very small domestic units; the unit most frequently encountered includes only two persons, and hearths of fewer than four persons constitute nearly 44 percent of the total; those of fewer than five persons, 58.2 percent. The columns of the histogram extend to the right in a long line of more expansive households, going up to around 25 persons. On the whole, however, hearths of more than six persons make up not even a fifth of the households; those of more than ten persons con stitute only 3.6 percent (see Figure 10.1).

If however we consider persons and not hearths, these populous households take on greater importance; an appreciable portion of the population shares the experience of a large family. In 1427 the population residing in hearths of at least six persons constitutes 52.5 percent of the total, and hearths of five persons shelter more Tuscans than any other category of household. Even the fringe of very large households, of 11 to 25 persons, still takes in 10.8 percent of the population. A Tuscan living in 1427 thus stood a good chance of residing in a domestic group much larger than that which simple mean size might suggest.

The average size of the household varies perceptibly with the residence, occupation, and social rank of its head. In the towns it falls to below four persons (3.91), to rise to 4.74 in the rural population as a whole (see Table 10.5). In Florence the average proves to be particularly low (3.80), and the distribution of households is extraordinarily skewed. The columns of the histogram show a summit to the left in the category of households including only a single person, and they fall off to the right in a long sequence of large domestic units. Analogous traits mark the households in all Tuscany's principal cities in 1427. Except for Arezzo and Cortona, however, none exhibits, as does Florence, a maximum frequency in the extreme left in the category of single-person households. Hearths including two persons elsewhere constitute the largest category (Pisa, Pistoia, Prato, and Volterra). Curiously, households of four persons are almost as numerous as those of three persons in Pisa and Arezzo; the former even exceeed the latter in Prato, Cortona, and Volterra. This last distribution with two summits characterizes above all the smallest towns of the group, those in which the portion of the inhabitants living from agricultural activities is the largest. The second summit, represented by households with four persons, no doubt betrays this rural presence within the urban communities.

A consideration of households in the towns and villages slightly softens these characteristics of the urban distribution. In these small communities, the bell is displaced more to the right, reaching its highest levels in house-

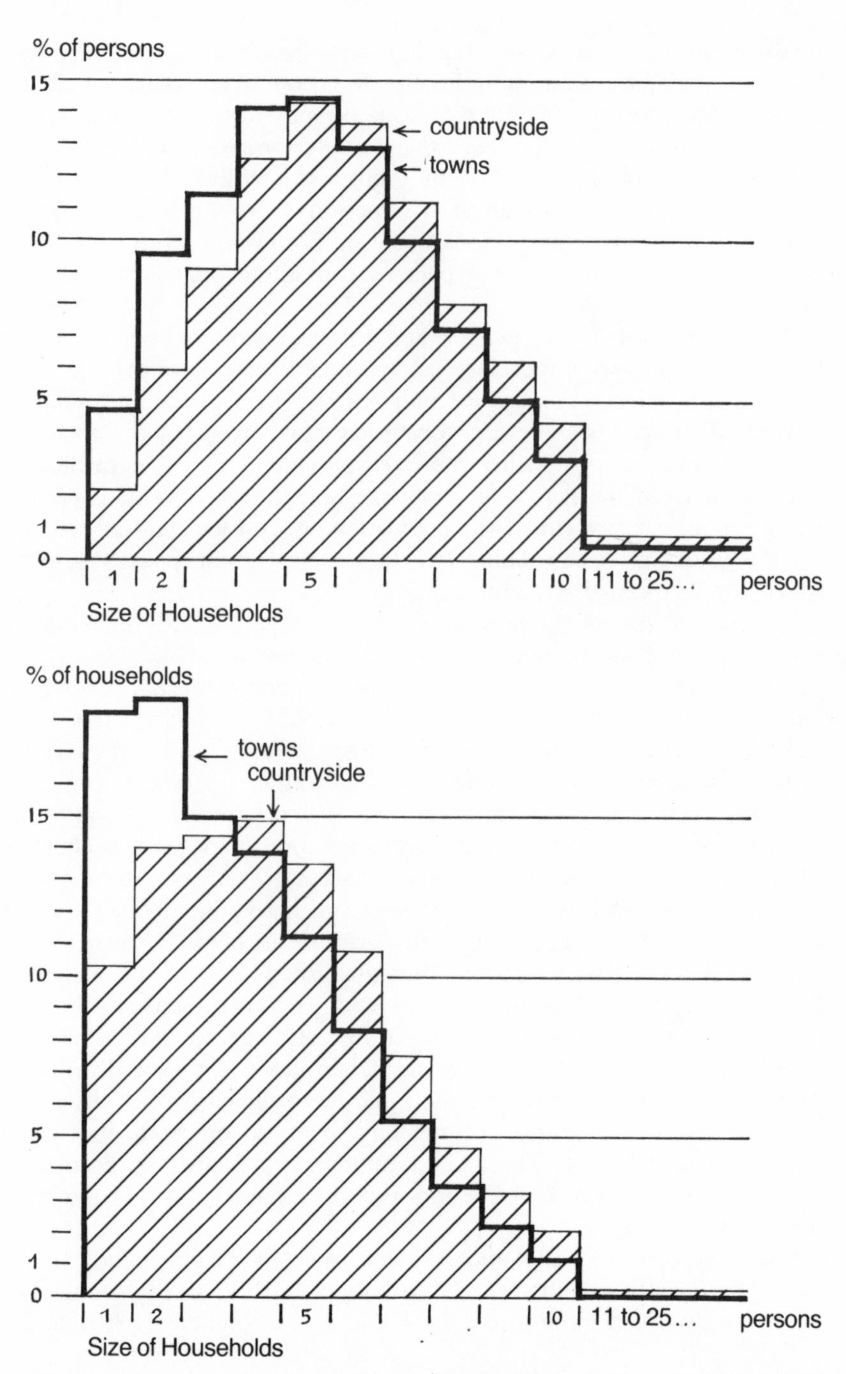

Fig. 10.1. Distribution of Households according to Size in the Towns and Countryside (Persons and Hearths)

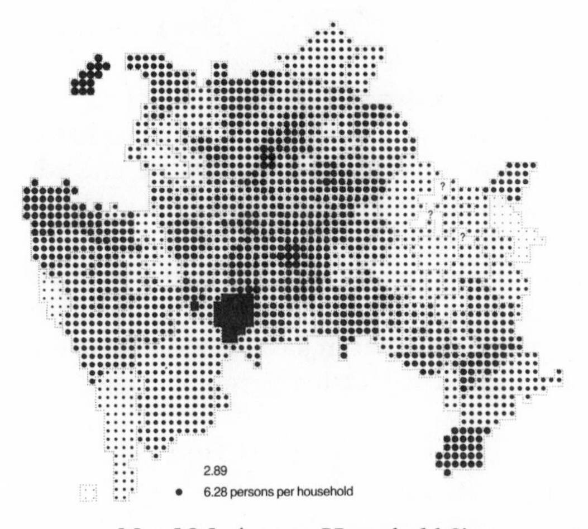

Map 10.1. Average Household Size

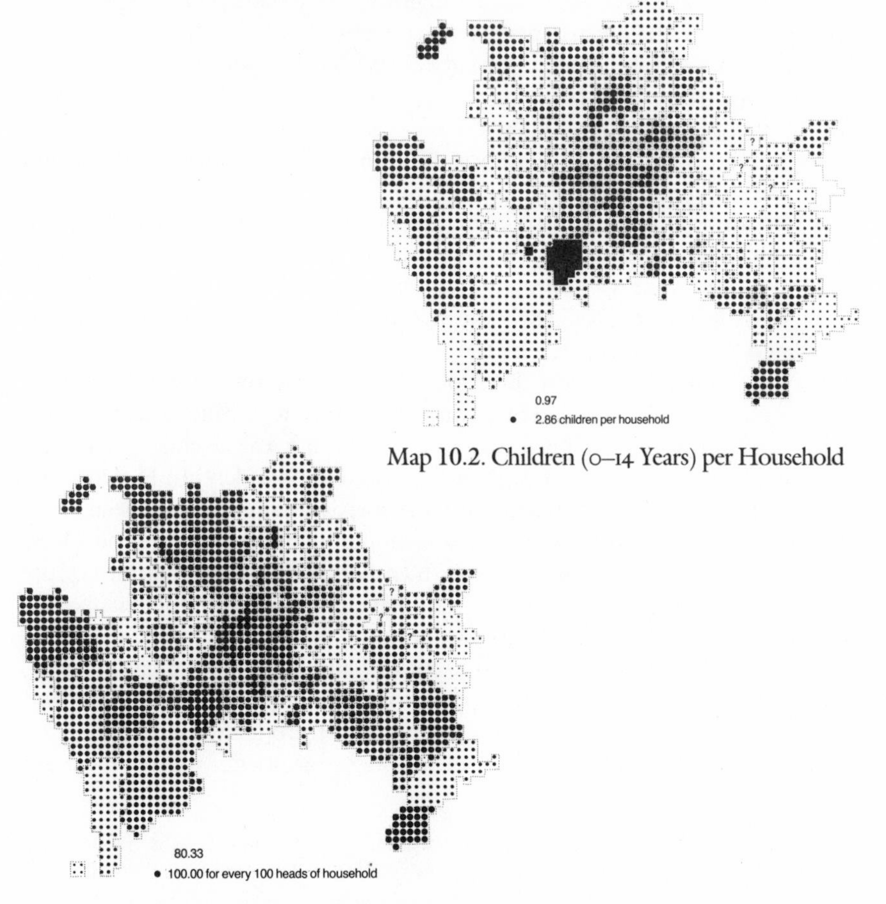

Map 10.2. Children (0–14 Years) per Household

Map 10.3. Male Heads of Household

holds with four or five persons.[11] In the countryside, the higher average size (in relation to the towns) is accompanied by a clear summit of households composed of five persons. There too, small domestic units are effaced; hearths of one to three members make up 38.7 percent of the total, as against 51.8 percent in cities. And large family groups make up a big proportion of the households; a third of the rural hearths include at least six persons. More than one-half (56 percent) of rural inhabitants are found in this last category. Large families, more prevalent in the contado than in the big cities, are also more typical of the center of the territory than of the periphery (see Map 10.1).

In both city and countryside, social and economic factors affect the average size of hearths. In the cities, the size of the hearth shows a clear, although not a linear, correlation with wealth. At Florence, when one passes from the lower or middle categories of wealth to the higher, the average size of the hearth begins to rise regularly. Nearly two-thirds of Florentine households with less than 400 florins in wealth show an average size of fewer than three persons; those with assets from 800 to 1,600 florins already include four; between 1,600 and 3,200 florins, hearths count on the average five persons; and the richest (with assets above 3,200 florins) claim six at least (Figure 10.2).

If Florentine households are arranged by the increasing number of members they contain and if the average wealth of these categories is calculated, then the coefficient of correlation between number of bocche and the average wealth is a high 0.87. The size of the household is thus strongly associated with its fortune, but the influence of the latter comes into play principally beyond a certain threshold which barely two in five Florentine households actually cross. These disparities tied to wealth affect in turn mean size according to professions, even though the average wealth of persons in the same occupational group could vary widely. In Florence the professions in which the average wealth surpasses the general mean (near 800 florins) also harbor the largest families. The group of professions which claim households of five or six members includes the majority of the major guilds—judges and notaries, Calimala, bankers, wool merchants, silk merchants—as well as the doctors of law, the *messeri*. Dyers, merchants of used clothing (*rigattieri*) goldsmiths, cutlers, and dealers in oil have comparably big households. The larger part of the minor guilds—tradesmen and artisans owning a shop and their own means of production—falls into the category of households with four to five members, where they are

11. Thus, at Castiglione Fiorentino, the largest numbers are found in hearths of four to five persons (288 and 290 residents belong to these categories); at Montepulciano, of five persons; at San Gimignano, of four persons; and so on.

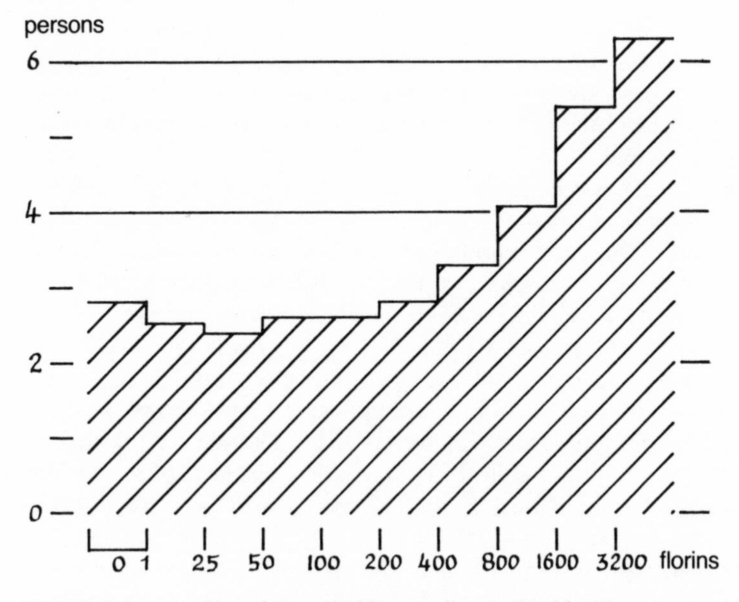

Fig. 10.2. Average Size of Households according to Wealth (Florence, 1427)

joined by those of the major guilds—spice merchants and furriers—who do not make it into the first group. Cloth workers, servants, employees of public or private institutions, soldiers, clerks teaching grammar and arithmetic to Florentine children, and other humble denizens of the city have households with fewer than four members. At the very bottom of this scale of sizes, marked both by their low average wealth and by tiny households, are found a few ecclesiastics, monks and religious women, who have strayed into the lay catasto. Also, there appear the sixty or so taxpayers who declare themselves to be domestic servants; their households have, on the average, fewer than two persons.[12]

With 51.3 percent of all households and 46.4 percent of the Florentine population, taxpayers who do not declare an occupation evidently have smaller hearths than the average—smaller than their neighbors' who claim to belong to a specific professional group (3.53 against 4.33). The reason for this is that servants, laborers, workers, unskilled journeymen, and widows (retired women, or domestics living alone in the metropolis) are numerous

12. At Bologna in 1395, butchers had the largest average hearths (4.63 persons), followed by messeri (4.45), linen merchants (4.39), leather dealers (4.38), wool merchants (4.32), notaries (4.31), tailors (4.17), and cordovan merchants (4.03). There follow porters (3.30), lavoratori (3.11), clerks (2.83), and spice sellers at the end (2.47). The figures are calculated on the basis of Montanari, 1966.

in this category. The same situation prevails in the other Tuscan towns. Where the proportion of female household heads is highest, for example, at Pistoia and Arezzo, the average size of the household falls below the general urban mean, and so also does the proportion of household heads declaring a profession.[13]

Wealth also influences the size of the domestic group in the countryside. In the rural quarter of Santa Croce, the correlation between size and mean wealth of families classified by number of members is even stronger than at Florence (0.91). As Figure 10.3 shows, the proportion of small households diminishes, and that of large households grows as wealth increases. However, these higher categories of wealth, and the bigger family sizes associated with them, characterize only a small number of rural households. Thus, the weak regional correlation of average wealth and average size (see Maps 4.1, and 10.1) should come as no surprise. The reason for this is evident: the resident population in the countryside owns little of the landed capital, the basis of taxable wealth; the citizens, who do not live on the land, possess it in largest measure.[14]

In the Florentine contado in particular, the extremely low average wealth of the indigenous population, subject to the regime of the mezzadria, is a misleading indicator. This is apparent in Figure 10.3, in which the first column represents rural hearths without any taxable assets; they comprise a fifth of all households in the countryside. This category exhibits a manifest irregularity in relation to the tendency which appears as we move up the scale of wealth. As a rule, the proportion of larger households increases as wealth advances. Now this category of seemingly destitute households includes numerous sharecroppers. Nearly a fourth of the mezzadri households in the east and a third in the west are devoid of taxable wealth, and they constitute 27 percent of the taxpayers in this category. It is therefore likely that sharecropping plays an important role in the maintenance of larger households among these country poor.[15] The distribution of households according to size by occupational category confirms this assumption (Figure 10.3). The category of sharecroppers shows a very low proportion of small households: 20 percent of them have fewer than four members, as against 35.5 percent among peasants of equivalent poverty. On the other hand, the

13. At Arezzo, 24 percent of household heads are women, and the mean size is 3.48; at Pistoia, the comparable figures are 21.7 percent and 3.54; on the other hand, at Pisa, 15.6 percent and 4.24; at Prato, 16.7 percent and 3.73.

14. See above, chap. 4.

15. The statistical method known as "factorial analysis of correspondences" has proved very useful in illuminating on the local and regional level the relations between demographic and economic phenomenona. See Klapisch and Demonet, 1972; idem., 1975.

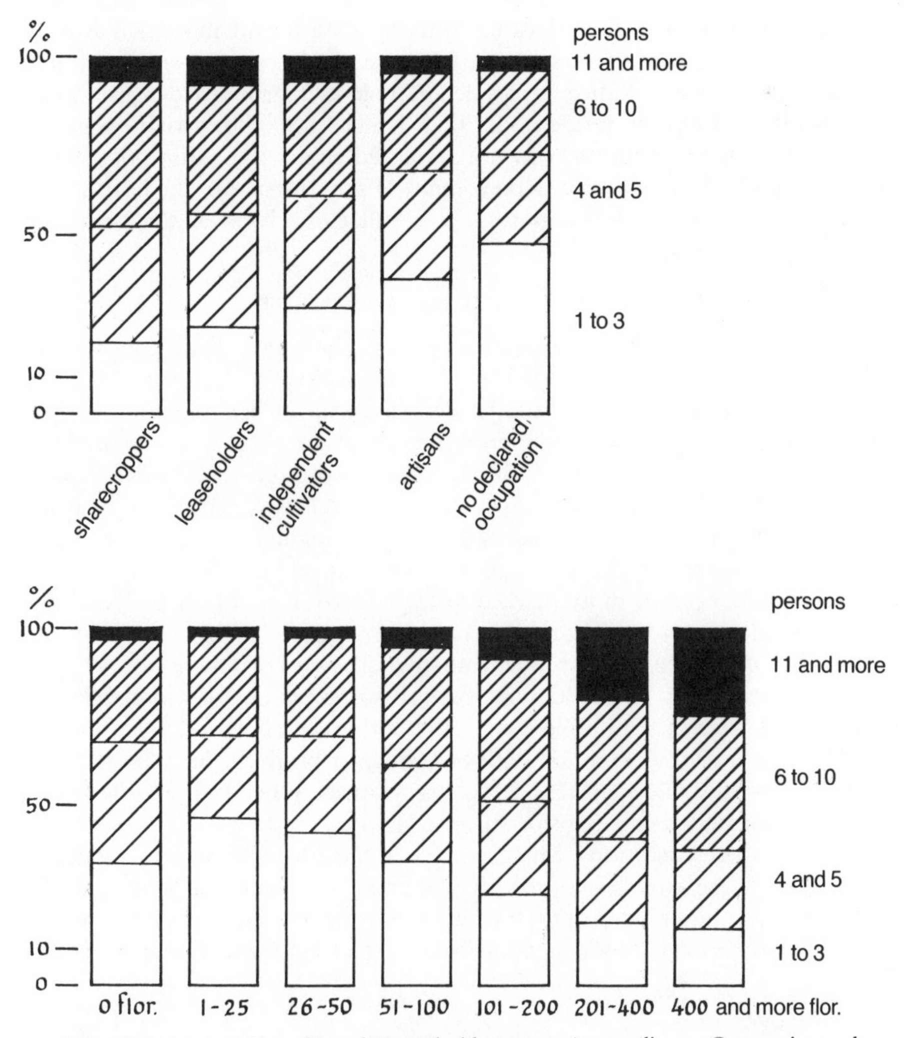

Fig. 10.3. Average Size of Rural Households (1427–30) according to Occupation and Wealth Category

portion of households with more than six members is larger here than in any other occupational group in the countryside. The unique family traits of the sharecroppers thus significantly disturbs the correlation in the countryside between wealth and the size of the domestic group. They also serve to explain the well-attested geographic correspondence between the center of the territory, the region in which the mezzadria system predominates, and the zone in which households attain an average size greater than elsewhere.

The domestic group in Tuscany thus shows a remarkably small average size. This trait seems to contradict what we would expect from the principle governing the choice of residence, that is, that married sons should normally continue to reside under their father's roof. But variations in size indicate that the principle was not respected across the entire population. Average size is, in any case, a poor index of the structure of the hearth. The Catasto, however, allows us to take a still closer look at that structure across Tuscan society.

STRUCTURE AND COMPOSITION OF THE HOUSEHOLD

The identification of household members in the pages of the Catasto confirms the preference accorded in Tuscan society to agnates. Marriage brought only the wife into the residential group of her husband. Affines, apart from the wife, are rarely encountered, or are altogether absent, from Tuscan families. At Arezzo, for example, 14 mothers-in-law, a single father-in-law, and three sisters-in-law (in all, an exiguous 0.43 percent of the town population) live with the husband of their daughter or sister. Similarly, only 1.5 percent of the households shelter an affine.[16] The exclusion of in-laws may be even more marked in the countryside.[17] Marriages resulting in a resident son-in-law are also extremely rare. In Arezzo, in only one instance does a husband reside with his father-in-law; there are six such configurations at Pisa, and only two at Florence, out of more than ten thousand households.[18] The wife, after losing her husband, occasionally returns as a widow to reside with her father or brothers, but almost never will a new husband join her among her relatives. When he does, the redactors of our documents register surprise.[19]

Under these conditions, Tuscans lived, in the great majority, in a residential group, the cohesion of which was based on patrilineal affiliation. In Florentine households, 73.7 percent of the members were related to the head. Among 9,753 residents connected to the head through marriage, 99.5

16. Only 0.48 percent of the residents of Pisa are related through marriage to the head of the household where they reside; 2.1 percent of the households include matrilineal relatives. The comparable figures at Florence are 0.15 and 0.5 percent respectively.

17. The proportions are 0.17 percent of the population and 0.76 percent of the households in the cortine of Arezzo; 0.28 and 1.23 percent in the Pisan contado.

18. We count two sons-in-law in the Pisan countryside, seven in the cortine of Arezzo. In all, sons-in-law and their wives represent only a tiny part of the children living with their parents: 0.6 and 0.8 percent at Pisa and in its contado, 5.1 and 3.8 percent at Arezzo and its cortine.

19. Thus, a family of San Donato a Paterno seems to have retained from one generation to another a resident son-in-law. In 1427, the lady Perpetua fu di Giannino lives with her son-in-law Neri di Francesco (AC 323, f. 158), who, some 15 years later (?), has taken for his patronym the name of his father-in-law, and lives in his turn with his son-in-law, who "è tornato mecho a generaticho per marito della A. mia figliuola per insino a dì 17 gennaio 1434," (AC 580, f. 22, declaration of Neri di Giannino).

percent were wives, daughters-in-law, or spouses of some sort. The cement of the Tuscan hearth in the early fifteenth century was incontestably membership in a group of agnates. It is, of course, possible that the taxpayers concealed their non-agnatic ties from the scrutiny of the tax officials. They may have believed that the officials would not accept the wife's relatives as legitimate mouths.[20] But it remains difficult to understand why the Catasto declarations, numbering in the tens of thousands, would have preserved so little trace of matrilineal relatives, if they were present in a significant number of hearths. On the other hand, the fiscal nature of the document at the base of our analysis may introduce a slight bias in favor of agnatic relationships.

How does this cohesion among agnates express itself from one generation to the next and within the same generation? Here is a initial observation: in this period of demographic recession and of high mortality, hearths joining persons who belong to more than two generations constitute a high percentage of the total. They make up 11.3 percent of hearths at Florence; between 13 and 21 percent in the six secondary towns; and 20.2 percent in the villages. These proportions rise still more as the communities grow smaller: 21.2 percent in the suburban villages of Arezzo, 24.7 percent in the Pisan contado, 26.3 percent in the Florentine. These figures emphasize the solidity of the intergenerational link.

We should not then be misled by the statistical predominance of the simplest forms of household structure. The most common residential group is without doubt the conjugal family, which is extended one time in seven by an ascendant (or more rarely by a descendant more removed than the son), and one time in fifty-four by a single brother or sister (see Table 10.1). This configuration, which predominates in the Tuscan population as a whole, gives way, in one case in six, to truncated forms of the domestic unit: widowers, or bachelors living alone, *frérèches*, households of orphaned children, or groups of seemingly unrelated individuals. In contrast to these small households is the slightly larger group (18.6 percent) of multiple households, usually bigger than the mean, in which several married males with their respective families share the domicile. They show two nuclei in 14.8 percent of the cases, three or more nuclei in the remaining 3.8 percent.[21]

20. See the note justifying the decision taken by the Ufficiali to exclude the niece, age 15, of a Pisan silk merchant, Agostino di ser Arrigo da Chianni: "no' glia s' a mettere ch'è da lato di femina." ASP, UFF 1532, f. 77; Casini, 1964, no. 756, 1:179.

21. We follow here the classification of Laslett and Wall, 1972, pp. 23–44. The nucleus corresponds to a couple (with or without children), a widower or widow with children. A nuclear, mononuclear, or simple household includes only one nucleus; a multiple, multinuclear, or complex household includes several. We shall reserve the term "frérèche" without other qualifiers for the joint family households of married brothers. We call vertical multiple households those which include several nuclei of different generations; lateral multiple households those in which authority is shared by couples belonging to the same generation.

Table 10.1. Composition of Tuscan Households in 1427

		Number	Percent
1	Solitaries	8,135	13.61
	a. Widowers	60	0.10
	Widows	3,980	6.66
	b. Unmarried	500	0.84
	Indeterminate	3,595	6.01
2	Without conjugal family	1,371	2.29
	a. Single brothers	959	1.60
	b.c. Unrelated or of unknown relationships	412	0.69
	1+2	9,506	15.90
3	Simple conjugal family	32,751	54.80
	a. Couples without children	6,130	10.26
	b. Couples with children	21,726	36.35
	c. Widowers with children	1,091	1.83
	d. Widows with children	3,804	6.36
4	Extended conjugal family	6,362	10.64
	a. Upwards (parent, grandparent, uncle, aunt)		
	b. Downwards (grandchildren, nephew, niece)	5,640	9.44
	c.d. Laterally (brother, sister, cousin) or mixed a,b,c,	722	1.20
	3+4	39,113	65.44
5	Multiple households	11,151	18.66
	a.b. Vertical upwards or downwards		
	with two nuclei	6,740	11.28
	with three nuclei or more	1,264	2.11
	c.d. Horizontal (*frérèches*)		
	with two nuclei	2,130	3.55
	with three nuclei or more	1,017	1.69
	5 =	11,151	18.66
	Grand Total	59,770	100.00

NOTE: The numbers refer to the classification of P. Laslett, 1972, p. 31. On certain of our choices, see notes 21 and 22.

Three out of five hearths that include two married couples (11.3 percent of the total) apparently are "stem families," which join a single married son to the married head. From an equally formal point of view, the patriarchal family, which subjects several married sons to the father's authority, takes in 2.1 percent of all households. The remaining multiple households (5.3 percent) are frérèches—joint family households composed of married brothers.

To render full account of these associations of parental couples and married sons, we should add the 13.4 percent of "vertical" multiple hearths, and the 9.4 percent of mononuclear households extended by an elderly ascendant, generally the old mother residing with her married son. We should note as well that a thousand households (1.7 percent of the total) are

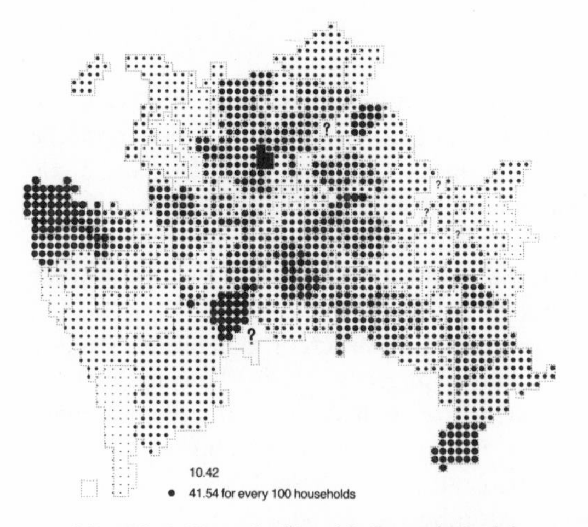

Map 10.4. Households with Several Nuclei

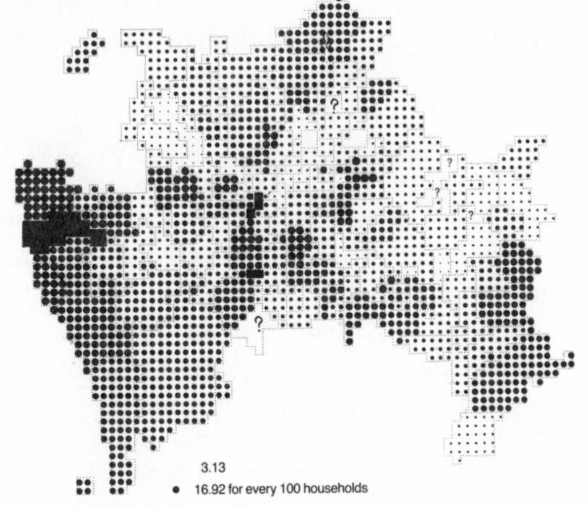

Map 10.5. Households Showing Lateral Extension

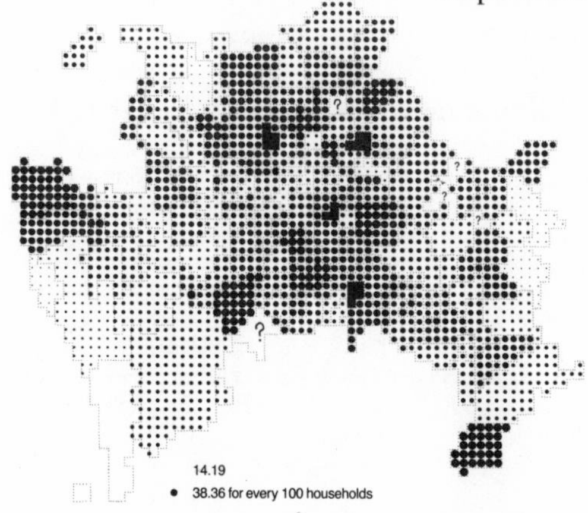

Map 10.6. Households Showing Vertical Extension

classed as vertical multiple households. They could as easily be classified as frérèches of adult males, of whom one at least is married, or better still, as extended mononuclear households including both an ascendant and a collateral relative.[22] These possible revisions underscore the limits of a too-rigid typology. But they do not fundamentally alter our conclusions, because, in all cases, the configurations affirm the strength of the bond which unites generations and encourages brothers to remain together.

Associations between couples belonging to different generations do not, in fact, exhaust the varieties of family aggregation in Tuscany in 1427. Households of married brothers, which we will simply call frérèches, make up, as we have said, more than 5 percent of all households; 3.6 percent include two fraternal couples, 1.7 percent at least three. Is the configuration as rare as this low proportion would indicate? In fact, fraternal solidarity is also expressed in the 1.2 percent of conjugal households in which a widowed mother and her adult married sons share the domicile. Finally, households we have characterized as patriarchal also include several married brothers.

Clearly, frérèches of more than two brothers and patriarchal households are the biggest of all domestic groups; some include 25 persons or more. Households of cousins who live together until the first cousins are grown are also quite populous.[23] The largest family group we encountered in Tuscany at the time of the first Catasto was the frérèche of Lorenzo di Iacopo, who lived in suburban Florence with his three brothers and with another man of the same generation whose relationship to the others is not known. Lorenzo's three sons and two nephews were married, and in the household there were 18 unmarried children or nephews and eight grandchildren or grand nephews. Apparently, under one roof (although it is not clear what kind of domicile contained this crowd) there were gathered ten conjugal families, or 47 members distributed over four generations. The mother of the last brother, the stepmother of the four others, was still alive at age 74, and she was not much older than the eldest of her stepsons.[24] An extreme example of this kind and the not negligible proportion of frérèches

22. More precisely, 991 households (1.66 percent of the total) include 908 (1.52 percent) with a married man, at least one unmarried adult brother, and the widowed mother; these last two thus could be considered either as forming a residual nucleus or as two extensions upward or to the side. A widowed mother with minor children, next to her married son, has been treated in our analyses as a normal nucleus. There can be added to these 908 households 83 hearths (0.14 percent) with two or more married men and a residual nucleus like the preceding.

23. The term, *fratelli cugini*, which in principle means first cousins, is frequently confused with *fratelli* and can even designate the association between an uncle and his nephews. See the examples in AC 251, f. 54, Antonio di Fanuccio; UFF 1542, f. 97, Piero di Guido e fratelli; UFF 1559, f. 54. Numerous cousin households are in UFF 1540, f. 530; UFF 1545, f. 236.

24. AC 172, f. 72, commune of San Cristofano a Novoli, quarter of S. Maria Novella, piviere of San Giovanni.

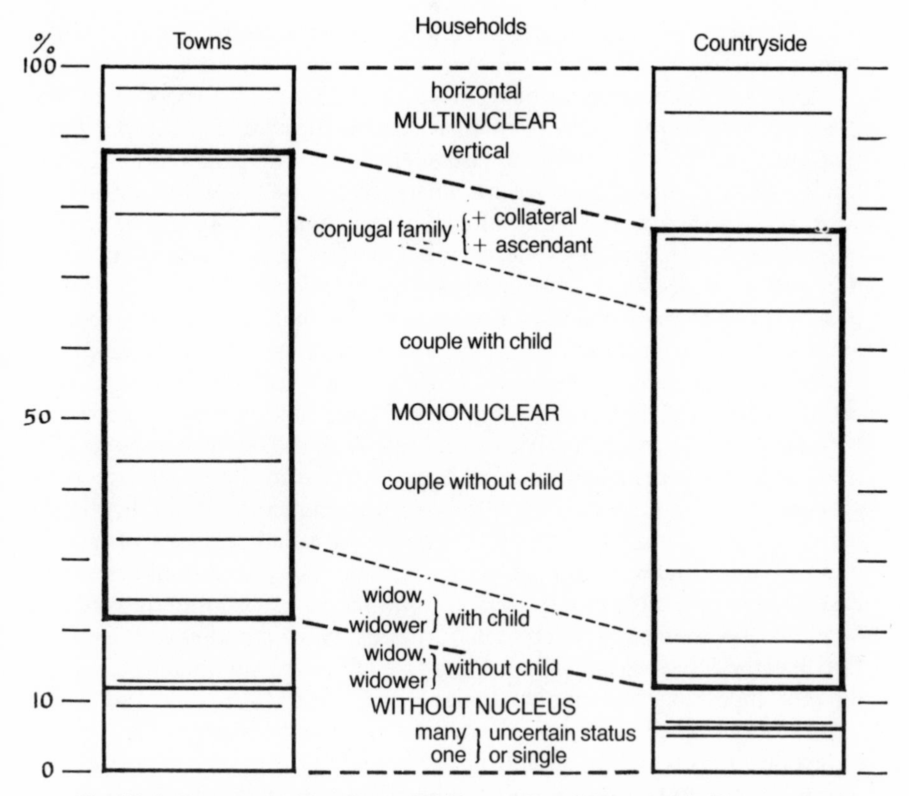

Fig. 10.4. Comparative Typology of Urban and Rural Households (Tuscany, 1472)

or of patriarchal hearths show that the Tuscan system easily admitted the coresidency of married male descendants and cannot be reduced to the model of the stem family. In the society as a whole, the Tuscan household therefore exhibits a rich variety of forms. Can we nonetheless distinguish some preference for a particular kind of domestic configuration within the many geographic and social sectors of the population?

In the cities and the countryside taken together, the proportion of mononuclear households remains approximately the same, but the proportions of extreme cases are inverted (see Figure 10.4). The percentage of rural multiple hearths equals that of truncated and single-person households in the towns. Even the core of mononuclear households points to this tendency toward aggregation in the countryside. There, one household in six belonging to this category includes at least one close relative, who is not the immediate descendant of the household head. The proportion of conjugal households lacking one partner is likewise greater in the towns, as is that of solitary widows.

The urban characteristics thus grossly defined are nonetheless more pronounced among the urban poor than among the rich. Figure 10.5 shows that there exists some similarity between the destitute Florentine households—those possessing no wealth whatsoever—and the wealthiest—those with at least 800 florins. In contrast to the humble folk of the middle classes, both rich and poor hearths include few solitary individuals, and they further show similar proportions of couples and of widowers or widows living with small children. Even couples housing a widowed ascendant are less common in these two categories of taxpayers. The basic difference touches on the relation between older couples and young people. The proportion of childless couples is in fact highest among the very poor, and very low among the rich; that of multiple households, including couples from different generations, is clearly concentrated in the upper categories of wealth. As for frérèches, they become more numerous above the threshold of 800 florins. The intermediate categories include persons of modest means, small artisans and shopkeepers, and pensioned widows; their hearths shelter many solitary persons, the remnants of formerly conjugal families, and more or less constant proportions of mononuclear families. But like the lowest strata of wealth, these levels are also characterized by the rare appearance of complex domestic groups.

In the countryside, the complexity of the domestic group is also linked, in certain measure, to the wealth of the household. But, like the mean size, the structure and composition of the hearth appear to depend above all on social status (and in this, wealth is only one of several contributing factors) and on its base in land (see Figure 10.5). Here again, the center of the territory surpasses the periphery in its greater proportion of multinuclear households; vertical links within households are also accentuated here (see Map 10.4). Thus, the zone of the mezzadria corresponds to a region not only of large, but also of complex, households. Table 10.2 does not, however, demonstrate clearly that the mezzadri are significantly different from other peasants, from small property owners or renters who lease the greater part of their holdings. All peasant hearths include few solitary persons, widowers, or young people. However, small property owners or tenants holding heritable lands under quitrent, anxious to avoid the dissensions that often followed marriages and divisions of the holding, include more households headed by a widower than do the mezzadri. The periphery, in comparison with the center, shows a similar pattern. The proportion of multiple households remains approximately the same (about 30 percent) for all the peasants. Sharecroppers, however, manifest a unique characteristic. In this group, only one couple in eight is childless; among other

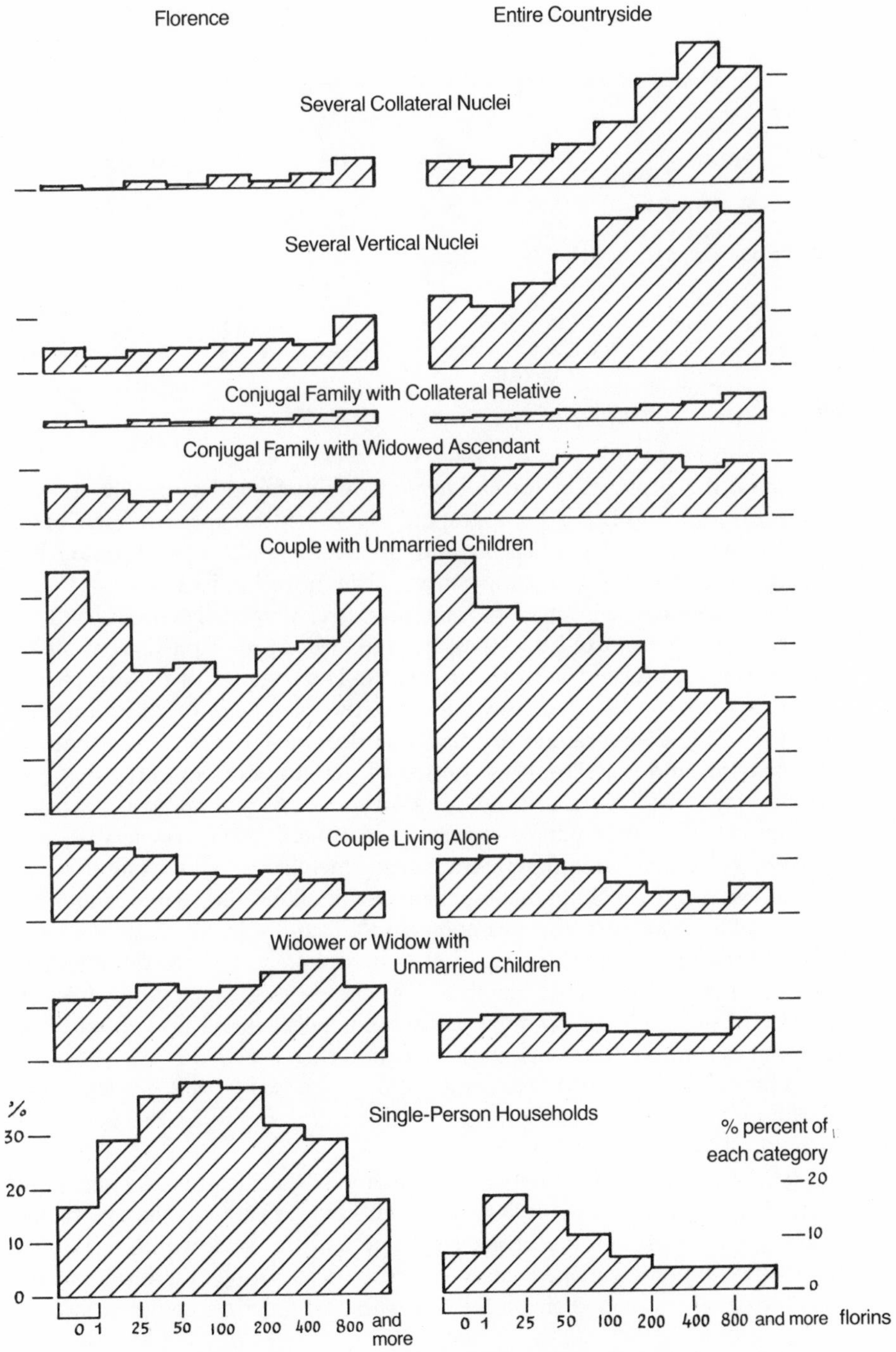

Florence

Entire Countryside

Several Collateral Nuclei

Several Vertical Nuclei

Conjugal Family with Collateral Relative

Conjugal Family with Widowed Ascendant

Couple with Unmarried Children

Couple Living Alone

Widower or Widow with Unmarried Children

Single-Person Households

% percent of each category

%

30 20 10 0

0 1 25 50 100 200 400 800 and more

20 10 0

0 1 25 50 100 200 400 800 and more florins

Fig. 10.5. Typology of Households according to Wealth at Florence and in the Countryside (1427)

Table 10.2. Typology of the Rural Domestic Group according to Social Category

Type of Household	*Mezzadri*	*Ind. Peasant*	*Renter*	*Artisans Shpkprs*	*No Occptn*	*Total*
Living alone	109	300	47	364	3,922	4,742
	1.5	4.3	2.9	16.6	19.6	12.5
Nuclear Households	3,995	3,628	919	1,151	10,518	20,211
	55.0	52.0	56.0	52.5	52.6	53.1
Extndd Nclr Hhlds	893	942	205	259	2,132	4,431
	12.3	13.5	12.5	11.8	10.7	11.6
Multiple households	1,656	1,521	346	305	2,413	6,241
vertical	22.8	21.8	21.1	13.9	12.1	16.4
Multiple households	610	586	123	114	1,005	2,438
frérèches	8.4	8.4	7.5	5.2	5.0	6.4
Totals	7,263	6,977	1,640	2,193	19,990	38,063

SOURCE: Catasto of 1427–30. Rural population only; towns excluded. Hearths without residents, and simple declarations of property are not counted.

peasants, the proportion hovers around one in four. The proliferation of the mezzadria diffuses a demographic vigor, which expresses itself in the youthfulness of the population and in a high child-woman ratio. This vitality is refracted in the composition of the household itself.

In the zones where small peasant property, perpetual tenures, and the rental of lands for fixed payments prevail, we do not find present all the family traits associated with the mezzadri. The complex of peasant characteristics seems even to dissolve toward the periphery of the Florentine territory. The demographic dividing line does not pass between landowning peasants and sharecroppers (nearly all the indicators of domestic structure so far considered show this), but rather between the settled peasantry and all other country people—agricultural wage laborers, owners of small parcels cultivated irregularly, craftsmen, merchants, and rural notaries. These last groups include many persons living alone and far fewer multiple households than does the peasantry itself (see Table 10.2). In the large group of people without occupation, where women are especially numerous the number of single-member households is greater still, while the proportion of large or complex households falls off. As household heads without occupation are much more common than declared peasants outside the Florentine contado (respectively, 56.9 as opposed to 29.5 percent), they deeply impress the social physiognomy of the family in the peripheral regions of Tuscany.

However striking the complexity of many Tuscan hearths, the phenomenon of the grand family still remains, in 1427, associated with particular social sectors, notably the urban patriciate and the landowning peasantry. Does the domestic distinctiveness of these social groups carry over to the last factor which helped shape the household: the person of the head?

THE HOUSEHOLD HEAD

To an administration seeking to ensnare it in its fiscal net, the household was first of all identified with the person who governed it, gave it his name, fulfilled its obligations—fiscal, military, political—and represented it before society.[25]

The head of the typical household in 1427, as the Catasto describes him, was a man in his 50s, married and presiding over a group then at its maximum size of five or six persons. Women rarely accede to this position, and only at an advanced age. Their significance regularly increases in the higher age brackets, as we can see from Table 10.3. Representing at age 30 only 5 percent of the total household heads, women increase their proportion to 17 percent twenty years later, and finally to 26 percent after age 67. These proportions are nearly two times smaller in the countryside, above all in the zone of the mezzadria, where women are almost never found in sole charge of a podere (only 0.5 percent of sharecroppers heading a family are women).

The population of household heads breaks into two more or less equal parts around the age category 48–52. At least one household head in two would thus have reached or passed age 50. Even if these ages are somewhat exaggerated (the *capi di famiglia* may have unconsciously wished to appear as patriarchs, and at all events they favored age 50), still fifty years is the age which primarily confers or confirms family authority.

Marriage, in other words, does not automatically confer upon the male the leadership of a household. To be sure, married couples are found at the head of the great majority of households, especially in the countryside, where hearths of widows, single persons, or those of indeterminate status are two times less common than in the towns (see Table 10.4). The distribution of household heads according to marital status is of course a subset of their distribution in the population at large. The one exception is the category of single persons. Evidently, the number of bachelor households heads can have little relationship with the distribution of children across the population. Married heads, on the other hand, like married people generally, are more numerous in the countryside than in the towns (respectively 44 and 38.8 percent), and more numerous too in the contado than in the district. A greater number of widowed heads, again like widows generally, take refuge in the towns.

Thus, the contrasting approaches to marriage in city and countryside partially explain why households are distributed differently according to

25. Household or hearth identifies the fiscal unit of residence, and we call the household head the person in whose name the declaration is filed; his name almost always appears at the head of the list of the household mouths.

Table 10.3. Distribution of Household Heads according to Sex and Age, 1427

Age	*Cities*						*Countryside*						*Total*					
	Men		*Women*		*Tgthr*		*Men*		*Women*		*Tghtr*		*Men*		*Women*		*Tgthr*	
Group	N	%	N	%	N	%	N	%	N	%	N	%	N	%	N	%	N	%
0–17	502	2.2	114	0.5	616	2.7	449	1.2	111	0.3	560	1.5	951	1.6	225	0.4	1176	2.0
18–27	1706	7.5	85	0.4	1791	7.9	2292	6.2	39	0.1	2331	6.3	3998	6.7	124	0.2	4122	6.9
28–37	3250	14.5	169	0.7	3419	15.0	4745	12.8	139	0.4	4884	13.2	7995	13.4	308	0.5	8303	13.9
38–47	3657	16.1	363	1.6	4020	17.1	6525	17.7	339	0.9	6864	18.5	10182	17.0	702	1.2	10884	18.2
48–57	3443	15.2	702	3.1	4145	18.2	6149	16.6	511	1.4	6660	18.0	9592	16.0	1213	2.0	10805	18.1
58–67	3188	14.0	982	4.3	4170	18.3	6396	17.3	806	2.2	7202	19.5	9584	16.0	1788	3.0	11372	19.0
68 +	2614	11.5	919	4.1	3533	15.5	6450	17.4	1047	2.8	7497	20.2	9064	15.2	1966	3.3	11030	18.4
Indt.	618	2.7	421	1.8	1039	4.6	677	1.8	367	1.0	1044	2.8	1295	2.2	788	1.3	2083	3.5
	18978	83.5	3755	16.5	22733	99.9	33683	91.0	3359	9.0	37042	100	52661	88.1	7114	11.9	59775	100

SOURCE: Catasto of 1427–1430.

Table 10.4. Distribution of Household Heads according to Marital Status

	Cities		*Countryside*		*Total*	
Marital Status	N	Prct	N	Prct	N	Prct
Married Couple	14,564	64.1	28,568	77.2	43,132	72.2
Widower	880	3.9	1,640	4.4	2,520	4.2
Widow	3,123	13.7	2,618	7.6	5,941	9.9
Celibate Male	592	2.6	598	1.6	1190	2.0
Celibate Female	143	0.6	134	0.3	274	0.5
Indeterminate Male	3,086	13.6	4,028	8.2	6,114	10.2
Indeterminate Female	343	1.5	252	0.7	595	1.0

SOURCE: Catasto of 1427–30.

the marital status of their chiefs.[26] But social factors also mediate the influence which these various types of behavior have on the structure of the domestic group. First of all, only 7.2 percent of single men or of indeterminate status living in the countryside are heads of households, as against 13 percent in the city. The contrast is most marked in the age category 23–27 years. These are the ages during which urban males could still escape the responsibilities of marriage in order to maintain a slightly higher standard of living. The city offered young people the chance to acquire economic (and residential) independence relatively early. These conditions of urban life, which acted to break apart the family cell, also strongly influenced the proportion of widows who, remaining in, or attracted to, the city by the promise of an independent life appear frequently as household heads.

The situation among young people in the countryside responds to an entirely different set of constraints, which result in a long delay between marriage and the establishment of an independent household. Figure 10.6 shows this clearly. It illustrates for each age group the proportion of married or widowed males, and then the proportion of those males who also appear as independent heads of their own households. The proportion of married heads of household is nearly the same for both city and countryside, in all age categories. On the other hand, neither the one nor the other includes the sum total of married men. However, the differences between proportions married and proportions heading their own households is especially pronounced in the countryside. Near age 25, more than 50 percent of male country dwellers are already married, as opposed to 35 percent of the citizens, and 17 to 18 percent head their own households. Nearly two

26. See above, chap. 7, pp. 221–22. Of rural residents, 55.4 percent are neither married nor widowed, 60.8 percent in the towns.

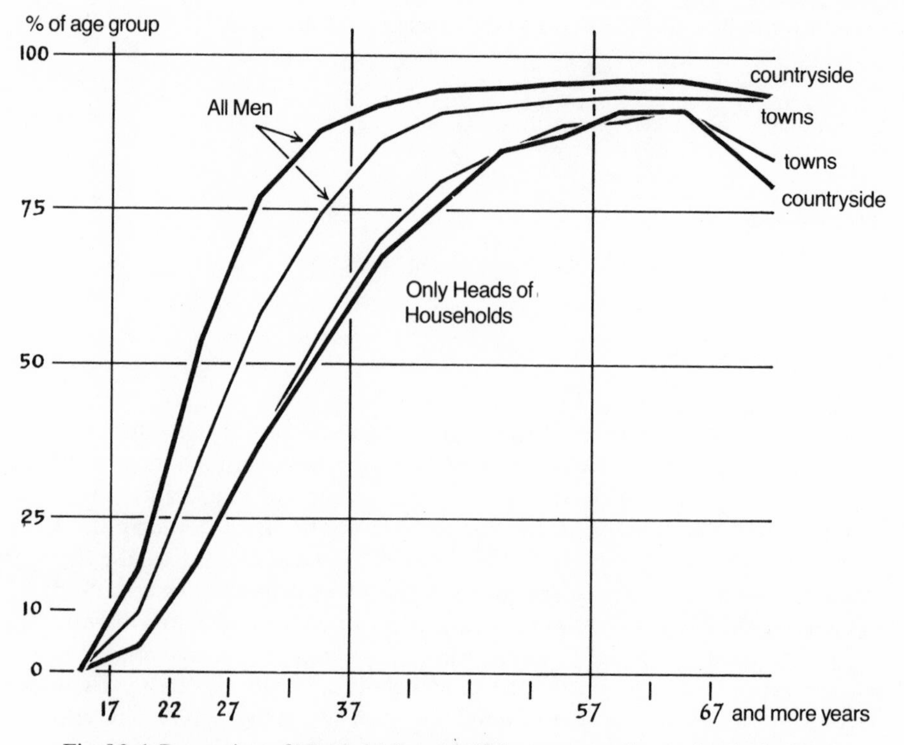

Fig. 10.6. Proportion of Married Men and Widowers according to Age in the Tuscan Population, 1427

thirds of the young married men in the countryside and one-half of those in the city thus remain subject to a paterfamilias, even though they have the responsibility of a wife and prospective children. This situation of dependency changes only gradually. Near age 40, when the figures for married or widowed men have reached their highest levels, the proportion of independent heads among them still remains considerably lower. About 20 percent of married men in the country are still, at this age, subject to a patriarch. In relation to the whole, married men who only belatedly achieve independence represent a sixth of urban males and a quarter of married peasants. Even if the more precocious and higher marriage rates in rural areas partially explain these discrepancies, clearly, cultural factors also intervene here: marriage and the establishment of an independent household do not coincide in Tuscany, and the domestic group is not reducible to the couple and its unmarried children. In order better to understand these differences between marriage and household formation, we shall now attempt to integrate the various characteristics of the Tuscan hearth which we have so far considered. We need to restore to our picture the short-term movements which make the household a continuing process. We will then be ready to look at them again from the point of view of long-term demographic movements.

II. The Household as Process

As the head of the household advances in age, the little domestic group he commands is slowly transformed. A static typology would not allow us to grasp this process, during which the hearth assumes different forms. Fixed categories cannot describe how the rules governing the organization of the residential group actually functioned. But our survey offers a means of imparting life to this typology. This is an exceptional advantage, which old censuses, and even those of the modern epoch, rarely convey. The age of the head, which is regularly cited, is in effect an excellent indicator of his position in the life cycle. On this basis we can seek to reconstruct the developmental cycle of the family.

THE HEARTH AND THE AGING OF THE HEAD

A good father of the family, a *massaio* or manager in contemporary terms, took as his ideal the promotion of the prosperity of his household. Basic to this task was the preservation and increase of the wealth which supported it. The familial patrimony thus changed according to the energy that he could expend and the charges which he had to meet at diverse moments of his life. Wealth thus constituted an important factor in the domestic cycle. Do its variations faithfully reflect the vicissitudes of the family's history?

At Florence, the youngest male heads of households—children or adolescents under 18 years—also possess the greatest average wealth. Only recently come into their inheritance, these orphans have not yet divided the paternal wealth. As we pass to the higher age categories, household wealth immediately diminishes; the category of taxpayers age 25 is distinctly the poorest of all (see Figure 10.7). From this age on heads of households progressively increase their wealth. However, the richest Florentines are not those over age 67. The apogee of fortune is reached near age 50; after 55 years, wealth substantially drops off, so much so that in old age (over 67) the head finds himself poorer than he was at 35. Thus, the oldest household heads posses no more than 9 percent of the total wealth of the city, while in the countryside the same venerable group owns 22 percent of the assets.[27] The composition of the urban patrimonies also varies with the age of the head. Between 25 and 55 years of age, the well-to-do Florentine increases the family wealth principally by enlarging his stock of movable assets. Simultaneously, however, he is converting part of his revenues into landed properties, the absolute, if not the relative, value of which increases steadily through his life. When he approaches or reaches age 55, he begins to transmit to his children, little by little, parts of his movable, though not yet his fixed, possessions; he sets his sons up in business and provides dowries for his daughters.[28] His income also tends to diminish as he grows older, and this too reduces his movable possessions. Patrimonies in the hands of the oldest Florentines testify, lastly, to a relative growth in shares in the public debt. These assets do not require close management and are therefore less burdensome to the elderly. The holdings of household heads over age 67 thus show a roughly equal division among movable goods and commercial investments, shares of the public debt, and land.

The tendency to accumulate or reduce debts also follows the life cycle of the family chief. In the towns, young adults near 25 years of age sustain the heaviest debts, which they repay as they age. In their maturity, many heads of family become the creditors of the young, lending as they themselves once borrowed. Credit linked to age thus constitutes an important channel by which the capital of the elderly flowed to support the enterprise of the young.

In the Florentine countryside, the richest heads are also the youngest (under age 18), but these form only a tiny group of heirs, no more than 1.2 percent of all households. Here, as we mount up the scale of ages, average wealth of households also falls, and the decline continues until the head passes into his 40s. From that point, wealth rises continuously with age. The richest peasants of the countryside have passed their sixtieth year. In rural society, dowries made up of movable property or of cash did not cut into the basic family wealth, its landed patrimony. But did not the establishment of sons on farms of their own, like the launching of an urban boy in a business career, pare the wealth of the peasant family? In reality it appears as if the cycle of wealth in peasant families is tied less directly to the life cycle of the head than it seems to be in the cities.

The wealth cycle in households with a female head is very different.

27. In the city of Florence, 735 hearths headed by a man older than 67 years possess 798,182 florins, out of the 8,947,440 florins representing the total taxable wealth held by male heads, or 8.9 percent. In the contado, the corresponding figures are 373,398 and 1,672,012 florins (22.3 percent).

28. Movable possessions constituted 42.1 percent of the wealth in families directed by a man between 53 and 57 years, 31.6 percent in those headed by a man of 63 to 67 years.

Hearths led by women constituted 9.1 percent of those in the countryside and 14.3 percent of those at Florence. But the proportion of the total wealth they absorb is slightly higher in the countryside than at Florence (6.4 and 5.0 percent, respectively). In fact, none of the biggest Florentine patrimonies in 1427 are under the control of women. Moreover, unlike males, female heads become increasingly impoverished as they age. At Florence as in the countryside, young orphan heiresses are roughly equal in wealth to their male counterparts. But women who become independent at older ages (they are in the great majority widows) also grow increasingly poor with time (see Figure 10.7). If they manage to stabilize their holdings when they have fewer children to care for, after 40 years, they nonetheless remain, on the average, considerably poorer than men of the same age, and they are destined inevitably for destitution in their final years of life. The gap between male and female wealth by age seems smaller in the countryside than at Florence, but the tendency otherwise remains the same.

The phases of increasing and diminishing wealth experienced by the family are linked to events which constitute its very life: progress in a career, but, also, growing obligations—births, divisions, emancipations, and the granting of capital to sons and dowries to daughters.

In the countryside, young people are more dependent on the help dispensed within the framework of the domestic community. The older generation retains control of property. At the death of the patriarch, sons enter into their inheritance, come of age, marry, and bring children into the world; the pressures on them simultaneously increase to divide their common patrimony. Divisions are usually accompanied by the physical separation of the adult sons. And continuing divisions reduce the average wealth of household heads through fairly advanced age categories. But subsequently each new head of household tends to increase his own wealth as he ages. At death, if he has resisted the demands of his sons, he should, in his turn, possess the largest fortune he has ever owned since achieving autonomy.

In the towns, the relation between the age of the household head and his wealth does not remain linear in the higher brackets. Urban families accord to the young a greater and more precocious independence than their equals can gain in the countryside; there, the families let the young take their leave and do not seek to maintain strict control over their doings. Urban fathers are older and have married later than the peasants; their sons are thus probably younger than heirs in the countryside when they divide their inheritance. Moreover, the commercial economy of the city favors individualism in property administration. The period during which the urban family gains in wealth is therefore shorter than in the countryside, and the rhythm of accumulation is reversed when the time comes to establish children in their own independent careers.

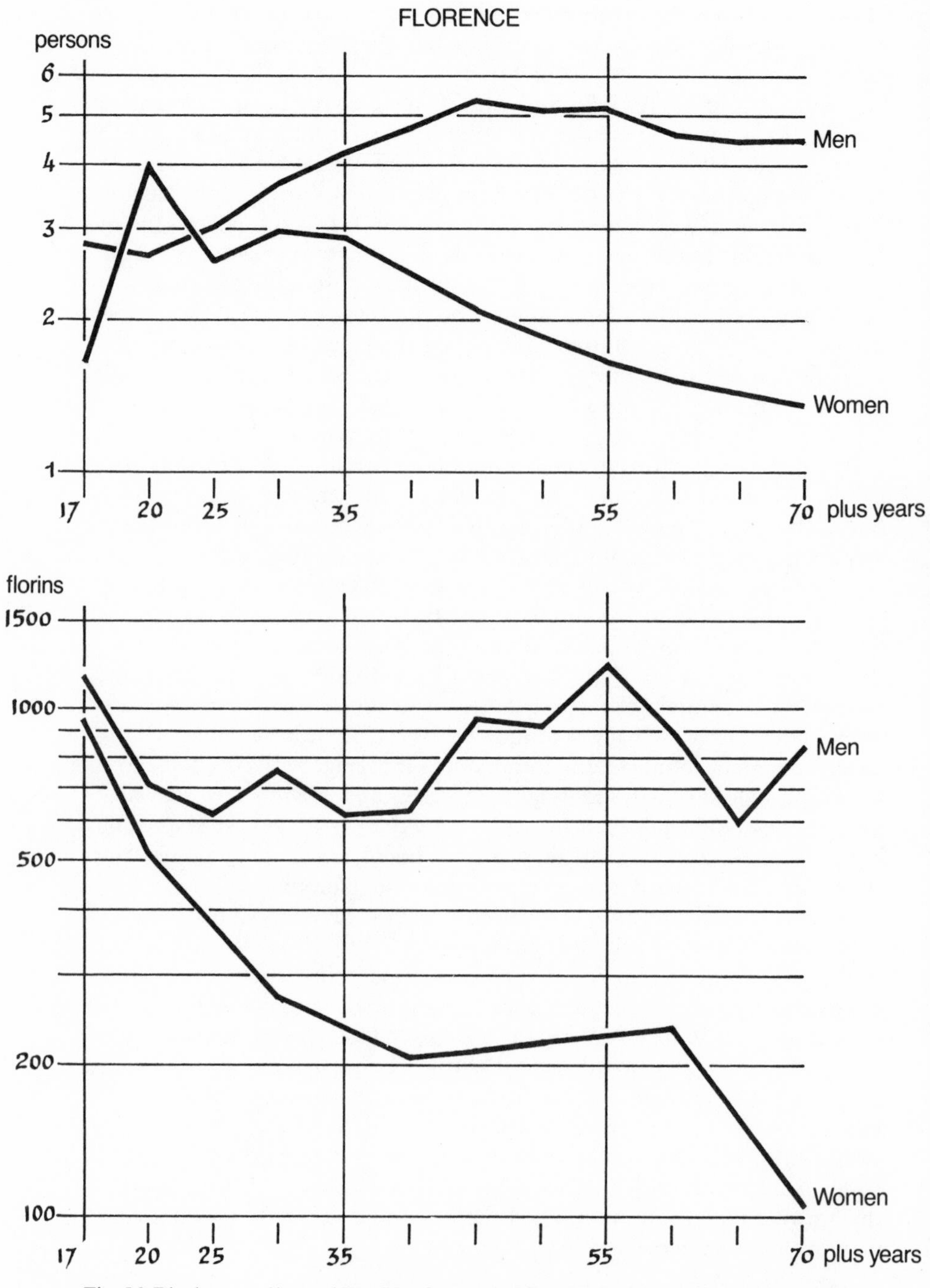

Fig. 10.7A. Average Size and Wealth of Households according to the Sex and Age of the Head (Florence, 1427)

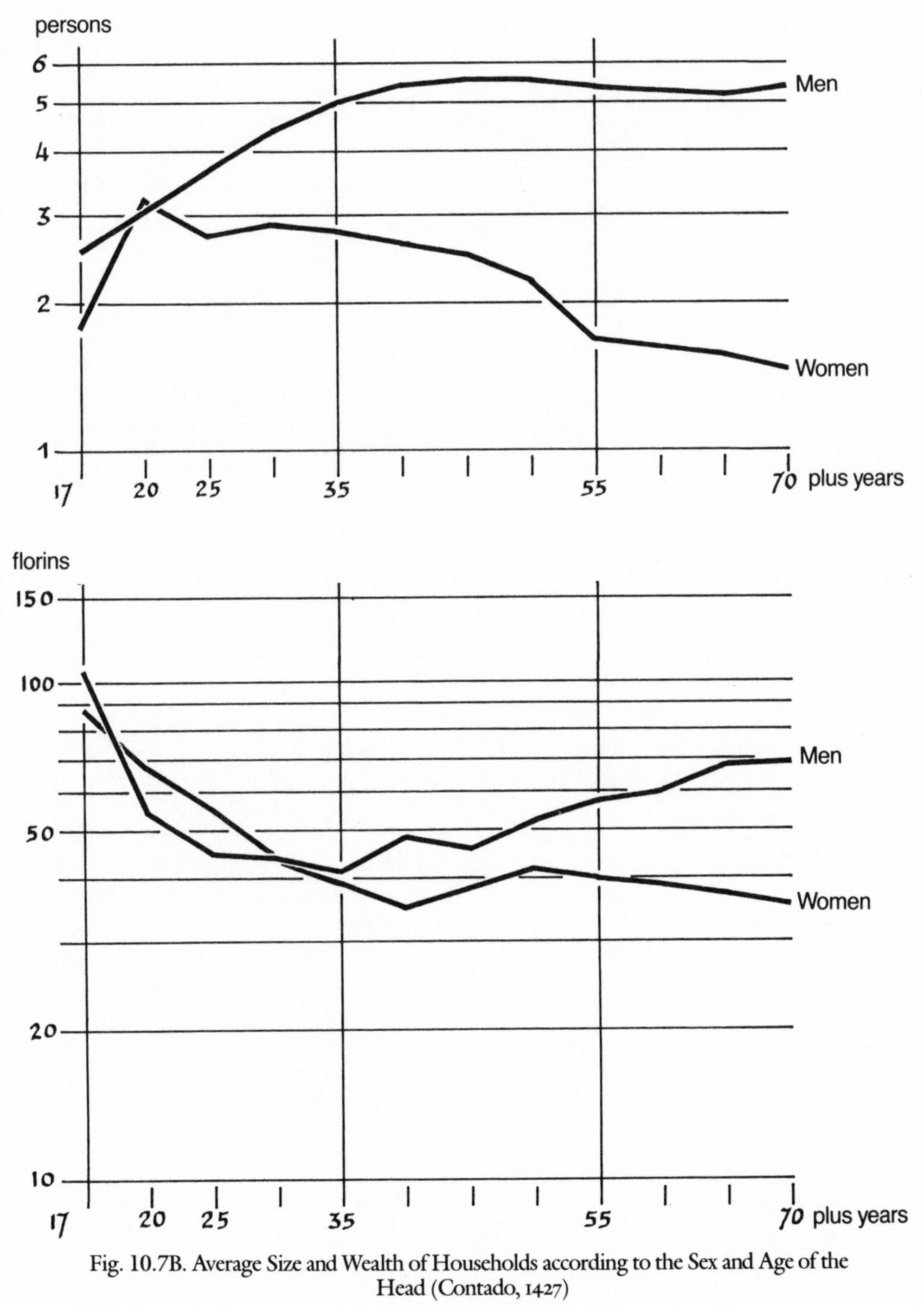

Fig. 10.7B. Average Size and Wealth of Households according to the Sex and Age of the Head (Contado, 1427)

Table 10.5. Household Size according to the Sex and Age of the Head

	Towns			*Countryside*			*All Tuscany*		
Age Group	Men	Women	Tgthr	Men	Women	Tgthr	Men	Women	Tgthr
0–17	2.51	1.66	2.49	2.51	1.72	2.37	2.60	1.69	2.43
18–22	2.71	3.13	2.73	3.02	3.17	3.02	2.88	3.14	2.89
23–27	3.16	2.36	3.12	3.69	2.70	3.68	3.47	2.46	3.44
28–32	3.68	2.75	3.64	4.36	2.83	4.33	4.09	2.79	4.05
33–37	4.25	2.74	4.16	4.99	2.75	4.91	4.68	2.74	4.60
38–42	4.77	2.57	4.59	5.40	2.60	5.28	5.18	2.59	5.03
43–47	5.20	2.35	4.90	5.51	2.45	5.33	5.39	2.40	5.17
48–52	4.96	1.94	4.46	5.50	2.18	5.25	5.31	2.04	4.95
53–57	4.98	1.77	4.42	5.39	1.68	5.10	5.24	1.74	4.83
58–62	4.60	1.65	3.84	5.23	1.61	4.80	5.03	1.63	4.45
63–67	4.49	1.44	3.88	5.14	1.56	4.77	4.91	1.50	4.44
68 +	4.49	1.42	3.69	5.34	1.44	4.80	5.10	1.43	4.44
Ind.	2.53	1.30	2.03	2.44	1.23	2.01	2.48	1.27	2.02
Total	4.34	1.73	3.91	5.03	1.73	4.74	4.78	1.73	4.42

SOURCE: Catasto of 1427–30.

A decline in membership accompanies this loss of material substance when the urban head of household reaches age 55. This is understandable: he disperses his wealth precisely to facilitate the departure of his children. Thus the life cycle of the couple conditions, in the last analysis, these phases of accumulation and dispersal and is itself revealed by the concomitant variations in family size.

Almost all households tend to grow in the period immediately following their formation. Table 10.5 and the curves in Figure 10.7 nevertheless reveal a major difference between hearths under male and female direction. Almost always smaller in size, households with a female head reach their maximum size relatively early. Households of young widows with their children account for this precocious maximum.[29] But they quickly give way to much smaller aggregations. By the time women who are responsible for their own taxes begin to represent a significant portion of all households, they no longer have children to rear and their hearths have shrunk to one or two persons.[30] It is remarkable that this continuous shrinkage in households directed by females should take an identical form in both city and countryside. Nevertheless, the total weight of these households is less significant in rural areas, where woman family heads are far less numerous.

In households directed by a male, on the other hand, the urban and rural trends over a period of time are widely divergent. The rural hearth is, to

29. They are very few: 44 in all, in their 20s, out of 7,096 feminine household heads and 59,770 heads of both sexes.

30. More than one half reached or surpassed their sixtieth year.

begin with, consistently larger than that of the citizen; it also reaches its maximum size at a later point in time. And the losses it endures in the last phases of its cycle are three times less significant than in the city. After age 40, a man living in the Tuscan countryside still directs a hearth including, on the average, at least five persons. Variations in this typical size remain minimal. In contrast, townsmen have authority over five persons only between ages 40 and 60. Urban characteristics are still more exaggerated in a large city such as Florence. Lower peak sizes accompany the generally small membership of the urban domestic group; the average size of families headed by very old men is very much reduced.[31]

These variations are obviously tied to events marking the life of the head and his spouse. Children multiply when the parents are in the prime of life, and they depart when the parents grow old. But it is striking that membership in the peasant hearth remains stable when the head of the household has reached age 60; even his patrimony continues to expand. The schema, according to which average size depends on the number of children brought into the world, raised in the family, and then let go to pursue their own careers, is not strictly applicable to rural hearths. Their example demonstrates to the contrary that the children present in a rural hearth are not always the offspring of its head, in the same way that marriage and household formation are not identical in the Tuscan countryside.[32] Can we, under these conditions, construct a cycle of family development in Tuscany which would adequately describe the experiences of both townsmen and peasants, both rich and poor?

THE TUSCAN CYCLE OF FAMILY DEVELOPMENT

The age of the head of the household in fact allows us to view more dynamically the rigid categories we have so far used. As Figure 10.8 shows, the young man promoted to the status of household head— a rather unusual event, as only 7.8 percent of rural hearths and 10.6 of those in towns are under the direction of men under age 28—will live alone or will have the charge of younger brothers and sisters or a widowed mother. These configurations are more frequent and last longer in town than in countryside. Near age 30, only 16 percent of young heads of rural households remain in this situation, while 31 percent of those in the city still live amidst the "debris" of an earlier conjugal family. The male reluctance to marry in an urban context helps to perpetuate these remnants of urban families.

31. See Herlihy, 1972c, Table 1, p. 22.

32. After a maximum (2.27) among fathers age 38 to 42 years, the mean number of children under age 14 per rural couple falls continuously (1.94 at 48–52 year, 1.08 at 58–62 years, 0.26 above 67 years. On the other hand, after a maximum (2.42) in the same age category, the mean number of children per rural household falls much more slowly.

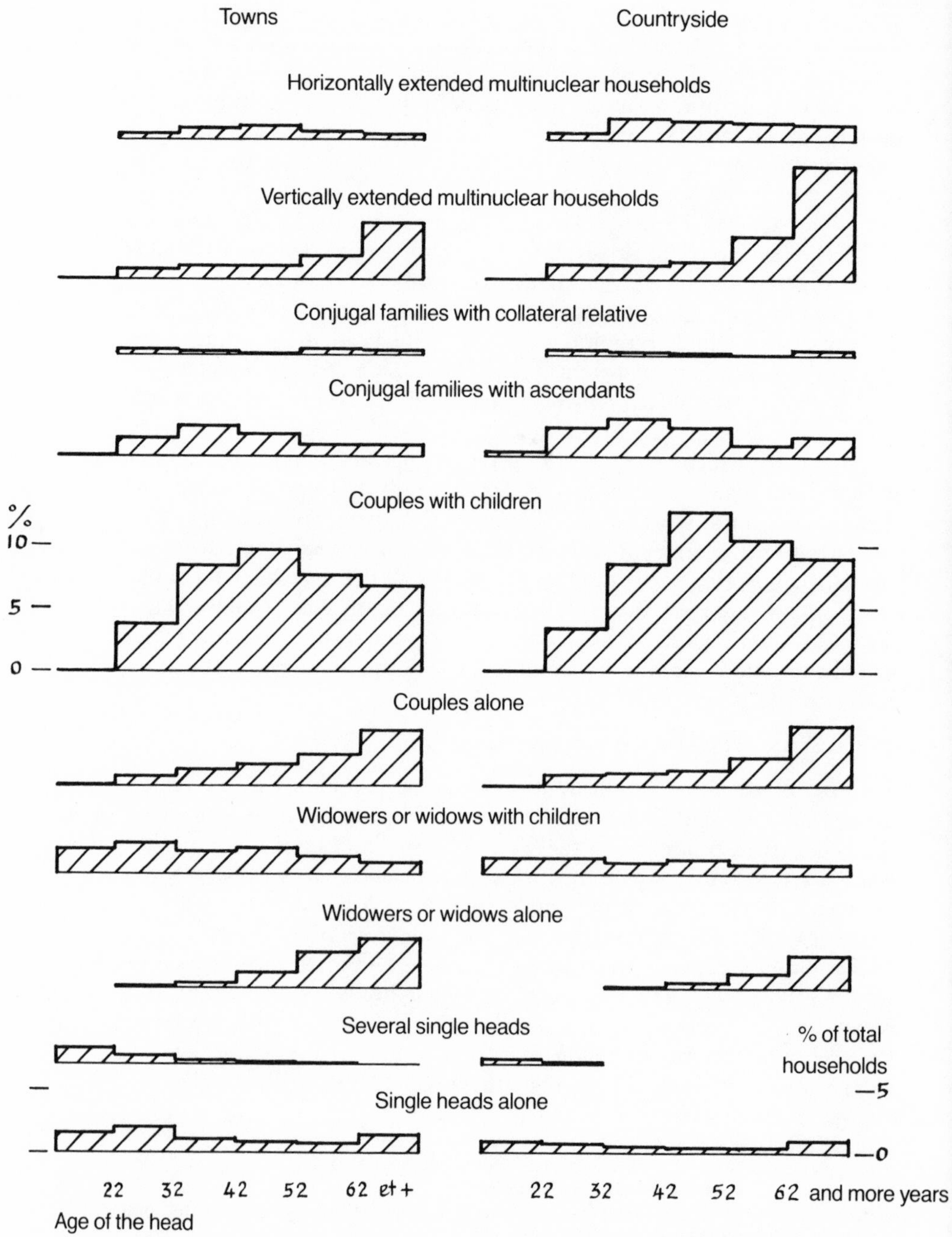

Towns

Countryside

Horizontally extended multinuclear households

Vertically extended multinuclear households

Conjugal families with collateral relative

Conjugal families with ascendants

Couples with children

%

10

5

0

Couples alone

Widowers or widows with children

Widowers or widows alone

Several single heads

% of total households

5

Single heads alone

0

22 32 42 52 62 et +

22 32 42 52 62 and more years

Age of the head

Fig. 10.8. Typology of Households according to the Age of the Head (Tuscany, 1427)

As soon as the head of the household has reached age 30, there begins to appear, especially in the countryside, an already significant number of households in which reside, alongside the widowed mother and her remaining single children, the young couple, the son and his new wife. Between ages 30 and 50, married couples with their children make up the majority of households; the presence of an old and widowed parent remains common, however, in the countryside. The roughly constant proportion of joint family households formed of married brothers (or of their offspring, cousins to one another) show that the peasantry at least freely associated the residential community with the maintenance of an undivided patrimony. After the head passes his fiftieth year, the association under the same roof of several married couples belonging to different generations shows a growing importance. In this last age category, the patriarchal family, which subjects to the authority of an aged man one or more married couples of the following generation, forms a third of all peasant hearths, but only one-fifth in the city. This for the reason that in the city, widowers, detached from their familial framework, in large part live alone.

In comparison with the urban family, the rural hearth is continuously marked, at all ages of its head, by a stronger cohesion between ascendants and descendants in the masculine line, and also between brothers and descendants of brothers. The city rather favors solitude: the solitude of the young in search of work; the solitude of widows or of old couples whose children have set up independent households or are already dead; the solitude even of the married couple caring only for its own children and not displaying, by a common residence, solidarity with brothers or other kin.

The distribution of household heads according to age is, as we have seen, very unequal; only late in life are the chances good that a male will accede to the position of household head, whatever his marital status. One-half of the households, the head of which has passed age 50 in the city, and 55 in the countryside, show a significant representation of those types of domestic groups which, as we have seen, are characteristic of the higher age brackets. Grand families under the leadership of the aged weigh more heavily on the aggregation of households than their clustering in the bracket of older heads might suggest. This further implies that at the core of each principal type of domestic group, the importance given to the lower age categories ought to be discounted. In fact, one-half of the multiple households including two generations have as their head a man older than 62 years in the countryside, and one-half of those with three nuclei are ruled by a man in his 70s. Also, one-half of the joint family households are under the authority of a man over 48.

Thus the rule of patrilocality and the tendency toward keeping the patrimony undivided, which responds to the custom of equal division among male heirs, work to limit the effects of the natural family cycle—expansion as long as children are born and are reared, and contraction when they reach the age when they can set up their own families.[33] The relatively high proportions of multiple households in the rural world of Tuscany confirm that the rules of residence visible in the ricordi of citizens were not exclusively the practice of the well-to-do urban classes, but also characterized peasant behavior in 1427. The young couple of the countryside settles on the paternal farm, just as the young Florentine townsman brings his bride to his urban home, usually that of his father. Given authorization to marry at age 25 or 30, the Tuscan male, probably the eldest son, can expect to remain for a number of years subject to his father's authority. Neither in the city nor in the countryside did the father abandon his powers or pass on his authority to a son living at home. Very few are the parents whose possessions are listed in the Catasto under a son's name, and who appear to be "retired" under their own roof.[34] But the eldest son (sometimes flanked by a brother), married while his father is still alive, stands a good chance of gaining, upon the latter's death, the dignified title of capo di famiglia. And this authority is strong enough to maintain the fraternal community at a more or less constant level (about 10 percent of each age group) among peasants between 40 and 60 years of age.

The tracking of specific family groups across the fifteenth century, from the Catasto of 1427 on, perhaps can show more concretely the fundamental characteristics of family development in Tuscany. We have attempted to do this for certain families from the rural parish of San Lorenzo al Corniolo, in the Mugello north of Florence. The Estimi or Catasti we use are those of 1426, 1428, 1435, about 1444, 1454, 1460, 1470–71, and 1480.[35] In 1428 the parish contained 64 families, but their number and their average size were severely reduced in the course of the fifteenth century.[36] In 1428 single-person households comprised 11 percent; mononuclear households, 53 percent; "vertical" multiple households, 28 percent; and frérèches, 7.8 percent of all households. The proportion of multiple households is thus higher than for Tuscany as a whole (23 percent) in this same period.

In 1460, a generation after the the first Catasto, households with only a

33. Italian inheritance custom did not admit primogeniture in the fifteenth century; see Tamassia, 1911, pp. 122–40; Fumagalli, 1912; Klapisch and Demonet, 1972, pp. 881–82. See also Berkner, 1972b.

34. For an example from the Pisan countryside, see Klapisch and Demonet, 1972, p. 889. Even at Pisa, there are only 15 retired fathers in the 1,750 urban households; in the surrounding countryside 66 in 3,900 households. At Arezzo, 7 in 1,200; in the cortine 9 in 1,200.

35. The register of the Estimo of 1426 is AC 166, and the village is surveyed from f. 97. For 1428, AC 323, ff. 9–57; for 1454, AC 762, ff. 29–64; for 1460, AC 882, ff. 46–135; for 1470, AC 970, ff. 13–92; for 1480, AC 1063, ff. 21–51.

36. See above, chap. 3, pp. 74–77.

single nucleus exceed two-thirds of the total, and persons living alone are two times more numerous than in 1428 (22 percent); multiple households make up no more than 11 percent of the group. The corresponding proportions in 1470 are 51, 32, and 17 percent. The overall trend, in this tiny parish, thus seems, over the fifteenth century, to have reduced the more complex family configurations. But, within this general context of a shrinking domestic group (which is probably not typical of the whole of Tuscany), nearly one-half of the households of the first and second Catasto still passed through a succession of forms similar to those of the cycle we have just described; at one time or another during the fifteenth century they also became extended.[37] A quarter of the mononuclear households of 1428 were profoundly changed in the following generation—they came to include several nuclei, whether because a married son was now living with his parents, or because a frérèche had taken the place of the earlier conjugal family. On the other hand, one-half of the multiple households of 1428 were reduced, 30 years later, to simple conjugal families, to couples or to isolated individuals. As for the 20 or so families that disappear after the middle of the century, they represented, with about two exceptions, simple conjugal families or isolated individuals, old persons for the most part, or marginal characters who had fallen under a fine or penalty and who had probably left the village.

The diagrams in Figure 10.9 show the evolution of some of these domestic groups between 1428 and 1480. When we first encounter them, numbers 3 and 4 are joint households of married brothers, with whom the aged mother still resides. In 1460, number 4 gives evidence of having passed through a curious intermediate phase during which an uncle, recently deceased, was living with his son, a nephew, and the children of another nephew; in 1470 a new frérèche is reconstituted around the son of one of the brothers of 1428. The frérèche represented in number 3 dissolves in 1460, to reform in 1470 as a vertically extended multiple household, joining a married uncle and a married nephew. The conjugal family of number 1 is already extended in 1428 by the presence of two brothers and a niece of the household head. It subsequently, near 1435, evolves into a vertical household, while still retaining a collateral relative attached to the couple; then, it collapses between 1470 and 1480 to a nuclear household, truncated by the death of the wife. With the fifth household, we pass from a conjugal family extended by a nipote (either a nephew or a grandson) to a stem family, then to a frérèche made up of the sons of the first couple, and finally to a frérèche of widowers. Here the community of brothers proves to be quite tenacious. In 1480, however, its chances of survival seem slim. Number 6 is

37. Compare the development of hearths at Prato, below pp. 325–27.

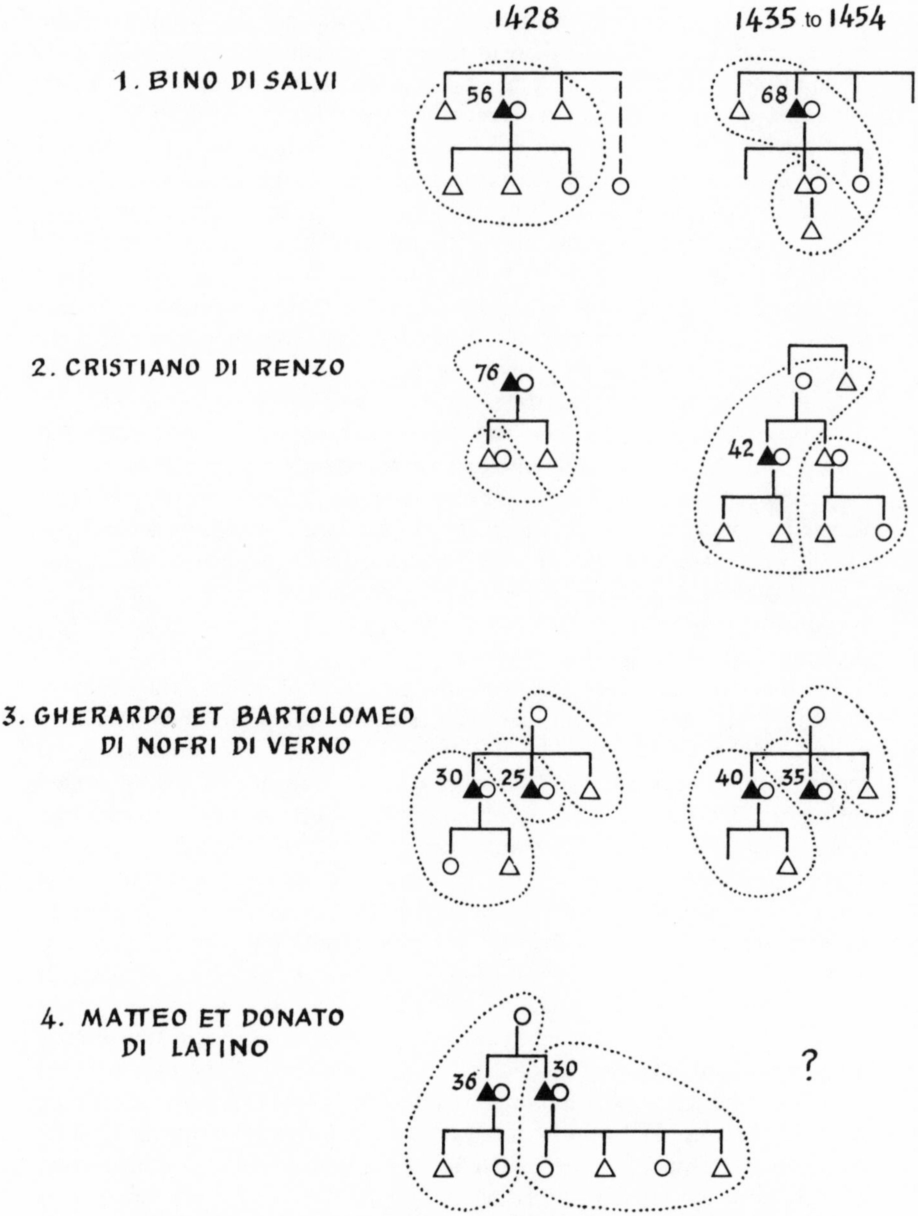

1428 | 1435 to 1454

1. BINO DI SALVI

56

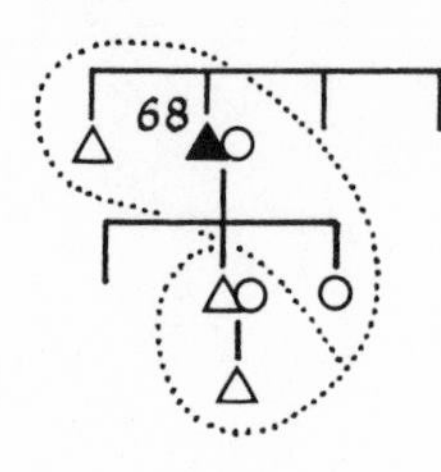

2. CRISTIANO DI RENZO

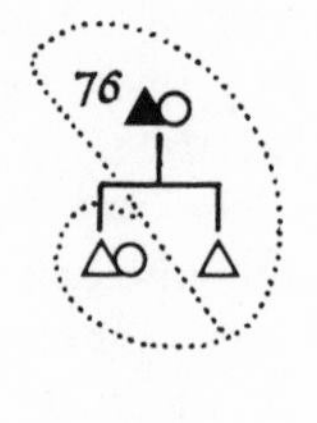

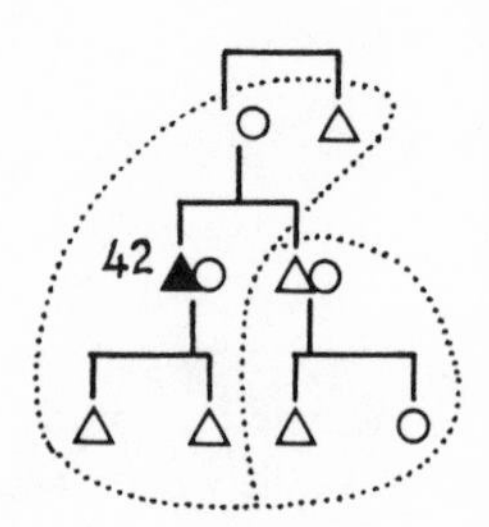

3. GHERARDO ET BARTOLOMEO DI NOFRI DI VERNO

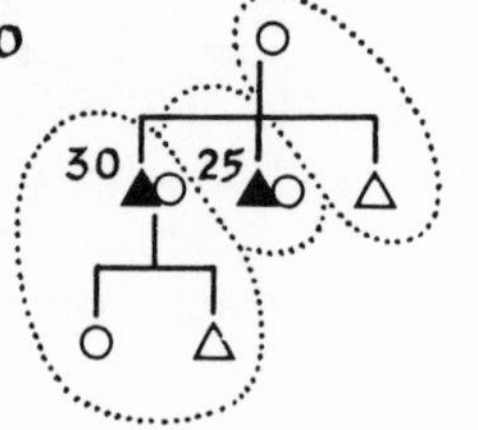

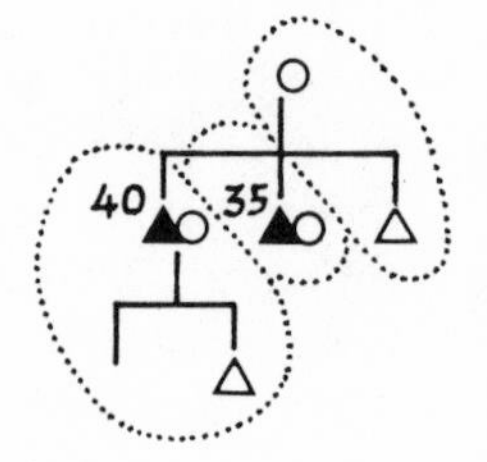

4. MATTEO ET DONATO DI LATINO

36
30

?

Fig. 10.9. The Development Cycle of Some Families at San Lorenzo al Corniolo (Fifteenth Century)

1460

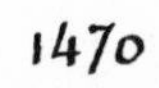

1480

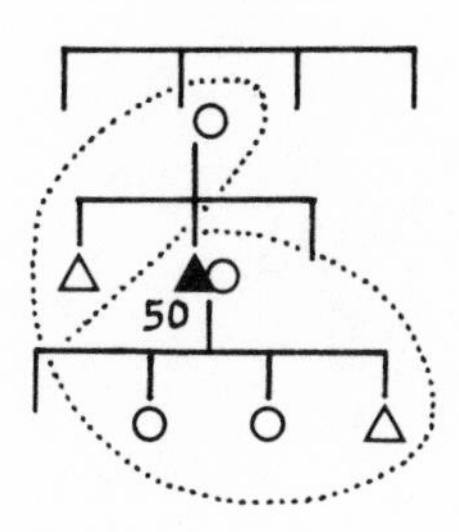

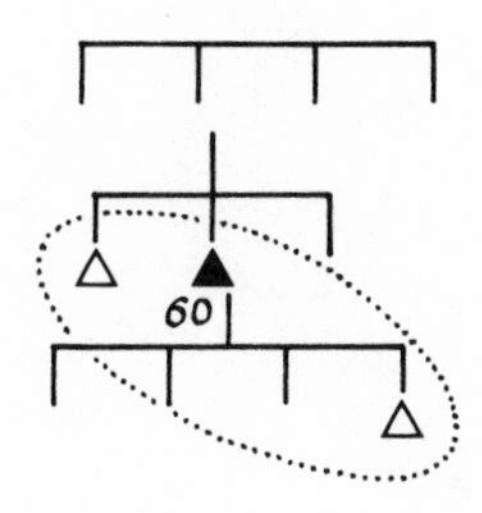

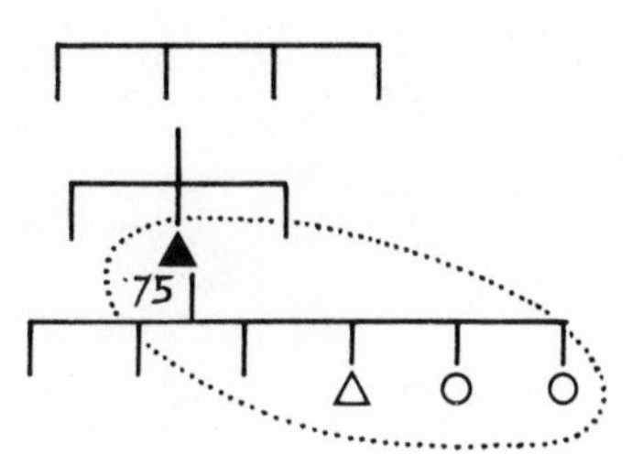

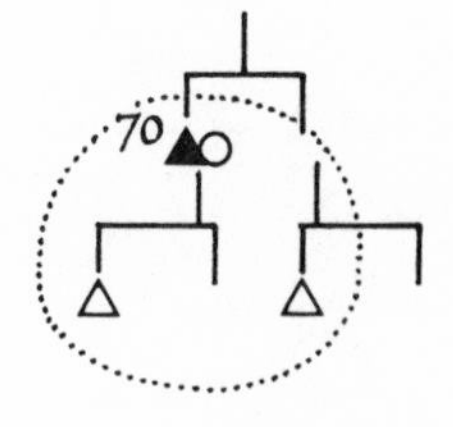

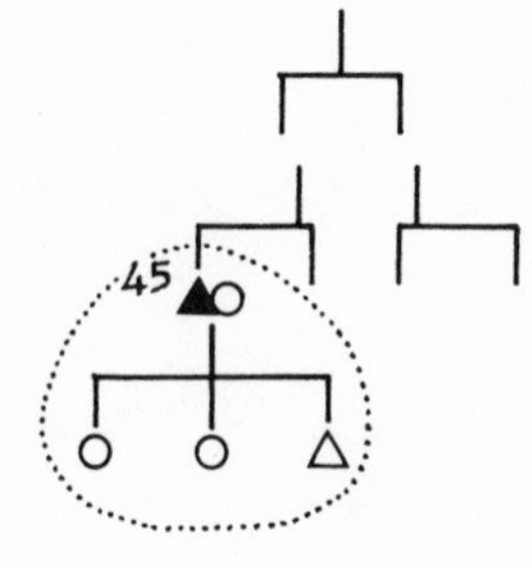

?

50

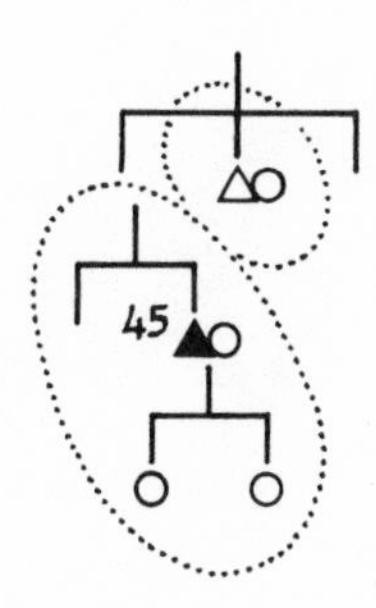

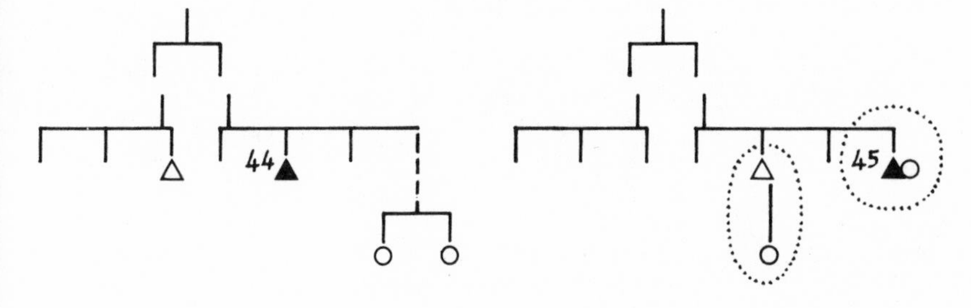

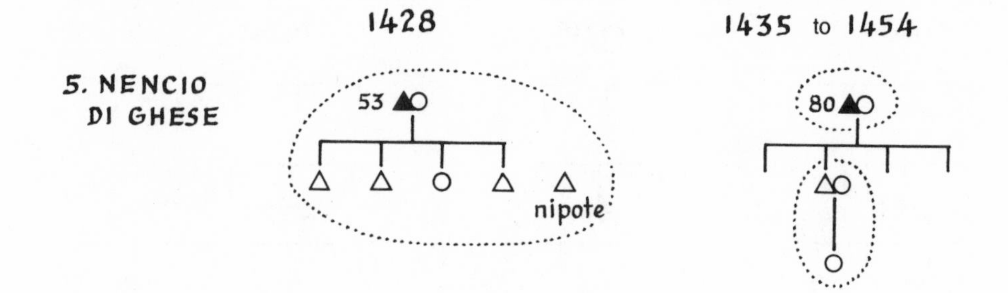
1428
1435 to 1454
5. NENCIO
DI GHESE
53
nipote
80

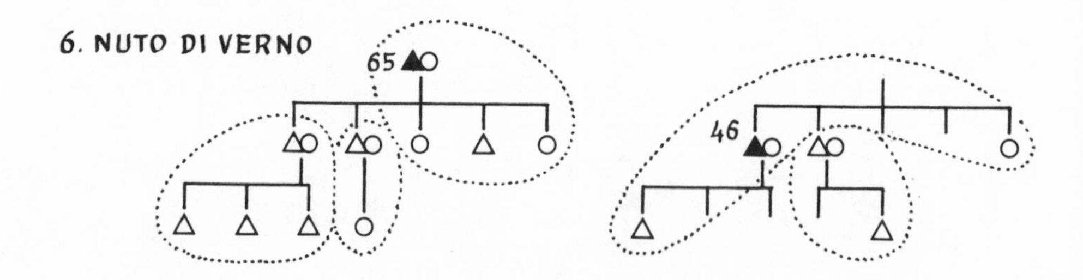
6. NUTO DI VERNO
65
46

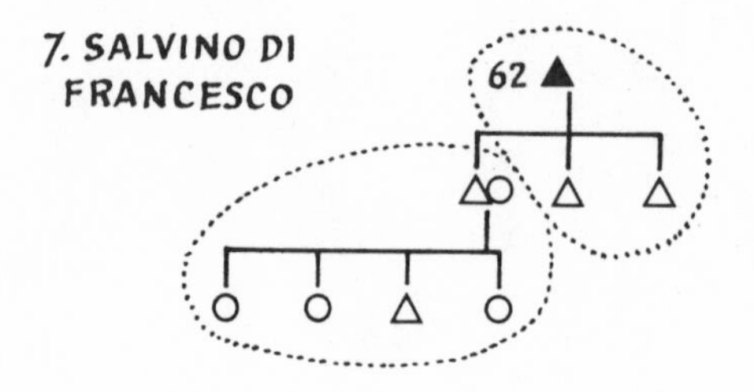
7. SALVINO DI
FRANCESCO
62

?

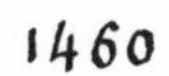

1470

1480

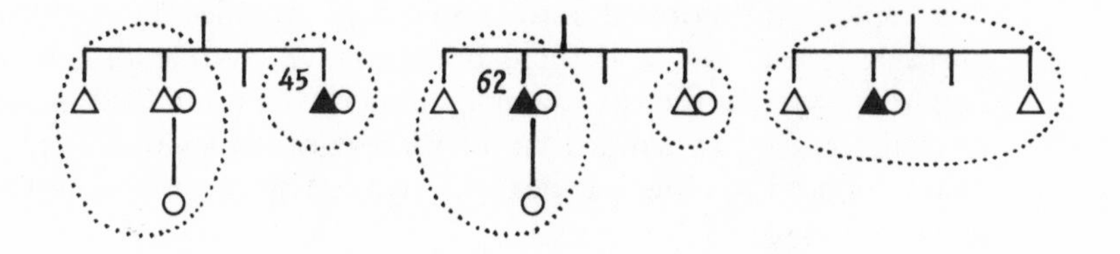

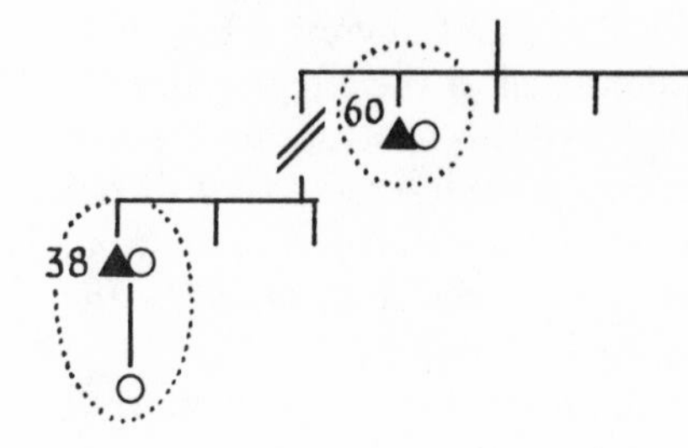

?

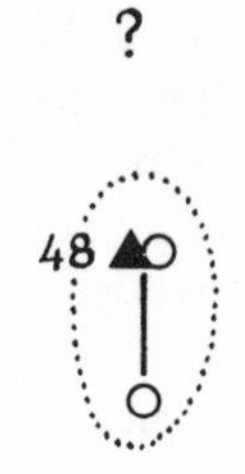

?

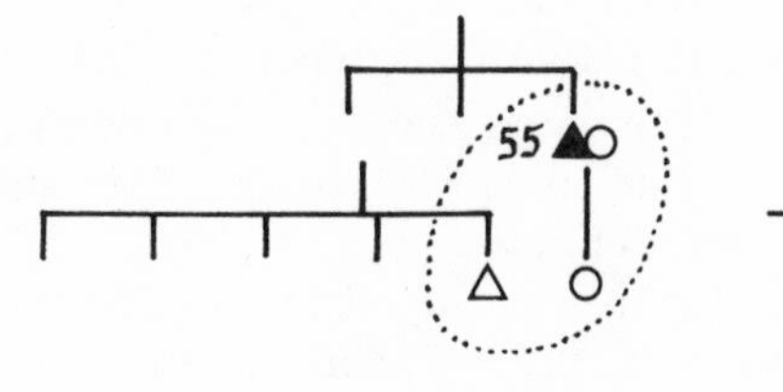

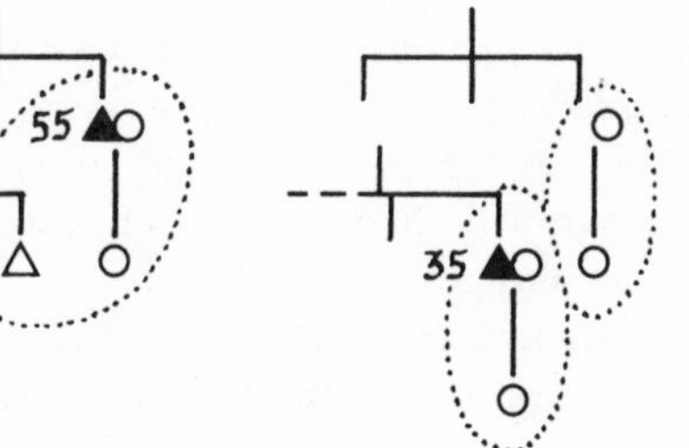

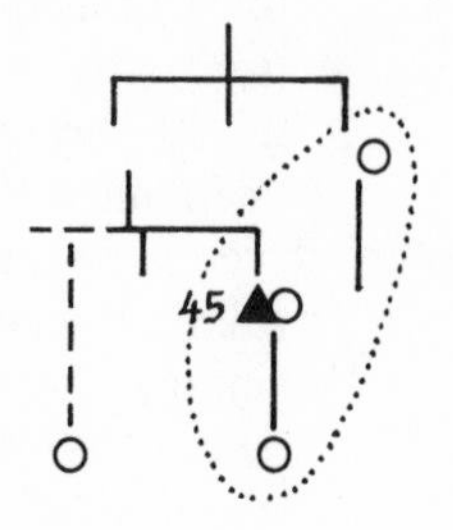

an example of a patriarchal family which evolves into a frérèche a decade later, after the death of the parents, and subsequently breaks into small nuclear families. Number 2, joining couples from different generations, is also rapidly transformed into a frérèche, extended by widowers of the previous generation, and then, by successive contractions, to a conjugal family in 1470. In the last example, number 7, a household including three generations evolves toward an association of uncles with nephews and is finally reduced to a nuclear hearth, extended by the presence of a niece and an elderly aunt.

These few examples are illuminating for several reasons. They clearly reflect the general trend toward simpler domestic configurations in the village; they also give expression to the cyclical sequence of forms, alernately enlarged and diminished, that our cross-sectional analysis of the Catasto led us to expect. There is an additional point of interest. They show the relative fragility of extended families; almost all of them represent only a phase in a cycle of development extending over two generations. At least in this pastoral zone (three of our seven examples are households of shepherds in 1427), family solidarity comes under stress in the second generation, even in domestic groups where, we might expect, solidarity would be the strongest, and it is almost always ruptured in the third.

With the help of similar materials from the Pisan Estimi and Catasti of the fifteenth century, Michele Luzzati has studied families in the commune of San Sisto al Pino e Musigliano, a tiny, suburban village in the county of Pisa. He shows that in a very different agricultural environment the largest and most complex family groups of 1428 were more easily perpetuated, and for a longer time, than small nuclear households.[38] Of the latter, four out five listed in the Catasto had disappeared before 1460, while the fifth retained the same simple structure. The four large family groups of 1429 maintained themselves, on the other hand, in an equally complex form and even grew in size between the first Catasto and 1491.[39]

Other scholars have undertaken similar analyses of urban families, specifically lineages and their various branches, belonging to the Florentine patriciate.[40] Family memoirs as well as fiscal declarations allow a reconstruction of the experiences of the extended family quite common in this social environment. F. W. Kent shows that the son of a Florentine family, if he intended to leave the house, generally departed before the birth of his children; conversely, a family of three generations, partriarchal or stem in

38. Luzzati, 1976, especially pp. 104–23. The village is located in the lower Arno valley; the peasants lease their lands from a multitude of owners.

39. This occurs within a growing population, which was not the situation apparently at S. Lorenzo al Corniolo.

40. Goldthwaite, 1968, pp. 36–37; Starn, 1971; Kent, 1977.

its configuration, had the best chances of survival for as long as the grandfather survived. His death converted the meńage into a household of brothers; but the burdens of maintaining a common home and frequent disagreements regarding the amount of support the brothers ought to provide their separate children (in dowries for daughters or capital for sons) usually led to its early dissolution.

Thus, the families of the Florentine patriciate, as well as those in the countryside, follow a cycle which takes them from simple forms—individuals living alone, widows and their children, young couples, and couples with children—to complex configurations, from a temporary stem-family type to the patriarchal household to the frérèche (or more rarely, an association of cousins), and then back again to simpler units. The cycle then renews. This theoretical cycle of development, stretched out over more than the lifetime of an individual, still does not describe even a third of the households in 1427.[41] We shall subsequently examine the demographic factors, which for a time could reduce the chances that many complex configurations would appear in the community. At all events, still other social factors played upon the developmental cycle to prolong or shorten its phases or to reduce or increase the statistical frequency of the forms it generated.

PEASANT AND PATRICIAN HEARTHS

The principal events in the life of the head of the household subjected his possessions, as we know, to a process of dispersal or accumulation, the steps of which closely paralleled the entries and departures of family members. Conversely, the wealth he possessed could induce the household head to quicken or slow down the process of family fission or aggregation.

In rural zones, for example, where the tenurial system is not based on peasant ownership or long-term leases, the cycle of family development does not often reach the phase of frérèches joining married men, and multiple hearths are more commonly patriarchal in character (see Map 10.6). In areas of mezzadria the exploitation of a usually large and compact farm, the podere, had a powerful influence on family structure. Thus, the family of sharecroppers had to be complete and its quality preserved to assure the proper performance of the agricultural labors.[42] The padrone wants the number residing on his farm to remain more or less constant (or at least the number of workers constant) in the interest of good cultivation. Unfortunately, the Catasto does not allow us to estimate the actual number of hired hands that sharecroppers may have taken on, at certain stages in the family cycle, in order to supplement temporary deficiencies in family

41. See Wheaton, 1975, for a discussion of the developmental cycle.
42. See above, chap. 8, p. 243–44.

Table 10.6. Average Size of the Florentine Hearth according to the Age of the Head and Wealth

Age Category	*Households*			
	Richest Half		*Poorest Half*	
	Ave. Size	*Index*	*Ave. Size*	*Index*
0—17	3.16	51.3	2.05	44.9
18–22	3.13	50.8	2.30	50.3
23–27	3.47	56.3	2.66	58.2
28–32	3.99	64.8	3.36	73.5
33–37	4.62	75.0	3.86	84.5
38–42	5.38	87.3	4.27	93.4
43–47	6.16	100.0	4.57	100.0
48–52	6.04	98.1	4.19	91.7
53–57	6.06	98.4	4.05	88.6
58–62	5.55	90.1	3.70	81.0
63–67	5.43	88.2	3.61	79.0
68 +	5.58	90.6	3.24	70.9

SOURCE: Catasto of the city of Florence, 1427. The age category with the largest average size is taken as base 100.

labor.[43] But most sharecroppers probably did not have the means to hire outside laborers. They therefore had recourse to near relatives in order to adjust the available labor force to the work demanded. It was better to retain a brother or married son, to draw on the labor of the elderly or of children, rather than neglect some part of the podere or hire a day laborer. On the other hand, joint family households joining brothers into frérèches are less common in regions of mezzadria, because there they did not have to serve the function of postponing the division of patrimonies. Thus, the mezzadria poderale, wherever it dominated the relations of production, contributed to the maintenance, or the reconstitution, of complete and complex familial groups; the system compensated for the lack of property or for poverty, which in other social sectors undermined domestic solidarity.

For its part, the example of the Florentine patriciate suggests that wealth powerfully influenced the course of the developmental cycle within an urban environment. The swollen size of rich hearths, noted above, indicates a protraction of the cycle of family development within the upper classes of urban society. We can at once verify in summary fashion this relation between wealth and the developmental cycle. Table 10.6 shows the variations in household size according to the age of the head, for the richest and poorest halves of the Florentine population. Always larger than than those of the poor, the hearths of the rich develop at a slower pace. Households in both groups attain their peak size in the same age category, but the rich arrive there in retarded stages. Then too, poor households shrink immedi-

43. Unlike the documentation used by Berkner in his seminal study, 1972a.

ately after their maxima; in contrast, the hearths of the wealthy show extraordinary stability. Right up to the extreme old age of its head, the rich household in the city keeps its big size, and in this it resembles the hearths of the countryside.

The belated inflation of Florentine households in the wealthier half of the community cannot be attributed to children born to the family head; he had, after all, already reached or passed his fiftieth year. Within the poorer households on the other hand, the cycle indicates that the relationship between the fertility of the couple and the size of the hearth was much more direct.

This crude division between the rich and poor has the limited merit of indicating that the households of the upper classes tended to compensate for the losses they experienced (through the marriages of daughters, in particular) through more or less equivalent additions. This process, which renders the domestic group more complex, is particularly pronounced at the highest levels of the social scale.

Among the 472 richest families of Florence (those possessing more than 3,200 florins in gross assets), 23 percent contain at least two family nuclei.[44] This is the same proportion which characterizes the entire rural population. Among the rich, isolated individuals are rare; nearly everyone appears integrated into a household. The small numbers of elderly couples living alone show that they too, like older couples in the countryside, tended to maintain common residency with their married sons. Among the urban rich (unlike the urban poor), a small or miserable domicile does not prevent the daughter-in-law from living under the roof of her father-in-law. He in turn retains administrative control over the patrimony until his death. Well-to-do citizens are, however, distinguished from the peasantry for this reason: the patriarchal family, uniting under the father's authority several married sons, appears less frequently in an urban context. At Florence only one out of ten multiple households, extended over several generations, includes more than one filial couple. The Florentine patrician delays as long as possible the marriage of his sons. If he must, in the interest of family survival, allow his eldest son to marry, at least he reduces the menace of partition by keeping the younger sons in prolonged bachelorhood. Younger brothers did not find this carefree state, in which they long remained, entirely objectionable, as an English traveler of the sixteenth century shrewdly noted.[45] The upper-class household at Florence thus seems, at first glance, reminiscent of the famous stem family in peasant society in which the old couple keeps under its roof one married son who will ulti-

44. See Herlihy, 1972c; Klapisch, 1972b.
45. See the text cited above, chap. 7, n. 30.

mately inherit the farm. The other children, who might strike out on independent careers, receive only minor support; but offspring who elect to stay at home must remain unmarried.[46] But this resemblance is in fact superficial. At Florence, this stem configuration represents only a passing phase. Family memoirs show that the bachelorhood of the younger sons was not permanent; after, and at times even before, the father's death, they were prudently and gradually married off as wealth allowed.[47]

The eldest brother who assumed the authority of the deceased father was likely to show the same reserve shown toward the marriages of his younger siblings. But he could not, in practice, prevent them from claiming their share of the inheritance and departing whenever they deemed his own power over them insupportable.[48]

The Catasto does not allow us to know what exact proportion of patriarchal households survived in the cities in the form of frérèches made up of married men. The ratio between these joint family households headed by a man close to age 40 (who had probably only recently lost his father) and patriarchal households with an old man at the head (who was likely soon to die), was approximately 1:2.[49] But this only indicates an order of magnitude, and the estimate rests on the questionable assumption that we can compare the numbers of hearths, the heads of which belong to widely different age cohorts.

At all events, frérèches formed at the death of the father did not last as long in the city as in the countryside. By the time the heads of a frérèche reached their sixtieth year, there survived at Florence only a quarter of the number that existed 20 years before, as opposed to one-half in the countryside. Often, the household divided only a few years after the father's death. Thus, the three sons, all adults, of Giovanni Niccolini, who died in July 1381, divided the paternal possessions from November 1382. The eldest brother, Niccolaio, took a separate residence, although still contiguous to the house of his two younger brothers, Lapo and Filippo. These latter lived under a common roof until October 1385, after their double marriage in the spring of 1384.[50] Richard Goldthwaite cites other examples of these divisions, occurring shortly after entry into an inheritance.[51] The sons of Sim-

46. For a discussion of the thesis of Le Play, see Laslett and Wall, 1972, pp. 16–28; Berkner, 1972a.

47. See above, chap. 7, pp. 226–28. Fumagalli, 1912, describes the law of partitions in urban fraternal communities.

48. Morelli, 1956, pp. 146–51, gives the example of his father Pagolo, who had long to contest the authority of his older brother Giovanni to secure his rights.

49. In this hypothesis, 50 percent of patriarchal households in the countryside, 58 percent at Florence, and 59 percent in all towns, were transformed into frérèches.

50. Niccolini, 1969, pp. 60–79; Klapisch, 1976b, pp. 955–59.

51. Goldthwaite, 1968, pp. 72 (Strozzi), 113 (Guicciardini), 159 (Gondi).

one di Filippo Strozzi, a contemporary of Lapo mentioned above, would continue after the death of their father, in 1424, to make common investments in a wool company. Still, according to the Catasto, in 1427 they were living apart and at that date no longer held undivided property.

A frérèche could, however, survive longer, especially if some of the brothers were still minors. The children of Piero di messer Luigi Guicciardini long remained together under the same roof after the death of their father in 1441. They divided the patrimony and separated the families a good twelve years later.[52] The sons waited until the youngest had reached adulthood before dividing the property. Often, the elder brothers had an interest in maintaining control over the shares of their minor siblings. Giovanni Morelli dwelt on the trials of his father Pagolo, whose elder brothers "had taken and combined everything with their own property, with little regard for Pagolo, still a minor. . . ."[53] But still in the fifteenth century, the bonds of affection nutured by long cohabitation during the lifetime of the parents occasionally survived their departure; a few brothers retained throughout life the affection and the intimacy formed in their youngest years.

The family memoirs from the period of the Catasto confirm the tendency of the privileged urban classes to hold parents and married sons together under the same roof. They had several reasons for preserving a common household, at least for a while. A too hasty division of paternal goods and commercial investments might disrupt the family business and bring the heirs to ruin.[54] (Of course, the desire to limit risk and commercial responsibities could also lead to a a quick division of patrimony.) The paring of households costs also favored the maintenance of these temporary frérèches. In Alberti's dialogue, the aged Giannozzo, apostle of patriarchal values, warned against divisions:

> . . . since it would be necessary to place two cloths on two tables, to burn two logs in two hearths, to hire two servants for two households, where only one is needed. . . .

He goes on in a similar vein:

> . . . it pains me to see families divided, to come in and go out through many doors; and I never allowed that my brother Antonio should live apart from me under another roof. . . .[55]

52. Ibid., pp. 123–24.
53. Morelli, 1956, p. 146.
54. This is the situation of the Guicciardini; see Goldthwaite, 1968, pp. 36–37, and the nuances added by Starn, 1971.
55. Alberti, 1960, 1:192.

Doubtlessly, disagreements and divergent ambitions often quickly sundered these fraternal unions. Still, the history of the Florentine patrician family from the end of the fourteenth through the fifteenth century does not seem entirely to contradict Alberti's ideas. The ancient sense of familial solidarity struck deep roots. "Let families," Alberti urges, "remain under the same roof and, if they grow so that one home cannot contain them, at least let them place themselves under the shadow of a single will."[56] In a strict sense, the vision of the family group which Alberti proposes—living together, earning together, consuming together in unity and discipline—was an outmoded, archaic ideal in the fifteenth century.[57] But not entirely. Members of a family who had to separate for lack of space still sought to live in neighboring houses; at times they kept a common entry, exactly as Giannozzo wanted. Groups of relatives showed their solidarity in many, often loose forms of association and of near residency; these linkages resist classification into firm categories.[58] If the lineage was no longer organized under a patriarch, the father of the family emulated, in more modest dimensions, this model of authority over his direct descendants. The patrician household with several generations came to be oriented downward, toward the immediate descendants, rather than backward, towards the *antecessori*.[59] The individual was no longer as dependent as he once had been on the help of a large lineage, on a common patrimony, and on family-based commercial networks. But he still drew benefits from a unified family group.

The developmental cycle of poor citizens differs sharply from that of the great urban families; this for the reason that it does not encompass a part of the married life of the sons. Among the poor and the miserabili, the "neolocal" establishment of married children predominates. Primarily for this reason the hearth shrinks in size after the head reaches maturity, and the number of couples living alone is larger here than in any other wealth category. The scant numbers of vertically extended joint family households indicate that formations of this type, which ought to have appeared after the marriage of a young couple, rapidly dissolved. Here, the harsh condi-

56. Ibid., pp. 191, 234 (see the text of the epigraph to this chapter), ". . . sotto uno tetto si riducano le famiglie, e se, cresciuta la famiglia, una stanza non può riceverle, assettinsi almeno sotto una ombra tutti d'uno volere."

57. The different definition he gives a few pages earlier (see above, n. 7) shows the ambiguity of Alberti's conceptions and the discordances between the narrow definition he offers of the domestic group and his ideal of the family community.

58. This is shown in the Catasto by the difficulties which the clerks sometimes show in identifying families, and by the many repetitions of data, shifts, and corrections. Later, many patrimonies would be, out of bureaucratic fatigue, registered together, even though the families no longer really lived together.

59. Goldthwaite, 1968, pp. 69–73; 269–75.

tions circumscribing the lives of the poor did not allow the underlying rule of patrilocal marriages to operate freely. Cramped lodgings, the often dispersed employment of the different family members, and other factors undermined the cohesion of the domestic group among the poor and gave it an abbreviated developmental cycle. Without a patrimony to defend, without the political and economic interests of a great lineage to advance, the conjugal family—or its remnants—largely prevailed in the poor urban classes. Only among the rich does the general system of marriage and residency work freely and effectively to shape their households and the course of the domestic cycle.

The same legal framework and the same rules of residence thus allowed domestic groups to react in very different ways to the pressures of their economic circumstances. The rule of patrilocal marriage did not command the behavior of the landless peasants, nor the rural artisans, nor the poor and humble city folk. On the other hand, wealth allowed the urban patriciate to come closest to forming Tuscany's ideal model hearth, to be emulated as far as possible by other social classes. There, authority remained firmly in the hands of wise old men; there, respectful sons submitted to the wishes of the elderly, even when they were well along on their course through life.

III. Time and the Tuscan Family

There is a further question: was the household displayed in the Catasto representative of a medieval stage in an evolution common to all Europe, or was it a regional creation, typical only of Tuscany, or at best, of Mediterranean areas? The question is hard to answer. Most detailed studies of the household bear upon the modern period.[60] The Catasto offers, in fact, the oldest comprehensive data on household organization found anywhere in the West.

The average size of the Tuscan hearth fluctuated widely between 1350 and 1550.[61] What governed these changes—shifts in household structure, or the brutal play of plagues? To judge, we make use here of several soundings, which can give us points of reference, between the last third of the fourteenth century through to the end of the fifteenth. Our sources here are the Estimo of Prato, city and countryside, from 1371.[62] We shall also use

60. Considerations of the modern period have dominated the examination of the historic hearth; see the communications in Laslett and Wall, 1972. However, for an example of the analysis of medieval documents, see Hammel, 1976.

61. See above, chap. 3, pp. 90–91.

62. See Klapisch, 1977.

samples from the later Catasti of Florence and its contado, dating respectively from 1458, 1469–70, and 1480.[63]

Age at marriage constitutes an effective modulator of demographic movements. Pushed upwards, it obstructs the formation of new families; pushed downwards, it boosts fertility and helps erase the losses suffered through epidemics. In 1372, in the wake of two major plagues (1348 and 1363), women of child-bearing age are nearly all married in the region of Prato; children younger than 15 years make up close to 47 percent of the population.[64] In 1427 the proportion drops to 36.7 percent and remains fairly constant at that level to the end of the fifteenth century. More frequent marriages in the years following the plague, true affirmations of life in the face of death, thus bore their fruit. In 1427, the age of marriage has begun to climb and the proportion of married women is slightly lower. Thus, the ratio between young children (from 0 to 4 years) and women from 15 to 44 years of age falls substantially, more than the ratio between married women of the same age group and the children.[65]

While the proportion of children in the total population is a function of nuptiality and fertility, the average family also shows a reduced burden of children. In all of Prato's dependent villages, the average number of children under 15 years falls slightly faster by hearth than by family nucleus. The household of 1427 contains a couple, or the survivors of a conjugal family, a little less frequently than in 1372, and consequently fewer children. As the hearth has continued to expand, even though slightly, over the same period, it follows that members who are not the spouse or children of the household head primarily account for the increase.

After 1427 a demographic recovery slowly gets underway. Normally, the proportion of children in the total population should gradually increase. In fact, in the city of Prato, it moves from 36.1 percent in 1427 to 38.7 percent in 1470; in the countryside, from 36.7 percent to 37.6 percent. The Florentine population contains 38.7 percent of children younger than 15 years in 1427 and 41.1 percent in 1458. Consequently, the category of unmarried children and grandchildren of the household head (all ages included) increases at Florence from 46.8 percent to 53.9 percent.

The greater number of children does not alone explain the growth in household size. The extension of the household in reality reflects the inclusion of relatives more removed from the head than his own children. About 1400 vertical ties gain greater prominence; at Prato, the proportion of households with three or more generations present doubles. Even in the

63. Based on a 10 percent sample of the households in these Catasti.

64. See above, chap. 6, for the pyramid of ages at Prato and its contado.

65. The child-woman ratio (children age 0–4 and women age 15–44) passed from 1.34 in 1371 to 1.05 in 1428; the ratio in regard to married women of the same age, from 1.36 to 1.23.

city of Prato, they form 8.7 percent of the total in 1371, 15.8 percent in 1427, then 14 percent in 1470.[66] In the surrounding countryside the comparable figures are 15.1 percent, 31.4 percent, and 32.6 percent respectively. Over the same years, leadership of the hearth passes to older men. Heads of households from 23 to 42 years of age form, in 1371, 52.3 percent of all household heads in the countryside of Prato, and only 25.7 percent in 1427. Heads older than 62 years trace an opposite evolution: comprising 9.4 percent of the total in 1371, they make up 27.9 percent in 1427. The same tendencies, slightly less pronounced, are visible also in the city.[67] The aging of the head and members of the hearth is partly a function of the general aging of the population; the community contains distinctly larger numbers of the old in 1427 than it did 55 years before.[68] But shifting age distributions do not alone explain these changes. The decline in the average duration of life, in the second half of the fourteenth century, did, in fact, limit the chances that the life courses of several generations could significantly overlap. Now, from the second quarter of the fifteenth century, as life expectancies improved, so also did the overlapping of generations. The deep trends of Tuscan household organization, which had been largely obstructed and obscured when fathers died young, once more showed their thrust and character.

Men in the early fifteenth century were still comparatively young at marriage, and they lived longer and were joined to healthy fathers, now not so much cut down by plague. The fathers also belonged to larger age cohorts than their sons. Comparatively few in number, the sons were destined to pass long years in subservience to their fathers, but they could also promise to their own children that they would know their grandparents. The probability that children under 15 years might live with one or the other of their grandparents doubled between 1372 and 1427 (respectively 19.7 percent and 44.8 percent of these generations lived with at least one paternal grandparent[69] At Prato in 1371, during early childhood (age 0 to 4 years), scarcely one infant in four lived with a grandparent, but one out of two did so in 1427. Over the same period, the chances that children would encounter, under the same roof, their grandparents daily almost tripled.[70]

66. At Bologna in 1395, households with three or more generations present formed 9.7 percent of the hearths. See above, n. 12.

67. Urban household heads belonging to the same age categories pass from 43.5 percent to 32.5 and from 10.2 to 23.2 between 1372 and 1427.

68. See Klapisch, 1977; at Prato, persons age 60 years or more formed only 8.5 percent of the population in 1372, but 15.2 percent in 1428.

69. The proportion of children living with a maternal grandmother did not reach 1 percent in 1427, as in 1372. The frequent remarriage of the grandfathers multiplied the number of grand stepmothers whose presence affect 0.7 percent of the children.

70. In 1372, 5.8 percent of the children in the countryside of Prato, as against 19 percent in 1427, live with a pair of grandparents; 5.9 percent and 21.5 percent respectively with a widowed grandmother.

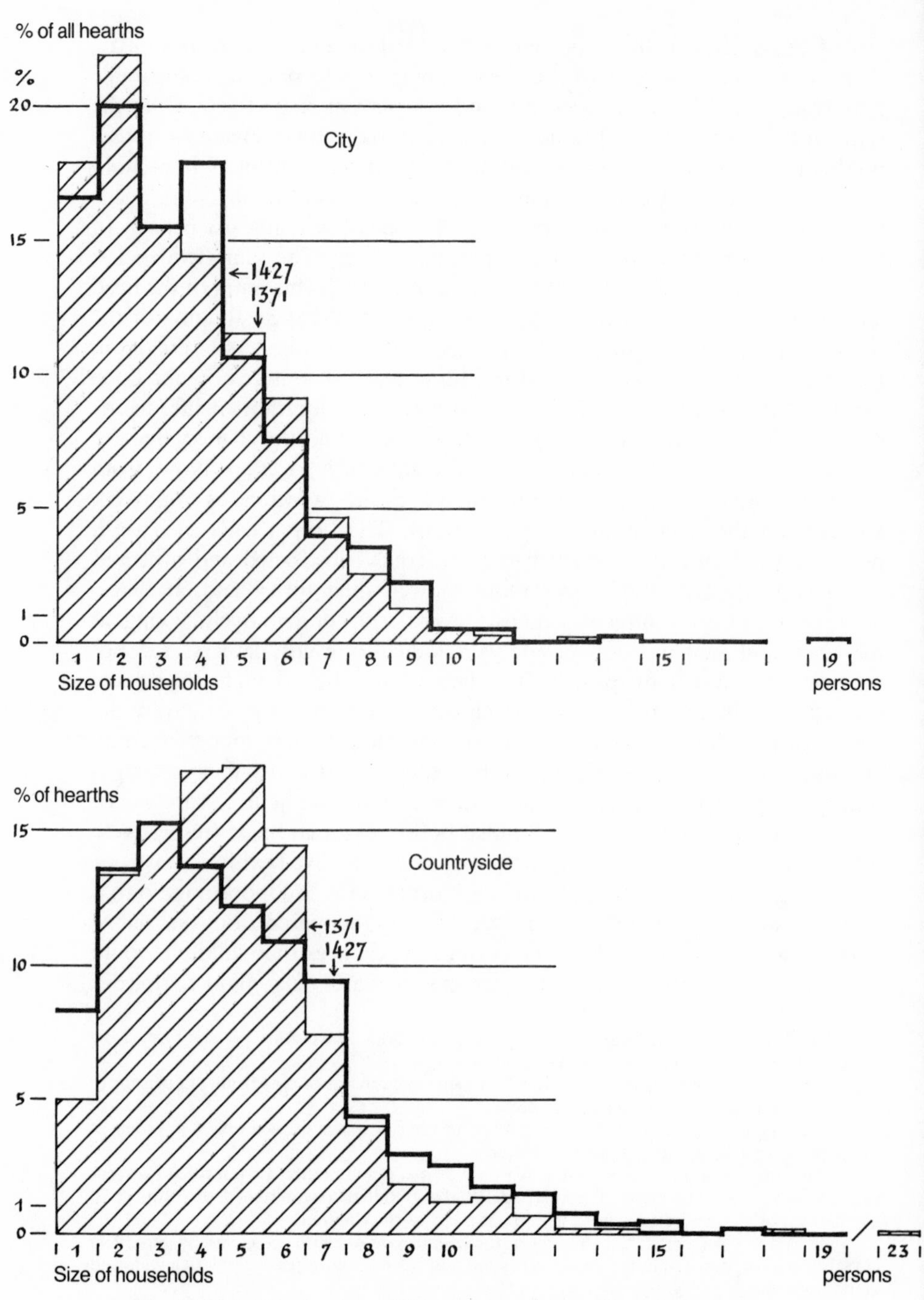

Fig. 10.10A. Distributions of Hearths according to Size at Prato (1371, 1427)

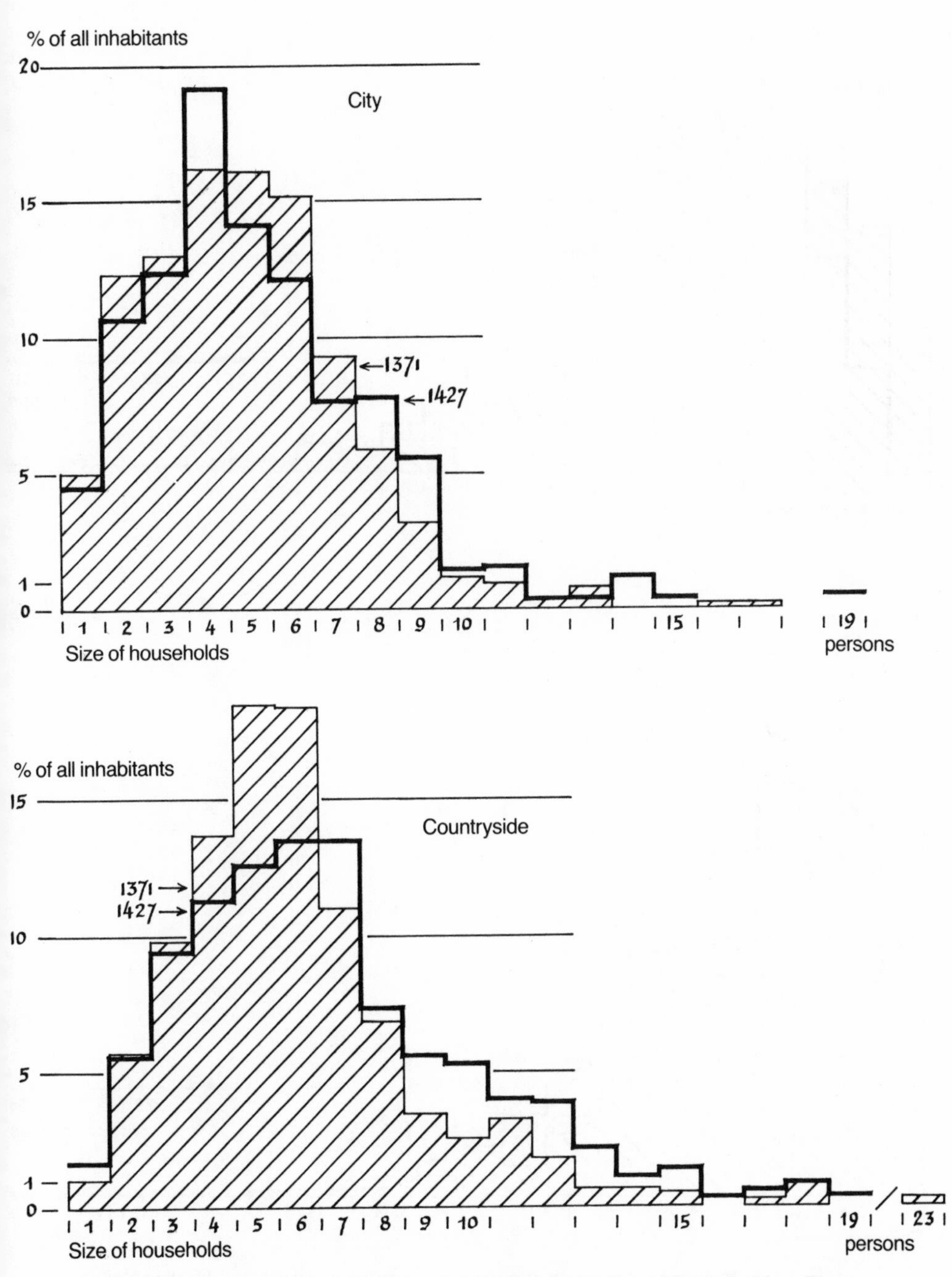

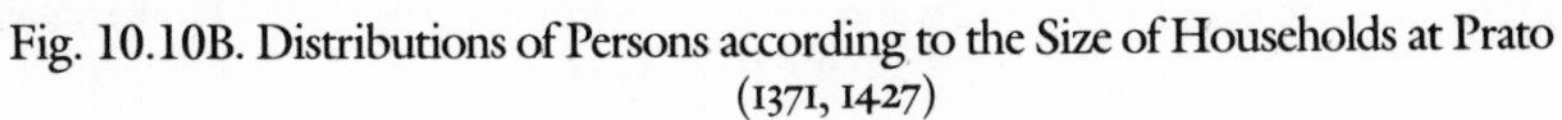
Fig. 10.10B. Distributions of Persons according to the Size of Households at Prato (1371, 1427)

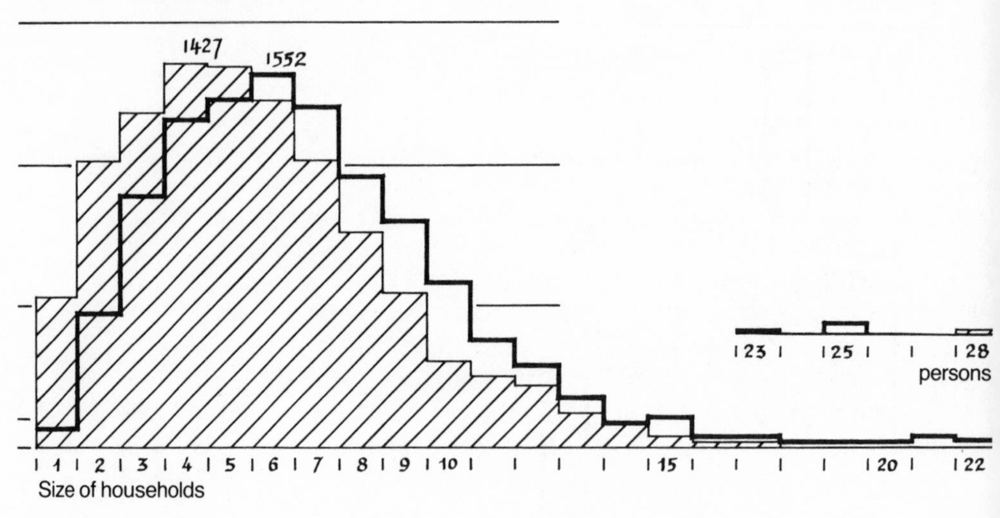

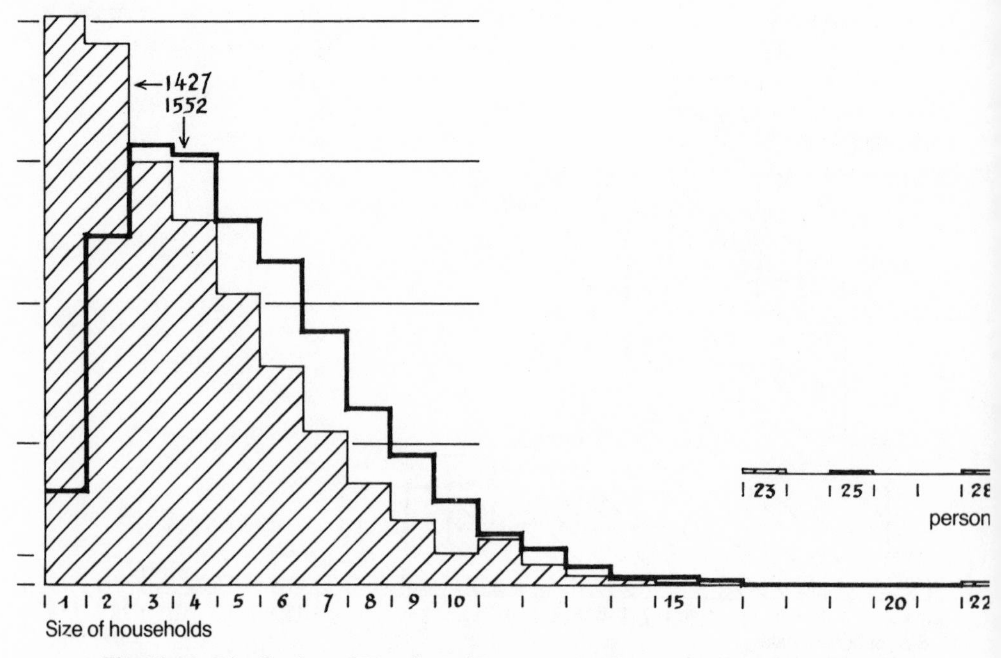

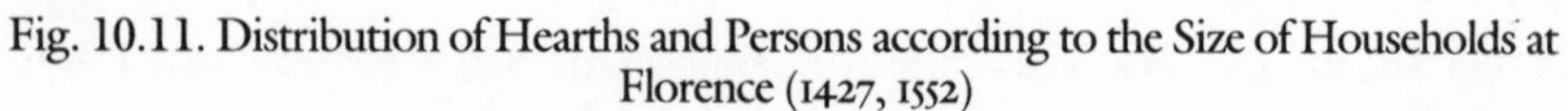
Fig. 10.11. Distribution of Hearths and Persons according to the Size of Households at Florence (1427, 1552)

Demographic movements thus were reinforcing the links between the generations.

Under the same conditions, the chances that multi-nuclear households would grow also improved considerably. In 1371, 14.3 percent of the rural households around Prato contained several families under the same roof. Two-thirds of these joint households were based on associations between father and son, and it is by no means rare to find two married sons. The others were frérèches. The proportion of hearths containing several families indicates, but in a less emphatic way than in 1427, the tendency to maintain a common life even after the marriage of sons—a tendency which, though weaker, also appears in the urban environment (see Table 10.7). Family cohesion shows even greater strength at the period of the Catasto. In the countryside of Prato, the number of multiple households has doubled since 1371 and constitutes close to 28 percent of all hearths. The vertical extension is even more predominant than at the close of the fourteenth century; the share of households with three or more nuclei has doubled (see Figure 10.12). The conclusions reached above thus win further support: the normal household in the Tuscan countryside is not based on the stem family; rather, it collects together, when conditions allow, the parents and several married sons.

Its cohesion is so strong that the fraternal community often survives for long after the death of the father. In 1470 more than a quarter of the hearths around Prato join families of a father and his son. One out of ten shelter brothers and their children. This means that the chances have increased that a peasant would pass all his life, or long years at least, in the domestic company of other relatives besides his wife and children.

Is the countryside of Prato somehow atypical? Perhaps here the general tendencies are pushed to extremes, while elsewhere the economic and demographic conditions do not allow them full display. Still, the grand lines of this evolution are met again at Florence and in the whole of its contado in the fifteenth century. Everywhere, the average number of conjugal families within the household grows over the course of the fifteenth century (see Table 10.7). The phenomenon is due at once to the fall in the proportion of solitaries and of households without family and to the increase in multiple households. The frérèches of the contado grow by a half, while the vertically extended households diminish slightly between 1427 and 1470. Even at Florence, households with more than two generations move from 11.4 percent in 1427 to 13.4 percent in 1480. Those containing collateral relatives, and at times their families, grow substantially (from 17.2 to 26.1 percent). Households uniting at least two conjugal families double between 1427 and 1480. A good part of this growth is attributable to the fraternalization of the hearth. Thus, if multiple households grow only by 50 percent, laterally extended households increase by three times their previous number. Close analysis shows that all Florentine households did not increase for the same reasons in the fifteenth century. The rich added more servants.[71] The poor produced more children.[72] The lateral extension particularly affected well-to-do or rich families, which came to shelter a growing number of the head's brothers, single or married. This evolution apparently continued between 1480 and 1552, though we must follow it through private records such as the ricordi. The number of servants registers fantastic growth up to 1552.[73] But apparently, the swollen size of the Florentine households also primarily reflects the refusal of younger males to marry, or to abandon the hearths in which they were reared.[74]

Thus, in the early fifteenth century, conditions were favorable to the reinforcement of vertical linkages within Tuscan families. Earlier, the brutal fall in life expectancies had dragged down the age of marriage, but this did not have immediate impact on the organization of the domestic group. Shortened life expectancies undermined the chances that parents and married children might live together. However, at the time of the Catasto, lowered mortalities and the great numbers of the aged raised the probabilities that fathers would be living when their sons reached adulthood. This offset the small increase in age at first marriage, occurring since 1371. Thus, the numbers of big, complex households increased quite rapidly, once prolonged life expectancies allowed the ties binding the generations to show their true strength.

Over the course of the fifteenth century, the factors which, during the period of demographic contraction, contributed to the appearance of vertically extended multiple households, tended to give way to factors favoring lateral extension. With a population reaching for stability at the time of the Catasto and finally attaining renewed growth in the last third of the fifteenth century, the proportion of the young grew larger within the community. And the age of marriage once more moved upward. The probability also increased that brothers even after marriage would maintain a com-

71. The coefficient of correlation between average wealth and number of servants increased from 0.716 in 1427 to 0.962 in 1458, indicating that at Florence, at least, the presence of servants was more tightly associated with wealth in 1458 than in 1427.

72. The correlation between wealth and number of children in the household weakens at Florence (and also in the countryside), going from 0.879 to 0.721; this shows that the poor had relatively more children (or the rich fewer) than before.

73. There are in the census 8,890 servants (but what exactly does the word mean in 1552?) 16.7 percent of the Florentine population, of whom 70 percent were women. Of households, 42 percent had at least one servant; Ridolfo Baglioni (from Perugia?) maintained an small army of 57 persons.

74. See above, chap. 3, pp. 91–92, and chap. 7, p. 220.

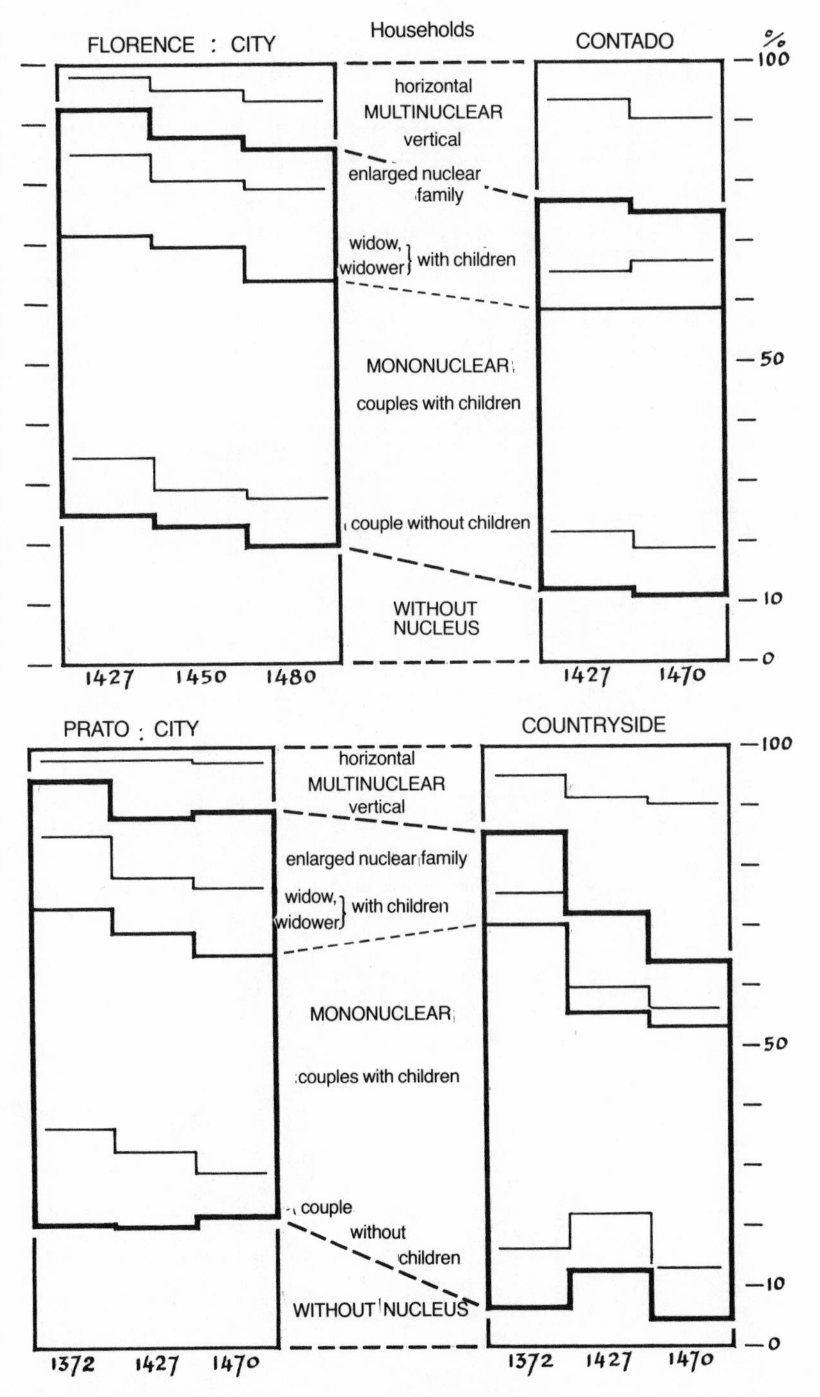

Fig. 10.12. Typology of Households at Prato and at Florence (Fourteenth to Fifteenth Centuries)

Table 10.7. Composition of Tuscan Households (14th and 15th Centuries) in Percentages

	City of Prato			*Contado of Prato*			*Florence*			*Contado of Florence*	
	1371	1427	1470*	1371	1427	1470*	1427	1458*	1480*	1427	1470*
Solitaries	18.5	17.2	20.9	5.2	11.4	3.3	20.3	16.2	14.8	10.9	8.8
No conjugal couple	2.1	2.9	1.2	1.2	1.3	1.0	4.8	6.8	4.8	1.5	2.2
Together	20.6	20.1	22.1	6.4	12.7	4.3	25.1	23.0	19.6	12.4	11.0
Simple conjugal families	64.9	58.4	54.7	69.1	47.0	52.3	59.7	57.5	59.4	53.1	56.3
Extended simple conjugal families	9.1	9.9	12.8	10.2	12.3	7.6	7.4	7.0	6.3	11.7	8.2
Together	74.0	68.3	67.5	79.3	59.3	59.9	67.1	64.5	65.7	64.8	64.5
Multiple households											
vertical	3.5	9.8	5.8	9.4	19.5	26.0	5.7	7.9	8.5	16.6	14.7
horizontal	1.9	1.8	4.6	4.9	8.4	9.8	2.1	4.6	6.2	6.2	9.7
Together	5.4	11.6	10.4	14.3	27.9	35.8	7.8	12.5	14.7	22.8	24.4
Total	100.0	100.0	100.0	100.0	100.0	100.0	100.0	100.0	100.0	100.0	100.0
Number of households analyzed	1806	943	86	1411	1088	92	9821	745	770	26566	2045
Average number of nuclei per household	0.86	0.93	0.95	1.10	1.23	1.52	0.84	0.92	0.99	1.16	1.22

SOURCE: Estimo 215 (Prato, year 1371); Catasti of the 15th century.
*Based on 10 percent sample.

mon household, both before and after the death of the father. This tendency is reflected in the growing proportion of laterally extended joint family households.

In sum, economic factors alone cannot explain the variations in household size and structure. Certainly, labor scarcity in the decades following the plague partially accounts for the high proportion of simple families found in 1371. Many young couples were then able to escape traditional restraints on marriage; they established themselves in autonomous fashion on empty lands, on the deserted farms which the owners were struggling to bring back under cultivation. But this proliferation of simple households still contrasts strangely with the familial system evident in 1427. Land had become, if anything, even more abundant than before. The Catasto overflows with complaints of property owners about the lack of laborers. But young people in 1427 do not seem to have taken advantage of this demand for their services, this opportunity for early marriage, as much as they had 55 years earlier. Many apparently preferred to remain under paternal authority. The shortage of labor does not therefore seem a sufficient explanation for this multiplication of simple nuclear families in 1371. Rather, high mortalities and shifts in the age distribution were limiting the chances that elderly parents and married sons might live together, as the domestic system recommended.[75]

Whether changing demographic or economic circumstances conceal it or reveal it, the tendency for married sons to live with their parents remains basic to the entire Tuscan domestic system. Less commonly, the formation of frérèches corrected for the scarcity and cost of labor in the period of slow demographic recovery. Preserving the cohesion of the domestic group after the death of its first founder, the father, the frérèche of married men also responded, well or badly, to the danger which equal inheritance posed for the fortune of every heir. But the frérèches still remained only an incidental phenomenon in a domestic system which primarily emphasized the bonds of the father with his sons, while allowing, on occasion, the eldest son to assume the paternal functions and power. On th other hand, the dimensions of the demographic collapse and powerful economic constraints deprived the system of free play and multiplied the numbers of fragmented households, those directed by children or by solitaries. This domestic "debris" strongly marks the family life of the late Middle Ages. Still, these traits appear chiefly at social levels which, amidst weak eco-

75. At least in the Tuscan countryside, the principles affecting the organization of households seem to have remained stable even into the eighteenth century. See Todd, 1975, who finds that the proportion of multiple households reached 42 percent (two-thirds were frérèches) at Pratolino in 1721.

nomic circumstances, do not organize their households in strongly patrilineal modes. Tuscan society of the quattrocento thus seemingly divides into two domestic systems. They reflect above all the reactions of different social classes, stricken by the fearful blows of pestilence and by the cruel loss of numbers, to the real menace of decline and extinction.

11
Kin and Affines

Con ciò sia cosa che l'uomo desideri di sapere di sua nazione e de' suo passati, e come i parentadi sono stati. . . .

For men wish to know their race and their ancestors and to know what marriage alliances were formed. . . .

Donato di Lamberto Velluti, *Cronica domestica*, 1367–1370

In fulfilling its many functions, the Tuscan family enlisted the support of larger groups of relatives, of kin and affines. These too administered to the needs, both material and spiritual, of their members. To be sure, groups based on descent or on marriage were not the only associations supporting the socialization of the young and the activities of the mature and the elderly. But the network of relatives surrounding each individual retained, in this society, a fundamental importance and exerted an almost daily influence.

Given its unwavering focus on the domestic community, the Catasto has only limited value in the study of these larger groupings. We here must chiefly rely on domestic ricordi and on writers who thought about and commented upon the social role of family and kin. The following pages must be reckoned a preliminary analysis, but still essential for an understanding of Tuscans of the quattrocento, and their families.

I. Kinship and Exogamy before the Thirteenth Century

In 721, the Council of Rome forbade Latin Christians to marry if they were members of the same kindred or descent group (*de propria cognatione*).[1] Roman law extended blood relations as far as the sev-

1. For a full exposition of the laws of the Church concerning consanguinity and affinity and their relationship with marriage, see Esmein, 1929–35, 1:371–92. The council of Rome decided that "Si quis de propria cognatione, vel quam cognatus habuit, duxerit uxorem, anathema sit"; Mansi, 1758–98, 12: cols. 262–67, cap. 9. The council of Rome adopted a conception which had previously been marginal, espressed in 527 or 531 by the council of Toledo. See Esmein, 1929–35, 1:376. On the meaning of the term *cognatus*, see Bullough, 1969.

enth degree; the Church in the eighth century thus assimilated the two domains of legal kinship and of relationships within which marriages were prohibited.[2] However, while retaining the traditional limit of seven degrees, the Church, before the end of the ninth century, adopted the German method of computing relationship; the canonical rule thus doubled the number of generations which had to separate the spouses from their common ancestor, as opposed to the Roman system.[3] The attempt to apply these draconian restrictions on the choice of spouses provoked considerable tensions. Sometime about 1063, the Italian reformer and saint, Peter Damian, composed a tract, "On the Degrees of Kinship," which reflects the conflicts engendered by divergent interpretations about the nature, extent, and significance of blood relationships.[4] A petition put forward by the Florentines before jurists at Ravenna gave Peter the occasion to clarify, or attempt to clarify, this tortured issue.

To set the stage for his argument, Damian discourses on the Church's concepts of the nature and function of the kin groups constituting human society. The vision of society which Damian's analysis puts forth is not original. It takes up ideas which had circulated in the Christian West since the time of Augustine and had been mediated by such writers as Isidore of Seville and Burchard of Worms.[5] Damian allows that in theory all human beings could follow the chain of their ancestry back to Adam and Eve; all people can therefore reasonably consider themselves to be members of a single descent group (*genus*). Significantly, God had created only one man and one woman, from whom all humanity is descended. God showed by this that all human beings should regard themselves as brothers and sisters.

However, in the course of extended time, the lines of descent constituting the human race continued to diverge, and their dispersion cooled and extinguished that brotherly love which should have prevailed; rivalry and discord threatened to disrupt human relations. "Even as kinship based on birth grew feeble as the generations passed, so also the flame of love, which human depravity deprived of fuel, grew cool. Then, to rekindle the spark of charity, marital alliances were contracted. . . . Where the strong links of consanguinity, which had bound blood relatives to one another, dissipate, marriage intervenes and reunites those who have drifted apart."[6] According to this traditional view, marriages act to reconstitute the binding, peace-

2. See Cimetier, 1932; Oesterle, 1949; Esmein, 1929–35, 1:376–80.

3. On the various methods utilized in the Middle Ages for calculating degrees of kinship, see, besides the works already cited, Champeaux, 1933. The text cited below, n. 17, shows that the Germanic method was already used in the Rhineland before 868.

4. Damian, 1853. For the date and the sources of this work, see Ryan, 1956, pp. 24–27.

5. See Ryan, 1956, pp. 24–27; Esmein, 1929–35, 1:93–96, 373.

6. Damian, 1853, col. 194.

preserving kinship of the dispersed lines which make up the great human brotherhood.[7] Damian emphasizes how the Church, in wisely encouraging marriage, promotes social peace:

> By promulgating its teachings, the Church has so well placed under its discipline the law of marriage that the ties of mutual love are necessarily preserved among men; I mean that, within the limits of descent groups, the affection born of a fraternal link supports love of one's neighbor. But when blood relation by birth (*genus cognationis*) begins to disappear, along with the terms that describe it, the law of marriage takes its place . . . and reestablishes the rules of ancient love among modern men. . . .[8]

The dignity of marriage is therefore not based on the satisfactions accruing to the couple; rather it derives from the vital social function marriage fulfills in bringing kin groups together and in preserving peace among them.

The lines of descent (*progenies*), dispersed in the course of time, thus lose the recollection of their common origins. They give way to aggregations less diffused and more conscious of their brotherhood. These kin groups are founded on the sentiment that the individuals within them descend from a common ancestor, male or female, and thus share a common trait, blood relationship (genus cognationis). At a given moment, these groups of cognates therefore include all those, of both sexes, who can follow the line of their ascendants to a common ancestor. Damian compares the solidarity of these blood relatives to the union of the parts of the human body:

> Just as the diverse parts combine and participate in the whole, in such a way that one may sensibly speak of a single body, so the various individuals who also descend from a common ancestor form, without any doubt, a single "race" (*genus*).[9]

The cement that binds together the members of the group is therefore their recognition of a common ancestor. Just as the eldest member in a group prevails over those younger than he, so the common ancestor, if he still lived, "could maintain under his authority all of these persons and could call them all 'children', in the legal meaning of the word."[10] The intermarriage of such *filii* would obviously contradict nature; the posterity of an ancestor could not therefore be endogamous. So the expansion of the

7. Compare the similar conceptions in St. Augustine, Isidore of Seville (early seventh century) and Burchard of Worms (early eleventh century), cited in Ryan, 1956, p. 25.

8. Damian, 1853, col. 193.

9. Ibid., col. 193.

10. Ibid., col. 199.

kin group (defined by the common ancestor) over a number of generations establishes the limits within which marriages are forbidden among descendants. The fraternal affection which should unite them excludes all possibility of sexual relations or of marriage between them.

The exogamous group of blood relatives thus finds itself identified with "filii in the legal sense of the term," with those persons who might be called upon to succeed one another. "For those who have the right to succession," Damian asserts, "are also related through common descent."[11] The capacity to inherit excludes the right to marriage with that person:

> . . . for one right eliminates the other, so that the woman from whom one can inherit cannot be taken as a legitimate wife, while those whom one may legitimately marry have no title to inherit.[12]

Inheritance or blood relationship and marriage alliance thus exclude one another, and, relying on this ecclesiastical postulate, Damian finds it easy to refute the jurists of Ravenna, who had argued that the fourth degree of kinship set the limits of marriage and the seventh those of inheritance.[13] The doctrine of the eleventh-century Church, rigorous as it was in Damian's interpretation, certainly presents itself in a clearer and more coherent form.

Before the Church, in the eighth century, made equivalent spheres of these two domains of kinship (defined by rights to inherit and prohibitions against marriage), genealogical memories could develop freely, as the attractiveness of an eventual legacy largely compensated for the matrimonial interdictions. The new canonical regulations meant that considerable pressure had to be exerted on the faithful to extend their genealogical memories. Italian chartularies and serf lists show in fact that even peasants enlisted mnemonic techniques to trace their filiation. These documents occasionally show chains of recurrent patronyms, and even matronyms, of great genealogical depth.[14]

For most people, however, the search back into time for a common ancestor could only have been supported by a vague sense of kinship. Realizing the inaccuracy of memory, the council of Worms in 868, following in this the dicta of Pope Gregory II 150 years earlier, admitted that:

> . . . in the marriages of the faithful, we do not fix the number of generations, but we declare that a Christian cannot take as a wife a

11. Ibid., col. 194: "Quod quibus est jus haereditatis, est et affinitas generis.

12. Ibid., col. 195.

13. Ibid., cols. 195–96. According to Pope Gregory II, even a vague knowledge of relationship excluded marriage: "Dicimus, quod oportuerat quidem, quamdiu se agnoscunt affinitate propinquos, ad huius copulae non accedere societatem." *MGH, Epistolarum* 3:275, dated 726.

14. On the use of patronymics and matronymics in charters of this period, see Herlihy, 1962.

> woman belonging to his consanguineal group or cognates if the common filiation (*generatio*) is known and remembered.[15]

Damian is shocked that some of his contemporaries cannot even track their ancestry to the third generation, which would permit them to respect the prohibited degrees of marriage under the Roman system:

> What in fact is the line of descent which is so obscure and of such low birth that its members cannot trace themselves back to their great-grandparents?[16]

He even deplores that some "live by the flesh, sneering that they are fecundated by the descendants of their nephews. . . ."[17] His words confirm that the Italians of the eleventh century, at least those of the popular classes, barely recognized and willingly transgressed (when they did not openly defy) the canonical incest prohibitions, which were still at this time not clearly defined. In another small work, *De gradibus cognationis*, Damian somewhat softened his definition of "generations"; he conceded that his previous interpretation had given rise to objections and complaints among the laity.[18] Many claimed that they could not observe so strict a rule.[19]

Did the descent group in its less extreme configuration have functions other than that of regulating exogamy? The notion that the solidarity of descendants disappears after the third generation is evident, it seems, in a type of agrarian contract we find throughout the Middle Ages, up to the thirteenth and fourteenth centuries, primarily in relatively backward regions with a poor and extensive agriculture. This rental contract, *ad tertium genus*, stipulated that the tenant and his descendants should retain the land for three generations and that the agreement should be renewed at the fourth. This type of agreement is common, for example, around Civitella, which at the time of the Catasto was part of the podesteria of Pieve Santo Stefano, in the north of the county of Arezzo. In 1305 the abbot of the monastery of Santa Maria al Trivio thus rents land to a certain Bonuzio di Ognibene and his wife Banta, as well as "to all the children of the said Bonuzio and Banta, and to their grandchildren, males and females, who

15. Mansi, 1758–98, 15: col. 875. Damian expresses this view in succinct form (Damian, 1853, col. 199): "Ut quandiu linea consanguinitatis agnoscitur, vel in memoria retinetur, nullus uxorem de propria cognatione praesumat accipere." On the history of this text, see Ryan, 1956, p. 27. The same council of Worms affirms further along (cap. 78, col. 882) that the fourth degree (computed by the German method, roughly the sixth in Roman terms) was within the prohibited limits and had to be reckoned from both the male and female lines.

16. Damian, 1853, col. 199.

17. Ibid., col. 199.

18. "Dissertatiuncula de gradibus cognationis," *PL* cols. 204–08, especially col. 205.

19. These ideas would, however, be adopted and restated with few changes by the canonists of the twelfth century, by Peter Lombard and Gratian.

descend or will descend from their legitimate union, down to the third generation; the agreement will be renewed at the fourth."[20] On these monastic lands, the system of land tenure apparently relied on descent groups extending for three or four generations, and they depended as much on filiation in the female line as in that of the male.

In communities of this sort, each individual belonged to several kin groups descended from a common male or female ancestor. These groupings were not perpetual. Their limits and contours varied with each case and at each new generation, when the name of the most distant ancestor, which had become useless, was forgotten. A less distant ancestor took his place and function, and the group effectively slid down one generation. As a new point of reference, he designated who among his descendants would constitute an exogamous group of blood relatives. These descent groups did not therefore grow larger at each generation; they did not retain, as did the later lineage, a fixed anchor in the past; nor did they possess, like a clan, a diffuse sentiment of common kinship. They merely circumscribed the domain within which individuals could inherit from one another but could not marry one another. These successive rearrangements of the limits and composition of the descent group, the genus cognationis, thus functioned in accordance with the demands of Church and state.

Damian's treatise gives us no indication of the real solidarity of this moving kin group. He only suggests that blood relationship would define groups, the salient characteristic of which would be hostility to other groups, similarly defined. But we are still far from the authentic lineage, to which Damian makes no specific allusion. He also avers that marriage alliances created new solidarities, but he does not identify the personal group of relations which could weave themselves around each individual. The relevance of the treatise for our purposes is the following. In this society, in which an undifferentiated rule of filiation prevailed, an extreme rule of exogamy forced the faithful to lose consciousness of their ancestry when they were not in a strong position to contravene the prohibitions openly. Too long and precise a memory threatened to make marriage an impossibility. How then could the lineage, only now becoming established in certain social strata, assert itself when the consequences for marriage were so disadvantageous?

II. The Appearance of the Lineage

As elsewhere in Europe, lineage began to make its appearance in Tuscany towards the end of the tenth, or the beginning of, the

20. ASF, Notarile, B 2816, f. 26, 31 December 1305. See also ibid., f. 68, 6 December 1306, contract given to "domine Flore filie condam Venture de Alfano . . . et suis filiis nepotibus et posteris ex ea recta linea descendentibus masculis et feminis legitimis usque ad suam tertiam generationem completam."

eleventh century. This unilinear group of filiation depends on the consciousness possessed by its members of descent from a specific common ancestor, through a line of ascendants of the same sex. The very length of the line is a sign of distinguished birth. A defined, organic, and cohesive group, the lineage is everlasting, and variations in its composition do not affect its existence; to signify its permanence and its unity, it generally acquires its own signs of identity, coats of arms, names, battle cries, a mythology, and so on.

FILIATION AND PATRIMONY

The agnatic lineage which emerges in Tuscany near the time of Damian's treatise differs in several significant aspects from the consanguine groups to which his theory refers. His theory of exogamous groups with a limited and constant genealogical depth—it is revised at each new generation—attaches as much importance to filiation in the female line as in the male line. As membership in a kin group and rights of inheritance are equated, women, as well as men, may inherit from other members of the group.

By contrast, within a lineage, filiation is constituted, in Tuscany, through men only. The men of a lineage, in effect, exclude from inheritance rights their sisters and their daughters, married and "adequately" endowed with dowries, along with their female descendants.[21]

In the eleventh century, internal and external factors conspired to threaten the wealth and status of propertied families. Beside divisions among heirs, including women, donations to the Church jeopardized the ancestral patrimonies. In the years preceding the Gregorian reform in the eleventh century, the Church maintained a rather lax control over its own lands; the great lay families profited from this in appropriating through favorable leases or simple usurpation more land than they donated. The Gregorian reform gave the Church much firmer control over its endowment. Propertied families responded not only by excluding sisters and daughters from the inheritance, but also by limiting their legacies to the Church.[22] This policy, which involved collective control of the patrimony and slowed its dispersion, at the same time reinforced the solidarity of the male members of the family and exalted their links to the past.

The appearance of the lineage is thus closely linked with growing concern over inheritance in family strategies. The inheritance right, which, *ex*

21. In Florentine wills preserved in the notarial chartularies from the thirteenth century on, fathers bequeath to their married daughters dowries (which they have already received) and often a small sum of money in addition, while insisting that they renounce all claim to any other property. On the rights of daughters to the paternal inheritance, see Bellomo, 1961.

22. On efforts to recover Church property in the hands of laymen in the territory of Lucca, see Herlihy, 1973a.

patrimonio, a male relative possessed, becomes the principal criterion of lineage membership.[23] Reciprocally, as inheritance rights and membership in a kin group were heretofore regarded as strictly equivalent, the married and dowered woman would from now on leave her father's lineage and take her descendants with her. If not she herself, at least her children and their descendants in the male line would belong to her husband's lineage.

The lineage, as a late development, for a long time influenced only a small sector of Tuscan society. An important text may mark its first appearance in our region. In two chartularies redacted in the thirteenth century by anonymous members of the cathedral chapter of Lucca, the compilers were able to identify the ancestors of the greatest Lucchese houses of the thirteenth century, going back as far, sometimes, as 991.[24] Thus, at least at Lucca, Tuscan lineages were crystallizing from around the year 1000.

Another form of family association which appears about the same time as the lineage and which is directly associated with it, is the *consorteria*, or association of coheirs.[25] As with lineages, we can find traces of them beginning in the eleventh century, but the majority of them were assembled in the twelfth. Many of these consorterie were composed of blood relatives only and at their origin may have included only brothers, as their names—*filii Roffredi*, *filii Melane*, to cite examples from Lucca—suggest. But many others were, or soon became, large associations with a complex constituency, which might include several lineages, not all related in the male line. The consorterie could collectively own property, particularly those powerful fortified compounds—towers or castles—which required considerable investment; thus the name, "tower societies," by which they were often known.[26] Even more striking is their success in imposing a rule of collective control over the private possessions of their members. They especially acted to prevent the transfer of real estate outside the group, a transfer for which women were notably responsible. The structure of these associations was frequently revised, usually through formal agreement.[27]

23. See the use of the term "milites et fratres militum ex patrimonio et predictorum militum filios et nepotes ex patrimonio," in the Statutes of Pistoia, *Statutum*, 1888, p. 177.

24. *Regesto*, 1910, p. 1, n. 39; p. 15, year 991. "Et nota," the thirteenth-century commentator remarks a propos of this text of the tenth century, "quod de isto Benedicto descenderunt filii Roffredi. . . . " See a similar remark, ibid. n. 58, p. 20, year 1001–02: "Hic fuit caput filiorum Meliane cum aliis suis capitubus." Also, n. 64, p. 22, 1 August 1005: "Hic fuit de filiis Ubaldi de Bocano," etc. On Lucchese families, particularly in the ninth and tenth centuries, see Schwarzmaier, 1972, especially pp. 262 ff.

25. On the appearance and nature of the consorteria, see Violante, 1977, especially pp. 118–25; Niccolai, 1940, pp. 116–47. On "clans" and lineages in medieval society, see Heers, 1974 or 1977. Our use of the terms clan and lineage follows anthropological usage. See Fox, 1967.

26. The fundamental study of tower societies remains that of Santini, 1887. On similar associations in Genoa, see Hughes, 1975.

27. The best picture of the internal structure of a consorteria can be found in the statutes of the "casa de' Corbolani" of Lucca. See the edition by Bongi, 1886.

The bonds, which, in propertied families, now associated kinship and property, and the continuity in management of the patrimony, which both the lineage and the consorteria sought to assure, deepened consciousness of filiation; it was now limited to the male line, but was projected as far back as possible in time.

LINEAGE MEMORY

In contrast to cognatic groups, the living members of a lineage derive their pride from a long chain of ancestors, limited only by the capacity of the member to retain their names and connections. Assisted by myth, the collective memory of the lineage does sometimes, it is true, extend itself too far into the past; for the longer the genealogy, the greater the prestige accorded to the descendants of the line.

It might be supposed that this new aspiration to anchor the lineage in the distant past no longer took account of what a long recollection of ancestors implied for marriages. In truth, a consciousness of lineage was able to take root in broader social circles only from the time that the Church, aware that its strict definition of incest could be applied only with difficulty, no longer predicated the prohibitions on a recollection of distant kinship. Instead, it defined the limits of exogamy at a fixed number of degrees and reduced their domain. The Fourth Lateran Council, in 1215, returned to the limit of four degrees, in which marriages were prohibited.[28] It then became possible to cultivate and celebrate a tree of ancestors; beyond the third ascending generation, one's forebears no longer constituted an impediment to marriage. The new canonical definition of kinship allowed anyone, who affected to copy the aristocratic manner of life, to indulge in the delights of genealogy. From the end of the thirteenth century, Florentine patricians took as one of their characteristic pastimes the construction of family trees.

One of the first Florentines to manifest this interest in the history of his lineage is Guido dell'Antella, who begins his ricordanze in 1299.[29] His personal memories go back to 1267 when, as a young boy of 13, he made a trip to Genoa. His own father had not kept memoirs (at least, Guido did not know of any), and the son had to rely on his mother's reminiscences to place his own date of birth (1254). Tuscan families, and especially Florentines, subsequently took a consistent interest in their ancestors and frequently succeeded in tracing the threads quite far back in time. Donato Velluti, who wrote between 1367 and 1370, Giovanni Morelli and Lapo

28. Mansi, 1758–98, 12: cols. 1035–38.

29. Guido di Filippo dell'Antella, 1843, pp. 5–24. The text of this ricordanze is reprinted in Castellani (ed.), 1952, 2:804 ff.

Niccolini, whose memoirs were composed around 1400, and many others, were able, through family archives, information gained from elders, and "origin myths" to carry their lineages back to the twelfth or the early thirteenth century.

What in their genealogies fascinated these domestic chroniclers? A knowledge of the deeds of their grandparents, of their supposed virtues, struggles and successes would, these writers hoped, inspire and guide members of the lineage as yet unborn. Velluti recorded the history of his house "for the perpetual memory of my descendants and for that of other members of the house of Velluti."[30] Morelli wished to recall the "virtue of our ancestors," and

> . . . to instruct our sons, or rather our descendants, by true example and by the things which have happened to us; if they reflect often upon these events, they will, by the grace of God, draw from them salubrious instruction, if not regarding everything—not all of these events are of great moment—at least regarding some things, with the help of God and of a sound mind."[31]

In sum, the solidarity of the lineage linked together the past, the present, and the future. But this adulation of the forebears also reflected the tensions of the society in which their descendants lived. As bourgeois chroniclers aspiring to an aristocratic demeanor, they felt threatened by upstarts, by new citizens who defied the older lineages, inventing, in their turn, a lengthy past. Morelli stated outright that in his day everyone was claiming the antiquity of race (*nazione*). He felt constrained to respond, by proving the validity of his own long lineage.[32] A novella by Franco Sacchetti, written toward the end of the fourteenth century, beautifully expresses the disdain with which the old families regarded the new arrivals. A vulgar craftsman came one day to the famous Giotto and asked him to paint his "arms," with no further qualification, on a shield. Taking him at his word, Giotto depicted the full suit of armor of a footsoldier. The incensed craftsman, railing at the sketch, was then scolded by the painter, who rebuked his pretensions:

> But who are you then . . . to tell me "paint my coat of arms"? If you were a Bardi, that would have been fine. But what are your arms? Of what house are you a member? Who were your ancestors? How is it

30. Velluti, 1914, p. 3. Pride of membership in a lineage is depicted and pilloried by Petrarch in his "Remedy for Both Sorts of Fortune", Petrarca, 1867, p. 101, "Della schiatta nobile."

31. Morelli, 1956, p. 85.

32. Ibid., p. 81.

> you are not ashamed? Better be born first before you talk about coats of arms, as though you were the Duke of Bavaria. . . .[33]

The craftsman sued, but the magistrates of the Grascia threw his case out of court; they agreed with Giotto. Sacchetti concludes:

> For every good-for-nothing wants arms and ancestry, when his father may have been nothing but a foundling in a hospice.[34]

NAME AND LINEAGE

The appearance of a collective and permanent *cognomen* to designate the kin group is in Tuscany directly related with the emergence of the lineage, which it generally follows in short order. The necessity to be recognized by society as a cohesive "house" made the adoption of a family name indispensible. When Morelli enumerated the series of his ancestors to a depth of eight generations, he attributed the collective name (de' Morelli), formed on the surname of his great-great-grandfather Morello, to all his ascendants; it was obviously impossible that they could have been so named.[35] Although often late in appearing, the name justifies and consecrates the cohesion and the continuity of the lineage throughout the generations. When a branch detached itself and gained independence from the principal lineage, it took care to signify both its connections to the older, and in some respects more prestigous, line by retaining its name, while proclaiming its autonomy through a differentiating patronym.[36] Thus, the Niccolini de' Sirigatti took the name of the founder of the commercial wealth of the family, who had settled in Florence at the end of the thirteenth century, while also retaining the old lineage of the contado, some members of which had immigrated into Florence toward the middle of the thirteenth century.[37]

The appearance of a permanent cognomen results from the increasingly intense interaction of family and community. Family names become frequent in Tuscan documents at the end of the twelfth century, among the great urban lineages which are often of rural and feudal origin; they become common in the thirteenth century within the merchant class.[38] In the

33. Sacchetti, 1946, nov. 63, p. 152.
34. Ibid., p. 152.
35. Morelli, 1956, p. 81.
36. Families of *magnati* in the Tuscan towns often changed their names when they assumed popular status. Thus, for example, the Montebuoni-Buondelmonti. Many branches of the prolific lineage of the Bardi did so. See the genealogies composed by Tiribilli-Giuliani, 1855, no. 25. The Ilarioni and the Angiolotti were branches of the Bardi who took new names when they changed their status.
37. The Florentine Sirigatti are at all events called consorti by the Niccolini. See Niccolini, 1969.
38. On this complex problem, see the old study of Gaudenzi, 1898. On Florentine names at the end of the thirteenth century, see Brattö, 1955; Castellani, 1956.

Table 11.1. The Use of Family Names by Tuscan Taxpayers, 1427–30

Residence	*Number of Taxpayers*	*Taxpayers Bearing Family Names*	*Percent*
Florence	9,821	3,608	36.7
Other towns	12,676	2,598	20.5
Countryside	37,029	3,471	9.4
Totals	59,526	9,677	16.3

SOURCE: Catasto of 1427–30.

early fourteenth century, Dante, and then a little later, Giovanni Villani drew up a catalogue of the great *legnaggi* or *casati* which, in the twelfth century, constitute the "flock of San Giovanni."[39] Dante's great-great-grandfather Cacciaguida, whom the poet meets in Paradise, names for the edification of his descendant the great Florentine houses, the ancestors of which he had known in his lifetime. In the poet's own day, those still in existence were proud that they were able to trace their origins, and frequently their name, to the first half of the twelfth century.

The diffusion of family names nevertheless remained severely limited in Tuscany, because lineages still involved so narrow a segment of society. Despite the ambition of new men to found casati, only a tiny minority of fifteenth-century Tuscans betray, through family names, consciousness of membership in an individualized and permanent group. The Catasto allows us to assess, at least in summary fashion, the diffusion of names and, through this, the import of lineages in the early fifteenth century.

When he presented his declaration to the clerks of the Catasto office, the head of family identified himself by his own Christian name and generally by that of his father; a few added a surname. Even in the fifteenth century, it is often difficult to determine whether this surname is an authentic family name, now fixed and passed on from generation to generation, a nickname, or a personal name borne by the single individual.[40] In any case, the frequency with which this third name appears in the declarations allows us to

39. *Paradiso,* canto XVI, 25–27: "Ditemi de l'ovil di San Giovanni / quanto era allora, e chi eran le genti / tra esso degne di più alti scanni." Villani, 1823, bk. 4, cap. 10–14, "De' nobili ch'erano nella città di Firenze al tempo del detto imperadore Currado." See also ibid., bk. 5, cap. 39, "Delle case e de' nobili che divennero guelfi e ghibellini in Firenze," for another list of Florentine lineages in the early thirteenth century.

40. In particular, the form "del —," which gives rise to many modern names but was still very fluid in the fifteenth century, is taken by us to be a family name, except when other indications show clearly that name following the "del" was the father. So also, a certain number of personal surnames or nicknames certainly figure among the "family names" in our machine-readable edition. When it could not be determined whether they were purely personal or already hereditary names, we preferred to include them, at the risk of increasing the number of family names.

Table 11.2. Family Names and Urban Communities

Town	*Number of Taxpayers*	*Taxpayers Bearing Family Names*	*Percent*
Florence	9,821	3,608	36.7
Pisa	1,729	409	23.7
Pistoia	1,245	387	31.1
Arezzo	1,189	152	12.8
Prato	943	179	19.0
Volterra	794	156	19.7
Cortona	877	88	10.0
Montepulciano	751	52	7.2
Colle (a)	573	74	12.9
Castiglion Fiorentino	391	42	10.7
Pescia (b)	427	253	59.3
San Gimignano (c)	369	115	31.2

(a) Town and countryside together
(b) Of which 42 are probably the patronym treated as a collective name.
(c) E. Fiumi, 1961, p. 179–83, allows an addition of some 15 names which he identifies from other sources.

discern in which social classes and in which regions family names were most widespread in 1427.

Table 11.1 presents the number and the proportion of taxpayers endowed with an apparent family name in the registers of the Catasto; it distinguishes between the capital, the secondary towns or important villages, and the countryside.

More than one Florentine household in three possesses a surname or cognomen in the campioni.[41] This proportion diminishes significantly in the secondary towns, where it claims no more than one-fifth of the taxpayers. Finally, it falls to less than a tenth of the households in the countryside. In sum, roughly one Tuscan in six at the beginning of the fifteenth century can attach to the line of his male ascendants and descendants a durable collective name. The proportion is low in comparison to that found in the large medieval towns outside of Italy.[42] It testifies to the fact that the appearance of a collective name is primarily an urban phenomenon. Table 11.2 shows that, *grosso modo*, the proportion of households carrying a permanent name decreases with the total size of the community. However, among populations possessing the same order of magnitude, towns situated in the eastern part of the region reveal proportions considerably lower than those in the west or center.

41. The portate occasionally give a family name which the redactor of the campioni failed to record. This fact is the more surprising as the fiscal administration was clearly interested in identifying taxpayers as unambiguously as possible.

42. See, for example, the study of Parisian names by Michaelsson, 1927–36.

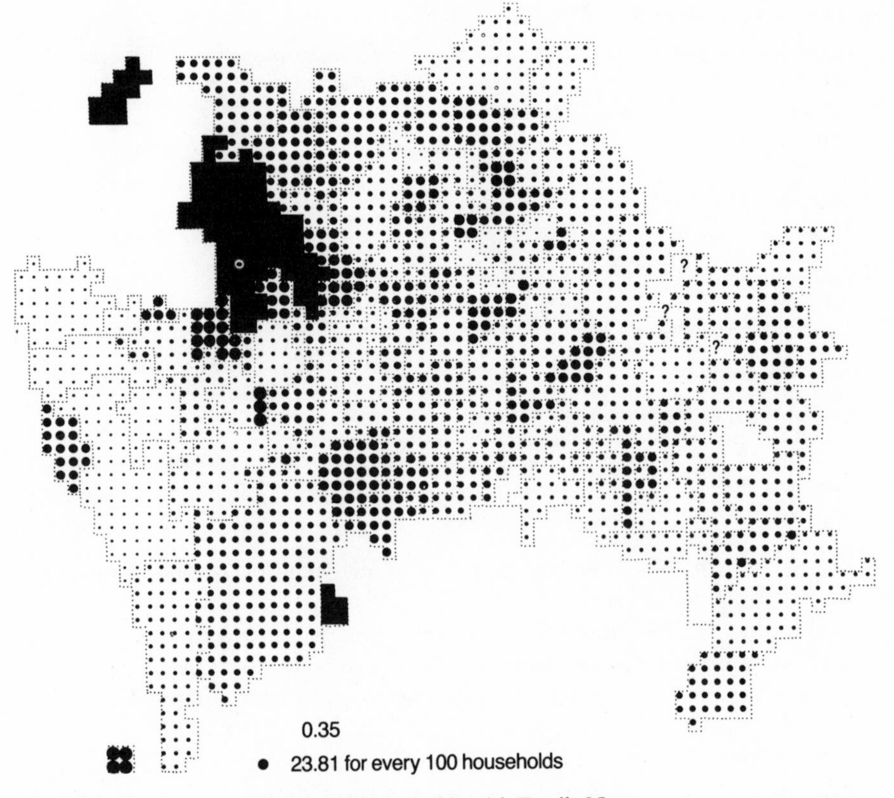

Map 11.1. Households with Family Names

Maps 11.1 and 4.1 show the proportion of rural households with a family name, and the distribution of wealth in the countryside. Households in the less strictly agricultural zones have both greater average wealth and make more use of family names.[43] Family names also appear more frequent in the northwest quarter of the territory, that is, in the contado of Pistoia, the Val di Nievole, the lower Arno valley, and in the Garfagnana, around Barga. It is true that the population in this area was concentrated in large villages of a semi-urban nature. Nevertheless, if we carefully examine these family names in the Val di Nievole and the county of Pistoia, perhaps we can better understand the processes by which they became fixed identifiers of lines of descent.

43. For example, at Castiglione della Pescaia, Livorno, Colle and San Gimignano, and in the Florentine suburbs.

In these northwestern areas, many family names seem to have been still in the process of forming. Probaby, the obligation to present declarations to the Catasto office hastened their crystallization. In the various versions of the Catasto, many heads of household present their own Christian names, then a patronymic, given in Italian, at times in the genitive form (Francesco di Marco, for example), but also at times in a form we might call plural (Francesco Marchi).[44] More rarely, the grandfather's name is so treated (for example, Giovanni di Francesco Marchi). In the Val di Nievole and at Pescia, the result is a doubling of the proportion of family names.[45]

By an analogous process—the fixation of a patronymic in the form of a Latin genitive or an Italian plural—many of the great Florentine casati had, two or three centuries earlier, acquired a permanent name, belonging to a near but already prestigious ancestor. The case of the Val di Nievole reveals how slowly family names diffused throughout Tuscan society. In the early fifteenth century, the practice spreads to parts of the countryside and to the common people of the towns. But the work of the demographers show that this crystallization of family names was not completed in some backward areas of Tuscany until the seventeenth century.[46] Perhaps we are witnessing the beginnings of this process, near the time of the Catasto, in one of the most prosperous areas of Tuscany, most open to exchange.

The development of the family name, while primarily an urban phenomenon, is also a mark of the wealthy and the powerful, of those who inevitably drew the attention of government and of other institutions. The city had attracted important families of the contado from the twelfth through the fourteenth centuries; they first formed lineages capable of defending their own interests and of imposing their policies on urban society. They were also first to adopt emblems attesting to their solidarity and power. In 1427 the highest concentration of family names is still to be found in the hundred wealthiest Florentine households (88 percent), while only 176 out of the 1,493 hearths without taxable property bear them.

Members of the poorer urban classes continued, in their vast majority, to rely on other forms of designation. Most referred only to their immediate ascendants.[47] A Tuscan not claiming membership in a great mercantile

44. On this debate, compare Gaudenzi, 1898, who sees in the form of Italian names ending in "i" a plural identifying all the members of the lineage or of the extended family. Most other later studies view it rather as a genitive, signifying the name of an ancestor, which comes to be fixed at a certain moment in time and borne by all his descendants. See Aebischer, 1947.

45. In the countryside of the Val di Nievole, the proportion falls from 46.2 to 27.8 percent; in the town of Pescia, from 59.3 to 49.4 percent; in the Garfagnana and at Barga, from 54 to 24.1 percent.

46. M. Livi Bacci, 1972.

47. Many examples may be found in the ricordi. See for example the peasants working the lands of Bernardo Machiavelli, 1954, p. 162 (1492): Francesco di Bettino di Tuccio and his sons Agnolo and Matteo; ibid., p. 164, Dino and Marco, brothers and sons of Lapino di Antonio.

house often gave, during the fifteenth century, three or four names: his own, that of his father, and occasionally that of his grandfather. When this sequence of names was not sufficient for unambiguous identification within a parish, one had recourse to supplementary indications, according to the circumstances: a profession or professional title (*ser*, *messere*), a nickname, or a personal characteristic.

It was customary also to repeat the Christian name every two generations and to give it to the first-born.[48] This practice derives from the belief, shared by many societies, that "a being who is born is always an ancestor reincarnated through a certain number of generations."[49] Reciprocally, in the common sentiment, the deceased whose name is reused will be in some fashion reincarnated in the new bearer, will remake himself, as was said in Tuscany.[50] This custom was reinforced as generations passed, as the stock of baptismal names continuously grew smaller.[51] Apparently the popular classes were satisfied with this short run of names; they were not seeking to assert, through a name, the solidarity and power of a leading family. The networks supporting the individual were based not upon the lineage, but upon his circles of close relatives, neighbors, and friends.[52]

III. Lineage and Marriage Ties in the Fifteenth Century

The agnatic lineage did not entirely eliminate the sentiment of kinship through women. Its function was primarily to defend the integrity of the patrimony against the forces seeking to disperse it. Marriages, and the formation of parentadi, continued to reestablish, as Damian envisioned, "the laws of old love among modern men." Thus, the term *parenti* continued to signify in Tuscany next-of-kin, both blood relatives and affines of Ego, those on whom he could primarily rely for help in business and in daily life.

48. According to the baptismal registers of San Giovanni at Florence, in January 1451, out of 89 male babies baptized, 15 were named after their grandfathers, and only one after his father. The line of Buonaccorso Pitti shows that the name of Buonaccorso was repeated every other generation from the thirteenth to the fifteenth century; see the genealogical table in Buonaccorso Pitti, 1905, p. 5.

49. Benvéniste, 1969, 1:235. The author shows how pairs of relatives can be designated by the same term; thus, the designation of the grandson, in Old French, "avelet," or "little grandfather," recalls this special relationship two generations apart that one finds in Tuscany.

50. Many examples may be found in the ricordi of families belonging to the mercantile aristocracy. A peasant example in the Catasto of 1469: "Morì e rifecilo," AC 934, f. 175. See Klapisch, 1980a.

51. If one compares the number of Florentine baptismal names in 1427 with those of 1260 (see Brattö, 1953) the impoverishment of the stock over 150 years is striking, since half of the Florentines in 1260 utilized 27 different names while half of their descendants only bore 12 in 1427.

52. Hughes, 1975, pp. 21–25.

MARRIAGE AND SOCIAL COHESION

Many lay and ecclesiastic authors of the fifteenth century repeat, to the point of boredom, the central idea of Damian's treatise: marriage, the social cement, unites not only two people, but two families. Francesco Barbaro thus observes that among the ancient Romans, marriage contributed to the cohesion of society:

> We are well aware of the origins of this ancient Roman custom, which forbade the taking of a kinswoman for a wife. It was feared that the love which rightfully binds us to our kin should remain enclosed within narrow limits and deprive, in certain measure, the descendants of the many advantages which they would gain from the zealous support of their affines. Thus, the union of families binds the city more tightly together, thanks to these marriages, which constitute so many bonds. . . . [53]

At the time of the Catasto, Bernardino of Siena similarly exalts the role that marriage plays in the maintenance of the social order:

> Matrimonial unions not only link many souls by the love which unite kin and reinforce their mutual affection, but they also bring enemies together in peace and harmony; they even unite kingdoms and entire countries.[54]

A little later, the Florentine humanist Matteo Palmieri describes, in his *Della vita civile*, the contradictory and complementary effects of the dispersion of lineages and of their reunification through the making of marriages and the formation of parentadi:

> In addition to the sons, the grandsons and all others born of our blood should be regarded as useful [members of the family]. At the beginning, a house is whole in itself; then, when its members have multiplied and a single dwelling can no longer contain them all, the lines of descendants, consorterie and vast families grow apart. But, by giving and receiving spouses in legitimate marriage, they gather in, through partentadi and through the love that unites them, a large part of the city. Thus, conjoined by kinship, men help one another in charity; they give counsel, favors, and assistance to one another, bringing to one another in this life capabilities, advantages, and abundant fruits.[55]

This sentiment remains commonplace in the later humanist commentaries on marriage. Toward the end of the fifteenth century, an unpublished

53. Barbaro, 1915–16, p. 44.
54. "De honestate coniugatarum," in Bernardino da Siena, 1950– 2:108.
55. Palmieri, 1825, p. 222

poem of the humanist Dario Tiberti, entitled *De legitimo amore*, proclaims that marriage "binds the world by covenant, love, and fidelity. It is true love, true peace and true harmony, true repose. . . . "[56] The same theme reappears in the imaginative literature of the age. *L'istorietta amorosa*, attributed to L. B. Alberti, deals with the Bardi and the Buondelmonti of Florence, "mortal enemies" for more than 200 years. After the marriage of Ippolito Buondelmonti and Leonora Bardi, "they became such friends in consequence of this alliance that they seemed all of the same blood."[57] Painting also draws upon the theme that marriage is the source of peace and reconciliation.[58]

CHOOSING AFFINES AND FRIENDS

Given the importance of the parentado, our writers discourse at length on the grave subject of the choice of a spouse. The foremost among the considerations to be weighed were the number and station of her relatives. Morelli emphasizes this:

> Take care to ally yourself with good citizens who are not in straitened circumstances and who are honest merchants. They ought to belong to the old families of the city, honored by the commune, blameless Guelfs. . . . [59]

And in the same vein, Alberti admonishes: "When one chooses a wife, one considers her beauty, her family, and her wealth."[60] Affines ought not to be of plebeian status, but ought to possess an appropriate fortune, engage in honorable activities, and have a reputation for sober and honest habits. Suitors, moreover, should avoid marrying into families which are considerably higher on the social ladder, "lest their grandeur overshadow one's own honor and position." And if a too powerful affine should fall on hard times, the moral obligation to help him out would threaten to ruin the husband as well. But neither should the wife's family be greatly inferior, because then too her relatives might make excessive demands for assistance: "Let them therefore be your equals," concludes Alberti, "and, as we have said, modest and civil."[61]

56. Cited in Resta, 1962, p. 109.
57. Alberti, 1960, 3:287.
58. Meiss, 1951, pp. 110–11 and fig. 107. The painting of Barna of Siena (at the Museum of Fine Arts, Boston), "Mystical Marriage of St. Catherine of Alexandria," was occasioned by the end of a private war, since the lower register shows two warriors laying down their arms.
59. Morelli, 1956, pp. 208–09.
60. Alberti, 1960, 1:110. The source of this remark may have been Isidore of Seville, 1911, bk. 9, chap. 7, "Item in eligenda uxore quattuor res impellunt hominem ad amorem: pulchritudo, genus, divitiae, mores."
61. Alberti, 1960, 1:112.

All these recommendations refer more or less explicitly to the heavy obligations incumbent on new affines, parenti of the husband by blood or marriage. In 1447 Marco di Parente wrote to his future brother-in-law, Filippo di Matteo Strozzi, calling him "very dear, like a brother to me." He declared that he wished to serve as his parente "to the full extent of my possibilities and power." He would spare nothing in accomplishing this service: "no effort to serve you and your affairs could be a burden to me".[62] The partners in a new alliance ought to help one another, in business as in public and private life—in all circumstances. In particular it was expected that the parenti would look after the interests of their common descendants, especially after the death of the father. Morelli urged his descendants to choose with care those among their wives' relatives in whom they could have confidence, in order that these parenti might assist the widow and watch over the patrimony of the children.[63] Indeed, his wife's near relatives could constitute a menace, and the father of the family ought to search out sincere supporters among them, "good relatives" who would help him defend the interests of his own children. Marriage brought together two families, but the risk remained, as Paolo da Certaldo phrased it, that the widow might betray her children for "her own relatives belonging to her lineage."[64] The precautions taken in the negotiation of marriage agreements thus continued to mark the relations between in-laws, especially after the father's death.

The relationships formed, when the survival of two patrimonies was in the balance, inevitably incited ambivalent feelings. In the best of cases, they engendered the fraternal sentiments expressed by Parenti. Alessandra Strozzi remarks in a letter dated 1449 that her own kin had accused her of heartlessness because she sent her twelve-year-old son to Naples.[65] These parenti were obviously worried about the well-being of the child, even though he was not a member of their lineage. Morelli, over several years of his childhood—the only period of his troubled life which he remembers fondly—also lived with his maternal grandfather after the remarriage of his mother; he was to him a "second father."[66] Straddling two *casate*, the wife often helped to maintain those bonds of affection and trust that marriages were supposed to engender; she continued to look after the interests of women in her natal lineage, as well as those of the family into which she had been received at marriage.[67]

62. Macinghi-Strozzi, 1877, p. 12. The letter is addressed to "Dilettissimo quanto fratello."
63. Morelli, 1956, p. 221.
64. Paolo da Certaldo, 1948, p. 239.
65. Macinghi-Strozzi, 1877, pp. 46–47.
66. Morelli, 1956, p. 497.
67. Chojnacki, 1974, well illuminates this situation at Venice; see also idem, 1975.

Nevertheless, the authors of the ricordi more than once express cynicism and mistrust when they reflected on the constraints and obligations of the marriage alliance. Morelli discourses at length on the ways of avoiding these obligations without antagonizing the soliciting party.[68] Alberti warns his readers against destitute affines who would pull down the house and bleed it mercilessly.[69] Despite these cynical remarks, "to make a good match" (*fare bel parentado*) remained the highest aspiration of well-born young people in the fifteenth century.[70] The influence a Tuscan might carry in the society of his day depended in large measure on the number and the quality of his affines.[71]

At the same time, to compensate for the failings of affines and to repair the losses through death which so frequently shredded the family cloth, the Tuscan of good family had to go beyond the circle of his relations to cultivate persons external to the family. Morelli warns his readers on several occasions not to place blind confidence in their parenti.[72] Alberti, for his part, regrets that certain members of the *gens Alberti*, whom he does not name, have neglected their only relatives in order to cultivate more advantageous connections, which he regarded as unworthy.[73] Apart from personal acquaintances, the Florentine patrician or bourgeois could also form useful friendships through membership in a faction, a party, or a confraternity. The evident strength of these associations in the Italian cities of the late Middle Ages is in part attributable to their functions as complements to the natural family.[74]

The career of Pagolo Morelli, father of the author of the ricordi, is a good example of the quest for friends. Pagolo lost his father, "never having seen him." He received neither the aid nor the affection of his three older brothers. According to his son, the resourceful Pagolo therefore determined

> . . . to win the friendship of upright men both virtuous and powerful. He went about with them, attesting to his great affection and serving

68. Morelli, 1956, pp. 237–41.

69. Alberti, 1960, 1:112.

70. Compare Alessandra Macinghi-Strozzi, 1877, p. 221: "Batista tolse donna, e ha fatto bel parentado, e n'è tutto lieto."

71. Compare the usage by Giovanni Dominici, 1860, p. 104: "Iudit nobile, ricca, bella, giovane, graziosa e molto imparentata . . . . "

72. Morelli, 1956, pp. 218–23. Morelli further affirms that the love of the father for his son is the only stable and enduring human affection.

73. Alberti, 1960 1:308: these Alberti were inclined "a più pregiare gli strani prosuntuosi che i suoi modestissimi e onestissimi."

74. See Trexler, 1974, especially pp. 234 ff. The author argues that religious sodalities at Florence admitting boys were designed in part to compensate for the weak masculine presence in the home.

> them in any manner possible, discussing with them their affairs, and thus demonstrating the trust and hope he placed in them; honoring them in offering meals and in other ways; serving as godfather at the baptisms of their children and in the various other more important capacities which present themselves when one is with people whom one wishes well.[75]

Thus, Pagolo was obligated to seek the help refused by his near relatives from influential friends whom he assiduously cultivated. "This same Pagolo," his son continues, "being young, destitute, alone, [was] without aid or counsel, apart from those of his friends." He got along through depending on the *amore* of carefully selected acquaintances. Similarly, the uncle of L. B. Alberti, Adovardo, who lived alone in Genoa without the support of a family, astutely made a pretense of falling in love with a young girl from a good family. This ruse captured the attention of the young nobles of the city. "I thus gained acquaintances and friends who have since then remained useful to me and to my children," his nephew reports him as saying.[76] "Friends are indispensable, if one wants to maintain a family and property," another Alberti, the elderly sage Giannozzo, remarks, "for they will give you advice and help you resist or escape from possible reversals of fortune."[77] Friendship wove the threads of a complementary network of solidarity in those areas in which kin and affines could not or would not play a role. In recognizing the limits of kinship, Florentines of the fifteenth century showed themselves to be highly conscious of the fragility of the associations based upon it.

STRATEGIES OF FAMILY SURVIVAL

The terrifying catastrophes of the fourteenth and fifteenth centuries instilled in many the fear that reversals of fortune could jeopardize the very survival of lineages.[78] The steep demographic decline, the caution of citizens in allowing their sons to marry (and their widows to remarry), aggravated, as we know, the dangers which laid siege to urban households. Echoing Dante, Petrarch lamented that "we have lost the recollection of so many families nowadays. How many families have you yourself seen reduced in a few years to almost nothing . . . ?"[79] Morelli devotes a large part of his ricordi to the analysis of the damages (*danni*) which the descendants

75. Morelli, 1956, p. 149–50, 152–53.
76. Alberti, 1960, 1:296.
77. Ibid., 1:185. On the recruitment of friends through serving as godparent, see Klapisch, 1976b, pp. 970–72
78. On *fortuna* and its remedies, *ragione* and *prudenza*, see Bec, 1967, pp. 301–30.
79. Petrarca, 1867, 1:103. The sentiment which animates the sixteenth canto of Dante's *Paradiso* is the same.

might suffer if the father died prematurely.[80] For each of these misfortunes, our merchant writer proposes appropriate remedies, which, in his estimation, would protect his posterity and lineage from ruin and extinction. The Dominican Giovanni Dominici was responding to worries of a similar sort when, in the first years of the fifteenth century, he wrote his *Regola del governo di cura familiare*. The book was intended to counsel a Florentine matron, Bartolomea degli Alberti, who was trying to rear four children alone, during her husband's exile.[81] All these works betray not so much a new way of perceiving the family, as a profound sentiment of its precarious existence. Chief among these treatises is the *Libri della famiglia*, which the scion of a great Florentine family, Leon Battista Alberti, composed in the 1430s.[82]

Ironically, Leon Battista was himself of illegitimate birth, the product of an unstable relationship. He never married, and never had the opportunity to put into practice the wise counsels he proffers. Nonetheless, he does give expression to a major preoccupation of his times, and this doubtlessly explains the tremendous success of his essay.

A consciousness of the disappearance or elimination of famous lines, the exile to which his own house had been subjected, and the scattering of its membership made him fear that the Alberti too might not survive:

> How many families in Italy and elsewhere, once prosperous and celebrated, are today almost empty and extinguished. . . . How many are today shredded and ruined?[83]

Even the memory of some of them had vanished.[84] To elucidate the factors that threatened their survival, Alberti, of course, points to the fierce epidemics of his day and the dangers which weighed upon the life of children from the moment of birth. But he blames above all the reluctance of young men to marry:

> According to the count I took a few days ago, no fewer than twenty-one young Alberti males are living without a partner, without a wife, and none of them is younger than 16 years of age, and none older than 36.[85]

The Catasto has already given us an indication of the dimensions of the problem to which Alberti is referring.[86] But are Alberti's apprehensions

80. Morelli, 1956, pp. 206–87.
81. Dominici, 1860.
82. The first three books were written at Rome in 1433–34; the fourth at Florence in 1443.
83. Alberti, 1960, 1:3.
84. Ibid., pp. 3–4.
85. Ibid., p. 34.
86. See above, chap. 7, pp. 215–16.

justified? At first glance data of the Catasto suggest that his fears were exaggerated. Most of the patrician lineages included several branches; among them, the richest members ruled the largest, most complex households and supported the largest number of children. It might thus appear that these great houses were among the most stable in the city; surely they enjoyed better chances of survival than the tiny families of the poor. But the data may here be misleading. If it is easy to observe the success of Florentines belonging to the great patrician households, it is more difficult to ascertain the risks which they had to confront before attaining, or retaining, their high position. In each generation, a good number, perhaps even the majority, of the branches of patrician lineages suffered a loss of wealth or status to the point of extinction. Poor households bearing great names are legion in the pages of the Catasto; they are poor in children as well as in property. The *Vita* of Saint Antoninus, bishop of Florence in the middle fifteenth century, records that the "shamefaced poor" of the city included a"great crowd of nobles." Antoninus himself, then a priest of San Marco, founded a confraternity called the *Buonomini di San Martino* in 1442, with an original membership of twelve citizens. Its purpose was to aid with charitable distributions the failed and ruined patricians and other "good citizens."[87]

At the end of a long period of reversals, suffered in business, politics, and in the bosom of his family, Giovanni Morelli gained the comfort of a vision. His deceased eldest son came to assure him that his own death would turn "to the salvation of your family and of you yourself."[88] But, at the death of another son, in 1421, fear again—the dread of watching his descendants die and *nostra nazione* extinguished—casts a somber shadow over the concluding, anguished sentences of his ricordi.

The concern which inspired Alberti's treatise thus seems well-founded. Nevertheless, the author maintains that the turns of fortune which ruin families are not all-powerful. The prudent man will find ways of parrying and defeating them. But he must understand the factors which increase or diminish the numbers, wealth, and honor of the household. This is Alberti's purpose in his essay, as one of his respondents clearly affirms:

> I only wish to recall the very perfect and useful rules which families ought to follow, in order not to come to ruin—quite agreeable and excellent rules, which will allow them to raise themselves and to find the greatest happiness and glory.[89]

87. ASS, I Maii, p. 440. The saint founded "hospitalis seu societatis s. Martini verecundorum pauperum mendicare erubescentium in civitate Florentiae, ubi magna ejusmodi generis nobilium multitudo alitur et fovetur. . . . " See Bargellini, 1972; Passerini, 1853a; pp. 501–15; and above all Trexler, 1973.

88. Morelli, 1956, pp. 515–16, 542. See Tenenti, 1973, pp. 132–33.

89. Alberti, 1960, 1:103.

The reader will be instructed how to breed and rear children, keep them in good health, how to persuade the young to marry, how to select a wife, manage a household, and acquire friends. Intelligent behavior can reduce, at least in part, the dangers which confront the domestic group; the family is the master of its own destiny, as is the individual who "can accomplish what he wants."[90]

Certainly this is one of Alberti's most original contributions to the social analysis of the family. Philosophers and moralists since antiquity were agreed in asserting that the family was a natural institution. In an epoch marked by demographic catastrophes and social strife, Alberti clearly recognized that nature—understood as a sequence of natural processes—does not alone guarantee the prosperity and survival of a lineage. Under the threatening pressure of circumstances, the head of the family must decide upon a strategy to assure the continuation of his line and must act in accordance with it. He must apply intelligence and energy to the enterprise. Whether in rearing children or choosing a spouse, in managing the household or cultivating friends (the four activities forming the themes of the four books), he must manipulate shifting conditions to his advantage and flexibly respond to circumstance. Is there not some similarity here between Alberti's view of the family, and the ideas concerning the prince and his state, which another Florentine, Niccolò Machiavelli, would advance at the beginning of the following century? Machiavelli also sought to lay bare the factors which contributed to the exaltation or debasement of the prince; he strove to bring them under conscious control. In considering their society, these perceptive Florentines recognized the fragility of fundamental human institutions; they also believed that reflection, intelligence, and wise behavior were the best remedies against adverse fortune.

90. "L'uomo può ciò che vuole," Alberti, 1960, 1:137.

Conclusion

The Catasto was a huge undertaking, which for three years engaged large material resources. Its redaction required a sustained effort on the part of the Florentine commune, and ran counter to many traditions, old procedures, and local privileges. On occasion it provoked violent resistance. Ending in relative failure, the reform did not radically or permanently change the methods of Florentine fiscal administration. The enormous data collected on the wealth of the Tuscan population remained largely unused; even the Florentine government did not know how to exploit this mine of statistical riches. The Catasto has remained a vast, unfinished account sheet; its redactors were unable to calculate the final total.

The computer now calculates that total. It thus displays the hidden characteristics of a population, already illuminated by numerous other fascinating sources. That population contains probably a larger urban component than anywhere else in medieval Europe; the distribution of its wealth is as much skewed and unequal as the distribution of its people. A metropolis of international visibility gathers one-seventh of the region's population, but two-thirds of the wealth held by laymen. The city dominates a countryside where the resident population is scattered across a dusting of farms and of hamlets; the pull of the great city powerfully affects their settlement, their possessions, and their productive activities. Even the towns of the periphery, set in the Florentine orbit since the middle of the fourteenth century, cannot offer a counterweight to the economic influence or to the demographic preponderance of the metropolis. Their partial effacement allows the Florentine commune, in this early fifteenth century, to build a territorial state, of which the redaction of the Catasto is itself an expression.

The analysis of the Catasto shows us a population which has just dropped to a demographic floor, and would remain stable for a another half-century. Only limited examples—from Prato, San Gimignano, and Pistoia—can measure for us the awesome dimensions of the decline which brought the Tuscan population to its shrunken state of 1427. The demographic collapse seems to have been more extensive than in other lands of Europe where judgment is possible, and its pace seems to have accelerated in the last quarter of the fourteenth century. Repeated catastrophic blows provoked by recurrent plagues brutally carried the population to a level, and imposed a structure, which made quick recovery difficult. The age pyramid at the time of the Catasto joins in remarkable fashion apparently contradictory characteristics: many old people, reduced numbers of adults and adolescents, but also, a large base of children. This structure reflects the fierce onslaught of plagues, the strength of which wanes only over the course of the fifteenth century.

To be sure, the data that we exploit are extremely heterogeneous, partial, and incomplete; they do not allow a rigorous comparison of the movements of births, marriages, and deaths. Still, the series of Florentine burials and baptisms that we have collected to supplement the Catasto give some indirect indications on demographic behavior. Thus, they afford us, really for the first time, a view of marriages across the entire range of a medieval community. We now know that Tuscan males were mature at first marriage, especially in the great cities and among the rich; and that their brides were, in contrast, very young. But is this a medieval and presumably fixed pattern of marriage? Our soundings between the end of the thirteenth and the end of the fifteenth centuries and the analysis of the Catasto show that masculine and feminine ages at marriage varied widely and responded to changing demographic and economic conditions. Shifts in marriage age clearly served to regulate the population's size. These fluctuations in the short-term and long-term evolution should warn us against hasty generalizations about the characteristics of medieval demography. A structural characteristic which seems, on the other hand, to mark Tuscan society continuously is the wide age difference between the marriage partners. Future research will show whether this is more Mediterranean than medieval. At all events, it exerted a powerful influence on behavior and mentalities within the family, and on images of authority in the domestic circle and in the larger Tuscan society.

The same questions—how stable, how Mediterranean or medieval are these patterns?—can be applied to domestic organization. The history of the family and household has grown prodigiously in recent years, not without confusion. Stimulated by demographic, sociological, and ethnographic studies, it has taken materials from everywhere, sometimes reviving old theories which the research pursued in other disciplines has largely rejected. At the center of the debate rests the idea that the domestic group has been progressively "nuclearized," collapsing around the married couple and their children. In undergoing modernization, the group allegedly falls in size and cuts itself off from the kinship or neighborhood ties which hitherto had served as its social extension and lent it material and moral support. But to judge from our Tuscan data, it is not possible to treat as a unity all households, without regard for their social situation and the changes which affected their structure across the late Middle Ages. Samples taken in the huge documentary mass from the fourteenth and fifteenth centuries allow us to draw domestic profiles, and this shows important similarities and continuities throughout the period; and it also shows that shifting levels of mortality and of nuptiality profoundly affected the structure of the residential group.

Also, the hearth, so sensitive to demographic conditions, does not offer a uniform image from the top to bottom of the social scale. It seems as if there were several types of families, shaped by their own distinctive developmental cycles and responding to different economic imperatives and perhaps also to different systems of value. Into one large category fall the families of rich citizens, set within a complex net of relatives and friends, and those of landed peasants, clinging close to their property and looking to maintain the solidarity of the group which farmed it; into another, the poor and miserable masses, and the small peasants or renters of dispersed parcels, always needy and insecure. In the first group, complex domestic forms and large families maintained themselves more easily than within the second, where the structure of the shrunken domestic group remained simple and easily fractured. Under these conditions, aggregate figures and averages show us little of the domestic system and the way it functioned. Can it be said without qualification that the principles of the patrilineal lineage dominated the Tuscan family in 1427? Strongly affirmed in the upper levels of society, these principles also underlay the developmental cycle of the peasant families; but they faded or even disappeared in the lower classes, where misery and mobility dissolved the solidarity of the domestic group and rapidly dispersed its members.

In this society which so strongly valued the masculine line and which included many elderly, the conduct of family affairs fell to aged males, in law and in fact. The *padre di famiglia* acquired—often late in life, to be sure—an authority which he retained until his death. He exercised it the more easily, as the years which separated him from his young wife and from children born to him in advanced years placed him in proud isolation, as did also the important activities he carried on outside the home. But death, as it thinned the ranks of these aged men, undermined this paternal preeminence; it often conferred, in spite of the stated ideal, the functions and responsabilities of family leadership on younger people, on offspring and women usually regarded as incompetent. The gulf of time which separated the father from his domestic kin worked paradoxically to exalt his authority during his life and also to shorten the period when it could be exercised. The disappearance that threatened the aging father doubtlessly inspired the sons, deprived of their natural guide, to exalt his image, drawing advantage in their turn from the prestige tied to the paternal office.

The computer thus allows us to explore these aspects of the Catasto of 1427. Without it, we could not have placed the many writings, which contemporaries devoted to the family, within their social and demographic context. For its part, a study limited to the Catasto of 1427 alone would have ignored the evolution over time, which seems to us one of the most remarkable aspects of the history of demographic and familial structures; a restricted study would have run the risk of freezing the image of the Tuscan population which the Catasto yields, and of imparting to its patterns a false aura of stability and permanence. In relating that image to the flow of demographic events and to the behavior and reflections of contemporaries, we hope that our research has uncovered, behind the mirror of seemingly static numbers, the profound currents which, in the fourteenth and fifteenth centuries, shaped and reshaped Tuscan society.

References

I. Sources

A. MANUSCRIPT SOURCES

The following abbreviations are used in references to manuscript sources:

AC	Archivio del Catasto
AODF	Archivio dell' Opera del Duomo di Firenze
ASF	Archivio di Stato di Firenze
ASP	Archivio di Stato di Pisa
CC	Camera del Comune
Not.	Notarile antecosiminiano
Provv.	Provvisioni
UFF	Ufficio dei Fiumi e Fossi

B. PRINTED SOURCES

Alberti, Leon Battista
1960 *Opere volgari*, ed. C. Grayson. 2 vols. Scrittori d'Italia, 218. Bari.
Aldobrandino da Siena
1911 *Le régime du corps de maître A. de Sienne, texte français du XIIIe siècle*, ed. L. Landouzy and R. Pépin. Paris.
Altieri, Marcantonio
1873 *Li nuptiali*, ed. E. Narducci. Rome.
Ammirato, Scipione
1641–50 *Istorie fiorentine*. 3 vols. Florence.
Antella, Guido di Filippo dell'
1843 "Ricordanze," ed. F. L. Polidori, *ASI*, ser. 1, 4:3–24.
Antoninus
1474 *Tractatus de censuris ecclesiasticis . . . ; de sponsalibus et matrimoniis*. Venice.
ASS *Acta Sanctorum quotquot toto urbe coluntur*. Paris, 1863–.
Barbaro, Francesco
1915–16 "De re uxoria," ed. A. Gnesotto. *Atti e Memorie della R. Accademia di Scienze Lettere ed Arti in Padova*, n. ser., 32:6–105.
Battagli da Rimini, Marco
1913 *Marcha*, ed. A. F. Massèra. RIS, n. ser. 16. Città di Castello.
Beccadelli, Antonio
1824 *Hermaphroditus*, ed. F. C. Forberg. Cobourg.
Bernardino da Siena
1880–88 *Prediche volgari*, ed. L. Banchi. Siena.
1950–[65] *Opera omnia*. Patres Collegii S. Bonaventurae. 9 vols. Florence.
Berti, P. (ed.)
1860 "Nuovi documenti intorno al catasto fiorentino, pei quali vien di-

mostrato che la proposta del medesimo non fù di Giovanni de' Medici," *Giornale Storico degli Archivi Toscani*, 4:39–62.

Boccaccio, Giovanni
1940 *L'Ameto. Lettere. Il Corbaccio*, ed. N. Bruscoli. Scrittori d'Italia, 182. Bari.
1965 *Opere in versi. Corbaccio. Trattatello in laude di Dante. Prose latine. Epistole*, ed. P. G. Ricci. La Letteratura Italiana, Storia e Testi, 9. Milan and Naples.
1967 *Tutte le opere*, ed. V. Branca. I Classici Mondadori. Verona.

Bongi, S. (ed.)
1886 "Statuto inedito della casa de' Corbolani," *Atti della R. Accademia di Scienze Lettere ed Arti* 24: 471–87.

Bracciolini, Poggio
1964 *Opera omnia*, preface by R. Fubini. Basel, 1538; reprinted, Turin.

Bruni, Leonardo
1847 "De Florentinorum Republica," trans. from the Greek by B. Moneta. In *Philippi Villani Liber de civitatis Florentiae famosis civibus . . . et de Florentinorum litteratura principes fere synchroni scriptores*, ed. G. C. Galletti. Florence.
1928 *Humanistisch-philosophische Schriften*, ed. H. Baron. Quellen zur Geistesgeschichte des Mittelalters, ed. W. Goetz, 1. Leipzig and Berlin.

Buoninsegni, D.
1637 *Storia della città di Firenze dall'anno 1410 al 1460*. Florence.

Cambi, Giovanni
1785 *Istorie fiorentine*, ed. Ildefonso di San Luigi. Delizie degli eruditi toscani, 20. Florence.

Capponi, Gino di Neri
1723–51 *Ricordi* (1420), ed. L. Muratori. *RIS*, 19, pp. 1149–52.. Milan.
1962 "Ricordi politici e familiari," ed. G. Folena. *Miscellanea di studi offerta a A. Balduino e B. Bianchi*, pp. 29–39. Padua.

Castellani (ed.)
1952 *Nuovi testi fiorentini del dugento*, ed. A. Castellani. 2 vols. Florence.

Cavalcanti, G.
1838–39 *Istorie fiorentine*, ed. F. L. Polidori. 2 vols. Florence.
1973 *The Trattato Politico-Morale. . . . A Critical Edition and Interpretation*, ed. Marcia T. Grendler. Geneva.

Cecina, A. L.
1758 *Notizie storiche della città di Volterra*. Pisa.

Chauliac, Guy de
1546 *Ars chirurgica*. Venice.

Cherubino da Siena
1888 *Regola della vita matrimoniale*, ed. F. Ambrini and C. Negroni. Scelta di Curiosità Letterarie Inedite o Rare dal Secolo XIII al XVII, 228. Bologna.

Colonna, Aegidio
1607 *De regimine principum*. Rome.
Coradini, F. (ed.)
1941 *Visita pastorale del 1424 compiuta nel Casentino dal vescovo Francesco da Montepulciano (1414–1433)*. Anghiari.
Corazza, Bartolomeo di Michele del
1894 "Diario fiorentino. Anni 1405–1438," ed. G. O. Corazzini, *ASI* ser. 5, 14:223–88.
Corsini
1965 *Libro di ricordanze dei Corsini (1362–1457)*, ed. A. Petrucci. Istituto Storico Italiano per il Medio Evo, Fonti per la Storia d'Italia, 100. Rome.
Cronache senesi
1934 Ed. A. Lisini. *RIS*, n. ser. 15, 6. Rocca San Casciano.
Cronica urbevetana
1920 Ed. L. Fumi, *RIS* n. ser. 15, 5, 1. Rocca San Casciano. Pp. 199–210.
"Cronichetta volterrana anonima"
1846 Ed. M. Tabarrini, *ASI*, App. 3:317–32.
Damian, Peter
1853 "De parentelae gradibus, ad Johannem episcopum caesenatensem," ed. J. P. Migne, *Patrologia latina*, 145, cols: 191–208. Paris.
Dante
1960 *Le opere di Dante. Testo critico della Società dantesca italiana*, 2nd. ed. Florence.
Dati, Gregorio
1902 *L'Istoria di Firenze dal 1380 al 1405*, ed. L. Pratesi. Norcia.
1969 *Il libro segreto (1384–1434)*, ed. G. Gargiolli. Scelta di Curiosità Inedite o Rare, 102. Bologna.
Delizie degli eruditi toscani
1778 ed. P. Ildefonso di San Luigi. Florence.
Deschamps, Eustache
1878 *Oeuvres complètes*, ed. M. de Queux de Saint-Hilaire. Paris.
Diario d' anonimo
1876 *Diario d' anonimo fiorentino dall'anno 1358 al 1389*, ed. A. Gherardi. In *Cronache dei secoli XIII e XIV*. Documenti di Storia Italiana, 6. Florence.
Dolce, Lodovico
1560 *Dialogo della istituzione delle donne*. 4th ed. Venice.
Dominici, Giovanni
1860 *Regola del governo di cura familiare*, ed. D. Salvi. Florence.
Dominici, Luca
1933 *Cronache di ser L. D.* 1: *Cronaca della venuta dei Bianchi e della Moria 1399–1401*, ed. G. C. Gigliotti. Rerum Pistoriensium Scriptores, 1. Pistoia.

Ficino, Marsilio

1522 *Consiglio contra la pestilentia. Consiglio di maestro Thommaso del Garbo contro la pestilentia*. Florence.

Francesco da Barberino

1957 *Del reggimento e costume di donne*, ed. G. E. Sansone. Collezione di "Filologia Romanza," 2. Turin.

Gaye, G.

1839 *Carteggio inedito d' artisti dei secc. XIV, XV e XVI*. Florence.

Gherardi da Prato, G.

1975 *Il paradiso degli Alberti*, ed. A. Lanza. Rome.

Giordano da Rivalto, Fra

1839 *Prediche del beato fra Giovanni recitate in Firenze dal 1303 al 1309*, ed. D. M. Manni. Milan.

Giovanni di Carlo

1698 *Vita beati Ioannis Dominici cardinalis*. In *ASS* II Junii. Antwerp. Pp. 401–18.

Giovanni di Lemmo da Comugnori

1876 *Diario dal 1299 al 1320*, ed. L. Passerini. In *Cronache dei secoli XIII e XIV*. Documenti di Storia Italiana, 6. Florence.

Giusti, M. and Guidi, P. (eds.)

1942 *Rationes decimarum Italiae nei secoli XIII–XIV. Tuscia*, 2: *Le decime degli anni 1295–1304*. Studi e Testi, 98. Vatican City.

Guasti, C. (ed.)

1867–73 *Commissioni di Rinaldo degli Albizzi per il Comune di Firenze dal 1399 al 1433*. Documenti di Storia Italiana, 1–3. Florence.

Guasti, C. and Gherardi, A. (eds.)

1866–93 *I capitoli del comune di Firenze. Inventario e regesto*. Florence.

Guicciardini, Francesco

1929 *Storia d'Italia*, ed. C. Panigada. Scrittori d'Italia, 120. Bari.

1945 *Le cose fiorentine*, ed. R. Ridolfi. Florence.

Iacopo da Porcia

1541 *De generosa liberorum educatione*. Basel.

Isidore of Seville

1911 *Etymologiae*, ed. W. Lindsay. 2 vols. Oxford.

Karmin, O. (ed.)

1906 *La legge del catasto fiorentino del 1427 (testo, introduzione e note)*. Florence.

Landucci, Luca

1883 *Diario fiorentino dal 1450 al 1516, continuato da un anonimo fiorentino fino al 1542*, ed. I. Del Badia. Florence.

Latini, Brunetto

1863 *Li livres dou trésor*, ed. P. Chabaille. Collection de Documents Inédits sur l'Histoire de France. Paris.

Libro del Biadaiolo

1978 *Il libro del Biadaiolo. Carestie e annona a Firenze dalla metà del '200 al 1348*, ed. Giuliano Pinto. Florence.

Machiavelli, Bernardo
1954 *Libro di ricordi*, ed. C. Olschki. Florence.
Machiavelli, Niccolo`
s.d. *Il principe . . . I discorsi sopra la prima decà di Tito Livio e gli opuscoli in prosa*. Florence: A. Salani.
1969 *Istorie fiorentine*, ed. E. Raimundi. Milan.
Macinghi-Strozzi, Alessandra
1877 *Lettere di una gentildonna fiorentina ai figliuoli esuli*, ed. C. Guasti. Florence.
Manetti, Giannozzo
1847 "Dantis, Petrarchae ac Boccaccii vitae." In *Philippi Villani liber de civitatis Florentiae famosis civibus . . . .* ed. G. C. Galletti. Florence.
Mansi, J. D.
1758–98 *Sacrorum conciliorum nova et amplissima collectio*. Florence and Venice.
Masi, Bartolomeo
1906 *Ricordanze di B. M., calderaio fiorentino, dal 1478 al 1526*, ed. C. Guasti. 2 vols. Florence.
Mazzei, ser Lapo
1880 *Lettere di un notaro a un mercatante del secolo 14*, ed. C. Guasti. 2 vols. Florence.
MGH *Monumenta Germaniae Historica*. Hanover, etc. 1826–.
Milanesi, G. (ed.)
1887 *Operette storiche edite ed inedite*. Florence.
Minuti, Vincenzo
1892 "Relazione del commissario Gio. Batt. Tedaldi sopra la città e il capitanato di Pistoia nell'anno 1569," *ASI,* ser. 5, 10: 302–31.
Monaldi, Guido
1845 "Diario." *Istorie pistolesi ovvero delle cose avvenute in Toscana dall'anno MCCC al MCCCXLVIII e diario del M.*, ed. A. M. Biscioni. Milan.
Montaigne, Michel de
1774 *Journal de voyage en Italie*, ed. and annotated by M. de Querlon. Rome and Paris.
Montanari, P. (ed.)
1966 *Documenti su la popolazione di Bologna alla fine del Trecento*. Fonti per la Storia di Bologna, 1. Bologna.
Morelli, Giovanni di Iacopo and Lionardo di Lorenzo
1785 *Croniche . . . .* , ed. Ildefonso di San Luigi. Delizie degli Eruditi Toscani, 19. Florence.
Morelli, Giovanni di Paolo
1956, 1969 *Ricordi*, ed. V. Branca. Florence.
Moryson, F.
1903 *Itinerary*, ed. C. Hughes. London.
Necrologio
1955 *Necrologio di Santa Maria Novella. Testo integrale dall'inizio (MCCXXXV) al MDIV*. 2 vols. Florence.

Naddo
1784 Naddo di ser Nepo di ser Gallo da Montecatini di Val di Nievole, *Memorie storiche cavate da un libro di ricordi . . . dall'anno 1374 all' anno 1398*, ed. Ildefonso di San Luigi. Delizie degli Eruditi Toscani, 18. Florence.

Niccolini, Lapo di Giovanni
1969 *Il libro degli affari proprii di casa di Lapo di Giovanni Niccolini de' Sirigatti*, ed. C. Bec. Paris.

Novelle
1796 *Novelle di autori senesi.* London.

Oderico di Credi
1843 "Ricordanze dal 1405 al 1425," ed. F. L. Polidori, *ASI* ser. 1, 4:53–100.

Palmieri, Matteo
1825 *Della vita civile.* Biblioteca scelta di opere italiane antiche e moderne, 160. Milan.

Paolino minorita, Fra
1868 *Trattato De Regimine rectoris*, ed. A. Massafia. Vienna and Florence.

Paolo da Certaldo
1945 *Il libro di buoni costumi, documenti di vita trecentesca*, ed. A. Schiaffini. Florence.

Petrarca
1867 *De' rimedii dell'una e dell' altra fortuna . . . volgarizzati nel buon secolo della lingua per D. Giov. Samminiato.* Collezione di Opere Inedite o Rare. Bologna.

Philippe de Novare
1888 *Les quatre âges de l' homme*, ed. M. de Fréville. Société des Anciens Textes Français, 27. Paris.

Pitti, Buonaccorso
1905 *Cronaca, con annotazion*, ed. A. Bacchi della Lega. Bologna.

PL
1841–64 *Patrologiae Cursus Completus,* Series latina, ed. J. P. Migne. Paris.

Pontano, Giovanni
1948 *Carmina, ecloghe, elegie, liriche*, ed. J. Oeschger. Scrittori d'Italia, 198. Bari.
1965 *I trattati delle virtù sociali. De liberalitate. De beneficentia. De magnificentia. De splendore. De conviventia*, ed. F. Tateo. Testi di Letteratura Italiana. Rome.

Quaresimale
1934–40 *Quaresimale fiorentino del 1424 e 1425*, ed. C. Cannarozzi. Pistoia and Florence.

Regesto
1910 *Regesto del capitolo di Lucca,* ed. P. Guidi and O. Parenti. Regesta Chartarum Italiae, 6. Rome.

Rinuccini, Filippo di Cino
1840 *Ricordi storici dal 1282 al 1460 colla continuazione di Alamanno e Neri suoi figli fino al 1506*, ed. C. Aiazzi. Florence, 1840.
RIS *Rerum Italicarum Scriptores*, new ed. Città di Castello, 1900–.
Rospigliosi, Antonio di Taddeo
1909 *Libro A di richordi (1459–1498)*, ed. G. C. Rospigliosi. Pisa.
Rucellai, Giovanni
1960 *Zibaldone*, 1: *Il zibaldone quaresimale. Pagine scelte*, ed. A. Perosa. Studies of the Warburg Institute, 24. London.
Sacchetti, F.
1946 *Il trecentonovelle*, ed. E. Li Gotti. Rome.
Salutati, Coluccio
1891–1911 *Epistolario*, ed. F. Novati. Fonti per la Storia d'Italia, 15–18. 5 vols. Rome.
Salvi, M. A.
1656–62 *Delle historie di Pistoia e fazioni d'Italia*. Venice.
Salviati, Jacopo d'Alamanno
1784 *Croniche e memorie dal 1398 al 1411*, ed. Ildefonso di San Luigi. Delizie deglie Eruditi Toscani, 19. Florence.
Savonarola, Girolamo
1879–80 "Libro della vita viduale." In ;Oeuvres spirituelles choisies, ed. E. C. Bayonne. 3 vols. Paris. 2:5–51.
1959 "De simplicitate christianae vitae." In *Edizione nazionale delle opere di Girolamo Savonarola*, ed. P. G. Ricci. Rome.
Singleton, Charles S. (ed.)
1936 *Canti carnascialeschi del Rinascimento*. Scrittori d'Italia, 159. Bari.
1940 *Canti carnascialeschi del Rinascimento (Nuovi-)*. Modena.
Sozomeno
1908 *Chronicon universale*, ed. G. Zaccagnini. *RIS*, new ed. 16, 1. Città di Castello.
Statuta
1778–81 *Statuta populi et communis Florentie . . . anno salutis MCCCCXV*. 4 vols. Freiburg.
Statuti
1910–21 *Statuti della Repubblica fiorentina*, ed. R. Caggese. Florence.
Statuti
1922 *Statuti dell' Arte de' medici e speziali*, ed. R. Ciasca. Fonti per la Storia delle Corporazioni Artigiane del Comune di Firenze. Florence.
Statuto
1946 *Statuto di Arezzo (1327)*, ed. G Marri Camerani. Florence.
Statutum
1888 *Statutum potestatis communis Pistorii*, ed. L. Zdekauer. Milan.
Statutum
1934 *Statutum bladi reipublicae fiorentinae (1348)*, ed. G. Masi. Orbis romanus, 2. Milan.

Stefani, M.
1903 *Cronica fiorentina*, ed. N. Rodolico. *RIS*, new ed. 30, 1. Città di Castello.

Tommaso da Celano, Fra
1904 *Saint Francis of Assisi according to Br. Thomas of Celano*, ed. H. G. Rosedal. London.

Vegio, Maffeo
1933–36 *De educatione liberorum et eorum claris moribus libri sex*, ed. M. W. Fanning and A. S. Sullivan. Washington, D.C.

Velluti, Donato
1914 *La cronica domestica scritta fra il 1367 e il 1370, con le addizioni di Paolo Velluti scritte fra il 1555 ed il 1560*, ed. I. Del Lungo and G. Volpe. Florence.

Venette, Jean de
1843–44 *Continuatio chronici Guillielmi de Nangiaco*, t. 2. Société de l'Histoire de France. Paris.

Vergerio, Pietro Paolo
1918 "De ingenuis moribus et liberalibus adulescentie" ed. A. Gnesotto, *Atti e Memorie dell' Accademia di Scienze e Lettere di Padova*, 34:75-157.

Vespasiano da Bisticci
1892 *Vite di uomini illustri del secolo XV*, ed. L. Frati. Bologna.

Villani, Filippo
1847 *Liber de civitatis Florentie famosis civibus . . . et de Florentinorum litteratura principes fere synchroni scriptores*, ed. G. C. Galletti. Florence.

Villani, Giovanni
1823–25 *Cronica*. 8 vols. Florence: Magheri.
1845 *Cronica*, ed. F. Gherardi–Dragommani. 4 vols. Florence.

II. Studies

Abel, Wilhelm
1966 *Agrarkrisen und Agrarkonjunktur . . . seit hohen Mittelalter*. 3rd ed. Berlin.

Aebischer, Paul
1947 "Les origines de la finale i des noms de famille italiens," *Onomastica* 1: 90–106.

AESC *Annales-Economies-Sociétés-Civilisations* Paris, 1946–.

Aleati, G.
1957 *La popolazione di Pavia durante il dominio Spagnolo*. Milan.

Alessandri, M.
1957 "La densità di popolazione nella Toscana meridionale negli ultimi secoli," *Rivista Geografica Italiana*, 64:224–43.

Alexander, J. W.
1959 "The Basic Non-Basic Concept of Urban Economic Functions." In

Readings in Urban Geography, ed. H. M. Mayer and C. F. Kohn., pp. 87–100. Chicago.

Anselmi, Gian-Mario, et al.

1980 Anselmi, Gian-Mario; Pezzarossa, Fulvio; and Avellini, Luisa, *La "Memoria" dei mercatores. Tendenze ideologiche, ricordanze, artigianato in versi nella Firenze del Quattrocento.* L'Esperienza Critica, 1. Bologna.

Ariès, Philippe

1965 *Centuries of Childhood: A Social History of Family Life.* Trans. Robert Baldick. New York.

1973 *L'enfant et la vie familiale sous l'Ancien régime.* 2nd ed. Paris.

1975 *Essais sur l'histoire de la mort en Occident du Moyen Age à nos jours.* Paris.

Arnold, Klaus

1980 *Kind und Gesellschaft in Mittelalter und Renaissance. Beiträge und Texte zur Geschichte der Kindheit.* Paderborn.

ASI *Archivio Storico Italiano* 1842–, Florence.

Auerbach, F.

1913 "Das Gesetz der Bevölkerungskonzentration," *Petermanns geographische Mitteilungen*, 59:73–101.

Banti, O.

1959–60 "Il vicariato e la podesteria di Vicopisano nel secolo 16. Note sull'amministrazione locale dello stato mediceo," *Bollettino Storico Pisano*, 28–29:319–92.

1964–66 "Ricerche sul notariato a Pisa tra il secolo 13° e il secolo 14°. Note in margine al *Breve collegii notariorum* (1305)," *Bollettino Storico Pisano*, vol. in honor of Professor O. Bertolini, 33–35:131–86.

Barbadoro, B.

1929 *Le finanze della repubblica fiorentina. Imposta diretta e debito pubblico (fino all'istituzione del Monte).* Florence.

1931 "Finanzia e demografia nei ruoli fiorentine d'imposta del 1352," *Atti del Congresso internazionale per gli studi della popolazione*, pp. 13–34. Rome.

Barbieri, G.

1966 *Memoria illustrativa della carta dell'utilizzazione del suolo della Toscana* (*Fogli* 9, 11, 12 *della carta*). Rome.

Bargellini, P.

1972 *I Buonomini di San Martino.* Florence.

Battara, P.

1935a "Le indagini congetturali sulla popolazione di Firenze fino al Trecento," *ASI*, 93:217-32.

1935b *La popolazione di Firenze a metà del '500.* Florence

Bautier, R. H.

1959 "Feux, population et structure sociale au milieu du XVe siècle: l'exemple de Carpentras," *AESC*, 14:255–68.

1965 "La valeur démographique du feu d' après les recensements de Chieri (Piémont), 1473–1500," *Bulletin Philologique et Historique du Comité des Travaux Historiques et Scientifiques (jusque 1610)*., pp. 235–46.

Bean, J. M. W.

1963 "Plague, Population and Economic Decline in the Later Middle Ages," *Economic History Review*, 15:423–37.

Bec, Christian

1967 *Les marchands écrivains. Affaires et humanisme à Florence, 1375–1430*. Paris and The Hague.

Becker, Marvin

1965 "Problemi della finanza pubblica fiorentina della seconda metà del Trecento e dei primi del Quattrocento," *ASI*, 123:433–66. Florence.

1966–67 *Florence in Transition*, 1: *The Decline of the Commune*, 2: *Studies in the Rise of the Territorial State*. Baltimore.

1968 "The Florentine Territorial State and Civic Humanism in the Early Renaissance." *Florentine Studies*, ed. Nicolai Rubinstein, pp. 109–39. London.

1981 *Medieval Italy. Constraints and Creativity*. Bloomington, IN.

Bellomo, Manlio

1961 *Ricerche sui rapporti patrimoniali tra coniugi. Contributo alla storia della famiglia medievale* (12°–13°). Milan.

1966 *Profili della famiglia italiana nell'età dei comuni*, 1. Catania.

1968 *Problemi di diritto familiare nell' età dei comuni. Beni paterni e pars filii*. Milan.

1970 *La condizione giuridica della donna in Italia*. Turin.

Beloch, K. J.

1937–61 *Bevölkerungsgeschichte Italiens*, especially *Die Bevölkerung des Kirchenstaates, Toskanas und der Herzogtümer am Po*. Berlin.

Bennassar, B.

1969 *Recherches sur les grandes épidémies dans le nord de l'Espagne à la fin du 16e siècle*. Paris.

Benvéniste, E.

1969 *Le vocabulaire des institutions indo-européennes, 1: Economie, parenté société*. Paris.

Bergin, Thomas G.

1981 *Boccaccio*. New York.

Berkner, L. K.

1972a "The Stem Family and the Developmental Cycle of the Peasant Household: An 18th Century Austrian Example," *American Historical Review*, 77:398–418.

1972b "Rural Family Organization in Europe: A Problem in Comparative History," *Peasant Studies Newsletter* 1:145–55.

1973 "Recent Research on the History of the Family in Western Europe," *Journal of Marriage and the Family*, 35:395–405.

1975 "The Use and Misuse of Census Data for the Historical Analysis of Family Structure," *The Journal of Interdisciplinary History*, 5:721–38.

Berry, G.
1961 "City-Size Distributions and Economic Development," *Economic Development and Cultural Change*, 9:573–88.

Berry, B. J. L. and Garrison, W. L.
1959 "Alternate Explanations of Urban Rank–Size Relationships." *In: Readings in Urban Geography*, ed. Mayer and Kohn, pp. 230–39. Chicago.

Besta, E.
1933 *La famiglia nella storia del diritto italiano*. Milan.

Biraben, J. N.
1963 "Conceptions médico-épidémiologiques actuelles de la peste," *Le Concours Medical*, pp. 619–2; 781–90.
1973 "Structures spatiales de la population et démographie historique," *Bulletin d' Information de la Société de Démographie Historique*, 9:19–21.
1975–76 *Les hommes et la peste en France et dans les pays européens et méditerranéens*, 1: *La peste dans l'histoire*; 2: *Les hommes face à la peste*. Paris.

Blalock, H.
1960 *Social Statistics*. New York.

Boase, T. S. R.
1972 *Death in the Middle Ages: Mortality, Judgment and Remembrance*. London.

Boffitto, G. and Mori, A.
1926 *Firenze nelle vedute e nelle piante*. Florence.

Böll, F.
1913 "Die Lebensalter. Ein Beitrag zur antiken Ethologie und zur Geschichte der Zahlen," *Neue Jahrbücher für das klassische Altertum, Geschichte und deutsche Literatur*, 21:89–145.

Bologna, L. M.
1924 "Origine e sviluppo della mezzeria toscana sino all'Editto Leopoldino," *Rivista di Diritto Agrario* 1:74 ff.

Bowsky, William M.
1964 "The Impact of the Black Death upon Sienese Government and Society," *Speculum*, 39:1–34.
1970 *The Finance of the Commune of Siena, 1287–1355*. Oxford.
1971 "City and Contado: Military Relationships." *Renaissance Studies in Honor of Hans Baron*, ed. A. Molho and A. Tedeschi, pp. 74–98. Florence.
1981 *A Medieval Italian Commune: Siena under the Nine, 1287–1355*. Berkeley.

Brandileone, F.
1906 *Saggi sulla storia della celebrazione del matrimonio in Italia*. Bologna.

Brattö, Olaf

1953 *Studi di antroponomia fiorentina: il Libro di Montaperti, 1260.* Göteborg.

1955 *Nuovi studi di antroponimia fiorentina. I nomi meno frequenti del Libro di Montaperti.* Göteborg.

Braudel, F.

1972–73 *The Mediterranean and the Mediterranean World in the Age of Philip II.* trans. Sian Reymonds. London.

1979 *La Méditerranée et le monde méditerranéen à l' époque de Philippe II.* 4th ed. Paris.

Braunfels, W.

1953 *Mittelalterliche Stadtbaukunst in der Toskana.* Berlin.

Brissaud, Y. B.

1972 "L'infanticide à la fin du Moyen Age: ses motivations psychologiques et sa répression," *Revue Historique de Droit Français et Etranger*, 50:228–56.

Brown, Judith C.

1982 *In the Shadow of Florence: Provincial Society in Renaissance Pescia.* New York and Oxford.

Brucker, Gene

1957 "Un documento fiorentino sulla guerra, sulla finanza e sulla amministrazione pubblica (1375)," *ASI*, 115:165-76.

1962 *Florentine Politics and Society, 1343–1378.* Princeton.

1971 *The Society of Renaissance Florence.* New York.

1972 "The Florentine *Popolo Minuto* and Its Political Role, 1340–1450". In *Violence and Civil Disorder in Italian Cities*, ed. L. Martines, pp. 154–83. Berkeley.

1977 *The Civic World of Early Renaissance Florence.* Princeton.

Brucker, Gene, and Becker, Marvin

1956 "The Arti Minori in Florentine Politics, 1342–1378," *Mediaeval Studies*, 18:93–104.

Bullough, D. A.

1969 "Early Medieval Social Groupings. The Terminology of Kinship," *Past and Present*, 45:3–18.

Burch, T. K.

1967 "The Size and Structure of Families: A Comparative Analysis of Census Data," *American Sociological Review*, 32:347–63.

1968 "Comparative Family Structure: A Demographic Approach," *Estadística*, 26:285-93

1970 "Some Demographic Determinants of Average Household Size: An Analytic Approach," *Demography*, 7:61-60.

Burckhardt, Jacob

1929 *Civilization of the Renaissance in Italy*, trans. S. G. C. Middlemore. London.

Callisen, S. A.
1937 "The Evil Eye in Italian Art," *The Art Bulletin* , 19: 450 ff.
Callmann, E.
1974 *Apollonio di Giovanni*. Oxford.
Canestrini, G.
1862 *La scienza e l' arte di stato desunta dagli atti ufficiali della repubblica fiorentina e dei Medici*. Florence.
Capponi, Gino
1875 *Storia della Repubblica di Firenze*. 3 vols. Florence.
Carpentier, E.
1962 "Autour de la Peste Noire: Famines et épidémies dans l'histoire du 14e siècle," *AESC*, 17:1062–92.
1963 *Une ville devant la peste. Orvieto et la peste noire de 1348*. Paris.
Carpentier, E. and Glenisson, J.
1962 "La démographie française au 14e siècle," *AESC*, 17:109–29
Casini, Bruno
1957–58 "I fuochi di Pisa e la prestanza del 1407," *Bollettino Storico Pisano*, 26–27:156–271.
1959–60 "Contribuenti pisani alle taglie del 1402 e del 1412," *Bollettino Storico Pisano*, 28-29:90 –318.
1961 "Il vicariato, la pretura e la delegazione di governo di Lari," *Bollettino Storico Pisano*, 3rd ser. 30:17–101.
1964 *Il catasto di Pisa del 1428–1429*. Pubblicazione della Società storica pisana, Collana storica, 2. Pisa.
1965 *Aspetti della vita economica e sociale di Pisa dal catasto del 1428–1429*. Collana storica, 3. Pisa.
Cassuto, U.
1918 *Gli ebrei a Firenze nel' età del rinascimento*. Florence.
Castellani, A.
1956 "Nomi fiorentini del Dugento," *Zeitschrift für romanische Philologie*, 72:54–87.
Cazelles, R.
1965 "La peste de 1348 en langue d'oil, épidémie prolétarienne et infantile," *Bulletin Philologique et Historique du Comité des Travaux Historiques et Scientifiques (jusqu' en 1610), 1962*, pp. 293–305.
Champeaux, E.
1933 "*Jus sanguinis*. Trois façons de calculer la parenté au Moyen Age," *Revue Historique de Droit Français et Etranger* , 4th ser. 12:241–90.
Chayanov, A. V.
1966 *The Theory of the Peasant Economy*, eds. D. Thorner, B. Kerblay, and R. E. F. Smith. Homewood, IL.
Cherubini, G.
1965 "La proprietà fondiaria di un mercante toscano nel Trecento (Simo d'Ubertino di Arezzo)," *Rivista di Storia dell' Agricoltura*, 5:49–94; 143–69.

1967 "Una famiglia di piccoli proprietari contadini del territorio di Castrocaro, 1383–1384," *Rivista di Storia dell' Agricoltura*, 7:244–70.

1968a "Pisani ricchi e pisani poveri nel terzo decennio del Quattrocento," *Rivista di Storia dell' Agricoltura*, 8:269–85.

1968b "La signoria degli Ubertini sui comuni rurali casentinesi di Chitignano, Rasino e Taena all' inizio del Quattrocento," *ASI*, 126:151–69.

1972a *Una comunità dell' Appennino dal 13 al 15 secolo. Montecoronaro dalla signoria dell' abbazia del Trivio al dominio di Firenze*. Biblioteca storica, 15. Florence.

1972b "La società dell' Appennino dal 13 al 15 secolo," *Modena* suppl. 6.: 23–26.

1974 *Signori, Contadini, Borghesi: Richerche sulla società italiana del basso medioevo*. Florence.

Cherubini, G. and Francovich, R.

1973 "Forme e vicende degli insediamenti nella campagna toscana dei secoli XIII–XV," *Quaderni Storici*, 24:873–903.

Chojnacki, Stanley

1974 "Patrician Women in Early Renaissance Venice," *Studies in the Renaissance*, 21:173–203.

1975 "Dowries and Kinsmen in Early Renaissance Venice," *Journal of Interdisciplinary History*, 5:572–600.

Cimetier, F.

1932 "Parenté," *Dictionnaire de théologie catholique*. Paris.

Cipolla, Carlo M.

1973 *Cristofano and the Plague. A Study in the History of Public Health in the Age of Galileo*. London.

Cipolla, Carlo M. and Zanetti, D. E.

1972 "Peste et mortalité différentielle," *Annales de Démographie Historique*, pp. 197–202.

Coale, A. J.

1956 "The Effects of Changes in Mortality and Fertility on Age Composition," *The Milbank Memorial Fund Quarterly*, 24:79–114.

1964 *Regional Model Life Tables and Stable Populations*. Princeton.

1965 *Aspects of the Analysis of Family Structure*. Princeton.

Coale, A. J. and Demeny, P.

1966 *Methods of Estimating Fertility and Mortality from Censuses of Population*. Princeton.

Cohn, Samuel Kline Jr.

1980 *The Laboring Classes in Renaissance Florence*. New York.

Commissione

1912 *Commissione per la pubblicazione dei documenti finanziari della Repubblica di Venezia (R.)* ser. 2a. Bilanci generali, I, 1: *Origini delle gravezze e dei dazi principali (976–1579)*. Venice.

Conti, Elio

1965 *La formazione della struttura agraria moderna nel contado fiorentino* 1:

Le campagne nell' età precomunale; 2: *Monografie e tavole statistiche, 15-19 sec.* Istituto storico italiano per il Medio Evo, Studi storici, fasc. 51 and 59. Rome.

1966 *I catasti agrari della Repubblica fiorentina e il catasto particellare toscano (sec. 14–19). La formazione della struttura agraria moderna*, vol. 3, Parte 1, sez. 1: *Le fonti.* Istituto storico italiano per il Medio Evo. Rome.

Corradi, A.

1865–94 *Annali delle épidémie occorse in Italia . . . fino al 1850.* 8 vols. Bologna.

Corsini, C. A.

1974 "Libri dei matrimoni e delle nascite. Nascite e matrimoni." In *Le fonti della demografia storica in Italia.* Comitato italiano per lo studio dei problemi della popolazione, no. 7, 1:851–952; 2:648–99. Rome.

Cristiani, Emilio

1962 *Nobiltà e popolo nel comune di Pisa dalle origine del podestariato alla signoria dei Donoratico.* Naples.

Croix, Alain

1974 *Nantes et le pays nantais au 16e siècle. Etude démographique.* Paris.

Cuvelier, J.

1912 *Les dénombrements de foyers en Brabant, 14e–16e siècles.* Paris.

Davidsohn, Robert

1962 *Storia di Firenze.* 2nd ed. Italian trans. 8 vols. Florence.

Delille, Gernard

1974 "Un problème de démographie historique: hommes et femmes devant la mort," *Mélanges de l' école française de Rome*, 86:419–43.

Del Lungo, I,

1905 *La donna fiorentina del buon tempo antico.* Florence.

1908 *Women of Florence*, trans. Mary C. Steegman. New York and London.

De Mause, Lloyd

1974 "Introduction," *The History of Childhood*, ed. L. de Mause. New York.

Desportes, P.

1966 "La population de Reims au 15e siècle," *Le Moyen Age*, 79:463–509.

Dini, F.

1902 *Le cartiere in Colle di Valdelsa.* Castelfiorentino.

Doren, Alfred

1901 *Die florentiner Wollentuchindustrie vom vierzehnten bis zum sechzehnten Jahrhundert.* Stuttgart.

1903 *Deutsche Handwerker und deutsche Handwerkerbruderschaften im mittelalterlichen Italien.* Berlin.

1940 *Le Arti fiorentine.* Italian trans. Florence.

Dorini, Umberto

1933 "Come sorse la fabbrica degli Uffizi," *Rivista Storica degli Archivi Toscani*, 5:1–40.

Duby, Georges
1964 "Dans la France du Nord-Ouest au 12e siècle: les 'jeunes' dans la société aristocratique," *AESC*, 19:835–46. Reprinted in G. Duby, *Hommes et structures du Moyen Age*, 1973, pp. 213–25. Paris.
1967 "Structures de parenté et noblesse dans la France du nord au 11e et 12e siècles," reprinted in G. Duby, *Hommes et Structures du Moyen Age*, 1973, pp. 267–85. Paris.
1978 *Medieval Marriage. Two Models from Twelfth-Century France*, trans. Elborg Forster. Baltimore and London.
1981 *Le chevalier, la femme et le prêtre. Le mariage dans la société féodale*. Paris.

Dupâquier, J.
1972 "De l'animal à l'homme: le mécanisme autorégulateur des populations traditionnelles," *Revue de l' Institut de Sociologie*, pp. 177–211.
1973 "Sur une table (prétendument) florentine d'espérance de vie," *AESC*, 28:1066–70.

Dupâquier, J. and Demonet, M.
1972 "Ce qui fait les familles nombreuses," *AESC*, 27:1025–46.

Emery, R.
1952 "The Use of the Surname in the Study of Medieval Economic History," *Medievalia et Humanistica*, 7:43–50.

Esmein, A.
1929–35 *Le mariage en droit canonique*. 2nd ed. Paris.

Fasano-Guarini, E.
1973 *Lo stato mediceo di Cosimo I*. Archivio dell'atlante storico italiano dell' età moderna. Florence.

Favier, Jean
1971 *Finance et fiscalité au bas Moyen Age*. Paris.

Febvre, Lucien
1947 "Une enquête: la succession des circonscriptions," *AESC*, 19:201–04.

Festa, G. B.
1910 *Un galateo femminile italiano del Trecento*. Biblioteca di cultura moderna, 36. Bari.

Fierro, A.
1971 "Un cycle démographique: Dauphiné et Faucigny du 14e au 19e siècle," *AESC*, 26:941–59.

Fineschi, V.
1767 *Istoria compendiata di alcune antiche carestie e dovizie di grano occorse in Firenze (1309–1335)*. Florence.

Fiumi, Enrico
1949 "Il computo della popolazione di Volterra nel medioevo secondo il 'sal delle bocche'," *ASI*, 107:3–16.
1950 "La demografia fiorentina nelle pagine di Giovanni Villani," *ASI*, 108:78–158.
1953 "Economia e vita privata dei Fiorentine nelle rilevazioni statistiche di Giovanni Villani," *ASI*, 111:207–41.

1956 "Sui rapporti economici tra città e contado nell' età comunale," *ASI*, 114:18–78.

1957 "L'imposta diretta nei comuni medioevali della Toscana." In *Studi in onore di A. Sapori*. 1:329–53. Milan.

1957-59 "Fioritura e decadenza dell'economia fiorentina," *ASI* 115:385–439; 116:443–510; 117:427–502.

1961 *Storia economica e sociale di San Gimignano*. Florence.

1962 "La popolazione del territorio volterrano-sangimignanese ed il problema demografico dell'età comunale," In *Studi in onore di A. Fanfani*. 1:248–90. Milan.

1965 "Stato di popolazione e distribuzione della ricchezza in Prato secondo il catasto del 1428–1429," *ASI*, 123:288–303.

1968 *Demografia, movimento urbanistico e classi sociali in Prato dall' età comunale ai tempi moderni*. Florence.

1969–72 "Popolazione, società ed economia volterrano dal catasto del 1428–29," *Rassegna volterrana*, 36–39.

Flandrin, J. L.

1973 "L'attitude à l'égard du petit enfant et les conduites sexuelles dans la civilisation occidentale: structures anciennes et évolution," *Annales de démographie historique*, pp. 143–210.

Fourquin, G.

1956 "La population de la région parisienne aux environs de 1328," *Le Moyen Age*, 11:63–91.

Fox, Robin

1967 *Kinship and Marriage. An Anthropological Perspective*. Harmondsworth, Eng.

Fumagalli, C.

1912 *Il diritto di fraterna nella giurisprudenza da Accursio alla codificazione*. Turin.

Gambi, Lucio

1956 "La popolazione della Sicilia fra il 1374 e il 1376," *Quaderni di geografia umana per la Sicilia e la Calabria*, 1:3–10.

Garin, E.

1958 *Il pensiero pedagogico dell' umanesimo*. Florence.

1968 *L' éducation de l' homme moderne. La pédagogie de la Renaissance*. Paris.

Gaudenzi, A.

1898 "Sulla storia del cognome a Bologna nel sec. 13," *Bollettino dell' Istituto Storico Italiano*, 19:1–163.

Geremek, B.

1973 "Il pauperismo nell'età preindustriale (sec. 14–18) In *Storia d' Italia*. 5:670–98, Turin.

Gigli, F.

1954 "La densità di popolazione in Toscana nei secoli 16 e 17," *Rivista Geografica Italiana*, 61:265–76.

Gilbert, C.
1967 "When Did a Man in the Renaissance Grow Old?" *Studies in the Renaissance*, 14:7–32.
Gioffrè, D.
1971 *Il mercato degli schiavi a Genova nel secolo XV*. Collana storica di Fonti e Studi, 2. Genoa.
Gluckman, P., Herlihy, D. and Pori, M.
1973 *A Spectral Analysis of Deaths in Florence, 1257–1500*. Typescript. Stanford: Center for Advanced Study in the Behavioral Sciences.
Goldthwaite, Richard A.
1968 *Private Wealth in Renaissance Florence. A Study of Four Families*. Princeton.
1972 "The Florentine Palace as Domestic Architecture," *American Historical Review*, 77:977–1012.
1975 "I prezzi del grano a Firenze dal XIV al XVI secolo," *Quaderni Storici*, 28:5–36.
1980 *The Building of Renaissance Florence. An Economic and Social History*. Baltimore and London.
Goody, J. (ed.)
1966 *The Developmental Cycle in Domestic Groups*. Cambridge Papers in Social Anthropology, 1. Cambridge, Eng.
1972 "The Evolution of the Family." In: *Household and Family*, ed. P. Laslett and R. Wall, pp. 103–24. Cambridge, Eng.
Goubert, P.
1961 *Beauvais et le Beauvaisis de 1600 à 1730*. Paris.
Greppi, C. and Massa, M.
1971 "Città e territorio nella Repubblica fiorentina." In *Un' altra Firenze. L' epoca di Cosimo il Vecchio. Riscontri tra cultura e società nella storia fiorentina*. pp. 1–58. Florence.
Grohmann, Alberto
1981 *Città e territorio tra medioevo ed età moderna. (Perugia, secc. XIII–XVI)*. 2 vols. Perugia.
Guidi, Guidubaldo
1981 *Il governo della città-repubblica di Firenze del primo quattrocento*. Biblioteca Storica Toscana, 20. 3 vols. Florence.
Haggett, P.
1973 *L' analyse spatiale en géographie humaine*. Paris.
Hajnal, J.
1953 "Age at Marriage and Proportions Marrying," *Population Studies*, 7:111–36.
1965 "European Marriage Patterns in Perspective." In *Population in History*, ed. D. V. Glass and D. E. C. Eversley, pp. 101–43. London.
Hammel, E.
1972 "The Zadruga as Process." In *Household and Family*, ed. P. Laslett and R. Wall, pp. 335–74. Cambridge.

1976 "Household Structure in 14th Century Macedonia." In *Mediterranean Family Organization*, ed. J. K. Campbell. Oxford.

Hareven, Tamara K.

1974 "The Family as Process: the Historical Study of Family Cycle," *The Journal of Social History*, 7:322–29.

1975 "Review of *Household and Family*, ed. P. Laslett," *History and Theory*, 14:242–51.

Heers, Jacques

1961 *Gênes au 15e siècle*. Paris.

1968 "Les limites des méthodes statistiques pour les recherches de démographie médiévale," *Annales de démographie historique*, pp. 42–72.

1974 *Le clan familial au Moyen Age*. Paris.

1977 *Family Clans in the Middle ages*, trans. Barry Herbert. Europe in the Middle Ages, 4. Amsterdam and New York.

Helleiner, Karl

1967 "The Population of Europe from the Black Death to the Eve of the Vital Revolution." In *Cambridge Economic History*, ed. E. E. Rich and C. H. Wilson, vol.4. Cambridge, Eng.

Henry, Louis

1949 "Le contrôle des recensements," *Population*,, 4.

1957 "La mortalité d'après les inscriptions funéraires," *Population* 12: 149–52.

1959 "L'âge au décès d'après les inscriptions funéraires," *Population*, 14: 327–29.

1967 *Manuel de démographie historique*. Geneva.

1972 *Démographie: analyse et modèles. Paris.*

Henry, L. and Gauthier, E.

1958 *La population de Crulai, paroisse normande. Etude historique*. Paris.

Herlihy, David

1958 *Pisa in the Early Renaissance. A Study of Urban Growth*. New Haven.

1962 "Land, Family and Women in Continental Europe, 701–1200," *Traditio*, 18:89–120.

1964 "Direct and Indirect Taxation in Tuscan Urban Finance, ca. 1200–1400." In *Finances et comptabilité urbaines du 13e au 16e siècle*, pp. 385–405. Brussels.

1965 "Population, Plague and Social Change in Rural Pistoia, 1201–1430," *Economic History Review*, 18:225–44.

1967 *Medieval and Renaissance Pistoia. The Social History of an Italian Town*. New Haven.

1968 "Santa Maria Impruneta: A Rural Commune in the Late Middle Ages." In *Florentine Studies*, ed. Rubinstein, pp. 242–76. London.

1969a "Family Solidarity in Medieval Italian History," *Economy, Society and Government in Medieval Italy*, ed. D. Herlihy, R. Lopez, and V. Slessarev, pp. 173–84. Kent, OH.

1969b "Vieillir à Florence au Quattrocento," *AESC*, 24:1338–52.

1970 "The Tuscan Town in the Quattrocento: A Demographic Profile," *Medievalia et Humanistica*, new ser. 1:68–81.

1971 "Editing for the Computer: The Florentine Catasto of 1427," *American Council of Learned Society Newsletter,* April issue.

1972a "Some Social and Psychological Roots of Violence in the Tuscan Cities." In *Violence and Civil Disorder in Italian Cities, 1200–1500*, ed. Lauro Martines, pp. 129–54. Berkeley, Los Angeles, and London.

1972b "Quantification and the Middle Ages." In *The Dimensions of the Past. Materials, Problems, and Opportunities for Quantitative Work in History*, ed. R. Lorwin and J. M. Price, pp. 13–51. New Haven and London.

1972c "Mapping Households in Medieval Italy," *Catholic Historical Review*, 58:1–24.

1972d "Marriage at Pistoia in the Fifteenth Century," *Bollettino Storico Pistoiese*, 7:623–47.

1973a "L'economia della città e del distretto di Lucca secondo le carte private nell'alto medioevo," *Atti del V. Congresso internazionale di studi sull' alto Medioevo*, pp. 363–88. Spoleto.

1973b "The Population of Verona in the First Century of Venetian Rule." In *Renaissance Venice*, ed. J. R. Hale, pp. 91–120. London.

1973c "Problems of Record Linkages in Tuscan Fiscal Documents of the Fifteenth Century." In *Identifying People in the Past*, ed. E. A. Wrigley, pp. 41–56. London.

1973d "Three Patterns of Social Mobility in Medieval History," *Journal of Interdisciplinary History*, 3:623–47.

1976 "The Medieval Marriage Market," *Medieval and Renaissance Studies. Proceedings of the Southeastern Institute of Medieval and Renaissance Studies*, ed. Dale B. J. Randall. Medieval and Renaissance Studies, 6, pp. 3–27. Durham, N.C.

1977a "Deaths, Marriages, Births and the Tuscan Economy, (ca. 1300–1550)." In *Population Patterns in the Past*, ed. Ronald Demos Lee, pp. 135–64. New York, San Francisco, and London.

1977b "Family and Property in Renaissance Florence." In *The Medieval City*, eds. Miskimin, Herlihy, and Udovitch, pp. 3– 24. New Haven and London.

1977c "The Distribution of Wealth in a Renaissance Community: Florence, 1427." In *Towns in Societies,* eds. Philip Abrams, and E. A. Wrigley, pp. 131–57. London.

1978a "Medieval Children," *Essays on Medieval Civilization. The Walter Prescott Webb Memorial Lectures*, ed. B. K. Lackner, and K. R. Philip, pp. 109–42. Austin and London.

1978b "Le relazioni economiche di Firenze con le città soggette nel secolo XV." In *Egemonia fiorentina ed autonomie locali nella Toscana nord-occidentale del primo Rinascimento: vita arte cultura*, pp. 79–109. Bologna.

1981 "The Problem of the 'Return to the Land' in Tuscan Economic History in the Fourteenth and Fifteenth Centuries." In *Civiltà ed economia agricola in Toscana nei secc. XIII–XV. Problemi della vita delle campagne nel tardo medioevo*, pp. 401–16. Pistoia.

Herlihy, David, and Klapisch–Zuber, Christiane
1978 *Les Toscans et leurs familles. Une étude du catasto florentin de 1427.* Paris.

Higounet, C.
1962 "Les *terre nuove* florentines du 14e siècle." In *Studi in onore di A. Fanfani.* 3:3–17, Milan.

Hilaire, J.
1973 "Vie en commun, famille et ésprit communautaire," *Revue Historique du Droit Français et Etranger*, 51:8–53.

Hollingsworth, T. H.
1957 "A Demographic Study of the British Ducal Families," *Population Studies*, 11:4–26; reprinted in *Population in History*, eds. D. V. Glass and D. E. C. Eversley, pp. 354–78, 1965, London.

Hughes, Diane Owen
1975 "Urban Growth and Family Structure in Medieval Genoa," *Past and Present*, 66:3–28.

Ildefonso di San Luigi
1785 "Istoria Genealogica de' Morelli," *Delizie degli eruditi toscani.* 19:i–clxxxiv, Florence.

Imberciadori, I.
1951 *Mezzadria classica toscana con documentazione inedita dal sec. 9 al sec. 14.* Florence.
1957 "I due poderi di Bernardo Machiavelli ovvero mezzadria poderale nel '400." In *Studi in onore di A. Sapori.* 2:836 ff. Milan.
1958a "Proprietà terriera di F. Datini e parziaria mezzadrile nel '400," *Economia e Storia*, 5:254–72.
1958b "Le scaturigini della mezzadria poderale nel sec. 9," *Economia e Storia*, 5:7–19.
1971 *Per la storia della società rurale: Amiata e Maremma tra il IX e il XX sec.* Parma.

International Classification
1969 *International Standard Classification of Occupations.* Revised ed. Geneva.

Jensen, R. and Dollar, C. A.
1971 *The Historian's Guide to Statistics.* New York.

Jones, Philip J.
1954 "A Tuscan Lordship in the Later Middle Ages: Camaldoli," *Journal of Ecclesiastical History*, 5:168–83.
1956 "Florentine Families and Florentine Diaries in the Fourteenth Century," *Papers of the British School at Rome*, 24. London.

1964 "Per la storia agraria italiana nel Medio Evo. Lineamenti e problemi," *Rivista Storica Italiana*, 76:287–348.

1968 "From Manor to Mezzadria." In *Florentine Studies*, ed. Rubinstein, pp. 193–241. London.

Kent, Dale

1978 *The Rise of the Medici. Faction in Florence, 1426–1434*. Oxford.

Kent, F. W.

1974 "The Letters Genuine and Spurious of Giovanni Rucellai," *Journal of the Warburg and Courtauld Institutes*, 37:342–49.

1977 *Household and Lineage in Renaissance Florence. The Family Life of the Capponi, Ginori and Rucellai*. Princeton.

Kirshner, Julius

1971 "Paolo di Castro on *cives ex privilegio*. A Controversy over the Legal Qualifications for Public Office in Early Fifteenth-Century Florence." In *Renaissance Studies in Honor of Hans Baron*, ed. A. Molho and J. A. Tedeschi, pp. 226–64. Florence.

1978 *Pursuing Honor While Avoiding Sin. The Monte delle Doti of Florence*. Quaderni di "Studi Senesi," 41. Milan.

Kirshner, Julius, and Molho, Anthony

1978 "The Dowry Fund and the Marriage Market in Early *Quattrocento* Florence," *Journal of Modern History*, 50:403–38.

Klapisch, Christiane

1969 "Fiscalité et démographie en Toscane (1427–1430)," *AESC*, 24: 1313–37.

1972a "Sources et méthodes de la démographie médiévale. Le catasto florentin de 1427–1430," *Annales de la Faculté des Lettres et Sciences Humaines de Nice*, 17:53–69.

1972b "Household and Family in Tuscany in 1427." In *Household and Family in Past Time*, eds. Laslett and Wall, pp. 267–81, Cambridge.

1973a "L'enfance en Toscane au début du 15e siècle," *Annales de Démographie Historique*, pp. 99–122.

1973b "Villaggi abbandonati ed emigrazioni interne." In *Storia d' Italia*. 5:311–69. Turin.

1975 "Le cadastre florentin et la quantification. Quelques méthodes d'analyse statistique appliquées à un corpus du Moyen Age." In *Actes du Colloque: Méthodes quantitatives en histoire*, pp. 219–35 (in Polish). Warsaw.

1976a "Exploitation démographique et anthroponymique du catasto florentin de 1427; problèmes de méthode." In *L' utilisation de informatique pour l' exploitation des documents textuels médiévaux*. Paris.

1976b "Parenti, amici, vicini. Il territorio urbano d'una famiglia mercantile nel XV secolo," *Quaderni Storici, 30:953–82.*

1977 "Déclin démographique et structure du ménage; l'example de Prato, fin 14e-fin 15e siècle." In *Famille et parenté dans l' occident médiéval*. Collection de l'école française de Rome, 30, pp. 255–68. Rome.

1979 "Zacharie, ou le père évincé: les rites nuptiaux en Toscane," *AESC*, 34:1216–43.

1980a "Le nom 'refait'. La transmission des prénoms à Florence (XIVe–XVIe siècles)," *L'Homme*, 20:77–104.

1980b "Genitori naturali e genitori di latte nella Firenze del quattrocento," *Quaderni Storici*, 44:543–63.

1981a "Mezzadria e insediamenti rurali alla fine del Medio Evo." In *Civiltà ed economia agricola in Toscana nei secc. XIII–XV: Problemi della vita delle campagne nel tardo medioevo*, pp. 149–65. Pistoia.

1981b "Célibat et service féminins dans la Florence du XV siècle," *Annales de démographie historique*, pp. 289–302.

Klapisch, Christiane, and Demonet, M.

1972 "*A uno pane e uno vino*. Structure et développement de la famille rurale toscane (début du 15e siècle)," *AESC* 27:873–901.

1975 "A Correspondence Analysis of a 15th Century Census: The Florentine Catasto of 1427," *The Journal of European Economic History*, 4:415–28.

Krause, J.

1957 "The Medieval Household: Large or Small?" *The Economic History Review*, 2nd ser. 9:420–32.

Kuehn, Thomas

1980 "Honor and Conflict in a Fifteenth Century Florentine Family," *Ricerche Storiche*, 10:287–310.

1982 *Emancipation in Late Medieval Florence*. New Brunswick, NJ.

Laribière, G.

1967 "Le mariage à Toulouse aux 14e et 15e siècles," *Annales du Midi*, 79:335–62.

La Roncière, Charles de

1968 "Indirect Taxes or 'Gabelle' at Florence in the Fourteenth Century." In *Florentine Studies*, ed. Rubinstein, pp. 140–92. London.

1973 *Un changeur florentin du Trecento: Lippo di Fede del Sega (1285 env.-1363 env.)*. Paris.

1974 "Pauvres et pauvreté à Florence au 14e siècle." In *Etudes sur l' histoire de la pauvreté (Moyen Age– 16e siècle)*, ed. M. Mollat. Publications de la Sorbonne, "Etudes," 8, pp. 661–765. Paris.

1976 *Florence, centre économique régional au XIVe siècle*. Aix-en-Provence.

Laslett, Peter

1969 "Size and Structure of the Household in England over Three Centuries," *Population Studies*, 23:199–223.

Laslett, Peter and Wall, Richard.

1972 *Household and Family in Past Time*. Cambridge.

Lastri, Marco

1775 *Ricerche sull' antica e moderna popolazione della città di Firenze per mezzo dei registri del battistero di San Giovanni dal 1451 al 1774*. Florence.

Le Bras, H.
1969 "Retour d'une population à l'état stable après une catastrophe," *Population*, 24:861–92.
1971 "Eléments pour une théorie des populations instables," *Population*, 26: 525–72.
1972 "La mortalité actuelle en Europe, I: Présentation et répresentation des données," *Population*, 27:271–94.
Ledermann, S.
1969 *Nouvelles tables-types de mortalité*. Institute National des Etudes Démographiques (INED), Travaux et documents, cahier 53. Paris.
Le Goff, Jacques
1963a "Au moyen âge: temps de l'église et temps du marchand," *AESC*, 15:417–33.
1963b "Le temps du travail dans la crise du 14e siècle: du temps médiéval au temps moderne," *Le Moyen Age; livre jubilaire*.
1964 *La civilisation de l' Occident médiéval*. Paris.
Le Roy Ladurie, E.
1969 "L'aménorrhée de famine (XVIIe–XXe s.)," *AESC*, 24:1589–1601.
1973 "Un concept: l'unification microbienne du monde (14e–17e siècles)," *Revue Suisse d' Histoire*, 23:627–96.
Litchfield, R. B.
1969 "Demographic Characteristics of Florentine Patrician Families, Sixteenth to Nineteenth Centuries," *The Journal of Economic History*, 29:191–205.
Livi Bacci, M.
1968 "Fertility and Nuptiality Changes in Spain from the Late 18th to the Early 20th Century," *Population Studies*, 22:83–102; 211–34.
1972 "Quelques problèmes dans le couplage des données nominatives en Toscane, 17e–18e siècles," *Annales de Démographie Historique*, pp. 232–33.
Lopes-Pegna, M.
1971 *Le strade romane del Valdarno*. Quaderni di studi storici toscani, ser. 6, quad. 4. Florence.
Lopez, A.
1961 *Problems in Stable Population Theory*. Princeton.
Lopez, Robert S.
1954 "Concerning Surnames and Places of Origin," *Medievalia et Humanistica*, 8:6–16.
1962 "Hard Times and Investment in Culture," In *The Renaissance. Six Essays*, pp. 29–54. New York.
Lot, F.
1929 *L' état des paroisses et des feux de 1328*. Bibliothèque de l'Ecole des Chartes, 90. Paris.
Lotka, A.
1943 *Théorie analytique des associations biologiques*. Paris.

Luzzati, M.
1976 "Estimi e catasti del contado di Pisa nel Quattrocento." In *Ricerche di Storia Moderna*, ed. M. Mirri, pp. 95–123. Pisa.

Luzzatto, M.
1948 "Contributo alla storia della mezzadria," *Nuova Rivista Storica*, 32.

Mallett, M.
1968 "Pisa and Florence in the Fifteenth Century; Aspects of the Period of the First Florentine Domination," In *Florentine Studies*, ed. Rubinstein, pp. 403–44. London.

Malthus, Thomas Robert
1798/1970 *An Essay on the Principle of Population (1798)*, ed. Anthony Flew. Baltimore.

Martines, Lauro
1963 *The Social World of the Florentine Humanists, 1390–1460*. Princeton.
1968 *Lawyers and Statecraft in Renaissance Florence*. Princeton.
1974 "A Way of Looking at Women in Renaissance Florence," *The Journal of Medieval and Renaissance Studies*, 4:15–28.
1979 *Power and Imagination. City-States in Renaissance Italy*. New York.

Mayer, H. M. and Kohn, C. F.
1959 *Readings in Urban Geography*. Chicago.

Meiss, M.
1951 *Painting in Florence and Siena after the Black Death*. Princeton.

Melis, Federigo
1966 *Tracce di una storia economica di Firenze e della Toscana in generale dal 1252 al 1550*. Florence.

Mengozzi, G.
1914 *La città italiana nell' alto medio evo*. Rome.

Merlini, D.
1894 *Saggio di ricerche sulla satira contro il villano*. Turin.

Michaelsson, K.
1927–36 *Etudes sur les noms de personnes français d' après les rôles de taille parisiens (1292, 1296–1300, 1313)*. Upsala.

Mira, G.
1942 "I registri d'estimo e lo studio dell'economia lombarda del sec. 15 e 16," *Rivista Internazionale di Scienze Sociali*, 13.
1955a "I catasti e gli estimi perugini del XIII secolo," *Economia e Storia*, 2:76–84.
1955b "I catasti perugini del 14 e 15 sec." *Economia e Storia*, 2:171–204.

Molho, Anthony
1971a "Jewish Moneylenders in Tuscany in the Late Trecento and Early Quattrocento." In *Renaissance Studies in Honor of Hans Baron*, pp. 99–118. Florence.
1971b *Florentine Public Finances in the Early Renaissance, 1400–1433*. Cambridge, MA.

Molho, Anthony, and Tedeschi, John. A., eds.
1971 *Renaissance Studies in Honor of Hans Baron*. Florence.

Mols, R.
1954–56 *Introduction à la démographie historique des villes d'Europe du 14e au 18e siècle*. 3 vols. Louvain.

Monti, G. M.
1927 *Le confraternite medievali dell' alta e media Italia*. Florence.

Muendel, John
1972 "The Grain Mills at Pistoia in 1350," *Bollettino Storico Pistoiese*, 3rd ser. 7:39–64.

Murdock, G. P.
1948 *Social Structure*. New York.

Neveux, Hugues
1968 "La mortalité des pauvres à Cambrai (1377–1473)," *Annales de Démographie Historique*, pp. 73–97.

Niccolai, F.
1940 "I consorzi nobiliari ed il Comune nell'alta e media Italia," *Rivista di Storia del Diritto Italiano*, 13:116–47; 292–342; 397–477.

Niccolini da Camugliano, G.
1925 "A Medieval Florentine: His Family and His Possessions," *The American Historical Review*, 31:1–19.
1933 *The Chronicles of a Florentine Family, 1200–1400*. London.

Noonan, John T.
1966 *Contraception, A History of Its Treatment by the Catholic Theologians and Canonists*. Cambridge, MA.

Oesterle, G.
1949 "Consanguinité," *Dictionnaire de Droit Canonique*. 4:231–48. Paris.

Origo, Iris
1955 "The Domestic Enemy: Eastern Slaves in Tuscany in the Fourteenth and Fifteenth Centuries," *Speculum*, 30:321–66.

Ottokar, N.
1958 "Gli scioperati a Firenze nel '300." In *Studi storici in onore di G. Volpe*. 2:703–07. Florence.

Ottolenghi, D.
1903 "Studi demografici sulla popolazione di Siena dal sec. 14 al 19," *Bollettino Senese di Storia Patria*, 10:297–358.

Pagnini del Ventura, G. F.
1765–66 *Della decima e di varie altre gravezze imposte dal comune di Firenze. Della moneta e della mercatura dei Fiorentini fino al sec. XVI*. Lisbon and Lucca.

Pampaloni, G.
1974 "Vita, società e organizzazione agricola di tre castelli della Maremma volterrana alla fine del Trecento e nei primi decenni del successivo Quattrocento." In *Storiografia e storici. Studi in onore di E. Dupré-Theseider*, pp. 747–83. Rome.

Panofsky, E.
1964 "*Mors vitae testimonium*. The Positive Aspect of Death in Renaissance and Baroque Iconography." In *Studien zur toskanischen Kunst. Festschrift für L. H. Heydenreich* . . . , eds. W. Lotz and L. L. Moller. Munich.

Pardi, G.
1916 "Disegno della storia demografica di Firenze," *ASI*, 74:3–84; 185–245.
1921a "La popolazione del contado fiorentino nel 1401," *Annuario Statistico del Comune di Firenze*, 15–16.
1921b "La peste del 1348 e la popolazione del contado fiorentino," *Bollettino dell' Unione Statistica delle Città Italiane*, 2–3.

Parenti, G.
1943–49 "Fonti per lo studio della demografia fiorentine: I Libri di Morti," *Genus*, 6–8:281–301.

Passerini, L.
1853a *Storia degli stabilimenti di beneficenza e d' istruzione della città di Firenze*. Florence.
1853b *Notizie storiche dello spedale degl' Innocenti di Firenze*. Florence.

Patzak, B.
1913 *Palast und Villen in Toscana*. Leipzig.

Peristiany, J. G. (ed.)
1966 *Honour and Shame. The Values of Mediterranean Society*. Chicago.

Petersen, W.
1969 *Population*. 2nd ed. London.

Plesner, Johann
1934 *L' émigration de la campagne à la ville libre de Florence au 13e siècle*. Copenhagen.
1938, 1980 *Una rivoluzione stradale del Dugento*. Acta Jutlandica, 10. Aarhus. New ed. by F. Papatrava. Florence.

Pollitzer, R.
1954 *La peste*. Geneva.

Pounds, N. J. G.
1970 "Overpopulation in France and the Low Countries in the Late Middle Ages," *Journal of Social History*, 3:225–47.

Pressat, Roland,
1966 *Principes d' analyse démographique de l' IDUP*. Paris.

Procacci, Ugo
1953 "Sulla cronologia delle opere di Masaccio e di Masolino," *Rivista d' Arte*, 28:3–55.

Prost, M. A.
1965 *La hiérarchie des villes en fonction de leurs activités de commerce et de service*. Paris.

Rasila, Vilgo
1970 "The Use of Multivariable Analysis in Historical Studies," *Economy and History*, 13:24.

Rauti, N.
1967 "Sistemazioni fluviali e bonifica della pianura pistoiese durante l'età comunale," *Bollettino Storico Pistoiese*, 64:75–98.

Reinhard, M., Armengaud, A. and Dupâquier, J.
1968 *Histoire générale de la population mondiale*. Paris.

Repetti, Emmanuele
1833–64 *Dizionario geografico, fisico, storico della Toscana*. 6 vols. Florence.

Resta, G.
1962 *Le epitomi di Plutarca nel Quattrocento*. Padua.

Rodolico, N.
1905 *La democrazia fiorentina nel suo tramonto (1378–1382)*. Florence.

Romano, R. and Tenenti, A.
1969, 1971 "Introduzione" to the edition of *I libri della famiglia* of L. B. Alberti, pp. vii–xlii, Turin; reprinted in: R. Romano, *Tra due crisi. L' Italia del Rinascimento*, pp. 137–68. Turin.

Roover, Raymond de
1963 *The Rise and the Decline of the Medici Bank (1397–1494)*. Cambridge, MA.

Rosenthal, J.
1973 "Medieval Longevity and the Secular Peerage, 1350–1500," *Population Studies*, 27:287–93.

Ross, J. B.
1974 "The Middle–Class Child in Urban Italy, Fourteenth to Early Sixteenth Centuries." In *The History of Childhood* ed. L. de Mause, pp. 183–228. New York.

Rossi, A.
1945–47 "Lo sviluppo demografico di Pisa dal 12° al 15° secolo," *Bollettino Storico Pisano*, 14–16:5–62.

Rossi, G. de'
1971 "Sviluppo economico e agricoltura." In *Un' altra Firenze*.., pp. 59–138. Florence.

Rubinstein, N.
1966 *The Government of Florence under the Medici (1434 –1494)*. Oxford.

Rubinstein, N., ed.
1968 *Florentine Studies. Politics and Society in Renaissance Florence*. London.

Rummel, R.
1967 "Understanding Factor Analysis," *Journal of Conflict Resolution*, 11:445–80.

Russell, Josiah Cox
1948 *British Medieval Population*. Albuquerque.
1965 "Recent Advances in Medieval Demography," *Speculum*, 40:84–101.
1972 *Medieval Regions and Their Cities*. Bloomington, IN.

Ryan, J. J.
1956 *Saint Peter Damiani and His Canonical Sources*. Toronto.

Salk, Lee
1973 "The Role of the Heartbeat in the Relations between Mother and Infant," *Scientific American*, 228:24–29.

Salvioli, G.
1894 "La benedizione nuziale fino al Concilio di Trento, specialmente in riguardo alla pratica e alla dottrina italiana dal sec. 13 al 16," *Archivio Giuridico*, 53:169–97.

Santini, E.
1910 "Leonardo Bruni Aretino e i suoi *Historiarum Florentini populi libri XII*," *Annali della R. Scuola Normale Superiore di Pisa*, 22. Pp. 169.

Santini, P.
1887 "Società delle torri in Firenze," *ASI*, 20:25–58, 178–204

Sapori, A.
1955 "La cultura del mercante medievale italiano." In *Studi di storia economica medievale*. 3rd ed. 1:53–93.

Schwarz, K.
1968 "Influence de la natalité et de la mortalité sur la composition par âges de la population et sur l'évolution démographique," *Population*, 23:61–92.

Schwarzmaier, H.
1972 *Lucca und das Reich bis zum Ende des 11. Jahrhunderts*. Bibliothek des deutschen historischen Instituts in Rom, 11. Rome.

Seronde, A. M. *et al.*
1970 *Tradition et changement en Toscane*. Cahiers de la Fondation nationale des sciences politiques, 176. Paris.

Shrewsbury, J. F. D.
1970 *A History of Bubonic Plague in the British Isles*. Cambridge, Eng.

Silva, P.
1909–10 "Pisa sotto Firenze dal 1406 al 1433," *Studi Storici*, 18:285–324.
1911 "Intorno all'industria e al commercio della lana in Pisa," *Studi Storici*, 19:329–400.
1912 "Il governo di Piero Gambacorta e le sue relazioni col resto della Toscana e coi Visconti," *Annali della R. Scuola Normale Superiore di Pisa*, 23:352

Slicher van Bath, B. H.
1966 *The Agrarian History of Western Europe, A. D 500–1850*. London.

Smith, T. L.
1960 *Fundamentals of Population Study*. New York.

Somogyi, S.
1950 "Sulla mascolinità delle nascite a Firenze dal 1451 al 1774,"*Rivista Italiana di Demografia e Statistica*, 4:460–70.

Sorbi, U.
1962 *Aspetti della struttura e principali modalità di stima dei catasti senese e fiorentino del 14°* e 15° secolo. 2nd. ed. Florence.

Stahl, B.
1965 *Adel und Volk im florentiner Dugento.* Graz and Cologne.

Starn, R.
1971 "Francesco Guicciardini and His Brothers." In *Renaissance Studies in Honor of Hans Baron*, pp. 411–44. Florence.

Stewart, C. T. Jr.
1959 "Size and Spacing of Cities." In *Readings in Urban Geography*, ed. Mayer and Kohn, pp. 240–56. Chicago.

Stradario
1913 *Stradario Storico di Firenze.* Florence.

Sudhoff, K.
1913 "Pestschriften aus den ersten 150 Jahren nach der Epidemie des schwarzen Todes 1348," *Archiv für Geschichte der Medizin*, 6:313–79.

Szabo, Thomas
1977 "Die Bedeutung der Kommunen für den Ausbau des mittelalterlichen Strassennetzes in Italien." In *Storia della città*, 2:21–27.

Tabarrini, M.
1892 "Le consorterie della storia fiorentina del medioevo." In *La vita italiana nel trecento*, vol. 1. Milan.

Tagliaferri, A.
1966 *L' economia veronese secondo gli estimi dal 1409 al 1635.* Biblioteca della Rivista Economia e Storia, 17. Milan.

Tamassia, N.
1911 *La famiglia italiana nei secoli decimoquinto e decimosesto.* L'indagine moderna, 15. Milan.

Tangheroni, M.
1973 *Politica, commercio, agricoltura a Pisa nel Trecento.* Pisa.

Tateo, F.
1967 "La disputà della nobilità." In *Tradizione e realtà nell' umanesimo italiano*, pp. 358–63. Bari.

Tenenti, A.
1957 *Il senso della morte e l' amore della vita nel Rinascimento (Francia e Italia).* Turin.
1973 "Temoignages toscans sur la mort des enfants autour de 1400," *Annales de Démographie Historique*, pp. 132–33.

Tiribilli-Giuliani, D.
1855 *Sommario storico delle celebri famiglie toscane*, ed. L. Passerini, 3 vols. Florence.

Todd, E.
1975 "Mobilité géographique et cycle de vie en Artois et en Toscane au 18e siècle," *AESC* 30:726–44.

Tolomei, F.
1821 *Guida di Pistoia per gli amanti delle belle arti.* Pistoia.

Toubert, Pierre
1973 *Les structures du Latium médiéval. Le Latium méridional et la Sabine*

du 9e siècle à la fin du 12e siècle. Bibliothèque des Ecoles françaises d'Athènes et de Rome, 221. Rome.

Trexler, Richard C.

1971a "Death and Testament in the Episcopal Constitutions of Florence (1327)." In *Renaissance Studies in Honor of Hans Baron*, pp. 29–74. Florence.

1971b "Une table florentine d'espérance de vie," *AESC*, 26:137–39

1971c *Synodal Law in Florence and Fiesole, 1306–1518*. Studi e Testi, 268. Vatican City.

1972 "Le célibat à la fin du Moyen Age: les religieuses de Florence," *AESC*, 27:1329–50.

1973 "Charity and the Defense of Urban Elites in the Italian Communes." In *The Rich, the Well Born and the Powerful*, ed. F. C. Jaher. Urbana, IL.

1973–74a "Infanticide in Florence: New Sources and First Results," *History of Childhood Quarterly. The Journal of Psychohistory*, 1:96–116.

1973–74b "The Foundlings of Florence, 1395–1455," *History of Childhood Quarterly. The Journal of Psychohistory*, 1:259–84.

1974 "Ritual in Florence: Adolescence and Salvation in the Renaissance." In *The Pursuit of Holiness in Late Medieval and Renaissance Religion*, ed. C. Trinkaus and H. A. Oberman, pp. 200–64. Leiden.

1975 "In Search of Father: The Experience of Abandonment in the Recollections of Giovanni di Pagolo Morelli," *History of Childhood Quarterly*, 3:225–28.

1980 *Public Life in Renaissance Florence*. New York.

1981 "La prostitution florentine au 15e siècle," *AESC*, 36:983–1015.

Un' altra Firenze

1971 *Un' altra Firenze. L' epoca di Cosimo il Vecchio. Riscontri tra cultura e società nella storia fiorentina*. Florence.

Varese, P.

1924–25 "Condizioni economiche e demografiche di Arezzo nel sec. 15," *Annali del R. Istituto magistrale di Arezzo (1924–1925)*.

Verlinden, Charles

1977 *L' esclavage dans l' Europe médiéval*, 1: *Italie, Colonies italiennes du Levant latin, Empire byzantine*. Ghent.

Villari, P.

1888 "Intorno alla storia di Girolamo Savonarola e de' suoi tempi. (A proposito d'uno scritto di F. C. Pellegrini)," *ASI*, ser. 5, 1:184–205.

Violante, Cinzio

1966 "Imposte dirette e debito pubblico a Pisa nel Medio Evo." In *L' impot dans le cadre de la Ville et de l' Etat*. Collection d'histoire, 13, pp. 45–95.

1977 "Quelques caracteristiques des structures familiales en Lombardie, Emilie et Toscane aux XIe et XIIe siècles." In *Famille et Parenté dans l' Occident médiéval*. Collection de l'Ecole française de Rome, 30. Rome.

Volpe, G.
1902 "Pisa, Firenze, Impero al principio del 1300 e gli inizi della signoria civile a Pisa," *Studi Storici*, 11:177–203.

Waley, D.
1968 "The Army of the Florentine Republic." In *Florentine Studies*, ed. Rubinstein, pp. 70–108. London.

Wheaton, Robert
1975 "Family and Kinship in Western Europe: The Problem of the Joint Family Household," *The Journal of Interdisciplinary History* 5:610–28.

Woehlkens, E.
1956 "Das Wesen der Pest," *Studium Generale*, 9:507–12.

Wolff, Philippe
1944–46 "Registres d'impots et vie économique à Toulouse sous Charles VI," *Annales du Midi*, 56–58:5–66.
1954 *Commerces et marchands de Toulouse (v. 1350 – v. 1450)*. Paris.
1956 *Les "estimes" toulousaines des 14e et 15e siècles (1335–1459)*. Bibliothèque de L'Association M. Bloch de Toulouse. Documents d'histoire méridionale. Toulouse.

Wrigley, E. A.
1961 *Industrial Growth and Population Change*. London.
1966 "Family Limitation in Pre-Industrial England," *Economic History Review*, 2nd ser. 19:82–109.
1968 "Mortality in Pre-Industrial England: the Example of Colyton, Devon, over Three Centuries," *Daedalus*, 47:546–80.
1969 *Population and History*. London.

Wrigley, E. A., ed.
1973 *Identifying People in the Past*. New York.

Zanelli, A.
1885 *Le schiave orientali a Firenze nei sec. 14°* e 15°. Florence.

Ziegler, Philip
1969 *The Black Death*. London.

Zipf, G. K.
1949 *Human Behavior and the Principal of Least Effort*. Cambridge.

Zuccagni Orlandini, A.
1848–54 *Ricerche statistiche sul Granducato di Toscana*. 5 vols. Florence.

Index

Family names beginning with Da, Del, and Della are classified under the place-name.

Abbreviations: fam., family; Flor., Florentine; loc., locality, city; mt., mountain; pod., podesteria; prov., province; r., river or torrent; sp., spouse; Tusc., Tuscan; wid., widow.